200

D0780844

KEY TO PLACES M[...]
EUROPE, AFRICA, [...]

1. Bog bodies, [...]
2. Star Carr
3. Stonehenge, Wiltshire barrows
4. Abbeville, Somme River
5. Koln-Lindenthal site
6. Lebenstedt site
7. Bylany site
8. Dolni Vestonice site
9. Lascaux Cave, Le Moustier, Abri Pataud
10. Terra Amata site
11. Mt. Circeo site
12. Pompeii
13. Adaura Cave
14. Parthenon
15. Mycenae
16. Palace of Minos
17. Troy
18. Çatal Hüyük
19. Ksar Akil Cave
20. Mt. Carmel caves
21. Jericho, Dead Sea Scrolls
22. Beersheba
23. Pyramids at Giza, Sakkara
24. Thebes, Luxor, Karnak
25. Aswan
26. Abu Simbel
27. Fulani tribe
28. Olduvai Gorge
29. Kalambo Falls
30. Bushmen tribe
31. Gwembe Tonga tribe
32. Nineveh, Nimrud
33. Jarmo
34. Diyala sites, Khafaje
35. Kunji Cave, Gar Arjeneh, Pa Sangar, Yafteh Cave
36. Deh Luran sites, Ali Kosh, Tepe Sabz, Chogga Sefid
37. Khuzistan, Chogga Zambil
38. Warka, Eridu, Ur (Sumerians)
39. Belt Cave
40. Mohenjo-Daro, Harappa
41. Swat, Pakistan
42. Pazyryk Scythian tombs
43. Anyang, Shang tombs, Choukoutien
44. Seoul, Korea
45. Java Pithecanthropines

AN INTRODUCTION TO
PREHISTORIC
ARCHEOLOGY

AN INTRODUCTION TO PREHISTORIC ARCHEOLOGY

Third Edition

FRANK HOLE
Rice University

ROBERT F. HEIZER
University of California, Berkeley

HOLT, RINEHART AND WINSTON, INC.
New York   Chicago   San Francisco   Atlanta
Dallas   Montreal   Toronto   London   Sydney

Copyright © 1965, 1969, 1973 by Holt, Rinehart and Winston, Inc.
All rights reserved
Library of Congress Catalog Card Number: 72–9584
ISBN: 0–03–005761–2
Printed in the United States of America
3 4 5 6   071   9 8 7 6 5 4 3 2

PREFACE

When we began this second revision we had the idea that only a minor amount of updating would be required; however, it soon became apparent that the changes in the field have been substantial enough since 1969 to necessitate a much more extensive revision through a restructuring of the text and the inclusion of new material. Our theme in this, as in previous editions, is to show how archeologists think and how they do archeology, rather than to tell what happened in the past. To accomplish this objective we have added considerable new material on the concepts and theories that underlie various aspects of the discipline. In the presentation of these ideas we proceed from the relatively simple to the complex, and a thorough understanding of the last part of the work that deals with interpretation depends on mastery of the material that has preceded it. Many of the ideas presented are familiar to students who have taken courses in anthropology and related fields, but it is important to stress that archeologists sometimes use familiar concepts in unfamiliar ways. We have tried to indicate these points of difference and to show that the concepts have been adjusted to take into account the particular needs of archeology.

Four chapters in the present edition are entirely new, although they each incorporate some material from previous editions. These new chapters, along with some reordering of the sequence of presentation, have, we feel, made the work a more coherent whole that will be easier to understand and to use as a text. A revised edition is inevitably a compromise between the need to update and to change, and the power of the earlier structure to restrain innovation in organization and presentation. In each of the revisions we have retained the basic content of the original work while making considerable additions and revisions in the organization. To a large extent these changes reflect changes in archeology itself, but we have been mindful that there are better ways to present material. The present edition takes both of these factors into account.

An Introduction to Prehistoric Archeology is divided into five parts, each of which deals with one aspect of the field. Even more basically, however, we might consider it a three-part work. The first chapters deal with the field itself and constitute an introductory survey of basic material. Next we deal with the acquisition and analysis of evidence; these chapters tell how we do archeology in the field and in the laboratory. The final section concerns interpretation and shows how we convert the raw data into statements about the past.

In a constant attempt to make their discipline more rigorously scientific, prehistorians employ a myriad of techniques and concepts. The last two decades have witnessed a burgeoning of technical applications that are useful in acquiring and analyzing data, and improvements of these techniques appear with regularity. The last decade has also seen a shift toward a more explicitly scientific conceptual view of prehistory, a shift that has been called revolutionary; in consequence the entire structure of archeology is undergoing change. The third edition of *An Introduction to Prehistoric Archeology* is our first attempt to deal systematically and at length with these new directions. Our two new chapters on the concepts that underlie modern archeology and the entire introductory part of the book are designed to make these conceptual changes clear in the context of archeology, science, and the modern world.

We are fully aware that the present edition is long and detailed and in consequence may not be suitable for all introductory courses. Nevertheless, we remain convinced that the work is the most comprehensive introduction available and that it serves a unique and useful purpose for instructors and serious students. Although the book can be used without outside reading, we have included an extensive, system of references at the end of each chapter for those who wish to pursue topics further. We consider the referencing and bibliography to be major strengths of the book, for it is a volume that can be used both as an introductory survey of the discipline and later as a source of references as the student grows in sophistication and develops special interests. In addition, the references may be used by instructors to direct students toward independent study for term papers or research projects.

Each teacher has his own method of presenting material, yet all must cover certain basic and fundamental topics. We recognize that many instructors prefer to let students read much of the background material on their own so that lectures can be used to emphasize points that are necessary to an understanding of topics presented in class. This book, with its coverage of the basic topics, may be used either as background reading or as the focal point of an introductory course.

Basically there are two kinds of introductory courses in archeology. The most common tells what happened in the past and in this sense is very much like a course in history. In these courses instructors may wish to use the present volume as supplemental and background reading.

Another kind of introductory course deals with how archeologists think, what the archeological process is, and how archeology relates to other disciplines. It is primarily for this kind of course that we have written the book. Following Rhys Carpenter, Stuart Piggott has written, "archaeological evidence is inevident." This is an extremely important point for both students and instructors to recognize. Taking this into account, one of the principal goals of this book is to show how archeologists convert the data of past cultures into coherent pictures of life in the past. In so doing we must in all honesty emphasize the difficulties; we would serve no useful purpose by ignoring them or by overstating our ability to deal with them. At the same time, when we recognize the problems inherent in dealing with prehistory, we challenge our ingenuity in attempting to solve them. This is part of the excitement of archeology.

This is not a wholly "original" work. A glance at the bibliography will indicate our debt to our colleagues. The way we have organized and presented the material is original, however, and is one of the major strengths of the third edition. A student attempting to piece together a coherent review of the field, its structure, its concepts and working assumptions, and its procedures would find the task extremely difficult. The third edition represents our attempt to present this coherent review from the thousands of articles and books that deal in their own way with the many facets of archeology. In this sense it is a personal work which reflects the views of the authors as to what is important. Nevertheless, we have attempted to present a balanced picture of archeology today by referring to alternative views. The references cited at the ends of the chapters include articles that cover the range of opinion on each topic and serve as a convenient guide to the significant literature.

F. H.
R. F. H.

ACKNOWLEDGMENTS

Although we take full responsibility for the form and content of the book, it is with a keen sense of appreciation that we acknowledge the contributions of many persons who have helped to make it better. Reviewers of the previous editions pointed out certain errors and shortcomings that we have tried to correct; and our colleagues who use the book and took the time to comment on parts that were especially useful or that required further elaboration and explanation have all contributed materially to this edition.

Among our colleagues we would especially like to thank Richard Blanton, Ann Brower, William Haviland, Gustav Konitzky, and Patty Jo and Richard Watson. The following students deserve special mention for their critical advice and for their help in the preparation of this revision: Allen Albee, Barbara Burger, Marion Hatch, Tom Hester, Bonnie Laird, Karen Nissen, and Caroline Sprague. To Mary Margaret Williamson, who checked and typed the final bibliography, goes our deep appreciation. One of us (R.F.H.) wishes to thank Ulla Kasten Rae for helping to read galley proofs while spending the year 1972–1973 at the Center for Advanced Study in the Behavioral Sciences. Finally, we thank Nancy Flannery, who drew Figures 41, 49, 54, 63, and 65.

CONTENTS

AN INTRODUCTION TO
PREHISTORIC
ARCHEOLOGY

PART 1

INTRODUCING MODERN ARCHEOLOGY

The field of archeology encompasses a broad spectrum of interests ranging from studies of the origin of man to the microscopic analyses of ancient tools and artifacts. It includes studies of the art and architecture of the higher civilizations of antiquity; it deals with the histories of peoples; it serves as an adjunct to written history; and it informs us of the ancient ways of man. Clearly the entire field of study is too broad to treat in a single volume, nor is it possible to indicate adequately the range of subjects that might be of some archeological interest. Instead, we review in the first three chapters the present status of archeology as it is practiced by American prehistorians for whom the discipline is a subfield within anthropology.

The first two chapters are an appraisal of the present state of archeology—what it is, ways it may be done, and what we may expect in the future. Modern archeology is then put into the perspective of its own history in Chapter 3. In so doing we make it clear that although this book treats prehistoric archeology as the anthropology of extinct peoples, it developed out of a background shared with other branches of archeology.

1

CHAPTER ONE

PREHISTORIC ARCHEOLOGY

WHAT IS ARCHEOLOGY?

In its broadest sense archeology is the study of man's past. It is also a set of methods for eliciting information and a manner of investigating the past that is a reflection both of the data that are available and of the academic training and theoretical orientation of archeologists. In America archeology is a sub-discipline of anthropology, a field that seeks to study man in his various aspects: physical, cultural, social, linguistic, and historic. Anthropologists are concerned with man's culture and with the culture of men; consequently, archeologists have been preoccupied with the changes in culture and the varieties of cultures. But archeology differs from most anthropology in that it deals with dead peoples—peoples who are often nameless—and with cultures in which individuals are seldom perceived. It differs in that archeologists study man's works—his artifacts and places of activity—rather than the people themselves. Thus, though archeology can never hope to be all that anthropology is, it can make important contributions to both anthropology and history by adding a time dimension that cannot be studied with living peoples. Archeology is part of, and ancillary to, anthropology; but its subject matter is different, its methods have little in common with general anthropology, and its interpretations tend toward the sweeping rather than the particular, concerned with processes rather than with static "slices of life."

That archeology is many things and that archeologists have a wide variety of interests can be seen from the fact they are found in departments of art, history, classics, languages, and anthropology. Moreover, archeologists are

3

employed by universities, museums, historical agencies, and the United States Park Service, and they frequently work on contract to the Corps of Engineers and highway departments. On occasion, archeologists are even employed as expert witnesses in legal proceedings. Archeology thus covers a broad range of topics and interests, and may be considered pure research on the one hand or applied technology on the other. With this range it is not surprising that many archeologists speak and write in almost mutually unintelligible professional languages. For this reason we cannot hope to describe systematically the full range of archeology's special interests; what we shall do is concentrate on that branch of archeology that is variously called prehistoric archeology, paleoanthropology, or just prehistory. At the same time it should be made clear that most of the principles described here pertain to all of archeology, even though particular techniques, processes, and subject matter differ among the branches.

Until recently it was widely held that archeology was not a distinct discipline, and many still feel this way today (for example, Watson, LeBlanc, and Redman 1971). The argument runs along these lines: archeology has its own data and a few techniques and concepts, but most of these are borrowed from geology, history, or anthropology. As one archeologist put it, "It is often, and I think rightly, held that archeology should not be counted as a separate field of study so much as a method of reconstructing the past from the surviving traces of former societies" (G. Clark 1954:7). Evidently Clark thinks of prehistory as an extension of history. A century and a half ago J. Hodgson (1822:xvi) had the same idea when he wrote,

> The vulgar antiquary, while he walks among the ruins of a city, is struck with wonder, and fixes his observation most upon their extent, their state of preservation. . . . He is an admirer of coins on account of their rarity, their age, the beauty of their rust, or from some accidental variety which marks them. . . . He values his collection of manuscripts . . . merely because they are old. . . . But the judicious antiquary considers the various objects of his contemplation with a learned eye; and imposes a value upon them in proportion to the quantity of light they throw upon the several departments of the history of the people to which they belong.

Walter Taylor (1948:43) once stated that archeology is no more than a method and a set of specialized techniques for recovering cultural information. "The archeologist . . . is nothing but a technician." In rebuttal to this, it is worth quoting Sir Mortimer Wheeler:

> I have no hesitation in denouncing that extreme view as nonsense. A lepidopterist is a great deal more than a butterfly-catcher, and an archeologist who is not more than a pot-sherd-catcher is unworthy of his *logos*. He is primarily a fact-finder, but his facts are the material records of human achievement; he is also, by that token, a humanist, and his secondary task is that of revivifying or humanizing his materials with a controlled imagination that inevitably partakes of the qualities of art and even of philosophy (Wheeler 1956:228–229).

Our own view was stated well by G. Isaac:

Archaeological studies are at their most significant when they attempt to elucidate the development of relations both amongst men, and between man and the material world. . . . Prehistoric archaeology is thus in its total aims not a natural science, a social science or a branch of the humanities; rather it is a distinctive pursuit in which all of these meet (Isaac 1971b: 123).

One of the objectives of this book will be to show that prehistoric archeology, at least, is a distinct discipline operating with a unique set of data that can be made to tell us about the development of humanity in the past through a set of interpretive techniques and integrative concepts specially combined and tailored for this task. At the same time we hasten to add that we are not attempting to build a wall around archeology but merely emphasizing its special characteristics.

PREHISTORY

We have used the term "prehistory" several times without explaining it. In the parts of the world where English is spoken it is usual to divide man's past into the historic and the prehistoric. If we define the historic past as that which has been recorded by writing, the prehistoric part is that which was not recorded by writing. The prehistorian, or archeologist, lacking the written records used by historians, must work with other artifacts that are usually uncovered through excavation.

The word "prehistoric" is so familiar and widely used that we might assume that the term has been in use for a very long time. This is not true, however; the first modern use of the word dates from just a little more than 100 years ago, in 1851, when Daniel Wilson used it in the title of his *The Archaeology and Prehistoric Annals of Scotland*. Somewhat earlier, in 1833, Tournal, proposed that the "Age of Man" could be divided into a "Prehistoric Period which extended from the time of man's appearance on the surface of the earth to the beginning of the most ancient traditions" and a "Historic Period which hardly dates beyond seven thousand years ago." T. Wilson (1899) wrote, in explanation, "Man may be assumed to be prehistoric wherever his chroniclings of himself are undesigned and his history is wholly recoverable by induction."

As a point of reference, history began about 3000 B.C., following the invention of writing somewhere in what is now modern southern Iraq. The language was Sumerian, and it was written in cuneiform on tablets of clay. The oldest tablets, those from Warka (Uruk) and from Jemdet Nasr, however, are pictographic (Fig. 1) and were hardly what we would call an effective medium of general communication. In fact, for several hundred years after its beginning, writing was used largely for keeping economic and administrative records. Full writing began around 2500 B.C. with the establishment of standardized signs and meanings. By 2000 B.C. most of Southwest Asia was

Fig. 1 Two sides of a clay tablet with pictographic signs found at Warka in southern Mesopotamia. Pictographs indicate people, things, and numbers and cannot be considered an effective form of general communication. (Redrawn from Falkenstein, *Archaische Texte aus Uruk*, 1936 Plate 10, No. 202.)

under the political influence of literate peoples. By contrast, England was prehistoric until the beginning of the Christian era, and because of the lack of readable pre-Columbian texts we must say that the prehistory of the American Indian ended only with the coming of Europeans in the sixteenth century A.D.

For practical purposes the line dividing prehistory from history is hard to define. Even in Southwest Asia, where writing began, only the major political centers were really within the sphere of literacy until fairly recently. Archeology is a major source of history in such places, even though the past several thousand years have been part of the historic era. If we stop to think about it, although written documents are the most important source of history, archeology can broaden our knowledge, even of the past in the United States. In recent years, for example, United States federal or state governmental agencies, or historical societies have investigated a great many sites occupied by non-Indians in the post-Columbian period.

As Deetz (1967:4) put it with regard to the colonists who landed at Plymouth,

> . . . no known historical documentation tells us exactly what animals were used for food by the Plymouth colonists, what types of dishes were used in the homes, when the first bricks were produced locally, or what types of nails, window frames or door hardware were used in constructing the houses. Archeological investigation of seventeenth-century house sites in Plymouth has given the answers to all these questions, fleshing out much of the bare bones of historical accounts.

Today information is recorded in diaries, books, magazines, newspapers, and official records, but still a vast amount goes unrecorded and will vanish from man's record unless it is recovered by a future archeologist. A hundred years ago, when paper was more costly and printing processes less mechanized, much more went unrecorded, and information that can supplement our written history still lies in the ground, awaiting an archeologist's interest. Thus archeology can contribute to knowledge of the whole of man's past; it need not stop where history begins.

To make the division of human history more precise, we can distinguish a period of protohistory. Protohistory is the study of peoples who were living after history began but who themselves did not have writing. When the

6

French coined the term *protohistoire*, however, they did not have the Australian aborigines or the Amazonian Indians in mind; they were concerned with peoples in western Europe, contemporary with, but not part of, the civilizations of the Mediterranean and Southwest Asia. Grahame Clark (1954) made a useful distinction in this regard when he described protohistory as "secondary prehistory," because it has to be studied with reference to the history of contemporary civilization. Archeology, which could be studied apart from civilization, was called "primary prehistory." By Clark's definition, this book is concerned with primary prehistory and the subject matter is world-wide.

HISTORY AND ARCHEOLOGY

Because archeology deals with man in the past, his culture seen in the perspective of time, it is natural to assume that archeologists have their closest intellectual relations with historians. For many, particularly European archeologists, this is true. The editor of *Antiquity*, Glyn Daniel (1967a: 170) states the matter forthrightly:

> We are all historians, we are all studying the past of man, whether we concentrate on Walpole, Beowulf, Stonehenge or Lascaux. Manuscripts, microliths, megaliths—it is all one. The past is the goal of the historian whether he is text aided or not . . . there are historians, in the strict sense of the word, who are frightened when they see archeologists advancing toward them with dirt on their boots and a brief case full of air photographs and Carbon 14 dates. Dugdale, Aubrey, Lhwyd and Stukeley did not think they were other than historians, and, for that matter, historians who could be members of the Royal Society. We have taken the distinction between a history that is mainly derived from material sources and one that is derived from the aid of texts, too far.

At the risk of belaboring a point, we should add that there are many ways of doing history, just as there are many ways of doing prehistory. At one extreme, the studies may be diametrically apart, although at the other they may share certain fundamental approaches. As we all know, history is concerned with more than a sequence of dates that denote events in the past; it is an ordering of knowledge about man's past into understandable contexts. In other words, history is an interpretation. In this very general sense, there are no grounds for differentiating between the goals of history and those of prehistory. Such differences as do exist seem to be based on the ways in which interpretations are made and in their presumed generality.

A much sharper distinction can be made between history and prehistory on the one hand, and humanism or antiquarianism on the other. Historians attempt to understand life in the past; humanists and antiquaries are concerned principally with objects, and especially in their esthetic value. An example of the differences comes readily to mind. A tourist who admires the

Obelisk of Luxor in the Place de la Concorde in Paris or, until it disappeared, the bust of Nefertiti in the Berlin Museum is not ordinarily experiencing a historical appreciation, nor were the persons responsible for placing these treasures far from their Egyptian context acting as archeologists or historians. Similarly, collections of arrowheads found in local museums contribute nothing to history unless the objects are placed in a human context. When objects —arrowheads or obelisks—are frankly placed to be admired in their own right, as objects, they have lost their historical value. As Dorothy Garrod has written (1946:27), "Man's tools are the instruments of his response to the world in which he lives, but they are much more—they are the weapons of his conquest of that world and the clue to its interpretation." Childe (1956:44–45) sees artifacts as the uniquely human means of satisfying the basic needs of securing food, shelter, and protection from enemies. In many museums, tools become works of art, and religious paraphernalia become treasures, all without value except their intrinsic worth or beauty. Mere collection and admiration of objects are not historical activities, for though they may deal with archeological remains, they stop short of cultural interpretation.

Archeologists trained in the United States often have little formal training in history and consequently feel little kinship toward these studies. Rather, they are ordinarily trained in general anthropology, the most inclusive of the various studies of man. In these departments, archeology is treated as a subfield of anthropology. We need not review all the reasons for this arrangement, but it should be noted that prehistorians usually deal with peoples whose closest living counterparts are studied by ethnologists. A liaison with ethnology and anthropology generally, rather than with history, is thus natural for archeologists who are prehistorians.

WHY STUDY ARCHEOLOGY?

Today many students question the worth of studying any particular subject and have even called into question the basic structure and rationale of education itself. Thus it is a fair question: "Why study archeology?" The question has been raised as well among archeologists themselves as we shall discuss later in this chapter. It has long been held that learning for its own sake is worthwhile, and there are many today who feel this is so. In this sense the study of archeology is no different from any of the scholarly disciplines, but there is something about it that makes it of more than esoteric interest. Grahame Clark (1970:4) in one of his characteristically perceptive essays expresses it well.

The study of prehistory stands in no more need of justification than exploration of the physical nature and mathematical properties of the universe, the investigation of all the multifarious forms of life, or for that matter the practice of the arts or the cultivation of speculative philosophy. Each in its own way enlarges the range of human experience and enriches the quality of human life.

Today when there is so much concern with the quality of life, these words are worth heeding, but there is more to it as G. Clark (1970:40–41) again says,

> Expressed in a sentence, the significance of world prehistory is the contribution it is able to make to widening the perspectives of history in accord with the needs of today. . . . Some concern with the past is basic to humanity itself in the sense that human groups are so constituted by virtue of inheriting specific traditions. The traditional lore shared by the members of particular societies served not only to heighten their sense of solidarity, but also to differentiate them from others in much the same way as do differences in plumage or song among birds.

Today we are witnessing a fractioning of the world into smaller and smaller national groups rather than into the larger political entities that were envisaged only a few decades ago. At the same time we are welding a technological and economic structure that is global in scope. The needs of the newly emerged nations to establish a cultural heritage along with their sense of participation in the oneness of humanity often can be accomplished solely through archeology, for in many parts of the world an indigenous history is only now beginning. In these situations, as G. Clark (1970:50–51) says,

> what we need, then, is anything but cultural nudity. On the contrary, we have to cultivate a reverence for the usages, history, and traditions of all peoples including our own—and not merely of all living peoples, but of all peoples who have ever lived. . . . Our survival depends on, among other things, our ability to view one another in a historical context appropriate to a world that shrinks in size and grows in potential danger with every passing year. History . . . is something which to a large degree determines how we behave. Let us view all histories and all prehistory in a world perspective; in honoring the achievements of our own and of all other peoples, we are after all acknowledging our own humanity.

As the historians of archeology (for example, Daniel 1971b) have rightly pointed out, we have been far too concerned with Europe and the influences of early civilizations in the Middle East. No less a figure than Gordon Childe was scarcely able to conceive of the indigenous cultures and civilizations of America, let alone those that flourished in other parts of the world. We badly need an education in world prehistory to place our own world in perspective, and this education can come about in many areas chiefly through archeology. Thus the value of studying archeology is hardly open to question, although one may correctly question the priorities that are given to different kinds of archeological projects.

Grahame Clark raised the issue of the role of tradition in the formation of modern cultures. To what extent does the past determine the present? Can we understand ourselves and others more acutely if we know the courses of events that led to today's world? That we can is certainly one of the principal tenets of both history and archeology, yet one finds the short-range view —essentially ahistorical—dominating most judgments. In this sense both archeologists and historians have failed to convey their messages, although the point is of fundamental importance.

Today there is a debate concerning the degree to which archeology can be scientific. Many argue that it should be, and a scientific approach would seem essential if we are to understand the processes in the past that led to the present orientation of cultures. The issues really are: What can we say with certainty? Are there principles of human behavior? Can we predict how people will behave given certain conditions? These and other questions are being raised by "New Archeologists," many of whom are concerned more with the general aspects of cultural development than with the particular details of any people's past. In any case, one can readily see that the interests of historically oriented scientists would be greatly aided by accurate statements of the processes that explain the historical development of a people or of peoples.

In the United States today, many question our national priorities, the direction of basic research, the uses to which the results of research are put, and the value of supporting specialist workers in a host of esoteric fields. In view of what we have said above, it should be clear that archeology does not fit neatly into a stereotype; it is done in many ways and may serve a multitude of purposes. Nevertheless, Fritz and Plog (1970:412) make a point that is valid for at least some archeological research when they say, "We suspect that unless archaeologists find ways to make their research increasingly relevant to the modern world, the modern world will find itself increasingly capable of getting along without archaeologists." This comment stands in sharp contrast with the optimism expressed by Grahame Clark and men of similar scholarly breadth and humanistic perspective, but it strikes a responsive chord in many of the restless and more narrowly specialized scholars in this country as well as with some of the public at large. In the future of archeology it is a factor to reckon with.

In our view the merit of archeology is that it can serve many purposes. It can produce for the aficionado objects of great beauty and grace; it can reveal the history of a people and of mankind; it can contribute toward an understanding of the present; and it may one day be used to test scientifically stated hypotheses about human behavior in general.

GOALS OF ARCHEOLOGY

There are different ways to look at the question of goals. We might consider the uses to which archeology may be put; the kinds of things that ought to be investigated; or the ways that archeology should be done, which would include the theoretical basis of archeology and the technical ways of doing it. To a large extent we must infer what the goals have been from the work that has been done, for goals change as our understanding of the past develops, as chance finds of great significance are discovered, and as techniques in ancillary fields are developed for application in prehistory.

P. Watson's (1972a) brief list is a resume of the uses to which archeology is put.

1. To furnish collectors' items and museum objects.
2. To furnish documentation for the study of art history or the history of architecture.
3. To attain knowledge of sequences of events and chronologies in the absence of written documents.
4. To help furnish data for much fuller historical studies (historiography, structural, or constructive history) with particularist/ideographic goals.
5. To furnish independent data that can be used to help test hypotheses . . . about cultural process; this has to do with generalizing/nomothetic goals and the general laws so confirmed provide us with understanding of history.

For the most part the first two goals cited by Watson pertain to classical and historic periods, and being largely self-evident, will not concern us here. It is toward the latter two goals that most prehistoric archeology is directed and about which there has been a considerable debate in recent years. Nearly everyone agrees that archeology can provide us with a kind of historical documentation of what happened in the past. Some may find this the central and most important goal of prehistory, but there are others who feel such activity is theoretically weak. Moreover they maintain that one can go much further—toward the explanation of prehistoric events rather than merely their chronicling.

"Archaeology ought to be what archaeology already is. The problem is how can we improve our ways of doing it" (Isaac 1971b:129). "Our aim now, surely, is to describe, as best we can with the material at our disposal at the time when we write, the life and times of prehistoric people" (Daniel 1971b:149). "One important goal is the explanation of particular events and processes in the past" (Watson, LeBlanc, and Redman 1971:171). "The understanding of past cultures, and the explanation of the differences and similarities found among them, is generally agreed to be the goal of anthropologically oriented archeology" (Watson, LeBlanc, and Redman 1971:ix). "Most will agree that the integrated field [of anthropology and archeology] is striving to explicate and explain the total range of physical and cultural similarities and differences characteristic of the entire spatial–temporal span of man's existence" (L. Binford 1962:217). "All archaeologists employ laws in their research. Those of us who are interested in processual analysis have made the formulation and testing of laws our goal" (Fritz and Plog 1970:405).

One might well recall Grahame Clark's thoughts: we must examine the past to understand how leading archeologists have arrived at such varied views of the goals of their field. Chapter 2 does this in outline form and our discussion of New Directions in Archeology in Chapter 2 likewise helps put this debate in perspective.

There should be no doubt in the reader's mind that most archeologists are concerned, as Daniel said, with describing the life and times of prehistoric peoples. This is now and always has been a central concern of prehistory, and it is certainly the foundation upon which it will continue to build in the future whether it reconstructs culture histories or tests hypotheses of lawlike generality. It should also be clear that the goals of archeology are in many ways similar to those of anthropology, except that archeologists deal with long spans of time and frequently encounter situations that are unique and unavailable for study in the laboratory of modern cultures.

With this discussion of general goals in mind it will now be useful to illustrate these points by referring to some of the kinds of projects that are now being carried out. This brief review illustrates the central concern with history among prehistorians and also suggests to students the opportunities for participating in archeology.

TYPICAL ARCHEOLOGICAL STUDIES

Sites

In the popular view each archeologist has his site or his notable discovery, but this is more characteristic of those who excavate enormous historic sites with their monumental tombs and architecture than it is of prehistorians who often devote their careers to digging and interpreting the remains of hunters and gatherers or simple villagers. Still, the excavation and interpretation of sites is at the core of archeology and is regarded by many as a goal in itself, for it is in the analysis of a site that one brings to bear all the aspects of archeological theory and technique. The excavation of a site provides the raw material of prehistory, but it also serves as the principal means for the training of students. The reasons for excavating a particular site will, in consequence, range from the role it is presumed to play in a key historical or theoretical problem to its value in teaching techniques of digging and methods of analysis.

Regional Studies

In contrast with the excavation of one site, which may occupy the attentions of archeologists over several generations (for example, the great mounds at Cahokia near St. Louis or some of the major cities in Southwest Asia) and become a focal point of vigorous and intensive research, are the more general regional surveys coupled with limited excavation. Although the layman usually thinks of the site and the dig and identifies an archeologist with it, professionals recognize the need for the more general areal overviews as well. Indeed the basis for intelligent work on any particular site depends a great deal on knowledge of its place among other sites and in its relationship to geographic features.

The overview may require extended fieldwork with very little return in objects for museums or even in immediate publication, and partly for these reasons the tendency has been to avoid it. However, in recent years there has come a growing appreciation of the importance of knowing patterns of settlement and of understanding them in relation to the social and physical environment of the prehistoric peoples (see Chap. 18).

Although we find the broad regional approaches increasingly popular, they are not new. What is new is the systematic manner in which they are now being carried out. Universities as part of their teaching programs, museums to augment collections of local culture, and to a lesser extent, amateur archeological societies sometimes set as their goal the discovery of the archeological resources of their state or region. During the Depression years extensive work of this kind was carried out by the Federal government, although the goals then were as much to provide jobs for the unemployed as to reveal prehistory. The effect, nonetheless, was to provide a corpus of systematically collected data about a region. Much of this work remains unpublished even today, although it has provided the basis of a number of regional surveys and is available for study.

In principle, regional studies set out to discover and record all the sites in an area. Follow-up work may include excavation of important sites in the attempt to build a coherent sequential picture of prehistorical occupation. Often there is little urgency to such survey, and it is not necessarily keyed to future excavation.

The selection of an area to survey may be carefully considered in advance with relation to a problem that interests a particular researcher, but often regional studies are simply carried out near where archeologists live or where there is a suitable supply of students or other manpower. The point is that regional studies, while they are of great importance in archeology, may be carried out with definite, problem-oriented goals, or they may simply be thought of as taking advantage of a local opportunity. (Further discussion of these matters is in Chap. 8.)

Salvage Archeology

In the past few decades there has been an increasing awareness that something ought to be done to rescue archeological sites from the onslaughts of modern construction. In the United States, where dams and highways are being built, responsible agencies frequently appropriate money to salvage the sites that will be covered with water or otherwise obliterated. Salvage archeology is a special and relatively modern example of archeology, but it is not entirely new. As early as 1627, Charles I of England officially declared that "the study of antiquities . . . is very serviceable to the general good of the State and Commonwealth." And positive action was being taken to preserve sites a hundred years ago in Britain when a Roman amphitheater was successfully saved from destruction because it stood in a railroad right-of-way. In 1899, when the Aswan Dam was built by British engineers, the proposed water level was reduced by 55 feet in order not to submerge the island of Philae with its magnificent stone temple (Ward 1900:256). This is one of the earliest examples of consideration being paid to archeological sites threatened by great engineering projects. The spate of dam-building in the United States in the past 35 years has inevitably led to the submergence of thousands of prehistoric archeological sites. Despite the concern of federal authorities over this loss and their efforts to recover materials, much more has been lost than learned. Regional archeological histories will forever be deficient to the extent that information was not obtained while there was still time.

Salvage archeology is usually based on the premise that some work is better than no work. As a result, certain methods are often used that would not be considered proper on more leisurely excavations. In many areas, salvage archeology has been the only systematic investigation, and it has contributed knowledge of enormous value. In this respect its methods should be emulated, but in two ways salvage archeology runs counter to practices that will be advocated here. First, salvage archeologists must be indiscriminate and take the sites as they come; it is not possible to be very selective on a rescue operation. Salvage archeologists must often set aside their scholarly interests in problems of their own devising for the general good of future archeology. Second, salvage archeologists working under the pressure of time may be forced to ignore many of the refined techniques of modern archeology. The resultant loss in information is offset by the fact that at least something was saved.

At the same time, we owe a great deal to salvage archeologists who, working under pressure, have developed techniques for survey and excavation that make even the normally paced digs easier. But perhaps their most important contributions have been to demonstrate the value of really intensive studies of whole areas and to illustrate the techniques and value of sampling sites. As was true of the River Basin surveys, where approximately 20,000 sites were found, it is possible to gain an accurate picture only through the use of sampling techniques to select sites for excavation that have a good prospect of being representative.

Ethnic History

It is often the more glamorous digs uncovering spectacular tombs or skeletons of early forms of men that capture the attention and imaginations of the public, but relatively little archeology is actually devoted to these ends. For the most part archeologists have shown a strong interest in tracing the paths taken by cultures, and when these paths approach the present, names of peoples can be attached to the archeological remains. Out of this we find a growing interest in ethnic history, or the history of a particular people. Indeed it is correct to say that recently archeology in some countries has been encouraged precisely to serve as an adjunct to history. In this sense it is national pride and ethnic identity that is served. Grahame Clark (1957:256–261) has discussed the interest in archeology displayed by the newly liberated countries of Europe following the First World War, and a similar interest is rapidly emerging in many of the world's developing nations. In consequence of this sense of nationalism, officials in some countries discourage "foreigners" from digging, feeling that the local prehistory belongs chiefly to the people who live in the country.

Ethnoarcheology has some decided advantages in that one starts from the present and works back in time, using such historic records as are available, with the keen appreciation of the local culture that only a native ethnographer or historian can have. Work of this kind is common in the United States whether we deal with Indians or early Anglo settlers. Incidentally, one of the side effects of the concern over ecology, especially the depletion of our natural resources, has been the stimulus to do historic archeology lest all tangible traces of our own ancestors be swept into spoil heaps or paved with asphalt.

A reaction to this kind of archeology has emerged in some areas including the United States where groups of American Indians are expressing their concern over what they feel to be the violation of the graves and living spots of their ancestors. Some Indians have attempted to prevent digging; however, most archeologists have felt it important to conduct scientific examination of Indian prehistory. Whatever the ethical merits of either side, the legality of the issues is being examined anew. Usually legal restrictions on disturbance of the dead cover only the remains of known persons or of bodies lying in marked graves, but efforts are being made in some areas to extend this protection to older aboriginal sites and native cemeteries.

Although some archeological studies may be stalled in the immediate future through moral suasion and legal means, it is safe to say that in the future more archeological attention will be paid to relatively recent remains and to remains that are relevant to a current sense of heritage than has been true in the past. For a perceptive discussion of what archeology means in today's world, see Pallottino's book (1968).

Key Problems in Human History

Although most archeology has been focused on single sites or relatively small areas, there have been some notable large-scale efforts to gain an understanding of the crucial turning points in man's history, which transcend modern cultural and geographic boundaries. These projects have a central theme and are carried out by investigators who, although they may or may not be working closely together in the integration of their separate projects, are nevertheless working on a well-defined problem of considerable generality. Two examples come readily to mind: the recent work by multinational teams of workers into the origins of man which has ranged from Africa to India with the most intensive work now being done in East Africa, and the investigation of the origins of agriculture that has been carried out in considerable detail in Southwest Asia and Mesoamerica.

One notable aspect of these projects is that they have included multi-disciplinary teams of scientists from the start and have achieved in the process a level of cooperation and mutual stimulation among the specialists that is unusual in archeology. Research teams have begun to replace the traditional one-man operation that has characterized and still characterizes much of archeology. Second, these projects have sought explanations for the crucial changes in human history. These explanations have tended to be phrased in terms of ecology: in the systematic interplay between man as a biological and cultural being and the physical and social environment in which he finds himself and to which he must adapt.

A similarly interesting problem, which has worldwide examples and consequently wide appeal, is the emergence of urbanism and the factors that gave rise to it. This is a subject that has attracted historians and philosophers as well as archeologists, but it is only now being investigated systematically in the field, which is surprising in view of the great amount that has been written to suggest the possible factors accounting for the phenomenon. Now that work on these problems is being carried out in earnest, it is apparent that the range of factors which may account for the developments is exceptionally broad; however there appear to be some that are more crucial than others. To determine this it was necessary to have constant interaction among the specialists, each working on his own facet of the problem but aware of the overall goals. The merit of this cooperative effort is seen in the wealth of new ideas that are expressed in print each year and in the way fundamental conceptions have changed. One sees a convergence of opinion on the methods of procedure, and it is conceded that the goal of understanding these major changes in mankind is within reach, once sufficient well-conceived and implemented projects have been carried out.

Perhaps one of the most remarkable aspects of these studies is that there has never been one person in charge of all the work, though it is easy to point to leaders who gave the initial stimulus and achieved some of the first important successes. It has been the challenge of intellectually interesting projects and the well-defined methods of approach that have attracted specialists out of various backgrounds into the common cause, resulting in exceptionally rapid attainment of important objectives. It is in these projects too that one can most readily find examples of the interplay between ideas, fieldwork, and experiment, together with innovation in analysis. In short, in these projects it has been the attractiveness of the problem rather than the lure of a particular site or regional history that has drawn specialists together, and in such team-oriented studies the melding of old and new archeology will be most effectively expressed in the years to come.

Testing Hypotheses

In Chapter 2 we discuss the theoretical interests that have spurred some of the most recent attempts to test hypotheses, but before we begin that discussion, we should recognize that archeologists have long gone into the field with an idea they want to test. Such ideas may be relatively simple or complex: the stratigraphic relationships among different groups of artifacts, the geographic regions where agriculture first took hold, or the role of irrigation in the origins of civilization. What is crucial today is the explicit statement of the relationship between theory and archeological data; that is, the setting up of an appropriate research design so that the results, like those from a good experiment, give definitive answers.

Some research may be directed solely toward the testing of an hypothesis, but it is much more common for this aspect of the work to be incorporated into the larger context of more purely historical interests. Thus we find a few instances of large-scale, nominally cooperative projects in which each investigator pursues his own interests but contributes as well to an overall goal of hypothesis-testing. The lead in these kinds of studies has been taken in the American Southwest where scholars who call themselves the Southwest Archeological Group plan to meet annually to frame hypotheses and to devise test implications that can be carried out by the various members in their own areas during their summer field sessions. Following the fieldwork the group plans to reconvene to discuss the results and then devise further projects for the next summer of work (Gumerman 1971).

Such an approach has the merit of incorporating the collective expertise and ideas of the members and the recycling of results immediately after the work has been completed. In this sense the group has achieved a more effective integration between members and more feedback between hypotheses and results than any other projects we have mentioned. Although there is no designated head of the group, an effective consensus as to approaches and methods is achieved through the regular meetings.

The Southwest Archeological Group has not been in operation long enough to have published substantial results, but we can mention some older explicit attempts to test hypotheses. One such hypothesis concerns dating by means of changes in artifacts. Brainerd (1951:304) states the theory that "each type [of artifact] originates at a given time at a given place, is made in gradually increasing numbers as times goes on, then decreases in popularity until it becomes forgotten, never to recur in an identical form." From this theory and from considerable data archeologists have deduced that there is a directional change (for example, from simple to complex) in the artifacts from any particular archeological sequence.

> It follows that each period is characterized both by its unique assemblage of artifacts and by the relative frequency with which each type of artifact occurs. . . . Hence, presence or absence and relative abundance of artifacts are two tools with which one can work in seriation . . . , [and] sites showing the greatest degree of agreement either in the occurrence of artifacts or in their frequencies will lie closest in time (Hole and Shaw 1967:4).

Most archeologists accepted the theory as fact and proceeded to carry out elaborate seriations of their data, thus presumably arranging them chronologically. What had not been done, however, was to test the theory against material of known age and with artifacts of different kinds. Critics of seriation were correct in saying that any data will seriate and there may be many reasons for changes in artifacts not related to the passage of time.

To test the hypothesis that seriation is a useful and accurate tool, Hole and Shaw used data from a well-stratified, long archeological sequence in which the chronological order of the material was known. They then seriated these data using various methods that had been proposed and found that in the test case some artifacts (most notably pottery) seriated very well while others (like flint tools) did not. Moreover, they found that some methods of seriation work better than others. Future studies can now build on these results and perhaps test some of their implications.

Another example of the testing of hypotheses is the study done by Robert McC. Adams (1962) of the relation between irrigation and the emergence of urban civilization in Southwest Asia. The hypothesis was that societies with complex administrative hierarchies arose in response to the need to organize and administer irrigation projects. What Adams found to the contrary was that complex societies arose long before the irrigation systems had developed to the point that they required elaborate administration. Although this point is disputed by some authors (Sanders and Price 1968) dealing with other areas, it appears to hold for Southwest Asia, and only similar testing in Middle America will tell whether the situation was the same there.

Experiments

A very wide range of studies may be considered experimental, but most of them fall into the category of "imitative experiments . . . in which matter is shaped and used, in a manner simulative of the past" (Ascher 1961a). Rather than using archeological materials directly, experimenters try to duplicate artifacts or archeologically known effects. Of these there are a great many examples. Another kind of experimentation is to examine the ways of modern peoples for the information this gives on how the tangible artifacts prehistorians may find relate to cultural behavior.[3] A third general type of experimentation is simulation in which one builds a model that is like a prehistoric situation in certain crucial respects and then allows the model to run through time so that the effects of different conditions built into the model can be observed.

Imitative experiments are the easiest to understand, and lend themselves to participation by almost anyone. They are especially useful as classroom exercizes. The best known such work concerns the methods by which prehistoric peoples made their stone artifacts (Graham and others 1972). Except for the making of gun flints and some use of stone tools by peoples in remote parts of the world today, the arts of chipping stone had nearly died out until some investigators began systematic studies. In this country the work of Don Crabtree at the Idaho State Museum has been particularly significant because he has been able to duplicate, after several decades of experimentation, the process by which Indians made fluted points. One may wonder how this information was lost because Indians were chipping flints when the first European colonists arrived, but by that time the arts of fluting had disappeared among even the Indians, as the use of bows and arrows had long since replaced spears and darts. Nevertheless, Crabtree found the decisive clue to the process from a historical record—from a Spanish priest who witnessed Aztec Indians making long knife blades from obsidian. Adapting the technique described—pressing a blade from the obsidian core with a t-shaped "crutch" placed against the chest to deliver pressure to a precise point on the edge of the obsidian core—Crabtree was at last able to remove the fine channel flakes from the bases of Folsom points. Since that discovery other modifications of the method have been developed. Figure 2 shows one such being carried out by Bruce Bradley, a student who worked with Crabtree.

In Europe the foremost flint knapper is François Bordes (1969), who is proficient in making most of the tools used by man in the various stages of the Paleolithic, using techniques for which there is absolutely no historical knowledge. As well as providing interesting data on the history of technology and laying to rest much fruitless speculation about how long it took to make tools, such work has been of great aid both in understanding the variation among tools and in the correct interpretation of the chipping waste that is found in most ancient sites.

Coupled with these imitative experiments are those that attempt to determine the uses to which the tools were put by examining wear patterns. To some degree this is an analytic technique, and to some degree experimentation, for one can only interpret the cause of wear if an experiment can be devised that will produce it. For example, experiments to produce the characteristic glossy sheen on the edges of flint sickles have been made from time to time over many years. It was the commonly held assumption that silica occurring naturally in the stems of grains and grasses polished the edges of the implements during prolonged use. Witthoft, who had been exposed to the phenomenon of a glaze appearing on the edge of a steel scythe during his youth, was unconvinced of the accuracy of the usual interpretation, because steel and flint are both harder than silica and could therefore not have been polished by it. Optical examination of the edges of sickles showed that abrasion was not the cause of the sheen, and examination of the cortex and fibers of the plants showed that silica was not the agent; rather, it was opal. His studies concluded "it results from frictional fusion of flint and dehydration and fusion of opal to flint surfaces. Thus the term corn gloss, originally used to describe polish on flint sickle-edges, seems especially appropriate" (Witthoft 1967:388).

Other kinds of experiments are being carried out with sites themselves in order to determine how they were built and what they mean in terms of the activities of the people. In the latter instance, one can work with modern situations as did Kim with a village near Seoul, South Korea. There he investigated the formation of a midden (refuse dump) in a modern rural

Fig. 2 (*top*) Bruce Bradley demonstrating a method of making obsidian blades, using a clamp to hold the obsidian core and an antler flaker to press off the blades. When the blades spring from the core they fall onto a rabbit skin. A pile of blades lies in front of the skin.

(*bottom*) Bradley demonstrating a method of pressure flaking, using an antler flaker on the edge of an obsidian biface.

community and compared its contents with the known ethnographic situation over a period of some 50 years, during which time there had been three major changes in the cultures that impinged on the inhabitants. His study is intended to focus on four points:

(1) the ratio of shards to utensils made of other materials found in the dump compared to the ratio in use in the community; (2) the ratio of unusual to common pottery types in the dump contrasted with the ratio in use in the community; (3) a theoretical reconstruction of the history and circumstances of the accumulation of the dump tested against the data obtained through community study; and (4) the significance of stratification as determined by the history of the community and reconstruction by the excavation team (Kim 1966:378).

The value of such a study will be readily appreciated by archeologists, who depended on samples of artifacts derived from middens for their reconstructions of the typical pattern of occurrence in an actual village.

A much more ambitious and long-term experiment is the construction (Ashbee and Cornwall 1961) in 1960 and the subsequent observation of the experimental earthwork on Overton Down, Wiltshire, England. The intent was "to study the changes which take place with time in a bank and ditch, and in selected materials buried within the bank" (Dimbleby 1965). After only four years, significant archeological implications had been derived, although the experiment is expected to run up to 128 years with partial excavation at regular intervals.

Working directly with modern peoples for the light their practices may shed on prehistory has become a current focus of research. Although ethnographic analogy (see Chap. 16) has long been standard procedure among prehistorians, it was used chiefly as an aid in the identification of objects found in the ground. Today the research is directed more toward the way archeological remains relate to things like social organization, burial practices, and particular activities. A recent issue of *World Archaeology* (1971) was devoted to the topic, archeology and ethnography. From that issue the article by Nicholas David is particularly apposite in the present context. David begins with the statement,

That a degree of fit exists between households and their domestic buildings is an ethnographic fact and an assumption necessary for the reconstruction of past social organization. . . . In this paper I attempt to demonstrate the fit that exists between compounds at the village of Be on the Mayo (River) Kebbi (N. Cameroon) and their settled Fulani inhabitants, and go on to discuss the problem facing the archaeologist who wishes to crack their building code (David 1971:111).

David's study was basically ethnographic in that he resided in the community and was able to determine the kinship of the people, their residence patterns, and activities, along with the tangible artifacts and remains that related to these practices. To augment his analysis he drew a map of the settlement and from this, another that shows only remains that would be potentially recoverable archeologically. He then invites the reader to try to interpret the significance of these remains much as an archeologist would try to interpret the plan of features at a site he has dug. The exercise, in other words, is not sterile but rather an important example of the kind of reasoning that every fieldworker goes through.

Much of David's paper is an explanation of the actual ethnographically known circumstances of the village. He then makes the point that it would be impossible for archeologists to make accurate interpretations of some of the features, though not of others. To cite a simple example of the failure of common sense expectation to be borne out, "wealth was never expressed in hut size." Rather he found hut size a function of "expected frequency of white ant infestation" (David 1971:126–127). "When a roof might be eaten in six months or less, the smaller the hut, and thence the roof, the easier it is to replace."

More complicated kinds of interpretations may lead to even greater imprecision.

> Even in the test case, doubly unreal since the rules were known and every-thing preservable and not easily portable was left without disturbance, impre-cisions, and ambiguities inherent in the data made accurate deductions of household groupings impossible or at least not unequivocally demonstrable. How much more so when a site is not protected by clean sand, but has been eroded, built over, pitted and plundered by later occupants, and tunnelled by rodents? (David 1971:128).

A study like David's provides a sobering appraisal, through "testing" a modern situation, of how much one can hope to infer from archeological remains. One should not, however, despair that any interpretation can be made. Rather his study provides us with a set of solid data to use in judging how far we may allow interpretations to go, and it extends our range of useful information concerning reasons houses may be of a certain size and duration, to cite only one example given by David.

Further removed from tangible reality than the cases cited above are the simulation experiments. This technique has been widely used in many fields of science and is coming into more general use for problems in social science where large populations and long times are involved. Of primary importance is the fact that such simulations are abstract models based on mathematics and are designed to operate with relatively few variables, largely because of the extraordinary mathematical difficulty of incorporating all possi-bly relevant variables and because of the difficulty in assigning a quantitative value to variables. Nevertheless, one may examine such single factors as popula-tion increase and its effects on demographic pattern. Such an example is given by Ammerman and Cavalli-Sforza (1972a) where they postulate that the spread of agricultural peoples because of increasing population (demic expansion) may be likened to a "wave of advance" that will progress radially at a constant rate. The authors contrast the wave of advance with colonization which could also be considered a result of population growth. In order to test which of the two hypotheses is correct in the instance of the spread of farming peoples into Europe, they needed to be able to plot the times at which farming peoples arrived at successively more distant points from the presumed origin. Thus they were able to plot points on the wave front to the center of diffusion and thereby estimate the radius of the wave front at various times. When they plotted these distances against time, if their wave of advance model were correct, the radius of the wave front should have varied linearly with time. This was found to be the case within the limitations of the data presently available.

The importance of the experiment lies not only in an explanation of the process by which Europe was colonized, but also in the deductions that may be made from using this model about other matters such as population densities at different places and times, or the genetic composition of populations involved in the spread. In short, while it has not been adequately tested as yet, and does not completely exclude other factors, the model has suggested a strong hypothesis to account for the process of population expansion and has provided some corollary hypotheses to test with archeological data.

We have seen how experimentation in archeology may take many forms and provide an opportunity for students having a wide variety of talents and interests to contribute to the field in ways that are not usually thought to be traditional. Indeed, it seems likely that much of the future of archeology will be closely linked with advances made through experimentation.

REFERENCES

General Works about Archeology: Bibby 1956; Binford 1962, 1965; Brion 1959; Caldwell 1966; R. Carpenter 1933; Casson 1939; Ceram 1958; Chang 1967a; Childe 1947, 1953a, 1956, 1962; G. Clark 1954, 1970; Cottrell 1957; Crawford 1953; Daniel 1950, 1959, 1962; Daux 1948; Deetz 1967; Fagan 1972; Gabel 1964; Gorenstein 1965; C. Hawkes 1957; Heizer 1959; Hudson 1967; Kenyon 1961; de Laet 1957; Laming-Emperaire 1963; Marek 1964; Meighan 1966; Müller-Karpe 1966; Piggot 1951, 1959a; T. Powell 1951; Pyddoke 1964; Robbins and Irving 1965; Sandars 1951; Silverberg 1966; W. Taylor 1948; Watts 1965; Wheeler 1956; Willey and Phillips 1958; Woolley 1953, 1959.

History and Archeology: Bagby 1963; Childe 1953b; Daniel 1967b; Finley 1971; Garrod 1946; Grimes 1954; Griffiths 1956; T. Jones 1967; Kroeber 1957a; McNeal 1972.

Goals of Archeology: R. Adams 1968; Binford 1962, 1965; Flannery 1967a; Hole 1972a; Longacre 1964; Swartz 1967; Trigger 1970; Willey and Phillips 1958.

Regional Studies: R. Adams 1965; Daniel 1955; Wauchope 1966; Willey 1953; Journals of local or state archeological societies; G. Daniel, ed., Ancient Peoples and Places Series.

Salvage Archeology: Brew 1961a, 1961b; H. Davis 1972; Heizer 1966; F. Johnson 1966; T. King 1971; McGimsey 1972; Petsche 1968; Wendorf 1962.

Historical Archeology (Ethnic History): Bennyhoff and Elsasser 1954; Cotter 1958; Fontana 1965; J. Harrington 1952, 1955; Hudson 1971; Toulouse 1949; Treganza 1956; Wertenbaker 1953.

Key Problems: Braidwood and Howe 1960; Hole and Flannery 1968; Hole, Flannery, and Neely 1969; MacNeish 1958, 1967a.

Some Examples of Experimental Archeology: Ammerman and Cavalli-Sforza 1972a and b; R. Ascher 1961a; Ashbee and Cornwall 1961; Bordes 1969, 1972; H. Bowen 1967; Childe 1937–1938; Coghlan 1940; Cosner 1951; Crabtree and Davis 1968; Curwen 1930; Cushing 1894; David 1971, 1972; Dethlefson and Deetz 1966; Dimbleby 1965; H. H. Ellis 1940; Eppel 1958; Farmer 1939; Harlan 1967; Harner 1956; Haury 1931; W. Hill 1937; Hole and Shaw 1967; Hough 1897; Isaac 1967; Iversen 1956; Jewell 1961; Jewell and Dimbleby 1966; T. Johnson 1957; Jorgensen 1953; Kim 1966; D. King 1966; Knowles 1944; Kragh 1951; Laudermilk and Kennard 1938; Lechtman 1971; Leechman 1950; Longacre and Ayres 1968; Lovett 1877; Lowery, Savage, and Wilkins 1971; McEwen 1946; McGuire 1891; Matson 1971; Neill 1952; Newcomer 1971; Nylander 1967; Outwater 1957; Pond 1930; Puleston 1971; C. Reed 1962; Ryder 1966, 1969; Semenov 1964; T. Shaw 1970; G. Smith 1891; Sonnenfeld 1962; Speth 1972; Squier 1953; Steele 1930; Steensberg 1943; Treganza and Valdivia 1955; T. Wilson 1898; T. Wiltshire 1859–1863; Witthoft 1967.

CHAPTER TWO

THE STRUCTURE
AND PROCESS
OF ARCHEOLOGY

Doing Archeology

"The Romance of Archeology" is a well-known phrase that sums up the attitude of many laymen about the field. How often are archeologists approached
at a social gathering by a bright-eyed questioner who says, "Oh Doctor, so
you're an archeologist! I don't know anything about archeology, but I would
surely love to do some." One can infer from these remarks, and from opinions
expressed by our colleagues, that most archeologists have fun digging. What
is ordinarily not pointed out, however, is that the archeologist enjoys what
he is doing in spite of a lot of unpleasant circumstances. The fact is that most
field work is rather physically hard on a person, and not a few workers have
suffered mental and emotional problems as a result of the physical and social
conditions of a field camp.

> There *is* a romance in digging, but for all that it is a trade wherein long
> periods of steady work are only occasionally broken by a sensational dis-
> covery, and even then the real success of the season depends, as a rule, not
> on the rare "find" that loomed so large for the moment, but on the information
> drawn with time and patience out of a mass of petty detail which the days'
> routine little by little brought to light and set in due perspective (Woolley
> 1932:1–2).

The accounts in the mass media usually stress the exotic setting of a
field camp, the hardships of chopping through a jungle or facing the desert

25

sands, and the story concludes with a major and valuable discovery, visible the moment it emerges from the earth. Nothing could be farther from the truth. The romance lies not in these spectacular ways. It lies, as John Platt (1962) says, in the excitement of science: the thrill of following out a chain of reasoning for oneself. The excitement of doing archeology is thus basically the same as the excitment of doing any science. Archeologists, like other scientists, have fun carrying out their research.

Doing archeology involves much more than fieldwork and much more than ordinarily meets the eye. In many respects doing archeology is like doing research in any field, but there are important differences along with the similarities. In order to make these matters clear we shall briefly review the process of archeology which is similar to any scientific research, and then discuss some of the factors that make archeological research inherently difficult. Our intent is not to make it appear that archeology is impossible to do but to give students a basis for appraising the field today and to stimulate innovations that will correct some of the problems.

Archeology is a process of taking and interpreting data from the ground so that they become a part of human history. As a process it is a logically ordered sequence of events that begins with a question or a problem and seeks its answer or solution. "What happened?" and "Why did it happen?" are the questions that impel most archeological research and ultimately provide the basis for the logical structure of research and interpretation.

As in any scientific field, archeological research is cyclic in the sense that it begins with the conception of a problem, seeks a method of investigating it, carries out the necessary fieldwork and analysis, and finally presents an interpretive report of the results. The results themselves frequently suggest new questions or problems and thus the cycle is ready to be repeated. The essential point is that one project should build on the results of the last so that research becomes cumulative. With this in mind we should say emphatically that one cannot know where he is going if he does not know where he has been. In any research the clues to the future are to be found in the past; we can only build effectively if we know our foundations.

The problems of knowing our foundations in archeology are manifold for a number of reasons having to do with the time it takes to complete research and with the nature of archeological interpretations. It serves no useful purpose to gloss over the problems inherent in archeology because they must be overcome ultimately if the discipline is to advance. It is probably true that most research in any field is at least partially inefficient, and although the point has been little stressed, it is a major problem in archeology (Hole 1972a).

The inefficiency lies in the fact that digging itself is time-consuming, in that the analysis of data is often difficult, requiring various specialized techniques, and in that interpretation may be subject to gross errors because the data have no evident modern counterparts. To determine what they are and what they mean is thus a matter of intuition and skillful use of scientific testing (see Part V for a full discussion of these matters). Add to this the problems of writing, editing, and publishing a monograph on the results, and we find that the entire cycle of even a relatively small project may have taken several years. Under less than optimum conditions a decade or more may pass before the work is completed and available to scholars. This is inefficient because in the time that has elapsed between the excavation and the publication other archeologists have been unable to build on the results.

The inefficiency of archeology can also be related to the way it is usually done. Until very recently most projects were carried out almost exclusively by one person who attempted to provide the scientific, administrative, technical, and editorial skills himself. With the advent of innovations in technical studies and in the broadening conceptions of what one may get out of the ground, it has become physically impossible for one person to master let alone carry out all the necessary tasks. Thus we are entering into an era of greater specialization that will affect the entire structure of archeological research.

The necessity of specialization has been emphasized, at least indirectly, in the writings of "new archeology." More explicitly it has been discussed in important articles by Stuart Struever (1968c, 1971). Nevertheless, the message has been only slowly accepted, perhaps in part because, as Struever pointed out, the academic structure under which archeology is usually carried out works against large, integrated research teams. Additionally it may relate to the teaching of archeology which has stressed general rather than particular skills and the integration of all aspects of the field rather than technical expertise in any one part. If the implications of Struever's article are acted upon, however, we may expect to find some shift in the way archeology is taught (Hole 1972a).

Since most archeology is supported by universities, museums, state governments, and various national governmental agencies, all of which have passed general budget cuts on to archeology in the past several years, it seems unlikely there will be any major growth in individual departments and laboratories of archeology in the near future. Nevertheless, the decade of the sixties saw an unprecedented number of archeologists trained, many of whom simply cannot find the support for a dig of their own. In effect, we have a relative overpopulation which may very well lead to the younger archeologists' choosing to develop their skills more highly in some aspect of the field so that they can contribute to work on a major excavation. If this is true we can predict a much more rapid development of archeology and a dramatic rise in the efficiency with which it is done.

Archeology is so diverse that it can accommodate students with many interests and talents. Nevertheless, the archeological curriculum is relatively standardized and in America is usually considered a part of general anthropological training. In many respects this is fortunate, for it exposes students to a worldwide perspective of cultures that he can use for analogy with prehistoric situations and to the general theories of human behavior that are relevant to an interpretation of archeological remains. In other respects, however, the training is unfortunate in that it is rather diffuse and ordinarily lacking in many of the details of archeology that are necessary for the practicing prehistorian in his research. And finally, while we have excelled in training persons with a general anthropological perspective, we have paid scarcely any attention to historical and humanistic studies that are thought by some to be equally important. Thus we find that few students can acquire expert knowledge of any of the technical fields that contribute so importantly to prehistoric research. To be sure, none of these strictures pertains to all graduates, but they are typical. To be realistic we should recognize that graduate training must have some limits and that a person can gain knowledge of areas lacking in his formal training through self-study. It would be impractical to try to teach everything.

The aim of graduate training in archeology is usually to prepare a person to teach and do research. For the former, the broad background is desirable, and for the latter, expert knowledge of an area of prehistory is essential. Perhaps at best we can hope for graduates to have the necessary background to carry out intensive self-directed studies in both of these areas after they receive their Ph.D.s. In fact, most of us remain students all our lives, continually reading, analyzing, and synthesizing, impressed less by what we know than by what we can learn.

If this is a fair statement of how archeology is taught and learned in the United States, it means that the deliberate and conscious learning of technical skills is left more to the initiative of the individual than to his professors. Consider the kinds of skills that are necessary to bring an excavation to its effective conclusion. The following outline merely lists the skills by the job title that ordinarily describes them (Hole 1972a).

Jobs Required to Carry Out an Archeological Project

Scientific
  theoretician
  integrator
  evaluator

Fieldwork
  dirt archeologist
  stratigrapher
  detective
  photo interpreter
  explorer

Ancillary Scientific
  botanist
  ethnologist
  geographer
  geologist
  palynologist
  zoologist

Editorial
  writer
  editor
  layout and design

Administrative
  executive director
  expeditor
  foreman
  politician
  secretary
  accountant

Analytic
  research assistant
  statistician
  computer programmer

Technical
  surveyor
  draftsman
  photographer
  restorer
  carpenter
  machine operator
  mechanic

To master any of the jobs outlined above requires both talent and training. Neither in assessing the talents required for these jobs nor in their teaching have graduate schools in the United States excelled. Partly for this reason we find reports which describe exciting research that has been executed with marked lack of skill, or we find reports which are poorly written, badly illustrated, or lacking the ancillary studies that would have made them meaningful in a broader context. The shortage of people who can do the necessary things with skill is apparent at every turn.

One need have little prescience to recognize the need for technical training. In the United States it has been customary for students to seek the Ph.D. degree with the end of taking a teaching job at a college or university. We have paid relatively little attention to training persons to do the technical jobs in archeology. Part of the reason no doubt stems from the fact that most archeology is carried out by persons associated with universities. These persons are also expected to teach. In such an academic structure there is little room for technical specialists, perhaps with B.A. or M.A. degrees, who can work in support of, but not in charge of, research. Yet if we look at a typical laboratory in engineering or in chemistry, we find glassblowers, electricians, machinists, laboratory technicians, and the like in some abundance. Research in many fields would be unthinkable without these persons working as part of a team. In archeology we have usually met these needs by using students, cooperative but usually overbusy professors, and on occasion, interested amateurs or persons associated with private industry. No wonder much archeology is inefficient and innovation slow.

Only rarely does one find an archeological research organization—like the United States National Museum (Smithsonian), the University of Pennsylvania, and perhaps a few other places in the United States—that can boast access to the necessary specialists within the institution itself, let alone within one set of cooperating laboratories.

The solution to the problem is obvious, but it will require a restructuring of popular conceptions of what archeology is and how it is done. Perhaps the university is not the place to initiate research laboratories. This is a matter that must be debated within the profession and that may be resolved ultimately in one or more of the following ways: through governmental assistance as an extension of national laboratories, through universities themselves as more emphasis is placed on archeology as a discipline that is distinct in many of its needs from anthropology, or through private enterprise initiated by groups of scholars and technicians who can form a pool of talent that can be drawn from for in-house projects or hired under contract.

Should such organizations be set up, one may find more attention paid then to the recognition and development of persons who have the requisite skills. It would seem then that academic training on the master's level or perhaps even on the undergraduate level might be directed toward this end. In this way we may find graduate programs tending as much toward the practical and applied aspects of prehistory as to the theoretical. In this way, too, we may find a growing rather than diminishing opportunity for persons to enter the field and become an important part of its development. Finally in this way we might expect to find archeology more rapidly approaching the ideals of science that are often expressed but only slowly realized.

COMMUNICATION

An essential aspect of archeology is the dissemination of information about particular excavations, theories, and technical innovations. The problem is at once difficult and relatively easy. The difficulty lies in the fact that prehistorians are rarely concentrated in great numbers in any one place; and the ease, in that there are relatively few archeologists. Both of these situations have changed in the last few years as we may see by referring to the *Guide to Graduate Programs*, published annually by the American Anthropological Association. According to the latest Annual Report (1971: Table 1), 73 persons with the M.A. or Ph.D. degree in archeology (most of them newly graduated) were seeking employment. To this we may add an additional unknown number of graduates who, at the time of the annual meetings of the association, had already found jobs. Such raw numbers are of little significance until one realizes that until the decade of the sixties, there were probably only a hundred or so professionally employed archeologists in the entire country, most of whom knew one another personally. The number of professionals is only a part of the picture, however. Most archeologists and serious students of archeology in the United States are members of the Society for American Archaeology. The membership list over the last 15 years shows significant increases. In 1957 some 950 persons were listed as members; in 1965, about 1500, and in 1972, nearly 4000. Although most of the members are not professional archeologists, the increase in membership does reflect a substantial increase in the number of person who are employed as archeologists either in teaching or in research.

The fact that a few decades ago there were relatively few archeologists made for an ease of communication among them through personal visits to sites, correspondence, annual meetings, and published reports. As the number of persons contributing to the field has increased, however, problems of communication have become acute. These problems are met, with varying degrees of success, in several ways. First, there have been founded in the last ten years or so a large number of specialist journals and newsletters that deal with narrower interests. Second, there has been a considerable increase in the number of sessions at local and national anthropological meetings that deal specifically with prehistoric topics. As well, it is common for groups of archeologists who have mutual interests to meet informally to share ideas and data. Thus while most archeologists are identified with a university, museum, or even a site, they do not work in scholarly isolation. In fact, one of the distinctive things about archeologists has always been their willingness to share ideas and to make data available to their colleagues.

With the greatly increasing numbers of practicing prehistorians, however, the informal cooperation inevitably has broken down to some degree, but the increased numbers have made it possible to work on larger problems cooperatively rather than to concentrate solely on one's individual interests. The formative years of American archeology saw regular meetings devoted especially to the problems of a region. Among the earliest of these was the annual Pecos Conference in the Southwest which resulted in the definition of ceramic types and chronology. Similar meetings held formally or informally around the country have shaped the character of regional studies in the last several decades.

In recent years, however, there have been a growing number of meetings that undertake to explore integrative rather than empirical subjects. For many years the Wenner–Gren Foundation has supported international symposia at its headquarters in Burg Wartenstein, Austria, on topics which were of wide interest and in which a substantial international participation could be assured. Perhaps more than any other single effort, these symposia serve to bridge the international boundaries that once separated archeologists as much as politicians, and they have paved the way for the modern era of international cooperation on field research projects as well. As a result of these and the periodic international meetings of prehistorians at large, archeology has become a truly international effort. No longer do we find leading archeologists unable to see beyond their own countries or continents, and this development has given rise to the discovery that local problems are only examples of larger, sometimes pancultural, phenomena. We now find archeologists working freely in more than one country, emphasizing interesting problems rather than being tied to particular sites.

As the means of communication improve and interaction increases, we find that advances in all aspects of prehistory are much more rapidly disseminated. The result will be that the field will grow much faster than it has heretofore. Because of these factors we may predict that the efficiency of archeology will improve, and we look forward to the many exciting developments that will ensue.

NEW DIRECTIONS IN ARCHEOLOGY

In the decade of the sixties, the concepts grouped under "new archeology" emerged as a potent force in archeology. Some (for example, R. Adams 1968:1187) call it a revolution in thought. The ideas behind the new archeology are as old as science itself, yet they came as a fresh breeze to a discipline whose leaders some had accused of being afraid to open their windows lest an idea waft in (Wauchope 1962). Science in fact, though not in ideal, has been slow to take hold in archeology, very likely because most prehistorians have not been trained as experimental or theoretical scientists, although many are well acquainted with the natural or inductive sciences. There is, however, a world of difference between zoological systematics and theoretical genetics, just as there is between accurately predicting the moon's eclipse and discovering the laws that govern the orbits of planets.

For years archeologists have talked of scientific archeology, usually contrasting it with the bungling attempts of amateurs. What most scholars had in mind was the technical control they exercised over an excavation. "We dug the site with strict scientific controls" was an oftheard phrase; or, "we made a rigorous scientific analysis of our pottery," when what they did was classify sherds. To be sure, strict control, accurate keeping of records, and classification are all part of good experimental or of natural science, but in themselves these technical operations are not science. Additionally in archeology there is a long tradition of numerical manipulation, whether it be the calculation of descriptive statistics, or the interpretation of frequency curves as artifacts change in time, or the use of inferential statistics and sampling that aid intuitive judgment. These are part of science but their use does not make archeology a science. Neither does the use of electronic calculators or computers which rapidly and accurately perform the routine calculations that so plague the empiricist make of archeology a science any more than it guarantees the accuracy of the inferences drawn from the calculations.

Science is not a set of operations but a reasoned, logical inquiry into a problem whose solution is within reach. Science is usually characterized by a series of sequential steps that lead to an answer, but these steps may be evaded and avoided on occasion as insight wins over logic, and impatience over routine. Still the test of a conclusion is its reproducibility and its capacity to take account of relevant factors that would negate the hypothesis or conclusion deduced from an experimental result.

New archeology, discounting its abortive attempts at birth (for example, W. W. Taylor 1948; Willey and Phillips 1958), really began with a spokesman who was able to discuss the issues of science with a generation of college students who had been trained, as an aftermath of Sputnik, in science to a degree that few of their elders had. This group, nominally headed by Lewis Binford, consists principally of young Ph.D.s from a few of the better-known graduate schools. This group, which comprises a numerically insignificant total of archeologists, was able to command attention largely by speaking bluntly and often of the potential of archeology and of the evils that had been masquerading as scientific work. An immediate reaction was one of defense by older archeologists who were being criticized and of renewed vigor in the attack by those who were winning the verbal debate.

The furor has now settled down. Surprisingly there is still only the most general consensus on what new archeology is. At this writing the most readable and thoughtful single volume expressing *a view* of new archeology is *Explanation in Archeology: An Explicitly Scientific Approach* by Watson, LeBlanc, and Redman. As they put it (1971:x), "If the term 'new archeology' is to be used, it should be equated with explicitly scientific archeology." The contrast with other forms of archeology "lies in the strong emphasis of the theoretically oriented archeologists on explicit definition of a problem, of data needed to solve it, and of techniques necessary to collect the data" (1971:120). In the same vein they say (1971:32), "Whatever one thinks of the sometimes pretentious expression of this insistence on self-conscious use of scientific method, one lasting beneficial result will be that archeologists henceforth will be forced to make their assumptions explicit." They agree (1971:159), however, that all archeologists need not be scientists. "There is no more reason for all archeologists to be scientists than for all historians to be sociologists, psychologists, or anthropologists."

The decade of the sixties saw the emergence of archeologists as philosophers of science, and during this time there was a great emphasis on the logic of scientific inquiry as it has been interpreted by philosophers, especially logical positivists like Hempel (1952, 1965, 1966), Hempel and Oppenheim (1948), and T. Kuhn (1962). Out of this came the belief— some call it dogma—that archeology can and should be science, done in one manner only. The crux of these discussions has been to develop consensus on the nature of explanation and the operations needed to achieve it. However, the arguments about explanation have waned and as Watson (1972b) puts it, "The 1970s should be devoted to the operationalizing of theory by the nomothetically-oriented prehistorian as excavator of the past."

Flannery (1972) sees two ways in which the ideas of science have been put to use already. Using colloquial terminology, he has characterized two approaches, both of them explicitly scientific, within new archeology: "law and order" and "serutan." In the former, especially espoused by Watson, LeBlanc, and Redman (1971), together with Plog (1968) and Fritz and Plog (1970), the goal is the formulation and testing of laws. The underlying assumption is that there are general (cover) laws that state causal relationships among factors that affect human behavior. If these laws can be discovered they will permit prediction and provide explanations of archeological evidence. These archeologists often assume a linear relationship between a cause and an effect. In structure the argument is: if A, then B. This approach to explanation, called Deductive-Nomological or D-N, has as one of its aims to produce a unity of science, but the authors of a useful review (Tuggle, Townsend, and Riley 1972) emphasize that the approach is only one of many and is not universally recognized among philosophers of science; indeed it is considered sterile by many. The strategy of the D-N approach is to devise cover laws or lawlike generalizations and to deduce from them implications that can be tested with archeological data (Watson, LeBlanc, and Redman 1971:9).

The direction of most of the research of the "law and order" prehistorians is in the testing of deductions implied by assumed cover laws. J. Hill (1971:407) stated the relationship between cover laws and the deductions made from them as follows:

> The deductive "cover law" model holds that phenomena are only satisfactorily explained when their occurrence can be deduced (predicted) from a

lawlike generalization . . . any satisfactory explanation is a general as well as a particularistic one. Given the specified conditions, the phenomenon to be explained can always be expected to occur because the processual relationships stated in the law imply it of necessity. . . . In the present state of our knowledge, the testing of many of our explanations will show their presumed cover laws to be false—but such testing is the only way to begin to build acceptable laws and higher-level theory.

In contrast with the D-N approach is the Hypothetico-Deductive (H-D) (Tuggle, Townsend, and Riley 1972:5). In this approach, one begins not with a cover law but with a major premise whose deductively derived implications can be tested archeologically. This characterizes most archeological inference today, although, as has rightly been pointed out, often the assumptions (hypotheses or premises) have not been made explicit, nor have alternatives been considered. One might say that archeologists have often found what they thought they should find—not because they were exceptionally prescient but because they have not looked at all the possibilities, especially those that might tend to negate their premises.

A serious debate concerns the ultimate origins of laws or hypotheses. This has been no less a concern in philosophy than in archeology. Although Fritz and Plog (1970:410) speak vaguely of "acquiring" a hypothesis, in fact hypotheses are usually suggested by data and by inconsistencies between results of analyses and theories.

> While research may sometimes begin with a particular hypothesis that has fallen into one's hands, we suggest that it usually begins with a problem (which may be derived from data observation conducted with an even more general problem in mind, or from the inadequacy of previous explanations or hypotheses). . . . A research design which is concerned with explanation in archeology should devote as much attention to the problem of hypothesis formulations as to other problem areas (Tuggle, Price, and Trigger 1971).

Disagreement with the emphasis on discovering laws through testing their implications and the necessity of invoking a relatively simple cause-and-effect relationship has turned many new archeologists in another direction. They disregard the search for laws entirely, preferring to concentrate explicitly on how things work. They are interested in the natural regulation of systems (hence, Flannery's term "serutan," the name of a popular elixir whose name spelled backwards is "nature") and find their inspiration largely in General System Theory. As we discuss more fully later, system theory was developed largely to deal with complex open systems in which there is a continual infusion of energy from outside. Such systems are characterized not by simple, linear, cause and effect relationships but by feedback and mutual interaction. Thus the kinds of correlations that are used to "prove" test implications by law-and-order archeologists are considered unsuitable by the systems group. These latter argue that the D-N model is itself inappropriate and that "mono-causal or causal chain explanations" are not adequate to explain the complexity of systems (Tuggle, Price, and Trigger 1971:7). Human life systems are complex. To be sure, there are relationships among tangible variables that may be described, but one must also account for certain intangibles—for example, goals or motives—that may profoundly affect the ultimate cause of a system. Although the operation of systems in general *may* be explained by a series of general laws described by a complex mathematical model, the operation of any particular system cannot be, for each is in some respects unique. It is this fact that makes archeology and history interesting to the public and challenging to the scholar.

Thus systems archeologists prefer to describe the workings of a system instead of seeking the causes of its working. In this way they can deal more effectively with its unique aspects. Any life system (whether in fact alive or found through archeological evidence) is a product of its history; for this reason if causes are sought, they may be only in the remote past and may not be evident in the momentary slice of time under consideration in an archeological study. To deal with this problem, many scientists (though few archeologists) are simulating systems by constructing a mathematical model of the relationships among the variables they think are important and then allowing the model to "run," via a computer, under different constraints to see what the effects of changes in input (for example, population increase) will be.

In essence then, the two approaches currently espoused by many new archeologists are quite different: one attempts to discover laws through testing of their implications; the other, to describe the inner workings of extinct cultural systems in terms of multiple causality and mutual effect. The former sees a linear relationship between cause and effect, the latter a circular relationship. In very simple terms, we refer to the paradox, "Which came first, the chicken or the egg?" Law-and-order archeologists would try to discover which came first, and the systems group would find the question meaningless.

Surely there are excesses in each camp but each has its merits. One thing is certain: human behavior is complex and to see all of it from either of the two contrasting viewpoints is very likely incorrect. To cite some simple examples we know there are some imperatives if human life is to be sustained. These have been described in *Man and Nature* by R. A. Watson and P. J. Watson (1969). They are the need for sustenance, for protection, and for reproduction. All species must deal with these effectively if they are to survive. Consequently some human activity must be directed toward ensuring that these imperatives are met. On the one hand, techniques of subsistence and housing, and the regulation of mating and caring for the young are caused by these biological needs and can be explained by a general law. On the other hand, the methods used to ensure that these conditions are met will vary with factors that have little to do with the rationale behind them. Thus the style of houses may vary with material available to build them, with the weather, and with the owner's wealth. The location of the shelters may vary with access to resources, with requirements for defense, with opportunities for trade or social interaction, or more accurately with all (and more) such things simultaneously.

While debate continues on the most appropriate set of concepts to use in scientific archeology, there is consensus that whatever assumptions are made must be stated explicitly. Perhaps it is in this agreement that new archeology offers its greatest innovation. No longer is it sufficient to discuss intuitively derived "probable" causes. If one is scientific, he can and must begin with an explicit statement of his assumptions, their implications, and the relationship of his data to them. In this way others can effectively judge the merits of the arguments, apply them to his own situations, and test them. The rationale behind this is given eloquently by J. R. Platt (1964) following T. C. Chamberlin (1965[1890]). In our view this approach offers a compromise to the extreme positions of new archeology and enables one to deal with a much wider range of situations without the necessity of defending one particular school of thought.

Much of the writing of new archeology has been concerned with the distinction between the inductive (nonrigorous, intuitive insight) and deductive (formally logical) approaches, but in truth scientists work with both. Some prefer to begin with data and to infer their meaning; this is induction. Others prefer to work theoretically, devising hypotheses or laws and then testing them with data. No one, however, can operate entirely without data in mind, for he would have not the least idea what kinds of laws or hypotheses he might test. By the same token, an inductive approach that begins with data, whether it be accidentally or deliberately derived, only achieves credibility for its hypotheses through adequate testing. By whatever means the hypotheses are ultimately derived, the procedure for testing them follows strict scientific method; the sequence for testing presented below follows Platt (1964:347):

1. devising alternative hypotheses;
2. devising a crucial experiment (or several of them), with alternative possible outcomes, each of which will, as nearly as possible, exclude one or more of the hypotheses;
3. carrying out the expirement so as to get a clean result;
4. recycling the procedure, making the hypotheses or sequential hypotheses to refine the possibilities that remain; and so on.

Steps 1 and 2 require intellectual inventions, which must be cleverly chosen so that hypothesis, experiment, outcome, and exclusion will be related in a rigorous syllogism. . . . It is clear why this make for rapid and powerful progress. For exploring the unknown, there is no faster method; this is the minimum sequence of steps. Any conclusion that is not an exclusion is insecure and must be rechecked.

Although this procedure is standard, many scientists (archeologists included) do not follow it because they become method-oriented or they fall in love with their pet theory. As Chamberlin (1965:755) put it,

The mind lingers with pleasure upon the facts that fall happily into the embrace of the theory, and feels a natural coldness toward those that seem refractory. . . . There springs up, also an unconcious pressing of the theory to make it fit the facts, and a pressing of the facts to make them fit the theory.

No point in either Chamberlin's or Platt's articles is as important as,

There is no such thing as proof in science—because some later alternative explanation may be as good or better—so that science advances only by disproofs. There is no point in making hypotheses that are not falsifiable, because such hypotheses do not say anything: it must be possible for an empirical scientific system to be refuted by experience (Platt 1964:350).

If we may characterize a compromise and scientifically sound approach for new archeology, it would be to postulate relationships among variables that can be tested using data derived from prehistory. A satisfactory explanation for the crucial data will then consist of the hypothesis that cannot be excluded after it has been tested along with alternative hypotheses. An explanation thus represents the best we can do at the present state of our knowledge.

TRENDS OF THE FUTURE

Glyn Isaac (1971b), in an article, "Whither Archaeology?," wrote, "It is safe to predict that branching and the establishment of liaisons with an ever widening range of disciplines will continue to be one of the most conspicuous trends." To this we may repeat our earlier comments that within archeology there will be greater specialization as students receive better training in technical aspects of analysis and in the ancillary supporting fields. In combination these two factors will make archeology at once more complicated and better able to contribute more accurate reconstructions and interpretations of the past.

Both of these trends will stem directly from the awakened appreciation of possibilities of doing archeology scientifically, but it is unlikely that an explicitly scientific approach will ever override the more strictly historic and humanistic aspects and rationale of archeology. The ability to discover the processes of culture and to establish laws of human behavior depends in large part on the capability of archeologists to make accurate assays of both the relative and the absolute time elapsed and to determine the nature of an archeological episode during a discrete segment of its history. The linking of these episodes through time by means of causal processes depends in large part on the primary data and will often come rather late in the archeological study of an area rather than at the beginning.

This fact, which has been expressed by various writers who have attempted to set forth a series of logical steps in archeological interpretation (for example, Willey and Phillips 1958; Swartz 1967), is a source of some frustration on the part of overly ambitious neophytes who would very much like to discover the major factors that have governed the course of human history as a first rather than as a last step.

In truth, of course, the basic acquisition of data and their initial interpretations through reconstructions of prehistoric lifeways must be done with the larger ultimate goals in mind or they will be done inefficiently and perhaps without the necessary controls. We see the increasingly complicated stages of prehistoric studies as an integrated set of operations no less necessary than they are time-consuming.

It is important to remember, however, that one of the chief attractions of archeology, both for archeologists and for the public who support it, is in the reconstruction of local histories and the display of the things people used. One may predict, therefore, the increasing popularization of archeology by archeologists themselves rather than by writers of fiction and the growth of displays and other educational media to convey the message of human heritage. For the larger part of the public the fascination of archeology is in the seeking and compiling of clues and in the deductions drawn from them. The reconstruction is very like the summation given by fictional detectives of the solution to an intriguing mystery.

We must remember that whatever archeology may become in the future, it depends on evidence that can be found in the ground. In many areas the very existence of such data is imperiled through thoughtless looting of sites, through natural erosion and degradation, and through various kinds of construction. Ironically the population increases that have spurred some of the recent rapid increases in prehistoric research have also created a need for more housing, more roads, and more industry, thus destroying the very subject matter of the field. Alarming statistics can be produced to show that sites are disappearing by the tens of thousands annually through these combined factors of attrition. Of these, perhaps only a fraction of a percent are excavated or even salvaged by professional archeologists. It seems clear, therefore, that a major thrust of archeology in the future must be in the attempt to salvage some record in key areas before it is too late. On balance, however, it is true there may be millions of sites in no danger, and in this sense the supply is nearly limitless. What is most distressing is that entire important regions may be stripped of their archeological resources before thoughtful investigation can proceed. Until survey is done, one can hardly judge the extent of the actual damage. And this damage can only be stated in terms of what we think is important today. It is professional archeologists who must assess these matters and take the necessary steps to correct the problems. It is not enough to cry "stop" to developers, unless compelling reasons can be given for doing so. It will be hard to convince many that an esoteric site report published 10 years after the excavation is sufficient justification either for the expenditure of funds to do the archeology or for the delay of construction progress to permit excavation.

In summary, if the trends we have outlined are correct, we may look forward to many more studies of modern peoples by archeologists who are concerned with understanding how human behavior is reflected in artifacts and other tangible remains that one may find archeologically. To this we may add the probability that there will be an increase in experimentation to discover methods of manufacture and the uses to which artifacts were put. The next decade will doubtless also see the invention or application of techniques that will aid in excavation, processing, and analysis. And finally we may expect to see many much more tightly integrated research projects designed to investigate problems that are considered of overriding importance.

REFERENCES

Doing Archeology: Atkinson 1954; Bordes 1972; R. Braidwood 1960; Childe 1956; G. Clark 1957; T. and T. Clark 1903; Coon 1957; Crawford 1921, 1953; Creel 1937; Heizer 1959; Heizer and Graham 1967; Hudson 1967; Judd 1930; Lloyd 1963; Piggott 1959a; W. Taylor 1948; Wauchope 1966: Preface.

Archeologists' Experiences: L. Braidwood 1953; C. Breasted 1947; Budge 1920; Ceram 1952; Crawford 1955; Daniel 1963; J. Evans 1943; Gann 1927, 1928; H. Kühn 1955; A. Layard 1853, 1903; Leakey 1966a; E. Lothrop 1948; A. Mallowan 1946; Maudsley and Maudsley 1899; A. Morris 1931, 1933; Petrie 1931; L. and G. Poole 1966; Rassam 1897; Stephens 1842; J. Thompson 1963; Von Hagen 1947; Wauchope 1966; Wheeler 1955; Woolley 1952, 1958, 1959.

Training of Students: Hole 1972a; K. Kenyon 1961; Rowe 1954; Strong 1952; Sturtevant 1958; R. Thompson and Longacre 1966. See training programs in archeology that are listed in the annual *Guide to Graduate Departments of Anthropology,* published by the American Anthropological Association.

New Directions in Archeology: R. Adams 1968; Bayard 1969; L. Binford 1962, 1964, 1965, 1968a, 1972; L. Binford and S. Binford 1968; Caldwell 1959, 1966; Deetz 1970; Flannery 1967a, 1972; Freeman 1971; Fritz and Plog 1970; Hammond 1971a, 1971b; Harriss 1971; J. Hawkes 1968; Higgs 1968; J. Hill 1971; Hole 1972a; Isaac 1971b; L. Johnson 1972; T. King 1971; Kushner 1970; Lamberg-Karlovsky 1970; Longacre 1970c; MacNeish 1967a; Martin 1970, 1971; Plog 1972; Redman and Watson 1970; Rouse 1972a and b; Sherratt 1972; Sterud 1972; Stickle and Chartkoff 1972; W. Taylor 1948; Thomas 1971; Trigger 1968b, 1970; Tuggle, Price, and Trigger 1971; Tuggle, Townsend, and Riley 1972; P. Watson 1972a; R. Watson and P. Watson 1969; P. Watson, LeBlanc, and Redman 1971; Willey and Phillips 1958.

Trends of the Future: Braidwood 1972; Hole 1972a; Isaac 1971b; Longacre 1970c; Struever 1968c, 1971; C. Thomas 1971; P. Watson 1972b.

CHAPTER THREE

A SHORT HISTORY OF ARCHEOLOGY

In the first two chapters we dealt with prehistory as it is done today. Although some of the approaches and techniques seem new, many of them were anticipated long ago. The present chapter, in briefly reviewing the history of archeology, attempts to set the modern activities in the field into their own context and perspective.

As an academic discipline, archeology has a history of only a little more than 100 years, but a few persons were practicing a form of archeology by the end of the fourteenth century. Early archeologists, spurred by an interest in ancient Greece and Rome, directed their work mainly toward recovering coins and objects of art. The emphasis was on collecting and cataloguing, usually for personal rather than for public pleasure.

It was out of this tradition of interest in the past that the concept of the romance of archeology was born. In fact, some of the finest tales of adventure and exploration stem from the romantic lure of discovering and collecting. The words of early travelers who happily faced privation, disease, and sometimes death as they sought their treasures across the globe quicken the pulse even today. This statement is true despite the fact that, as Wheeler (1956:241) remarked, ". . . romance is merely adventure remembered in tranquillity, devoid of the ills and anxieties, fleas, fevers, thirst, and toothache, which are liable to be the more insistent experience."

Without doubt, the most persistent motive throughout the history of archeology has been to collect antiquities. Sometimes excavation was needed; at other times, not. Sometimes collection was an end in itself; at other times it was a step toward a broader end. Whatever curious turns archeology has taken, collection has traditionally been at its center. But the emphasis has shifted. Today private collecting is done mostly by amateurs and persons of means, and is actively shunned by professionals.

Although collecting is a central activity of archeology, it does not fully describe the subject. When artifacts—whether they be cuneiform tablets, Greek statues, flint tools, or bits of pottery—are collected, archeologists must describe, classify, and record the information recovered. When this work is done, the data are interpreted. The differences among the various kinds of archeology are largely in the geographic areas and particular times studied, and in the way the data are interpreted. The following sections will be concerned with describing four broad subjects of archeology.and telling something of their development historically.

DILETTANTES, BARGAIN HUNTERS, AND DEEP-SEA DIVERS

The history of "treasure hunting" is highlighted by cultivated gentlemen of the arts, brash performers for fame and prestige, highwaymen with official backing, cowboys, and submarine adventurers. At their best, these men stirred the imaginations of a complacent self-centered world; at their worst, they wrought irreparable damage to the record of man's past.

The history of treasure hunting must be viewed against the slow development of archeology, the emergence of a conscience about how it should be done, and the appearance of an educated public and appreciative governments who acted to protect their ancient remains from destruction. We shall want to judge the men involved, but we must remember that our criticisms of their work depend on knowledge not available a hundred or more years ago. Were we to judge work done in 1800 or 1900 by the standards of today, we should generally find it damnable.

The earliest record we have of archeology was actually discovered by archeologists of a much later day. The first archeologist who appears in history is Nabonidus, last of the kings of Babylon (555–538 B.C.) and father of Belshazzar. Nabonidus became intensely interested in the past of Babylonian culture and conducted excavations of ancient buildings, saved what he found, and established a museum in which his discoveries were displayed.

Tombs, with their lure of buried riches, have long attracted both looters and archeologists. In fact, excavation for the jewelry and precious metals contained in princely tombs began far before the advent of anything approaching archeology in Egypt. As W. Emery (1961:129) neatly observes, the Egyptians believed "you could take it with you," and as a result they buried a wealth of materials with their dead. Belzoni and others of his ilk were doing nothing new when they entered these tombs, for they often found they were several thousand years too late to salvage the prizes they sought. The ancient Egyptians themselves were always conscious of the temptations that royal tombs offered to looters, and they took elaborate precautions to protect them. The state of affairs is realized when one reads that in 1120 B.C. there was an official investigation and list of tomb robberies made in Egypt. But the practice of robbing was worldwide; to mention only a few, there are interesting accounts of looting of Shang tombs at Anyang in China; of the ship tomb of the Viking queen Oseberg; of the log tombs of the Scythian chieftains at Pazirik, Siberia; and of the royal tombs of Ur.

The historian Strabo mentions that when Julius Caesar established a Roman colony for veterans of his campaigns on the site of ancient Corinth, former cemeteries were discovered and looted for bronze vessels, which were sold to Roman collectors who prized items of Greek manufacture. The Spanish conquistadors in Mexico, Panama, and Peru soon learned that they could "mine" ancient cemeteries for gold objects, and they proceeded to do so as soon as the native peoples were conquered. Fernandez de Oviedo, a Spanish chronicler, wrote a detailed report on the opening of a tomb in Darien in 1522, and if we are willing to call this archeology, his is one of the earliest archeological reports from the New World.

In the fifteenth century, 2000 years after Nabonidus, the large-scale collecting of art treasures began in Italy and flourished, especially in Rome, under the example of popes like Sixtus IV (1471–1484) and his immediate successors. To supplement the techniques of merely removing standing monuments, Alexander VI, who was pope between 1492 and 1503, began excavating to add to his collection. During the fifteenth century it became fashionable for influential men of affairs as well as of the church to furnish their homes with the abundant ancient statuary. These men of the Italian Renaissance were known as dilettanti, to describe their delight in the fine arts.

The collector's spirit did not remain confined to Italy. With the spread of the Renaissance, collectors from all over Europe began to accumulate objects that would later become the nuclei of many of the world's famous museums. It was during this time that the city of Herculaneum, buried under a thick deposit of volcanic material thrown out of Vesuvius in A.D. 79—at which time Pompeii was also buried—was "mined" for Roman sculptures, which were sold to rich collectors.

When Thomas Howard, the Earl of Arundel, visited Italy in the early seventeenth century, he began his extensive collection of art from Greece, Italy, and Southwest Asia. His example of travel and collection was not lost on other young Englishmen of means who, for the next 200 years, were to follow Howard to the Mediterranean. The extent of Arundel's zeal can be seen today in the Ashmolean Museum, which retains the nucleus of his once much larger collection of marbles. Howard's collection, not appreciated by his descendants, was partly destroyed and then dispersed.

By the beginning of the nineteenth century, the scene of large-scale collecting had begun to shift to the site of the most ancient civilizations. It was on the desert valleys of the Nile, Tigris, and Euphrates that the great feats of treasure hunting were performed. Until the end of the eighteenth century, the Western world knew little of the riches that awaited discovery in Southwest Asia. A few mud bricks with undecipherable inscriptions on them, a handful of cylinder seals, and tales of certain imposing cities in ruins were all that had reached Europe after the Crusades. The establishment of a British consulate in Baghdad in 1802 marked the opening of Southwest Asia for the Western world and its treasure hunters.

The occupant of the British Residency in Baghdad for most of its first 25 years was Claudius Rich, a precocious student of languages and an astute politician. Rich's wide interests were shown in his careful surveying of prominent archeological sites and especially in his collecting. After his untimely death in 1821, some 7000 pounds of antiquities—including ancient coins, Syriac manuscripts, and about 1000 pounds of clay tablets, cylinders, and bricks with cuneiform inscriptions gathered by him—were deposited in the British Museum.

These early excavations in Mesopotamia were, of course, not very carefully conducted, and undoubtedly as much information was ignored or lost as was recovered. But they were remarkable feats of accomplishment when we consider that they were carried out with very small amounts of money (Layard paid his workers 6 cents a day), in sites of impressive size (Kuyunjik covers 1850 acres; the Khorsabad palace, 25 acres; Nippur, 445 acres), among warring Arab tribes (witness the destruction of Peters' camp and equipment at Nippur in 1889), and at a time when medical knowledge was minimal (C. Bellino, C. Rich, and G. Smith died in the middle of their fieldwork from cholera or dysentery) (Lloyd 1955; Pallis 1956). Books by Layard—as much about adventure as about archeology—became bestsellers in their day.

A contemporary of Claudius Rich, Henry Creswick Rawlinson, was a British (Indian) Army officer, horseman, adventurer, and student of ancient inscriptions. With remarkable energy and devotion, Rawlinson visited virtually every ancient monument of consequence in what is now modern Iran. His interest was mainly to collect samples of the ancient writing that had not yet been deciphered. As evidence of his travels one frequently finds Rawlinson's name carved into cliffs that were once reserved for the inscriptions of kings. But Rawlinson's fame lies not in his arduous journeys nor in his artistry with a chisel, but in his recording and translating of the long-lost inscriptions that describe Persia's former opulence. By 1837, working in his spare time, he had accomplished the translations that were to gain him the title, "Father of Cuneiform."

In Egypt, collecting of antiques was begun during the fifteenth century by Italian humanists who were interested in the religious texts that the Romans had reported being on the obelisks. A by-product of these activities was the pillaging of sites and tombs. This interest in the ancient Egyptian language received its biggest boost with the discovery of the Rosetta Stone in 1799. It was discovered by one of Napoleon's field officers, André Joseph Boussard, who was directing excavations for fortifications at Fort Rachid (later Fort Julien) about 7 kilometers from Rosetta (near Alexandria) in the Nile delta. The Greek inscription was soon translated by archeological experts attached to the French forces, and it was thus learned that the stone referred to a general synod of Egyptian priests at Memphis in honor of Ptolemy V. The importance of the stone was realized, and it was entrusted to General Jacques François de Menou, who kept the stone for safekeeping, in his house. The British army in 1801 forced the surrender of General Menou; included in the articles of capitulation was the provision that all Egyptian antiquities collected by the French should be delivered over. General Menou, in an attempt to save the Rosetta Stone, claimed the stone as his personal property, but the English commander, Lord Hutchinson, through his envoy, Turner, ignored this nicety and seized the stone, which was taken off to England in 1802, where it was deposited, with Elgin Marbles, in the British Museum.

Rubbings of the trilingual inscription of the Rosetta Stone were made by the French before it passed from their hands; they provided French scholars with what they needed. While the British worked hard at finding the key to the Rosetta inscriptions, so also did the French, and the answer was finally provided by Champollion in 1822.

The earliest archeology had been done by men whose primary business lay along quite different lines, but by the middle of the nineteenth century archeology received an impetus that it had not hitherto enjoyed. Both the French and British, sensing the great treasure that awaited the enterprising, supported men whose sole job was to recover antiquities.

One of the first of these men was Austen Henry Layard, who, under British auspices, undertook to dig the site of Nimrud, Mesopotamia, one of the ancient Assyrian capitals. (Actually he had mistakenly identified the site as Nineveh.) As Layard approached the task, his expectations mounted and he recorded a dream he had as follows: "Visions of palaces underground, of gigantic monsters, of sculptured figures, and endless inscriptions, floated before me. After forming plan after plan for removing the earth, and extricating these treasures, I fancied myself wandering in a maze of chambers from which I could find no outlet" (Lloyd 1955:126). When two palaces were discovered during the first day of excavation, the news spread rapidly, and soon the French entered the scene. With the lure of gold for the taking, agents of the two countries frantically dashed around, staking claims on sites about whose contents they knew nothing.

In spite of the promise of treasure for the British Museum, Layard, in contrast to his French counterpart, Paul Emile Botta, was never able to finance properly a really serious excavation. He was reduced to an expedient more the rule than the exception in those days. It can be stated simply: "to obtain the largest possible number of well-preserved objects of art at the least possible outlay of time and money" (Lloyd 1955:133). Though he sorely regretted it, as he dug through Nimrud, Layard saw many of the treasures disintegrate before his eyes. Frescoes, sculpture, and metal work frequently crumbled to bits when exposed to air and handling. Layard, in common with his competitors, had no knowledge of how to preserve the priceless objects and no time in which to experiment on techniques of conservation.

In the ensuing years French and British archeologists even vied with each other at the same site. In 1853 a British subject, Hormuzd Rassam, who was Layard's successor, enviously saw the French diggers approach a particularly likely looking spot on Kuyunjik, one of the palace mounds at Nineveh. Rassam took his workmen and had them excavate at night, stopping at dawn before the French came on the scene. By this simple subterfuge Rassam's men discovered a picture gallery and library in the palace of Ashur-bani-pal, an Assyrian king who lived between 669–633 B.C. Lacking time and funds, the men hacked their way through the palace, preserving little that was not intact and thereby losing much. Rassam (1897:395–396) wrote,

> Early the next day I . . . examined the localities where collections of unbaked clay tablets had been discovered, and was glad to find that important relics had crowned our labors. I found, to my great vexation, that a large number of the records had crumbled to pieces as soon as they were removed, as they were found in damp soil impregnated with nitre. Had I had an Assyrian copyist with me, we might have preserved, at all events, the history of the documents, though part of the originals would have been lost.

Rassam later learned that mud tablets could be baked and thus preserved, and wrote, "Our excavations at Aboo-Habba were caried out without much interruption for eighteen months altogether, during which time we must have discovered between sixty and seventy thousand inscribed tablets, a large number of which fell to pieces before we could have them baked."

The great public interest in these ancient records written in cuneiform on clay tablets made them particularly desirable to collect, and the Arab workers were quick to realize this. The natural result was large scale plundering of Mesopotamian sites by local people searching for tablets which they sold to dealers in Baghdad who in turn sold them to archeologists and museum collectors. G. Smith bought 2000 tablets from Sippar in 1876; Budge in 1890 purchased 9500 tablets which had been illegally dug from Dêr, and after Sarzec's departure from Telloh in 1900 the local natives opened up the tablet chambers (that is, libraries and record rooms) and were able to procure 35,000 tablets in sufficiently good condition for dealers to purchase. The search for the tablets continued, and in 1931 it had gotten so out of hand that Royal Air Force planes were used to drive away the Arab plunderers (Pallis 1956:284).

As an example of the manner in which digging was done more than a century ago in Mesopotamia, we quote Loftus' (1858:52–53) account of his efforts to collect glazed coffins from the site of Warka (Uruk) in southern Mesopotamia:

The object of my second visit to Warkah was to collect a series of such antiquities as it afforded, and more especially to obtain one of the glazed coffins which might be sent to the British Museum. As the colour of those near the surface is affected by exposure, I tried to procure a good specimen from below; but, the deeper I dug, the more saturated with moisture and brittle they became, so that, the moment an attempt was made to move one, it fell to pieces. Finding it impossible to succeed at any depth, I came to the conclusion that the only chance for me was to try at the surface. As the Arabs were much more adept at digging with their spears and hands than with the spades which I had brought with me, I permitted them to follow their own mode of searching. Their cupidity is attracted by the treasures contained within the coffins, to procure which many hundreds are broken and searched every year. Their method of proceeding is simple enough: they pierce the loose soil with their spears, until they chance to strike against some solid substance: by the vibration produced, the Arab knows at once whether he has hit upon a coffin or the vault containing one. The spear is then thrown aside, and, after the fashion of a mole, the wild fellow digs a hole with his hands. If an obstacle presents itself, the spear is again had recourse to, and in this manner perseverance secures the object of search. When the coffin is rifled, a hole is broken through the bottom to ascertain if there be one below. In riding or walking over mounds considerable care is requisite on account of the innumerable holes made by the Arabs, who of course never take the trouble to fill them up again.

FIG. 3 Transport by V. Place on the Tigris River in 1855 of Assyrian sculptures. The *kelek* rafts are made of inflated animal skins decked with logs. The entire shipment of about 300 cases, except for a colossal bull sculpture and a winged figure now in the Louvre, was lost when the rafts were sunk by Arab brigands. Illustration from V. Place, *Nineve et Assyrie*. Paris, 1869.

During every day of my stay several coffins were uncovered, and numerous expedients adopted to remove one unbroken: but notwithstanding every precaution, they broke with their own weight. Pieces of carpet and Arab abbas were tied tightly round them, the earth inside was either partially or wholly removed, and poles were placed below to give support; all however to no purpose.

But as if these feats of looting and mass destruction were not enough, a crowning blow to Assyriology occurred in 1855 with the destruction by Arab vandals of some 300 cases of antiquities collected by Place from the Palace of Sardanapalus. Disappointed in the cargo, the Arabs capsized the rafts carrying it as they were about to enter the Persian Gulf below Baghdad, and there they await recovery by some enterprising archeologist who can locate and raise them from the mud (Fig. 3). An expedition was organized in 1972 to search for and recover this precious body of material.

Lloyd (1963:35) described the great despoiled Near Eastern site of Khafaje, which, "when we first visited it, looked like a battlefield. The main mound . . . was completely honeycombed with holes large enough to be shell craters, surrounded by mountains of discarded earth." Lloyd also records that since 1930 in the Lurish province of western Iran between 400 and 500 burial grounds, each containing about 200 graves "have been excavated commercially [for bronze objects] without any assistance from acheologists" (Fig. 4).

The looting of ancient graves for the valuables they contain has been practiced for thousands of years. As scientific interest in antiquities developed, much material which was of no interest to tomb robbers began to acquire pecuniary value. Egyptian mummies (the word derives from "mumiya," the Arabic word for raw pitch) were much in demand in the fifteenth and sixteenth centuries in Europe where they were ground into powder and taken as medicine. Mark Twain in *Innocents Abroad* reports that on the Egyptian railway "the fuel they use for the locomotive is composed of mummies three thousand years old, purchased by the ton or the graveyard for that purpose, and . . . sometimes one hears the profane engineer call out pettishly, 'D——n these plebians, they don't burn worth a cent—pass out a king.' " We remind the reader that this is humor, not fact.

No tale of treasure hunting should fail to mention one of the most extraordinary persons ever to be called an archeologist. Giovanni Battista Belzoni was perhaps the most outrageous and audacious looter of them all. Working in the early 1800s, partly under the auspicies of the British Consul in Cairo, Belzoni capped his richly varied life as circus strong man and hydraulic engineer by dedicating himself to robbing tombs. Belzoni, whom Mayes (1961:296) somewhat inappropriately described as "the man who laid the foundations of an English Egyptology," was a giant of a man whose deeds assumed gigantic proportions.

Belzoni's career in Egypt began in Thebes. His first efforts are described as follows: "Every step I took I crushed a mummy in some part or

Fig. 4 In the foreground is an archeological site in western Iran that was systematically looted of the bronzes in more than 1000 graves. The site is pockmarked with vertical shafts that lead to the tombs, leaving the site worthless for archeological exploration.

other. When my weight bore on the body of an Egyptian it crushed like a bandbox. I sank altogether among the broken mummies with a crash of bones, rags and wooden cases . . . I could not avoid being covered with bones, legs, arms and heads rolling from above" (Daniel 1950:155–156). Moving from tombs to outdoor projects, Belzoni excavated Abu Simbel, he opened the Second Pyramid, he recovered the 8-ton head of Rameses II from Thebes, and he probably would have succeeded in the prodigious engineering feat of sending the Philae obelisk out of the country had he not been intercepted by a better armed band of brigands who claimed it for themselves. But Belzoni was not altogether a crude wrecker and collector, if we may judge him by his time-consuming efforts to make wax castings of the interior of two elaborate Egyptian tombs with the aim of bringing them back to Europe and making exact reproductions for showing to the public. Belzoni was not the seed from which British Egyptology sprang but the autumn brilliance of a leaf that was soon to wither and fall. Howard Carter, famous for his excavation of the tomb of Tutankhamen in 1923, had this to say about Belzoni's day: "Those were the great days of excavating. Anything to which a fancy was taken, from a scarab to an obelisk, was just appropriated, and if there was difference with a brother excavator, one laid for him with a gun" (Carter and Mace 1923–33: Vol. I, p. 68).

In 1842 Austen Layard's equipment was plundered by Arabs. After appealing to the authorities, a procedure which had no effect, he took matters into his own hands. Bonomi (1853:34) describes how he handled the matter:

> In three or four days he learned who were the robbers, and he determined to make them feel that they were not to carry their incursions into his quarters with impunity. Taking with him two trusty Arabs, expert at their weapons, he came upon the guilty sheikh in the midst of his followers, and politely asked for the missing articles, some of which were hanging up in his sight. When the sheikh and his party had stoutly denied the possession of the goods in question, one of Layard's two attendants handcuffed the old man in a moment, and, jumping on his horse, dragged him out of the encampment at a most uncomfortable pace. The suddenness of the performance paralyzed the by-standers, who were well supplied with arms. The sheikh was carried to Nimroud where he thought it wiser to make a full confession than to journey to Mosul and confront the Pasha. Next morning the missing property, with the addition of a kid and a lamb, as a peace offering, made their appearance: the sheikh was therefore liberated, and Layard had no subsequent reason to complain of him or his tribe.

Experiences of this sort were the rule rather than the exception in the early days of archeology in the Middle East, and we can only admire the fortitude and capability of these early excavators.

By the end of the nineteenth century, archeologists had come to recognize the part that texts would play in unraveling the history of the area, and they began to dig primarily to recover the ancient writings. Some of the inscriptions were on stone and clay, but others (especially from Egypt) were papyrus rolls containing Egyptian texts as well as Greek and Roman literary writings. With this change in emphasis, archeology took a historical bent and became more leisurely and scholarly than it had been in the days when the museums were empty (as also were many of the excavators' heads).

A fascination with the extreme age of cave-dwelling man, whose remains dated from the latter part of the Pleistocene, or Ice Age, developed just over a century ago in western Europe. By the end of the nineteenth century many sites, the scenes of occupation lasting thousands of years, had been systematically "quarried." Gangs of workmen were hired to obtain the few carvings of bone and ivory, figurines of clay and stone, and superbly made tools of flint and bone that had been produced so many thousands of years before. The lure was not so much the intrinsic value of the artifacts as it was the great age that they implied. In recent years, in an attempt to salvage what remains, many of the dump heaps outside the caves left by unscientific diggers of the nineteenth century have been systematically reexcavated in order to recover the tools that were overlooked or discarded by the earlier diggers. In this way some idea of the total assemblage that occurred in the cave or shelter can be determined, though the material is lacking in associational context. Men such as Otto Hauser, a Swiss dealer in antiquities, became wealthy collecting and selling material to the museums that would bid the highest. In 1908 he sold a skeleton from Le Moustier for 100,000 gold marks to the Museum of Ethnology in Berlin. All over the continent and England as well, gentlemen spent their holidays excavating in the local sites. But these looting operations gradually died out as the historical importance of the antiquities was recognized.

There was a time when public interest in ancient cities was so great that in 1840 J. L. Stephens, acting privately, though an official of the U.S. government, made a serious effort to purchase the Classic Maya site of Palenque (Heizer 1969:219–226), and J. E. S. Thompson (1963:222) quotes a letter from Lord Palmerston to Frederick Chatfield, British representative to the five Central American republics, asking him to make an attempt to secure some of the famous carved stelae of Copan, saying,

> It appears that these ruins are held in little or no estimation by the natives of the country, and it seems possible, therefore, that the chief difficulty to be encountered in removing specimens of the sculpture would consist in providing means of transporting them to some place of embarkation. You will be careful, therefore, that in making inquiries in pursuance of this instruction, you do not lead the people of the country to attach any imaginary value to things which they consider at present as having no value at all.

Fortunately neither Stephens nor Chatfield succeeded in removing the antiquities of Palenque or Copan, two sites now generally agreed to be the most beautiful of all Maya cities.

A happy and early exception to the prevailing rule was the famous and successful research team of Henry Christy, an English banker, and Edward Lartet, a French magistrate who abandoned the law for paleontology. Between 1863 and 1865, when Christy died from an illness contracted in digging a cave in Belgium, the two men excavated in the famous French paleolithic sites of La Madeleine (from which the Magdalenian culture was named), Le Moustier (type site of the Mousterian culture), Les Eyzies, Laugerie Haute, and others. Their cooperative work was intelligently done, and among their important accomplishments were the first recognition of paleolithic engraved art, recognition and definition of the Upper Paleolithic as distinct from the

Lower Paleolithic, and the first classification of paleolithic cultures based on associated fauna.

In the United States there was a similar pattern of events. When the West had been wrested from the Indians and opened to cattle grazing, cowboys became pioneers in archeological discovery. At the successful conclusion of the Mexican War, engineers of the United States Army were dispatched to the newly acquired territories of the southwestern United States, and their reports contained descriptions of prehistoric sites that were soon to encourage American archeologists to investigate them. In the late 1800s members of the Wetherill family, early settlers in Colorado, discovered at Mesa Verde some of the most impressive and best-preserved prehistoric remains in the Western Hemisphere. In 1888 Richard Wetherill and Charley Mason, looking for a stray herd, came upon one of the largest cliff dwellings ever built—"Cliff Palace." After their discovery the Wetherill brothers explored the Mesa Verde canyons in detail, and archeologists soon followed suit. A Swedish archeologist, Baron Gustav Nordenskiold (1895), wrote the first comprehensive account of the ruins in 1893, and, in retrospect, this seems to have been an open invitation for looters to try their luck also.

Meso-America and Peru, centers of the New World civilizations, have been the scene of even greater looting. There is scarcely an art shop or decorator's atelier in the United States that does not feature some pieces of pre-Columbian art, usually finely modeled pottery, stone sculptures, or jade carvings. These antiquities are smuggled out of the countries of their origin; conveniently, the rural natives dig them up in their free time, thus sparing a modern collector the burden of becoming a latter-day Belzoni.

The attitude that the importation of antiquities to America is not only moral but necessary today is expressed by Andre Emmerich, a dealer in pre-Columbian art, who was quoted by Ann Holmes in a feature article in *Zest*, the Sunday supplement to the *Houston Chronicle* (May 14, 1972, p. 37):

> I believe totally in the preservation of the art of the past. But I do not support the narrow nationalism, the possessiveness involved in the position of some of these countries. Is Homer only for the Greeks? . . . Is Shakespeare only for the English? Rembrandt only for Dutch eyes? . . . Should descendants of the Turks who ran the Greeks into the sea be the sole possessors of the Greek treasures found there? . . . The United States has bought its art and has not acquired it by conquest. We have paid our moral debt, furthermore, by sponsoring and paying for many important archaeological explorations and by contributing about 75 percent of the literature on pre-Columbian art.

In response to the statement of Harvard University, which controls the Dumbarton Oaks Museum in Washington, to the effect that it will work to eliminate black market purchases, Emmerich said, "Certain museums in the east can be pious about things like that. They are already overflowing with fine examples. But what about the empty museums of Texas and California?"

Our response to such nonsense, which is merely that of a commercial dealer in antiquities trying to justify his activities, is that laws prohibiting unauthorized export of antiquites should be observed by everyone as a matter of principle. The commercial trade in antiquities has and continues to encourage the destruction of evidence. If Texas and California museums remain empty of stolen contraband objects from other countries, we will be, as Texas and California citizens, happy. If the antiquities dealers go out of business or get thrown in jail, we will not be saddened.

One more aspect of treasure hunting should be considered. As practiced underwater to recover objects long since sunk, it has been called with some derision "archaeological salvage" (de Borhegyi 1961:44). Particularly in the Mediterranean, where traders have been moving goods by ship for thousands of years, there are numerous wrecks lying in relatively shallow waters that are easily accessible to divers. Soon after the invention of the aqualung in the 1940s, a growing group of sportsmen-adventurers discovered that treasure awaited their search. It was exceedingly simple. For example,

> As soon as word got out that an archaeological discovery (a sunken ship) had been made at Antheor, amateur divers rushed from all parts of the French Riveria and with thoughtless enthusiasm carried off hundreds of souvenirs of their visit. One day in 1949 an American yacht anchored over the wrecks, and the owner arranged a special show for his guests. He put the davits of his ship at the disposal of the divers swimming there so that they could bring up heavy articles from the sea bottom (de Borhegyi 1961:10).

We do not wish to imply that all underwater archeology is disreputable; in fact, in recent years there have been some exciting results as a consequence of the development of adequate techniques of recovery and recording. Long ago the potential of underwater archeology was recognized. Sir Charles Lyell (1872, 2, Chap. 46) cites a considerable number of known instances of submarine archeological materials, and his list of the numbers of British vessels wrecked between 1793 and 1829 provides a hint of the possibilities for archeology that exist on the ocean botton. Lyell concludes by saying, "It is probable that a greater number of monuments of the skill and industry of man will, in the course of ages, be collected together in the bed of the ocean than will exist at any other time on the surface of the continents." For an early account of traditions, some of them probably based on fact, of settlements below the present surface of lakes or the ocean, see the Lord Bishop of St. David's account (1859).

Underwater discoveries can even be made inland. During the exceedingly dry winter of 1853–1854, when lake levels fell far below normal, the pilings of Neolithic and Bronze Age houses were found on the exposed margins of certain Swiss lakes. In order to retrieve additional similar remains, archeologists sometimes resorted to draining lakes. As we now know, especially from such magnificently preserved sites as Burgaschisee-Süd in Switzerland (Müller-Beck 1965), an enormous amount of unique material was lost before adequate techniques for preserving waterlogged wood were developed.

For persons living in the fifteenth or even during much of the nineteenth century, looting was a wholly respectable practice, but as soon as it was shown that serious archeological study could pay dividends in knowledge ultimately far greater than the price an object alone might bring, educated persons engaged in looting have found themselves working against the main stream of public conscience. When measured against the life history of archeology, looting is the activity of thoughtless children; adults are expected to be better informed and to set a creditable example. Evidence of man's past is destructible and, once destroyed, can never be restored.

TEXTS, TEMPLES, AND TOMBS

The title of this section recalls the previous one, for most of the treasure hunters were dealing with temples, texts, and tombs. But the important thing is the purpose toward which the work is directed. Here we shall deal with studies of the ancient civilizations and their immediate antecedents. Such work is usually done by persons trained in the humanities.

Classical archeology received its greatest impetus from Heinrich Schliemann, though he did not originate scientific classical studies. In fact, some would deny that his methods should be dignified by the term archeology. Schliemann's impatience with getting to the bottom of sites left him with little taste for working out precise stratigraphic associations. In his later years his associate, Dörpfeld, and more recently, Mellaart, brought a certain order to his digs, but his early work amounted to little more than the recovery of objects. By contrast, Schliemann's predecessor, Giuseppe Fiorelli, who excavated Pompeii in 1860, attempted to restore a picture of the whole Roman city. Fiorelli said that the discovery of art objects was of only secondary importance; yet it was Schliemann, not Fiorelli, whose work was followed by the world and whose example was emulated by later workers. Although Schliemann's excavation methods left much to be desired, they were nevertheless far better than the work of his predecessors in the eastern Mediterranean area.

Childhood reading about the sacking of Troy during the Homeric period so impressed Schliemann that after he made his fortune as a merchant, he began to study ancient history and set as his archeological task the finding of Homer's Troy. In his several seasons of excavation between 1869 and 1889 he was successful in finding a convincing Troy (Hissarlik) in western Turkey, and other great sites. In Mycenaean shaft tombs, he found treasure that was described then as being "one of the most important discoveries of past human civilization that has ever been made" (Daniel 1950:138). He also found remains of an even earlier, previously unknown, prehistoric Greek life and so opened a whole new world for classical scholarship. But Schliemann's influence was most effectual in that he opened the eyes of the world to the possibilities of excavation directed toward solving problems rather than solely toward the recovery of objects of art.

The recent history of Classical archeology has been one of continuing discovery and interpretation. The Egyptian hieroglyphs had been deciphered by Schliemann's time, and Greek writing could be read, but other ancient scripts have not been deciphered to this day. A pre-Greek civilization, Minoan, was responsible for two forms of writing, the more recent of which, Linear B, was shown only in 1952 to be a form of ancient Greek. The earlier form, Linear A, is still to be deciphered adequately. Early cuneiform inscriptions from Mesopotamia, writing on Hittite documents from Anatolia, and the written Mohenjo-daro script of the Indus Valley civilization still cannot be read.

Classical archeologists are often students of ancient languages. In this respect their work is to supplement written history by combining archeology with philology. Note, for example, the map of Homeric Greece, and the outlying Mediterranean regions that it has been possible to draw solely from geographical details contained in the Iliad (Page 1959). Archeologists who deal with the Mesopotamian and Egyptian civilizations, however, are often trained in art or architecture rather than languages. Their job is as much to discover facts of prehistory as to add to knowledge of written history. The persons who transcribe the ancient texts are called epigraphists; usually they do not participate in the actual excavation of a site.

We do not wish to overemphasize the differences between Classical archeologists and their colleagues who deal with prehistoric periods, because there are many notable examples of fruitful cooperation between the two disciplines in Europe, especially with regard to Roman sites.

Writing is not the only concern of Classical scholars. Art fascinates many students, and some study coins (for several unusual and highly interesting publications that deal with cultural rather than financial or numismatic aspects of coins, see the recent work of Zeuner [1963] on domestication of animals; M. Grant [1958] on Roman history as illustrated on coins; and D. Allen's [1958] excursion into life in the late pre-Roman times in Britain as illustrated by devices on Belgic coins); others prefer architecture; and, of course, there is the old mainstay of most archeology, pottery, which serves as a means of determining chronology as well as cultural connections between different societies. In spite of the diversity of topics and approaches, when ancient civilizations are studied, the emphasis usually rests on the esthetic qualities of civilization—art in its various forms, monumental architecture, and literature.

Schliemann's work set the tone of what is still being done. The significant changes since his time have been in the development of more precise techniques for acquiring information. As knowledge has accumulated, it has been possible to plan excavation more intelligently. As better techniques for excavating, recovering, and preserving antiquities have been developed, archeologists have been able to learn more. Classical archeologists have defined their aims and devoted their time to recapturing history in ever more sophisticated ways. It is not stretching a point to say that more scientific skill and technical aid have been expended in classical archeology than in any other branch in the last decade. For a review of these techniques, see Part III of this book.

PROTOHISTORY

Christian Jurgensen Thomsen, curator of the National Museum in Copenhagen in 1836, devised a method for sorting and displaying the antiquities in his charge. His method was to keep separately the objects of stone, bronze, and iron. This was the birth of the Three-Age System that has plagued more constructive archeological thought to the present day. Nevertheless, it soon became apparent through the excavations carried out by Thomsen's associates, among them J. J. A. Worsaae, that in Denmark there was an actual stratigraphic succession of flint, bronze, and iron. With this clue it was natural for archeologists to conclude that man had gone through these three stages almost everywhere.

The principle of superposition or stratification (sometimes called Steno's Law) was first devised by Nicolaus Steno (1638–1686), a Danish medical doctor attached to the court of Ferdinand II, Grand Duke of Tuscany. Steno's *Prodromus* was published in 1669. When the principle of stratigraphic succession was applied (it has been used consistently only in the last 70–80 years), archeology could be used to extend local history by recording evidence of past cultures in their proper chronological order. Building on this foundation, enterprising archeologists in Europe turned their attention to uncovering their national past and in the process gathered information that showed the spread of civilization across the Western world. Without writing that can be deciphered, archeology becomes what Albright (1957:49) calls "anepigraphic" (the science of unwritten documents), or what C. Hawkes (1954) calls "text-free." This kind of archeology discovers lost or forgotten civilizations such as the Minoan of Crete, the Hittite of Asia Minor, and the Harappan of India—it literally creates these. The Scythians of South Russia who had no writing were, however, pretty well described by Herodotus, and by combining Greek documents and archeology, we know a great deal about them. Unlike their colleagues who were working with Greek and Roman materials, archeologists in western Europe could not readily name the peoples whose past they were excavating. True enough, the British had historical knowledge of the Celts and the Angles and Saxons, but before them, nothing. And in most of Europe there was no knowledge at all of who the early inhabitants had been. Modern national names would not describe the peoples who, thousands of years earlier, had not been grouped into those transitory political allegiances. With nothing to fall back on, archeologists named prehistoric people after some of their most characteristic artifacts. Thus we have the curious spectacle of the "Beaker-folk," whose movements have been traced to the Rhineland, Holland, and finally, by about 1800 B.C., to the British Isles.

Another group, perhaps having its origin in the steppes of central Asia, was named the "Battle-axe Culture." Somewhere in Europe the Beaker-folk and the Battle-axe people met, and both seem to have entered Britain at about the same time. It is anybody's guess what these people called themselves or what their language was. Although they lived at a time when civilization thrived in the Mediterranean, they were effectively out of touch and are usually regarded as prehistoric.

In most areas it was when the people took to farming rather than hunting that they came under the influence of the Mediterranean and Southwest Asian civilizations, and these centers continued to influence the outlying areas for much of their history. Accordingly, it has been natural for scholars concerned with peripheral areas to study their material in terms of the influential civilizations. How otherwise could they compare one area with another, or interpret fragmentary data that were only complete in the centers of diffiusion? As early as 1836 Thomsen saw clearly that the later prehistory of northern Europe would have to be understood as derivative from the Mediterranean area of civilization, although this view reached its extreme form in Childe's *The Dawn of European Civilization* (1957). Dawkins (1880:447) also saw the possibility of dating the later prehistoric cultures of Europe by referring them to the dated remains of the Mediterranean area when he wrote,

> . . . it is a question equally interested to the historian and to the archeologist, to ascertain the extent to which the light of their culture (that is, of Egypt, Assyria, Etruria, Greece, and Phoenecia) penetrated the darkness of central, western, and northern Europe, and to see whether it be possible . . . to bring the Historic period in the Mediterranean region into relation with the Prehistoric period north of the Alps.

This relation was not understood until G. Montelius in the last decade of the nineteenth century effectively tied the two chronologies together. Montelius carefully studied artifacts from both Europe and the Mediterranean and worked out a chronology based on the types of tools. His division of the Bronze Age into chronological segments numbered I–V enabled archeologists working from the British Isles to the Aegean to date their material relative to one another. Recent assessments of radiocarbon dating (Renfrew 1970b), however, show these correlations to have been incorrect (see Chapter 12).

Archeology in the biblical lands has made clear many brief or cryptic references in the Bible to sites, people, customs, and historical events, with the result that archeology in this particular actually has been able to add a great deal of specific detail to the historical documentation. In the Migration period (or Dark Ages), after the decline of Rome in the third century A.D., northwestern Europe lost direct contact with the literate Mediterranean world, and for a period of about half a millennium lapsed back into what was essentially a "nonhistorical" phase, which we know mainly from traded goods found in archeological sites rather than from documentary evidence. The study of protohistory has therefore been closely allied to the humanistic traditions that produced the classical scholars. In contrast, prehistoric archeology is concerned with peoples who lived before or beyond the influence of civilization.

Piggot (1959a:Chap. 5) has provided us with an excellent discussion of the degrees to which societies can be called historic. Peoples lacking writing (or whose writing cannot be deciphered) but who lived in the penumbra of literate civilizations may be known to us by name, and something of their history may have been recorded by their neighbors. The Scythians of South Russia, described by Herodotus and Strabo, the occupants of the Land of Punt (Somaliland), with whom the Egyptians traded and whose customs they recorded, and the Celts of Europe, known from writings of Caesar, Tacitus, and others, belong to the category of nonliterate barbarians living beyond the borders of the civilized world where writing and reading were practiced. But the fact that they are named and described, and the knowledge that certain events of ancient history involved them, bring them into focus as "real" and identifiable people rather than as people belonging to that shadowy, nameless kind of group (so familiar to the prehistorian) whose very existence is a fact discovered by archeologists. This kind of knowledge about preliterate societies is not limited to the peoples living on the fringes of the Greek, Egyptian, and Roman worlds, but indeed is equally true of all the primitive cultures of the Old and New Worlds that are known to us from the writings and museum collections compiled by travelers, explorers, and ethnologists. Christopher Columbus and Hernando Cortes wrote, or caused to have written, records of societies whose traces now are solely archeological, and in so doing they were instrumental in permitting these now extinct groups, in the last moments of their lives, to enter into the historical arena and, as a result, avoid the fate of so many human groups of prehistory, which was to live and die anonymously.

In the New World the great native empires of the Aztecs and Incas, which were brought to a sudden and bloody end by the Spanish conquest in the early sixteenth century, managed to incorporate some of their history in Spanish accounts. These "histories" take the form of traditional genealogies of important families and main events in the lives of certain individuals, including the ruling dynasties. Thus for the Peruvian rulers there are lists of emperors that are very useful in identifying and dating archeological sites of the late Inca period. The Homeric epic was a memorized tale that happened to get recorded in writing while it was still remembered in detail, and it has been argued that the Iliad describes an actual historical situation referring to the end of the Bronze Age. Piggott (1959a:104) uses the term "conditional literacy" to characterize the surviving written records of societies such as that of the Mycenaeans in Linear B script—tablets that are almost exclusively bookkeeping accounts recording the amount of production or inventories of goods. These official business records, made by clerks who were a specialist minority in the society, can tell us a great deal about the economic and political structure of the Mycenaeans, but they do not contain literary or historical accounts. The famous Peruvian knotted-string mnemonic records called "quipus" were probably similar in function. The surviving books (codices) of the Maya and Aztec peoples, though known to represent only the barest fraction of such records existing at the time of the Spanish conquest, are of the greatest importance in our understanding of the later history and calendars of these societies. Thus a variety of situations is involved when we refer to a society as historical.

ADAM AND BEYOND

In contrast to other kinds of archeology, prehistory is not primarily aligned with humanistic or even historic disciplines. Rather, prehistory has always been closely allied with anthropology, which developed at about the same time, and with geology, which supplied the evidence of the great age for man. From the beginning, then, prehistorians have attempted to develop a scientific study of mankind by using the concepts of the social sciences and the methods, concepts, and techniques of the natural sciences. A concern with history enters because we trace the careers of extinct cultures, but this concern takes two forms: evolutionary studies that deal with the development of culture generally and studies of the culture history of archeologically identifiable groups of people.

The geological ideas of the great age of the earth and the concepts of biological evolution have a fairly long history, but they really became important for archeological studies only after the time of Darwin.

Quite by chance the year 1859 marked both the publication of Charles Darwin's great book *On the Origin of Species,* which presented the theory of evolution by natural selection, and the birth of Paleolithic archeology. In that year several British geologists (John Evans, Prestwich, Flower, and Falconer) visited Amiens, France, where they verified the claims made by Jacques Boucher Crêvecoeur de Perthes (Fig. 5) that rude flaked stone implements (Fig. 6) occurred at great depths from the present surface in the Pleistocene (then called "antediluvian") gravels of the Somme River. Such ancient and crude tools fitted well with the idea implied (but not stated) by Darwin of the progress of man from lower forms. No primitive fossil human bones were known in 1859 except for the first of the Neanderthal skulls, discovered in 1856, about which a controversy was raging over whether it was the skull of a primitive form of man or that of a pathological idiot.

The early prehistorians recognized that the remains they were digging up had their closest counterparts among living primitives rather than among civilized peoples. It was natural for them to turn to anthropologists, and especially ethnologists, who were gathering information on primitive peoples, rather than to historians and humanists, for their inspiration and interpretation. The development of man's technology from simple to complex over the

FIG. 5 Jacques Boucher Crêve-coeur de Perthes (1788–1868), the father of Paleolithic archeology, who attributed flint implements found in the gravels of the Somme River to the work of ancient man.

FIG. 6 *(left)* The first published illustration of a hand ax (scale 1:2). (Hearne's [1715] edition of Leland's *Collectanea* 1:lxiv). This implement is described in the Sloane Catalogue: "No. 246. A British weapon found, with elephant's tooth, opposite to black Mary's, near Grayes Inn Lane" (as quoted in J. Evans 1897: 581).
(right) The same hand ax reproduced as a woodcut in J. Evans, *Ancient Stone Implements* 1897: Fig. 451 (scale 1:2).

long span of his existence was readily attributed by writers like G. de Mortillet (1867) to cultural evolution. As a result, many prehistorians have been more concerned with discovering and interpreting the universal trends of culture evolution than with working out the details of short-range local sequences of cultures. The earliest attempts at describing cultural evolution were based largely on analogy with living primitives, who were thought to exhibit various "stages" of cultural evolution. Though this notion has been persistent, detailed work on particular sequences has demonstrated that human history has been remarkably varied and cannot be described by any single system of stages of development.

Generally speaking, the further back archeologists push into the past, the harder it is to recover evidence about the people of the times. Even though geology provided archeology with certain fundamental ideas about the age of the earth and in particular about the concept of stratigraphy, it offered no direct methods for recovering archeological material, or for interpreting the physical conditions of times past. These ideas and techniques were provided by an array of other sciences, some of which were also facing the problem of reconstructing the ancient world. Kidder (as quoted by Wauchope 1965:157) put it this way:

> . . . [Archeologists] will find that other sciences are grappling with the problems of plants and animals, of weather and rocks, of living men and existing social orders; collecting, classifying, winnowing detail, and gradually formulating the basic laws which render this perplexing universe understandable. Beside and with them the archeologist must work if his results are to be more than the putterings of the antiquary.

Archeologists have, therefore, grown accustomed to cooperating in research projects with chemists, physicists, botanists, zoologists, geographers, geologists, geomorphologists, and even astronomers when the special knowledge of these scientists can be made to reveal information about prehistory. The same is true of the cooperation with physical anthropologists who are interested in the physical characteristics of extinct populations, with human evolution, and with other biological characteristics of man. Because man's early history of development is more closely tied to biology than to culture as we know it today, archeological interpretations of fossil man as frequently draw on theories of biology as they do on anthropology. The extent to which cultural and biological evolution have gone along side by side, and the way in which culture has helped to shape man's body, are neatly discussed by Washburn (1959, 1960) and Washburn and Howell (1960).

American archeology can be considered a somewhat special case of the development of prehistory generally. Because the earliest men to reach America were modern physically, there is no major current interest in the biological evolution of the American Indian, although numerous detailed studies of the physical characteristics of ancient skeletons have been made. However, there is considerable interest in the Indian's cultural evolution because his culture underwent striking changes in the 15,000 years or so that he has occupied the continent. Nevertheless, the main effort in American archeology has been to work out regional sequences of occupation (Jennings and Norbeck 1964). These are clearly of considerable value and provide the basic information that must be used in a consideration of pancontinental development of culture, especially as it relates to the development of civilizations and their influence thereafter. The publications by Jennings (1968), Jennings and Norbeck (1964), Meggers (1972), Sanders and Marino (1970), Willey (1955, 1960, 1966, 1971), and Willey and Phillips (1958) illustrate the wider consideration of New World cultural development.

No detailed history of the development of American archeology has yet been written, but the interested student can learn something about the subject by consulting Ceram (1971), J. Griffin (1959), Hallowell (1960), Jennings (1968:31–37), R. F. Lee (1970), Longacre (1970b), McGregor (1965), W. Taylor (1954), Willey (1968a), and Wilmsen (1965).

Prehistory can be contrasted with treasure hunting, art history, philology, history, and even protohistory in its goals and methods. This contrast holds in spite of the fact that the ends of these studies—to understand man's past—are superficially the same. We have therefore entitled this book *An Introduction to Prehistoric Archeology* rather than *An Introduction to Archeology*. The aims, methods, and results described in the remainder of the book pertain for the most part to prehistoric archeology.

LANDMARKS IN ARCHEOLOGY

There have been many landmarks in technical innovation and in theoretical orientation in the hundred or so years of the history of archeology. Progress in the two areas has run neither smoothly nor coordinately, and it seems that one is often out of phase with the other. This probably results from the fact that the leaders in these two areas are ordinarily different people. The "idea people" tend to be impatient with the tedious task of meticulous excavation and recording of data, and the "technical people" regard the theorists as wide-eyed visionaries whose heads are in the clouds. In fact, most archeologists probably have some interests in each area, but the balance is rarely equal, as the following quotations from Wauchope's obituary of A. V. Kidder will illustrate.

About his early career and his Ph.D. dissertation, Wauchope (1965: 152) says, "Although Kidder is best known during this early period (ca. 1915) for his stratigraphic and typological techniques and space-time reconstructions, here we see what may be even more remarkable for the time: hypotheses regarding the sociocultural significance of ancient pottery." Wauchope (1965:157–158) also cites Kidder's own words:

> Study of the Maya from the earliest times to the present involves consideration of age-long and world-wide problems: the relation of man to his habitat, the spread and interaction of nascent cultures, the origin of higher civilization,

the decay and fall of social orders, the clash of native and European races, the adjustments between conquerors and conquered, the impact of Twentieth Century ideas upon backward peoples.

And another quotation:

> In the past many facts appeared to be mutually contradictory. Modern learning, however, shows that all truths are interrelated. Chemistry and physics are striking downward to common fundamentals; zoology and botany are rapidly merging and the resultant newer biology is joining hands with the physical sciences. Similar tendencies are becoming manifest in the human field, where geography, ethnography, sociology, and psychology are constantly drawing closely together.

Later he spoke of the time when we shall "be in a position to approach the problems of cultural evolution, the solving of which is, I take it, our ultimate goal" (Wauchope 1965:159).

In view of Kidder's perception of the goals of archeology, which are strikingly modern, we may be surprised to learn that "he did not attempt to answer these questions or to marshal his data bearing on them . . . . He was certainly aware of anthropology's concern with specific culture processes and specific cultural dynamics, but he was obviously not interested in them sufficiently to investigate them empirically and in depth himself" (Wauchope 1965:163). Rather, Kidder pioneered in and provided archeology with excellent examples of field technique and methods of analyzing artifacts.

We may be tempted to look at Kidder's perception of goals as an illustration of the idea that even great men cannot do everything, but at least we can consider the possibility that Kidder may simply have been too far ahead of his time. Platt (1962:17) put it this way: "It is just as sure a recipe for failure to have the right idea fifty years too soon as five years too late." Max Planck (1949:33–34) made a similar point: "A new scientific truth does not triumph by convincing its opponents, but rather because its opponents die, and a new generation grows up that is familiar with it." As we indicated in Chapter 1, the time for the ideas is now.

In Kidder's time the greatest strides were being made in technique, and especially in gathering new data. Archeology paralleled anthropology generally in this sense and in this concern. Improvements in these areas were easy to conceive and to execute, whereas few men could see the ways to approach the goals of understanding culture processes. Such latter problems have certainly been very difficult to deal with, but we take the position now that the time is right to work as diligently in theory as in technique. To put our contention into some historical perspective, we shall review some of the landmarks in each area.

Our discussion of landmarks in technique and interpretation is sketchy and makes no pretense at being exhaustive, and certainly no attempt is made to find every relevant source. The authors who are cited have had considerable influence on the thinking of their fellow archeologists, but they were not necessarily the only archeologists who could have been mentioned, nor were they necessarily the first in their field to have stated the ideas. Readers who wish to examine the history of archeological thinking should consult some of the histories of archeology that are cited in the references.

A casual visitor to archeological excavations in 1860, 1910, and 1960 might not detect many changes in technique, but if he observed the operations carefully he would recognize several fundamental differences. Superficially excavations remain the same: archeologists dig in the ground to recover the artifacts and information that lie therein. The differences in the last hundred years have come from the ways archeologists dig and in the kinds of information they think they will be able to extract. There is mutual interaction between these two parts of the operation. Better techniques enable us to recover more information, and as we do so we develop new techniques to give us still more and different kinds of information.

Historically, the most important technique was that of stratigraphic excavation, but, though the principles of stratigraphy were learned early, they were inconsistently applied, and one still finds them ignored in isolated instances. Apparently Thomas Jefferson in 1784 was one of the first, if not the first, to apply the principles of stratigraphy in excavation (see Heizer 1959:218–221 for Jefferson's own account of this work), but as Wheeler (1956:59) notes, "Unfortunately, this seed of a new scientific skill fell upon infertile soil." The same author, in describing the excavation of the Roman town of Silchester in the 1890s, says, "It was dug like potatoes" (Wheeler 1956:150), and he quotes Petrie's comment about certain excavated sites in the Near East that are "ghastly charnel houses of murdered evidence" (Wheeler 1956:112). It was not until 1914 that American archaeologists routinely began to excavate in such a way that the stratigraphic relations of buried materials could be demonstrated (N. Nelson 1916).

As we discuss later, the importance of stratigraphy is that it enables archeologists to keep things from different periods separate. Our understanding of stratigraphy has come a long way in recent decades, partially as a consequence of the use of new techniques for discerning it, and partly in the recognition that sites can be dug by their natural levels. The increased sophistication in the use of stratigraphy can probably best be exemplified by reference to work now being done in paleolithic sites where, in the absence of convenient strata or structures, levels as thin as a few centimeters, representing brief encampments by hunters, are now being peeled off. This is sometimes termed micro-stratigraphy, and it illustrates the close interaction between the development of techniques and theory. It had been customary to dig paleolithic sites by the gross recognizable layers that were separated by marked changes in color or composition, but when it became necessary as a result (for example) of archeologists asking new kinds of questions about the size of groups occupying the sites and about the differences in kinds of artifacts in several parts of the same site, it was then necessary to devise methods of isolating artifacts from smaller and smaller spatial and chronological units of the site. The goal now sought, and being reached in some instances, is to isolate each separate occupation. Armed with data from such digs, archeologists can now enter an entirely new realm of interpretation. It is safe to predict for the future that there will be even more refinements along these lines. In Part III of this book we take up these issues more fully.

The second area of technical development concerns the invention and routine use of processes for preserving artifacts and for analyzing them. The greatest innovations have come since 1950 with the advent of radiocarbon dating and the interest that scientists in physics and chemistry have displayed in applying their skills to archeological problems. These topics are treated more fully in Parts III and IV of this book; thus they will not be described here. It is useful to note, however, that the fascination with technical applications of several types of unusually complex apparatus has probably tended to diminish interest in more theoretical things. Archeologists have suddenly become overwhelmed by the wealth of data now available or potentially available, and it is not surprising that they have turned to the use of computers to help manipulate them. It will be a long time before the impact of new techniques can be fully evaluated; this appraisal will have to wait until more archeologists have used the techniques and found which will be of real value and which are merely expensive toys. We can judge the activity in technical applications by the quantity of publications and even of research institutes that have grown up to report new developments and experiments with better devices.

TECHNIQUES

Somewhat less obtrusive, but still of fundamental importance, are techniques of survey and sampling. Again, these are examples of feedback between the need for new kinds of knowledge and the development of techniques to obtain it. Modern archeologists recognize the value of extensive and detailed surveys, especially of settlement patterns and their relation to geography, trade routes, sociopolitical structure, and the like, but they did not become customary until recent decades. An early example is Braidwood's survey of the Amuq, but the full power of the techniques was appreciated only in such studies as Adams' *Land Beyond Baghdad* (1965), which undertook to relate settlement patterns to hydrological, social, and historical factors. Here again, however, the future holds more promise as surveys become more detailed and exact with respect to the kinds of information desired. It should be added that Adams' survey depended heavily on the use of aerial photography, a technique that received its greatest impetus during World War II.

Sampling can also be regarded as an important technique in both excavation and analysis. This topic will be taken up in various contexts in later chapters, but we can point out here that the use of sampling techniques stems from ideas about patterning in culture. Sampling techniques are used in two ways: to help select sites for excavation, and to obtain reliable groups of artifacts for analysis. They are important because they enable an archeologist to make intelligent decisions about what, where, and how much to dig as well as about the quality of his data.

A final area of innovation is the use of multidisciplinary teams in archeological research projects. Although it has long been acknowledged that archeologists must draw on the advice and information of specialists in other fields, it is a relatively new technique to include these people in a field party. The newness of this concept can be sensed by reading Wheeler's (1956:153) statement: "The staff of an archeological excavation on any considerable scale includes a director, a deputy director, a supervisor for each area under excavation, a trained foreman, a small-find recorder, a pottery assistant, a photographer, a surveyor, a chemist, a draftsman, and, according to need, an epigraphist or numismatist." Naturally, Wheeler would change the composition of the group somewhat for a dig in the paleolithic, but it is noteworthy that he did not include a botanist, a zoologist, or a geomorphologist. These people, and more, are now being included almost routinely in modern large-scale operations. Although as he notes (Braidwood 1972), he was not the first to use them, it is largely to Braidwood that we can attribute the rise of the multidisciplinary approach; and the reasons should be clear. He was concerned with the origins of agriculture, a topic that no archeologist could hope to solve on his own. As research projects have become more "problem-oriented" they have come to include more and more of the specialists without whose help the problems cannot be solved. We must also mention that it is necessary to have these people work in the field with the archeologists so that each person can evaluate the problem on the spot. It is hard to overestimate the degree to which congenial colleagues seeking a solution to a common problem can stimulate one another to more penetrating insights and consequently to better results.

INTERPRETATION

This brief discussion of landmarks in the history of ideas serves to put the ideas into their proper historical context, but they will be discussed in greater detail in Chapter 4. We may view the current directions in prehistory, outlined in Chapter 2, as a logical outgrowth of the pioneering efforts cited below.

All archeology is based on the idea that there are ancient remains of human activity to be found. This may sound simple-minded, but, considered in the context of the history of archeological theory, it is basic. Until people knew there was a human past long enough to be interesting, there could be no archeology. Thanks to history, educated people were aware of some antiquity long before archeology started, but they commonly held the notion that the earth is only about 6000 years old. They had little knowledge of people vastly different from themselves in the modern world, let alone in the ancient, and consequently no interest in digging to expose the past. Had this situation prevailed, archeology would have developed as a branch of history with a special interest in the civilizations of the Mediterranean and Near East. Schliemann and others of his time were digging to find things they knew once existed. The real intellectual breakthrough came when scientists found that the earth is millions rather than thousands of years old, and when they discovered that life in the remote past was far different from life today.

Geologists and paleontologists were responsible for these ideas, which became important for archeology when the stratigraphic association between crude stone tools, geologic age, and extinct animals was demonstrated. Hard on the heels of this discovery came the ideas of biological and cultural evolution. When these ideas had taken hold, they showed scientists the potential of archeology and gave them a goal to seek: the missing link. A rash of activity followed, particularly in Europe, which resulted in the first syntheses of Pleistocene prehistory in the late 1880s.

Although techniques of digging saw little improvement during the first 50 years of archeological activity, the important concept of *sequence* (itself borrowed from geology and history) had become clear and was effectively used in the early general accounts. The seminal idea was that the sites contained continuous records of change that could be arranged chronologically to give an idea of the development of cultures. These records were pieced together from evidence that was recovered stratigraphically, although the stratigraphy was crude by modern standards. The discovery of sequences led naturally to an awareness of differences between areas, and this awareness in turn to the idea of distinct archeological cultures that prehistorians likened to modern "tribes."

By virtue of hindsight we can see two important concepts implicit in these findings. Both concern culture systems. First, there is the idea of cumulative and directional change in the technologies of the ancient peoples, and, second, the idea that because each culture has its distinct set of traits the boundaries of separate culture systems can be inferred. The use of these concepts can be seen clearly in such archeological classics as Breuil's *Les subdivisions du paléolithique supérieur et leur signification* in 1912 and A. de Mortillet's *La classification paléthnologique* in 1908. Both of these works had a profound influence on archeological thinking in Europe.

With the results of the preceding decades' work compiled into a systematic chronological-developmental form, the way was paved for making inferences about intangible aspects of prehistoric life. The artifacts of the paleolithic referred to hunters, and it was assumed that these people led lives analogous to those of modern people who had the same technology. But the aspect of prehistoric life that attracted most speculation was their art. The early prehistorians avidly excavated—and sometimes looted—sites to recover engraved bones and stones, and caves were systematically searched for paintings. When the splendid polychrome paintings on the ceiling of Altamira were discovered in 1879, they stimulated a chain of speculation about the intellectual capacities and interests of prehistoric man, a subject that still intrigues a number of authors, as we can see from the quantity of books that not only illustrate the art but attempt to interpret its mental, religious, magical, and technical aspects.

Although these ventures into the spiritual life of early man are ingenious and interesting, they can scarcely evoke the ring of credibility that studies of diet and even of social organization can. Grahame Clark's pioneering work, *Prehistoric Europe: The Economic Basis,* published in 1952, showed the way for investigations of subsistence, settlement, and technology that continue today. But Clark did more: he effectively integrated concepts of ecology into archeology by showing how economy is "an adjustment to specific physical and biological conditions of certain needs, capacities, aspirations and values." He says,

> There are thus two sides to the equation—on the one hand the character of the habitat, itself to a greater or less degree influenced or even conditioned by culture, and on the other the kind of life regarded as appropriate by the community and the resources, in the form of knowledge, technical equipment and social organization, available for its realization. The relation between man and external nature is thus a dynamic one and the development of culture viewed in its economic aspect is indeed one of man's growing knowledge of and control over forces external to himself (G. Clark 1952:7).

The importance of these concepts is that they treat man as a variable in a natural world—one element in an ecosystem—and that man's culture, as seen in artifacts, is adaptive. The idea of culture as an adaptive system thus emerges, and with it a sense that the artifacts can be viewed as tools used by man to cope with his world. A change in emphasis could then be made from the delineation of technical sequences, which had often been viewed as examples illustrating evolution, to an interpretation of the processes by which this evolution had taken place. Archeologists continue to use these concepts, and they have been reiterated in a number of books that explicitly use the term "ecology" in the title.

The next step, which is being developed today, is to attempt to reconstruct the social systems operative in the past. To do so, ecological theory and a thorough knowledge of the way modern social systems work are required. Archeologists can thus make use of their reconstructions of the physical environmental conditions, their knowledge of prehistoric settlement patterns, and the hunting or gathering practices of the people, to make a number of reasonable inferences about the kind of social organization. The inferences stem from the idea that under specified conditions people have a limited range of cultural possibilities (or responses); then it is often possible to make more specific inferences and say what these responses are.

These concepts partly stem from, and partly lead into, an interest in general systems that force archeologists to look at ever-wider geographic areas to try to reconstruct the interplay of people in the several separate groups comprising an effective network of interaction. The view thus shifts from the local group in isolation to the local group in a context of both natural and social environments. What we see today in archeology represents a gamut of interests from collecting artifacts and building up local sequences of technological change to interpretation of internal differences in sites, to the reconstruction of broad cultural systems, with the emphasis on what people were doing to cope with their immediate situations. These latter concerns lead to attempts to understand the processes by which cultures operate. Here it is that the logical position shifts from working first with archeological data and attempting to make inferences about them to phrasing testable hypotheses about culture systems and attempting to test them with archeological data. This area has yet to be exploited, but we shall give a number of hypotheses in Chapter 21 that lead in this direction. The lead in proposing such changes in orientation is taken by archeologists who are aware of relevant theory that has been developed in other fields. Just as early prehistorians took their cues from historians, today archeologists read works by geographers, communications and learning theorists, and biological ecologists. By virtue of their incompleteness, prehistoric data are unlikely to lead to the generation of new theories except where they come into conflict with models of what "should" be that have been derived from other fields in the social sciences. A priori archeologists assume some uniformitarianism in human behavior, at least since the later Paleolithic (that is, for the last 35,000 years). In other words, we assume that people were basically the same as, though technologically inferior to, us today. Accordingly, it is assumed that we can use theoretical principles that have been deduced from a study of modern behavior. On the social or cultural level of inference, uniformitarianism may not be true, but in a biological sense it is presently taken for granted. It seems reasonably clear now that men are faced with the same kinds of situations that face the other living organisms studied by ecologists. Thus we now assume that man's behavior is an aspect of his adaptation and the mechanism of his interaction with the environment; our source of possible doubt is that we can infer the specific behavior from what we know of people today.

It is worth emphasizing here that the use of such hypotheses does not mean that we regard them as proved. Hypotheses are used to organize our thinking and direct our questioning; it remains for archeologists and others in the behavioral sciences to try to put them into the form of questions that can be answered by explicit research programs. This task becomes the domain of research strategy, an area that will be dealt with later in this book.

REFERENCES

General Works on the History of Archeology: Breuil 1941; Casson 1939; Ceram 1958, 1971; Daniel 1950, 1967b; Eggers 1959; Hamy 1870; Harriss 1971; Heizer 1959, 1962a, 1969; Laming-Emperaire 1963, 1964; Longacre 1970b; Lynch and Lynch 1968; Oakley 1964a; Shorr 1935; Wace 1949; Zehren 1962.

Dilettantes and Bargain Hunters: D. C. Allen 1960; Belzoni 1820; Clair 1957; Creel 1937; Dannenfeldt 1959; W. Emery 1961; J. Grant 1966; Lloyd 1955, 1963; Loftus 1858; Lyell 1872; Mayes 1961; Parrot 1939; Peet 1943; Poole and Poole 1966; Rassam 1897; Woolley 1958; T. Wright 1844.

Deep-Sea Divers: Bascom 1971; Bass 1963, 1966; de Borhegyi 1961; Dumas 1962; Frost 1963; Goggin 1960; Holmquist and Wheeler 1964; Olsen 1961c; Ryan and Bass 1962; Silverberg 1963; Trockmorton and Bullitt 1963.

Texts, Temples, and Tombs: Budge 1920; R. Carpenter 1933; Chadwick 1961; Cleator 1962; Doblehofer 1959; M. Grant 1958; Mellaart 1959; Page 1959; D. W. Thomas 1961; Zeuner 1963.

Illicit Traffic in Antiquities: R. Adams 1970a; Beals 1971; Coggins 1969, 1970; Daniel 1971a; R. Ford 1971; Robertson 1972; *Society for American Archaeology* 1971.

Protohistory: Albright 1957; Bibby 1956; Childe 1957; Dawkins 1880; Griffiths 1956; C. Hawkes 1954; Hood 1967; Locke 1912; Piggott 1959a; Rowe 1944, 1945.

Adam and Beyond: Jennings and Norbeck 1964; G. de Mortillet 1867; van Riet Lowe 1950; Washburn 1959, 1960; Washburn and Howell 1960; Wauchope 1965; Willey 1955, 1960; Willey and Phillips 1958.

Technique: (Chaps. in Parts III and IV) R. Adams 1965; Braidwood 1960; Brill 1971; Dittert and Wendorf 1963; Heizer and Graham 1967; Hudson 1967; Papworth and Binford 1962; G. Schwartz 1967; Wheeler 1956; Willey 1953; E. Wood 1963.

Interpretation: (Chaps. in Part V) Breuil 1912; Childe 1944a, 1944b; G. Clark 1952, 1957; Mortillet 1908; South 1955; L. White 1947, 1959a.

European Paleolithic Art: Bandi 1961; Breuil 1952; Brodrick 1948; Burkitt 1955; Graziozi 1956, 1960; Laming-Emperaire 1962; Lantier 1961; Leroi-Gourhan 1964, 1967, 1968; Poulik 1956; T. Powell 1966.

Dictionaries and Encyclopedias of Archeology: W. Bray and Trump 1970; Cottrell 1960.

PART 11

THEORY AND DATA

Any scholarly discipline has its own set of theory and concepts as well as its typical subject matter or data. The two, along with the goals or central problems, are inextricably interrelated. In Chapter 1 we listed some of the goals of archeology and in Chapter 2 we discussed how archeology is being done today. Our historical review in Chapter 3 pointed to some landmarks in ideas and methods. In these initial chapters we mentioned a number of concepts without further explanation and it is essential now to elaborate on these key ideas. This we do in Chapter 4. In this chapter we discuss the basic concepts that relate to prehistory, to man, and to his culture. Both our appreciation of the evidence of prehistory and the ways we deal with it depend on these concepts. We reserve until Part V a discussion of the concepts that pertain primarily to interpretation of the evidence.

CHAPTER FOUR

BASIC CONCEPTS IN PREHISTORY

It is sometimes said that anthropology and archeology are fields in which theory is poorly developed. This is a fair criticism if we take it to mean that the fundamental concepts have not been adequately defined, consistently used, and systematically taught. It is not going too far to say that as archeologists we have failed to get our concepts across to many students. That this is true is apparent when students who have sat in class for a semester and mastered all manner of trivial data cannot conjure up any reasonable statement of how these data can be used, much less how one converts data in the form of artifacts fresh from the ground into statements about people who lived in the past. The problem seems to be that few archeologists say much about how they arrive at their conclusions. This point has been stressed repeatedly in the writings of new archeology: we must make our assumptions and procedures explicit. If archeology is to develop as a rational science that follows orderly procedures it is absolutely essential to make the underlying assumptions clear. For students and professionals alike, this means continually asking: What do we know? How do we know? And what difference does it make?

Throughout this book we try to explain why archeologists do the things they do. Many of the concepts we use are derived from other fields and adapted for use in prehistory. We have borrowed from geology, anthropology, and biology, to name only a few, and it is to these fields that one must turn for supplementary reading on points that we discuss only briefly here. Students who have substantial backgrounds in these fields may consider our treatment of the concepts overly simplified, but it is in the way the concepts are used rather than in their substantive content that we are interested. Thus, we do not belabor our discussion of biological processes; instead we try to show to what degree they are analogous to cultural processes. Similarly, we look at the biological and cultural aspects of man for the purpose of illustrating that archeological interpretation depends on which among the concepts we choose. As research in biological and cultural anthropology continues, some of the concepts will change and archeologists will change their ideas accordingly. It is important, therefore, to show in this chapter what concepts are currently accepted and how they are put to use.

ANTIQUITY AND CHANGE

We discussed in Chapter 3 the slow development of the idea that man has an antiquity that goes well beyond recorded history. This is a profound concept and essential to all prehistoric archeology, but the concept itself is not obvious. Although most peoples have a sense of the past through kinship lines and perhaps through seeing ruins of structures built by forgotten peoples, they usually feel that the past was very much like the present and that it was not very long. Consequently the past holds little interest for most persons. It is fair to say that most people are more concerned with the present and the future than they are with the past.

Coupled with the idea of antiquity is the idea that man has changed, that he has not always been as he is today. From history one knows of changes in the political fortunes of peoples and of changes in technology, but the idea that man was once fundamentally different was not apparent until some chance finds were correctly interpreted. Without prior knowledge that the earth is very old and that it, too, has undergone major changes, it would not have been possible to interpret the finds of ancient tools and human fossils correctly. As we mentioned earlier there was considerable debate about these; most scholars believed that the tools belonged to early historic times, or were natural phenomena, and that the fossil bones were those of abnormal modern people. Archeology did not invent the ideas of antiquity and change, but when they had become sufficiently well-established in geology to overcome the prevailing beliefs, it capitalized on them.

Geologists could see landforms changing, and they rightly postulated that the processes responsible had been going on since the earth was formed. continual deposition on earth as things are discarded and as soils erode from

Similarly, paleontologists were able to discern differences in the fossils in strata of different ages. As the fossil record became clearer, it could be seen that species replaced species and that forms of life greatly different from those of today had once roamed the earth. It was but a small step to apply these concepts to man himself. It remained to discover the mechanisms that govern such changes, but after Darwin most scientists accepted the possibility of the evolutionary development of all forms of life. After this time man's past took on an entirely new interest for scholars.

Today there are still some who do not accept human evolution. For these persons studies of fossil man are meaningless, and for them a major portion of prehistory does not exist. Thus they would deny archeological interpretations that depend on ideas of great antiquity and fundamental changes in form or quality. It is important to point this out because it illustrates very well how dependent we are in any kind of analysis on initial premises. Before we can study anything we must make as an operating hypothesis that it exists and that it has certain properties. The existence and properties of anything are observed or deduced, and until our conceptions of them are confounded by the evidence, we continue to accept them.

STRATIGRAPHY AND SEQUENCE

Closely related to ideas of antiquity and change is the concept that there is a continual deposition on earth as things are discarded and as soils erode from higher land and are laid down at lower elevations. The deposition takes place in orderly layers that chart the sequence of events. Thus if one digs through these layers, he encounters successively older material as he goes deeper. In archeology this is important because we can put things in their proper chronological sequence if we can isolate strata that lie above one another. This concept leads to one of the principal methods of relative dating (see Chaps. 7 and 15). It was largely through the use of stratigraphy that geologists were able to deduce the antiquity of the earth. By analogy with modern events, they could see that it took a long time for layers to build up and for changes to occur.

UNIFORMITARIANISM

Without the concept of uniformitarianism—that the present is a guide to the past because the *processes* of geology (for example, uplift, erosion, deposition) are constant—geologists would not have been able to infer that it had taken millions of years for the layers now seen on earth to have accumulated and changed. The same principle is applied by prehistorians who regularly use analogy with modern peoples as a guide to interpreting prehistoric ways of life (Chap. 16). With regard to human behavior in the past, however, it is now acknowledged that it may have no exact counterparts among modern peoples. This is especially true with fossil forms of man. Behavior aside, if we look at the processes of biological change, scientists agree that the same processes affect all forms of life and have been constant since life began. Thus the principle of uniformitarianism applies directly to studies of human evolution.

CUMULATIVE CHANGE

An underlying tenet of anthropology is that human culture is learned and transmitted from one generation to the next. This means that changes in culture can be and often are cumulative. Thus we find cultures changing in the course of human history from simple to more complex. There are also those who believe that life systems in general change in similar fashion, from relatively undifferentiated toward more diversified (Chap. 21).

These concepts are useful to prehistorians chiefly as an aid in relative dating, especially when change can be expressed in artifacts. Thus sites with simpler assemblages of material are likely to be older. That this is not necessarily true is explained later (Chap. 15). The concepts have value as well in stimulating consideration of the question why change tends to be toward increasing complexity through diversification and specialization. It is in the principles of ecology and general system theory that we find the explanatory working hypotheses in use today.

The concepts mentioned above make the discipline of prehistoric studies possible and set forth certain rules of procedure. Below we raise concepts that define the subject matter of prehistory and serve to differentiate it from related fields like history. These concepts also set the stage for the interpretation of man's behavior in antiquity in terms used by ethnologists and ecologists. Much of the work being done today in American archeology depends on concepts derived from ethnology and biological studies. This text is not the place to give a thorough review of these studies, but we will briefly mention those that are important in the present context. Concepts that relate specifically to interpretation will be discussed in Chapter 16.

A number of basic concepts concern the nature of man. We are accustomed to repeating that he is both a biological and a cultural being, and to this we should add that man in the singular, if not necessarily collectively (and there is some debate on this point), has his psychological, intellectual, spiritual, and mystical characteristics as well. Together these comprise the facets of mankind that we can presently perceive and hope to analyze. In prehistory most analysis focuses on aspects of man's material culture.

BIOLOGICAL ASPECTS OF MAN

Like other animals, man must deal with the problems of eating, protection, and reproduction. Because he reproduces through mating between the sexes, offspring share the characteristics of both parents. For this reason biological change between generations is inevitable, although within any population over the short run it may not be noticeable. In the long run the random combinations of genes in a population will introduce changes that are noticeable. Thus, even if we were to assume biological continuity, no population today would resemble one of 5000 years ago in the total configuration of genetically controlled characteristics. Even if closed breeding populations had been maintained over such a long time, no population today could be identical with any 5000 years ago. It is not implied that such changes are for the better or worse, only that differences must exist.

The chief factors that cause changes in the biology of populations are genetic drift, mutation, and natural selection. Genetic drift is a change in the gene frequencies in a population. Mutation is the unpredictable spontaneous alteration of genetic material which would eventually bring about some changes in the genetic structure of populations even if drift were not a factor. Although most such mutations are thought to be deleterious and consequently have a low probability of remaining in the gene pool, others may be inconsequential or even beneficial and thus be heritable. Many feel that mutations create the potential for adaptation to circumstances of stress in populations by providing the genetic material that preadapts a segment of the population for survival under conditions of change. The final factor, natural selection, works by culling out that segment of the population that cannot reproduce rapidly enough to keep it viable. The result is that certain genes may be eliminated from a population. Organisms are said to be well adapted when they can maintain their breeding population at a high enough level to support stability or growth. It is through natural selection that mutations may be removed from a population or increased at the expense of other, less adaptive, genes.

These various factors ensure that there will be changes over time in the genetic makeup of human populations. Some maintain that culture removes much of the pressure of natural selection and consequently allows greater genetic diversity to exist, but one may also make the case that the biological organism must adapt to culture itself. In the history of mankind culture, with its accumulating requirements, has probably acted upon the genetic makeup of populations through favoring the survival of persons with greater intelligence and manipulative skills, to name just two obvious traits that have some biological basis. It is likewise true that people may select mates according to physical characteristics, and if this were systematically observed, it would serve to cull out certain "undesirable" genes.

Throughout this discussion of biological factors we have stressed populations, for it is only in dealing with them that we can see genetic factors at work. The science of genetics is based on populations and on the probability that one thing will lead to another. It does not in any way deal with the certainty that anything will happen to an individual.

ADAPTATION

As far as prehistory is concerned, the most important concept currently in use is that of adaptation. Many authors, especially those interested in the processes of culture, see changes in the archeological record as evidence of adaptation.

What is frequently not stated is that the evidence consists of artifacts which relate to cultural events; these are only loosely analogous to biological processes. Moreover, in emphasizing adaptation, archeologists often neglect to consider that changes may be maladaptive or neutral. To state that change is necessarily adaptive is to prejudge the case, a matter that we discuss more fully in Chapter 21.

The fact of biological change as evidenced in the fossil record is a matter of great concern in interpretation, for it raises the possibility that early forms of men did not have the same biological capabilities as men of today whose behavior is usually used for purposes of analogy. To deal with this problem some anthropologists have undertaken studies of other primates: chimpanzees, gorillas, and especially baboons, which are the easiest to study and which occupy an ecological niche similar to that of early forms of men. The assumption is that the earliest forms of men were more similar than modern man in mentality and in behavior to those nonhuman primates which have only the most rudimentary "culture."

Recent research in this branch of anthropology is taking an even more biological turn as it investigates the degree of genetic relationship between species and attempts to determine the sequence and chronology of events that led from ancestral forms to modern man and apes. These studies will no doubt have considerable bearing on the kinds of archeological analogies that will be made in the future and on the kinds of interpretations that will be considered useful about the behavior of fossil men.

In brief resume, prehistorians, for the most part, take man's biological heritage into account only peripherally. This is an area of theory that badly needs further consideration so that the assumptions that are usually made implicitly become explicit and amenable to serious discussion and testing.

PSYCHOLOGICAL AND INTELLECTUAL ASPECTS OF MAN

Archeologists have usually ignored psychological and intellectual factors in their interpretations of man's history. For that matter, the subject is not very popular in anthropological studies of any kind, partly because the factors are extremely difficult to assess and because they pertain more to persons than to populations. In contrast, humanists often invoke creativity and decadence in explanation of phenomena under their investigation. Others have attempted to attribute success or failure of a culture to biological factors that affect intelligence and creativity. None of these approaches has found much support among anthropologists or even among geneticists. Likewise, statements about peoples' accepting or declining challenges, or about their acting in accord with some vision of self-determination, have been severely criticized by historians and anthropologists alike. Nonetheless the persistence of such ideas suggests there is something to them, if not in fact, in that people believe them to be true. We might compare this with current findings of psychologists that children whose teachers are told they are smart are likely to do much better in school. The interpretation is that the teachers "saw" and attempted to nurture the talent they believed was there, when, in fact, they were deliberately misled about the test scores of students for purposes of the psychological experiment. In these and perhaps in most cases students performed up to their teachers' expectations.

Seldom are historical explanations phrased in such rational terms, however, and it is this that makes them so difficult to handle systematically. The same is true if we deliberately try to discover rationality in human behavior. Much of new archeology is dedicated to finding the rational basis of human behavior, either through laws that govern such behavior or through a mechanical description of the ways in which various behaviors affect one another. When one postulates relationships between definable and measurable variables, he can test their correctness with appropriate experiments. But the concept that underlies such hypotheses is that the relationships are in some way determined and rational. Thus the postulated relationships must conform to logic. The alternative is seldom mentioned.

Ultimately, science can hardly afford to dismiss out-of-hand factors that are thought by most people to be important, even though they do not lend themselves to easy analysis. However, in the present state of archeological science, we must work with the kind of data we have and can hope to control. There will be work aplenty for future generations as we accumulate well-founded concepts and results.

CULTURE

To begin, we must make a distinction between *culture* as an abstraction and *cultures* as particular groups of people who are named. For example, we speak of culture in general, of American culture, or Hopi culture, or in archeology, the La Tene or Adena cultures. Because the same word is used for three rather different concepts, we must define each separately. This initial discussion will deal with culture in the general sense as a distinctly human phenomenon.

It is often said that humans have culture whereas animals do not, but the distinctions between the two have become less clear with intensive studies of nonhuman primates and other forms of life which behave in noninstinctive ways. To clarify the nature of culture we may contrast it with strictly biologically controlled behavior. Culture has been defined as "historically created designs for living, explicit and implicit, rational, irrational, and non-rational, which exist at any given time as potential guides for the behavior of man" (Kluckhohn and Kelly 1945:97). Humans have many of these socially transmitted patterns of learned behavior while animals' behavior is more genetically controlled and instinctive (W. Bray 1972). Animals cannot pass learning from one generation to another except by example, and they are relatively inflexible in learning itself. On the other hand, some human behavior is thought to be instinctive so one might express the distinction between the species in the proportion of behavior that is controlled through either learning or instinct. However, there is no simple gradation between humans and animals; there is a vast difference.

At the base of this difference is the fact that culture is transmitted by symbolic communication (abstract thought through speech). This fact has two important implications: culture is uniquely human because other animals are not equipped for symbolic communication, and cultures (in the specific sense) may change abruptly in ways that appear to defy our generalization that it is learned from preceding generations. It is symbolic communication that allows the rapid transmission of knowledge and experience from one group of people to another, so that, for example, the Manus Islanders studied by Margaret Mead can leap in one generation from the Stone Age to the twentieth century.

The contrast with biologically transmitted behavior lies in the fact that biological information depends on the reproduction of matter, while culture depends on the transmission of learned behavior and is not constrained by the same physical laws. Thus the mechanisms of biological change and evolution do not pertain except metaphorically to cultural change and evolution (Huxley 1955:16–22).

Very little archeological discussion concerns culture in the general sense. Indeed anthropologists have argued whether there is any validity to the concept at all (Mellor 1972). Still most of us accept the existence of culture even though it may be an abstraction constructed out of experience and intuition. L. A. White (1949) and others have written extensively of this intangible concept and made it a central focus of anthropological studies. In archeology we are much more concerned with the particular cultures and the ways they change or the reasons they are different. In order to discuss these matters, however, we must consider the properties that culture (in the general sense) is thought to have.

Pattern. Culture is usually thought to be patterned, or ordered in a systematic way such that the component parts fit together harmoniously. Looked at this way, culture consists of various subsystems: technological, social, religious, ideological, and economic. The underlying assumption is that these subsystems interact in ways that are mutually supporting or at least not harmful. We may infer from this that people must behave consistently so that they do not upset the working of the system. When people behave consistently, we may say that their behavior is patterned. Finally people in different cultures behave in somewhat different ways.

Archeologically we see evidence that these concepts are valid in the way artifacts are distributed in sites. The artifacts themselves show patterning, a fact that has been tested through the use of various analytical techniques. To demonstrate that patterning exists is only the first step, for archeologists would like to use this fact to infer what behavior causes it. This is not easy and it must ultimately depend either on direct ethnographic analogy or on general hypotheses about the relationship between artifacts and behavior that are themselves derived from a study of the modern world.

Change. Another property of culture is that it changes. The ways it changes are loosely analogous to the ways biological organisms change, but there are important differences. We have already mentioned that culture is transmitted through extracorporal means, which allows for rapid and dramatic changes. We should also remember that the anthropologists' conception of culture was inferred from observation of peoples' behavior and the discussion of a particular culture usually focuses on an ideal set of patterns. In the beliefs of any people there are proper ways to behave and proper ways to manufacture things. To some degree, people who are brought up (enculturated) in that culture adhere to these ideals, but there is typically a considerable range of variation in their actual behavior. For this reason we find what we may call *random change,* a process that is analogous to genetic drift. The learning of appropriate or ideal behavior patterns cannot be perfect, so there will inevitably be some differences between generations which may not be noticeable in the short run but which may accumulate over time as long as populations remain somewhat isolated.

Diffusion is one of the primary mechanisms of cultural change. Because culture is transmitted largely through symbolic communication, it is possible for aspects of it to be exported over long distances as in the case of the Manus Islanders. Although it would be rare for entire cultures to be so transmitted, certain patterns of behavior and customs may be introduced into another culture and adopted. Conversion of peoples to foreign religions is a case in point; here a set of behavior of foreign origin replaces or mixes with native traditions. There is no direct biological counterpart to this kind of change, although hybridization is somewhat analogous.

Invention is also a primary mechanism of change. The usual implication is that people consciously and purposefully invent things they need. That invention need not be deliberate, however, was discussed at length by A. L. Kroeber (1948) in an article that attributes many inventions to man's delight in play. Manipulative and intellectual "play" is fun and sometimes results in inventions of importance. However, whether inventions are deliberate or not, insofar as the things invented become a part of a culture and affect the overall cultural patterns, we may say that the culture has changed.

Accidental discovery is closely related to invention and can be considered an agent of change if the value of the discovery is recognized and the resultant invention put to use. Accidental discovery is analogous to mutation and is probably only infrequently of value or recognized to be of value and hence retained as part of culture.

The importance of the processes enumerated above is that they produce variability, which, like genetic diversity, may be crucial to survival of the species under rapidly changing circumstances. However, unlike biological change, the material out of which changes can be effected need not lie in the culture itself, but can be borrowed from another culture. Thus, the ability to transmit and borrow useful behavior from outside one's own culture is extremely important for humans, and has resulted in the exceptionally rapid development of the inventory of culture. We may say that the pace and magnitude of cultural evolution today far outstrips the pace of biological change in the human species.

Adaptation. Aside from its ability to transmit information through extrasomatic, symbolic means, culture is seen primarily as an agent of human adaptation in much the same way as the ability to run fast may confer a selective advantage on certain animals. In this sense, culture is a biological phenomenon (G. G. Simpson 1964). Ordinarily, however, culture is seen as standing between biological man and the physical and organic environment that surrounds him. Today it is unthinkable for man to exist without culture, for he is no longer equipped to survive solely through his biological equipment. His basic needs of subsistence, shelter, and reproduction are largely satisfied through learned behavior and effected through the spoken communication with his fellow men that leads to cooperation.

Consider how ill-equipped the newborn infant is; even if he were of adult size and strength, he could not cope with the world about him. He lacks the basic tools for survival. Compared with the predators who would find him succulent quarry, he lacks the speed, size, and strength that would help him defend himself, and he would find it hard to keep warm and obtain suitable safe shelter. Man survives because of his culture: tools, equipment, social behavior, skills, and knowledge, and these are learned after birth. To say that culture is adaptive does not imply that people always behave adaptively, but only that without culture they would not survive. The adaptive aspects of culture are a matter that will be explored in greater detail in Chapters 16 and 21.

THE RELATION BETWEEN BIOLOGICAL AND CULTURAL PROCESSES

It is incorrect to argue that biological change is no longer important in man simply because culture can take care of most biological problems. What should be said is that there is feedback between biological and cultural change, each affecting the other. Washburn (1960), Washburn and Lancaster (1968), and others (for example, Bordes 1971) have made a strong case that increments of culture had a profound effect on man's early development, and this position is not seriously challenged today. What has been debated is whether biological change is important today or whether, in fact, man is changing biologically. A fair assessment of the situation points to the probability that culture has altered the adaptive value of certain genes. For example, it is no longer essential to have good eyesight, or the ability to run fast, or to hear or smell well. People with gross deficiencies in these abilities can survive, breed, and consequently add to the relative numbers of persons with these problems. On the other hand, in industrial cultures there is increasing dependence on the ability to use the mind, to communicate effectively, and to manipulate things with dexterity. One might think that selection would favor persons with these skills, but success in a culture need not be only in the biological sense of reproduction. In fact, the biological analogy fails, for, as Simpson says, "Natural selection solely and always favors relative efficiency in reproduction. Artificial [cultural] selection may, and usually does, favor other and conflicting goals (and here they *are* goals)" (G. C. Simpson 1964:151). That is to say, people are at least as concerned with matters like quality of life as they are with quantity of offspring, and the former goal competes with the latter.

As examples of the interplay between biology and culture, W. Bray (1972) enumerates a number of cultural factors that may affect biological change in man: (1) population size, (2) assortive mating, (3) the degree of interpopulation mobility, (4) control and regulation of childbirth, (5) disease, and (6) alteration of mutation rate (for example, through use of drugs). "Genetic changes have brought about increased ability for adaptation by cultural means, and this cultural adaptation has changed environmental conditions in such a way that new selective pressures have arisen, giving rise to further genetic changes in the population."

ARCHEOLOGICAL CULTURES

The preceding discussion concerned culture in general; of much greater relevance to archeologists is the concept of the archeological culture. It follows from the principle of uniformitarianism that if modern man is a cultural animal and people today have cultures, there were also cultures in prehistoric times. In archeology we deal not with patterns of behavior (including customs, language, and speculative thought) but with artifacts, and from them we must infer the existence of cultures. V. Gordon Childe (1947:51) defined the relationship in the following way.

> An archaeological culture is an assemblage of artifacts that recurs repeatedly associated together in dwellings of the same kind and with burials of the same rite. The arbitrary pecularities of all cultural traits are assumed to be concrete expressions of the common social traditions that bind together a culture. Artifacts hang together in assemblages, not only because they were used in the same age, but also because they were used by the same people, made or executed in accordance with techniques, rites or styles prescribed by a social tradition, handed on by precept and example and modifiable in the same way.

Thus for archeologists, cultures exist in the form of tools, pottery, burials, styles, ornaments, and art, because these things are repeatedly found together. Artifacts are part of a people's material culture, but an ax is not culture, nor is a burial or a house. It is only when certain kinds of axes, burials, and houses are found together in several sites that archeologists refer to the repeated associations of artifacts as evidence of a culture. All these statements imply a kind of grouping an ethnologist would call a "tribe," or a "people," or a "society." We expect that people who occupy a common territory and share a common material culture will also share such things as language, ideas about right and wrong, preferences in art, religion, and other intangible traits. These elements of nonmaterial culture are not recovered by prehistoric archeologists, but every effort is made to make inferences about the social or nonmaterial aspects of the remains they examine. In this sense archeology is "paleoethnology."

In most archeological writing, cultures consist of things that are found in excavation. The most important of these units are usually termed "artifacts." Artifacts are then ordinarily classified into types that serve to identify their variety and to simplify their description. An archeologist can then characterize an excavation by the kinds of artifacts it produced. Should the artifacts be different from those found in other excavations, he may decide to let them stand for a culture and give it a name. This method is not precisely the same as that used by ethnologists to identify cultures, because it does not take into account such intangible and important considerations as language, religion, or political relations; nor does it imply any knowledge of the way the culture was organized. The closest analogue to this procedure is the drawing up of trait lists in ethnology in order to determine which people are related most closely. The judgment in this instance would be based on the number of items that two or more groups of people shared without any particular weighing of the importance of the artifacts held in common. The definition of an archeological culture in this way is traditional and serves important functions for comparing excavations, but it does not necessarily lend itself to the kinds of questions that archeologists now think relevant.

It is possible to deal, as Childe did, with culture largely as a taxonomic device for ordering his archeological evidence in time and space, but modern approaches emphasize the behavorial aspects of prehistoric cultures. What were the people doing? What were they like? Why did they change?

There is consensus among archeologists that artifacts—tools and other things made or used by man—are "fossilized" evidence of human behavior. If this operating assumption is true, it follows that we *may* (but not necessarily will) be able to infer the behavior from the artifacts. As Binford (1962: 219–220) has pointed out, there are three kinds of behavior on which artifacts may inform: technological, sociological, and ideological. If all artifacts relate to one or more of these kinds of behavior, we may be able to infer the behavior if we can correctly identify to which uses the artifacts were put. In his study of artifacts a prehistorian interested in behavior will keep in mind the possible relevance of his data to these categories and thus establish a structure to his analysis. However, although one can easily conceptualize three important areas of behavior, and in specific instances relate artifacts to them, it is quite another problem to verify the relationship between most artifacts and the behavioral context within which they were used. Logically we cannot do this solely with archeological material for we would only be correlating assumed evidence with assumed behavioral patterns. We could hardly fail to find ourselves correct. Instead what we must do is study modern peoples to see how their behavior relates to the tangible traces that can be found archeologically. The study by David (1971) referred to earlier is one example, and *Approaches to the Social Dimensions of Mortuary Practices,* edited by James Brown, goes into considerable detail on the possibilities of making inferences about the intangible aspects of culture from one set of commonly found data. However, even in regard to burial practices which have been described and analyzed since the early days of anthropology, there has not emerged a systematic set of concepts and procedures for their analysis archeologically in behavioral terms.

In shifting the emphasis from cultures to cultural practices, we avoid one dilemma but raise some problems. We avoid labeling archeological remains with names of cultures that imply distinct social groups when we have not the slightest idea whether such groups are manifest in the criteria we use to identify them. To confess the lack of tangible support for such labeling casts into doubt all the historical reconstructions that speak of migrations, wars, and other kinds of interaction among prehistoric peoples. This does not suggest that such activities did not occur, but only that the identity of the groups—their sociocultural characteristics as well as their distribution in time and space—is in question.

If instead we speak of cultural practices, we raise another problem; namely, to determine the relationship between archeological data and the behavior. What we gain, however, is precision of focus and the possibility of discovering the relationship through a study of living peoples. This we cannot do if we wish to talk about prehistoric cultures because many of the criteria on which cultures today are defined are intangible. The archeological culture thus remains a typically archeological construct in which validity can be tested only with reference to the concepts that underlie it. In short, archeological cultures are not analogous to the cultures an ethnographer describes and should not be treated as if they were.

The concepts discussed in this chapter are basic to an understanding of archeology as distinct from history and the humanities. Archeologists, like anthropologists, take the view that man is only one part of the organic world, and he exists in a context that is both social and physical. The thing that sets man apart is his culture, but that too can be seen as a biologically based phenomenon in the sense that people have the biological capacity to symbolize through speech and thus transmit abstract thoughts. Still, in important ways man is an animal, and his biological and cultural qualities affect one another through mutual interaction.

In order to understand the special nature of archeology, one must recognize that the data themselves to a large extent determine the kinds of things archeologists can investigate. It is commonplace to assert that archeological remains represent only a portion of the things used by people in a culture, and that even if we were to include all things, we would still omit a great deal of the essence of a culture. Under these circumstances archeology cannot be all that anthropology is nor can it routinely employ concepts of anthropology. Prehistorians must adapt these concepts to their particular data; for example, an archeological culture is analogous to, but not the same as, an ethnographic culture.

Because of the problems inherent in dealing with archeological material, some prehistorians have preferred to deal with archeological data exclusively in their own terms. One could, for example, develop a science of artifacts without any reference to the peoples who made and used them. This would, however, be a rather sterile and unsatisfying study, unrelated conceptually to anything of social consequence. One could arrange the artifacts in time and space and study their characteristics, but the question would inevitably be raised, "so what?" Much archeological research has been conducted essentially on the level of a self-contained study of artifacts, but prehistorians inevitably use these studies as the basis for making inferences about the behavior of peoples. It is at this point that the need for accurately stated assumptions, to which a great deal of archeological research should be directed, becomes critical.

REFERENCES

Culture: Bagby 1953; Cohen 1968; Halloway 1969; Kroeber 1948, 1952, 1963; Kroeber and Kluckhohn 1952; Mellor 1972; L. White 1959b.
Culture and Biology: D'Aquili 1972; Eisenberg 1972; Emlen 1967; Laughlin 1968; Washburn 1960; Washburn and Lancaster 1968.
Physical Anthropology and Human Evolution: B. Campbell 1966; Dobzhansky 1955; Dolhinow and Sarich 1971; Downs and Bleibtreu 1972; Hulse 1965; Lovejoy, Burstein and Heiple 1972; Schaller and Lowther 1969; G. G. Simpson 1967; Washburn and Jay 1968.
Primate Studies: DeVore 1965; Dolhinow 1972; Jay 1968.

CHAPTER FIVE

PRESERVATION OF ARCHEOLOGICAL EVIDENCE

ARCHEOLOGICAL EVIDENCE

For the most part archeological evidence is tangible. It can be excavated, handled, weighed, measured, photographed, and described. Such evidence consists of artifacts (any objects made or used by man) and of the sites in which they occur, the strata or levels in the site, and distributional maps of their spatial occurrence. Data may also consist of counts, measurements, and descriptions of the primary evidence. Evidence is found in the earth itself, in pollen contained in it, in the bones of animals, and in various forms of economic and industrial waste found in sites. Data also consist of the relationships between and among things. What is archeological evidence to one excavator, or at one time, may not be considered as such for another. Thus carbonized wood was not usually saved as data for dating until the radiocarbon process was invented. Similarly, until techniques of flotation were developed, archeologists overlooked the seeds that might occur in the soil. What constitutes data thus depends on what the archeologist thinks is data as well as on its actual occurrence. We can usefully make three categories: (1) raw data as they appear before analysis; (2) analytic data that concern the physical, numerical and relational aspects; and (3) conclusions that give the meaning of the raw data as they have been interpreted by a prehistorian after analysis.

What are considered data, regardless of the techniques available for obtaining them, depend also on the goals an archeologist has set for his project. When we reviewed the history of archeology, we gave many examples of excavations that were carried out with the single goal of recovering objects for display in a museum. In the case of most nineteenth-century excavations these objects were simply quarried from the sites and few records were kept of their context. In the museums objects from many sites and many cultural periods were often displayed together so that a viewer was able to gain no appreciation of the range of material that was found in any site or at a single period. The objects were considered valuable as works of art and examples of craftsmanship rather than as sources of information on a wider range of interests. When objects are removed from sites and treated in this manner, a great deal of what archeologists with other ends in view would regard as data is ignored. When collectors import artifacts from sites that have been looted of their monuments and art objects, they thus heedlessly continue these old practices and contribute to the destruction of primary archeological evidence. Once removed from their context, such objects may no longer be of much archeological value, however much they may be prized as objects for display.

We stress the matter of the nature of archeological evidence because it emphasizes the difference among the approaches used by the various disciplines that study the past. We especially deplore the wasteful looting that now seems rampant throughout the world. It is a little ironic that as we develop better ways to recover and interpret archeological evidence, it is disappearing at a frightful rate.

WHAT IS PRESERVED?

Accurate reconstruction of prehistory depends on the preservation of archeological evidence. The amount of evidence that is preserved depends on the conditions it has been exposed to and the ability of an archeologist to recover it. Data that lie in the ground but cannot be recovered by an archeologist are, for practical purposes, unpreserved. In a given environment we can predict what kinds of things may remain after a certain time; yet frequently, by accident, only a small part of the potentially preserved materiál will remain; also frequently, from the viewpoint of archeology, the wrong things will be preserved. Man lives in a world composed of plants, animals, minerals, and other people (societies or cultures), and we are looking for data that will help us understand their interrelations. Naturally, of these, minerals are the most likely to be preserved under any conditions, but even metal may oxidize and fired clay may disintegrate. With the exception of stone and gold, very few inorganic artifacts last under adverse conditions. It should be clear, therefore, that archeologists are literally at the mercy of the elements and that only their sophisticated understanding of natural destructive processes and their ingenuity in designing technical aids for the recovery of evidence give them a chance of success in their more complicated endeavors. To illustrate what we mean, today's large buildings, being framed with steel, will soon disintegrate if left untended; our automobiles will be reduced to window glass and spark plug insulators; our tools will rust, our books and papers will rot, our landscapes will be littered with imperishable plastic containers, and "throwaway" bottles rather than beer cans. Without historical records, an archeologist in 50 or 100,000 years would have to use a great deal of imagination to recapture a reasonably accurate picture of what life is like today. The reader interested in how modern cultures or sites might be reconstructed by future archeologists can consult Nathan (1960), Slosson (1928), and O. Lancaster (1949). Wylie (1959:106–107) in his excellent book on the disposal of modern wastes, writes,

> Times change and the character of refuse changes with changing habits in home and industry; the stream of refuse flowing from any community provides material from which a comprehensive record of the life and interests of the people could be written. Local and national newspapers still clean and legible would furnish relevant facts, while these along with periodicals and magazines would reveal reading habits and interests. The quantity of tins would indicate a decline in home cooking and to the economic strain that is forcing an increasing number of housewives to go out to work. The quantity of coal and ash and cinders would surely indicate the inefficiency of the open fire and the certainty of a polluted atmosphere. Bottles and, still more revealing, their metal caps, would establish drinking tastes while scraps of food, decaying vegetable wastes would reveal what the people ate. Discarded clothing, household furnishing, and odd surprising things would supply all the evidence required to complete the story.

But under some conditions our cities would survive virtually intact. The best environments for preservation of organic remains are the very wet, the very dry, and the very cold. If oxygen can be excluded, very wet environments may even preserve metal. The worst environments are those that are alternately wet and dry, hot and cold. Preservation thus depends on environment. There is a complicated and little understood chemistry that determines how the environment will affect particular artifacts. From the standpoint of preservation, the tropics have the worst environments. Their heavy rains, acid soils, warm climate, vegetation, insects, and erosion combine to destroy almost everything built or dropped by man. Because of this, even spectacular monumental architecture and art has been destroyed in Southeast Asia. Even with any conceivable techniques, the archeologist will never learn very much of prehistory from that area.

Destruction does not take long. Archeologists clear jungle from Mayan temples only to watch them disappear back into the forest after a few years. W. H. Holmes (1897:102) records that the site of Chichen Itza in Yucatan was cleared for a hacienda in the last century, but in 50 years the jungle growth had completely covered it again (cf. Fig. 7). As vegetation takes hold, its prying roots slowly tear the structures apart. Heavy rains have long since washed most of the plaster façades from the buildings, and paintings are rarely preserved.

FIG. 7 The ruins of a palace at Palenque, a Maya site, have been partially cleared of the jungle vegetation that rapidly engulfs a site and gradually destroys it (Rickards 1910:10).

Occasionally some fluke will preserve a fact of prehistory that would normally have been lost. Surprisingly, for example, some Maya paintings have been preserved just because of the humidity. At Bonampak, water has deposited a thin film of lime that excludes air and dirt from the paintings. The same thing happened in southern France with some of the 10,000–20,000-year-old cave paintings at Lascaux. But nature is fickle on this score, for if too much lime is deposited, paintings are obscured or obliterated. In Mayan Guatemala a few wooden lintels remain, but little other organic material has been preserved. Archeological knowledge of the Maya comes largely from their buildings, stone tools, a few metal artifacts, tombs, as well as from interpretation of the codices—the books written in an unintelligible script.

The tropics are wet, and the ground in which artifacts lie is usually very acid. The best remains, preserved by moisture, have come from northern Europe, Scandinavia, and the Arctic, where bogs have sealed artifacts in a wet and airless tomb, or low temperatures have prevented decay. Whole bodies have been found in bogs. The Tollund man, buried with the noose that strangled him still around his neck, is a famous example (Glob 1954). His preservation was so perfect that the species of plants he ate for his last meal could be identified in the contents of his stomach. Schlabow and others (1958) describe in detail two bodies found in a bog at Windeby in Schleswig-Holstein, Germany: one, a female who still wore a blindfold (Fig. 8); the second, a male who met death by strangulation with a hazel-root rope. The

90

FIG. 8 *(right)* Head of Windeby Bog-body No. 1 with blindfold. (K. Schlabow and others, "Zwei Moorleichen Funde aus dem Domlandsmoor," *Praehistorische Zeitschrift,* Vol. 36.)

FIG. 9 *(below)* Tattooing on the body of a man from the Pazyryk burial ground, in the Altai Mountains of Russia. (A. Mongait, *Archaelogy in the U.S.S.R.,* Moscow Foreign Languages Publishing House.)

circumstances suggest that the persons were put to death for transgression of laws, probably those dealing with adultery, and were buried in graves dug into the swamp. They date from the early post-Christian Iron Age in the second or third century A.D. In addition to the archeological recovery, the article referred to contains detailed information of the anatomical, histological, and roentgenographic examination of the bodies. Of special interest are the discussion of the well-preserved brains and references to a surprisingly large number of other prehistoric brains. In Switzerland and neighboring countries the remains of villages once situated on lakeside marshes but now found beneath the water surface have remained waterlogged and well-preserved for several thousand years. The evidence recovered from the mucky slime of one such well-preserved site may give more information than that from hundreds of poorly preserved sites.

A remarkable example of how man unwittingly helped nature comes from Russia, where tombs of warrior horsemen yield the complete burial furnishings. Two thousand years ago Scythian inhabitants of the Altai buried their leaders in tombs more than 12 feet deep. After the tombs were lined with logs and covered with rocks, moisture rapidly filled the shafts and froze during the first winter to such a degree that it never completely thawed during the summer. The deep freeze thus created has preserved even the most fragile silk, felt, wood, leather, metal, and, of course, the bodies of men and animals that were interred with them (Rudenko 1970). The preservation of human bodies was so perfect that the designs of complicated tattooing could be readily copied (Fig. 9).

Another instance of unusual preservation of wooden materials is that of the thousand-year-old Oseberg Viking ship in Norway. The entire ship, 65 feet long, used as the coffin of a Viking queen, was buried beneath a mound of earth. Excavated in 1904, it yielded wooden sledges, four-wheeled carriages, a bed, a chair, buckets and two female skeletons, one of which is believed to have been a bondwoman who was selected to accompany her royal mistress into the afterworld (Fig. 10). The ship burial is dated at 800 A.D. (Brogger, Falk and Schetelig 1917).

It is commonplace to find wooden structures dating from our era in Europe, but it is rare to find wood more than a few thousand years old, because most areas that are now wet have been so for only a relatively short time; bogs in Europe are usually a direct outcome of Pleistocene conditions. Occasionally wood is preserved from sites occupied during the Ice Age. Dawkins (1880:269–271) gives us the details of a remarkable find of a complete wooden house of the Neolithic period in Ireland. This famous discovery, made in 1833, is called the Drumkelin house after the name of the bog in Donegal County where it was found. Even more extraordinary are a few examples of wooden spears in Europe that may be more than 100,000 years old. A possible wooden club and large pieces of a tree, together with pollen, seeds, and nuts, have been recovered by J. Desmond Clark from Kalambo Falls in Northern Rhodesia in an environment that has remained wet for

Fig. 10 *(top)* The Oseberg Viking ship when first uncovered. *(center and bottom)* A wagon and sledge from the Oseberg ship.

93

50,000 or more years. We have no way of knowing how many such localities there are, and must depend on accidents of discovery just as much as we depend on accidents of preservation. A particularly interesting example of preservation is the several footprints of Lower and Upper Paleolithic man impressed in the mud floor of Basua Cave in Italy and in several French caves (Vallois 1928; Blanc and Pales 1960; de Lumley 1966). These foot imprints are of great interest to physical anthropologists because they are the only evidence of the fleshy proportions of these ancient humans who are otherwise known only from their bony remains. With footprints and other impressions, preservation depends on the site's not having been used regularly, if at all, until the imprints had hardened. Similar footprints in mud have been found in Salts Cave, Kentucky, but they are more recent than the European cave examples mentioned above (P. Watson 1969:62).

Another unusual example of nearly total preservation comes from Poland where a woolly rhinoceros of the type hunted by man during the Pleistocene was found impregnated with oil and salt. The beast had been washed into a pool by a flooding river and then buried with silt. By luck, this pool was saturated with crude oil and salt from a natural oil seep. The body was thus sealed from oxygen, and decomposition could not occur. In Siberia whole mammoths have been found in the places where they were frozen many thousands of years ago. Contrary to earlier popular opinion, the animals were not trapped by an overnight change of climate; evidently they fell into crevices in the snow and eventually were buried by silt in a natural icebox. We have yet to find the body of a Paleolithic man preserved under either of these extraordinary conditions.

Almost perfect preservation also occurs in exceptionally dry environments. Even without mummification, Egyptian bodies would have been well-preserved by the dry atmosphere of much of Egypt, as we can see from the naturally preserved bodies that have been found in the American Southwest in caves, and in graves along the coast of Peru. In all these places the most fragile textiles, basketry, and wood and leather objects may be preserved. Possibly the most spectacular example of mass destruction and preservation with it occurred in A.D. 79, when Vesuvius erupted, burying Pompeii and Herculaneum in a flood of mud and ash. Although bodies were not preserved, their casts were. Inorganic objects remained in a perfect state, and the carbonized remains of complete loaves of bread, so perfectly preserved that they still bear the name of the baker stamped on them, have been recovered. Sometimes, as was true of the scrolls found in 1753 at Herculaneum and those found by Bedouin in dry caves near the Dead Sea, suitable techniques for unrolling them, preventing them from decomposing, and even of reading them with the aid of ultraviolet light had to be devised before they could truly be said to be preserved.

A unique situation came to light at the site of Jericho, where Zeuner (1955a; also K. Kenyon 1960) was able to determine the reasons for the preservation of cloth and wooden furniture in Bronze Age tombs. The tombs had been cut into limestone, the burials and offerings deposited, and the tombs walled up. Carbon monoxide and methane gases seeping into the closed tombs through cracks in the rock replaced the normal air that would have permitted bacteria to live. As a result, organic materials that would normally have decayed within a few years after being deposited were preserved. Most archeologists work with poorly preserved sites, even in very dry areas, such as Southwest Asia and the American Southwest, where very little is preserved unless it has been isolated from the small amount of moisture that does occur. To witness the torrential rains and flash floods that seasonally soak such areas makes one appreciate how accidental is preservation. In areas of extreme cold, if there is any thawing at all, rot will occur, and if wet areas should dry, new oxygen will enter and with it destruction. A fact that is sometimes not appreciated is that in an area such as the Near East, rains fall during the cooler winter months when the effect of the small amount of precipitation is relatively much greater than it would be during the hot summer months.

Most open sites are subject to alternate wetting and drying, and organic materials disintegrate or are destroyed by bacteria in a fairly short time. If one counts the number of objects recovered from a dry cave in the western United States, he cannot fail to be impressed with the large amount of perishable items made of horn, leather, or vegetal materials that would rapidly disappear in an open site (Fig. 11).

Table 1 presents the count of items recovered from six sites where dry conditions have preserved organic materials that would normally have disappeared. The two sites from Chile are from the very dry north coast where conditions of preservation are similar to those prevailing along the narrow Peruvian coast. The two sites in New Mexico are from protected caves in a dry region where conditions of preservation are optimal, and the same situation holds for the two Nevada cave sites. The average annual rainfall in these areas ranges from less than 1 inch to not more than 8 inches. Table 2 summarizes the counts in Table 1 and presents the proportional amounts in percent of total number of items of perishable and imperishable pieces. It is easy to see how deficient our knowledge of material culture items would be for an open site in Nevada, for example, where not more than 10 percent of the items that find their way into the trash layers are of durable materials.

In the dry deposits of Lovelock Cave, Nevada, cordage was perfectly preserved, and details on the size and mesh of nets could be determined. One hundred forty-two pieces of braid gave evidence that the prehistoric occupants of the cave knew how to braid, 3, 5, 6, 7, 16, and 18 strands; and 404 knots proved to belong to 8 types (mesh or sheet-bend, overhand, reef, granny, slip, clove hitch, "necktie" or timber-hitch, and wrap knots). Details of the methods of stringing shell beads were also preserved (Fig. 12). This listing of some of the details observable about cordage illustrates clearly the degree of complexity in one single aspect of prehistoric technology that is ordinarily totally absent in open sites.

If a technique or type of artifact does not make its appearance after

FIG. 11 (*a*) Three flint knives in wooden handles from Humboldt Cave, Nevada. Length of specimen on the left is 22.4 cm.

FIG. 11 (*b*) Three prehistoric fishlines from a single cache in Humboldt Cave, Nevada. The string is Indian Hemp (apocynum); the hooks have bone barbs and wood shanks. Note the similarity of the three composite structures as well as the variation in details. Length of wood shank of center example is 9.0 cm.

TABLE 1

	Playa Miller, Chile	Punta Pichalo, Chile	Cordova Cave, New Mexico	Tularosa Cave, New Mexico	Humboldt Cave, Nevada	Lovelock Cave, Nevada
Imperishable						
Stone	494	6389	1577	1546	87	95
Metal	17	1				
Pottery	28,871	1414	751	5470		
Shell	1	222	2	4	2	7
Bone	29	228	23	55	272	530
Antler			8	1		
Perishable						
Wood	55	945	394	762	113	310
Rush, cane, twine basketry	323	1552	628	3473	2982	7535
Skin, wool, feather	750	442	40	594	49	320
Vegetal food	299	48	2000	28,000		
Hoof, horn				3	15	20

Occurrence in six dry open or cave sites of perishable and imperishable objects. Two Chilean open sites from Bird (1943:191–216, 253–278); two New Mexico cave sites from Martin and others (1952); two Nevada cave sites from Loud and Harrington (1929); Heizer and Krieger (1956). Unworked stones of various kinds reported as found are included; unmodified food animal bone is counted; human burials (2 at Playa Miller, 42 at Punta Pichalo, 2 at Tularosa Cave, 32 at Lovelock Cave) are counted each as one bone. (We are indebted to Mr. Ronald Weber for preparing this and the following table.)

TABLE 2

	Imperishable		Perishable	
Sites	No. Items	Percent	No. Items	Percent
Playa Miller	25,412	95	1427	5
Punta Pichalo	8253	73	2987	27
Cordova cave	2361	43	3062	57
Tularosa cave	7296	19	33,832	81
Humboldt cave	361	10	3159	90
Lovelock cave	632	7	8285	93

Summary of Table 1, showing total numbers of imperishable and perishable items from six sites. In many open sites perishable items are totally absent. The two largest figures (at Playa Miller and Tularosa Cave) are ascribable, respectively, to the great abundance of potsherds and maize cobs.

FIG. 12 Beads recovered from Lovelock Cave, Nevada, showing details of their stringing. The dry environment of the cave preserved organic material, in this case the actual vegetal cord on which the beads are strung, that would ordinarily be absent from archeological sites. (Loud and Harrington, "Lovelock Cave," *University of California Publications in American Archaeology and Ethnology,* Vol. 25, No. 1, 1929.)

a considerable amount of archeological investigation has been carried out in an area, it may be permissible to suggest that the prehistoric peoples did not know or possess that technique or tool. If the technique or implement is of the kind that would not leave any palpable trace, even under relatively favorable conditions, the archeologist would then admit that there was no way of telling whether it may or may not have once occurred in the area he is interested in. For example, slings made of cordage were widely known ethnographically in the New World, but they had not appeared archeologically up to 1960 in North America, even in collections secured from dry cave deposits. Arguing from this negative evidence, one author proposed that the sling was introduced to the Indians of North America in historic times. Although this explanation seemed unlikely, there was no way (except possibly through linguistic analysis, which was never done) to verify or disprove the recent spread of this weapon. Now, however, at least three prehistoric North American slings (all from dry caves in western Nevada) are known, and the theory of historic introduction is shown by archeological facts to be incorrect. Inferring that culture traits are absent simply because they are not proved to be archeologically present must be made with judgment and only after consideration of all relevant evidence.

A discussion of the preservation of artifacts should not omit consideration of the history of the sites. Ideally, for archeologists, the occupants of a site would decide on the spur of the moment to abandon their homes and forthwith walk off, taking nothing with them and leaving everything where it lay. The site would then become rapidly buried; when excavated after many years, an archeologist would discover everything just as it was left on the day of abandonment. As we have pointed out above, this ideal is a fantasy, because objects disintegrate. We have not mentioned, however, the effects of man and nature on the sites themselves (Fig. 13).

Without trying to give an exhaustive list of the ways in which nature manages to disturb and disarrange archeological sites and strata, we may mention the natural soil-building process that tends to bury objects lying on the surface of the earth; the burial of settlements by drifting sand in Africa,

FIG. 13 The people who lived in ancient settlements contributed to the destruction of the sites whenever they dug into the ground. The picture shows Tlatilco, a pre-Classic site (about 1300 B.C.) in the valley of Mexico, in which early burials were cut through by later grave diggers who chanced to dig in the same spot.

Europe, and Asia; burial under volcanic ash as at Pompeii, and certain Pueblo sites in Arizona; covering by molten lava that hardens to solid basalt, as at the pre-Classic site of Cuicuilco on the outskirts of Mexico City and at certain locations in Europe. Settlements on the edge of the sea may become destroyed as the ocean wears away the shore; the shoreline may subside, allowing encroaching water to engulf a settlement; floods may bury occupation sites under thick deposits of mud; and a recent instance is provided by the 1962 avalanche in Peru that caused the death of 3500 persons. A well-known example of the destruction of a site is that of the Palace of Minos in Crete. An earthquake, perhaps, combined with conquest, was followed by fire. The year, 1400 B.C., has been determined, and even the month (March) as evidenced by smoke stains that could only have been caused by the Notios, the strong southwest wind, which achieves maximum force in that month (A. Evans 1921–1935:4:942–946). An earthquake recorded as occurring in 27 B.C. threw down the upper half of the northern colossal statue on the western plain of Thebes (that is, Luxor) which had been sculptured and erected at the order of the Egyptian pharaoh Amenhotep III about 1450 B.C. (Fig. 14). After the statue was damaged, it made a noise as the first rays of the sun struck it, and it became the center of the Cult of Memnon, who in Greek mythology was the son of Aurora (or Eos), goddess of dawn. Either as a pious act or to suppress the cult, the Roman emperor Septimius Severus in 197 A.D. ordered the statue reconstructed, and it is this reconstruction that we see today (Bataille 1952).

A final example of the way geological forces have acted on archeological remains is in the detached section of sandstone cliff with a weight calculated at 30,000 tons which reared threateningly over the great communal settlement of Pueblo Bonito in Chaco Canyon, New Mexico. The prehistoric occupants of the site had built a massive stone-mud mortar buttress beneath the undercut edge of this block, apparently successfully, to restrain it from toppling over on the settlement. Judd (1959a) traces the history of the braced-up cliff which finally did collapse in 1941.

WHAT IS WILLFULLY DESTROYED?

As we have seen in the robbing of ancient tombs, man himself destroys many sites and artifacts. His destructive powers have probably never been greater than now, however, with the building of networks of highways, the spread of urbanism, and the construction of dams, not to mention the continued practice of looting archeological sites. During the Paleolithic, when the numbers of men were not great and the economy was based on hunting and collecting, there may not have been very profound changes imposed by man on the earth's surface. But when he became a farmer and acquired a tool kit that allowed him to quarry stone, dig ditches and pits, and domesticate animals— which in some areas turned wooded country into deserts by overgrazing— man began to make profound changes in the earth's face.

FIG. 14 The northern ("Vocal") colossal statue of Memnon which stands on the western plain of Thebes (Luxor), Egypt. This, with its duplicate, represents Amenhotep III of the Eighteenth Dynasty. The upper half of the colossus was reconstructed in Roman times.

Fig. 15 Prehistoric sculptured basalt doorways from the site of Tiahuanaco removed for reuse in the nearby modern village.

As Claudius Rich (1819:40) wrote, "A ruined city . . . is a quarry above ground." The unfortunate truth of this pithy statement can be documented by hundreds of instances of the pillaging of ancient buildings for construction materials. Some sites where stone was employed have been leveled and others so greatly damaged that they are like the Abbey of St. Martin in Tours, of which Henry James in *A Little Tour of France* says, "What we see today may be called the ruin of a ruin." The Greek Temple of the Giants at Agrigentum, Sicily, was destroyed in the eighteenth century to provide material for a breakwater, and in about 1800, great sculptures of Nineveh were broken up to furnish materials to repair a bridge. The great pre-Inca site of Tiahuanaco in the Bolivian altiplano near Lake Titicaca contained immense quantities of beautifully sculptured stone blocks. The nearby village by the same name consists of houses with sculptured doorways taken from the ancient site (Fig. 15), and the large church, built in the seventeenth century by Pedro de Castillo, is constructed entirely of stones carried from the nearby ruins. When the railroad was built between La Paz and Guaqui, Bolivia, on the shore of Lake Titicaca, the site of Tiahuanaco provided a convenient source of stone for building bridges, and Posnansky (1945:166) records the fact that "an immense statue around which there was entwined a snake from the chest to the feet, was divided and set in cement in bridges." Many of the stones at Tiahuanaco proved to be too heavy to transport (some weigh 100 tons), and, it being beyond the imagination of the local people after the Spanish conquest to understand how such

102

large stones had been brought from distant sources, the belief grew that these colossal stones were made of concrete and must contain gold. Accordingly, many of the great blocks were split open with steel chisels in order to find the gold. A few failures did not seem to be sufficient evidence that the story was untrue, because everywhere on the site one can see scores of these sundered blocks. The lure of gold was so great, the Tiahuanaco site so impressive, and the imagination of ignorant people so active, that a Spanish miner in the seventeenth century went to the great effort of digging a hole more than 20 feet deep, 120 feet wide, and 250 feet long in the top of the Akapana, a great, flattopped mound of earth. Local recollection of this activity having been lost, the pit (which contains water) is now believed by the townspeople to be the ancient reservoir that served the prehistoric occupants of the city.

Winlock (1942:11) found clear evidence of the nearly total destruction of an immense mortuary temple in ancient times at Deir-el-Bahri, Egypt, and it is recorded in Egyptian texts that the magnificent mortuary temple of Amenhotep III of the Eighteenth Dynasty was destroyed in the reign of his successor. Archeologists have excavated the temple area and found only some column bases and fragments of shattered statues.

In southern Utah, J. W. Powell (1961:107–108), in referring to a three-story pueblo ruin at the mouth of the Kanab River where it enters the Colorado River, wrote, "The structure was one of the best found in this land of ruins. The Mormon people settling here have used the stones of the old pueblo in building their homes and now no vestiges of the ancient structure remain."

Wars have caused immense destruction to ancient sites. One of the best-known instances is the Parthenon in Athens, which, while being used in 1687 by the Turks as a powder magazine, received a direct hit by a Venetian shell, which blew out the interior.

When religious iconoclasm inspires the destruction of the sacred monuments of other religions, it leads to destruction of archeological evidence. Moorehead (1961:109) describes the defacement of Egyptian monuments by Coptic priests, and Duignan (1958) records that by 1531, roughly 10 years after the conquest of Mexico by Hernando Cortes, the Franciscan priests had torn down 500 Aztec temples and broken up 20,000 stone idols. Inca religious sites in Peru suffered a similar fate, and a book by Father Joseph de Arriaga, in 1621, records the destruction of large numbers of various types of native temples and shrines: 477 Chapkas, 603 main Huacas, 3410 Konopas, 617 Halkis, 45 Mamazuras, 180 Huankas, and so on. By contrast, religious sanctity of a spot may serve to protect a site. Rawlinson (1850:419) wrote that an ancient site opposite Mosul, Iraq, had not been excavated because "the spot, indeed, is so much revered by the Mohammedans, as the supposed sepulcher of the prophet Jonas, that it is very doubtful if Europeans will be ever permitted to examine it." On the other hand, Layard at Nimrud noted that his Arab workmen were continually trying to batter out the eyes of sculptured animals and persons because they were the idols of unbelievers. Stephens (1842:187) tells a tale of the President of Guatemala, who about 1810 received a present of a small gold image from the archeological site of Santa Cruz de Quiche. Intrigued with the possibility of getting gold, he ordered "a commission" to explore the site for hidden treasure, and in the process the palace was destroyed. The Indians, roused "by the destruction of their ancient capital, rose and threatened to kill the workmen unless they left the country."

One continuing cause of the loss of archeological information lies in the increasing number of collectors of ancient art objects. Such collecting goes back to Classical times, but today, among wealthy persons who can afford it, very high prices are paid for prehistoric stone sculptures, metalwork, and ceramic vessels. The availability of a market encourages surreptitious and illegal digging, often by needy local people who usually realize very little for their labors. The looting of cites is a regular business, both in the New World—in Mexico, Guatemala, and Peru—and in Egypt and the Middle East. Although the objects found may be preserved, in the course of changing hands through dealers and collectors, their context may be forgotten. Then identification of their source and age can be determined only by referring to similar pieces in archeological reports or museum collections. Most countries have very strict laws governing the excavations, and prohibiting the unauthorized export, of archeological materials, but these regulations usually are observed only by reputable archeologists. On the other hand, antiquities dealers encourage unauthorized digging and manage quite successfully, through the simple expedient of bribes, to remove vast quantities of material to their galleries in New York, San Francisco, Los Angeles, London, Paris, Rome, and other capitals of the art-conscious world.

Professional anthropologists in the United States, through resolutions approved by the membership of such organizations as the American Anthropological Association and the Society for American Archaeology, have taken a position against the illegal traffic in antiquities. UNESCO has formally approved a resolution on the Means of Prohibiting and Preventing the Illicit Import, Export, and Transfer of Ownership of Cultural Property. These are all steps in the right direction, and ultimately the abolition of the marketing of contraband antiquities will lead to the cessation of plundering of sites. One may also applaud the editors of the widely read journal titled *Archaeology* published by the prestigious Archaeological Institute of America for recently changing its practice of printing advertisements of antiquities dealers and galleries offering such illicit and contraband materials for sale.

WHAT IS RECOVERED?

Much is preserved that is not recovered from ordinary excavations. Belzoni, or even Schliemann and Layard, recovered only a small part of the available information. When Sir Leonard Woolley went to Mesopotamia in 1922 to excavate at the great site of Ur, he found the Royal cemetery within a few

Fig. 16 The Queen's harp from Ur as it was reconstructed by L. Woolley. Height is 1.07 m.

weeks, but kept it secret until four years later. It took Woolley all that time to train his men and himself so that he was confident of doing a good job. His excavation stands as a tour de force of technical skill. In one instance he was able to restore a completely disintegrated harp by filling with plaster the open cavity in the ground where it had lain (Fig. 16). But for all his skill, he still discarded much that might have been saved. In another example, Creel (1937:41–42) has shown by astute reasoning based on indirect evidence that bamboo books existed in Shang Dynasty times in China in the third millennium B.C. No actual remains of such books have ever been found, but there is no question that they once existed.

For all the palaces and tombs that have been excavated in the centers of early civilization, there has been little attempt to discover how people lived. Sometimes, though, such information comes almost by accident. A number of Egyptian tombs have now been excavated in which there are models of houses, and other buildings: carpenter shops, butcher shops, bakeries and the like, all stocked with the tools of the trade and figures of the artisans going about their tasks. These models, together with some of the elaborately decorated scenes on the walls of noble tombs, give us an unusually complete picture of some of the more mundane aspects of life (Fig. 17). But the more

Fig. 17 Wrestling scenes and warfare depicted on a painting at Beni Hasan, Egypt, and dating from about 2500 B.C. The wrestling scenes depict two Egyptians, one painted in a clear red, the other of a red-brown hue, probably so colored in order to distinguish the entwined arms and legs of the two men. Although these rows of individual scenes are not precisely like a motion picture film strip, nevertheless in a number of cases it is clear that a continuous series is represented. (P. E. Newberry, *Beni Hasan*. Archaeological Survey of Egypt, Egyptian Exploration Fund, London, 1893, Part II, Pl. XV).

usual situation is that we do not even know what the people ate, let alone anything about such intangible realms of inquiry as the effects of civilization on the lives of the common people. The available information about the early civilizations comes mostly from texts and sometimes from pictures, but only rarely from the excavation of houses. This preoccupation with one kind of information—art, architecture, epigraphy—implies a corresponding blindness about other kinds of data.

We should not like to give the implication that prehistoric archeologists are not blind sometimes too, but theirs is a blindness that comes not so much from a lack of interest in all kinds of information as from a lack of knowledge that such information exists or can be extracted.

To illustrate this point—that there is no preservation unless adequate techniques for removing buried material are available—we can take the excavation of Ali Kosh in Iran. There, after making a test pit into the mound, Hole and Flannery reported (1962:125) "plant remains were scarce at Ali Kosh." The few seeds that did come to light were found accidentally in the cleaning of a radiocarbon sample, but the clue that they might be found in ashy deposits raised the possibility that more such remains could be found if the ash were treated by water separation. Fortunately, considerable pioneering work in this technique was being carried out in the early 1960s, and in a subsequent season of work at Ali Kosh hundreds of ashy samples were poured in water to separate the carbonized organic material from the silty matrix. As a result, tens of thousands of seeds were found in deposits where they had not been noticed before and where they could rarely be seen even by careful separation of the dry material (Hole and Flannery 1968; Struever 1967). A simple recovery technique thus resulted in the effective preservation of invaluable clues to the history of agriculture.

The foregoing examples have dealt mostly with the recovery of artifacts, but there are other kinds of data in sites. It is just as important to record the spatial distribution of artifacts with respect to the stratigraphy of the site and with respect to one another as it is to pick them out of the ground and count them. These data are often ignored, but they are essential if we are to reconstruct the uses of artifacts and of different areas within the site, or the ages of different structures. Moreover, as was true of the seeds, there are "nonartifactual" remains that will yield information. Men trained to pick up bronzes and potsherds will blithely hack through bones, charcoal, and fragmentary traces of perishable material (Fig. 18). Hired laborers or students under the supervision of an unimaginative archeologist will more often than not miss just the kind of information that we need for modern analysis.

Just as an archeologist must take care to recover what is preserved, he must preserve what is recovered. Countless objects have been destroyed within a few hours of their excavation because they dried out or fell apart. Metal will often turn to dust; in fact, it may appear only as a rusty stain in the ground. Basketry, textiles, and wood may dry out and disintegrate. Almost all excavated objects are damp when first taken out of the ground, and a few minutes in the hot sun may destroy them. Objects taken from bogs are subject to shrinking and cracking that can be countered by proper use of preservatives. Bones that threaten to fall apart can be reinforced with plaster, papier-mâché, glue, or plastic compounds. There is no lack of techniques for preservation, but the excavator must know enough to use them.

WHAT IS REPORTED?

If there is a big difference between what is preserved and what is recovered, there is a bigger difference between what is recovered and what is reported. Archeologists are notoriously slow in reporting the results of their excavations. Many reports are never written, and many that are written are never published. It is safe to say that there is much more excavated material unpub-

FIG. 18 A workman at Chogga Sefid, Iran, carefully exposing the inorganic traces of a floor mat that remain more than 8000 years after the fibers had decomposed.

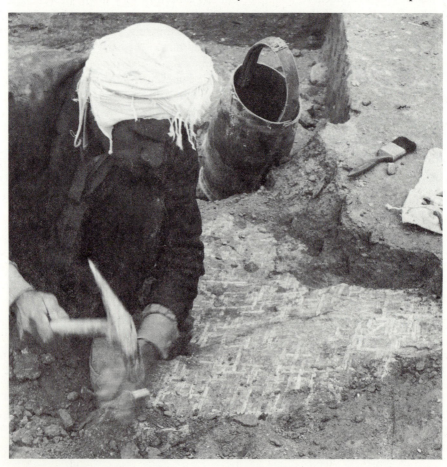

lished than published, and for practical purposes this information is lost. Because the sites were destroyed in the process of excavation, if there is never a publication, the information is lost forever.

It is not uncommon for an excavator to publish only part of his material. He may do the pottery or temples, or may report on only the very finest objects from among a large group. In this regard it is common to see a group of artifacts labeled "typical" or "characteristic" of the site in question, but it would often be more accurate to say that they were the finest, the most elaborate, or the most exotic. Mud bricks are typical; gold pins are not. Another archeologist might dig for years and never find one of the so-called "typical" objects. Such reporting can be a misleading weighting of the evidence.

Archeologists may also fill in blanks without explicitly saying so. They may guess that such and such happened and report it as fact, or they may leave out material that does not fit their preconceptions. More will be said about excavation technique and report writing in other chapters; this short discussion should point up that what we understand about prehistory is based on many variables. Part of the archeological context is the human filter through which information about preserved antiquities must pass before it is eventually described in print.

REFERENCES

Techniques of Preservation: Biek 1965; Bruce-Mitford 1968; G. Clark 1954; Delougaz 1933; A. Evans and Fenwich 1971; FitzHugh and Gettens 1971; Gettens and Usilton 1955; Helbaek 1953; de Laet 1957; Leechman 1931; Parkinson 1951; Plenderleith 1956; Plenderleith and Werner 1971; Rowe 1953; Seborg and Inverarity 1962; Vynckier 1966.

Examples of Unusual Preservation: Barrington 1783; H. Bennett 1806; Bird 1943; Blanc and Pales 1960; Broholm and Hald 1940; Colton 1932; Creel 1937; Cummings 1933; Dawkins 1880; H. Ellis 1847; A. Evans 1921–1935; Freeman and Echegaray 1970; Glob 1954, 1969; Heizer and Krieger 1956; Hole and Flannery 1962, 1968; K. Kenyon 1960; Loud and Harrington 1929; de Lumley 1966; Mairui, Bianchi, and Battaglia 1961; Movius 1950; Rudenko 1970; Schlabow and others 1958; Tanzer 1939; Thorvildsen 1952; Vallois 1928; P. Watson 1969; Zeuner 1955a.

Examples of the Destruction of Sites: J. Matthews 1965; Posnansky 1945; J. Powell 1961; Rich 1819; W. Thomas 1956; Winlock 1942.

Archeology of the Future: O. Lancaster 1949; Nathan 1960; Slosson 1928; Wylie 1959.

Traffic in Antiquities: R. Adams 1970a; Beals 1971; Coggins 1969, 1970; Ford 1971; Society for American Archaeology 1971.

CHAPTER SIX

ARCHEOLOGICAL SITES

In reading prehistory we find references to cere-
monial sites, hill forts, graves, trading centers, and camps. Looking at the
modern world we have no doubt there is diversity among the settlements.
Some may be primarily manufacturing centers, others market towns, still
others suburbs or rural hamlets. We also have centers of transportation and
of fishing or agriculture. Still, for the most part people live in all these sites
and they are multipurpose to serve the needs of their residents. How would
you characterize New York City? Is it a center of industry, of commerce, of
shipping, of transportation, or of population? It is all of these and more
depending on what aspects you want to emphasize. Why is it then that we
confidently ascribe specialized functions to prehistoric sites?

We do so for two reasons. First we have a conception of how people
live and behave. Through ethnography we know that some contemporary
peoples with simpler ways of life actually have complex settlement systems.
In the course of a year one group of people may use a number of sites that
principally serve specialized functions. Hunters frequently observe game from
lookouts; religious activities are often carried out in places of solitude and
obscurity; winter villages may be placed with protection from wind and the
availability of fuel in mind, and summer encampments may be in quite other
parts of the territory. People who travel continually may have favored overnight campsites as well as sites for their permanent villages. Manufacturing
may typically be carried out near sources of raw material. One could expand
this list indefinitely, but the point should be clear that before most people

were permanently settled and before rapid and efficient transportation and communication were possible, people took themselves to the things they needed. Today we bring the products to the people. Thus, we reason, in antiquity there were far more specialized sites than today. Ethnography also tells us what kinds of sites we may expect to find among people who have ways similar to our primitive contemporaries.

Secondly, we may examine the contents of the sites themselves. That Gar Arjeneh rock shelter in western Iran served as a butchering station or that Yafteh Cave (see Fig. 20) was a base camp can be inferred from the kinds and quantity of material left by their inhabitants (Hole and Flannery 1968). It would be even more obvious to find a fort with arrows imbedded in the walls and the bodies of slain defenders in testimony of the last battle. In the absence of domestic refuse and with the geographic context in mind (perhaps on a defensible ridge away from evidence of settlements) we could infer a very specific use of the site. Although more examples are ambiguous than obvious, we do have good reason to ascribe singular functions to many sites in prehistory. This chapter summarizes the kinds of sites that have been described.

KINDS OF SITES

A site is any place, large or small, where there are to be found traces of ancient occupation or activity. The usual clue to a site is the presence of artifacts. There are millions of sites on the earth, some of which are as large as a city, others as small as the spot where an arrowhead lies. The number and variety of prehistoric sites are limited only by the activities of prehistoric men who lived and left their equipment scattered over the full breadth of the earth, and by conditions of preservation.

A person could hardly comprehend prehistory if he regarded each site as unique; archeologists therefore customarily group sites into convenient categories. A reader of a general work on archeology will see reference to paleolithic sites, early Bronze Age sites, or Desert Culture sites. These sites have been classified by the kinds of artifacts that are found in them: stone tools, bronze tools, and a variety of milling stones and hunting equipment, respectively. Another way to classify sites is to emphasize their locations. Thus one sees reference to open sites (villages), cave sites, lakeside sites, and valley-bottom sites. The activity represented by the remains can be expressed in such designations as kill site, camp site, quarry site, and living site, and the duration of the occupation as permanent, seasonal, or intermittent. Finally, one can refer to the archeological context of the sites; for example, stratified, nonstratified, or surface find. These designations could be expanded, but no one of them can account for all the possible kinds of sites. To help the reader appreciate the variety of archeological sites, we shall describe a number of different kinds of sites that are grouped by the activities they represent.

It takes a study of all kinds of sites relevant to a particular research objective to give a rounded picture of the social system operative in prehistory; therefore it is somewhat meaningless to say that some kinds of sites are of more value than others. It is fairer to say that some kinds of sites yield a greater range of information than do others, and that consequently these are the sites most often studied. Useful listings of the various kinds of antiquities, arranged by category, or organized by means of an outline of the different sorts of cultural inferences that can be drawn from these antiquities, have been presented by N. C. Nelson (1938:146–148) and V. G. Childe (1956:129–131).

Habitation Sites

The most commonly sought and excavated sites are the places where people lived, for the simple reason that these sites were a focal point of prehistoric activities. In a sense, all archeological sites imply habitation, though it may have been relatively short, but for convenience here, a habitation site is one around which a group of people centered their daily activities. Habitation sites that were occupied the year round frequently have the remains of houses, but the dwellings may be caves or rock shelters (Figs. 19, 20) or even open areas in which no trace of a permanent shelter remains. Seasonally occupied sites generally have fewer traces of architecture. We know by ethnographic analogy that prehistoric men found shelter in various sorts of constructions ranging from temporary brush windbreaks, lean-tos, and tipis to semisubterranean houses made of logs and earth that could be lived in year after year, mud-brick or rough masonry houses, and so on. Some pictures of modern settlements and prehistoric sites that illustrate this variety are found in Figures 7, 21, 25, 44. In areas where shelters were not needed, habitation sites may show nothing more than the remains of fire and a scatter of refuse and artifacts. What may be the most ancient structure known, an arc-shaped pile of stones, which perhaps served as the floor or foundation of a windbreak, has recently been discovered in Olduvai Gorge, Tanzania, by L. S. B. Leakey. By the potassium-argon dating method this shelter, if it is correctly identified as such, is nearly two million years old (Leakey and Lawick 1963:147).

Sites that are ordinarily close to settlements are agricultural fields and terraces, irrigation canals, roads, bridges, aqueducts, and cemeteries. Occasionally habitation sites served the dual purpose of dwelling and defense, although defensive structures are relatively rare in prehistoric times; however, from the locations and construction of some communities we may infer that defensive structures did exist. Such examples include the cliff dwellings in Mesa Verde (Fig. 21), and the remains of actual fortresses in the Mexican and Peruvian highlands certainly attest to recurrent warfare between local groups. Many Iron Age sites in Europe and Africa evidently served the dual purpose, as did the palisaded villages, such as Aztalan, Wisconsin, of later prehistoric times in eastern United States. All these attest to the social practice of serious warfare and the need for living in defensible villages.

Trading Centers

Trading centers have been reported from a few places, though they are hard to recognize with certainty. Trading on a scale large enough to necessitate trade centers must have been unusual for prehistoric peoples. Sites centrally situated between the Maya and Aztec areas have been identified as ports of trade, though of course they were habitation sites as well. In Turkey, archeologists have found a site on nonarable land that was favorably placed for the salt and obsidian trade, and the widespread trade in the latter commodity and in copper raises the possibility of finding definite evidence of mining and manufacturing sites if they are deliberately sought. Cleared pathways across open ground, or roads such as the Roman roads of Britain and Inca highways are features related to trade. At the great prehistoric metropolis of Teotihuacan near Mexico City, a site which covers about 20 square kilometers (8 square miles) and held a population estimated by some to be as high as 125,000 persons, there are certain groups of buildings where foreign pottery (from the Gulf Coast, Yucatan, and Oaxaca) is abundant and where the archeologists think that merchants from these distant areas may have lived (Millon 1970).

Quarry Sites

Sites in which a great variety of minerals were mined (often for trade) are common throughout the world, although there is seldom any excavation of them. Examples include the Alibates Ranch in Texas, where prehistoric men quarried for a widely used multicolored flint; flint mines, dug into the chalk deposits at such places as Grimes Graves are well-known sites in England. Mining for metal ores has also left sites. In grim testimony of the dangers of certain prehistoric activities, archeologists have uncovered the bones, and sometimes the bodies, of miners who were crushed by falling rock. Quarry sites may be workshop areas where ores were smelted, flint was chipped, or soapstone was worked into bowls. Analysis of raw material from quarry sites has helped answer the question of where a particular product was mined, and a study of the distribution of finished artifacts made from the stone may tell the archeologist a great deal about ancient trade relations. Examples are the petrological analysis of British stone axes of the Neolithic and Bronze Ages and of the determination by trace element studies of obsidian and copper in the Near East.

Kill Sites

It is common in the United States to find *kill* sites, places where one or more animals were killed by hunters, some of whom may have had no permanent dwellings. At kill sites archeologists find the bones of the animals, projectile points used for killing them, and the tools for butchering. In some cases where the bone material has been well preserved the pattern of butchering the animals can be reconstructed in considerable detail. For example, see Wheat (1967); Builday and Parmalee (1962).

Frequently there is associated a fireplace in which the meat was cooked. Outside the Americas it is less common to find kill sites, though certain remains from the Acheulian and later periods, situated at the edges of rivers and lakes, must have been combination kill and habitation sites. We should

FIG. 19 A typical rock shelter that was used some 15,000–25,000 years ago by hunters in West Iran. The shelter, Pa Sangar, offers minimal protection from the elements, but it affords a panoramic view of the valley below where the food supply lived.

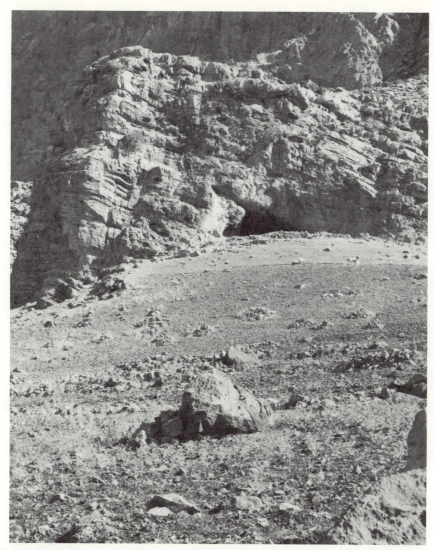

Fig. 20 Yafteh Cave in West Iran was used as a base camp by hunters some 35,000 years ago. The cave is large enough to accommodate about 20 persons, and it overlooks the length of the Khorramabad Valley.

remember, however, that hunters usually have a home base from which they wander in pursuit of game and often bring back only the edible portions of butchered animals. The amount of bone and stone tools in these sites suggests seasonal, or perhaps permanent year-round camps. Archeologists usually call these sites "living floors."

Ceremonial Sites

Ceremonial sites include the imposing megalithic construction at Stonehenge, which is rivaled by the much older caves in France and Spain where remark-

FIG. 21 A cliff dwelling at Mesa Verde. Masonry houses were built on ledges in the vertical sides of the mesas. Although defense may have been an important consideration in the placing of these settlements, most of the population lived on top of the mesas or in other easily accessible places.

able paintings, carvings, and reliefs are found. Chogga Zambil, in southwestern Iran, an Elamite ziggurat of the thirteenth century B.C., is one of the largest known religious structures ever built, and the enormous ceremonial precincts in Meso-America evoke admiration the world around (Fig. 22). Ceremonial centers need not be attached to habitation areas, but if they are monumental in size they cannot have been far from a supply of labor. Ordinarily, however, there are no dwellings other than those of political or religious officials and their retainers within the area of a ceremonial site. For example, La Venta, a large Meso-American ceremonial center, was erected some distance away from the area where the population lived.

Burial Sites

Burial sites have attracted looters since early historic times, and many archeologists concentrate their efforts on cemeteries because they often contain useful information about social practices (Chap. 19). Burial sites range from isolated burials in shallow holes to elaborate masonry constructions, earth mounds, and megalithic monuments. Their variety is illustrated by the mounds used by the Hopewell Indians of Ohio, the platform burials used in the northern woodlands, simple cremations in the Cochise site of Cienega in Arizona, the Neanderthal burials at La Ferrassie, France, the royal tombs of Ur, and most remarkable of all, the pyramids of Egypt, which were simultaneously imposing funerary monuments and housing for royal tombs. It was long thought that the pyramids of the New World served only as elevated platforms on which to build religious temples, but the discovery in 1950 by Ruz, the Mexican archeologist, changed this opinion. At the Classic Maya site of Palenque in the state of Chiapas, Mexico, the pyramid and Temple of the Inscriptions were built over a great burial chamber, and subsequently several other examples of tombs in the pyramids have been found. M. Coe (1956) has argued that the main purpose of Meso-American pyramids may have been to house tombs of high priests and kings, and the round fluted pyramid at the Olmec site of La Venta is thought to have served as an elevated spot from

FIG. 22 View of the Pyramid of the Moon, Teotihuacan, Mexico, a site built and abandoned during the Classic period. This enormous city and ceremonial center covers approximately 8 square miles.

which to observe astronomical phenomena, its height being sufficient to provide an observer standing in its summit an unobstructed view of the horizon over the high canopy forest (Hatch 1971). The La Venta pyramid may also contain tombs according to a magnetometer survey of its interior (Morrison, Clewlow, and Heizer 1970).

Burials may also be found in the garbage dumps of large villages; they may be under the floors of houses; or they may occur singly, away from habitation sites. At times certain cemeteries, or sections of a cemetery, may have been reserved for persons of one sex or age or social rank. Usually, however, cemeteries contain a sample of the whole population that died in the period of the cemetery's use. Examples of special cemeteries are those for children in Pennsylvania (Farabee 1919); separate cemeteries for men in the Desert Fayum (Caton-Thompson and Gardner 1934); the Roman cemetery at Ziegelfeld in upper Austria, where special areas were reserved for children, for victims of epidemics, and for persons belonging to "an elevated social group, very like the clergy" (Kloiber 1957); and the Carter Ranch site in eastern Arizona, where the burials were grouped by descent line and status (Longacre 1964).

Surface Scatters

Surface scatters are sites that have a geological or geographical context (Chap. 7) but no archeological associations. The numerous finds of flint tools in river gravels around the world can sometimes be classified as surface scatters. Usually such tools were secondarily deposited by water that moved them from the spot where they were dropped by prehistoric men. In these sites flint tools are found alone, without associated fireplaces, houses, or bones. In fact, the first ancient tools of man to be identified as such were found in river gravels by Jacques Boucher Crêvecoeur de Perthes, a customs official of Abbeville, France, who exhibited his finds in 1838. His work began the systematic search for objects of the European Paleolithic period. In the United States knowledge of the distribution of early big-game hunters is based largely on a plotting of isolated projectile points and other artifacts found by farmers while plowing in their fields or by persons who accidentally came upon them while walking. Although most such sites cannot be classified by activity, flints are sometimes found on the surface in situations that suggest activities. For example, in West Iran, in hilly country on the edges of large valleys, one frequently finds flints on the tops of hills, as though hunters had waited and watched for their quarry there.

Petroglyphs and Pictographs

Petroglyphs and pictographs are pecked and painted pictures of animals, men, mythical beings, or geometric and curvilinear designs whose meaning has not been interpreted with any reliability. They are usually found on exposed, flat rock surfaces, either in the open air or on the protected walls of caves and shelters. Pecked or painted designs are spread over most of the world, and vary from the great painted caves of France and Spain, such as Lascaux and Altamira, and the marvelous painted art of South Africa to rude designs pecked on boulders in the western United States and some quite remarkable painted caves in Texas and California. In general these painted or pecked designs seem to have been associated with magico-religious activities rather than being pure expressions of artistic-aesthetic impulse (C. Grant 1965; Heizer and Baumhoff 1959; Ucko and Rosenfeld 1967). We are all familiar with the propensity of tourists to carve, scratch, or paint their names on monuments, public walls, and the like. The practice was apparently just as common in antiquity, and the inscriptions of Spanish and American explorers on the cliffs of Morro Rock, New Mexico, actually constitute a valuable historical record. When the inscriptions scrawled on Egyptian monuments by Bonaparte's soldiers had been studied, they provided information not otherwise known. The ancient Egyptian habit of inscribing signatures on monuments has often proved valuable to archeologists, who can sometimes date sections of sites, determine for what length of time the walls were standing in good condition, or identify architects by name. The 107 inscriptions, often in poetic form, written in Greek or Latin on the lower legs of the northern Colossus of Memnon at Thebes have been collected and studied for their historical and religious interest (Bernand and Bernand 1960). In the same way an intimate insight into the life of the common people at Pompeii is afforded by a careful study of the graffiti on the walls of that city. A graffito copied from a wall in Pompeii and inscribed there about 2000 years ago (Fig. 23) reads: "Successus the weaver loves the innkeeper's maid servant, Iris by name. She, however, does not return his love. But he begs her to take pity on him. Written by his rival. So long" (Tanzer 1939:87).

Large "intaglio" figures of animals, humans, or geometric forms constitute a special kind of pictographic site, as do the giant desert figures along the lower Colorado River, the "medicine wheels" and effigy figures in the Great Plains, the immense figures on the coastal desert of Peru, and the giant, turf-cut figure in Wessex illustrated by J. Stone (1958: Plate 72).

HOW IS A SITE MADE?

Perhaps the two questions most frequently asked of archeologists are, "How is a site made?" and "How do you know where to look for sites?" In principle, the answers to both questions are easy, but sometimes a little explanation and illustration are required to put across the point.

Sites are the result of human activity, and as a consequence, one might think they would be easily recognizable, but so few persons have seen an archeological site that they very likely would not recognize one. It is easy to recognize and understand the pyramids and mounds that were built as

FIG. 23 A grafitto from a wall in Pompeii. (See text for translation.)

tombs and memorials to the dead, but it is sometimes impossible to see, and it is much harder to understand, how some sites came to be "buried." "How deep did you have to dig?" and "Why is there so much dirt on top of the site?" are two related questions that reflect a lack of general understanding about the processes that have left archeological sites in their present condition. How, for example, does it happen that human refuse in a cave may attain a depth of 50 feet, or a village leave a mound that rises 100 feet above its surrounding plain, or that a settlement is buried under several feet of sterile dirt? Each of these is a separate situation and requires its own explanation.

Take the case of caves and rock shelters where continued occupation over thousands of years left a layered deposit of debris some tens of feet in depth. What caused this deposition? At first it may be hard to understand how persons, living a normal life, could eventually pile up so much dirt. The answer, though, is really very simple. We should recognize, to begin with, that ancient cave dwellers were ordinarily less particular about cleanliness than we are, and secondly, that through natural geological processes, dirt is continually added to the floor of a cave. The accumulation of debris in caves thus can be explained as the joint result of man and natural processes. A family moving into a cave might bring in some branches or grass to cover the damp, hard floor where they wanted to sit and sleep. They might even bring in some rocks to sit on. They would bring in wood and branches to build fires. The hunters would kill animals and bring their bodies into the cave. When they had finished their meals they would throw the bones to one side. On muddy days they would track in dirt. They would never sweep out the cave. As natural erosion of the cave or rock shelter took place, bits of rock and dirt would flake off the ceiling. Sometimes a major rockfall would bury the whole floor. Dust carried by wind might add appreciable quantities of fine soil over long periods of time, and water-carried sediments might also add to the filling process. If occupation together with natural events continued for thousands of years, the cave might finally be filled to its top.

Somewhat similar to cave deposits are refuse heaps, or middens. Some of these have been thoroughly analyzed; by way of illustrating what they may contain we can cite an example from California, where E. W. Gifford screened samples of 15 shell mounds and determined the relative proportions of fish and mammal bone, marine shell, charcoal, ash, stone, and fine soil. He determined (1916:15) that the average mound contained the following percentages: fish remains, 0.031; other vertebrate remains, 0.055; shell, 52.07; charcoal, 0.22; ash, 12.27; stone, 7.5; residue (soil earth), 27.84. These deposits are made up of the day-to-day leavings of people living on the spot.

The great mounds (*tells*) that have accumulated in some parts of the world, especially in the Near East, represent a similar story, except that natural processes have done more to take away than to add material (Fig. 24). There are mounds in Turkestan that were occupied between the tenth and seventh centuries B.C., where the depth of deposit is as much as 34 meters (about 114 feet). At Ur in Mesopotamia, Woolley dug more than 90 feet to

FIG. 24 The mound of Farukhabad rises some 22 meters above the Deh Luran plain. The sharp profile on the right has been caused by the adjacent river undercutting the mound. Farukhabad was occupied intermittently for about 4000 years beginning about 4000 B.C.

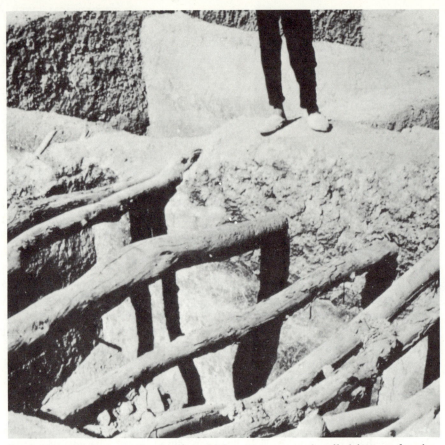

FIG. 25 Detail of a recently abandoned Near Eastern mud-walled house, showing the position of roof beams.

reach the base of the great mound, and Sultantepe in Anatolia rises to a height of more than 150 feet. How do such huge accumulations form?

These mounds occur in parts of the world where the chief building material is mud. The people make bricks or layers of sun-dried mud and they lay poles across them to form a roof on which they pile brush or matting, and cover the whole with a thick layer of mud that is practically impervious to what little rain falls in these arid regions (Fig. 25). Despite the low rainfall and consequent slow rate of erosion, the houses do deteriorate and eventually become unsafe for continued use. Then thrifty villagers scavenge the scarce poles used in the roof and reuse them in a new structure. After this, the bare walls standing there against the wind and rain rapidly disintegrate and eventually leave a featureless mound where the old house stood (Fig. 26). After minor leveling, new houses are often built on the same location, frequently several feet higher than the original house. One may wonder why people—as they customarily do in the Near East—chose to build on top of old houses rather than pick a spot on level land. The reasons seem to be that, with

FIG. 26 Mud brick and stone walls gradually eroding and forming a mound of rubble of the type that constitutes many archeological sites.

agricultural fields beginning at the edges of the settlements, there was no room to expand, and often defensive walls were built around the towns, preventing lateral expansion except at the cost of extensive renovation of the circumvallation. A diagram that illustrates how mounds grow is found in Lloyd (1963: Fig. 1).

The mound is such a conspicuous feature of the landscape in Southwest Asia and so conspicuously absent by comparison in the rest of the world that one must ask why. Childe (1962:56) says that there "are no tells in the woodland zone of Eurasia, north of the Po valley and the Hungarian plain." There are at least two reasons for this. First the building material in Europe was usually wood; and, second, the sites in Eurasia generally have not been occupied for so long as those in Southwest Asia. In Europe, outside of caves, an occupation of 1000 years duration is almost unknown. Where wood is used in building, it disintegrates and does not leave a mound. Where stone is used, it is frequently reused for new buildings; therefore there may not be the constant addition of new material. Under these conditions only small mounds accumulate. In modern cities, when old buildings are razed, they are rarely leveled to their original surface. In the course of repaving, street levels are raised. And so, even in the United States, mounds are growing. J. C. Wylie (1959:9) calculates that in our own civilization "every thousand people . . . discard nearly a ton of rubbish every day of their lives." Some of the refuse remains in the living area and thus adds to the rising surface of our cities.

123

FIG. 27 Plan view of summit of mound in the Southeast United States, showing the remains of superimposed buildings. The entire village, of which this mound is a part, was surrounded by a defensive stockade. (T. M. N. Lewis and M. Kneberg, 1946, *Hiwassee Island*. By permission of the University of Tennessee Press.)

FIG. 28 Section through mound at Hiwassee Island, showing the successive stages of construction. (T. M. N. Lewis and M. Kneberg, 1946, *Hiwassee Island*. By permission of the University of Tennessee Press.)

This discussion has so far excluded the conscious building of mounds by the deliberate heaping up of dirt or stone. The practice of building mounds on which to place houses, public buildings, and temples was common in the eastern United States as well as in Meso-America (Figs. 27, 28, 29). Indians in the Upper Mississippi Valley region of the United States often made mounds for purposes of burial, some of them being in the form of animals, birds, and serpents.

For a variety of reasons some locations are more attractive than others, and these spots may be continuously occupied or frequently reoccupied. A common cause of the successive use of the same spot may lie in its presumed religious sanctity. Often a shrine or church existed there, and later peoples, perhaps of a different religion, took advantage of the same site to build their religious structure. Immediately following the Spanish conquest of Mexico in the first quarter of the sixteenth century, the major Aztec shrines were razed, and important Catholic churches were built on their sites. In Europe, nearly without exception, the great cathedrals stand on the sites of pre-Christian shrines or temples. In Denmark it is commonly noted that flattopped tumuli occur within churchyards. This association of prehistoric sites and Christian churches is explained by the early belief that the heathen precepts were thus rendered harmless (Andersen 1951a, 1951b:133).

The modern Marsh Arabs have their island villages in the great drowned areas of the lower Tigris and Euphrates rivers. The same land has not always been covered with water, but in the last few centuries, when the ancient system of dikes fell into disrepair, the land became inundated. In ancient times the land was dotted with towns and cities, and it is the tops of the *tells* or mounds, rising above the marsh waters, that are now occupied by the Arab villages (Salim 1962:7, 95). Any still-existing structure dating from classical antiquity is likely to have had a history of multiple successive uses from the time it was first built and served its original purpose. Take, for example, the Roman amphitheater at Arles, in Provence, France. It was built just before the beginning of the Christian era; it measures 134 meters long by 106 meters wide and seated 30,000 spectators. In the fifth century A.D. the Visigoths transformed it into a fortress by filling the arches, adding towers, and excavating an encircling moat. Then, in the Middle Ages, the poor took possession of the arena and in it built houses that accomodated 2000 occupants (Fig. 30). The little city also had its own chapel. In the nineteenth century the amphitheater was cleared of squatters, their houses torn down and removed, and 20 feet of refuse removed that had accumulated over the original floor. Today this great structure has been restored and is used as a bullfight arena. Examples need not be multiplied; those given above are cited merely to illustrate some of the ways in which successive occupation may come about.

These examples show how mounds come into being. The other problem is how sites become buried. In the category of buried sites are most of the so-called Early Man sites in the Americas, as well as such examples as Olduvai Gorge, where the early African hominids (early forms of man) have

Fig. 29 North-south section of pyramids within Pyramid A-I Complex at the site of Uaxactun, Guatemala. *a*, Sanctuary; *b-c*, Cists; *d-f*, Crypts; *g*, a burial; *h*, cache of five pottery vessels beneath Stela A-7; *i*, Cist; *j*, empy hollow cut in limestone bedrock; *k*, Stela A-7; *l*, Stela 7; *m*, Altar; I-XIII, pyramidal platforms; 1-6, floors at bases of pyramids. (From Carnegie Institution of Washington Publication No. 456—Smith, Plate 10.)

Fig. 30 Roman arena reoccupied by a medieval town, Arles, France. (Cie. des Arts Photomécaniques, Paris.)

been found. These are covered by geological strata, and the circumstances of burial are often very similar the world around (Fig. 31). As typical examples, consider sites like Naco and Lehner in the American Southwest. There, some 9000 years ago, hunters killed mammoths alongside a stream. They left part of a carcass at the edge of the water, where it was buried as the river flooded and deposited a load of sand or silt over the bones. In time, as the river aggraded its regime, it buried the site under many feet of dirt. Thousands of years later, when the river began to degrade its channel, the site was exposed again, this time in the vertical bank of the new stream.

It should be obvious from this example that the absolute depth of a site below the modern surface has no bearing on its age. The question, "How deep did you have to dig to find a site that old?" is meaningless. The depth of deposit over a site is related to geomorphological processes, whereas the depth of accumulation of human refuse within a site reflects a combination of cleanliness, type of material used in structures, the desirability of the site for continued settlement, and such natural processes as the disintegration of cave ceilings, and the washing or blowing in of sand or dirt.

RECOGNIZING ARCHEOLOGICAL SITES

A wide array of techniques, ranging from walking to aerial photography to magnetic prospecting, can be used to find sites. Fortuitous discovery of sites will always be important, though perhaps not so dramatic as that of Adaura cave near Palermo, Sicily, which was opened by the demolition of artillery ammunition during World War II, and that of the hitherto unknown sites on the northeast coast of Nuka Hiva in the Marquesas Islands, which were exposed by the action of a tidal wave.

FIG. 31 Air view of the central portion of Teotihuacan, showing the principal pyramids and the Street of the Dead. The Pyramid of the Moon and the Street of the Dead are shown here unexcavated. For a comparison of the pyramid restored see Figure 22. The masonry structures at Teotihuacan gradually disintegrated as vegetation took root, thus creating soil and trapping windblown sediments. Eventually the features of the site disappeared under rounded mounds. (Photo courtesy of Museo Nacional de Antropologia.)

FIG. 32 Edible seeds of thorny plants that ripen in late summer and fall in the dense forest in the Oaxaca valley, Mexico, were harvested by food collectors. Fruit of the organ cactus, prickly pear, and the pods of several leguminous shrubs and trees provided a varied and abundant source of food. Sites of the prehistoric people are caves, rock shelters, and open camps. Compare the terrain and vegetation with Figures 20 and 34, where hunting rather than gathering plants was the principal occupation.

If an archeologist wishes, however, he can bypass the serendipitous approach and deliberately look for sites. There are two approaches he can use. He can start with an area that he likes and ask, "What kinds of sites are there?"; or he can begin with a kind of site in mind and ask, "Where can I find one?"

To begin to find sites in certain areas, a person must first familiarize himself with the landscape and its potential for supporting different kinds of human activities. It is helpful also to have some general ideas about the kinds of sites that are likely to be found. For example, a person would normally look in somewhat different places for sites of hunters and for sites of farmers (Fig. 32). Moreover, he would know that hunters usually lived in relatively small camps, in impermanent dwellings, that they moved regularly in pursuit of game, and that such sites as they did occupy would have been in places where water, game, and perhaps fuel could be obatined. Farmers, by contrast, ordinarily lived in permanent settlements and chose their sites with an eye toward arable land.

Armed with this kind of knowledge, a person can then survey the landscape for suitable places. Then comes the difficulty. How do you recognize a site when you see one? A person who takes the time to familiarize himself with an area will soon learn what is natural there: how the hills look, how the grass grows, where the trees are, and the location of sources of water. If he pays attention, he will begin to notice when things look out of place. An unnatural contour to a hill, an unusual kind of vegetation growing in a particular spot, or soil differing in color from that of the surrounding areas are all clues to sites (Fig. 33). In short, the observer must train himself to look for the unusual. Direct inspection of suspicious or "unnatural" features of the landscape should then tell whether or not a site is present. If the unusual contour is strewn with flint or pottery, or is a heap of shell, it indicates an archeological site. If the grass grows more luxuriantly in the outlines of a rec-

FIG. 33 An ancient irrigation canal is recognized by the growth of grass in the filled-in channel. A test pit has been dug across the canal to reveal its size and shape.

tangle, it may mark the borders of an ancient ditch or house, and occasionally the walls of houses may be exposed on the surface (Fig. 48).

Some archeologists get in the habit of watching wherever building involves the moving of a lot of dirt. But we need not always wait for construction crews to expose sites. Rivers may do the same thing. Perhaps the most spectacular such site is Olduvai Gorge in Tanzania, where many hundred thousand years of hominid occupation along the edge of a lake can be seen in the sides of the eroded gorge. As one goes from the top to the bottom of the gorge, each successive layer is older than the preceding one. Similar finds, though less impressive, are often made in the United States by persons who scan the cut banks of streams looking for flints, bones, and layers of charcoal that may be weathering out.

Caves should also be examined. Men usually lived toward the front of caves, sometimes leveling a terrace in front to give themselves room to work in the daylight. If the archeological deposit has been covered by rockfall or soil after the abandonment of occupation, artifacts will at times be found just below the cave, where they are eroding out of the steep or rocky slope. Caves of hunters are often situated on hillsides or cliffs where the men could survey the surrounding countryside (Fig. 34), but caves occupied by gatherers of plant food are located where the food is and may offer no attractive vistas for overlooking the landscape (see Fig. 32). Cave dwellers were not much interested in deep and dark underground caverns such as Mammoth Cave in Kentucky, except for special ceremonial purposes.

Instead of random searching, many archeologists decide what they want to find and then go out to find it. A discovery comparable to Schliemann's finding Troy was made by a Dutch doctor, Eugene Dubois, who went to Java in 1890 to find a fossil man, and did—*Pithecanthropus erectus* (now included in *Homo erectus erectus*) (Lasker 1961:91f). Ordinarily, deliberate discovery of particular kinds of sites depends on careful evaluation of available information.

An example taken from modern archeological research is the seeking of sites that will shed light on the origins of agriculture. In these investigations archeologists have worked closely with botanists and zoologists to determine where the most likely spots in the world to find out about the history of agriculture would be. Obviously, maize had to be domesticated somewhere near where it grew in the wild, and the same is true for wheat or for goats or cattle. The process is one of eliminating the areas where domestication could not have occurred and then trying to narrow the field still further by identifying the most favorable locations within the possible areas remaining. Then it is time for field work, beginning with surface survey to see if relevant sites can be discovered. If they can, excavation ordinarily follows; if they cannot, it is necessary to reexamine the premises on which the areas were selected.

Here is where archeologists must depend on the talents of specialists in other fields. When our knowledge of the present does not lead us directly to knowledge of the past, it is usually because the natural environment has

FIG. 34 *(top)* Kunji Cave in West Iran was a base camp that housed hunters more than 40,000 years ago. *(bottom)* From the cave entrance hunters could scan the valley floor on which wild oxen, onagers, and elk grazed. These animals, plus the goats that scaled the cliffs above the cave, comprised the bulk of the diet for the hunters.

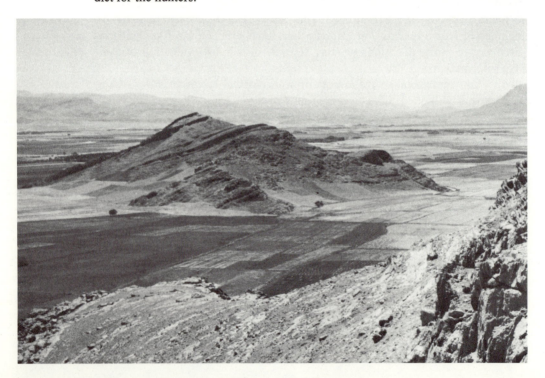

changed. The world's present climatic pattern is only a few thousand years old, and what is now pleasant country may have been under ice during the period we are interested in investigating. Or land that is now grassless rock and sand dunes may have been well watered not too long ago. Archeologists, therefore, must know not only in what kind of environment sites would be found, but also what kind of environment existed when the sites would have been occupied. For information about prehistoric environments archeologists depend on geologists, paleobotanists, and paleozoologists, who study plants and animals and the countryside in which they lived. An interesting example plotting winter and summer conditions in the Pleistocene and using these maps to suggest available food resources lying within a 6-mile radius of occupied sites is provided by Higgs and others (1967), Vita-Finzi and Higgs (1970), and Higgs and Webley (1971).

REFERENCES

Kinds of Sites: There is no point in listing references to examples of habitation and burial sites; students can easily find them as they read general reviews of prehistory or basic site reports. For examples of quarry sites, see W. Holmes 1919. For kill sites, see Wheat 1967; Haury, Antevs, and Lance 1953; Haury, Sayles, and Wasley 1959; Kehoe 1967; Warnica 1966. For Meso-American ceremonial sites, see Drucker, Heizer and Squier 1959. For other kinds of sites see Alexander 1970: Part II.

How Is a Site Made?:   Andersen 1951a, 1951b; Childe 1962; Crawford 1953; E. Gifford 1916; Haury, Antevs, and Lance 1953; Haury, Sayles, and Wasley, 1959; Heizer 1960; Heizer and Graham 1967; Judson 1961; Lloyd 1963; Montgomery, Smith, and Brew 1949; North 1937; Pyddoke 1961; Salim 1962; Schmid 1969; Solecki 1953; Woodward 1933; Wylie 1959.

Recognizing Archeological Sites: Atkinson 1954; Blanc 1953; Gorenstein 1965: Chap. 2; Heizer 1959: Chap. 7; Heizer and Graham 1967; North 1937; Ruppé 1966; Solecki 1957.

CHAPTER SEVEN

ARCHEOLOGICAL CONTEXT

Context is the environment within which things (artifacts, sites, and even cultures) are found or within which they operate. Consequently, part of the definition of archeological things is a specification of their context. It is only when we can specify the three major contextual variables—time, space, and human activities—that we can make inferences bearing on historical problems. For other kinds of problems we may need to know only one or two of the contextual variables. For example, if we wish to describe a sequence of technical innovation we need only know time and space. To make inferences about the uses of artifacts we find that space and behavioral context become relevant, whereas time may be largely irrelevant.

All sites have geographical context (that is, context in space), and if the sites or the artifacts in them can be dated, they have context in time. The archeological culture represented in the sites is defined in terms of the kinds of artifacts found, their date, and the location of the sites.

A single arrowhead found on the surface ordinarily cannot be dated, nor can it be associated directly with other artifacts, even though it is of a named type (for example, Folsom). It therefore has, properly speaking, no archeological context. By contrast, all objects found and recorded as occurring in one level of a cave can be related to one another and to other finds in the levels above and below. Such an association of artifacts may also be referable to similar associations at other caves. It is easier to interpret the significance of an assemblage when there are other similar assemblages from several sites. It should be clear, therefore, that the context in which any artifact is found determines the extent to which one can make interpretations about it.

134

STRATIGRAPHY AND STRATIFICATION

In excavation one attempts to place the evidence in time and space. Speaking particularly about artifacts, the principal source of temporal and spatial information is stratigraphic excavation. These excavations allow archeologists to relate separate sites to one another and to make inferences of cultural significance. A recording of strata allows us to determine the time and space coordinates of artifacts in the following way: if there are layers, those laid down first will be found on the bottom. This idea is so simple that most authors give only passing reference to it; yet interpretation of stratification is one of the most difficult jobs for the excavator (Fig. 35). All serious

FIG. 35 One of the earliest instances of the recognition of stratigraphy in American archeology. The painting, done in 1850, shows a Mississippian mound being excavated under the supervision of Dr. Montroville Dickeson. (Courtesy of the City Art Museum, St. Louis.)

students should read Wheeler's (1956) and Pyddoke's (1961) discussions of the subject. As Wheeler puts it, "The first rule about stratification is that there is no invariable rule" (Wheeler 1956:62).

The words "stratigraphy" and "stratification" are often used interchangeably, but they have somewhat different meanings. We consider stratigraphy to be the actual sequence of events in a site, whereas stratification refers to the levels (natural or arbitrary) that are excavated. Stratigraphic layers in a site may consist of many things. In a cave or rock shelter, debris from daily living may accumulate as it is packed down under foot. If the cave should be abandoned for some time, chips and flakes falling from the roof and walls as a result of natural weathering will cover with a sterile layer the debris left by people, or wind or water may wash in a layer of soil that contains no artifacts. The result is a series of superimposed natural and cultural layers that can be seen as the cave is excavated. Occupational debris, likely to be rich in organic matter and to contain charcoal, is usually dark in color, whereas the sterile accumulation deposited by nonhuman agency is generally lighter colored (Fig. 36).

One must remember that even occupation sites may not have been lived in continuously, or that the occupations shifted from one part of the site to another. Under such conditions the stratigraphic record will have gaps or temporal discontinuities, and the archeologist may or may not be aware of these lacunae from a simple visual inspection of stratigraphic profiles. His chief hint of a discontinuity may come from his analysis of the artifacts that are known, or assumed on other grounds, to follow a different pattern of change. Phillips, Ford, and Griffin (1951:233) were thus able to identify gaps in their ceramic sequence in a stratigraphic pit, and a particularly interesting example of the recognition of a stratigraphic gap is provided at the site of Jericho (K. Kenyon 1960:198; Zeuner 1954), where an occupational hiatus between the Neolithic and Bronze Age settlements was marked by an immature soil. The time required for development of this immature soil was estimated by Zeuner at 300±100 years on the basis of soil development at Jericho after its abandonment in the Byzantine period, whereas Kenyon, on other grounds, calculates this time lapse at about 180 years (1580–1400 B.C.).

Archeologists working at several sites in Palestine before World War I failed to recognize chronological gaps, with the result that the chronology was not only incomplete but compressed. Such failures to recognige hiatuses in a sequence are of course usually more common in the early stages of investigation of an area. They do illustrate the important point, however, that archeologists should work systematically toward establishing a chronological sequence before they tackle other tasks.

In open sites, if there have been permanent buildings, the layers are usually made of house floors, and because they are successively rebuilt, there is usually a discernible gap between them. The floors thus serve to isolate and demarcate material below them. Frequently in such sites there are also

Fig. 36 Excavation of Kunji Cave, Iran, showing the clear-cut layering of the deposits. The dark bands were caused by the decomposition of organic material, whereas the lighter strata are composed largely of disintegrated stone from the roof of the cave. The age of these layers extends back more than 40,000 years.

dump areas. One may find an ashy layer lying under dirt from disintegrated buildings that, in turn, is under a floor or wall foundation (Fig. 37). These are all examples of layers that, taken together, comprise the archeological stratigraphy of a site.

The closure of cave openings either by the accumulation of occupation trash or by natural deposition, at times allows dating of the contents. J. Hawkes and Woolley (1963:199–200) cite a number of examples of trash deposits that either covered paintings or engravings on cave walls or blocked entrances to caves whose walls bear paintings of Upper Paleolithic age.

The words "layer," "level," and "horizon" are used by various authors to denote the stratigraphic context in which artifacts are found. There is no uniform size or time duration to a level; it may be only an inch thick or several yards thick, depending on the circumstances; it may represent the accumulation of a day or of a millennium. Levels are set off from one another by the fact that they look different from adjacent levels (that is, are darker or lighter or are composed of different materials), or by the fact that they are sealed off from other levels (by a rockfall or a floor), by the fact that they

FIG. 37 Stratification in Tepe Ali Kosh, Iran. Dark layers are composed of organic material, and the lighter layers of clay from the disintegration of houses. The dark, ashy deposit can be seen butting up against the partly collapsed brick wall of a house in the lower right. On the left side, next to the shovel, the ash layers rode over the eroded stub of a wall and eventually became horizontal as erosion of exposed features and filling in of depressed areas on the site proceeded. After the house had been abandoned for some time it was completely covered by layers of trash as the village continued to be occupied.

Fig. 38 Deposits at Gar Arjeneh, Iran, showing the lack of visible stratification that is common to rock shelters of this sort. The bulk of the deposit is composed of disintegrated rock that has fallen from the overhang. Tools and bones are interspersed throughout. The deposit is partly contemporary with that in Kunji Cave (Fig. 36).

are a certain depth (that is, arbitrary levels), or by the fact that their analyzed contents differ from those found in adjacent levels. The word "level" and its synonyms thus mean several things. One must be careful to understand how they are being used in each instance. As "level" is used here, it refers to the demarcation of associated remains by natural (geological), cultural (for example buildings), or arbitrary events (excavation techniques), and to the discrimination of different associations of artifacts.

Some sites do not have visible natural stratification, but consist of homogeneous deposits that are essentially the same from top to bottom (Fig. 38). These sites are often referred to as "unstratified," the term here meaning that they do not evidence natural stratification. If analysis of artifacts that have been collected with information on their place of occurrence shows that there is a difference between types of objects found at different depths, the archeologist may then speak of cultural phases or levels. At the bottom of the site there may be an early cultural phase that is different from a late cultural phase found in the upper deposits. One may even go so far as to speak of the site as being culturally stratified, although this use of the term is not common.

When an archeologist deals with an unstratified deposit in which he can distinguish no differences in texture or color, what must he do? Does he treat the entire deposit as a single unit of deposition and simply record his finds as occurring within this homogeneous matrix? If he did so, he would be following too literally the recommendations of Wheeler (1956: Chap. 4) to dig by natural levels. The method widely used by archeologists in excavating such sites is to establish arbitrary levels and to treat each level, which may be as thin or as thick as he deems desirable, as though it were a natural stratigraphic level. It is a method of establishing some kind of stratigraphic control, even though it be an arbitrary one, in the absence of visible layers. One of the authors (Hole) has seen rock shelters in Iran with as much as 15 feet of archeological deposit, representing thousands of years of occupation, which have no apparent natural stratigraphy. Any cultural succession in such sites is demonstrable only by analysis of the artifacts, which have been collected by arbitrary levels, or by plotting layers of artifacts which are separated by layers of dirt in which there are no artifacts.

Wheeler (1956: 70) refers to the method of arbitrary or metrical stratigraphy as an "old outworn system," and he is absolutely correct in saying this if the system is employed in archeological deposits that are composed of distinguishable natural levels or layers. He is not so correct, and in fact, may be wholly wrong, in referring to the system as outworn if he is referring to unstratified deposits. Collections made and recorded by arbitrary levels, when analyzed, often show differences in type or frequency of types from level to level. These differences, which result from differences in cultural practices, are as "real" as anything that can be determined by following natural layers.

After identification of separate levels in a test pit, archeologists can then proceed to remove layers over a wide area. Archeologists use the findings from test pits or trenches to guide them in recognizing the layers they will expect to encounter when they clear an extensive area. A variation of this procedure is to use balks or stratigraphic control walls between pits or areas (Fig. 39). Wheeler discusses this technique and illustrates it with two photographs of sites in India (Wheeler 1956: Chap. 5, Plates 4, 5). In digging the very large tells in the Near East, effective use has been made of the step trench, a technique that allows archeologists to plumb the total depth of the mound with a relatively small excavation, without the disadvantages of digging a vertical-sided shaft that would be dark, dangerous and difficult

FIG. 39 Excavation of the Cerro Colorado refuse midden at Taltal, northern Chile, where a test trench revealed the slope of natural strata. When the stratification had been determined, a large block of the midden was isolated and stripped layer by layer, as shown in this photo. (Photo courtesy of Junius Bird.)

to remove dirt from at any great depth. The step trench starts toward the center of the mound with a pit of convenient dimensions. This pit is dug down to either an arbitrary or a natural building level and then shifted slightly toward the edge of the site, where the new area is taken down another level. This ultimately results in a long trench whose interior face is a series of steps that gradually move outward until sterile subsoil is encountered (Figs. 40, 41).

A good deal of archeology is small-scale work, however, and if an archeologist is limited with regard to funds, size of work crew, or time, he may be able to excavate only a series of test pits or a trench. Lloyd (1963:64) describes the method of one archeologist who covered sites with test pits. Although these pits were dug with great care, and all finds were meticulously recorded, Lloyd concludes that "this process could have been prolonged indefinitely without any prospect whatever of coming to understand the anatomy of the mound." The choice of the two alternatives (area exposure or test pitting) is clearly stated by Kathleen Kenyon, a leading British archeologist, who says (1957:41–43),

Fig. 40 A step trench 45 meters long and 5 meters wide was used to expose successive levels at Chogga Sefid over a vertical depth of some 18 meters.

There was a phase in Palestinian archaeology in which expeditions set out with the aim of excavating a site completely, and of removing each occupation level over the whole site from the uppermost to the lowest. This was a reaction against earlier methods in which pits or trenches were sunk which never gave an adequate idea of any of the phases discovered. The aim of this total clearance was to gain a complete picture of each successive period. There is something to be said for this idea. But it has two serious disadvantages. Scientifically, it has the disadvantage that nothing is left for posterity. I have already stressed the fact that archeological methods are always improving, and should continue to do so. Therefore, material should be left for future excavators to test the results of their predecessors on all sites of major importance, though the complete excavation of smaller sites is desirable in theory. The second serious disadvantage is that though a number of long-term plans have been made to carry out the complete excavation of a large site, no single one has ever been carried through. Changes of circumstances, in the resources available to the expedition, or due to political events, have always suspended operations, with the result that much time has been spent on preliminaries and in dealing with less important superficial areas and the really interesting levels have hardly been reached.

We have now come back to the idea of more limited excavation. But the limited excavation must be to a set plan. We must decide what problems we hope to solve and how that solution can best be attained. I have already referred to the problems which were uppermost in our mind in deciding upon Jericho as a site for excavation. They concern in fact the beginning and end of

142

FIG. 41 Profile of one side of the step trench in Tepe Sabz, Western Iran. The trench began at the highest point on the site and was stepped back toward the outside of the mound to permit easier access to the trench but still maintain a continuous stratigraphic sequence. After the trench had been stepped back five times, the remaining depth was removed via a shaft 5 by 3 meters in extent and some 5 meters deep. The profile shows the way successive stratigraphic levels were grouped into cultural phases, each with subunits called zones. Each phase is characterized by a unique assemblage of artifacts. (F. Hole, K. V. Flannery, and J. A. Neely, *Prehistory and Human Ecology of the Deh Luran Plain.* Museum of Anthropology, University of Michigan, Memoirs [1969].)

ancient Jericho, the question whether the end of the Bronze Age occupation could be ascribed to the period of Joshua, and the examination of the extremely early occupation revealed by Professor Garstang. In between lay many long centuries in which Jericho was a very important town, on which our excavations would undoubtedly throw light, but our initial operations were planned to throw light on these two main problems.

As Kenyon points out, important sites must be restudied as techniques improve, and this survey can be done most effectively if an undisturbed block of the original stratified deposits remain. Museum collections from archeological sites may easily be restudied whenever the occasion requires, but, from reexcavation, new insights can be secured that inspection of already collected material can never supply because it has been divorced from its context.

There are several examples of sites that have been excavated by the two methods—arbitrary levels and natural layers—and the reader may find it worthwhile to compare the occurrence of pottery types collected by digging arbitrary levels in Tularosa and Cordova caves, New Mexico (P. Martin and others 1952:Fig. 26, Table 2), with the profile of stratigraphic layers (Martin and others 1952:Fig. 25), noting that there is a general correlation of the two, but also that collecting of potsherds by natural layers would have produced a much sharper ceramic sequence. At the site of Pachacamac on the central coast of Peru, Strong and Corbett (1943) excavated two large "cuts" (that is, trenches) in the refuse deposits and collected materials by what they call "stratigraphic blocks," each of which was 1 meter long, 1 meter wide, and ½ meter thick. When the excavation was finished, the actual stratigraphy exposed on the vertical wall of the trench was recorded (Strong and Corbett 1943:Fig. 5). After analysis of the pottery recovered from the trench, the proportions of each ceramic style were indicated on a grid diagram of the stratigraphic blocks (Strong and Corbett 1943:Fig. 20). By comparing the two figures, one can see that there is a very rough correlation of ceramic styles, as they occur in stratigraphic blocks, with the actual stratigraphic layers. The example is instructive in showing that greater accuracy in recovering context would have been effected by collecting pottery by natural stratigraphic layers.[1] Willey (1939) reports on an investigation of a village site in Georgia where he began collecting potsherds by arbitrary 3-inch levels. The percentages of Swift Creek to Lamar pottery in successive levels suggested that Swift Creek was earlier.

These figures, however, were not conclusive. Obviously pits, roots, and other intrusive features had disturbed the natural midden deposits to such an extent that artificial three-inch levels would not give a true time-depositional picture. . . . To correct this, a technique was employed whereby each sherd was plotted in relation to the soil strata and to other sherds. This was done in

[1] Strong in 1932 excavated the Signal Butte site in Nebraska by proper methods. He writes, "The deposit was taken down layer by layer, according to (grid) squares and each layer was carefully cleared off prior to excavation to prevent mixture of artifacts." We do not know why Strong did not employ the same technique at Pachacamac, but it was not because he was ignorant of the proper method.

the usual manner, isolating a block for stratigraphic purposes by cutting a narrow trench on the four sides of a ten-foot square. Beginning on one face, the soil profiles were recorded and then a one-foot strip the length of the block was peeled down from the top.

Willey's report illustrates the necessity of assessing results as an excavation progresses so that methods can be changed to suit the circumstances. After changing his techniques, Willey was able to affirm definitely that Swift Creek preceded Lamar.

In most instances where natural stratigraphy exists it is wrong to dig a large area by arbitrary units, because no horizon in any site is absolutely level throughout its extent. Contemporary houses may often be built on different absolute levels; thus excavation by arbitrary depth units will cut through strata of different ages and mix them (Fig. 42). The inappropriate use of a system of absolute levels has been effectively depicted by Wheeler (1956:Fig. 11). In Wheeler's drawing, pits have been dug into lower levels. Later filling of the pits introduced more recent material at the same level as older artifacts.

A method that has been used to great advantage is the technique of isolating a block. By this method a square trench is excavated in such a way that there is left standing a block of deposit on whose four sides the natural layers can be clearly seen. The block is then peeled down layer by layer. For

FIG. 42 A horizontal exposure in the step trench at Chogga Sefid, Iran, reveals the foundations of houses and work areas. The trench is 5 meters wide.

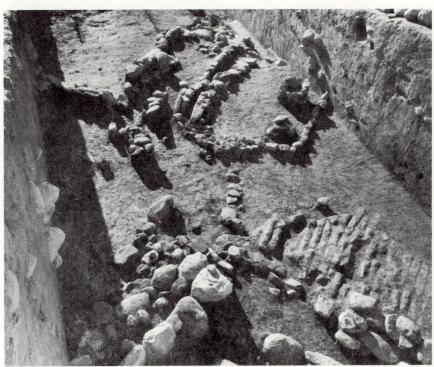

examples of the use of this technique see Bird (1943:253, 257, Fig. 24), Schmidt (1928), Troels-Smith (1960:Plates 1–3), and Webb and de Jarnette (1942:95ff., Fig. 27, Plate 162). One advantage of this method is that samples of artifacts from an area of constant dimensions can be secured. The samples make it easier to compute the proportions of artifacts and lead to interpretations that would otherwise not be possible (cf. Heizer 1960:101–102).

As a check on results it is sometimes useful to be able to refer back to the stratigraphy after the excavations have been concluded. To facilitate this, soil scientists have developed methods of securing a vertical sample of stratification by attaching a heavy cloth or board to the sides of the excavation, fixing the soil to this backing with an adhesive, and then removing the backing with a thin layer of soil attached. The vertical panel can then be removed to the museum and used to check texture, color, and other features of the original profile at leisure.

DERIVING STRATIGRAPHY
FROM STRATIFICATION

A practical problem for all field archeologists is to decide what the observed stratification indicates. Does it accurately reflect the sequence of cultures? Are two or more cultural horizons mixed, or are the strata reversed?

A striking example of reversed stratigraphy was found in the American Southwest, where, at the large site of Chetro Ketl in Chaco Canyon, New Mexico, the prehistoric people excavated their garbage dump in order to build a large semisubterranean ceremonial chamber. The excavated garbage dump, thus overturned, formed a new dump that had the most recent material on the bottom and the oldest on the top (F. Hawley 1934, 1937). N. M. Judd (1959b: 176–177) cites a similar instance of partly reversed ceramic stratigraphy at Pueblo Bonito, New Mexico. Judd, who knew in general what to expect in the way of ceramic stratigraphy from the work of earlier investigators, accidentally selected the prehistoric dump as a spot at which to make a stratigraphic pit. Recognizing that pottery types were not appearing in their correct sequence, he sought for, and found, the cause of the reversal in the kiva pit that had been excavated nearby. It is fortunate that N. C. Nelson, who carried out the first systematic stratigraphic examinations in refuse heaps in the American Southwest did not happen to select an overturned refuse dump to demonstrate the method!

Although reversed stratigraphy is rare in archeological deposits, archeologists can expect it to occur in a variety of circumstances. Winlock (1942: 75ff.) describes an apparent instance of Eleventh Dynasty Egyptian materials overlying deposits of the younger Eighteenth Dynasty. The "reversal" of order resulted from a misinterpretation of the sequence of the construction of two buildings. An unusual example of reverse stratigraphy was found at the site of Muldbjerg in Denmark (Troels-Smith 1960). The site had been built on peat at the edge of a lake. When the water level in the lake rose, the peat rose with it, breaking away from the bottom of the lake. In this instance, artifacts from the site were found on top of and below the peat, although the peat itself, which was sandwiched in the middle, was older than the site. Another situation that is often found on relatively shallow but extensive sites is that the settlement has shifted from place to place. Under such conditions we find "horizontal" stratigraphy, which can sometimes be disentangled by observing pits or other features dug through floors of previous houses, or by noting the occurrence of different kinds of artifacts. Two quite different examples of horizontal stratigraphy are to be found in Abri Pataud, a paleolithic site in France, and in Bylany, a neolithic village in Czechoslovakia (Movius 1966:317–318, Soudsky 1967:29–32). Such examples point up the fact that unless careful attention is paid to the possibility of horizontal stratigraphy the erroneous conclusion that the entire site represents a contemporary settlement may be reached.

Discussions of the various proceses by which mixing and disruption, including reversal of normal stratigraphy, can occur are found in H. Colton (1946:297ff.), Dietz (1955), E. Gifford (1951), W. Holmes (1893:238–239), J. Matthews (1965), Pyddoke (1961:85), Rowe (1961), and Tolstoy (1958:8–9). Burrowing animals may cause translocation of artifacts by moving them above or below their original level; dead trees may fall and bring up to the surface buried soil locked into the root network, men may dig holes for storage pits or graves and cause mixing of materials of different ages.

We may appear to be laboring the point of stratigraphy, but it is nevertheless extremely important to recognize that normal deposition of layers is subject to a wide variety of disturbance. For this reason, the examples cited above are well worth reading and bearing in mind. We should like to impress upon the reader that archeological deposits must be carefully studied; assumptions that relative age of materials can be determined from relative depth may be misleading. Depth in itself tells nothing about age (Figs. 43, 44).

In the absence of floors or rockfalls, differences that show stratigraphy may be subtle. In villages where houses were built of dirt taken from around the site it is often hard to distinguish layering. In these instances only freshly exposed and slightly damp layers may be visible, except to the well-trained observer. In the glare of the noonday sun subtle changes in stratigraphy are often lost because of the intense reflections or because the dirt dries out. A water-spraying device (like a pressure garden sprayer) can be used to keep the profile moist (Fig. 45). A special photographic technique employing infrared sensitive film is often successful in providing pictures that show contrast between layers not visible to the naked eye (Buettner-Janusch 1954). Deetz and Dethlefsen (1963) have outlined a method of detecting nonvisible stratigraphic differences in an apparently homogeneous or unstratified midden profile by making pH determinations at fixed points.

Fig. 43 Abandonment of kiva (ceremonial chamber) at Pecos during black-on-white phase is shown by skeleton 924, whose burial pit is cut into the floor of the kiva. Subsequent filling of the kiva and the placing of burials into the fill continued during the Glaze I, II, and III phases. Note, however, that the depth of burials below the surface is no true indication of the age. Skeleton 764 of the Glaze III phase is the same depth below the surface as skeleton 803, which belongs to the Glaze I phase. (A. V. Kidder, "Pecos, New Mexico: Archaeological Notes." *Papers of the Robert S. Peabody Foundation for Archaeology*, Vol. 5. By permission of the R. S. Peabody Foundation and the Trustees of Phillips Academy.)

FIG. 44 The upper meter of deposits at Yafteh cave, West Iran, shows natural horizontal layers, but inspection of the profile shows four pits dug through the layers from the surface; one mass of rocks that fell from the ceiling can be seen in the center of the picture. The pits introduced younger material into the same horizontal plane as that of the older material; if the pits had not been seen, a mixing of artifacts of different ages would have occurred during excavation. The upper ash layers are of historic age, whereas below the string are darker deposits that date back approximately 25,000 years.

Because of difficulties in analyzing stratigraphy, archeologists must use the greatest caution in drawing conclusions. Almost all interpretations of time, space, and culture contexts depend on stratigraphy. The refinements of laboratory techniques for analysis are wasted if archeologists cannot specify the stratigraphic position of their artifacts. Pyddoke (1961:17) writes,

> The vertical side of any excavator's trench displays a section through super-imposed strata, and almost every archaeologist today will record the thickness and extent of these layers and carefully note the exact position of his "finds," but an excavation report is not complete unless the writer sets out to explain the manner in which the layers were deposited. To understand his site properly the stratigrapher must always ask himself how his finds reached the position in which he discovered them; his little sequence of strata can no longer be regarded just as a heaven-sent means of separating cultural levels, nor can

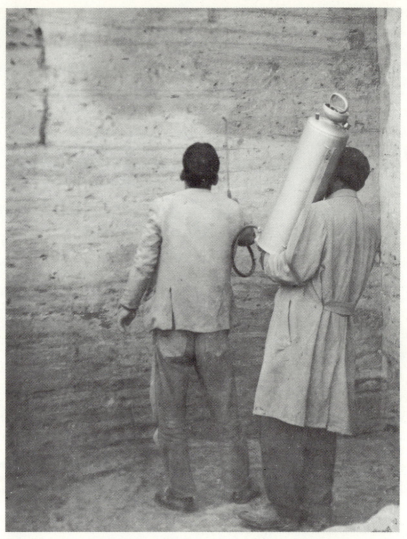

FIG. 45 Use of a water spray brings out color differences in strata at Chogga Sefid, Iran. When the soil dries after digging, finely layered strata are difficult to see.

deposits be regarded as meaningless and "barren" simply because no recognizable artifacts or organic remains are discovered in them. They are equally important parts of the continuing record.

A further point should be stressed. Once the stratification has been determined, it is still necessary to verify the association of the objects in each horizon. We generally assume, usually correctly, that objects found associated together at one level in a particular layer in an archeological site were made and used at the same time. By "the same time" is meant, of course, a period such as 10 or 15 years or even a person's lifetime. If this were not true, association of objects would mean little to the archeologist.

The rule that associated objects are contemporaneous may be upset, however, by the preservation of heirlooms or curiosities that finally come to rest in association with much younger objects. In certain societies valued goods are handed down from generation to generation. The Yurok tribe in northwestern California passed valuable obsidian blades from father to son, and it is conceivable that examples of these blades seen by ethnologists around 1900 may have been a century old. On the other hand, Foster (1960b) conducted an "age census" of pots used in the households of the Mexican Indian town of Tzintzuntzan and found only one vessel whose age was as great as 40 to 50 years. Foster's observations bear out the assumption made by archeologists that pottery vessels have a relatively short life. Examples of the use of antiques are in the occurrence of prehistoric projectile points in historic period Seneca graves in New York (W. Ritchie 1954: 67–68) and ceramic vessels of Nazca type in Middle Ica period graves on the Peruvian coast (Kroeber and Strong 1924:116). The reuse of stelae and sculptured monuments of earlier manufacture by the Maya builders of Piedras Negras is mentioned by W. R. Coe (1959:155). A similar instance of the modern use of ancient pieces is seen in the collecting of Babylonian cuneiform cylinders as good luck charms by Persian pilgrims who were visiting Moslem shrines (Rich 1819:58).

Two instances of the deliberate copying of ancient artifacts serve to illustrate another possible source of confusion for archeologists. In the Late period in the seventh century B.C., in Egypt there was deliberate imitation of Old and Middle Kingdom relief carving and literature dating from 1000 to 2000 years earlier (W. S. Smith 1958:240–241; Aldred 1961:155). The modern Eskimos of Point Barrow were observed by Ford (1959:220) to copy a prehistoric boot pattern that was shown to them by an archeologist, and we have here another instance of a revived form. An archeologist might assume that the ancient quarries were still being worked in the fourteenth century A.D. when he found a Cairo mosque built of the same limestone that covered the great pyramid—an assumption that would be wrong because it is known that Sultan Hasan, in A.D. 1356, stripped off large amounts of the outer limestone casting of the pyramid of Cheops to build the mosque. R. B. Dixon (1905:136–137) noted that the Maidu Indians of northern California used stone-bowl mortars to grind acorns in, but that these mortars were always archeological pieces which they had found on ancient sites. A final example is that provided by Gadow (1908:17), who observed Mexican Indians making clay figurines in prehistoric molds and selling them to tourists.

It is generally assumed that the objects found in graves represent pieces that were made and used during the lifetime of the person buried. Ordinarily this assumption is true, but a special situation is presented by family tombs or collective sepulchers that may have been used as a depository for corpses for a period of several generations. In this instance, even though the offerings placed with the bodies may pertain to a long period, it will be difficult to isolate the styles of artifacts typical of any particular part of the period, because they will be mixed indiscriminately. The use of grave lots (material contained in a single grave) as a means of developing a sequence of types has been discussed by Rowe (1962), who takes up the special problem of collective tombs.

TIME

When an archeologist asks, "How old is it?," his question is more than a matter of idle curiosity. For many analyses one must know the position in time of what has been found. After an archeologist identifies and describes his artifacts, he usually compares them with artifacts from sites dated relatively older or younger than the one in question. The study of culture change and of evolution, for example, depends on knowing which find is the earlier. The question of age is vitally important also in evaluating the cultural significance of two things. For example, the similarity of two objects of the same age at different sites may imply trade, whereas the similarity of two objects of widely different ages may suggest a long cultural tradition. The discovery of the Tartaria tablets in Romania illustrates the importance of knowing relative ages. The question, still unanswered, is whether they precede, are contemporary with, or follow the tablets from Warka in Mesopotamia, where the first traces of writing are traditionally said to occur. The article by Hood (1967) concerning the tablets is a splendid example of the use of several techniques of dating to try to arrive at reasonable conclusions of great cultural and historical importance.

Knowing the relative ages may also help establish association, as was clearly seen when the famous Piltdown hoax was uncovered; here part of the proof of the deception depended on the fact that the skull and jaw, which were claimed to have been found associated, were not of the same age (Weiner 1955). An archeologist may find an ambiguous specimen and want to know to which of two cultures it belongs. If he can date one or the other he may be able to solve his problem. These and many more practical applications of dating constantly face the archeologist; therefore he must know the relative ages of sites and artifacts before he can make intelligent judgments of their cultural significance.

At the outset it should be noted that two kinds of time—relative and absolute—are important in archeology. In fact, this is only a convenient distinction, for all dating is *relative*. Absolute dates are those that are keyed to our modern calendar. Our calendar is based on recurring astronomical events, but it is arranged relative to the date of Christ. The ancient Maya for example, had a different system that was just as absolute as ours.

A relative date tells us simply that one thing is older than another; in archeology, material is dated in relation to other archeological material. For example, the Piltdown jaw was dated as relatively younger than the skull. Absolute dates automatically give relative ages; thus, by reading the birth dates of George Washington and Abraham Lincoln, we can tell immediately that, relative to Washington, Lincoln was more recent.

There are differing degrees of accuracy in all dating, whether we call it absolute or relative. With some modern techniques we are able to give dates that are expressed in terms of the Christian calendar, but such dates are absolute only within a mathematically expressed margin of error. Sometimes, because of the possible error, the dates would be less useful to archeologists than sound relative dates would be. For example, when two closely similar sites are found, it is useful to know which is earlier. If the absolute date (carbon-14 years before present) of each site (for example, 5200 ± 200 and 5100 ± 200) has a margin of error of 200 years more or less, the archeologist can never be really sure which is earlier, because the true date in these illustrations will fall between 5000 and 5400 years in one instance and 4900 and 5300 years in the other, the overlap being between 5000 and 5300 years. By contrast, if the archeologist can find some way to date one site relative to the other, rather than relative to the Christian calendar, he can tell which is the older.

Besides the methods for dating one must also consider what is to be dated. The best method is to date the article—a site or an artifact in the site—itself. Another method is to date the immediate context in which the artifact or site lies. For example, it may be possible to date the beach deposit in which a site is found, or the hearth in which an artifact is found. If so, we then infer that the artifact is the same age as its context. The third, and least accurate, method is to date similar occurrences. Thus, if the beach in which a site is found cannot be dated, a similar site elsewhere may be dated; or sometimes the geological stratum in which a site is found can be dated some miles from the site; or, in some instances where geological formations have been traced around the world, it may be possible to get a date from another continent that will give an estimate for the age of a site. In short, although absolute and relative ages can be given for many archeological occurrences, the dependability of these age determinations may vary considerably. An interesting example of geological cross dating comes from Java, where tektites (also called billitonites)—small, chemically distinct drops of glass of cosmic origin—fell during the Middle Pleistocene. Conveniently for archeologists, they have been found in the upper Trinil beds in Java, where Pithecanthropus fossil human remains were found, and also in the Philippines in association with the teeth of stegodons and elephants (von Koenigswald 1956: 104–105). The age of the tektites of Java has subsequently been determined because some of them underlie the basalts, which by the potassium-argon method can be shown to be 500,000 years old (Gentner and Lippolt 1969: 82). Pithecanthropus and the stegodons and elephants, therefore, are older than 500,000 years.

CULTURAL ASSOCIATION AND SPACE

In Chapter 4 we discussed the concept of culture as it is used in archeology. In most instances we speak of archeological cultures or of the way artifacts relate to behavior; we will call this "cultural association" to emphasize that we are inferring from our data an abstraction that is something like what anthropologists call culture or cultural behavior. As prehistorians we associate our data with these concepts. This important distinction should be kept in mind in the following discussion.

Cultures exist only in a context of time and space. As stated before, the one thing that keeps a Parisian or a tourist from enjoying a historical appreciation of the obelisk of Luxor is that it has been removed from the context that would have given it correct historical meaning and placed instead in the middle of the heavy Paris traffic. In Luxor the obelisk was among the ruins of which it was a part. Enlightened probing of these ruins has revealed the cultural context into which the obelisk fitted. In addition, at Luxor there are the sun and the sand and the Nile; these comprise the geographical context. Inserted into the contexts of culture and geography, the obelisk has far different meaning and evokes far different appreciation than it does in Paris surrounded by fountains, palaces, motorcars, and tourists. As Childe (1956:5) put it, with a different example (the Elgin Marbles) in mind, "Indeed we tear down the frieze from a temple in a sunny clime and set it at eye-level in a room in murky London to appreciate its beauty."

An archeological culture (the reconstruction we make from archeological finds) represents a social system that existed in a definable area and whose members shared certain artifacts, ways of life, and ideas. The contextual variables of time and space are thus intimately linked when we deal on the level of cultures, but if we want only to describe the distribution of boat-stones, let us say, we can ignore culture. If, however, we wish to interpret the distribution of the boat-stones or to examine the nature of these artifacts, we must infer the way they were used. It is only when we treat space as uninterpreted geographic data that we can ignore culture. This use of the spatial context is so obvious that it requires no further discussion; accordingly, we shall focus on cultural association as a dimension of archeological context.

A normal procedure in archeology is to lay bare a level in a site and plot the occurrence of artifacts with respect to one another and to the other features in the stratum. We do this for two reasons: to discover the kinds and numbers of artifacts in a particular assemblage, and to enable us to infer their uses. These goals follow from our ideas that culture is patterned and that artifacts are tangible evidence of prehistoric behavior (chap. 4).

Moreover, we assume that most artifacts were used for a rational purpose or at least one that we may be able to infer from their context within the sites. Characteristic sets of artifacts will have been manufactured and used at the scenes of the activities to which they pertain. A careful examination and analysis of context and associations will therefore tell us about the activities carried out by the prehistoric peoples.

Moving from the general to specific cultures, we can find other uses to which the concepts of archeological culture and space are applicable. When assemblages from contemporary sites are compared, some are more alike than others. Accepting the ideas that cultures are patterned and transmitted symbolically, it follows that sites having more similar assemblages of artifacts are likely to have been more closely related so long as they are found within a restricted geographic space. These similar assemblages are then conventionally taken to be representatives of archeological cultures, a term that is akin to the popular use of "tribe" when it is used to describe modern peoples. There is considerable question regarding what constitutes similarity among assemblages, but we shall ignore this problem for the time being. It is worth noting, however, that there may be exceptions to the rule that related cultures are found within restricted geographic areas. Recent mass migrations and exportation of ways of life negate the generalization. However, it is to be doubted that in prehistoric times one could find a parallel to transplanted modern English culture in such widely spaced places as Hong Kong, Nairobi, Sydney and Victoria, B.C.

In the absence of history, an archeologist must give an arbitrary name to the cultures. He may name them after the region in which they are found (for example, Desert Culture), after the site in which the assemblage was first identified (Badarian after the Egyptian site of Badari), or after a characteristic artifact industry in the assemblage (Beaker Culture after the kind of pottery). As a person goes back in time he finds he can distinguish fewer and fewer separate cultures. The reasoning is that at each period man has a limited fund of knowledge and technical skills, and he must draw on these when he invents new things. The farther back in time we go, the smaller the inventory of possibilities man had. The earliest forms of men naturally had the smallest inventory of ideas from which to draw; so they were exceedingly restricted in what they could do. As the inventory grew larger with passing time there was more possibility for innovation; and as men spread across the earth they faced different problems, which required unique solutions. Groups of people in separated locales therefore developed somewhat different habits and skills. Cumulatively, the inventory of ideas increased slowly, but significant differences can be seen during the Middle Pleistocene between peoples living in Africa, Europe, and Asia. These differences are in contrast to the earlier situation, when the artifacts are very similar wherever they are found. In the earliest times, we can identify only one archeological culture, whereas later we find striking differentiation. (See Chap. 4 for a fuller discussion of the reasoning.)

Countering tendencies toward divergence, and acting to increase the stockpile of ideas of each separate group, was diffusion of ideas, which took place either through imitation, symbolic communication, or migration. But the pooling of ideas made it possible for more divergence, a fact that becomes especially noticeable in recent times as people developed highly specialized ways of dealing with local situations. We find as we approach the present that differentiation proceeds more rapidly and that archeological cultures become more restricted geographically. The tendency has only recently been counteracted with the invention of rapid communication and transport, with the result that many cultures are losing their uniqueness and being subsumed under more dominant, expansive cultures.

Many of the cultural differences that we observe now in Europe between people living in various countries might not be obvious archeologically. Evidence of such things as dress, language, and art—in the absence of graphic arts—would not ordinarily be preserved. Even though people over most of Europe used similar tools during the early stages of the last glaciation and are therefore hard to differentiate archeologically, we have no reason to assume that they spoke the same language, told the same legends around their campfires, believed in the same gods, or painted their faces in the same way. *As archeologists we can distinguish cultures only when we can distinguish differences.* Many peoples in the past left us very little with which to distinguish differences. Specific ways for identifying cultures from artifacts, and the ways to interpret archeological data in cultural terms, are given in Part V of this book.

The boundary lines we draw between cultures are arbitrary. People living along the Rhine share elements of French and German culture; in many ways they are not typical of other groups of French or Germans living further west or east. For every culture there is a center in which it finds its clearest expression. Groups on the geographical edges may grade indistinguishably from one culture to another; there are few clear-cut lines. All archeologists could read with profit Kroeber's (1936; 1963:46) and Driver's (1962) discussions of the problem of defining culture areas, how to draw boundaries between culture areas, and how to define the climax group within a culture area.

In summary, context, with its aspects of time, space, and culture, is central in archeological studies. The use of stratigraphy to establish associations and relative ages of artifacts allows interpretations to be made about culture. An archeological culture consists of repeated associations of artifacts as they occur in time and space, and archeologists use the concepts of culture generally to help them understand the processes that led to the development of archeologically identified cultures.

REFERENCES

Stratigraphy and Stratification: Bird 1943; Fryxell and Daugherty 1963; Heizer 1960; Heizer and Graham 1967; K. Kenyon 1957, 1960; P. S. Martin and others 1952; P. Phillips 1970: Part 2:575–576; Phillips, Ford, and Griffin 1951; Ore 1968; Pyddoke 1961; Schmidt 1928; Strong and Corbett 1943;

Troels-Smith 1960; Webb and de Jarnette 1942; Wheeler 1956; Willey 1939; Zeuner 1954.

Preserving Stratigraphic Profiles: Dumond 1963; Franken 1965; Shorer 1964; H. Smith, McCreery, and Moodie 1952; H. Smith and Moodie 1947.

Deriving Stratigraphy from Stratification: Aldred 1961; Buettner-Janusch 1954; W. Coe 1959; H. Colton 1946; Deetz and Dethlefsen 1963; Dietz 1955; Dixon 1905; F. Ellis 1934; Ford 1959; Foster 1960b; Gadow 1908; Gifford 1951; F. Hawley 1934, 1937; Hole and Shaw 1967; W. Holmes 1893; Judd 1959b; Kroeber and Strong 1924; Matthews 1965; Movius 1966; Petrie 1899; Rich 1819; W. Ritchie 1954; Rowe 1961, 1962; W. Smith 1958; Soudsky 1967; Tolstoy 1958; Winlock 1942.

Time: (References to chapters in Part IV) Gentner and Lippolt 1969; Hood 1967; Oakley 1946b; Oxenstierna 1967; J. Thompson 1950; von Koenigswald 1956; Weiner 1955; Woodbury 1960.

Culture and Space: Driver 1962; Driver and Massey 1957; Kroeber 1936, 1963.

PART III

ACQUIRING THE FACTS OF PREHISTORY

The prehistoric past exists in the form of archeological remains, but each item and each fact must be discovered and recorded before it can be said to exist meaningfully.

Man, the biological species, first appeared and made simple but recognizable stone tools as long ago as 1,750,000 to 2,600,000 years (Curtis 1961; Isaac, Leakey, and Behrensmeyer 1971; Le Gros Clark 1967). Since that time he has changed biologically, behaviorally, socially, and, in the largest sense, culturally (J. Lancaster 1968; Washburn 1959, 1960, 1968; Washburn and Howell 1960), and by this extraordinarily complicated process of change through time he has expanded in numbers and colonized all the inhabitable portions of the earth. Wherever man has been he has left some evidence of his presence. It is the archeologist's first job to locate the places where this record of the human past occurs. The search for these locations is called "site survey." Many sites are found by accident rather than by deliberate search; others are discovered by applying certain general principles that archeologists have learned by trial-and-error method. Careful inspection for surface remains by persons walking over the ground is the most widely used method of site survey. We should guess that any fairly active archeologist has, between the age of 20 and 50, walked about 4000 miles looking for sites. There are special techniques such as examination of aerial photos for discovering site locations, but these are usually applicable only in certain areas.

Once sites are found, their age and contents must be determined—not in detail, but to the extent that their general chronological position and what kind of materials are contained in them can be estimated. Artifacts found on the surface will provide some clues of the site's contents. Its size, depth, or location may give a hint whether it is recent or ancient. There are devices that can, as it were, look beneath the surface and inform the operator about buried walls, housefloors, stone sculptures, and the like. The magnetometer is one of these pieces of apparatus that provide information on what lies buried beneath a site's surface. Everything learned about sites on a survey is recorded in notebooks, and at the conclusion of the survey the archeologist is in a position to select for excavation any sites that seem to offer the greatest amount of information of the sort he is interested in.

Excavation that follows survey is a complicated, usually expensive, and time-consuming procedure. There are well-developed methods for digging small open sites, closed occupation cave sites, large open sites, sites with abundant architectural remains, shell mounds, and so on. Each kind of site requires a particular approach, but all sites are dug in the same way to the extent that the investigator must dig from the top down to the bottom and thus be digging backward in time. Systematic exploration is always necessary, and it involves due attention to recording the occurrence of everything found so that when the excavation is concluded the site as such (or that portion of it which was dug) has been translated into the photographs, notebooks, maps, and specimen catalogue that the excavator makes.

Once an excavation is finished and the archeologist is back at his home base with his records and collections, he will write a report on his findings and provide his opinion on how they contribute to the understanding of the regional development of prehistoric culture. Archeological reports are difficult and time-consuming to prepare, and a year's fieldwork may require three years of careful study and writing before the archeologist can tell himself that the project has been completed. In this process of studying his finds the archeologist proceeds systematically, and usually treats different classes of objects separately. Pottery, stone tools, architectural remains, bone implements, animal bones used for food, and similar objects are presented in a separate section of the report. Trade, probable site-population numbers, social organization of the prehistoric inhabitants, hunting and collecting, or farming patterns are also discussed from the standpoint of what inferences can be drawn from the excavation data. Animal bones must be identified by a competent zoologist; vegetable remains, such as burned seeds or charcoal or pollen, must be studied by botanists; stones used for tools or in building construction will be studied by a petrographer in the hope of discovering the geological sources of the various kinds used; chemists, physicists, and pedologists may also be consulted to give their opinion on some aspect of material or soils.

The archeologist's main activities can be summarized as those of finding sites, excavating them, making records of all finds, analyzing in a systematic way (usually through application of typology) the materials recovered, and writing a report to interpret the human occupation at the site or sites he has investigated.

CHAPTER EIGHT

SURVEY

Archeology is a source of history, and for the most part the evidence is concentrated in sites. Except when they have been discovered previously, the archeologist's first problem in the field is to find sites. He usually begins with a survey. But before he takes to the field, he should decide exactly what he wants to accomplish. The kind of survey he will make, as well as where he will make it, depends on the kind of information he wants to obtain.

THE PROBLEM

Modern archeologists are concerned about general problems of history. They want to learn about and preserve knowledge of man's past. Because excavation is destructive, conscientious archeologists weigh the probable value of their efforts against the loss resulting from them. We can no longer justify excavation to recover art objects or texts alone, if such excavation destroys much other information. Most archeologists, today, whatever their personal interests, take care to recover as much information as they can that is of interest to other archeologists as well.

There are other factors that determine what archeologists do. Today, after more than a century has been devoted to the careful collection of prehistoric materials from thousands of sites whose ages cover more than a million years of man's activities, and from every continent, there is increasing interest in trying to fit the facts of prehistory into a perspective of world history. In doing this, it becomes apparent that important segments of human history are unknown. To discover whether this missing evidence exists, and is recoverable, archeologists tend more and more to define the problem, select an area where they think the information to solve the problem will be found, and go there and excavate for the evidence. At times an archeologist who could just as readily obtain funds for excavating a site with elaborate architecture, rich tombs, and fancy pottery, will secure a grant to investigate an area where the archeological materials are scanty and unelaborate. Many, probably most, archeologists are more interested in the problem they are working on than in the objects they find. The uninformed public may think that the archeologist who spends the summer digging an open site under the hot summer sun in Nevada is doing less important work than he would be doing if he spent the same amount of time in central Mexico, digging up temples and tombs containing beautifully decorated pottery. Both kinds of investigation are important, and the choice of one of a series of options is often made by the archeologist in the hope that he can thus contribute more to filling out gaps in our understanding of the human past. Many considerations enter into the choice of where to work. Available funds, number of assistants, ease of moving about, political situations in foreign countries, the amount of time that can be spent, how long one's family can or should be abandoned, and many other factors must be weighed in choosing a problem to devote oneself to. Most archeologists dream about carrying out some big project, which may never be realized because the favorable balance of factors is never realized.

KINDS OF PROBLEMS

Universities, museums, or amateur archeological societies sometimes set out to discover just what the archeological resources of a country or a state are. Their aim is to survey intensively and plot all sites within certain geographical limits. There is no urgency to such survey, and it is not necessarily keyed to future excavation. Local surveys aimed at recording all known archeological sites provide a relatively inexpensive and useful opportunity for student training. Interested nonprofessionals who are often invited to contribute their efforts are frequently able to make substantial contributions because of their more intimate acquaintance with the area. The follow-up to such studies usually depends on the personal interests of individual archeologists. Regional studies are the firmest ground work for future excavation. In fact, serious archeology is predicated on such surveys (Chap. 15). Sometimes areas to be surveyed are selected for a definite reason. A small valley may be chosen because the archeologist thinks a full story of its prehistory will contribute more toward understanding the general history of an area than scattered work might do. There are excellent examples of just such work, and their benefits have been proved. Unfortunately, they are rare, because such programs are expensive and are usually scheduled to be carried out over a period of three to five years.

Most people are interested in the histories of their regions. But there is perhaps less concern with history in the Americas than in Europe, because the American past is Indian history. However, in Europe and other parts of the world, prehistoric people are usually considered part of a people's national identity. Sites are thus sought specifically to contribute toward understanding the national past. The history of the peoples who make up present-day Europe has been traced in detail, and it is being pushed farther back in time as new data from prehistory are uncovered.

The prehistory of particular non-European peoples, such as the Incas or the Mayas or the Aztecs, can also be discovered through archeological investigations, and the details of the culture history of identifiable peoples, such as the Egyptians, the Celts, Scythians, and Chinese, to name only a few, can be discovered by archeology. Each history of a population over time provides us with one more bit of the history of mankind.

Archeologists may be interested in problems that require finding special kinds of sites. For example, since World War II there has been extensive effort in Southwest Asia to discover how, when, and where domestication of animals and plants began. As mentioned earlier, similar work has been done in Meso-America. Richard MacNeish's work in Mexico on the origins of maize agriculture is a good example of how an archeologist and botanists, working on the solution of an important problem in culture history, were able after several years of work to narrow the choice of possible places to look until they are now confident that they have found the place where domestication of corn began. The archeological reconnaissance that preceded the intensive excavations in the Tehuacan Valley reached nearly the geographical limits of Mexico and entailed relatively little intensive digging. In both instances, it was necessary for archeologists to define the area in which it seemed most probable that domestication first occurred. They then had to go to the areas to find sites that could be excavated. Other archeologists have attempted, like Schliemann, who excavated Troy, to find sites for which historical records existed. In all such instances, it is first necessary to eliminate areas in which one need not look.

Many sites are dug to train students in the proper techniques of excavation. In Great Britain, Roman sites are used; in the United States, Indian sites. Usually the sites are chosen for the training that students will receive in certain techniques rather than for the light the location may shed on archeological problems. At the same time, although such student-training digs may be carried out at a site where it is anticipated that no outstanding or new discoveries will be made, it is still necessary that the work be done with due care and that all materials and records be properly collected and preserved. There are some exceptions to this rule, among which the archeological field-school operated by the University of Arizona is one. There, in addition to training students, the archeologists are attempting to develop new techniques for excavation and analysis that will help in the solution of particular kinds of archeological problems.

HOW TO FIND SITES

Whatever the reason for wishing to find sites may be, there is the practical problem of how to find them. The methods used in a survey depend on the kind of sites desired, the terrain in which they lie, and the ingenuity of the archeologist. Laming-Emperaire (1963:80) estimates that 25 percent of known archeological sites are discovered by chance or accident, more than 70 percent by systematic search, and not more than 2–3 percent by all the various methods that are called "scientific," among which are included aerial photography, electrical prospection, and so on.

Most sites are found when someone walks over them. Archeologists usually grid an area and systematically work back and forth across it, examining the ground. The best method for searching is to walk, but in some regions most of the sites can be found by crisscrossing the area by horse or jeep, stopping to examine and record suspicious features. In Iraqi Kurdistan, R. J. Braidwood and B. Howe (1960) found that a foot survey produced the most complete record. They employed as site locators local men who had herded sheep as boys and had, in this work, observed spots where potsherds and flints occurred. Most archeologists who work in the United States depend heavily for leads to site locations on information given them by interested amateurs or landowners who have observed evidence of Indian occupation.

In addition to collecting artifacts, a surveyor will map the position of sites and make notes about them. This information is best recorded on standardized forms. The design of the forms will vary, depending on the kind of base maps available for the area, the amount of work done previously, and the expected total of sites. An example of such a form is in Figure 46. Other examples are shown in the handbooks on field archeology. Although these record forms differ in details and arrangement, they are all rather similar because the same kind of information is being noted.

Occasionally there are no artifacts on the surface of sites to give a clue that men once lived there. Such spots can sometimes be recognized as sites through the use of special techniques. On occasion they can be detected by noting the vegetation. In semiarid lands, vegetation will grow best where water collects. Old canals that have silted in to the level of the surrounding land may retain subsurface moisture better and allow a more luxuriant growth of grass (see Fig. 33). Buried buildings may alter the soil chemistry or drainage so that certain kinds of plants will grow where they will not grow in the unaltered landscape. Zeiner (1946) has written a most interesting report on the botany of the Angel Mounds site in Indiana. At this site, by observing the pH of the soil and counting the frequency of different species of plants, it was determined that the precise course of the palisade wall that enclosed the village could be plotted without excavation. (References to published papers on site-vegetation type correspondences are given at the end of this chapter.) The slight difference in number or species of plants growing on the surface

ARCHEOLOGICAL SITE SURVEY RECORD

1. Site .... 2. Map .... 3. County ....

4. Twp. .... Range .... ¼ of .... ¼ of Sec. ....

5. Location ....

....

.... 6. On contour elevation ....

7. Previous designations for site ....

8. Owner .... 9. Address ....

10. Previous owners, dates ....

11. Present tenant ....

12. Attitude toward excavation ....

13. Description of site ....

....

14. Area .... 15. Depth .... 16. Height ....

17. Vegetation .... 18. Nearest water ....

19. Soil of site .... 20. Surrounding soil type ....

21. Previous excavation ....

22. Cultivation .... 23. Erosion ....

24. Buildings, roads, etc. ....

25. Possibility of destruction ....

26. House pits ....

27. Other features ....

28. Burials ....

29. Artifacts ....

....

....

30. Remarks ....

31. Published references ....

32. UCMA Accession No. .... 33. Sketch map ....

34. Date .... 35. Recorded by .... 36. Photos ....

FIG. 46 An example of an archeological site survey record form.

above buried walls or ditches often shows up clearly on aerial photographs. Not only must an archeologist have an eye for the unusual, but he must also be in the right spot at the right time; in many places the critical differences in color or type of vegetation are detectable for not more than a few days or weeks.

Aerial survey is one of the most useful means of finding sites, especially where there is a minimum of vegetation and where large areas are to be surveyed. Photos taken at the proper altitude and time of day show things that are not visible to anyone on the ground. It is often possible to map many of the buildings and streets of a town or city directly from the photos. When used in conjunction with surface inspection, aerial photos give information that could otherwise be learned only by excavation.

One of the most sucessful uses of aerial photos to plot the distribution of sites was made in southern Iraq and Iran, where the dry plains are suited to the technique. In several seasons of work, Oriental Institute archeologists have mapped hundreds of sites, covering 7000 years of history. The aim of the survey was to discover the relations of irrigation canals to sites and distribution of population. Aerial photos not only speeded the work tremendously but revealed many features that would probably not have been seen from the ground. Willey utilized aerial photographs most effectively in plotting the location, main features, and extent of archeological sites in the Viru Valley, Peru, as a preliminary to the actual field work. Not only was time saved, but more accurate and complete maps were secured. This particular method is best suited to large, open areas without heavy vegetal cover.

The interpretation of aerial photos is a specialized job that requires knowledge of what will appear on photos and what kinds of traces sites will leave. Sites frequently show up as nothing more than dark spots in otherwise gray fields, or gray spots in otherwise dark fields. In most instances, it is necessary to walk over the areas noted on the photos to verify them as sites. Even though an on-the-spot inspection to make a detailed record and to gather surface collections may be required, there is a great saving of time in being able to locate the sites from aerial photographs.

In some areas, photos will reveal very ancient sites. In other areas the usefulness of the method decreases sharply with the age of the sites. In Europe, plowing and other intensive land use have gone far toward obliterating surface traces of ancient sites. By contrast, in Southwest Asia, where erosion and cultivation have not affected the land surface so greatly, sites will show unless they have been buried. There, on the Mesopotamian alluvial plain, the accumulation of silt has probably covered most of the very early sites, and accidental discovery (usually through the digging of canals) will continue to be the principal means of finding the oldest and buried settlement areas.

Although natural processes of alluvial deposition that covers archeological sites may make discovery of such places difficult, this earth-covering also protects the materials. The process of erosion by wind or water may remove the overlying earth and bring buried sites to light. Sites exposed by surface wind deflation are often called "blowout" sites. Gullying by water may cut through alluvial layers and expose buried remains. In the American Southwest, many of the Early Man sites now known have been discovered either in erosional gullies or in blowout locations.

JUDGING THE CONTENTS OF SITES

Structural Features

On-the-ground survey and aerial photography are used to find sites. Once a site is located, there are at times, depending on the nature of the site itself, ways to determine what features are in it, without having to excavate to discover them. One way is to use magnetometry, usually called "magnetic surveying." The proton magnetometer is a sensitive instrument that measures the intensity of the earth's gravitational field directly below the instrument. When readings are taken at intervals across a site, the presence of underground archeological features is indicated in the form of variations in the strength of the magnetic field. A plot of the readings will show a profile of "peaks and valleys" that can be interpreted as archeological features (Fig. 47). The interpretation usually requires some test excavation to determine the precise nature of the magnetic anomaly, because one cannot tell a priori whether a ditch or a wall will have the higher value, and thus appear as a peak on the profile.

Magnetometry depends on the fact that protons act as miniature bar magnets and gyroscopes. In the presence of a magnetic field, the protons align themselves with the magnetic field, which attracts just as a magnet does, except that the protons are slowed in this act by the gyroscopic action. As they incline toward the desired alignment, they gyrate at a rate that is directly proportional to the magnetic intensity. The magnetic intensity thus shows in the gyration rate.

A disadvantage in using magnetometry is that pieces of metal, whether in the ground or on the operator's clothing, or in the form of underground wires, overhead power lines, automobiles, buildings, pipelines, or other artifacts will affect the instrument. On the other hand, this very disadvantage makes it possible for the device to detect metal objects below the surface. Deeply buried metal hoards can be readily located with this instrument.

In archeological sites, differences in humic content from one place to another are responsible for differences in the intensity of the magnetic field. Thus, when buried pits are filled with organic material, they register a greater intensity than does the ground into which they were dug. The shape of the underground features also determines their magnetic intensity. Magnetometry has great potential for special applications, but wider testing under varying field conditions will be necessary before the tool becomes a standard item of archeological equipment, especially because such instruments are expensive. A detailed magnetometer survey of the La Venta pyramid in Mexico was carried out in 1969. Clear indications of stone constructions inside the large earthen mound were secured, but their nature remains to be determined by actual excavation (Morrison, Clewlow, and Heizer 1970).

Another method for locating features within known sites is to measure the electrical resistance of the earth. This method, called "resistivity survey- ing," is dependent on water content of the soil; thus it lends itself well to archeological sites where there are several kinds of subsurface structures. For example, stone walls have a higher electrical resistance than the surrounding

FIG. 47 Magnetometer survey of a ring ditch at Stanton Harcourt, Oxon. A magnetic contour diagram is given with a sample magnetic profile and sketch- ditch section. The ditch was cut down into natural gravel and filled with mixed gravel (dashed) and then uniform loamy earth (solid black). (R. E. Linington, "The Application of Geophysics to Archaeology," *American Scientist*, 51 (1963): 60.)

soil or clay has. The equipment needed is more cumbersome, and its application generally more time-consuming, than that for magnetometry.

The technique involves placing electrodes in the ground at regular intervals and sending an electric current through one of them. The amount of resistance in the ground between two electrodes is measured as the ratio of voltage across the electrodes to the current flowing through them. The system requires the use of at least four electrodes, an electrical source, and a measuring device. When operated by two persons, this method is as efficient as magnetometry.

There have been relatively few applications of resistivity surveying, although in theory it should be useful in many circumstances. The major problems are that rain-soaked ground and a high water table will seriously affect the readings. Natural geological phenomena may also cause trouble. For example, pockets of clay or soil in surrounding rock may be indistinguishable from archeological features. Rocky soil also causes trouble, because the interference caused by rocks may be taken for archeological features.

Other methods have been used for discovering what is below the surface of a site. The probe is a simple device made of a rod of spring steel with a ball bearing welded to its tip. When the experienced operator pushes the probe into the ground he can often tell the kind of object he strikes by its feel and sound. The probe is especially useful for finding pits and stone walls. An auger may also serve to test the depth of a refuse deposit or to determine the position of subsurface features (Ford and Webb 1956:21). Another method is to thump the ground with a large wooden mallet and listen to the sound. If site soils are lying over compact soil or bedrock, a practiced thumper can tell by the sound where the walls and pits are. Solid core drilling can provide information on construction layers of large earthen mounds. Such a drilling project was performed in 1965 in Illinois when 340 cores were secured from the great Monks Mound at Cahokia near St. Louis, and from these a good idea of the internal structure was secured (N. Reed, Bennett, and Porter 1968).

Cameras have been used to examine the interiors of unexcavated underground Etruscan tombs. When a tomb is found, a hole is drilled in its top and a miniaturized camera with a flash gun is lowered to take pictures of the interior (Lerici 1959). When the contents have been thus revealed, one can decide whether or not to excavate.

In some instances it is also possible to map the visible features on a large site and attain a good idea of the sort of site it is. This approach is especially useful where walls are visible as courses of stones flush with the surface, but where it is hard to perceive the plan from ground level (Figs. 48 and 49). Or, if a site is obscured by heavy vegetation, it is possible to plot buildings that are hidden from one another in such a way that the observer cannot see the layout of the site from one position. To do such plotting requires two persons, one with a tape, protractor, and compass, and one with a drawing board. By taking compass bearings and measuring distances and

FIG. 48 Surface indications of a house in the Deh Luran valley, Iran. The upper part of the walls, made of clay, have completely eroded away, leaving only the stone foundations. See Figure 49 for a plan drawing of the house.

FIG. 49 Plan of a house mapped from the surface of a site in the Deh Luran valley, Iran. The man in Figure 48 is examining what would be the upper left-hand corner of this plan.

PLATFORM ?

PLATFORM ?

DOOR PIVOT STONE

0 2 4 6 8
FEET

172

plotting these on paper, the necessary information for a map can be secured. One person with a compass stands at the corner of a building and sights the second person with the drawing board, who is also at a corner. In this manner, by shooting from a known position to an unknown position, a whole town can be mapped expeditiously and with fair accuracy.

Whenever possible an accurate map made with a transit or telescopic alidade is made of the site and its immediate environs. Site maps should, of course, be made before excavation is begun in order to record original surface contours and features and to provide datum points for a grid system.

Age and Cultural Association

Another object of survey is to collect artifacts that will identify the contents of sites. If an area is archeologically unknown, it is necessary to collect a representative sample of the material on the surface. This material can later be compared with other collections. One assumes that the sherds or other artifacts in the surface collection represent each of the archeological cultures in a site. This assumption is not always well founded, but it is used as a general guide. It is also assumed that the finds made on the surface of sites having similar contents will be similar. Comparison should thus reveal how many sites of each culture are present in the surveyed area.

The kinds of artifacts found on the surface vary with the age of the site, soil chemistry, climatic conditions, vegetation, and previous survey. Caves that have been abandoned for hundreds or thousands of years may have few or no artifacts lying on their surfaces. The upper part of the fill may be sterile rock, dirt, and, as is so often the situation in many parts of the world, dung dropped by animals that are kept penned in the shelter. In order to find surface indications of human occupation, it is often necessary to crawl on hands and knees for some time before finding the first signs of human habitation. As one walks up to caves and rock shelters, it is usually best to begin the search for occupation evidence on the talus, a good bit below the cave opening. Flints and sherds that are deeply buried are more likely to be exposed on eroded talus slopes than on the present exposed floors of the caves. The surface finds may be few and unencouraging, but their paucity is not necessarily an indication that the cave's yield will also be meager. If the caves were cleaned out by ancient occupants, *all* the artifacts from deposits that were formerly part of the cave fill may have become part of the talus. Sometimes previous occupants swept out the dirt. It is necessary to excavate to find out.

The surface signs on open sites may also be misleading. Mounds or middens may be covered with pottery and flint, or their mass may be barren. In Southwest Asia it is usually hard to find artifacts on mounds that are covered with close-cropped turf. Centuries of trampling by sheep and goats have usually beaten the surface into a hard layer and broken all sherds into small pieces. But it is not always easier to find sherds in newly plowed mounds. In fact, we have surveyed mounds of which one-half was recently plowed and the other fallow, and found no consistency to tell us which half contained the greater amount of material. We have also seen mounds that by shape, size, and position must have resulted from human habitation, but on which no artifacts could be found. In order to interpret his findings, the archeologist must try to explain why one site has abundant artifacts and another very few.

Conditions for collecting also depend on whether a site has been looted or eroded. If graves have been looted, pottery is frequently thrown out onto the surface. Sites situated along streams may be cut by the water; fresh sections, thus exposed, usually yield good examples of pottery.

The degree to which precise information about the age and cultural contents of sites can be learned from surface materials has been hotly debated. In an effort to make surveys more dependable, special sampling techniques have been worked out. For a number of reasons these techniques have not been generally used. Most workers prefer to look for "type artifacts" rather than attempt random sampling. An alternative method is to dig small test pits to try to obtain more artifacts than occur on the surface and to find out their stratigraphic relations. If time allows and the archeologist has reasons to think that important information can be secured, he will make his surface collection and dig one or more test pits. A detailed description of the collecting techniques (both surface and test pitting) that were followed in the project of the archeological survey of the lower Mississippi Valley is provided by Phillips, Ford, and Griffin (1951:Sections II, V, VI).

In the past the most common technique of surface collecting was to gather materials selectively. Today many archeologists try to collect everything on the surface that is of human origin. On large sites where there is abundant material this is a very wasteful procedure although it may be necessary to obtain an adequate sample on smaller sites. To save time and to obtain accurate information on the distribution of material on the surface, archeologists also use various sampling techniques. In this way they avoid the necessity of picking up everything, and they gain control over the location of the material they find. This then enables them to infer wherein the site material of a certain age or function occurs.

Whatever the specific method used in making the collection, the artifacts must be analyzed. Often this is done on the site immediately after collection, particularly if a selective sample was collected to determine the ages when a site was occupied. If the archeologist has any knowledge of the area, he will be able to recognize certain types of pottery and stone tools. His selection will emphasize items that he recognizes. Thus painted sherds will sometimes be more valuable in identifying the culture and date of a site than unpainted sherds are. The principle behind the use of the type of artifact is that certain well-defined types occur within sharply defined limits of time. Although painted designs on pots are likely to change rapidly through time, unpainted utility pottery may change very little over long periods. If an archeologist knows the area well, he will be able to tell with fair accuracy just how long a site was occupied and what its relations to other areas are. The total collection from the surface can thus be broken into smaller, dated units (parts of assemblages), each of which is defined by the diagnostic type artifacts.

The other survey technique consists in trying to obtain a "random sample" of the sherds on the surface. The reason is that deliberate selection of type artifacts can lead to undue emphasis on certain types and neglect of others, possibly leading to misinterpretation. Furthermore, when there are no easily datable type artifacts, changes through time may be best seen in the relative frequencies of different types. For example, during the early occupation of a site, artifacts of type A may have been most abundant, with type B in the minority; later type B may become dominant, with some type A remaining and some type C beginning to appear. Still later, all type A may be gone, type C dominant, and types B and D minor elements. The differences between the phases are seen in the differences in the frequencies of types. On the surface of a stratified site it would be very difficult to separate assemblages, but where sites were occupied for only a short time, it may be possible to determine the frequency of the various types for one moment in time. It is not possible to do so by deliberately selecting only the most attractive or familiar examples.

The usual method for systematic sampling is to grid the site and pick up only the pottery within certain grid squares. All pottery in these selected grids is collected. When the material has been lumped, the percentages of various types can be calculated. It is assumed that pottery of all types was distributed at random across the site and that it occurs on the surface in the same proportion as in the ground. But even random sampling, which is designed and carried out in such a way as to eliminate the subjective element in collecting, may not produce all the types of materials that could be recovered, nor does it give an accurate estimate of their relative abundance. Examples of deceptive results from random sampling are provided by Dorwin (1971), who prefers the method called "stratified cluster sampling." This technique has rarely been used on very large sites that had a long occupation.

The problems of collecting a good sample, by whatever method, from Near Eastern tells that are at times a mile or so in circumference, 50–100 feet high, and that were occupied for 5000 years, are tremendous. Archeologists studying what is probably the largest prehistoric site in the New World, Teotihuacan, near Mexico City, drew a map of the ancient city from aerial photographs; they found that it covered an area of about 8 square miles. The map was then gridded, and collecting teams gathered potsherds from each square. Millions of sherds have been collected, and it will be a matter of years of classifying, tabulating, and seriating the ceramic data before the story of the growth of the city, as evidenced in the testimony of the pottery, will be concluded (Millon 1964, 1970).

Any student who plans to conduct a site survey and make surface collections of pottery sherds (or any other artifacts that occur in great abundance) should read the published discussions on the theory and practice of sampling before he goes into the field (see references at the end of this chapter).

Percentages of types are usually calculated from raw numbers of sherds. Sometimes relative percentages are based on weights of various sherd types, and some archeologists count only rim sherds, or pieces from different pots where two or more sherds can be fitted together. The problem with these various statistical sampling techniques is that some sherds weigh more than others because the pots from which they came were thicker. Others break more easily. A calculation of weight or raw number is thus useful only in special circumstances (Baumhoff and Heizer 1959; Solheim 1960).

There has developed a general agreement among American archeologists that a surface sherd collection of at least 100 fragments will contain representatives of the pottery types present at the site, but settling on this number as an adequate sample does not appear to rest on any demonstrable evidence. Sites containing a large number of types can scarcely be characterized with a sample as small as 100 sherds.

No serious archeologist would contend that the surface of a site is always a microcosm of its contents. The only way to tell whether it is, is to sample the surface and then dig the site. A few archeologists (among them Spier, Tolstoy, and Ford) have examined in particular—by comparing surface potsherd collections with collections made from test pits dug in the same sites —the assumption that the surface materials do represent a sample of the pottery contained in the deposit. From our own experience, we believe that the presence of artifacts on the surface is dependent on so many variables, both natural and cultural, that it is unwise to use surface indications as more than a rough guide to a site's contents. Even preliminary test examination of a refuse deposit may not yield a sample that is representative. There are accounts of instances where an original excavation was followed by a second exploration with rather different sampling results (cf. Greengo 1954, on shell species represented in the 1948 and 1952 excavations of the Monagrillo shell mound in Panama; cf. Kroeber 1925:932, Table 17, on artifact class frequencies from the 1902 and 1906 excavations of the Emeryville shell mound on San Francisco Bay; cf. Phillips, Ford, and Griffin 1951:233, on problems in recovering a normal sequence of pottery types from refuse deposits in Mississippi Valley sites). It should be assumed that buried materials will move both up and down because of later disturbance by people digging pits (for disposal of garbage, corpses, storage, and so on) and by animals burrowing.

A technique to supplement surface survey is to test-dig a site; in other words, to dig a small exploratory pit that plumbs the depth of the site. Its purpose is to find out the stratigraphic relations of artifacts and to provide a basis for judging whether the site is worth extensive excavation. This is a particularly valuable technique to use in caves where surface material may be sparse. Furthermore, in caves one usually cannot tell, from looking at the cave walls and the surface of the infilling, how deep the deposit is. One should not plan a season's dig at an untested cave; it might contain only a few inches or many feet of debris. The greatest care should be exercised to make as full a record as possible of the position of all finds made in such an exploratory pit, because, if the site is later dug systematically, the pit materials will have to be considered together with the rest of the finds, and their positions and presence in one or another layer must be determinable.

Techniques for surveying are of variable dependability, and their use depends on the archeologist's needs. No survey can substitute for excavation; there is too much guesswork, and there are too many gaps in surface survey. This is especially true with magnetic or resistivity surveying, because one has a hard time translating the readings into specific archeological features. These systems are of no value in deciding questions of age, nor are they of value when more than one level is present. Magnetic or resistivity surveying cannot sort out superposition. Such information comes best from artifacts, and artifacts with context are secured by proper excavation.

SYSTEMS FOR SITE DESIGNATIONS

Every site that is of sufficient importance to be mentioned in publication or recorded for a file of archeological data must have a designation. Usually sites are given the local name or the name of some geographical feature nearby.

In some areas archeologists have worked out a uniform site designation system for large areas, such as counties, states, or countries, in order to achieve some degree of uniformity. In the United States the most widely employed system is that developed by the Smithsonian Institution in connection with the River Basin Survey program of archeological salvage. In this system, a hyphenated, three-unit symbol is employed, the first being a number representing the state (for example, California is number 5); the second is a three-letter abbreviation representing the county within the state (for example, in California SJo signifies San Joaquin County); and the third, a number representing the order of assignment of numbers to sites within each county, usually in the order of their being entered into the permanent master file of sites. Thus the 53d site recorded in San Joaquin County, California, would be rendered 5-SJo-53. This system, with the admission of the new states of Alaska and Hawaii, has caused an alteration in the alphabetical order of states; California, for example, moved from number 4 to 5 position after the admission of Alaska. It has been suggested that the official U.S. Post Office abbreviations for states (for example, CA, California) should be used rather than numbers, in order to prevent confusion (Heizer 1968a).

For Canada, a grid system of the site designations has been proposed by Borden (1952), and a system of geographical coordinates has been proposed for site reference in Switzerland (Staub 1951). Uniform site designation systems are probably necessary to record large numbers of sites, but at present and for some time to come, important sites will be more familiarly known by the names that have been selected for them by the archeologist who excavates and reports on his findings. Alternative systems for designating sites have been proposed, and reference to these is made at the end of the chapter.

REFERENCES

Methods for Site Survey and Some Examples of Intensive Regional Surveys and Excavation: R. Adams 1962; Beals, Brainerd, and Smith 1945; R. Braidwood 1937; Brunett 1966; Dibble and Prewitt 1967; Dittert and Wendorf 1963; Drucker 1943; Drucker and Contreras 1953; Ford and Willey 1949; Gumerman 1971; Hayes 1964; Heizer and Graham 1967:Chap. 3; Hinsdale 1931; Kellan 1958; MacNeish 1958, 1964, 1967a; Meggers and Evans 1957; Mellaart 1963; N. Nelson 1909; Phillips, Ford, and Griffin 1951; Rouse 1952; Ruppé 1966; Sayles 1935; G. Schwartz 1967; Tolstoy 1958; Trigger 1965; Wedel 1967; Willey 1953.

Archeological Histories of Specific Populations: Childe 1958; M. Coe 1962, 1967; Rice 1957; J. Thompson 1945a; Wedel 1936, 1938.

Archeological Information on Earliest Animal and Plant Domestication and Their Diffusions: R. Adams 1962; R. Braidwood and Howe 1960; R. Dyson 1953; Flannery 1965, 1968; Gabel 1967; Harlan 1971; Helbaek 1959, 1966, 1969; Herre 1963; Hole and Flannery 1968; MacNeish 1964; Mangelsdorf, MacNeish, and Galinat 1964; C. Reed 1960, 1961; C. E. Smith 1965; Ucko and Dimbleby 1969.

Plant Associations on Archeological Sites: C. Brown 1936; Chikishev 1965; Dimbleby 1967; Heizer 1958b:207–213; Helbaek 1966, 1969; Hrdlicka 1937; Meigs 1938; Murray 1970; Struever 1962; Yarnell 1964, 1965; Zeyner 1946.

Aerial Photography for Site Survey: R. Adams 1962; Bradford 1957; Chevallier 1957, 1964; Crawford 1954; Edeine 1956; Itek Corp. 1965; Jacobsen and Adams 1958; Kedar 1958; Miller 1957; Reeves 1936; St. Joseph 1951, 1966; Solecki 1957; The War Office 1958; Whittlesey 1966a, 1966b; Willey 1953.

Examples of Sites Exposed by Deflation (Blowouts) and in Erosional Washes: Clewlow 1968; Gebhard 1949; Haury, Antevs, and Lance 1953; Haury, Sayles, and Wasley 1959; Judson 1953; Wendorft and others 1955.

Magnetometry and Resistivity Used in Detecting Subsurface Archeological Features: Aitken 1961, 1969; Andersen 1951a; Archaeo-physika, 1965; Black and Johnston 1962; Breiner 1965; Hesse 1966; R. Johnston 1964; Lerici 1962; Linington 1961, 1963; H. Morrison 1971; *Prospezioni Archeologiche* (Fondazione Lerici, Rome) Vol. 1 (1966), *et seq.,* issued periodically; Rainey and Ralph 1966; Stirling, Rainey, and Stirling 1960.

Archeological Map Making: Atkinson 1953; Debenham 1947; Detweiler 1948; K. Kenyon 1961:115–122; Schwarz 1967; Spaulding 1951; The War Office 1956, 1958.

Surface Sampling and Seriation: Alcock 1951; R. Ascher and M. Ascher 1965: 248; L. Binford 1964; G. Cowgill 1964, 1970, 1972; Dorwin 1971:354–366; J. Ford 1962; Gelfand 1971; Gumerman 1971; Krumbein 1965; P. Phillips 1970:Part 2:pp. 575–576; Ragir 1967; Redman and Watson 1970; Rootenberg 1964; Spaulding 1960; Vescelius 1955; Willey 1961.

Comparisons of Surface Artifact Samples with Excavated Samples: R. Braidwood and others 1971; P. Phillips, Ford, and Griffin 1951:228ff; Spier 1917; Tolstoy 1958.

Systems for Site Designations: Cole and Deuel 1937:22–24; W. Gladwin and H. Gladwin 1928a; Hadleigh-West 1967; Heizer 1968a; Rowe 1971; Shaeffer 1960; Solecki 1949.

CHAPTER NINE

EXCAVATION AND RECORDING

Archeologists select sites for excavation that they hope, usually for good reason, will provide information to illuminate some inadequately known part of prehistory. The only justification for excavating a site is that new information can be secured from it. The clever use of advanced techniques for excavation and analysis is wasted if it is not directed toward, and designed for, the solution of a particular problem. The suitability of approaches and the scope of the dig should develop naturally out of an archeologist's intention. As R. J. C. Atkinson says in *Stonehenge* (1960), in a review of the development of archeological thought about this impressive site, "It is now no longer considered sufficient, or even justifiable, to excavate a site in a repetitive manner, merely waiting, like Mr. Micawber, for something to turn up. On the contrary, every excavation and every part of one must be planned to answer a limited number of quite definite questions." W. H. Sears (1961), in an attempt to draw inferences about the social and religious systems of prehistoric North American Indians, found that the older literature is grossly deficient in relevant information. His study points up the fact that archeologists should excavate to answer problems rather than simply to observe and collect what comes to light, or dig for information on chronology to the practical exclusion of other information. Before an archeologist can estimate a site's potential worth, he must have a thorough knowledge of the area and past excavations in it. He can tell how what is on record from each site relates to what is known and what is not known. To be able to choose a site to excavate means that he must first have read everything published that could have any bearing on the problem he is interested in, as well as studied all of the available earlier collections that have relevance to the period or sites where he intends to pursue his studies.

Sometimes many sites in an area are worth digging, and the problem of selecting one becomes difficult. Some archeologists compare archeology to a military campaign because of the many factors that must be balanced before the best approach can be selected. Starting with a problem and some sites that will help solve the problem, the archeologist has to consider the size and difficulty of digging each site, the time available for excavation, sources of equipment, cost, and the number and quality of workmen and supervisors available. After these factors have been considered, one or more sites will then be selected as best suited for digging. The presence of a good access road or permission to dig from a landowner may tip the balance in favor of a particular site. Often the choice is not so clear-cut, but it is unusual to have a number of equally promising sites. It is especially important to pick a job that can be carried through to completion. Many sites cannot be excavated in a single season, but must be revisited repeatedly, as in the instance of Pecos Pueblo, New Mexico (Kidder 1958), which was excavated in 10 field seasons between 1915 and 1929, or Pueblo Bonito, New Mexico (Judd 1954), which was worked annually in each field season from 1921 through 1927. Perhaps the longest continuously excavated site in the world is Susa, Iranian Khuzistan, where field parties have been in residence since the 1880s. Very large sites, like Teotihuacan in Mexico or Tiahuanaco in Bolivia or the Angel Mounds in Indiana, may be investigated by a successsion of archeologists, each one being interested particularly in different kinds of problems. In the course of years, the chronology and history of the site begin to unfold.

The elements of a military organization are evident in the actual excavation: there is the training of labor; the orderly assignment of the men and supervisors; the procurement of equipment and supplies; and the recording of data. Above all, the job should be done with precision. As M. Wheeler (1956:80) noted, it is axiomatic "that an untidy excavation is a bad one." In order that the excavation be carried out smoothly, efficiently, and without loss of information, there must be enough trained supervisory personnel on hand. In a dig where college students are providing the labor, trained supervision may not be a problem, because students can be readily trained to observe and record finds or to ask for assistance when they need it. In Mexico or Egypt or Peru or Africa, however, where untrained labor is available in quantity and the pay scale is low, the archeologist may be able to carry off an excavation of rather larger magnitude than in an area where labor is expensive. But with the larger crew of workers, the head archeologist will need more assistants to supervise and maintain a careful watch on the progress of the excavation. Big digs are always more difficult to carry out than small ones, and anyone who has managed an excavation with 50 or 100 pick-and-shovel workers has learned that shirking, stealing finds, labor agitation, internal dissension among the workers, which must be adjudicated, and a dozen other problems tend to eat up precious time and cause frayed nerves. By the end of such a dig the archeologist is usually willing to swear that he will never return to the same area and submit to such frustrations another time. But when all is done, and in retrospect, such experiences seem worth while, and it is not six months before our archeologist is planning a follow-up dig.

Sites are not dug merely to find out what they contain. If this were true, a bulldozer pushing earth into a hopper at the bottom of which a screen awaited to catch all objects would be enough equipment and technique to ensure reasonably complete recovery of objects. Preferably, archeologists try to do two things in an excavation, regardless of the size of the site, its type, or how large an excavation is planned. They want to discover the cultural sequence in the site and to expose, collect, and record details of whole cultural levels separately. They do this to find out how the people lived during each cultural period. Their procedure is to find the vertical relations of one cultural level to another, and the horizontal relations of objects within each cultural level. To accomplish these ends, the archeologist must maintain careful stratigraphic control. The purpose of the dig and the resources available to carry it out determine how large an area will be dug and the techniques that will be used. There is no general rule that will apply to all situations. Students interested in learning how different kinds of sites in different areas are excavated can best do this by reading a series of firsthand excavation reports.

KINDS OF EXCAVATIONS

Test Pits and Trenches

Many excavations begin with test pits, and in fact many end with test pits. Test pits (or soundings, *sondages*) are used to find out quickly and cheaply what sort of things are in a site. They may be used to determine the depths of occupation deposits in various places, the sequence of levels, and the location of particular features. They may be used to obtain a larger sample of material than is possible from surface survey alone. Often certain kinds of things are found on the surface of a site, and these may indicate to the archeologist that there may be something of quite particular interest that occurs below the surface. He will probably make a test excavation in the hope of verifying his suspicions; if successful, he may then decide that this is precisely the site he has been searching for. Of course, even though he does not encounter in the *sondage* the type of evidence he hopes to find, he may not be discouraged, because a small test in a large site may not reveal very much. In short, test pits provide hints; they are not ends in themselves. Test pits cannot be expected to provide a sample of the site's contents sufficiently large or representative to enable archeologists to say with any confidence how typical or unique the materials are that they secure from it. There is no rule about what percentage of a site must be dug, or how many burials must be uncovered, or how many potsherds or flint tools must be collected before archeologists can say that they have a representative sample. How much of a site is excavated will rest on the availability of time, funds, labor, weather, and the archeologist's judgment about whether he has a large enough sample to solve the problem he set as his goal.

Rectangular pits may be dug into the site wherever an archeologist thinks they will give him useful information. Some persons may wonder why archeological pits are always dug with straight edges and vertical profiles; it is simply to make easier the recording of the location of objects and features. What is more, the stratification can be seen much more readily in a vertical, cleanly cut profile (see Fig. 37). The pits are used to establish the depth of deposit in various places and to find out what the stratigraphy is. Test pits must be large enough to enable the workers to reach the undisturbed subsoil. Even ground water should not prevent the pit from being excavated to the bottom of the cultural deposits. M. Wheeler (1956:73) notes that at Arikamedu, in India, pits were successfully dug to base 11 feet below sea level, and at Mohenjo-daro, with the use of pumps, a depth of 10 feet below the water table was reached. Test pits are dug to prevent expensive and time-consuming excavation in the wrong place and to solve specific problems of stratigraphy. There is no way to generalize about how many pits should be put into a site. Some sites will not require exploratory pits, others may need several. Archeologists often dig 5 by 5 foot pits, but much larger units are required in the large, deep sites of the Near East and India. Wheeler (1956:83) suggests making the sides of the squares equal in length to the anticipated depth of the site. In loose and water-soaked soils there is constant danger of cave-ins, and all archeologists who have found it necessary to dig very deep trenches or pits have experienced the concern that unstable walls may fall and bury workers. Long trenches are often used to find buried buildings or walls, though they may also be used to correlate stratigraphies in various parts of a large mound.

A variation, the step-trench, is often used on large sites (see Figs. 40 and 41). A step-trench runs from the top of a mound to its base (Lloyd 1963: Plate 2). At the base it will cut into sterile soil to establish the depth of deposit. As the trench cuts in toward the center of the mound, steps are left so that the bottom of the trench does not reach sterile ground. The trench is designed to find both early and later materials. The oldest should be on the bottom, but, once it is found, there is no point in digging it repeatedly by trenching from the summit to the base. In fact, on a large site it would be impossible to dig a narrow trench straight down from top to bottom. The step-trench is a compromise that permits sampling of the entire stratigraphic sequence; it is reasonably safe and can be worked with numbers of men stationed on different steps along its course. What is only a special kind of test pit is a trench that is cut across the site.

Excavation of Large Areas

Any large-scale dig will aim at exposing wide areas so that a good bit of each cultural level may be seen. When a village is being dug, archeologists usually try to expose several houses and special work areas if they are present (Fig. 50). The object of this procedure is to learn about the range of activities going

FIG. 50 Plan of the Coombs Site, Utah, showing the excavation of an extensive area to obtain the layout of the village. (R. H. Lister, J. R. Ambler, and F. C. Lister, "The Coombs Site," *University of Utah, Anthropological Papers*, No. 41.)

Figure labels visible within the map:

GG-B C-F G-L M-Q R-U V-Y

1-4
5-9
10-14
15-19
20-24
25-29
EE
FF

GG. HH A B   C D E F G H K L M N P Q   R S T U V W X Y Z

Approximate edge
of cultivation of mound

JARMO

Area of gray ash
concentration

Area of relatively
featureless brown
buff silt, upper 2.0 m.

Concentrations
of pot sherds

Contour interval = 5.0 m.

Scale = ⸺ 20 m.

FIG. 51 Plan of the excavated areas at Jarmo, Iraq. Broad coverage of the entire
site was attempted by means of digging a grid of squares. (R. J. Braidwood and
B. Howe, *Prehistoric Investigations in Iraqi Kurdistan,* Fig. 6.)

on in various parts of the settlement at the same time. Frequently, and generally where the site is large, more than one large area will be dug. Detailed
plans of the distribution of artifacts and various classes of refuse exposed in
large area excavations in Old and New World sites are given by Dorwin
(1971: Figs. 16–39), J. D. Clark (1967), J. D. Clark and Haynes (1970);
and Binford and others (1970).

As with test pits, there is no rule that will tell how large an area to dig.
An interesting but not wholly successful attempt to combine the advantages
of test pits and excavations of large areas was Braidwood's at Jarmo, in Northeast Iraq (R. Braidwood and Howe 1960:Fig. 6). The excavators gridded the

184

whole site and dug a checkerboard of squares (Fig. 51). They hoped to correlate the levels in one square with those in another by interpolating through
the unexcavated squares. Unfortunately, because of the undulating stratigraphy
so common in a large mound, they were unable to accomplish their intent; in
this instance the experiment was therefore a failure. Braidwood and Howe
(1960:39) say, "The underlying strata of the archeological sites may pitch and
toss in ways which their present surface contours seldom suggest; the conven-
tional lecture-hall analogy of archeologists that the layers in a mound are like
the layers of a cake is a vast over-simplification." Phillips (1970:Vol.2:574–
576) discusses the same problem of matching layers shown in the vertical
profile of a series of discontinuous and scattered test pits, his example being
Lower Mississippi Valley floodplain sites.

In the excavation of large areas, the entire expanse should never be
completely cleared and exposed; rather, standing exposures (pillars, walls,
or balks) must be left for back-checking on stratigraphy (Fig. 52). It is not
advisable to excavate any site completely if there is a chance to leave part of
it untouched for future workers. The more common use of sampling techniques today has the double advantage of enabling a person to choose intelligently what areas to dig, and of ensuring that a portion of the site remains for
future examination. New techniques that will surely be developed in the
future can then be applied to important sites with the prospect of gaining new
kinds of information. Archeologists have long been aware of the desirability
of leaving undug some part of the site for future reinvestigation. French
archeologists of the last century made it a practice to leave such undisturbed
portions, which they called "silent witnesses." But frequently, where this was
done, illicit collecting (that is, looting) has since destroyed the important
remnants, and one can conclude only that unless the site can be protected
from destructive pillaging, it may be best to excavate as much of it as possible.

HOW TO DIG

"There is no method proper to the excavation of a British site which is not
applicable—nay, must be applied—to a site in Africa or Asia" (M. Wheeler
1956:36). Lloyd (1963:30) disagrees with Wheeler's statement on the
grounds that British and Near East sites may be so different that quite different
methods of excavation must be employed. Lloyd also disparages "American
expeditions with their multiple card indexes and photographic kite-balloons,
often seeming to be involved in trying to apply a kind of methodism under
obstinately unsuitable circumstances." Surely this criticism cannot be generally applied to all American archeological expeditions to the Near East. Because
many American overseas research projects are well financed, the expeditions
may tend to be somewhat liberally supplied with equipment, and at times this
may include photographic kites or balloons and multiple card indexes (by
which is probably meant a cross-reference card catalogue of objects), but,
notwithstanding these "drawbacks," a very large amount of first-rate excava-

FIG. 52 General view *(top)* and close-up *(bottom)* of the excavations at Tia-huanaco, Bolivia, showing the technique of excavating large areas and leaving regularly spaced balks to preserve evidence of stratigraphy. (Centro de Investigaciones Arqueologicas en Tiwanaku.)

tion and reporting has been done there by American workers. Another archeologist (G. Clark 1954:7) suggests that all archeologists, whether working with the paleolithic or with Greek art, should have training in prehistoric archeology, because it requires greater discipline to recover a maximum amount of data. In spite of these bits of advice, there are no rules for digging a particular site except that care must be used to apply the best techniques for digging and recording. The way a site is dug depends on the archeologist's capabilities, the resources at his command, and on the site itself. As G. Clark (1957:108) says, the archeologist must have powers of observation, pertinacity, and adaptability.

If care combined with observation, pertinacity, and adaptability is a necessary requirement, then how is one to dig? This depends on the situation. Bulldozers are often used to clear sterile overburdens from deeply buried sites or from sites that must be dug quickly because of impending construction. On the other hand, some European paleolithic sites are dug from top to bottom with no tool larger than a screwdriver bent in the shape of a hook (Laming-Emperaire 1963:95–106).

The tools used vary with a person's preference. In the United States long-handled shovels and trowels are the most popular. In Great Britain, many use a cultivating fork instead of a shovel. In Southwest Asia, the pick is a universal instrument. None of these is necessarily better than the others for loosening dirt. Aside from the basic earth-moving tools, there is an assortment of ice picks, dental tools, hooks, brushes, knives, spatulas, bellows, trowels, and scrapers to choose from. Again, the use of any of these depends on the excavator's preference and the job to be done. Digging in other lands where one employs local laborers may pose problems. For example, one of the present authors found that in southeastern Mexico many of the pick-and-shovel men hired to do the digging on a large site did not know how to use either tool; they had to be instructed in their use. In many instances, the local laborers will have some method of moving earth that they are familiar with and would prefer to use rather than push a wheelbarrow. Thus, Arab diggers in Mesopotamian sites prefer to carry out earth in baskets; though this may seem inefficient, when the men are allowed to indulge their preference they may do more work than when they are forced to adopt another means.

Basically, there are two ways to expose a site (Fig. 53). One is to strip an area horizontally. To make this exposure the surface is scraped with a shovel and the area is peeled down by thin layers. The advantage of this method is that it enables the worker to see features in their extent. Differences in soil color, which indicate archeological features such as pits or postholes, appear in their proper position. To offset such advantages, it is hard to recognize and keep track of subtle stratigraphic changes when one comes down on top of them.

The second method is to dig into an area against a vertical face. That is, the workers begin by cutting a trench into a level and then proceed across the area by cutting away at the vertical edge. They can in this way see the area being excavated in section, and as a result it is easier to recognize and follow changes in stratigraphy. When loose, ashy levels are being followed across an area, this is an ideal method, and it is the only way possible to dig in very hard ground. When the soil is too compact it cannot be easily scraped off with a shovel or trowel. Complete reliance on following a vertical face may mean that features that are most easily seen from the top will be missed. There are two ways to get around these problems.

When one is stripping an area horizontally, it is advisable to dig what Wheeler calls "control-pits." These are small pits dug within the larger area. The object is to see ahead of time what is below, a form of "peeking," as it were, so that stratigraphy is anticipated and will not be missed in stripping a level. The other method makes up for the problems of excavating against vertical face. The edge against which the workers are picking or shoveling will usually be 6–9 inches in height if they are working through an area that may contain houses, fireplaces, or other features. When each level is finished, the surface should be scraped with trowels or shovels and then brushed to remove loose dirt. This procedure brings out details of soil-color changes, and it is often possible to see features that might otherwise be missed from the narrow perspective of a vertical face. The control pit is usually used even with the vertical face—again, so that stratigraphy can be forseen.

"How deep should each level be?" is a question the archeologist must ask himself and decide. The answer depends on what a level is. In a site where there are well-defined buildings, each rebuilding can be considered a level. The number of buildings that can be referred to such "time-based" levels will depend on the site. A cultural level is one that contains a contemporaneous assemblage. A cultural level may include several phases of rebuilding, but an archeologist cannot always determine this when still in the field. It is better at first to consider stratigraphic levels separately, and to combine them later if appropriate. The standard method of recording stratigraphy of a section is described by Atkinson (1953:154, 166–170), Heizer and Graham (1967:Chap. 7), and Wheeler (1956:68–79).

The advisability of excavating by arbitrary levels has been debated, but there is no other method to use in the absence of stratigraphy. The size of the levels depends on the tools used and the archeologist's experience in guessing what may be significant. Arbitrary levels in a thin refuse deposit that has accumulated over a very long period of time may be no more than 2 or 3 centimeters thick, because rather fine vertical differences in occurrence of artifacts will need to be known. In a deep refuse deposit that has been built up in a short period of time, the arbitrary level thickness may be as much as 30 centimeters. There is no rule that can be applied beyond the one of common sense. Where there is a great deal of fill in rooms or buildings, and where stratigraphic levels may be several feet or even yards apart, digging usually proceeds by levels that the workers can easily manage. The digging levels then would not be the same as the recognized stratigraphic levels; that is, they would be thinner.

At times, when working in unstratified deposits, one will find levels where tools or bones are concentrated and other levels that are relatively sterile. Here the archeologist will keep the levels with artifacts separate, even though he cannot discern any visible differences in the deposit itself. If artifacts are plotted as they are found, it may be possible to reconstruct the existence of nonvisible natural levels after the dig has ended.

The method for dealing with particular kinds of features is well

FIG. 53 Plan *(top)* and block *(bottom)* diagram of the Cienega Site, Arizona, showing the deposits both horizontally and vertically. The block diagram summarizes the sequence of cultural features in relation to the geological stratigraphy. Excavators must establish controls on the digging that will allow them to reconstruct the deposits in this manner. (E. W. Haury, "An Alluvial Site on the San Carlos Indian Reservation, Arizona," *American Antiquity,* Vol. 23.)

described in the handbooks on excavation, but it can be learned only by actual experience and practice. It is sufficient to say that there are special techniques for excavating bogs; shell mounds; sites having brick, mud, stone, or wood walls; pyramids; temples; for clearing burials and tombs; and even for sunken ships lying on the sea bottom.

Under certain circumstances, tunnels have been driven into large archeological sites in order to learn something about superposition of structures. Layard's tunneling operations of 100 years ago at Nineveh could not be justified today as good technique, for he dug tunnels in order to make as many discoveries of sculptures as posisble in a limited time. At the great pyramid of Teotihuacan in the Valley of Mexico, a tunnel was driven into the center of the structure at ground level in order to determine whether the pyramid had been built at one time or whether it consisted of a series of superimposed structures, each later one encasing the earlier surfaces and increasing the size. A similar tunnel driven into the great earth pyramid of Cholula, in the Valley of Puebla, Mexico, yielded rich results, showing that no fewer than five superimposed structures were present. Several of the large, pyramidal structures with temples on the summit at the lowland Maya site of Tikal, Guatemala, could be examined only by tunneling, because to dissect them by excavation would have caused their destruction. For any very large, solid construction, such as a Mesopotamian ziggurat, a Meso-American pyramid, or a large Bronze Age European burial mound, the only practicable means of getting any information on internal features is by means of tunnels. Recent attempts to discover hidden chambers in the interior of the great Fourth Dynasty stone pyramids at Giza in Egypt have not succeeded at the time of this writing, but the complex apparatus being used to try to detect open chambers in the apparently solid masses of masonry is set up in the ancient tunnels that penetrate the pyramids (Alvarez and others, 1970). No apparatus has yet been devised to enable archeologists to conduct nondestructive examinations of the details of the internal features of large solid architectural masses. Few excavators will ever be required to explore sites by tunnels, but it is of interest to know that, if this is the only method available for sounding a huge, solid structure, it can, when properly applied, provide extremely useful information about the interior.

EXCAVATION RECORDS

Because excavation destroys primary evidence, it is essential to keep good records. There is no point at all in excavating carefully if accurate records are not made and preserved.

Mapping and Plotting

All excavated sites should be mapped, but the kind of mapping that must be done before and during excavation varies with the site. A basic plan of the site will show its relation to roads, streams, towns, and so on. A more detailed plan should show the contours of the site and the areas excavated. On very large sites it may be necessary to use surveying equipment, but on smaller sites plotting with a compass, tape, and hand level is ordinarily sufficient. The use of a transit on small and simple sites is usually unnecessary, though it may be essential to use this instrument to record the complicated stratigraphy and features in a large mound.

Plans of sites are usually approximations, because without total excavation it is difficult to tell the limits of a site (see Fig. 50). However, the recording of objects within the excavation must be done with precision. Permanent features, such as walls, floors, hearths, concentration of stones, graves, and so on, are ordinarily plotted in three dimensions. To facilitate recording, most archeologists first establish a single reference spot which they call the "Datum Point." All measurements, both horizontal (distance) and vertical (elevations), are ultimately keyed to this one fixed reference spot. They then proceed to lay out a square grid with stakes driven to mark the corners of squares, which may be 3 or 5 or 10 feet (or 1 or 2 or 3 meters) on a side. One side of the grid has letters (*A, B, C, D*) for each row of squares, and the other side numbers the rows (1, 2, 3, 4, and so on), so that each square can be identified (for example, square *M* 18) by the conjunction of a letter and number at a designated corner. Measurements can be taken laterally from the stakes. Thus walls of houses can be measured relative to the sides of the excavation and their depth below a datum point on the surface of the site. If walls must be removed to get at something lower, a three-dimensional record enables an archeologist to restore their location later, either in a model or on a drawing. Special artifacts may also be recorded in this way, though it is more usual for such things as flint tools and potsherds to be removed and a record made of the level and grid square in which they occurred (Fig. 54). Thus the archeologist will record the fact that a certain group of sherds came from a particular level and square, but he will not know precisely where each item lay with reference to the others unless he records these facts during excavation.

Whether all finds should be recorded with equal precision depends on the archeologist's judgment about what is important. As a practical matter, objects that occur in great quantity or are so small that they cannot be seen easily during excavation, but are caught when the dirt is screened, will be recorded only by level. When very small objects are anticipated, all dirt is screened after it is removed from the excavation. Such a practice precludes recording the precise location. If the archeologist encounters an unusual cluster of flints, sherds, or rock, he ordinarily leaves them all in place until he can judge whether their position is of special significance. It is always wise to err on the safe side, though it is hard for an archeologist to justify leaving every find in place for very long if this tends to slow down an operation already pressed for time or money.

A neat excavation is essential to accurate recording. If possible, the

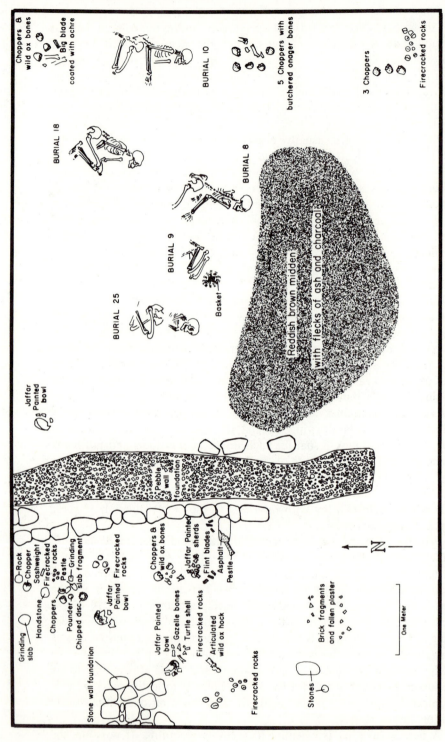

FIG. 54 Artifacts, skeletons, and architectural traces are all plotted where they were found in Ali Kosh, Iran. The distribution shows household debris inside the house and burials in what was probably a courtyard. Some of the burials had been partly destroyed by later people, who used the eroded mound for a cemetery. (F. Hole, K. V. Flannery, and J. A. Neely, *Prehistory and Human Ecology of the Deh Luran Plain*. Museum of Anthropology, University of Michigan, Memoirs [1969].)

walls of the pits should be kept straight. The only exception to this is when vertical sides will not hold. In certain loose soils—shell mounds and sand—edges may not hold. If the side of the pit or trench will hold vertically for only several feet, it is possible to step it in and begin another vertical cut. In no instance where it can be avoided should the sides slope toward the bottom. Keeping the sides vertical makes it easier to keep accurate records. It is very difficult to plot the true positions of artifacts and features against a sloping side. The comparability of levels is also reduced if the area at the bottom of a pit is much smaller than at the top.

It is of little use here to give specific descriptions of methods for numbering levels or bagging artifacts, except to note that it is customary to number levels from the top down. Level 1 will therefore be the first dug, and some larger number will indicate the last and oldest and deepest level reached. In other words, the numbering reverses the order in which the levels accumulated and follows the order in which they are excavated.

As an excavation progresses, the records of stratigraphy in the form of diagrammatic profiles of sections accumulate (see Fig. 41). Archeologists should take care to correlate their drawings of stratigraphic sections while they are in the field; otherwise they may return home and find that they have failed to make a record of how the levels in one section relate to those in another. Few archeologists, while they are engaged in the excavation, succeed in making notations of all relevant points, but these errors of omission should be kept at a minimum. It is better to have more notes than necessary than too few.

Photographing

Photography is a necessary part of recording. Used in conjunction with drawn sections, it helps show the stratigraphic relations of various features and levels. Photographs add to the plans of the levels a measure of reality that drawings can never achieve (see Figs. 36 and 37). It is regular practice to photograph all sections and features. Often drawings can be made directly from the photos, but in any event they serve as useful checks on the drawings. No matter how diligently an archeologist tries to observe and record everything of significance in his profiles, he often fails to recognize, until he returns home, the importance of some aspect of the exposure. On many occasions clear photographs of the vertical section in question will answer his questions. Both black-and-white and color photographs should be taken for the reason that features not apparent on one photograph may show up on the other.

Many stratigraphic exposures show clearly distinguishable color differences between the layers when they are first excavated, but after a time dust collects on the exposed face, and the once apparent color differences fade. Exposures should be brushed or scraped, working from the top down, to clean them of loose dust and scalings. A hand bellows or air pump and a sharp trowel will serve equally well for this purpose. If the cleaning is done with care, features exposed in the vertical wall, such as post molds, pit outlines, or boundary lines between the levels, can be lightly incised with the tip of a trowel to make certain that they will appear in the photograph. Care must be taken not to unduly accentuate such lines or to emphasize doubtful points lest this amount to falsification of evidence. Original color distinctions in the profile may often be reconstituted by spraying a fine mist on the face with a pressure sprayer of the type that home gardeners use to spray pesticides on garden plants (see Fig. 43). It is very important to keep a notebook record of photographs taken while an excavation is in progress. The date a picture was taken, location of the section, feature or activity being photographed, and a memorandum about what the photograph is intended to record will be the greatest help to the archeologist when he is once more back home and writing his report.

Any dig at certain times will become "messy," and a fair amount of constant housekeeping is required to keep tools, bags, boxes, and other items picked up. A messy dig may lead to inadvertent loss of specimens or tools that are set aside and covered. When photographs are taken of an excavation, it is good practice to remove paper bags, boxes, tools, and dirt piles, in addition to cleaning the vertical faces and straightening out bulges or unsquared corners. There are several useful guides to archeological photography that deal with the special kinds of equipment (cameras, film types, flash attachments) needed and provide advice on how to secure good photographs of the kinds of things archeologists usually wish to record.

It would be possible to map an excavation entirely by photographs. A tripod of sufficient height to include the total area of an excavation unit could be placed over the unit when needed. All photos would thus be of standard scale and from the same perspective. A series of such photographs taken over the entire site could be made into a mosaic in the same manner that aerial photos are mounted. Use of this sort of system might result in recording some features that might otherwise be overlooked, but it is also true that photos may miss important features. The photo technique is valuable when portions of a site are excavated at different times. Some features that are visible only when seen over the total area may not show up on a map but will be evident in a photo mosaic.

Infrared film can often provide a much sharper contrast than can regular panchromatic film. It has proved useful in photographing rock paintings, soil profiles, and large surface areas of sites.

Photographs taken of the whole site from a distance will provide a permanent visual record of the relation of the site to local features of the terrain. Usually at least one such photograph appears in every full archeological report. Such pictures may be taken from a high elevation in the vicinity or from a low-flying airplane or helicopter.

Examples of poor photography and poor photographic reproduction in publications are as common as poorly done sketches and plans. Mapping and photography are necessary to good recording, but unless the operator has sufficient skill to use the equipment, its use is no guarantee that the records will be good. The capabilities of the archeologist and his staff will be judged in part by the attention they pay to the technical aspects of excavation and recording. Poorly illustrated reports are all too often an indication that the excavations were poorly recorded and that the reports are second rate.

PRESERVATION OF ARTIFACTS

Excavation and preservation of artifacts go hand in hand. It sometimes happens, as at Ur, that objects must be "fabricated" in the ground before they can be excavated. It was only after Sir Leonard Woolley had poured plaster into holes in the ground and then excavated the resulting casts that he could be sure of what had lain in the ground. Sometimes archeologists uncover bones in a very bad condition, and they must often take great pains to solidify them. Once bones or artifacts are protected, they can be taken to a laboratory for final excavation and restoration. In such instances excavation merely means getting the things out of the ground safely. Full exposure, cleaning, and repair take place under the better controlled and more leisurely conditions of a laboratory. The archeologist should be aware of the fact that cleaning of objects is both subjective and destructive. He may clean a specimen to the point where he has altered it, and if he removes the oxidation or patina from a stone or metal object he may be removing something that could provide valuable information. Cleaning and restoration should not be done casually; it is better not to do anything than to do too much. The magnitude of the problem of preservation should not be underestimated. In each area where work has been done, archeologists have developed special techniques for preserving artifacts. The techniques are developed best in Europe and Great Britain, where perishable and especially fragile materials are more likely to be preserved than elsewhere. It is beyond the scope of the present work to attempt to describe the varied methods for preservation of materials in the field or their repair and restoration in the laboratory. An extremely useful source of information is the volume of abstracts of publications (Gettens and Usilton 1955) dealing with the technical methods employed in treating organic and inorganic objects of artistic or archeological nature.

Waterlogged artifacts may be preserved by one of several methods. Furniture from the Oseberg Viking ship in Norway was preserved by one of these (see Fig. 10). This ship-tomb was filled with remarkable grave furniture, including elaborately carved sleighs, one of which was fragmented into 1068 pieces of wood, each of which had to be treated separately. The procedure was to boil them in an alum solution, dry them, and then soak them with linseed oil. In this way the pieces kept their original shape and size and could be fitted back together. Another method recently described is to treat old waterlogged wood with a solution of polyethylene glycol that reduces shrinkage and hardens the material. At the mesolithic site of Star Carr in England, the excavator, G. Clark, devised a large vacuum tank in which animal bones were impregnated with preservative solution.

Artifacts that come out of the excavation in good shape can be sent immediately to a museum. Unfortunately, loss may also occur in storage. Items that were dry may rot; others may disintegrate in shipment if they are not properly packed for transport or are roughly jostled; and some specimens are affected by heat, insects, or dirt.

Even though an archeologist's immediate responsibility is to remove artifacts from the ground safely, he must not overlook their future well-being. Instances of improper preservation in the field, resulting in later destruction, are legion. For example, bones may be coated with various substances that at first appear to preserve them; later, when they are unpacked in the laboratory, they may have disintegrated. Varnish applied over damp bone is notorious in this respect. Other preparations may harden bone, but be unremovable in the laboratory except with destruction of the bone.

Preservation is not limited to techniques for keeping things from rotting shrinking, and disintegrating. It also means recovering a maximum of data. It means examining sherds or lumps of clay for possible impressions or "casts" of plant seeds. One can learn (from an article by Helbaek 1953; see also G. Clark 1957:193–194) how, by identifying and counting casts or impressions of seeds in clay, Helbaek discovered what particular cereals were being cultivated and what the relative importance of the different species was. Preservation means saving charcoal for possible or planned radiocarbon dating, and plant and animal remains for identification. It sometimes happens that an archeologist does not know that something, like preserved seeds, is in a site when he digs it. A case in point is at Tepe Ali Kosh in Iran, where Hole found seeds quite by accident in the ashy matrix of a carbon-14 sample he was cleaning. Subsequently, using a technique called "flotation" or water separation, to remove charred organic material from soil, he recovered several thousand seeds. Preservation means plotting associations. In short, it means throwing away nothing that might provide a lead to cultural interpretations. An archeologist may be primarily interested in architecture or flints, but if he ignores making records of the rocks on which people sat or with which they boiled water, he is missing—and therefore not preserving—relevant archeological data. The same is true of keeping records. Records keep track of association. Artifacts and samples that turn up in the laboratory without records of their locus and associations have, for practical purposes, been lost.

At times an excavation produces more material than can be saved. Preliminary analysis in the field is often sufficient to enable an archeologist to discard a weighty collection of flint scrap, potsherds, grinding tools, or whatnot, whose characteristics have been sufficiently recorded and which are impractical to save. Such excess materials are best abandoned at the site where they were excavated, but it is essential that these modern caches or hordes of prehistoric materials be abandoned in such a way that some future archeologist will not mistake them for anything except what they are. One way of doing this is to mix in with the redeposited materials several modern coins, or a few glass bottles, and thus mark the deposit as a secondary one. A statement that such leavings have been buried should be entered in the notes as well as in the publication. Judd (1956b:212–213) has provided a detailed description of wall repairs made at Pueblo del Arroyo in New Mexico in the seasons of 1923–1926; it will prove a valuable record to future students of Pueblo masonry in allowing them to distinguish between reconstructed and original masonry sections. Visitors to the great Peloponesian site of Mycenae are always impressed by the encircling cyclopean walls of the citadel, which look as though they had stood since the site was abandoned in the twelfth century B.C. The walls are, however, very heavily constructed, and what is original and ancient and what is rebuilding can be learned only by a careful reading of the archeological reports published by excavators of the site over the last hundred years. In the same vein, it will be useful to future students if authors of reports will state clearly which surveyed areas have no sites, as well as tell which areas have not been looked at. Archeologists who reexcavate a site examined earlier will be grateful to find a published record of the location of dumps since these may cover cultural deposits which are of interest to later workers. An instance is provided by Winlock (1942:155) who reports that he had to remove more than 50,000 cubic meters of rubble which Naville in 1893 had dumped into what he had assumed to be an ancient empty quarry pit.

THE STAFF

The composition of the supervisory and technical staff of an excavation is one of the most important matters to be arranged (Alexander 1970). Most digs consist of an archeologist and his assistant, with varying numbers of workmen. Technical help, advice, and analysis are usually obtained catch as catch can. This is not an ideal situation, but on some digs such a staff will suffice. At the opposite extreme, Wheeler's staff for large digs consisted of "a director, a deputy director, a supervisor for each area under excavation, a trained foreman, a small-find recorder, a pottery assistant, a photographer, a surveyor, a chemist, a draftsman, and, according to need, an epigraphist or numismatist" (M. Wheeler 1956:153).

Wheeler was concerned with historical sites. For prehistoric sites he would have had to add a zoologist, a paleobotanist, a palynologist, a geologist, a mineralogist, a pedologist, and possibly others as well, and could have left the epigraphists and numismatists at home. There is not less need for specialists at prehistoric sites; indeed, there may be need for a greater variety, because the prehistorian must rely on the natural scientists for recovery and interpretation of basic information much more than on the historian. On a practical basis, one person may well control two or more specialities, so that a mere listing does not indicate the number of persons involved. For examples of archeological projects on which a number of specialists in different fields cooperated, and whose reporting includes contributions from the several specialists, we cite the Boylston Street Fishweir in Boston (F. Johnson 1942); an Early Man site in Wyoming (J. Moss 1951b); Braidwood and Howe's (1960) survey and excavation in Iraqi Kurdistan; the Deh Luran project (Hole, Flannery, and Neely 1969); and the Tehuacan project (Byers 1967).

It is only under especially fortunate circumstances that a prehistorian can take such a team of specialists to the field with him. Most analyses are made by technicians in their home laboratories, though it is common for them to visit sites being excavated. In fact, it is important that these persons have a chance to do work at archeological sites. Only in this way will they be able to appreciate the conditions under which samples are obtained. At the site they can also make valuable suggestions about collecting samples and preserving specimens. Furthermore, as a guide to what is happening in the site, an archeologist will find useful a running analysis of the plants and animals encountered.

Excavations are chronically understaffed. For most sites the deficiencies lie, not so much in labor, but in too few supervisory personnel and in inadequate numbers of specialists who can identify such things as animal species from bones, pollens extracted from soils, and so on. In Wheeler's organization, like a military chain of command, each man is assigned responsibility for a certain segment of the operation and supervision of a certain number of workers. However, no matter how the staff is organized, care must be taken to ensure that someone is present at all times in all areas under excavation. In this way proper records can be kept. Routine excavation is often dull work, which requires little supervision, but, when the unexpected occurs, prompt and efficient supervision is necessary. Under loose supervision an incalculable number of artifacts have been broken or thrown away by careless workmen or stolen by dishonest ones.

Like every archeological operation, the selection of a staff must be planned with due regard for the unique circumstances of each dig. No factor is as important to the outcome of an excavation as the cooperative efforts performed day after day by the group of individuals who, collectively, comprise the staff.

Most excavation reports do not inform the reader on the day-to-day events, happenings in camp, and how the archeologist lives while conducting a program of investigation. Such records usually exist in the form of a daily journal kept by the excavator, but they are personal and are not published. A few books written by archeologists toward the end of their careers, or by wives of archeologists, are cited at the end of Chapter 2.

REFERENCES

Use of Earth-moving Equipment to Clear Sterile Overburden: Wedel 1951.
Tunneling of Pyramids to Examine Interior Construction: Atkinson 1967; Mil-

lon and Drewitt 1961; Millon, Drewitt, and Bennyhoff 1965; Perez 1935; Reed, Bennett, and Porter 1968.

Handbooks, Manuals, and Guides to Excavation Techniques: Alexander 1970; Atkinson 1953; Barker 1969; Bernal 1952; Biddle and Kjølbye-Biddle 1969; R. Braidwood 1960; Franken 1965; Fry 1972; Goodwin 1953; Gorenstein 1965; P. Hammond 1963; Heizer and Graham 1967 K. Kenyon 1961; Laming-Emperaire 1963; Noel-Hume 1969; Olsen 1961c; Papworth and Binford 1962; Potratz 1962; Robbins and Irving 1965; Schwarz 1967; Webster 1963; Wheeler 1956.

Mapping and Recording with Photographs: Colwell 1956; Crone 1963; Heath 1957; McFadgen 1971; Merrill 1941a, 1941b; Nylen 1963; Schwarz 1965; D. Simpson and Cooke 1967; Straffin 1971; Whittlesey 1966a, 1966b.

Archeological Photography: Blaker 1965; Buettner-Janusch 1954; Cameron 1958; Cookson 1954; Dorwin 1967; Frantz 1950; Heizer and Graham 1967: Chap. 12; John 1965; de Maré 1962; S. Matthews 1968; Noel-Hume 1969: Chap. VII; D. Riley 1946; P. Ritchie and Pugh 1963; Schwarz 1967:152–167; J. Wiltshire 1967; F. Wood 1945.

Aerial Photography; Remote Sensing: Beazeley 1919; Capper 1907; Chevallier 1964; Deuel 1969; Eardley 1942; Gumerman and Lyons 1971.

Infrared Film in Archeological Photography: Buettner-Janusch 1954; W. Clark 1946; Itek Corp. 1965; Schaber and Gumerman 1969.

Technical Examination, Repair, and Restoration of Artifacts: Biek 1963; Dowman 1970; Heizer and Graham 1967; Hodges 1964; Leechman 1931; Lucas 1962; Orchard 1925; Plenderleith 1956; Rathgen 1926; Rowe 1953; Seborg and Inverarity 1962.

Planning and Directing an Excavation: Alexander 1970; Gorenstein 1965:52–56; P. Hammond 1963:Chap. 6; Wheeler 1956:Chap. 11.

CHAPTER TEN

CLASSIFICATION AND DESCRIPTION

When the archeologist has finished with the digging of a site and has returned to his home base with aching back, equipment, notebooks, maps, photographs, and artifacts, he has accomplished only the first half of his research. The second half is to write a report. Actually, considerably more time is required to analyze material and write reports than to excavate a site. A conservative estimate is that it takes from two to three times as long to prepare a good report. In the report all the finds must be described and illustrated, and the site map and stratigraphic profiles must be presented and discussed. The report should also provide information on the age of the cultural materials found, and the culture disclosed should be compared with other archeological cultures in an effort to determine how similar and how different it is. The report, when published, makes the particular body of information available to everyone interested. Some archeologists would rather dig and discover than write reports of their findings, but those who fail to do the latter are avoiding a responsibility. Archeological data that are not reported may just as well have been left in the ground. Although the archeologist may be studying the bones and tools of men who lived hundreds or thousands of years ago, and who never had any form of writing, when he writes about his excavation he is writing history—the story of people who lived at some point in time and whose culture was learned from generations that lived earlier and was passed on to generations that lived later. If the site being described was lived on for a long period of time, a long run of its history may be evidenced in the successive layers laid down over the years and centuries by the human occupants. Before he can write any kind of history, an archeologist must put his information into a cultural and chronological context (Rouse 1953, 1955). This procedure is discussed in Chapter 18.

An archeologist works with three kinds of data: artifactual; nonartifactual (for example, bones, soils, and charcoal); and the geographical or chronological positions of the site. After he has analyzed and interpreted these data, an archeologist can write a history, but the first step is analysis. Classification—which for the most part means identifying and naming artifacts—and a description of all data are basic to archeological analysis.

CLASSIFICATION

In order to bring system and order to a chaotic assemblage of data, the archeologist must put all items into convenient categories. With animal bones from a Neolithic site in Greece, putting into categories means placing the sheep in one pile, the cattle in another, but this is only one kind of classification. If the archeologist is sorting materials from a California coastal shell mound, he will start by separating deer bones from sea-mammal bones, and chipped-stone tools from ground-stone implements. Classifications are also used to describe tools, houses, burials, and even sites. Archeological classifications are intended to simplify making comparisons among artifacts from several sites so that chronological and cultural relations can be readily established. A *type* is the most frequently used unit of comparison with artifacts. By the word "type" we mean a particular kind of artifact (for example, arrow-point, house floor, metate, scraper, bone awl, and so on) in which several attributes combine or cluster with sufficient frequency or in such distinctive ways that the archeologist can define and label the artifact and can recognize it when he sees another example.

Classification is a tool that can be made to work for many purposes. Theoretically, there is an almost infinite number of typologies for any body of material. Different typologies can help in understanding chronology, the relation of one part of a site to another, or the relations among sites or areas. Unfortunately, as G. Clark (1952:1) says, "The overwhelming proportion of archeological evidence has been gathered rather by accident than by design, and studied more as an exercise in classification than as a source of history." It is quite possible to get lost among the trees of typology and never see the forest of which they are a part. There has been considerable controversy over typology among American archeologists; much less among Europeans. Most of the discussion has centered on what the type is or should be.

The foremost question is, "What kind of information is desired?" Is a simple description of what is present the aim, or information about chronology or technical skill? Different goals may require that different types be discerned. Ordinarily there are few obvious ways to proceed at the beginning; the archeologist therefore looks for everything with the view to making "trial" types. After a preliminary analysis he may decide to alter his types so that they will more nearly help him solve his problems. There are several issues involved in deciding what a type is. First, how much difference should there be among types? The process of classification in archeology is similar to that of defining a species in biology or paleontology. With a few conspicuous exceptions, members of different biological species can be interbred. In paleontology, of course, this crucial test cannot be applied; skeletons do not interbreed under any circumstances. Even with the criterion of interbreeding, some workers lump a great many variants into single species, whereas others maximize the differences and distinguish many species. The same distinctions can be made with artifacts. There is no way to establish rules for the amount of difference that separates types of artifacts because, as with the fossil animals, the makers of the tools are dead and cannot indicate to us today what types they recognized and intended to fashion.

The recognition and naming of types serve many purposes. First, as we have said, they are a means of introducing order or system into a varied assortment of objects. The array of archeological materials recovered thus becomes capable of being understood and handled in a meaningful way. Second, artifacts and nonartifactual materials from an archeological site are the concrete and palpable evidence of human action, because all of these items had to be carried to the living area and were then modified by men in some way. Let us illustrate this by taking two excavated items. A flint projectile point may have involved the following actions: obtaining the flint at its geological source; carrying it back to camp; securing a chipping implement (hammerstone); shaping the rough material by flaking into the finished weapon tip; mounting it on the end of the projectile shaft; searching for game; shooting the animal. The leg bone of a deer, not in itself an artifact, may have come from an animal whose taking and utilization may have involved these actions: killing of the animal by a hunter (or team of hunters) who used a deer-head decoy disguise; the killing effected with a bow and arrow; the dead animal skinned and butchered; the skin and carcass parts carried to camp; distribution of part of the meat to village mates; cooking the meat in baskets by heated stones or roasting it over the open fire; eating the cooked meat; dressing the skin and sewing it into a garment; use of some of the animal's bones to make tools (scrapers, awls, harpoons, and so on); ritual disposal of certain bones; using the food scraps to feed camp dogs—the list is almost limitless. We can see from these two constructed and much abbreviated examples that an object found in an archeological site is in reality an historical document of past human action. Who made the projectile point, why it came to be buried in the site, and who killed and ate the deer, are questions one can ask of these stones and bones but not have answered by them. But more general questions of what *people* used projectile points and what they killed and ate for food can be answered, and typology is a useful aid in framing such questions. As typologies become more refined, the archeologist learns that at a certain time in prehistory, which he may label as Period IV, a certain group of people, which he may label the Olmec Culture or Beaker Culture or Folsom Culture, used a certain series of forms or, in other words, made and used certain things in certain ways. In a later period, the archeologist observes that new or modified forms are being made and used. He will look for the reasons for typological changes and may discover that they are caused by altered habits resulting from changes in climate, which in turn led to altered requirements in tools, to different cultural practices such as the acceptance of farming, or simply to quite arbitrary modifications in style that arise through the mental activities of their makers. Changes in type over time are therefore a main road to studying the course of events in prehistory.

Functional Types

Archeologists find it easy to classify a bow and arrow if they are lucky enough to find them preserved. They are able to recognize and know their use because they know that similar tools are used by living peoples. However, if they should find several variations of bows and arrows at one site, they will have a hard time trying to decide whether they should take notice of the differences. They will wonder whether variously shaped arrowheads were used for different kinds of game or resulted from accidents in manufacture or from the preference of their makers. In short, once archeologists get beyond very gross classification of material or known use, they run into difficulty. Classification of stone or bone tools is even more difficult. One can call a piece of chipped flint a "knife" and still be in doubt whether it was really a knife, a javelin tip, a scraper, or something else. It is common for some archeologists to name artifacts after their presumed use, even though there is no way to check the guess. This practice has resulted in a great deal of misunderstanding by uncritical readers. Furthermore, giving an artifact a name carries the implication that it served a particular use; this kind of attributed function often leads to inaccurate comparison. For example, when a person reads the term "knife" in several reports, he is likely to assume that the same implement is being described in each instance. A check of accompanying illustrations may reveal that very different objects are being described by the same term.

The greatest pressure for giving functional names to artifacts comes from people who know the material the least. More and more, professional archeologists are shying away from such commitments *in their basic reports.* Interpretations about use should properly come after an artifact has been described in such terms that it can readily be comprehended and compared. After the basic descriptions have been made, the analyst should try to discover what functional types are represented. Only when the use of an artifact is unmistakable is it appropriate to name functional types. The distinction between basic description and interpretation of function should always be clearly made.

Convenient Types

An opposite approach to naming functional types is to define types as being whatever variations of artifacts can be used to make comparisons. Sir Flinders Petrie (1901), for example, was less concerned over what the ancient Egyptians were thinking about when they made different styles of jar handles than over the fact that he could set up a chronology based on changes in the form of jar handles. Similarly, when American archeologists describe projectile points, they go to great lengths to discern differences that may help define geographical and chronological versions of cultures. An aborigine who was given a handful of different "types" might, unlike an archeologist, see no noteworthy differences among them. However, the aborigine's opinion is irrelevant because typing helps the archeologist. As Jennings (1957:98) remarks, "I view . . . types not as synonymous with cultural truth but as an invention of the analyst for his own convenience."

A distinction has been made by certain American archeologists between "designed" and "discovered" types. A designed type is said to be empirically derived, and to serve the purpose of helping to distinguish—by means of forms or shape—different segments of the cultural continuum. Designed types are arbitrary and are imposed by the classifier on the objects without consideration of the purpose the object may have served its maker (MacWhite 1956:12). Discovered types are, therefore, "real," and reflect forms that are assumed to have been culturaly significant to their makers. A similar idea was expressed some years ago by Burkitt (1955[1933]:59) when he wrote,

> The classification of gravers [burins] is a matter of some controversy. They can be classified according to type, or they can be classified according to the method of their manufacture. Neither of these systems is perfect, and, indeed, the student must always remember that he is not making rules for prehistoric man, but deducing laws from facts. He is in the position of a grammarian, not of the inventor of a language.

Daniel (1960:87) observes that there was a large amount of "hybridization of ideas and plans" of Breton Passage Graves, and says that "too exact a classification of the wide variety of Breton monuments can only be, at worst, an academic exercise, and at best, a learned arrangement of observer-determined categories."

Convenient ("designed") types are probably the most commonly used in archeology. Whenever a report lists types without giving any basis for them, the reader is justified in assuming that the archeologist finds it convenient to group his material in such fashion; he probably has no other rationale behind his classification. This sort of typology has definite limits and is gradually being replaced by other methods. The use of purely arbitrary types results in different archeologists' choosing various types to describe the same assemblage. Because of this, more than for any other single reason, it is hard to compare archeological data. Most archeologists assume that they are doing a good job and that other archeologists understand what they are doing. Unfortunately, this is not always true. A person who wants to sum up the results of many excavations must himself handle the material or at least be sufficiently familiar with the excavators and their techniques to make judgments about what they report. Too often synthesizers overlook the extremely variable quality of reporting; this in addition to the very variable quality of excavation.

Cultural Types

Persons make things (artifacts) the way they think things ought to be made. Some archeologists try to discover the ideal that the makers were trying to copy. "The term *type* is intended to represent the perfect example, exhibiting all the characteristics which differentiate it from other types" (Byers and Johnson 1940:33). Ideal types ("discovered" types) are assumed to be those that the makers of the artifacts themselves recognized while engaged in the actual production of the items. In practice, however, the ideal is rarely achieved. When flint breaks oddly or a pot fires faultily or a metal casting is imperfect, the artifacts vary somewhat from the ideal. Making due allowance for such aberrations, archeologists try to find the ideal to which a series of artifacts conforms. These types are commonly established by visual inspection of the ranges of variation in an artifact industry. Except as a preliminary assessment of a small assemblage, ideal types cannot be described on the basis of one example. In the basic description, ideal types are not functional types. Deetz (1967) suggested one way to look at the cultural type when he related artifacts to language. In his view the makers of artifacts have a "mental template" that tells them what a tool should look like. The finished object is made up of many parts (attributes) whose occurrence in combination makes the tool a particular type of object. Deetz likened the attributes to elements of language, morphemes and phonemes, which speakers combine to produce meaningful communication. Deetz, like Burkitt (1933:59), thinks that if we analyze the "grammar" of artifacts we shall be able to learn more than if we look just at finished pieces.

Another way to discover cultural types is to use statistical analysis to discriminate clusters of attributes that occur in significant frequencies. The method depends on the fact that people do things by habit and preference; that is, they have an ideal in mind when making artifacts. Most artifacts are the result of several separate stages of manufacture. Very likely there are alternate ways to accomplish each stage, and the way chosen may have no significant bearing on the use to which the artifact is put. The particular way a piece is made can, to a large degree, show the peculiar notions the maker had about how the job ought to be done. Some methods of manufacture are characteristic of individuals or groups of people. If archeologists can distinguish these differences in method of manufacture and end result, they have an easy way of distinguishing between cultural groups *even though to all intents and purposes the finished artifacts are functionally identical.* In many instances the archeologist may pay more attention to the attributes of artifacts, for example, to shell tempering of pottery or the lost-wax casting process, than to the whole pieces, because it is the technique rather than the object that helps him solve his particular problem.

To discover types statistically one must first describe artifacts by their attributes. Attributes are recognizable features such as size, shape, color, material, and decoration. A single pot may have many attributes. In one industry there may be several shapes and sizes of pots, two or three different kinds of tempering material, and a dozen or more kinds of decoration. Analysis attempts to discover which combinations of attributes are found in association in such frequency that they are probably not accidental. Archeologists look for "a consistent assemblage of attributes whose combined properties give a characteristic pattern. . . . Classification into types is a process of discovery of combinations of attributes favored by the makers of the artifacts, not an arbitrary procedure of the classifier" (Spaulding 1953:305). According to Spaulding, types discovered by cluster analysis "cannot fail to have historical meaning."

Many archeologists have shied away from using statistical techniques, partly because of the sampling problems in any excavation and partly because the limitations and opportunities of statistical techniques are poorly understood by them. Statistical treatment is invaluable in the simultaneous handling of many variables. It will yield data, but as Spaulding has pointed out, the archeologist still must interpret them. The increasing interest in multivariate statistical analyses by means of computers may be mentioned here because coding of the data on artifacts must be very precise and, to be generally useful, standardized. In other words, the present loose methods of typology must be considerably refined before attributes will become encodable. References to published papers on this subject are given at the end of this chapter.

Archeological data are destroyed by nonhuman agencies as they lie in the ground; they are destroyed by man during excavation and handling; and to one degree or another they are altered again as they pass the filter of archeological analysis. To help overcome analytical looseness, a concern with methodology has developed in American archeology and, to a lesser but increasing degree, in European archeology. In practice, most archeologists use several approaches to typology because no one method is useful all the time. But the most useful tool is always the archeologist's brain.

DESCRIPTION AND ILLUSTRATION
OF ARTIFACTS

Description of artifacts goes hand in hand with classification. Good descriptions should be brief, readily understood, and comparable with other descriptions to the extent that essential information is provided. All too often, for example, an archeologist will forget to inform the reader of the kind of stone an artifact was fashioned from. When describing the artifacts, the archeologist tries to think about what features other students may be interested in learning about.

All descriptions begin with words. Purely verbal descriptions, however, are easily misunderstood even by speakers of the same language. Translations to other languages are even more difficult, because descriptive terms frequently have no direct counterparts in other languages. Verbal descriptions are best when they define the attributes of artifacts.

Graphic Descriptions

The most common, and in some ways the best, kind of discription is a drawing or photograph of the artifact. However, the ideal sought is seldom attained. To draw artifacts requires the hand of a skilled draftsman, just as photographs require the skilled use of a camera. Reports are filled with poor examples of each technique, and one looks far to find good examples of either. Archeologists are ordinarily not capable of doing first-class pen-and-ink illustrations themselves. Often the funds required to pay an illustrator will be the largest cash outlay spent in preparing a report.

Drawings can show details that will not appear on photographs, but they are highly susceptible to personal interpretation. Artists usually emphasize the features that seem most important to them. Their interpretation may be entirely correct, but the reader has no way to judge for himself. Sometimes an archeologist insists that the drawings emphasize or, in some notorious instances, create certain features that he desires.

It is difficult to make good photographs of artifact. Success or failure depends on the kinds of light, perspective, focal length of lenses, background, and developing and printing techniques used. In the hands of a skilled operator the camera can be made to do what the archeologist wishes, but like a drawing, a photograph can misrepresent.

If the shape of an artifact is important, it is common to represent it by an outline, which is a stylized description. Stylized drawings are ordinarily taken to be ideal types. They may not duplicate the outline of any single specimen. Such drawings are easy to make and easy to understand. But many artifacts cannot be understood by their shape alone. For these, one must use a more representational technique. The usual practice is to draw particular artifacts as faithfully as possible (Fig. 55).

FIG. 55 The style to be used in illustrating tools depends on their important attributes. Outline drawings are sufficient when the gross shape of a tool is important; techniques of chipping can be depicted best by a careful drawing of the details; a photograph shows texture and color differences.

The use of outline drawings is relatively new and is usually coupled with some sort of tabulation or statistical treatment (Bohmers 1956; Kleindienst 1961). In this technique, types and their variants are outlined and keyed to columns in summary tables (Fig. 56). The reader can look in the table to find that x number of Type A, variant n, were present in level 7. If the classification is accurate, this is as good a method as drawing all the artifacts from level 7 or even all those of type A.

Whether photographs or drawings are used, there must be a good set of representations of the artifact types. Without them no report is very intelligible. This remark does not necessarily mean that drawings must accompany each report, but descriptions must refer to readily available sources.

In all illustrations of artifacts it is absolutely necessary to indicate their size, either with a scale or by stating the size in the caption below the illustration.

Statistical Descriptions

Statistical descriptions may be simple tabulations of data or descriptions of the combinations of attributes of artifacts. All reports that present basic data should contain a numerical listing of artifacts, and most will also have a calculation of the frequencies in which various artifacts occur. The use of statistical techniques often permits more exact description than do words or illustrations alone, and may help to discriminate between associations of attributes or artifacts that are not readily observable by any other method. Moberg (1961) has discussed the great variety of quantitative methods presently available for archeological description and analysis.

Mention has been made of the use of statistics in discovering artifact types, a process that follows logically after basic description. However, statistics are also used for basic description. For example, it may be useful to describe the size of certain artifacts. Statistics may describe the range, the

FIG. 56 Chart illustrating technique of graphically representing changes in frequency of projectile points of various types in relation to time. (M. L. Fowler, "Summary Report of Modoc Rock Shelter," Illinois State Museum, Report of Investigations, No. 8, 1959.)

209

mean, and the standard deviations in size. These three statistics may be sufficient to describe an artifact type or may help to discriminate between variations of a type found at different sites. That is, even though the same type may have been used at different places, two different sizes of the type may have been made, and the demonstration of this fact may lead to significant cultural interpretation.

Statistics can also help tell whether the observed variations seem to be random and accidental, or nonrandom and purposeful. This information is especially useful because it will help the archeologist avoid the error of emphasizing attributes that are the result of accident rather than design.

Less complex numerical techniques have been used to describe entire industries. For example, a segment of the French Paleolithic has been described by classifying all the flint tools into types and plotting their frequency in each site on a cumulative histogram (Sonneville-Bordes 1960). Visual comparison of the histograms shows how closely one site conforms to another in terms of relative frequencies of various types. Bohmers (1963) describes a method of comparing the percentages of a series of clearly defined artifact types whose mean measurements are represented graphically. These data, represented by a series of vertical histograms, are ranged next to one another for convenience of visual comparison.

By far the most common kind of statistical description is the simple listing. With these basic data it is possible to carry out many additional analyses. For maximum potential in analysis, however, one needs information about all the attributes of all the artifacts. The labor involved in measuring, listing, and tabulating attributes is prohibitive unless the results to be gained are obvious beforehand. It is possible to do too much refined observation, just as it is possible to do too little, about attributes of artifacts. An example of the complexity of attributes that can be identified in one class of artifact, projectile points, is to be found in the list published in L. Binford (1963). How much warrant there is for each detailed observation can be decided only after archeologists have put the typology into practice and have determined whether meaningful results have been achieved.

Application of statistical methods to determine chronology from artifacts has been done for approximately the past 50 years by American archeologists. No effort is made in the present work to describe the several methods, their applications, and results. References to published works are given at the end of this chapter.

Symbolic Descriptions

There has been considerable concern over whether it is possible to describe artifacts entirely objectively. Statistics have been used to help achieve objectivity. The main problem is not over the philosophical or technical possibilities of description, but that all workers are not consistent in their use of basic terms.

Ignoring the question of whether true objectivity can ever be achieved, several workers conclude that, to the extent to which each analyst can understand and apply a standard terminology, the resulting descriptions will be comparable. The easiest way to achieve agreement of description is to define the most minute attributes of artifacts in the simplest fashion. Measurements of length, width, shape, and weight are examples of attributes that can be easily defined. It is also possible to define design elements, and combinations of elements, by using a symbolic notation. When description has been reduced to a formal language of symbols, it is easily handled mechanically and readily compared with other similar descriptions (cf. Whiteford 1947; L. Binford 1963).

The most ambitious attempts to make such descriptions have been at the Center of Documentary Analysis for Archaeology in Paris. The initial work of this group includes the classification and recording of such diverse data as epic tales, bronze axes, and linear elements of design. As attributes in each of these areas were observed, they were given symbols, and their occurrence was recorded on edge-punched cards. The basic data thus stored can then be recalled by inserting sorting needles into stacks of the cards and withdrawing those on which certain attributes or clusters of attributes occur. Although the French did not do so initially, business machines and computers have since been used by them and other workers.

The advantage of recording each artifact mechanically is that unlimited numbers of attributes can be accommodated and that the data, readily available for retrieval from the file, can easily be extracted. If one is interested in learning the association of axes with convex bits, holes for hafting, and trapezoidal sections, one can quickly do so by inserting and lifting three needles in a stack of edge-punched cards. Cards picked up by all three needles provide the worker with what is in effect a statistical correlation. By this method it is possible to change the constitution of types without a basic reanalysis of the artifacts. Each worker can select whatever attribute clusters he wishes, and no change will have been necessary in the basic description.

Archeological reports are filled with descriptions of variable quality that add up to an enormous bulk. The use of a coding system coupled with mechanical handling of data would eliminate long verbal and graphic descriptions and greatly facilitate the comparison of material. Today large libraries are required to store the basic data, which exist in the form of published articles, monographs, and books. With punched cards, it would be possible to store the same data in a relatively few cubic feet and at much less expense (Hymes 1963).

The advantages of mechanical recording and statistical analysis are obvious. As archeologists become more aware of their possibilities, they will be used more frequently. It takes a great deal of time to create the descriptive system on which basic recording must be based and for each analyst to learn the system. For the present, these are the two most important obstacles that prevent universal adoption of such techniques. Some individual attempts, using manageable bodies of data, have been made in the United States to record and analyze archeological field data on edge-punched cards. Dr. F. Johnson directed the project of the Radiocarbon Dates Association in which several thousand carbon-14 age determinations were recorded on edge-punched cards (for illustration, see Heizer and Graham 1967:Fig. 29). Two attempts, both unfortunately abortive, have been made in the United States to secure by the cooperative efforts of archeologists a collection of systematized or coded data on projectile points (Krieger 1964; Weyer 1964; Swanson and Butler, 1962). To achieve such projects, however useful, would represent a staggering amount of effort, and it seems likely that complete files of coded data on the artifacts from any area where collecting has gone on for a long time can be realized only by governmental auspices. But until archeologists become sufficiently aware of the need for complete files of data they will probably continue to work singly or in small groups, each working in his own way and without particular regard for what others have done earlier or will do in the future. Few would argue against the proposition that archeology has now secured such a mass of material that no individual can study all the available items of even one class of artifact, such as projectile points, pottery, basketry, and so forth. The compilation of complete files provides one of the directions in which the present authors think archeology will move.

In spite of archeologists' traditional preoccupation with classification, a universally accepted system has never been devised. Until one is developed, archeology will continue to be plagued by descriptions that are not comparable with one another. It is clearly worth the effort to develop and learn better methods of handling basic data.

DETERMINING THE USE OF ARTIFACTS

Identifying the use of objects that were made by prehistoric peoples is often a real problem for archeologists. In fact, sometimes it is not even certain whether or not a piece is natural or man-made. Even if we are certain that an object is an artifact we must recognize that it may have served many purposes. We cannot always be certain when we identify a chipped, pointed, flint implement as an arrow-point that it did not also serve as a scarifier, graver, awl, toothpick, or punch. A hand-stone (mano) used for grinding seeds may on occasion have been used to crack open bones to remove the marrow, to cast at a camp dog stealing food, to break firewood, to grind a lump of red ocher into red paint powder, to pound a tent-peg into the earth, and so on. Multi-purpose uses probably were experienced by most tools made by primitive peoples, even though a primary function may have led to their manufacture.

We must also contend with objects that are not clearly one tool or another. For example, flint knives, points, and scrapers may be very similar in shape and size. Finally, and still more difficult, are objects about whose

FIG. 57 An object of undetermined use found at Ali Kosh, Iran, dating between 6500 and 6000 B.C. (scale in centimeters).

purpose we can make no reasonable guess. Judd (1959b:290) has written: "Unusual pieces are the sore thumbs of an archeological collection. There is no taxonomic pocket into which they can be dropped conveniently. Their very uniqueness makes them conspicuous and tempts the finder to speculation." As a result of speculation, one frequently finds these artifacts labeled "ceremonial object" in archeological reports. An example of an artifact of unknown use is illustrated in Figure 57.

For typological analyses it is not necessary to know the use to which objects were put, but for inferences about the activities of prehistoric peoples it is required. Unless the uses of objects are unequivocal—and they are rarely so—one usually begins by comparing them with similar objects in use today among primitive peoples.

Inspection under a microscope of the edges of stone tools may show use-wear evidence which can be interpreted in terms of what purpose the tool served. This kind of investigation is fairly new, and although the evidence of wear patterns on stone tools may be clear, it is often difficult to prove what kind of cutting or scraping was anciently practiced and often it is impossible to prove whether the tools were being used to work wood, bone, hide, or some other material. Perhaps it will be only after the analysis of some of the large museum collections of ethnographic stone tools, whose method of use is definitely known, that we will be able to identify positively the distinctive wear patterns occurring on meat-cutting flint knives, skin-dressing tools, fiber-shredding implements and the like. (Frison 1968, T. Hester 1970, 1972; T. Hester and Heizer 1972; Semenov 1964; Wilmsen 1968a, 1968b; Witthoft 1955).

Ethnographic Analogy

Items made and used in a certain fashion by primitive peoples provide the archeologist with an analogue of an item that is similar in form and material to one that has been recovered from a prehistoric site. He may thus identify the prehistoric object by its similarity to the more recent one whose function is known. By observing modern primitives as they fashion these materials we can gain an understanding of how stone was worked by grinding or chipping; how clay was fashioned and fired to make pottery; how holes were drilled in stone; and how shell, wood, and leather were shaped to produce artifacts. A large number of published ethnographic accounts contain descriptions of native industrial methods and material culture. Not only should the student of archeology read monographs on the material culture of aboriginal societies whose homes lie in arctic, desert, tropic, mountain, coastal, and forest areas, but he should study museum collections of artifacts, and if possible spend time in a nonindustrialized culture (cf. R. Ascher 1962; Gould 1968b; Oswalt and Van Stone 1967; J. White 1967). When the archeologist thinks about the functions his ancient artifacts served in a once-living society, he is being a prehistoric ethnographer.

MacAlister (1949:99), in a book on the archeology of Ireland, makes excellent use of the method of ethnographic analogy in interpreting prehistoric materials. He says:

> It is not too much to say that a study of the contemporary cultural ethnology of the South Sea Islands must now be regarded as a *necessary* preliminary to any serious study of the cultural ethnology of Ireland down to at least 1500 years ago. A student of Prehistoric Ireland may go to school under the instruction of a lowly Arunta of Central Australia, without the least sense of incongruity; and he will assuredly come back from his teachers enlightened with an illumination which he could never have drawn from any other source.

Père Lafitau in his *Moeurs des sauvages americains comparées aux moeurs des premiers temps* (1724) produced one of the first attempts at a systematic comparative ethnography by comparing the American Indians' tools and customs with those of "antiquity," by which Lafitau meant mainly the peoples described in Homer's *Odyssey*.

Native pottery making has been frequently observed and recorded in publications, and from such detailed descriptions of preparing the clay, fashioning the pot, and firing it archeologists can gain valuable suggestions about how to examine and test their prehistoric examples in order to understand the details of the pottery's manufacture. By studying prehistoric pots (for example, Balfet 1965; Foster 1948, 1960a), several ethnographers who are interested in native pottery making have offered useful suggestions to archeologists, and, in the hope of better understanding the technological process of prehistoric ceramics, a number of archeologists have lived with modern native pottery-making groups and observed their techniques (for example, R. Thompson 1958a).

Our knowledge of flint chipping comes primarily from firsthand observations of native peoples engaged in the act. By long practice and experimentation, certain persons today have been able to become extraordinarily expert in the manual art of pressure and percussion flaking of stone, and through this knowledge are able to determine from ancient chipped-stone implements the methods by which they were fashioned.

Grahame Clark (1953a:355) proposes that identification of prehistoric forms by ethnographic analogy be restricted to cultures having a similar subsistence level as well as approximately the same ecological background, and Childe (1956:51) and Willey (1953:299) concur. One would not compare prehistoric Eskimo artifacts with those used by the modern desert Bushmen of Southwest Africa and expect to learn much about the uses of bone snow knives and sea-mammal harpoons. Nor would an archeologist compare the tool inventory from a Stone Age prehistoric site in the arid North American Great Basin with that of the metal-using cultures of the tropical west coast of Africa, for the reasons that the two cultures are too dissimilar in level of technological development and occupy markedly different environments.

We are on much surer grounds in interpreting the way or ways in which a prehistoric object was used or the processes by which it was produced when there has been historical continuity of culture. In Europe, the study of prehistory is considerably aided by citing persistences, in the peasant or folk cultures in the modern period, of forms or practices that are similar to archeological occurrences (E. Evans 1956). G. Clark (1951, 1952) has applied this method with excellent results, and Gunda (1949) gives us examples of the persistence of plant collecting in the economic life of Eurasia. In the United States the "direct-historical approach" (discussed above) provides the opportunity, if one works back in time from historic village sites occupied by identified tribal groups, to determine historical continuity of culture complexes that have been ethnographically identified. An archeological example is Kehoe's (1958) attempt to settle the problem of the function of rings of boulders found in the Great Plains area. By gathering ethnographic examples he is able to demonstrate that the stone circles are tipi rings.

Wilmsen (1968b:982) observed that "archaeologists must assume that, other things being equal, . . . processes which structure the ethnographic record have also structured the archaeological record."

In many instances where traits have persisted in one area over a very long period of time, we may conclude that there has been continuity of culture. Winlock (1942:193, 207) calls attention to the identity of basket forms found in Dynastic Period Egyptian graves and modern baskets made at Edfu in Egypt and Nubia, and the same situation exists with regard to special techniques of hairdress. W. Emery (1948:34, plate 35c) notes an ancient, round leather shield with a central boss found at Qustul, Nubia, which is identical with shields still in use by the modern Beja tribes of the Sudan; a camel saddle with an antiquity of 1500 years, which can be precisely duplicated by modern examples in Nubia; and Nubian graves, dating from 2270–1600 B.C., containing pots with water and food, that are exactly like modern Nubian graves. The persistence of certain pottery vessel forms and manufacturing techniques in Mexico has been studied by Durand-Forest (1967). Creel (1937:174) refers to the modern persistence in China of the ancient semilunar slate knife in the same form but of a different material (iron). The ritual importance of the macaw (*Ara macao, A. militaris*) among the Zuni Indians of New Mexico has been abundantly attested to on the prehistoric time level in the Puebloan Southwest since the Pueblo III period. Judd (1959b:263–267) discusses the persistence of the macaws in ritual in the area and gives evidence of their occurrence in archeological sites. A rather similar situation obtains in California, where certain raptorial birds (hawk, condor, eagle) have been employed in a ceremonial context for the past 4000 years (Heizer and Hewes 1940; Wallace and Lathrap 1959).

Context

Occasionally the archeologist has the rare good fortune to find artifacts in various stages of completion. When an archeologist finds such items, he can arrange them in a series from unshaped raw material to the finished form. With this arrangement it is often possible to show that unusual pieces, which might otherwise be put into a separate type, are really unfinished or discarded examples of an abundantly represented type. For example, see a study of the processes of the manufacture of C-shaped fishhooks by Hamy (1963) and the production of flint tools and steatite bowls by Holmes (1919, especially Figs. 50, 104).

Sometimes the position of an artifact in the ground gives a clue to its use. This possibility again points up the need for careful digging and recording. W. Emery (1948:62, plate 34b) illustrates a specialized kind of tool found in Dynastic Period tombs in Nubia and explains that these objects were previously thought to be mace heads, but that in fact they were an archer's "arrow loose." He was able to make the identification after he found the artifacts attached to the hand and thumb of skeletons in tombs.

A better knowledge of context might help in the identification of an upper-paleolithic antler tool, named "baton de commandement" by a French prehistorian of the last century because he believed they were rods of authority possessed by chiefs. They have also been identified as "shaft-straighteners," as "thong-stroppers" (R. Braidwood 1967), as "drumsticks" (Kirchner 1952), and as "twitches" used to hold an animal's lip (Eppel 1958). Actually, these are all guesses, because we do not know with any certainty what function these artifacts served. On the other hand, the "banner-stones" of eastern United States archeology were once believed to be ceremonial objects, but the finding of such pieces in context in graves in Southeastern sites (Webb and Haag 1939:50; Webb 1946:320–323), associated with antler pieces, allowed them to be correctly identified as parts of throwing-sticks (atlatls, spear-throwers). Whether they were purely decorative or helped to balance the implement when the spear was cast has not yet been decided to everyone's satisfaction.

Replicative Experiments

Experiments in duplicating artifacts will provide a rational explanation of how they were made. Although the ability of an experimenter today to reproduce an ancient form does not by itself prove that the object was in fact made in just this way, the procedure demonstrates how the artifact may have been produced. We cite the following examples—which are not by any means a complete listing—of experiments to reproduce artifacts or to learn the way in which tools were used, or to learn their degree of efficiency. A considerably expanded list of replicative experiments can be found in Heizer and Graham (1972) and Graham, Heizer, and Hester (1972).

Experiments in using stone axes to cut down trees have been performed and reported on by J. Breasted (1935:36), J. Evans (1897:162), Iversen (1956), Jorgensen (1953), Leechman (1950), E. Morris (1939: 137), Nietsch (1939:70), G. V. Smith (1891), and Woodbury (1954: 40–42). Stone working by flaking or abrasion (pecking), resulting in the reproduction of "prehistoric" objects, has been carried out in modern times by Skavlem (Pond 1930), H. Ellis (1940), Kragh (1951), Knowles (1944), McGuire (1891), Neill (1952), Treganza and Valdivia (1955), and T. Wiltshire (1859–1863). An early experiment by Lovett (1877) attempted to determine the methods of manufacture of prehistoric flint implements by analogy with recent production of gun flints at Brandon, England. Other kinds of experiments involve earth-oven cooking (N. Layard 1922); cooking in a skin (Ryder 1966); copper smelting (Coghlan 1940); iron smelting (Wynne and Tylecote 1958); stone-drilling methods (Rau 1881); stone sculpture with stone hammers (Powell and Daniel 1956:28; Heyerdahl 1959; Heyerdahl and Ferdon 1961); American Indian pottery making (Griffin and Angell 1935; Waring 1968:320); arrowshaft straightening (Cosner 1951); woodcarving with native tools (McEwen 1946; Müller-Beck 1965); pigments used in South African cave paintings (T. Johnson 1957); efficiency of and use-evidence on primitive harvesting implements (R. Braidwood 1967:110; Witthoft 1967; Steensberg 1943; Curwen 1930); transport of heavy stones with human labor (Atkinson 1960:99–110; Heyerdahl 1959: 132–134); the method of notching atlatl-dart foreshafts for stone points (Cosgrove 1947:52, Fig. 71a–e); time-tool wear study of manufacture of simple wooden implements with flaked stone tools (Crabtree and Davis 1968); the serviceability of notched animal ribs and scapulae as fiber-extracting tools (Morris and Burgh 1954:61–62); preparation of yucca fibers (Osborne 1965); evidences of use-wear on the working edges of stone blades used for digging (Sonnefeld 1962); experimental production of the glaze on stone walls ("vitrified forts") by burning timbers that were used in their construction (Childe 1937–1938); cutting wood with an obsidian-edged wooden saw (Outwater 1957); determination by experiment of the method used to extract the live animal from the conch shell (*Strombus gigas*) by means of a small hole punched in the upper part of the spire (de Booy 1915:79–80); the planned destruction of a mud-hut village in Waziristan (D. Gordon 1953); reproducing minute drilled holes in stone beads with a shaft drill tipped with a barrel cactus thorn and employing sand abrasive (Haury 1931); reproduction of native copper artifacts (Cushing 1894); testing the belief that bevel-edged arrow-points turned in flight (T. Wilson 1898). One of the very earliest of these experiments was performed by Eduard Lartet (1860; see also Heizer 1962a: 107), who reproduced cutting marks on bone made by flint implements and thereby was able to offer proof of the coexistence of man and the extinct animals; he did so at a time, a century ago, when many were unwilling to accept the idea.

Another way of understanding how an artifact was fashioned is to dissect it. This cannot be done for most solid pieces, but, especially for textiles that are woven together of separate pieces, this kind of dissection can be performed. In illustration, we cite two sling pockets (Heizer and Krieger 1956:102–105; O'Neale 1947) from dry Nevada caves, and O'Neale's (1937) analysis of textiles of the Early Nazca period in Peru. The same technique of analysis can be used with basketry. Occasionally pictorial records of technological processes are found. Childe (1944a) has made excellent use of Egyptian tomb paintings of Egyptian metalworkers at work in a survey of copper and bronze metallurgy in the Old World.

An unusual experiment now being carried out in England concerns the building of an earthwork in 1960 in Wiltshire (Jewell 1961; Ashbee and Cornwall 1961). The bank and ditch will be studied through future years to determine rates and processes of denudation of the bank and silting-in of the ditch (Jewell and Dimbleby 1966).

Isaac (1967) has reported on an experiment in South Africa, where (1) scatters of cement casts of Acheulian handaxes and flakes were systematically placed in the bed of an ephemeral stream of wash; (2) bone refuse was placed in the open; and (3) bones of domestic animals were exposed to the air under a screen protection. Periodic examination of these three experimental layouts provides information on rearrangement by water, removal by scavengers, and decay caused by weathering. The information secured from this experiment could be of aid to the archeologist in interpreting an actual prehistoric find.

Social Correlates

Identifying an object is not the same as understanding its use. Many objects that we regard as mundane and worthy of no special attention are involved in seemingly esoteric rites of which we could have no guess without firsthand knowledge. For most of prehistory, these social correlates are, of course, lost to us, but when we read some of the modern ethnographic accounts we can imagine that they did exist. In illustration, we cite the paper by Sandin (1962) on the "Whetstone Feast" of the Iban of Sarawak. Among the Iban, after several bad harvests or because new families must have ceremonially blessed whetstones to sharpen iron farming tools, perhaps 30 separate rituals are performed during the ceremony. The events that together form the "feast" include making offerings to the good spirits; bloody sacrifice of pigs and chickens; making small ceremonial huts for storing farm tools; collecting and offering worn out household tools to the spirits; washing, cleaning, and oiling of old whetstones; playing music; singing and dancing; combing the hair of live pigs; feasting and wine drinking; bathing of pigs; and divining future argricultural success from the whetstones. This ceremony may be taken as one example (how typical it is we do not profess to know) of the complexity of social action that can involve a simple tool which the archeologist would normally assume to be merely utilitarian. The complicated ritual of the Iban would not be in the least inferable, either as a general fact or in any detail, from the whetstones as archeological specimens. Only if the institution of blessing whetstones by farming people was widely observed would an archeologist have reason even to suggest the possibility that the Iban whetstones (if they were found as archeological examples) may have been ritually sanctified, but even this would be the sheerest guess. The only hint we would have, and this is a very slim one, would be the recorded fact that whetstones are sequestered in the loft of the house after the farming season is over. Archeologically speaking, the association of the whetstone with the house-floor might come about with the abandonment and disintegration of the house, provided, of course, that the occupants of the house did not take with them their sacred whetstone when they moved out.

NATURAL OR MAN-MADE?

In some instances we must seriously question whether an object was made by man. This question is especially vital to students of very early man who made crude stone tools. By looking at the history of archeology we can see that for only a little more than 100 years has the human origin of hand axes found in the gravels of European rivers been acknowledged. Tools made by relatively modern people, the polished stone axes of Neolithic and later times, found on the surface or dug up by accident in Europe, were until the sixteenth century thought to have been formed by the action of lightning when it struck the earth (Blinkenberg 1911; Heizer 1962a:61–69). Their true identification came when European explorers found primitive peoples making and using stone bladed axes to cut down trees.

The way to recognize an object as an artifact rather than a fortuitously shaped piece produced by natural processes can be learned only from experience. Warren (1914), Barnes (1939), and Leakey (1960:45–48) have tried to set forth the differences between stones flaked by man and those fractured by nature, but written explanations of distinctions that can best be appreciated with a practiced eye do not suffice. Remember, experience is the only proper teacher. Flaking of stone (or, more properly, spalling) by lightning is discussed by Farmer (1939) and Laudermilk and Kennard (1938). Harner (1956) has investigated the action of heat in producing spalled rocks or flakes that might be—and sometimes actually have been—taken to be artifacts.

Nature can cause stones to break or chip in such a manner that it is very hard to decide that the pieces are not man-made. Indeed, Leakey's account, referred to earlier, admits that in some instances natural and man-made flakes cannot be distinguished. Although an experienced archeologist usually can make a definite decision on whether a bone or stone or piece of shell that he digs up has been modified by human action, there will occasionally arise situations where the amount of human interference is so slight that it cannot be clearly differentiated from a flake or groove or scratch or bit of polish that may equally well have been caused by some natural action. It is in such situations that there may arise claims of the existence of very ancient but extremely simple tools. American archeology has had its full share of such claims. About 15 years ago, G. F. Carter (1957) argued that he had found fire hearths and crude tools in geological deposits along the coast of Southern California that might be as much as 100,000 years old. A number of experienced archeologists are of the opinion that these stones are naturally fractured rocks and cannot be identified as artifacts. The proposal has at present few adherents. A more recent instance is that of the recovery of several hundred stones that are taken to be "unquestionably" or "possibly" artifacts from an alluvial fan in the Mohave Desert, Southern California (Leakey, Simpson, and Clements 1968). Opinion is divided on whether the stones are of human manufacture, especially because "the age of the fan is over 40,000 years but probably less than 120,000 years, with a probable age of 50,000 and 80,000 years." Opinions on whether the fractured stones are artifacts or "naturfacts" can probably never be resolved to the complete satisfaction of every "expert" who examines the stones. The reason is that we may have an actual instance of the sort envisaged by Leakey (1954:46) when he earlier wrote about the difficulty of deciding whether simply flaked stones were natural or man-made; "How, then, can these results of pressure flaking by natural agency be distinguished from humanly made tools? Often they cannot. Consequently, many specimens that *may* be due to human workmanship, but which have been obtained from a geological stratum, have to be discarded as doubtful specimens." In the Mohave Desert example in question Leakey has apparently opted for a decision that the specimens were humanly produced, but other and equally expert prehistorians who have studied the material take the opposite view. Everything considered, the extraordinary age of these fractured stones, which are from four to twelve times as old as any acceptably dated definite stone tools found so far in North America, will require that proponents of the existence of Mohave Desert Pleistocene man secure general agreement on the artifactual nature of the fractured stones before their claim can be taken seriously. This recent discovery is all too similar to the proposal made by Carter (1957), mentioned earlier, which was an echo of the century-old invention of the Eolithic that saw in naturally flaked stones the opportunistic recognition by ultrasimple cultured (or protocultural) men in the Pliocene of the utility of sharp stones for cutting and hacking.

The reader is referred, for studies of naturally fractured stones or bones that have at one time been alleged to be artifacts, to the publications of Breuil (1943), J. D. Clark (1958, 1961), and Watanabe (1949); to Dart's (1949, 1957) claims that *Australopithecus* of South Africa used bone tools (the "osteodontokeratic culture"); to N.C. Nelson's (1928) demonstration that the alleged bone tools from Pliocene deposits in Nebraska were natural; to Pei's (1938) careful analysis of the activities of animals in breaking or otherwise modifying animal bones that might be taken to be implements; and to T. Harrisson and Medway's (1962:336, Plate 1) analysis of broken bones of large mammals from Niah Cave, Sarawak, which do not show signs of grinding, polishing, decoration, or use-wear. Such bones are at times considered to be primitive tool types, but Harrisson and Medway are able to demonstrate convincingly, by the experimental smashing of fresh bones with a large stone, that similar shapes are readily produced by this means. Dart (1960), on the other hand, reports on the experimental breaking of fresh sheep femora to show that spirally broken antelope limb bones in the Makapansgat cave were presumably intentionally rather than accidentally produced, and thus sees in these experiments support for the osteodontokeratic culture of the Australopithecines. Dart and Kitching (1958) compare what are undoubtedly human-fractured bones from the Kalkbank site, South Africa, of middle Stone Age date (ca. 15,000 years old) with the osteodontokeratic tools from the Australopithecine deposits at Makapansgat.

We must be careful *not* to assume that unmodified bones or stones were *not* used as tools, because a handy cobble that would serve as a hammer must be considered a universal human tool type. Unmodified lower jaws of ungulates also provide ready-made implements. Waugh (1916:Plate 6c) pictures a deer jaw used by the Iroquois for scraping green corn from the cob, and Swanton (1942:Plate 16) illustrates an unmodified deer jaw that has a handle attached at right angles to the ramus. This piece is said to have been used by the Caddo as a sickle, probably for cutting grass. Bison scapulae were widely used as hoes for cultivating maize in the Great Plains area, and these were employed without alteration but show signs of abrasion and polish resulting from use (Dunlevy and Bell 1936:244). Deer antlers used as picks provide us with another example of the utilization of unmodified animal remains.

It should be clear from the foregoing that archeologists must take great care in identifying the uses of artifacts. We should also stress here that many artifacts are not well made and that archeologists must be careful not to discard them solely because they look natural at first glance. Finally, the absence of prepared tools for certain jobs does not mean that there were no such tools.

As an aside, we mention here another aspect of interpretation of archeological materials. Archeology has had more than its share of uninformed theorists who have proposed an incredible variety of hypotheses accounting for the routes of entry and culture stock carried by the ancestors of the American Indians. These crackpot theories variously proposed that metal-seeking Egyptian prospectors, refugees from sunken Mu or Atlantis, wandering Israelite tribes (ten were "lost" and still remain unaccounted for), Alexander's fleet under Admiral Nearchus, Vikings who lost their way, Egyptians in reed boats, Phoenecians, Welsh, Paleolithic North Atlantic voyagers, and a half-hundred more people at different times came to the New World. None of these theories has been proved to have any basis in fact, and none is likely to. For some of these proposals and the arguments against them, see H. Gladwin (1947), C. Gordon (1970), Jennings (1968:44–45), Mertz (1964), Wauchope (1962).

In a different category are studies carried out by reputable anthropologists who are fully aware that trans-Pacific or trans-Atlantic culture connections are possible although generally believed to be highly improbable. The few serious attempts to prove the case by such students as Ekholm (1946b), Estreda, Meggers, and Evans (1962), Greenman (1963), Moran and Kelley (1969), and Riley and others (1970) have not been generally accepted. The problem in deciding whether geographically separated cultural similarities are the result of culture contact (diffusion) or independent parallel inventions (convergence) exists because there are no hard-and-fast rules that can be applied to test the data. We can recommend, as an introduction to the ways in which anthropologists study such problems, the following papers, selected from a much larger body of relevant literature: Caso (1965), R. Dixon (1928), O'Brien (1968), Rands (1953), Rowe (1966), Tolstoy (1966).

REFERENCES

Classifying Archeological Materials: L. Binford 1962, 1963; Cahen and van Noten 1971; Epstein 1964; J. Ford 1954b; Hole 1971; Krieger 1944, 1960; de Paor 1967:36–43; Rouse 1960a, 1960b; Whallon 1972a.

Statistical Analysis to Discover or Define Cultural Types: Clarke 1962, 1967; Driver 1961; Fowler 1959:66–69; Kroeber 1940a; Lorandi di Gieco 1965; McPherron 1967; Sackett 1966; Tugby 1965; Whallon 1972a, 1972b; Witherspoon 1961.

Theories, Procedures, and Terminology Used in Defining Convenient ("Designed") Types: Bell 1958; L. Binford 1963; Black and Weer 1936; Bordes 1950; Finkelstein 1937; J. Ford 1954a; J. Clark and others 1966; Garcia Cook 1967; de Heinzelin 1962; Jelinek 1967:88–111; Jennings 1968:17–19; McKusick 1963; P. Phillips, Ford, and Griffin 1951:61–68; Pope 1960; Renaud 1941; W. Ritchie 1961; Rouse 1960b; Suhm and Krieger 1954; Swanson and Butler 1962; Wauchope 1966:Chap. 5.

Discussions and Arguments for Discovered ("Real") Types: Deetz 1967; Ford 1954b; J. Gifford 1960; Krieger 1944; Ritchie and MacNeish 1949; Rouse 1960a; Spaulding 1953.

Computer Applications to Archeology: M. Ascher and R. Ascher 1963; Chenhall 1967; G. Cowgill 1967a, 1967b; Craytor and Johnson 1968; Doran and Hodson 1966; Hodson 1969; Hole and Shaw 1967; Hymes 1963, 1965; Kendall 1969; Kuzara, Mead, and Dixon 1966.

Describing Artifacts and Techniques for Illustrating Archeological Reports with Drawings or Photographs: Blaker 1965; Bryant and Holtz 1965; Grinsell, Rahtz, and Warhurst 1966; Heizer and Graham 1967:Appendix I; Hope-Taylor 1966, 1967; Isham 1965; Kobayashi and Bleed 1971; Piggott 1965; Ridgway 1938; R. Smith 1970; Staniland 1953; Webster 1963:142–143, 153–163.

Application of Statistical Methods to Determine Chronology of Artifacts: Belous 1953; Brainerd 1951; J. D. Clark 1964; G. Cowgill 1968, 1972; Dempsey and Baumhoff 1963; Gelfand 1971; Hole and Shaw 1967; Jelinek 1962a; Johnson 1968; Moberg 1961; W. Robinson 1951; Spier 1917; Troike 1957; Tugby 1965; Wissler 1916; Woodall 1968.

Use of Edge-Punched Cards or Optical Coincidence Cards for Recording Archeological Data: Biek 1963:Fig. 12; Bordaz and Bordaz 1966; J. D. Campbell and Caron 1964; Christophe and Deshayes 1964; E. Davis 1965; Gardin 1958; Nagel 1966; Shepard 1957:322–332; Soudsky 1967; Voss 1966; *Inventaria Archaeologica* (International Council for Philosophy and the Humanities, UNESCO); *Index de l'outillage* (C.N.R.S., Paris).

Graphs, Pie Diagrams, and Histograms to Show Comparisons of Artifacts from Different Levels in One Site or between Sites: Bohmers 1956, 1969; J. Clark and Howell 1966; Sonneville-Bordes 1953, 1960.

Determining the Function of Prehistoric Artifacts through Ethnographic Analogy: K. Anderson 1969; R. Ascher 1961b; Custance 1968; Heider 1967; Heizer 1951a; Hester and Heizer 1972; Holmes 1913; Service 1964; M. A. Smith 1955; R. Thompson 1956.

Primitive Technology and Material Culture: Blackwood 1950; Daumas 1962; *Dictionnaire archéologique des techniques 1963–1964*; Feldhaus 1914; Forbes 1955–1958; Hiroa 1930; Hodges 1964; O. Mason 1891; Sayce 1963; Semenov 1964; Singer, Holmyard, and Hall 1954–1958; *World Archaeology* 1971.

Ethnographic Descriptions of Native Pottery Manufacture: Conklin 1953; Fischer 1963; Fontana and others 1962; Foster 1948, 1955, 1956, 1960a; Griffin and Angell 1935; Guthe 1925; Hayden 1959; W. Hill 1937; Rogers 1936; Stanislawsky 1969; R. Thompson 1958a.

Firsthand Accounts and Technical Descriptions of Aboriginal Stone-Flaking Methods: Bordes 1947; H. Ellis 1940; Gould 1968a, 1968b; W. Holmes 1919; Knowles 1944; Kragh 1951; Leakey 1954; Mewhinney 1957; Mitchell

1949; Oakley 1950; Pond 1930; Squier 1953; W. Watson 1950.

Analysis of Attributes: Irwin, Hurd, and LaJeunesse 1971; Movius and Brooks 1971; Movius and others 1968; Parkington 1972; Sackett 1966; Whallon 1972a, 1972b.

Modern Flint Flakers' Efforts to Reproduce Prehistoric Forms: Crabtree 1966; Crabtree and Davis 1968; Custance 1968; Graham, Heizer, and Hester 1972; Metraux 1959; Neill 1952.

Experimental Reproduction of Prehistoric Artifacts as a Lead to Determining How They Were Made: R. Ascher 1961a; Crabtree and Davis 1968; Heizer and Graham 1967:Chap. 11.

Artifact Recognition: Methods for Distinguishing Naturally and Humanly Modified Stone and Bone: R. Ascher and M. Ascher 1965; Barnes 1939; Bourdier 1953; Breuil 1943; J. D. Clark 1958, 1961; Farmer 1939; Greenman 1957; Harner 1956; Koby 1943; Lacaille 1931; Laudermilk and Kennard 1938; Leakey 1960:45–48; McCrone and others 1965; N. Nelson 1928; Pei 1938; Warren 1914, 1923; H. Watanabe 1949.

CHAPTER ELEVEN

TECHNICAL ANALYSES OF ARTIFACTS AND SITES

Most of the interpretations archeologists make about culture are based on artifacts because, as was pointed out in the last chapter, artifacts are direct material clues to human action. These interpretations sometimes depend on technical analyses that must be made by metallurgists, chemists, physicists, geologists, botanists, and zoologists. Usually, technical analyses are made to discover methods of manufacture and to identify the mineral or chemical composition of artifacts. These data can be used as evidence of trade between areas and to indicate the technical processes and skills of artisans. Other kinds of analyses can be applied to sites and to noncultural materials. Analyses of the physical condition of sites may tell how they were formed, how long they were occupied, and perhaps what they contained if visual traces are gone. Analyses of plant and animal vestiges in the form of pollen grains, carbonized vegetal elements, and bones may give information on prehistoric diet, climate, land use, and chronology.

There are literally dozens of highly sophisticated laboratory and instrumental analytical techniques available for examination of artifacts. Because we can mention only a few, the reader is referred to the sources listed at the end of the chapter for suggested reading.

ANALYSIS OF POTTERY

Classification of ceramics depends on knowledge of their attributes. Such attributes as shape, texture, and design are readily identified visually by an archeologist, but there are other qualities whose presence may be equally valuable for identification. Among these are the way pots were made, firing conditions, nature of the paste or glaze used, and other surface finishing. Such data may help to distinguish among wares at one site, or to determine the place where the pottery was made. Other qualities, such as hardness, porosity, luster, strength, color, and mineral content, can also be readily determined, but often such details are of little use to archeologists. Technical analysis is worth the time and trouble only when it helps to solve an archeological problem.

The main tools used by a ceramist are binocular and petrographic microscopes. With these he can identify most of the culturally important attributes of sherds. For preliminary analysis, a binocular microscope is necessary for identifying paste and tempering material. Often nothing more is needed. If more detailed analysis is required, the petrographic microscope will reveal the mineral composition of the tempering material used in the pottery. These analyses can help establish whether pots were manufactured locally. With sufficient information from other areas, it may also be possible to find the place of origin of pots that were made elsewhere. As a case in point, A. Shepard (1963:21–22; see also Judd 1954:235), who noted the abundance of a painted pottery with sanidine basalt temper of nonlocal origin at Pueblo Bonito, New Mexico, proposes that the pottery may have been manufactured at a source some 50 miles distant. Although large-scale import from such a distance is possible, the alternative possibility that foreign potters came to Pueblo Bonito carrying temper material (rather than bulky and breakable pots) and made their distinctive pottery on the spot might be considered. This is the kind of problem that the archeologist sees; it could be settled by determining whether the fine clay or paste of pottery from the two localities is the same or different. A good example of petrographic analysis of potsherds is the report of Williams (1956) on the tempering materials in the pottery of several sites in central Mexico.

Other techniques depend on the use of chemical reagents to test the presence or absence of certain chemicals in sherds. These tests can often be made by archeologists, but if quantitative determinations are desired, it is usually necessary to turn to a chemist or a ceramist. Spectrographic analysis and differential thermal analysis are two other techniques for identifying the chemical composition of sherds.

A widely used standard for recording the color of pottery is the loose-leaf Munsell Soil Color Charts (Munsell Color Company, Baltimore, Maryland), which contain color chips that permit close matching of hue. When archeologists use the same color reference system exact comparability is assured when pottery from two areas is being analyzed.

ANALYSIS OF METAL AND STONE

Quantitative chemical analysis of metal artifacts can yield valuable information about techniques of manufacture and composition. Similar analyses can be made on the composition of the stone in artifacts. Such knowledge can lead to information about where the artifact was made and where the stone or metal or ore was obtained. Techniques of analysis are varied, and the investigator chooses the one that promises to provide information needed to solve the problem. Relatively simple chemical analysis may be sufficiently precise to enable the technician to determine the relative proportions of the major components of a smelted metal object. Such data may be of small value, however, if the archeologist, in the hope of showing whether a single find may have been secured by trade, wishes to compare a metal object found in one region with those found abundantly in another region. Here a more precise quantitative analysis of a series of elements present will be secured either by the neutron-activation analysis or x-ray fluorescence methods. The place of origin of copper artifacts can be determined by identifying a similar trace-element composition in copper ores.

It is equally interesting to learn how metal artifacts were made. Details of manufacture that cannot be determined by simple visual inspection may be discovered by photomicrographic examination of portions of artifacts. Such discoveries go a long way toward enlarging our knowledge of the technical skills of prehistoric peoples. As an example, we can cite the study made by Prof. Cyril Smith, Massachusetts Institute of Technology, of a copper bead dating back to about 6500 B.C., found in Tepe Ali Kosh. Because it is one of the earliest copper artifacts known, a study of its manufacture is of considerable interest. Metallographic and microscopic analyses clearly show that the artisan cold-hammered a lump of native copper into a thin sheet, that was then cut with a chisel and rolled to form the bead. In other words, the technology involved was very simple and required no knowledge of metallurgy. In some instances it is possible to identify the work done by individual smiths or factories because of peculiarities of manufacture that are not easily seen with the naked eye. The spectrographic analysis of faience beads found in tombs of the Wessex culture, England, by J. Stone and Thomas (1956) proved that these beads were of Egyptian origin, known to date from about 1400 B.C., thereby providing the English archeologists with an important fixed date in British prehistory.

A highly technical method of petrographic analysis called "fabric analysis," employed by L. Weiss (1954), can prove that two fragments of marble once were part of the same sculptured stele, and some important matchings of what were considered fragments of separate stelae have been made by application of this technique.

The identification of places where stones were secured for making tools, ornaments, or large sculptures can tell the archeologist something about ancient procurement activities. If the source for a certain kind of flint occurs in an outcrop 10 miles away, he concludes that the local people simply walked there when they needed more implement material. If the source proves to lie at a distance of 200 miles, he will probably assume that the material was secured through a system of intertribal trade. Extensive studies of obsidian in the Near East have provided similar detailed information about the sources from which the stone was derived and the pattern of its distribution. From this kind of evidence archeologists have gained clues about the relations among early sites—clues that were not at all apparent but that may have considerable value in helping to understand the spread of agricultural communities. Similar work is beginning in North America, and some results are now in hand for Meso-America and California. British archeologists and petrologists, working cooperatively, have made a special investigation of the distribution of neolithic stone axes manufactured from rock whose sources are known, and from their studies have reached certain conclusions on the extent of trading routes used. The stones of one of Europe's most impressive ancient monuments, Stonehenge, have been traced to their sources. The so-called blue stones of the inner circle are now known to have been originally secured in southern Wales, at a distance of approximately 160 miles. Most of the sculptured altars, stelae, and colossal heads of the Olmec culture found at the site of La Venta in southeastern Mexico are known to be made of stone secured in the Tuxtla Mountains, about 90 miles distant (Williams and Heizer 1965). These sculptures range in weight from 4 to more than 36 tons, and they date from the first half of the first millennium B.C. An important cultural fact can be derived from all these details; namely, on this early time level in Meso-America the Olmec people were sufficiently organized socially, and had the required engineering skills, to be able to move both by land and water these very heavy weights (Heizer 1966). Another example of the extent to which the Olmecs went to obtain material is described by Flannery and others (1967). The excavators found that magnetic mirrors of a type occurring in Olmec sites were being manufactured at a site near Oaxaca, in the Mexican highlands. Although it seems clear that long-distance trade for exotic materials was being carried out, the mechanism of transmission and the kind of objects traded in return remain in question. It has also been demonstrated through x-ray fluorescence analysis of obsidian from the La Venta, Tres Zapotes, and San Lorenzo Tenochtitlan sites that this natural glass was being procured by trade from the Guatemalan highlands to the south and from the state of Hidalgo, Mexico, to the north (Stross and others 1968; Hester, Heizer, and Jack 1971; Hester, Jack and Heizer 1971; Jack and Heizer 1968; Cobean and others 1971). From these several examinations referred to above, we bring into focus the "geography of the Olmec world" of the first half of the first millenium B.C.

Examples could be multiplied, but enough has been said to show how facts of cultural history can be deduced from the information provided by the petrographer.

ANALYSIS OF WEAVING

In dry refuse deposits of occupied caves or rock shelters of the American West, in dry desert areas such as Egypt or the Peruvian coast, or in acidic peat bogs, woven cloth and baskets may be preserved even though made of ordinarily perishable materials. The imprints that textiles leave on wet clay that was later baked may provide information about prehistoric cloth or basketry.

Analysis of textiles can provide a wide range of information. To begin with, it is often possible to identify the material used. Study of the fibers may lead to conclusions about whether plants or animals were domesticated. Identification of the fibers may show that they are not native to the area. Analysis of the dyes tells a great deal about the technical skill of prehistoric man, and may also give several clues about trade if the pigments are identified as originating in an area other than that in which the textiles were found. Study of the kind of weaving and type of loom used to produce a kind of cloth gives data on technical skill and, in many instances, on cultural relations. Where actual basketry that was once present has not survived, impressions or casts of basketry may be recorded on soft clay that was later fired, and by a study of these imprints a great deal about the basketry techniques may be learned. In the Tehuacan Valley sites it was found that, as time passed, people learned different techniques of knotting and basketry (MacNeish, Nelken-Terner, and Johnson 1967).

Basketry and matting are studied in similar ways. Classifications of basketry techniques have been devised by O. Mason (1904) and Balfet (1952).

ANALYSIS OF SOILS

Analyses of soil help date sites, indicate how deposits were formed, and tell something of the environment at the time of formation. The persons who study soil are called pedologists, but similar work may also be done by geologists, geographers, and geomorphologists.

It is often evident how a site accumulated and was buried; if not, the information may be obtained through detailed analysis of the sediments. In most instances one can discover whether sites resulted from natural or man-made deposition; the pedologist can distinguish among water-laid, wind-laid, and man-laid deposits. This analysis is important because it helps to show whether the articafts are *in situ* and provides information about the environment at the time of deposition.

Through analysis of buried soil horizons, one can tell something of the climatic conditions that produced them. In some instances (for example, on the Mediterranean coast) one can correlate some of the buried soils in caves with those in dunes and thus arrive at a rough relative chronology (Howell 1959; H. Wright 1962), However, identification of these soils is a job for a specialist who must be familiar with the chemistry of soil formation. Two soils having the same appearance may result from different causes. Facile nontechnical comparisons based on visual observation by an archeologist are generally undependable. Rates of soil weathering and development of soil profiles offer a promising lead for archeological dating.

The sediments in caves will at times give additional information on climate derived from other sources. For an extended discussion of this question as it relates to a specific series of sites, see Movius (1960).

Pedologists, through chemical analysis of the soil, may also be able to tell whether an observed feature in the earth is natural or man-made. For example, there may be a question whether a hole once held a post or resulted from a burrowing animal, or perhaps just from the digging by the inhabitants of a site. Analysis of the humic content of the pit compared with soil nearby may tell whether a wooden post rotted there. In acid soils, bone is usually destroyed by chemical action. Solecki (1953:382–383) was able to show in the Natrium site, West Virginia, from a very high phosphate concentration in what were believed to be grave pits—but in which no visible signs of bone were apparent—that the pits had at one time contained burials. Bone ordinarily will not be preserved in soil whose pH (hydrogen value) is 6.3 or less. A pH value of 7.0 is neutral; values of over 7.0 indicate basic or alkaline soils; those below 7.0 are acid. In soils with a pH greater than 6.5, pollen will not be preserved (Dimbleby 1957).

Human organic wastes are rich in nitrogen, phosphorus, and calcium, and where people of minimal sanitary practices have lived these elements will be concentrated in the soil. There will be a gradual loss of these constituents over time in an open-air site; therefore quantitative differences in soil chemistry may be a means of relative dating (Cook and Heizer 1965).

Just as with other technical analyses, those of soils can produce far more information than the archeologist can use. Such analyses are useful only when the problems they can help solve are well defined.

The soil is a very important part of the ecosystem (Hyams 1952), and as the physical base on which man lives and works, may be expected to be modified by addition or subtraction of physical and chemical constituents in accordance with the specific practices followed on the spot. Thus a living site will ordinarily experience the addition of inorganic and organic trash incidental to the occupation process. The high proportion of nitrogen, phosphorus, and calcium is for the most part attributable to human body wastes, which are disposed of in the nearest convenient spot (Cook and Heizer 1965). It can be computed that a model living group of 100 persons will produce in body wastes each year 915 pounds of introgen, 137 pounds of phosphorus, and 55 pounds of calcium. It is therefore not remarkable that the soils of California Indian villages which have been studied chemically are very high in all these elements. It may be safely presumed that similar chemical enrichment of the soils of spots lived on by aboriginal peoples with similar living habits will be demonstrated.

Soils of fields that have been cultivated by simple farmers in the New World can be rated on a scale of excellent to poor according to soil fertility and permeability, and some impression therefore gained relating to the efficiency of the ancient system of agriculture (Judd 1954:59–61; U. Cowgill 1961, 1962).

Every single item of organic origin that has once been present in a site in complete form but has decayed into a formless chemical residue can, theoretically, be determined by chemical anlysis. The present authors believe that chemical techniques now available could be used to analyze the soils of prehistoric sites and could produce information on the kinds, and to some extent the quantities, of perishable items once present. Practically nothing has been attempted along this line, and it stands as one of the great opportunities for future development in prehistory. For example, it is known that the maize plant has an affinity for absorbing zinc, copper, and aluminum in the form of trace elements from the soils in which the plants grow. If the population of a site ate large quantities of maize, the soil of the living site should show higher than ordinary levels of these trace elements. There are numbers of large and important prehistoric sites in Meso-America where it is assumed that maize was the staple food item, but no concrete evidence (pictorial, carbonized seeds, and so on) has been recovered. If trace-element concentrations could be established, we might be able to follow the chemical trail back in time to sites where maize was first being eaten and thus know we were dealing with people who were the first corn farmers.

ANALYSIS OF ANIMAL AND PLANT REMAINS

Aside from artifacts, the largest source of information about prehistoric life and times comes from studying the bones of animals that people ate and the plants they ate or otherwise used. Identification of faunal and floral vestiges are made by zoologists and botanists.

Most analyses of bones are simply identifications of the species present (Cornwall 1956; A. Olsen 1961a, 1961b). Many site reports include such a listing but all too often fail to describe the implications of the presence of these species for prehistoric man. If we know the species present, we can determine the meat diet of prehistoric man, and, by computing the frequencies of animals, we can get an idea of the relative importance of each species. Calculating the minimum number of animals of any species present in an archeological site can be done by counting either the left or right of one particular bone. By knowing the number of animals that were brought to the area where people had their houses and cooked their meals it is possible to estimate the amount of meat available. T. E. White (1953b) does this by estimating the dressed weight of game animals.

We should mention at this point that conclusions regarding total number of individual animals may be incorrect because of the disappearance through chemical action or mechanical breaking of certain of the bones. The example of the Solutrean 4 layer in the site of Badegoule in southern France (Bouchud 1954) is given here. The layer produced 2577 adult reindeer teeth that theoretically should have shown the following proportions:

$$
\begin{array}{ll}
1032 \text{ incisors} & \text{(normal incisor-premolar ratio of 3/2)} \\
\left.\begin{array}{l} 774 \text{ premolars} \\ 774 \text{ molars} \end{array}\right\} & \text{(normal premolar-molar ratio of 1/1)} \\
\overline{2580}
\end{array}
$$

The teeth recovered show the following actual distribution:

$$
\begin{array}{ll}
144 \text{ incisors} & \text{(actual incisor-premolar ratio of 1/7)} \\
\left.\begin{array}{l} 989 \text{ premolars} \\ 1444 \text{ molars} \end{array}\right\} & \text{(actual premolar-molar ratio of 17/25)} \\
\overline{2577}
\end{array}
$$

The newborn reindeer has 4 incisors and 3 premolars in each half of the jaw. The 186 teeth of newborn animals found should therefore have had the following proportions:

$$
\begin{array}{ll}
104 \text{ incisors} & \text{(normal incisor-premolar ratio 4/3)} \\
\underline{78 \text{ premolars}} \\
182
\end{array}
$$

The teeth actually found are divided as follows:

$$
\begin{array}{ll}
12 \text{ incisors} & \text{(actual incisor-premolar ratio 1/15)} \\
\underline{174 \text{ premolars}} \\
186
\end{array}
$$

Apparently in this instance there has been differential disappearance of certain teeth, which has skewed the normally expected proportions. Because the teeth of reindeer did not, so far as known, serve as material from which artifacts were made, the imbalance of expected numbers of kinds of teeth cannot be attributed to cultural practices by the persons who killed the reindeer for food. The ritual disposal of bones of food animals observed by some hunting peoples may effectively eliminate from occupation refuse deposits certain bones of species that are considered important (cf. Elmendorf and Kroeber 1960:145; G. Foster 1945: 181; Heizer 1951b). In extreme cases this can lead to great scarcity of bones in sites where it is known from other evidence that hunting was a major economic pursuit (Oswalt and Van Stone 1967:70–73, 101).

Another caution about interpreting the number of animals is that the presence of 25 mice, a horse, and a deer does not mean that the people were primarily mouse eaters. In the first place, 25 mice yield considerably less meat than a baby deer. In the second place, small rodents probably inhabited most archeological sites and often died natural deaths in the deposits. Others were probably killed as pests. It is not reasonable to assume that they were ever a very important part of the diet of prehistoric man, although such allegations have been made. In the Great Basin area of the Far West, large rats were regularly hunted for food, but because they may weigh up to 1 to 2 pounds, they deserve being classed as game. To illustrate, in 1859 Captain J. H. Simpson of the Corps of Topographical Engineers in eastern Nevada encountered a Shoshone Indian and talked to him through an interpreter, "I asked him if his country was a good one. He said it was. He liked it a good deal better than any other. I asked him why. Because, he said, it had a great many rats." Similarly, the infrequent listing of birds, snakes, and miscellaneous scavenger carnivores in the site gives little clue to the diet of man; their presence in the archeological deposits may not have been due to a human agency. Jewell (1958) shows that concentrations of the bones of water voles in Wiltshire barrows in England does not, as might easily be assumed, indicate a wetter situation in the Bronze Age at the site, but that the bones were introduced into the site by roosting birds who disgorged pellets containing the bones of animals caught elsewhere. Matteson (1959) has shown that terrestrial snails may live and die on refuse middens and leave their shells to be discovered by an archeologist who may assume incorrectly that they provided part of the diet of the human occupants. An explanation for the abundant presence of the bones of gulls, bald eagle, and condor in the Five Mile Rapids Site, Oregon, is that probably the birds were attracted to the place where people were drying fish. Because the birds are all scavengers and are not usually eaten, it is probable that the bones are those of birds killed to prevent them from robbing the fishermen of their catch. At the Mousterian site of Lebenstedt in Germany bones of muskrats, wolves and vultures are interpreted as remains of scavengers that died or were killed in the refuse heaps (Butzer 1964:381–382).

On the other hand, V. Watson (1955) has sounded a cautionary note in calling attention to the situation in New Guinea where meat resources are rare and considerable reliance is placed on small feral mammals, worms, and insects that would not leave any bones. Thus, to infer that because no animal bones were found in archeological sites the people did not eat meat, or had a protein-deficient diet, would be incorrect. The example points up once more the incompleteness of the archeological record and reminds us that there may be a number of alternative explanations for either the presence or absence of some element in the refuse deposits of an archeological site.

Special feasts may leave evidence whose nature would be difficult to interpret from archeological evidence. For example, in the Mt. Hagen district of New Guinea great feasts are held at intervals of several years. At these times numbers of pigs are killed, roasted, and eaten. There is a record of 1100 animals being killed at one such feast (Riesenfeld 1950:425; Salisbury 1962). Because pigs are eaten only on such festive occasions, the great accumulation of discarded bones that one supposes results from such a feasting orgy would refer to one single event of this sort. Only certain villages hold such feasts; therefore there would eventually be a great concentration of pig bones in these sites and not in others.

If the data secured from bones are properly weighted, a great deal of information can be derived about diet. We have mentioned how, by calculating the sizes of various species, one can tell approximately how much meat could have been consumed. By noting which parts of the body are represented, one can tell whether the hunters brought whole or partial carcasses back to camp (for example, Hole and Flannery 1968; W. Wood 1968; Fitting 1968:54–64). This information must be taken into account in any calculation of the amount of meat available. One can also tell, by examining the bones how many animals were butchered. In some instances meat was separated at the joints; in others, long bones were simply hacked through. Interpretations of the cultural significance of fragmentary animal bones in refuse deposits must be made with caution, because the archeologist does not know what cultural practices (Grahame Clark calls these "social choices") may have been involved in hunting, butchering, bringing back the kill to the site, or in disposing of the bones after the animal was eaten. Kehoe and Kehoe (1960) present a detailed analysis of bones recovered from a bison kill site in Montana and demonstrate that they can distinguish activity patterns of different cultural groups and whether such a kill site is ascribable to hunters sent out from villages or nomadic hunters. Actually, archeologists often reach a conclusion that seems to be supported by the data they have recovered from the excavation, but the conclusion may not be nearly so correct as the archeologist implies. In illustration, note the paper by J. Davis (1959) in which he critically examines the evidence for certain conclusions made by Southwestern archeologists on changes of diet in successive prehistoric cultures; he finds that many interpretations proposed are actually contradicted by other data. Flannery's (1967b:171) study of the frequency of vertebrate food animals utilized between 8000 B.C. and A.D. 1500 in Tehuacan Valley, Mexico, is another example. He shows that, by plotting numbers of animals caught, the chart illustrates hunting activities by man, but that a graph using the same data (which shows available amounts of meat) would obscure the picture of the variety of meat-securing activities by overemphasizing deer, which was the largest animal killed and eaten.

The kinds of animals and plants present in a site may give information about the climate that prevailed while the site was occupied. As indicators of climate, the large animals are not always as sensitive as small animals may be. For inferences about climate, plants and snails seem to be sensitive indicators. Bones of microfauna (such as mice), although of little value in determining diet, must be saved for the climatic clues they can give. Plants and animals are often found within narrow ecological zones. When these zones are known, it is possible to infer that flora and fauna found in sites came from similar or different zones. Inferences can be made from pollen, impressions of plants in clay, and from preserved plants. It is more difficult to make inferences from small mammals, because they are often burrowers and may have entered a site long after its abandonment. Their presence, although an indication of climatic conditions, may be related to a climate quite different from that prevailing while the site was occupied by man, if it can be shown that these burrowers are intrusive in postoccupation times. Some of the animal bones found in an archeological deposit may represent individuals killed, brought home, and eaten. Some bones, particularly those in cave or rockshelter deposits which offer protection to animals as well as men, may have been brought there and left by scavengers or simply may be remains of animals that died in the cave or shelter when man was not living there (Hole and Flannery 1968). Thus, cultural remains associated with animal bones may result from quite different depositional processes, and it is the archeologist's problem to recognize and distinguish these. At times serious errors of interpretation can result from the failure to recognize this problem, as is illustrated in the case of certain cave deposits in Nevada (Heizer and Baumhoff 1970; Heizer and Berger 1970). The problem of distinguishing bones of animals used for food from those finding their way into a cultural deposit by natural means is discussed by Heizer and Cook (1960:135–138) and D. H. Thomas (1971).

Both flora and fauna can give information that a site was occupied at a certain time of year. When caches of ripe seeds are found, one infers that the site was occupied during or soon after the harvest season. If animals of a certain age are found, it may indicate seasonal slaughter or that the animals were domesticated. When migratory birds are found, one can determine the seasons when they would have been present and killed. It is easier to tell when a site was occupied than to say that it was not occupied at a particular time. A great deal of what we know about the history of domesticated animals has been learned from bones dug up in archeological sites. Zoologists who cooperate with archeologists, both in the field and at the home laboratory, are slowly learning how men in the Mesolithic and Neolithic came to protect and encourage the multiplication of animals for economic ends.

Valuable clues to diet may also be derived from analysis of human feces. These are preserved in desiccated form in dry sites and may contain the bones of small mammals, fish, or insects, together with seed and vegetal matter that can be identified. This is a field of investigation that has been badly neglected. For analyzing coprolites preserved in dry archeological sites, E. O. Callen of McGill University, Canada, perfected a technique of soaking for 72 hours in a 0.5 percent aqueous solution of trisodium phosphate. The softened mass is then sedimented, and a detailed microscopic examination and separation is made of all the solid matter that remains. Studies of human coprolites from cave and shelter deposits in Mexico, Peru, Nevada, and Kentucky (cited later) have shown that extraordinarily detailed information on dietary patterns can be secured. Examination by an ichthyologist of the bones and scales of fish in 1000-year-old coprolites from Lovelock Cave, Nevada, led to some interesting observations about dietary amounts. One coprolite whose original (dry) weight was 25.0 grams yielded 5.8 grams of fish bone representing no fewer than 101 small chubs whose total live weight is calculated at 208.4 grams (7.4 ounces). This was the fish component for one particular meal for one person.

Coprolites of humans and other animals preserved in dry deposits usually contain pollen grains. The pollen evidence may indicate the season of the year when the feces were voided as well as provide an indication of the variety of local flora.

Only in parts of the Old World has enough information been collected to enable prehistorians to write general studies of special hunting pursuits such as fowling, seal hunting, and fishing (G. Clark 1946, 1948a, 1948b). The general overview of the history of man's economic pursuits in Europe by G. Clark (1952) has not, for some reason, stimulated anyone to attempt a similar synthesis of data for North America, and such a work would be very helpful if available.

Occasionally an archeological report listing bony remains of deep sea (benthic) fishes will interpret their presence as the result of deep sea fishing by the people in whose refuse middens the bones occur (for example, Fitch 1969). This interpretation may be correct, but the archeologist should be aware of the alternative possibility that deep-living fish may be cast ashore by giant waves of gale force. This occurred in February, 1960, near Monterey and large numbers of fish with habitat ranges between 50 and 200 meters deep were thrown on shore (Follett 1970). In prehistoric times such a "windfall" would doubtless have been exploited by local peoples, with the result that the bones of these fish would find their way into the occupation refuse.

Not only would the archeologist usually like to know what the dietary range was—that is, the list of edible materials available to and exploited by the people he is studying—but in addition he would like to know the relative amounts of each food resource. He probably can never hope to secure very precise data on these subjects, but he should at least go as far as he reasonably can toward this end when collecting and interpreting the archeological facts. There are studies reporting the percentages of animal and vegetal foods in the diet of modern hunting peoples who live in a similar environment and follow a way of life similar to prehistoric people. These studies (Table 3) provide the archeologist with data which he can compare to

TABLE 3 PERCENT OF MAIN DIETARY RESOURCES IN FIVE NORTH AMERICAN TRIBES (data from Driver (1957), Powers (1877), Stefannson (1937), and R. White (1963)).

	Agricultural products	Wild plant products	Fish	Animal products
Colorado River Yuma	.40[1]	.35[2]	.15	.10[3]
South California[4] Inland Luiseno	—	.75[5]	.05	.20
South California[4] Coastal Luiseno	—	.40[5]	.50	.10
Pyramid Lake Paiute, Nevada	—	.25	.50	.25
Arctic Eskimo	—	—	.30	.70

[1] Maize, beans, pumpkins
[2] Mesquite, screwbean, river and desert plants
[3] Rabbits, wood rats, ducks
[4] Estimated from variable percentages
[5] Includes acorns, seeds, greens

those he has recovered from excavations. Dry cave sites, of course, will offer nearly ideal conditions of preservation so that by combining food residues found in refuse deposits with information on diet from coprolites, as was done at Lovelock Cave, Nevada (Ambro 1967; Heizer and Napton 1970) and the Tehuacan Valley caves, Mexico (Callen 1967; MacNeish 1967b), a reasonably complete picture of ancient diet can be reconstructed. Data on economy from open sites are much more difficult to amass because only exceptional circumstances of preservation, such as carbonization of seeds or imprints of grains on the base of pottery vessels before they were fired (for example, Helbaek 1953), provide us with evidence which ordinarily has vanished. Thus, to cite one instance, Dorwin (1971:366–369) makes good use of the information on the amount of meat available to the occupants of the Bowen site in central Indiana, but he cannot assess the importance of vegetable food because this kind of evidence was not recovered. In the American Southwest, Hough (1930) estimated that prehistoric Puebloan peoples' diet consisted of the following proportions: maize (85 percent), other vegetal foods (9 percent), animal food (5 percent) and minerals (1 percent). Fairservis (1967) provides a table of daily dietary items that he believes may have been eaten in ancient times at Mohenjo-daro.

Much has been written about what is termed "ecology," the interaction between man and his natural environment. Man as part of the ecosystem, by which term is meant the triple combination of biome (plants and animals), habitat (soil and climate), and culture, must never be lost sight of in the study and interpretation of archeological materials. All general archeological reports employ the ecological approach, whether or not the author uses the word, because it is not possible to write about culture and what people did without referring to the biome and habitat. Economic systems are a result of the direct application of culture (hunting or farming tools, types of crops grown, kinds of animals hunted, and the like) to the conditions and available plant and animal life (biome). Size of the human population in an area is a reflection of the existing natural features exploited through the use of tools.

CHEMICAL ANALYSIS OF RESIDUES

At times qualitative analysis may lead to the identification of certain residues that an archeologist recovers. By way of example, we cite the chemical analysis of cheese residues in Egyptian tubular jars of the First and Second Dynasties (W. Emery 1961:212), the determination that mercury poisoning was probably responsible for a prehistoric death (Aitken 1961:169; E. T. Hall 1963:195), chemical analyses of Egyptian beer and yeast residues (Lucas 1962:5–13; Winlock 1942:193), demonstration by microscopic examination of residues that wheat beer and mead had been contained in two north German drinking horns found in a peat bog (Grüss 1932), analyses of wine residues in Egyptian pots (Lucas 1962:20), chemical analyses of "bog butter" (adipocere) preserved in wooden casks of Scottish bogs (McAdam 1882, 1889), and verification of the supposition that fat was used as fuel in lamps of the Ertebolle culture of Denmark through chemical analysis of scrapings from the basins of lamps (Mathiassen 1935). A similar demonstration that certain vessels from Irish sites were lamps was made by R. Moss (1910). An effort to determine by chemical analysis of "cakes" or "dottels" whether supposedly prehistoric "Puebloan tobacco pipes" were pipes for smoking tobacco was inconclusive (R. Dixon and Stetson 1922).

It may one day be possible, by use of chemical analyses, to determine the kinds of activities that were carried out in particular spots within a site. Research has not yet progressed to the point where this has been done, but in a large site, with sufficiently refined qualitative chemical techniques, it might be possible to identify areas where grain was ground, acorns were leached, pottery was made, animals were butchered, and so on. Biek (1969) has provided the best review yet made of techniques that would be applicable to this kind of investigation. This as yet untested kind of analytical archeology already has a number of proposed problems to work on when someone with the necessary technical knowledge, time, money, and interest goes to work on them (for example, Heizer 1960:99; Hester and Heizer 1971; Isaac 1969: 12). As a guess we think that some of the ultrarefined methods already developed in geochemistry, criminology, and forensic medicine may be applicable directly to archeological problems.

ANALYSIS OF SITES

Sites themselves, irrespective of the artifacts within them, may be analyzed. The discovery of buried sites has been facilitated by chemical analyses of the soil. Where analyses of soil have been taken at short intervals over a wide area, sites may be recognized by their distinctive chemistry (Cook and Heizer 1965). High percentages of phosphate within a site may also indicate the former presence of bones (Solecki 1953). Finally, sites may be examined for the clues they give to age and past climate.

In North America geologists are often consulted by archeologists who have discovered evidence of Paleo-Indian implements in alluvial deposits. As examples, the reader may wish to consult Antevs' studies of the geology of the Naco and Lehner sites in southern Arizona, where flint implements were found associated with bones of mammoths (Antevs 1953b, 1959); the geological study of the San Jon site in eastern New Mexico by Judson (1953); the geomorphological study of the Lime Creek area in Nebraska (Schultz, Lueninghoener, and Frankforter 1948); and the geological studies by J. Moss (1951a, 1951b) and G. Holmes (1951) of early man sites in the Eden Valley, Wyoming. These studies, which lead to conclusions about the age of sites and the prehistoric climate, are paralleled by similar work in Europe (Bordes 1954 and Müller-Beck 1957:5–23).

Because sites are often too large to warrant complete excavation, sampling techniques requiring the least amount of energy or wasted effort have been devised to secure a reliable sample of surface materials or buried objects. In California shell mounds and earth middens, and the contents of excavated pits, have been screened, the constituents sorted and identified, and calculations made of the total amount present in the site mass of each class of material (stone, bone, and the like). Although it is assumed (or better, hoped) that such sampling does provide a reliable body of information, there is reason to believe that it does not, because the sampling has not been properly performed. The theory and practice of archeological sampling are too complex to attempt to discuss here; the student is encouraged to read several of the published works cited at the end of this chapter.

Technical analyses are ancillary aids to archeology (Brothwell and Higgs 1963; Hammond 1971b). In themselves they provide data that only archeologists can interpret. Before archeologists begin to dig, they should have a clear idea of the kinds of information they may be able to recover, and if they are adequately "briefed" they will have a better chance to recognize what they see, because its appearance will suggest some human action in the past. For this reason the archeologist should have read as widely as possible the findings of other excavators, so that, when he digs, as little as possible will escape his eye. This suggestion is particularly appropriate for archeologists who analyze chemical vestiges, which may not appear to be important by themselves, but which, after they are analyzed, may provide important information.

THE PROBLEM OF HOAXES AND FAKES

Most archeologists will not be bothered with the "planting" in their site of specimens that do not belong there. Occasionally, however, a malicious individual or a person who does not understand the serious nature of archeological investigation will play a practical joke and bury, for later "discovery" in apparently undisturbed ground, a specimen that he found elsewhere. Most archeologists will simply not stand for this kind of horseplay, and, if discovered, the practical joker will be told to leave. The most notorious instance of faking and planting of objects—in this instance, human bones—in a deposit is that of Piltdown Man. The story of this hoax has been told by Weiner (1955), who, with admirable courtesy, restrains himself from drawing the logical conclusion and naming the perpetrator. The demonstration by analytical chemical methods that the bones were forgeries was made by K. P. Oakley and his colleagues in the British Museum. An earlier instance, in which a human lower jaw was said to have been discovered in Pleistocene gravels, involved the father of paleolithic archeology, Boucher de Perthes, Having offered a reward for finds of bones to the quarry workers in the Moulin-Quignon pit, the temptation was too much for one worker who, in 1863, presented the jaw to Boucher de Perthes and claimed, and received, his reward. The jaw was finally shown, by application of fluorine test, to be more recent than it was alleged to be (Oakley 1964a:111–116). What is probably the earliest instance of an attempted archeological hoax in the New World concerns the sixteenth-century planting of Roman coins in a site, "discovering" them, and citing these as evidence to bolster the theory of the Old World origin of the American Indians (Castellanos 1589:Canto sesto:19). A more recent example of planting artifacts was at the Domebo mammoth kill site in Oklahoma—an attempt fortunately unsuccessful, but which unfortunately led to rumors that all of the projectile points found at the site were planted (Leonhardy 1966:preface).

Many forgeries make their appearance in museum collections, where they may be taken as genuine until somone becomes suspicious of their authenticity and examines them from a new viewpoint. It was actually for this reason that the Piltdown hoax was exposed, because it became increasingly difficult to see how the morphological anomalies of the bones could be reconciled with what was otherwise known of human evolution. More recent examples are the discovery that the remarkable Etruscan terra-cotta warrior statues in the Metropolitan Museum of Art in New York are recent forgeries (Von Bothmer and Noble 1961) and that a well-known cast gold figurine representing Tizoc, an Aztec lord, proved to be of modern manufacture (Easby and Dockstader 1964).

An increasing amount of faking is being done, mostly for financial gain. The forgers often work hand in hand with dealers who sell to private collectors and museums. Archeologists are often asked to give their opinion on whether a piece is genuine or fake. If an archeologist is willing to provide such an opinion, he must base it on his knowledge of what he has seen of undoubtedly genuine pieces that the specimen in question resembles. Often the proof that a piece is genuine depends on complicated, time-consuming, and often expensive chemical and physical testing. The archeologist should not forget that in ancient times there were also copiers and forgers (Partington 1947).

REFERENCES

Laboratory and Instrumental Analytical Methods of Artifact Examination: Aitken 1961; Beck and others 1971; Biek 1969; Brill 1971; Brothwell and Higgs 1969; Frison 1968; Heizer and Graham 1967:127–129; Hodges 1964; Jones, Weaver, and Stross 1967; Johnson and Stross 1965; Key 1963; Levey 1967; Lucas 1962; MacDonald and Sanger 1968; Movius and Brooks 1971; Movius and others 1968; Pyddoke 1963; Römisch-Germanisches Zentralmuseum zu Mainz 1959, 1965; Rosenfeld 1965; Semenov 1964; Tite 1972; Wilmsen 1968; Yao and Stross 1965. See also the journal *Archaeometry.*

Analysis and Description of Pottery: Alvarez, Franco, and Escobar 1967; Chase 1971; H. Colton 1953; Hodges 1964:Chap. 18; March 1934; Matson 1951, 1960, 1965, 1971; Olin and Sayre 1971; Perlman and Asaro 1971; Sayre and Chan 1971; A. Shepard 1956, 1966, 1971.

Analysis and Examination of Metals; Comparison of Metal Artifacts with Ore Deposits: Bastian 1961; Biek 1963; Britton and Richards 1969; Caley 1949, 1971; Carter 1971; Coghlan 1940, 1960; Dougherty and Caldwell 1966; Drier 1961; Fields and others 1971; Friedman and others 1966; Gordus 1971; Hall 1971; Pittioni 1960; Samolin 1965; Schroeder and Ruhl 1968; C. Smith 1971; Wertime 1964; Yao and Stross 1965.

Identification of Sources of Obsidian and Other Stones through Petrographic and Other Methods of Analysis: Cann and Renfrew 1964; Castiglioni, Fussi, and d'Agnolo 1963; J. Dixon, Cann, and Renfrew 1968; Gordus, Griffin, and Wright 1971; Green, Brooks, and Reeves 1967; Heizer and Williams 1965; Heizer, Williams, and Graham 1965; Jack and Heizer 1968; Jope 1953; Keiller, Piggott, and Wallis 1941; Negbi 1964; Parks and Tieh 1966; Renfrew 1968a; Renfrew, Cann, and Dixon 1965; Renfrew, Dixon, and Cann 1966; Shotten 1969; Stevenson, Stross, and Heizer 1971; E. Stone 1924; Stross and others 1968; Stross and others 1971; H. Thomas 1923; Wallis 1955; Williams and Heizer 1965a, 1965b; G. A. Wright 1969.

Preservation of Cloth and Basketry and Technical Analysis of These Materials: K. Dixon 1957; I. Emery 1966; Heizer and Krieger 1956; Henshall 1951; W. Holmes 1881; I. Johnson 1967; MacNeish, Nelken-Terner, and Johnson 1967; Miner 1936; Morris and Burgh 1941; Munger and Adams 1941; Rachlin 1955; Weltfish 1930, 1932.

Soil Analysis: Analytical Methods, Dating, Interpretation of Archeological Sites: G. Arrhenius 1931, 1954; O. Arrhenius 1934, 1963; Atkinson 1957; Biek

1969; Carter 1956; Cook 1950, 1964; S. Cook, Brooks, and Ezra-Cohn 1961; S. Cook and Heizer 1962, 1965; Cornwall 1958, 1960, 1963; U. Cowgill 1961; Dauncey 1952; Deetz and Dethlefson 1963; Dietz 1957; Eddy and Dregne 1964; Lee 1969; Limbrey 1972; Lotspeich 1961; Lutz 1951; R. Parsons 1962; Ruhe 1965; Saucier 1966; Simonsen 1954; Soil Survey Staff 1962; Sokoloff and Carter 1952; Solecki 1951; Van der Merwe and Stern 1972.

Identification of Animals Secured and Used by Prehistoric Peoples (Methods, Examples, Cultural Significance): Biesele 1968; Brainerd 1940; Chaplin 1965, 1971; G. Clark 1954:70–95; Cornwall 1956; Dawson 1969; Flannery 1967b; Gabel 1967; Glass 1951; Higham 1968; Lawrence 1951; Lehmer 1952; Leroi-Gourhan 1952; Lorch 1939; MacNeish 1967b; M. Martin 1936; Olsen 1961a, 1961b, 1964, 1971; Payne 1968; Perkins 1960; C. Reed 1963; T. White 1952, 1956; Ziegler 1965.

Calculating Minimum Number of Animals of Individual Species Present in an Archeological Site (Methods, Body Weights): Einarsen 1948; Flannery 1968; Hole and Flannery 1962:126–127; Hole, Flannery, and Neely 1969: 262–330; E. Kuhn 1938:256; Lehmer 1954:170; McPherron 1967:190–200; Murie 1951; Perkins 1969:177; Sheldon 1933; W. T. Stein 1963:216–219; Wettstein 1924; T. White 1953b.

Archeological Contributions to the History of Domesticated Animals: Angress and Reed 1962; G. Clark 1947; Coon 1951; Drew, Perkins, and Daly 1971; R. Dyson 1953; Flannery 1965, 1969; Murray 1970; Perkins 1969; C. Reed 1960, 1961; Ucko and Dimbleby 1969; Zeuner 1963.

Inferences about Climate Based on Animal Bones in Archeological Deposits: Bordes and Prat 1966; Bouchud 1954; Garrod and Bate 1937:I:139–153; Hargrave 1939; A. Harris 1963; Higgs 1965; Hokr 1951; MacNeish 1958; Soergel 1939, 1940.

Snails and Molluscs from Archeological Sites as Ecological Indicators: Allen and Cheatum 1961; F. Baker 1937; Barreis 1969; Burchell 1961; Cunnington 1933; Emiliani and others 1964; Germain 1923; Geyer 1923; Lambert 1960; Matteson 1959, 1960; Richards 1937; P. Sears 1952.

Determining through Plant and Animal Remains whether a Site Was Seasonally Occupied: G. Clark 1954; Heizer 1960; MacNeish 1964; Meighan and others 1958:9–10; D. Thompson 1939.

Analysis and Constituents of Prehistoric Human Coprolites: Callen 1965, 1967, 1969; Callen and Cameron 1960; Colyer and Osborne 1965; R. Cowan 1967; Follett 1967; Heizer 1967; Heizer and Napton 1970; Napton 1969; Roust 1967; Samuels 1965; P. Watson and Yarnell 1966; Yarnell 1969.

Pollen Analyses of Animal and Human Cave Coprolites: P. Martin 1961; P. Martin, Sabels, and Shutler 1961; P. Martin and Sharrock, 1964; Napton 1969.

Ecological Approach in Archeology: P. Baker 1962; Bennett 1944; Burnham 1972; Childe 1946; J. D. Clark 1965; Coe and Flannery 1964; E. Evans 1956; A. Hawley 1944; Helm 1962; Hole 1966, 1970; Hole and Flannery 1968; Hole, Flannery, and Neely 1969; Meighan and others 1958; Sanders 1965; P. Sears 1953a, 1953b; Thenius 1961a, 1961b; Watanabe 1966.

Screening Soils and Archeological Sites to Identify Kinds and Amounts of Economic and Industrial Refuse: Ambrose 1967; Barghoorn 1944; S. Cook 1946; S. Cook and Heizer 1951, 1962; S. Cook and Treganza 1947, 1950; Green and others 1967:201–215; Greenwood 1961; Heizer 1960:94–99; J. Hester and Conover 1970; Meighan and others 1958; Niemeyer and Schiappacasse 1971; Rappaport and Rappaport 1967; Struever 1968a; Terrell 1967; Treganza and Cook 1948.

Theory and Practice of Archeological Sampling: L. Binford 1964; G. Cowgill 1970; J. Hill 1967; Ragir 1967; Rootenberg 1964; Vescelius 1955.

Detection of Fakes and Hoaxes: Cooney 1963; Easby and Dockstader 1964; Ekholm 1964a; Gettens and Usilton 1955; Keisch and others 1967; Peterson 1953; Plenderleith 1952; de Pradenne 1932; Randall 1908; Reith 1970; Stross 1960; Vayson 1932; Wakeling 1912.

General Surveys of Natural Science Applications to Archeology: Aitken 1961; Archaeo-physika 1965; Biek 1963; Brill 1971; Brothwell and Higgs 1969; Judson 1961; F. G. Rainey 1966; Rainey and Ralph 1966; Royal Society of London 1970; Stross 1971. See also the journal *Archaeometry* published by the Oxford University Research Laboratory for Archaeology and the History of Art (Vol. I, 1958–Vol. XIII, 1971) and *MASCA Newsletter* (No. 1, 1965) published by the Museum, University of Pennsylvania.

PART IV

DATING
THE EVENTS
IN PREHISTORY

Many important problems in archeology cannot be solved at present because our techniques for deriving chronology are not well enough developed to give results of sufficient precision. This difficulty is immediately evident to anyone who has worked on a problem whose solution depends on precise dates. Such problems have to do with origins, influences, diffusions of ideas or artifacts, the direction of migrations of peoples, rates of change, and sizes of populations in settlements. In general, any question that requires a definite statement of the type, *A* is earlier than *B*, depends on dating. Then, if it can be shown that *A* is earlier than *B*, and not contemporary with or later than *B*, the two alternative hypotheses can be ruled false. An enormous amount of ambiguity in archeology would be removed if answers to such apparently simple questions could be obtained readily. Unfortunately, often they cannot.

The recent corrections in radiocarbon dating give a good example of the degree to which changes in dates themselves affect interpretations of cultural developments. Renfrew (1969, 1970 a, and b) discusses some of the ways in which corrected radiocarbon dates have entirely changed conceptions of the relationship between the Neolithic and Bronze Age cultures of Europe and those of the Aegean. For example, it had been customary to interpret the building of megalithic tombs in western Europe in terms of colonization and influence from the Mediterranean. Now it is known that these structures *preceded* those that were thought to be the prototypes. For example, the final building of Stonehenge and the nearby Wessex burials in southern England had been attributed to Mycenaean influence; now they have been shown to be some 500 years older. The reversal of relative dates thus requires a complete change in the theories that are offered in explanation of the building of these structures. "The moral which we should not fail to draw, however, is that the new dates should not simply change our chronologies. They render meaningless so much that has been written in recent years that there must have been serious inadequacies in our whole approach to the past, not simply in our chronology" (Renfrew 1970a:209).

Archeology is unique with respect to the other branches of the social sciences and humanities in its ability to discover, and to arrange in chronological sequence, certain episodes in human history that have long since passed without the legacy of written records. But the contributions of archeology to this sort of reconstruction depend largely on our ability to make chronological orderings, to measure relative amounts of elapsed time, and to relate these units to our modern calendar.

Few cultural interpretations in archeology and none that have unique interest with respect to anthropology generally can be made without reference to time. Moreover, none can have demonstrated validity if the chronology used is not accurate and appropriate—accurate in the sense of correct, and appropriate in the sense of applicable in the situation under study. This remark is unfortunately not trite, because there are examples in most archeological journals where its tenets were ignored. It is not pedestrian nit-picking to ask that time be controlled when it is a priori obvious that many answers (all of them if they have historical implications) depend absolutely on it. We would go further and say that there cannot be "proof" of a theory about cultural process unless time can be controlled.

Time is treated in most serious general works on archeology, but the discussion usually centers on the technical aspects of its determination; for example, how to do tree-ring, radiocarbon, or cross dating. Relatively little attention is paid to exploring the properties of time derived from each method. Because of the pronounced differences among the premises on which the various methods of dating are based, it is useful to discuss briefly the nature of archeologic time and its implications for interpreting the past.

Concepts of Chronology

Most authors (for instance, Oakley, 1964b) make a basic distinction between relative and absolute chronology, but this is actually irrelevant for all uses except establishing rates of change; otherwise one always wants relative chronology, and absolute dates are decidedly secondary, if of any real interest at all. Absolute or chronometric dates state the age as the exact number of years that have elapsed since a fixed beginning date, in the fashion of a calendar. Thus the year George Washington entered the White House as President was 1789; the year Abraham Lincoln entered the White House was 1861. Second are *relative* or *indirect* dates where the age is given, not in terms of years, but as "younger than" or "older than" some other event. For example, we can say that relative to Lincoln, Washington's presidency was earlier. Stating this relation does not tell us how much earlier, but the two events are fixed *in their proper sequential position*. Most archeological datings are of the relative type, where it is known that Culture *A* is older than Culture *C*, but how old *A* and *C* are, or how much later *C* is than *A* in terms of number of years, is unknown.

For purposes of discussion we can distinguish four bases on which all dating methods stand. Three are as follows: cyclical events such as the movements of the sun and moon on which most calendars are based; constants such as the speed of light or the rate of vibration of quartz crystals (at the moment of no particular interest in archeology); and progressive or cumulative change as in the decay of C^{14} molecules, the cumulative increase in the hydration layer of obsidian, or changes in the form of artifacts. A fourth basis for dating is stratigraphy. Because the relation among dating methods is not always obvious, we shall try to point out what the implications of their use in archeology may be.

Absolute Time

All of us are familiar with calendars and clocks that are based on the observed periodicity of certain natural events. Calendars give elapsed time measured relative to the movements of heavenly bodies; clocks are ultimately related to the same cycle, and time consists essentially of subdivisions of it. The important point about these measurements (and more precise measurements now in use) is that they depend on the repetition of events at uniform intervals In this sense, a day is a day without regard to the year in which it occurs.

With calendric and horologic time, it is easy to date the succession or synchrony of events anywhere in the world. It permits placing of chronologically succesive but geographically separate events, and ultimately establishes the basis for studies of rates of change, differential development in separate areas, and the identification of the geographic sources of widespread cultural influences. Analogous use of time in our daily lives allows contest judges to award the prize to the first entrant with the correct answers and to pick the fastest runners in three separately run heats.

Cumulative or Progressive Change

Several of the dating methods described in Chapters 12 and 13 are based on natural phenomena whose changes can be measured and made to yield a date. The most familiar of these is radiocarbon dating, which depends on the fact that the C^{14} isotope decays at a known rate. Knowing the rate and the amount present in a sample enables one to calculate how many radiocarbon years have elapsed since the death of the organism whose remains are being dated. Obsidian-hydration dating also depends on progressive change: that the hydration layer on glass is added to continuously. A measurement of the hydration layer is thus a statement about age and can be translated into either relative or absolute dating, depending on the circumstances.

The important thing to remember about dates that are based on progressive change is that they need not be, and usually are not, directly translatable into calendric years. These are dates in their own system, and it is a matter for further investigation to determine the correlation between such dates and the calendar.

Relative Dating

The use of stratigraphy is ultimately the most important method for establishing relative dating (Chap. 4). It depends on the fact that earlier deposits lie under later deposits. Usually stratigraphy gives the relative ages of deposits only within a single site, although special circumstances (such as the deposition of ash layers from a single eruption of a volcano) may allow one to relate the stratigraphy of two or more sites with as much precision as one can ordinarily attain within one site.

Although stratigraphic levels give chronologic relations, they tell very little about absolute amounts of elapsed time or even of relative amounts of elapsed time. A statement that one find is "older by a foot or two" (Napier 1964:88) tells nothing about elapsed time. Stratigraphic levels represent unequal lengths of calendar time, and two such units are only accidentally of the same duration. The kind of chronology that one can derive from stratigraphy is thus limited to telling which unit is earlier, and one can infer only the barest information about relative lengths of time. Thick layers *may* have taken longer to accumulate than thin layers, but this is not always true. It should be evident that stratigraphic units in themselves cannot be related to calendars.

If the archeologist is unable to relate levels in several sites to one another by stratigraphy, he must turn to other methods, of which the most important is known as *cross dating*; it involves the comparison of artifacts found in the stratigraphic levels (Chap. 13). Stated in its simplest form, the idea behind cross dating is that similar artifacts are approximately contemporary. The greater the similarity, the closer the ages. Cross dating depends on the fact that certain artifacts—coins, types of pottery, and arrowheads—have a limited occurrence during the life of any culture. When "identical" artifacts are found at separated sites, the principle of cross dating states that the two sites are roughly the same age, namely, within the span during which the artifact was used. Some artifacts have a much shorter life span than others have, and as a consequence are better "index fossils" or "horizon markers."

Using the occurrence of artifacts, and/or their frequencies, one can compare isolated stratigraphic units and judge whether they approach contemporaneity. In the absence of a known stratigraphic sequence somewhere, however, it may not be possible to tell, from the artifacts alone, what the relative ages of the deposits are. It is thus necessary to use stratigraphy and cross dating together to determine relative ages of sites that are separated; that is, there must be some way independent of the two occurrences in question to decide on the relative ages.

It often happens that *trends of change* can be distinguished in the archeologic record. The trend from the use of stone to bronze to iron is a simple illustration. A site in which one found flint arrowheads would ordinarily be judged earlier than a site in which one found bullets. Knowing trends of this sort, one can resort to "typological" dating, at times an exceedingly useful technique for ordering materials that are temporally exclusive and distinct in time.

Segmenting Time

Archeologists are accustomed to dividing time into periods, phases, levels, and the like; for example, "all are of Mousterian or Acheuleo-Mousterian age" (Boule and Vallois 1957:375). Periods and phases ordinarily include deposits that have several levels—in other words, the larger groupings are usually based both on stratigraphic breaks and on the changes in the content of the levels. Most students of history would agree that although change is continuous there are times when its rate or impact is increased or lessened. The exploitation of a new power source, a period of warfare, and similar discontinuous events provide criteria that enable one to recognize distinct periods in a cultural continuum.

For historical periods, it is not necessary to use periods or ages except as a shorthand device to denote a certain kind of activity within a certain range of time. Archeologists, however, frequently use their periods as though they were equivalent to units on a calendar. A phase comes to be thought of as we think of a decade or a century, except that instead of being so numbered, it is usually named.

Implications of Archeological Time

In fact, there is no such thing as *an* archeologic time. From the preceding discussion, the reader can see that there are many kinds of time that range from years of known and constant duration, to the life span of an artifact type that is of unknown and unpredictable duration, to the stratigraphic levels of a site whose principal chronologic significance is that they demarcate earlier from later strata. In practical terms, archeologists use and must interpret dates from a wide variety of sources whose degree of precision is highly variable and whose correlation to absolute chronology is uncertain and not mutually commensurable. Much of archeological dating, in other words, represents more a statement of faith than a sober appraisal of proved evidence. It can hardly be stressed too strongly that this is a sad statement of affairs for scientists whose chief claim to fame is their ability to interpret unique and long-forgotten records of man's past. It is not going too far to say that many professional archeologists have overstepped the bounds of credibility in assigning relative and absolute dates to sites that on closer inspection have yielded only the most tenuous evidence of age. It is especially true that many interpretations that absolutely depend on accurate dating assume a precision that is far greater than warranted. It is also true that archeologists have begun to pose questions that require far more accurate dates. The chapters that follow will describe the present state of the art of dating archeological remains. But by this time the student should be sufficiently warned that, in spite of occasional impressive sophistication in techniques, most dating methods are far too imprecise to help us much with a number of the most important problems we now pose. Even today, despite a full century of digging, analyzing materials, and publishing their findings, archeologists are not in possession of enough facts to do more than sketch the history of man in any except the broadest terms. Only now are we seeing the first attempts at writing the history of man and his culture (J. Hawkes and Woolley 1963; G. Clark and Piggott 1965; G. Clark 1961), but these are only outlines.

CHAPTER TWELVE

DATING BY PHYSICAL-CHEMICAL METHODS

R ADIOCARBON DATING

For archeologists, one of the most important discoveries of the twentieth century was made just after World War II. In 1949 a method for determining the absolute age of certain ancient and previously undatable organic materials was announced (Arnold and Libby 1949; Kamen 1963). The method was devised to measure the amount of low-level radioactivity of carbon remaining in ancient and dead material of organic origin. With this measurement it was possible to tell how long ago the once living plant or animal died. Thus archeologists could learn the approximate year in which a tree was cut for a house beam, how long ago a man represented by a mummy had died, or when the fire had been burned in a fireplace. The immediate enthusiasm of archeologists went far beyond the limits of the method as it was first developed. Most archeologists had had "guess dates" for their materials, and they were aware that a system of absolute dating would probably invalidate some of their guesses. Unfortunately, some of the new dates were so far off the expected, and many so internally inconsistent, that some archeologists simply chose to ignore them. After this pendulum swing of enthusiasm, more sober judgments prevailed, and the "bugs" in the system were largely worked out. The radiocarbon method for dating has proved itself useful when the laboratory uses all possible care and the archeologist supplies material that has been collected with proper methods. In view of its importance, carbon-14 (C^{14}) dating will be described in some detail.

In essence, radiocarbon dating is based on the following argument. Neutrons produced by cosmic radiation enter the earth's atmosphere and react with the nitrogen isotope N^{14}. The reaction produces a heavy isotope of carbon, C^{14}, which is radioactive and has a half-life of about 5730 years.[1] Libby's (1955:2) equation describing the reaction is

$$N^{14} + n = C^{14} + H^1$$

Chemically, C^{14} seems to behave exactly as ordinary nonradioactive carbon, C^{12}, does. Thus the C^{14} atoms readily mix with the oxygen in the earth's atmosphere, together with C^{12}, and eventually enter into all living things as part of the normal oxygen-exchange process that involves all living plants and animals. As long as matter is living and hence in exchange with the atmosphere, it continues to receive C^{14} and C^{12} atoms in a constant proportion. After death the organism is no longer in exchange with the atmosphere and no longer absorbs atoms of contemporary carbon.

After the death of an organism the C^{14} contained in its physical structure begins to disintegrate at the rate of one half every 5730 years; thus, by measuring the amount of radiocarbon remaining, one can establish the time when the plant or animal died. Half-life (t ½) is measured by counting the number of beta radiations emitted per minute (cpm) per gram of material. Modern C^{14} emits about 15 cpm/g, whereas C^{14} 5700 years old should emit about 7.5 cpm/g. In the disintegration the C^{14} returns to N^{14}, emitting a beta particle in the process. Thus:

$$C^{14} = B - + N^{14} +$$

There were several assumptions about the process that had to be verified before it could be used with confidence. For example, it was necessary to verify that the rate of cosmic radiation through long periods of time has remained constant; that the concentration of C^{14} in the reservoir of exchangeable carbon on the earth and in the atmosphere has not changed; and that C^{14} is distributed evenly throughout the atmosphere and living matter. Verification of these assumptions involved such things as possible errors in the calculation of a half-life, instances of differential levels of C^{14} among living things, the effect of atom bomb explosions on the production of C^{14} by atmospheric enrichment ("atom bomb effect"), and the effect on the ratio of C^{14} to C^{12} of burned fossil fuels such as coal and oil, which add nonradioactive carbon to the atmospheric reservoir ("Suess effect").

---

[1] The original Libby value for the half-life of C^{14} was 5568 ± 30 years. Research currently being carried on at several laboratories will result in final agreement on determination for this constant. For the present, the Fifth Radiocarbon Dating Conference, Cambridge, 1962, has accepted 5570 ± 30 years (the original value) as the half-life of radiocarbon, and made the decision to use A.D. 1950 as the standard for computing dates B.P. (Before Present). The best value now obtainable for the half-life is, however, 5730 ± 40 years. To convert published dates to new half-life, multiply them by 1.03 (*Radiocarbon* 5, 1963, "Editorial Statement").

For a number of years it was thought that the possible errors mentioned here were of relatively minor consequence, but more recent intensive research into radiocarbon dates, compared with calendar dates, shows that the natural concentration of C^{14} in the atmosphere has varied sufficiently to affect dates significantly, especially for periods older than 1500 B.C. The principal variables in the production of C^{14} are thought to be solar activity, climatic change, and variations in the magnetic dipole of the earth. Because scientists have not been able to predict the amount of variation theoretically, it has been necessary to find a parallel dating method of absolute accuracy to assess the correlation between C^{14} dates and the calendar.

The latest research in radiocarbon dating has centered on the attempt to correlate the dates with tree rings. At the present time it has been possible to extend a correlation back as far as 7100 years, although the data for more recent times are much more complete. The older dates depend on the few trees of great age, principally bristlecone pines, that still remain. The corrections that are presently available (Table 4) show that radiocarbon years and calendar years begin to diverge significantly after 1500 B.C., and from then until the limits of the correlation method are reached, the radiocarbon dates get progressively younger with respect to calendar dates. Thus a radiocarbon date of 2200 B.C. is about 500 years too young, according to the best estimated calendar age. There is some question whether the trend shown in the radiocarbon dates can be extrapolated to still older periods; if it can we may expect to find an error of 20–30 percent, or 2000–2500 years in the dates of older samples. It is important to stress, however, that *"it is presently impossible to determine on theoretical ground, what the relationship is between a radiocarbon date and the true age of a sample"* (Stuiver and Suess 1966:536). Thus we should adopt the habit of dating events in *radiocarbon years* rather than in calendar years, except when it is possible to use the correction factor. In all cases, however, the radiocarbon date should be included so that the reader will be aware that correction has been applied.

Radiocarbon dating depends on a number of other assumptions as well. For example, it had to be assumed that it was possible to obtain dependable samples of carbon from archeological contexts. Early results indicated that it was possible. One of the first samples run was a piece of wood from an Egyptian boat that had been dated by archeologists at 3750 years before the present. The date was based on texts and other archeological evidence. The average age of three runs of the radiocarbon sample was 3621 ± 180 (C-81)[2] (Fig. 58). After a series of confirmatory results had been secured, there seemed little reason to question the essential validity of the assumption that

[2] All radiocarbon dates are numbered in a lineal series by each laboratory. The laboratory is identifiable by the prefix letter(s); thus, for example, C=Chicago; Y= Yale; GRO=Groningen. Since 1959, dates from all laboratories are published in *Radiocarbon* (Vol. 1, 1959; Vol. 2, 1960, etc.). A list of all radiocarbon dates secured annually between 1950 and 1965 is available (Deevey, Flint, and Rouse 1967). See also Jelinek (1962b) and Movius (1960).

TABLE 4 MASCA CORRECTION FACTORS SUGGESTED METHOD OF ADJUSTMENT OF RADIOCARBON DATES TO CALENDRIC DATES BASED ON THE DETERMINATION OF AVERAGE DEVIATIONS FOR 250-YEAR PERIODS IN THE A.D. AND B.C. ERAS EXCEPT FOR THE FIRST AND LAST TWO PERIODS WHICH SPAN LONGER INTERVALS OF YEARS. C^{14} DATES ARE CALCULATED WITH THE 5730 HALF-LIFE (Michael and Ralph 1971:28, Table 1.5).

Time Period Represented by Radiocarbon Dates	Average Deviation of C^{14} Dates (+ = younger, − = older)	Calendric Period Represented by Precisely Dated Tree-Ring Samples	Number of Samples
A.D. 1525 – 1879	+ 50	A.D. 1500–1829 (329 years)	12
A.D. 1250 – 1524	0	A.D. 1250–1499	7
A.D. 975 – 1249	0	A.D. 1000–1249	8
A.D. 700 – 974	− 50	A.D. 750– 999	4
A.D. 450 – 699	− 50	A.D. 500– 749	11
A.D. 200 – 449	− 50	A.D. 250– 499	9
25 B.C.–A.D. 200	− 50	A.D. 1– 249	7
225 B.C.– 26 B.C.	0	249– 1 B.C.	7
450 – 226 B.C.	+ 50	499– 250 B.C.	7
675 – 451 B.C.	+ 50	749– 500 B.C.	7
900 – 676 B.C.	+100	999– 750 B.C.	8
1125 – 901 B.C.	+100	1249–1000 B.C.	10
1325 – 1126 B.C.	+150	1499–1250 B.C.	4
1550 – 1326 B.C.	+200	1749–1500 B.C.	9
1750 – 1551 B.C.	+200	1999–1750 B.C.	6
1900 – 1751 B.C.	+300	2249–2000 B.C.	12
2050 – 1900 B.C.	+400	2499–2250 B.C.	4
2225 – 2051 B.C.	+500	2749–2500 B.C.	6
2450 – 2226 B.C.	+550	2999–2750 B.C.	6
2650 – 2451 B.C.	+550	3249–3000 B.C.	7
2850 – 2651 B.C.	+650	3499–3250 B.C.	5
[3700 – 2951 B.C.]	+700	[4395–3645 B.C.] (750 years)	11
[4366 – 4060 B.C.]	+750	[5116–4810 B.C.] (306 years)	9
		Total	176

archeological materials could be dated with fair precision. Research since Libby's original announcement has gone far in an effort to achieve better laboratory techniques in the preparation and counting of samples.

In the predictable rush of enthusiasm, archeologists began to submit samples to Libby and others for dating. After large numbers of dates had been released, it became apparent that the system was creating as many new problems as it was solving. The dates could not always be justified on archeological grounds. As the evidence was examined, several likely sources of error were pointed out (E. Anderson and Levi 1952); none of them, however, involved the fundamental assumptions about the nature of C^{14}.

It has been thought that anomalous radiocarbon ages of shells of

FIG. 58 W. F. Libby's first results in testing the reliability of radiocarbon age measurements with samples of known age from Egypt (W. F. Libby, *Radiocarbon Dating*, Fig. 1).

fresh-water molluscs are caused by the incorporation of inactive carbon deriving from humus carried in solution in the water. A single radiocarbon date for an archeological level should be accepted with reserve, and efforts should be made to verify such single dates with additional check runs or by other methods for dating. Wood charcoal and pottery associated together may not be of the same age, and a radiocarbon date of the charcoal could be misleading if applied to the ceramics. An instance of this occurred at the site of Cuicuilco, in the Valley of Mexico, where charcoal from preceramic earth fill gave an age of 6715 ± 90 years but was associated with pottery known on other grounds to be 2700–2300 years old.

The ideal material for radiocarbon dating is wood charcoal burned at the time the archeological site was occupied. Bone burned at the time the site was inhabited can also be dated. Unaltered wood from dry sites, soot, grasses, dung (animal and human), well-preserved antler or tusk, paper, calcareous tufa formed by algae, lake muds (gyttja), parchment, peat, and chemically unaltered mollusc shells all contain enough C^{14} to allow them to be dated. Unburned bone contains a substance called collagen, which is rich in carbon, and this can be extracted and dated. The amounts of organic material required to make a reliable age determination vary with individual laboratories. For example, Geochron Laboratories (Cambridge, Mass.) operates as a commercial service,[3] having a fixed charge per age determination. It recommends the following amounts of material: charcoal, 8–12 grams; wood, 10–30 grams; shell, 30–100 grams; peat, 10–25 grams; bone, 20–100 grams. (For more complete lists, see Polach and Golson 1966: Table 3, and Ralph 1971.)

It is possible for a sample to become contaminated after it is removed from the ground. The first archeologists to submit samples often put them in paper boxes or padded them with cotton for shipping. This practice frequently resulted in mixing older with more recent carbon as a result of the fact that the modern cotton or rubbed-off paper became mixed with the sample. Other archeologists treated samples with an organic preservative to keep them from falling apart, thus introducing young radiocarbon into the old sample. It was also found that modern rootlets had frequently penetrated the charcoal as it lay in the ground. In some instances it was found that older carbon had been present. For example, where tar was used to coat wood, it had introduced older carbon into the sample. Another source of error lay in the fact that humic acids from the surface soil sometimes percolate into underlying archeological horizons. Here again, modern carbon can be introduced into an old sample. By the time archeologists began to recognize the many possible sources of contamination, physicists and chemists had begun to improve on the original techniques for preparing the samples by a rigorous cleaning process. All the recently developed methods for counting samples use similar techniques for their initial preparation. Washing samples in strong acid and alkali solutions and subsequently burning them have added considerably to the dependability of the determination. This important fact must be considered when one uses dates run between 1950 and 1955, the period when sample preparation did not always include the removal of contaminants.

Libby's original apparatus was primitive compared to that now in use. He used what is called the "screen-wall" technique, in which he reduced the organic material to carbon and then smeared it on the inner surface of a specially built Geiger counter. By contrast, modern methods change the carbon to a gas—carbon dioxide (CO_2), acetylene (C_2H_2), or methane (CH_4)— and count it in a proportional counter (for photos of apparatus, see Briggs and Weaver 1958). There has been a considerable gain in accuracy and reliability over the older technique, because the sample is not handled after it has been made ready for conversion to a gas. Thus the danger of radioactive contamination from the atmosphere, a disruptive factor introduced by atomic bomb tests, has been eliminated. With the gas-proportional counters, a much smaller sample is needed to make an age determination.

Two other methods are now being used by laboratories making radio-

---

[3] A complete listing of laboratories, including those that do commercial contract dating, may be found in *Radiocarbon*.

carbon determinations. One involves using CO_2 in a Geiger-Muller counter rather than solid carbon, as Libby first tried. The other uses the liquid scintillation spectrometer. Neither of these methods has yet proved better, for routine work, than use of the gas-proportional counter.

Another important refinement is isotopic enrichment. With the original methods, the effective range of radiocarbon dating was about 30,000 years. With the more modern systems, 50,000 years is the practical limit, but for samples of great importance an elaborate, expensive, and time-consuming process of isotopic enrichment can be carried out that will enable the scientist to ascertain the age of material as old as 70,000 years (Haring, deVries, and deVries 1958). On a practical basis, however, with isotopic enrichment the problems of contamination become much greater the older the sample is. A practical example will make this clear.

> The addition of 1 percent of modern carbon to a sample that is 5570 years old increases the specific radioactivity by 2 percent, so that the measured age of the sample is too small by 160 years, an error of 3 percent. For a sample that is 23,000 years old, the addition of 1 percent of modern carbon increases the specific radioactivity by 16 percent, corresponding to 1,300 years, an error of 5 percent. But for a sample that is 67,000 years old, the addition of 1 percent of modern carbon makes the radioactivity 40 times what it should be. The indicated age would be 37,000 years; this bears no relation to the true age and depends only on the degree of contamination (Aitken 1961:97).

Quite apart from matters of possible contamination, no sample is worth dating unless it is archeologically dependable. Archeologists must make sure that their samples are from undisturbed deposits. They should be prepared to tell the laboratory technicians how the sample was collected, the kind of deposit in which it was found, the kind of pretreatment they have given it—washing or sorting out of foreign material by hand—whether there were roots or humus-rich soil horizons near the sample, and anything else that might bear on its dependability. Here the responsibility rests squarely on the shoulders of the archeologists, who must take care to submit only samples of high quality.

It is necessary before leaving the subject of radiocarbon dating to mention two more topics. The first is the statistical expression of the dates and what it means (Spaulding 1958; Polach and Golson 1966). All dates are expressed in terms of a plus-or-minus factor. Thus the date for the Egyptian boat mentioned above was given as 3621 ± 180 years before the present. The plus-or-minus 180 is the range of one standard deviation; it indicates that 68 percent of the time the true age of the sample will lie between 3441–3801 years—that is, $3621 + 180/3621 - 180$—before the present. If we double the plus-or-minus factors, there will be a 95 percent probability—19 chances of 20—that the true age lies within these limits (that is, 3261–3981 years before the present). But "there are *no* limits within which the true age lies with absolute certainty" (Aitken 1961:98). We thus see that although the radiocarbon method is usually referred to as a method for securing absolute dates, it is in fact not an exact or precise time-determination method. At best, it provides dates that are more probably correct than wrong within the plus-or-minus sigma of error.

The second matter is the use of B.P. (Before Present) as opposed to B.C. (Before Christ) or A.D. (Anno Domini) when stating the age of a sample. For archeologists, the use of B.P. dates makes little sense. The machines count the years that have elapsed since the time the organism died, but archeologists need not. When dates are written B.P., persons reading them must continually update them. The compromise adopted in 1962 by the Fifth Radiocarbon Dating Conference to use A.D. 1950 as the standard for computing dates B.P. is not entirely satisfactory, although it is decidedly preferable to using a constantly changing date. The main problem that will arise from using A.D. 1950 is that dates published before the agreement have to be adjusted. (The new index to radiocarbon dates assembled by Deevey, Flint, and Rouse [1967] makes this adjustment.) A second problem is that archeologists as well as nonprofessionals have difficulty adjusting their thinking about the past when they must use several time scales. The mistakes made when one must shift between A.D. and B.C. are annoying at best.

Jelinek (1962b) has provided a very useful list of radiocarbon dates of archeological materials. In an annual volume entitled *Radiocarbon*, published by the American Journal of Science, appear lists of dates determined by the half-hundred active radiocarbon laboratories, and an index to these for the years 1950–1965 has recently been published (1967). Since 1969 an annual index has been published in *Radiocarbon*.

OTHER RADIOACTIVE DATING METHODS

Several other methods of dating depend on radioactive decay of elements. Many of these techniques cannot be applied to archeological materials because they are only effective on extremely old material or because they are based on material ordinarily not found in archeological sites. One method that may become valuable for dating very old archeological deposits is based on the decay of potassium-40.

Potassium–Argon Dating

Measurement of the ratio of potassium-40 (K^{40}) to the gas argon-40 (A^{40}) in many minerals extends the range of absolute dating far beyond the limits of radiocarbon. This method depends on the fact that radioactive K^{40} decays at a known rate (t $\frac{1}{2} = 1.3$ billion years) to form A^{40} By measuring the ratio of K^{40} to A^{40} in a mass spectrometer, one can calculate the age of the rocks. K-A dating also depends on these assumptions: that no argon was added or lost during the lifetime of the sample, and that measuring techniques are accurate. Of the three assumptions, the second is known to be incorrect in many instances; certain rocks leak argon at a greater rate than others do. For example, mica retains 80–100 percent of its argon, whereas feldspars retain 40–85 percent. Accurate dating of some of these minerals must await clearer definition of the factors that cause the leaking.

The value of the K-A dating is that potassium-rich rocks or ash deposits laid down by natural means before or following occupation of a site may be dated. Thus far the major application of the method on archeological materials has been at Olduvai Gorge in Tanganyika, where L. S. B. Leakey has found some of the oldest known fossil hominid bones. At Olduvai the beds containing the fossils are composed of volcanic tuffs (consolidated volcanic ash) alternating with clays. It appears from the freshness of the tools and bones that vulcanism occurred repeatedly while the site was being occupied, and that the material was covered by tuff soon after it was laid down. The tuffs make excellent dating material. The K-A dates from the lowest levels at Olduvai average 1,750,000 years. This age is much greater than would have been expected by many workers, and it has been questioned on stratigraphic and technical grounds (Howell 1962a). More recently stone artifacts excavated from what is interpreted as a former ground surface within a volcanic tuff layer east of Lake Rudolf, Kenya, have been dated by the K-A content of pumice pebbles enclosed in the tuff which provides an age of 2.1 ± 0.26 million years (Isaac, Leakey, and Behrensmeyer 1971). These are the oldest dated stone tools recovered through excavation.

Most archeological sites cannot be dated by K-A. It would do no good to date rocks brought into a site by man because they might well be millions of years older than the site. The major application of this method to archeology would seem to be only at sites where there has been vcolcanic activity that has caused the deposition of potassium-rich materials either shortly before or shortly after occupation by man.

Thermoluminescence

In 1960 Kennedy and Knopff announced a potentially useful method of dating archeological materials. This method was based on the fact that objects such as pottery that have been heated more than 400–500°C in the past could be dated by measurement of their thermoluminescent (TL) glow. Although the principle of thermoluminescence was well known, it was necessary to verify the practicality of routinely dating archeological materials. The theory seemed sound enough, but attempts to apply it to dating ancient pottery were unsuccessful in so many instances that the high hopes of many archeologists, having been raised by overconfident (and at times quite uninformed) persons, were dashed. As has occurred so often in natural science studies, what was required to develop a reliable procedure had to proceed at a slow step-by-step pace where each of the variables could be identified and compensated for, so that gradually a controlled technique would result. Such is often the way of success in science when an idea is conceived, the theoretical basis is examined, and enthusiasm over anticipated results exceeds early test-findings. Then sets in a period of reaction when optimism ebbs, but the effort at making the proposition prove out continues. Finally, with one small gain after another, the method is perfected and everyone is once more happy. The opposite, of course, may occur, when continued effort at correction fails at every step and the matter is then abandoned as beyond the technological capabilities of the generation to make the theory successfully applicable.

So, in a rough way, it has been with thermoluminescence dating, but now, after more than a decade of laboratory experiment, some reliable dating results have been achieved (Winter 1971: 133–146).

By way of explaining the principles of TL dating we quote from Mazess and Zimmerman's (1966) article:

> Thermoluminescence (TL) is the release in the form of light of stored energy from a substance when it is heated. The phenomenon occurs in many crystal-from nonconducting solids, and has been suggested as the basis of a dating technique for rocks and minerals. Naturally occurring radioactive elements in these materials are a nearly constant source of ionizing radiation. It is assumed that some of the electrons excited by this radiation become trapped in metastable states, a few electron volts above the ground state. Released from their traps by heating, the electrons return to the ground state, emitting light.
>
> Pottery accumulates such trapped electrons with time, and the amount of natural TL produced by a sherd therefore depends on the time elapsed since its last firing. The amount of natural TL also depends on the amount of ionizing radiation present, and on the nature and number of electron traps in the material (which determine the material's sensitivity to radiation-induced TL). By taking these factors into account, natural TL has been used for dating limestones, lava flows, ice, and pottery.

There are still many problems with the method, and various laboratories have taken different approaches to their solution. As one might expect under the circumstances, there is no standard set of methods for processing and analyzing ceramics, nor is there general agreement on whether the method should be used for relative or for absolute dates. Among the problems currently under investigation is the possible contamination of the sample by the addition of radioactive particles from the soil in which it was buried, or from exposure to cosmic rays. Other studies are aimed at using thermoluminescence for the dating of nonceramic materials. There has been some success in dating obsidian from El Chayal, Guatemala, but experiments with glass show that its potential depends heavily on the amount of uranium it contains (Ralph and Han 1971).

Aside from dating, one application of the method is in detecting modern ceramic fakes, because it is easy to determine that a pot was recently made when it fails to show an accumulation of TL.

At the present time active research on thermoluminescence is being carried out in laboratories at the following institutions: The University Museum, Philadelphia; the University of California at Los Angeles; the University of Wisconsin; the Research Laboratory for Archaeology, Oxford;

Nara and Kyoto Universities in Japan; and the Danish Atomic Energy Commission, Roskilde, Denmark.

Natural Low-Level Radioactivity (Beta Activity)

Buried archeological materials will vary in low-level radioactivity in the form of beta and alpha activity measured with a proportional-flow counter. Correlations between radioactivity of the soil-matrix environment and the material (bone or teeth are excellent subjects) can be determined.

The method shows great promise as a means of making distinctions in the relative age of two finds, of detecting intrusion of recent bones in older deposits, and of checking archeological materials for their fit with postulated climatic history.

Applications of the method have been made to a number of alleged or possible finds of early human remains in order to learn whether they are contemporary with the soil layer where they were (or are said to have been) recovered, or whether they are later intrusions. Such finds as the bones of Midland Man, Texas; the Piltdown bones; Arlington Springs Man, Santa Rosa Island, California; human osseous remains from the Llano Estacado, Texas; and the Lagow Sandpit remains from Texas have been examined by radiometric assay, and sometimes the results have enabled the investigators to decide that the bones are either ancient or relatively recent.

Lead-210 with a t ½ of 22 years is present in recently refined lead, which is a source of paint pigment. A number of forged old masters have been detected by age-dating the Pb-210 content of the paints used (Keisch 1968). This technique has no readily applicable archeological utility but is interesting from the methodological standpoint.

Fission Track Dating

A method for dating glassy materials such as obsidian which was exposed to high heat in ancient times, glass, or pottery glaze

> depends on the spontaneous fission of U^{238} atoms contained in glass taking place at a constant rate, and leaving fission tracks (that is, detectable damage trails of nuclear fragments). Once formed, the fission tracks in a glass disappear if the glass is heated above a critical temperature. It may be assumed that the density of spontaneous fission tracks of U^{238} atoms in a glass is proportional to the lapse of time after the glass was either produced or last heated above the critical temperature, and to the density of U^{238} atoms contained in the glass. The latter can be determined from the density of U^{238} atoms which are induced by bombarding the glass with a known dose of thermal neutrons. Then the lapse of time is given approximately by the simplified formula [Time= $6.12 \times 10^{-8} \times$ dose of thermal neutrons $\times$ (density of U^{238} fission tracks ÷ density of U^{235} atoms)] (Watanabe and Suzuki 1969).

An application of this method to the dating of archeological pottery has been carried out by Zimmerman (1971).

FIG. 59 Secular variation—London, Paris, Rome, and Boston. The time scale is indicated by dots at 20-year intervals. The curves up to 1900 are those obtained by Bauer (1899), who used recorded observations of declination and dip to determine an empirical formula. Bauer's extrapolations into periods when only declination was measured have been omitted. Subsequent to 1900 the data have been taken from Vestine and others (1947). (M. J. Aitken, *Physics and Archaeology.* Courtesy of John Wiley & Sons, Inc., 1961.)

PALEOMAGNETIC DATING

Magnetic dating can also give absolute dates. Variations in the angle of declination between magnetic north and true north and in the angle of dip of a magnetic needle have been recorded for 400 years in London and for shorter periods in other cities (Fig. 59). These measurements have shown that the magnetic field of the earth, as expressed in terms of angles of declination and dip, has changed, although not in easily predictable ways. Other studies have shown that a record of past angles of declination and dip is trapped in baked clay. In unfired clay the magnetic fields of the magnetite and hematite grains occur at random. When clay is fired, the grains are aligned with the magnetic field of the earth surrounding them. On cooling, the alignment of grains is "frozen" and can be recorded as long as the clay is preserved intact. This permanent alignment of grains is called thermo-remanent magnetism. Where records of past angles of declination and dip have been kept, it is possible to compare the values obtained from a piece of clay with the plotted values of historic records and arrive at the date of the archeological specimen of fired clay.

In practice the method is severely restricted by inadequate records. In addition, for any given time the angles of dip and declination vary considerably from place to place. Reference to Figure 59 will show how the values for the same years in Boston, London, Rome, and Paris differ. Thus one must not only have good records of change but also have them for areas near archeological sites. One thousand miles is a maximum distance for extrapolation of data, but there are ways of getting around this limitation.

The problem for the archeologist is to obtain samples of baked clay that can be dated by radiocarbon or some other means. When a number of such samples from one area has been recorded, one can plot a curve that shows the variation in angles of dip and declination through time. When a series of clay samples of known dates has been measured, one can measure samples that have no independent dates. By comparing these with the scale, one can calculate their age.

Research has focused on Japan, Central Europe, South America, Mexico, Arizona, and Canada where considerable data concerning the meanderings of the earth's magnetic poles have been obtained. Many of these data are presented in tabular or graph form in Bucha (1971). In summary, Bucha (1971:84) says,

> The application of the archaeomagnetic method is still restricted to those areas for which the archaeomagnetic curves have been determined, but it has been extended to Mexico and Arizona on the basis of fundamental geomagnetic characteristics . . . covering the past 3000 years. In this area, the method can improve the dating of the sherds of unknown age and substantially facilitate their classification.

Magnetic dating has thus proven useful in a number of instances and will gain in importance as the basic data on shifts in the magnetic poles are gathered for more areas and over longer periods.

There are many difficulties in magnetic dating. Some of these result from the problems of accurate declination-and-dip measurement and some from the nature of thermo-remanent magnetism. For example, the best material for dating is that remaining in the precise position where it was fired. Fireplaces and pottery kilns are ideal. Bricks have ordinarily been removed from the place where they were fired. It is thus difficult to align them in their original positions so that the deviation of the angles of declination and dip can be calculated. By the same token, pottery rarely can be used to establish declination unless it has remained in the kiln where it was fired. In fact, pottery is often a poor medium for measuring because it was frequently traded over great distances. On certain types of pots, however—glazed pots or those with considerable plastic decoration—it is possible to measure the angle of dip because they were probably fired standing on their bases and hence on a fairly level surface. Nevertheless, their angles of declination cannot be measured because there is no way of knowing what their alignment with respect to geographical north was when they were fired. In one instance it was possible to take a large series of pots made over a long period of time in a city in China and measure the variation in angle of dip. Scientists thus arrived at a simplified approximation of a dating standard (Aitken 1961: 152).

The measurements themselves are usually made in a laboratory with special equipment. Only two determinations are made in the field. One is a calculation of geographic north; the other, a determination of magnetic north. Both of these readings are recorded while the sample is in undisturbed position in the ground and before it is sent to the laboratory for measurement of thermo-remanent magnetism. Measurements in the laboratory are done with several kinds of sensitive magnets. Under certain circumstances there may be some alteration of the thermo-remanent magnetism. Laboratory methods have been worked out to allow for these and to determine whether the sample is suitable for measuring.

CHEMICAL ANALYSIS FOR FLUORINE AND NITROGEN

The most important of the chemical techniques are the analyses of the fluorine and nitrogen contents of bones. Quantitative differences in the amount of fluorine and nitrogen may permit archeologists to reach a decision on the relative age of buried bones, and in many instances, where there is an apparent association of the bones of extinct animals with those of man, to determine whether the human and animal bones are of the same or different ages. Buried bones and teeth gradually absorb fluorine from the ground water. The absorption of fluorine occurs through the alteration of hydroxyapatite, the phosphate of which bones and teeth are mainly composed, with the result that a chemically stable compound, fluorapatite, is formed. The amount of fluorine can be determined by chemical analysis or through the x-ray crystallographic method. McConnell (1962) has questioned the reliability of the fluorine method as a means of determining the age of bones. Whereas the fluorine content increases with age, nitrogen, by contrast, decreases in amount with prolonged burial, owing to the disappearance of collagen in bone. The conditions of burial of bones at different depths, in different soils, and in different places make it impossible to establish a rate for fluorine uptake or nitrogen loss. Therefore no generally applicable dating method can be devised that is based on quantitative determination of these elements in buried bones.

Laboratory methods for extracting collagen (gelatin) from ancient bones have been devised, and this collagen is suitable for dating by the radiocarbon method. Oakley was able to extract a small amount of collagen from the Piltdown bones, and H. de Vries of the Groningen Radiocarbon Laboratory determined from this organic extract that the mandible was 500±

100 years old and the Piltdown skull 620 ± 100 years old (Oakley 1959). Fifty years ago Lyne (1916) examined the Piltdown mandible by x-ray. This examination should have shown that the characteristic roots of ape teeth were present, but radiographic techniques at this time were not sufficiently perfected to make this feature clearly apparent on the plate. A reexamination by x-ray in recent years would surely have shown the nature of the teeth clearly, but such tests were not made.

Analyses of organic material help to determine the relative ages of bone specimens from one place. Because of the complicated and poorly understood chemistry involved in the absorption of organic elements by bone or in the disappearance of organic matter, it is not possible to compare specimens from different places with accuracy. Bones, teeth, and antlers may take up fluorine at variable rates. It is known that temperature and humidity affect the chemical action, and environments differ greatly in their chemical makeup. In spite of the many limitations, chemical analyses may be very useful in helping to establish stratigraphy or association of one bone with another. There is as yet no method for deriving an absolute chronology from chemical analyses.

Schoute-Vanneck (1960) describes a method of relative dating of coastal shell middens. Shells of mussel (*Mytilus*) are dissolved in acetic acid, and the ratio of conchylin (a substance similar to chiton) to calcium carbonate (lime) is determined. There is proved for South African coastal sites a progressive loss of conchylin over time. The method is now useful for relative dating, but if in the future the rates of decrease of conchylin can be determined, an absolute or chronometric dating method could be devised.

Progressive chemical changes occurring in animal skin (or leather) are claimed to follow a rate by which the age of ancient skin can be determined. Burton, Poole, and Reed (1959) describe a technique where collagen fibers extracted from ancient skin are mounted for microscopic viewing. When the fibers are heated, they begin to shrink, and the older the specimen, the lower the shrinkage temperature. Fragments of the Dead Sea Scrolls, written on parchment, were found to produce "collagen fiber shrinkage temperature dates" that agreed with paleographic and radiocarbon-age determinations. In theory, almost any ancient preserved material will differ in its chemistry from modern material. Sometimes the process of change can be invested with a rate or tempo and thus provide a means of calculating the age of older materials. At other times all that can be said is that there are differences between what are clearly older and clearly younger materials. But even this knowledge can be useful because it provides a means of relative dating.

Mention may be made here of attempts to determine the blood groups of ancient populations from their bones. Thieme and Otten (1957), in a review of earlier work, have concluded that the results achieved are undependable; on the other hand, M. Smith (1960) and Glemser (1963) feel that presently known techniques of paleoserology will yield useful and dependable results.

PATINATION

It has long been observed that the surface of rocks exposed to the atmosphere undergoes chemical alteration. The altered surfaces are said to be *patinated*. Many writers have suggested the possibility of using the amount of patina on stones as an index to their age. A recent evaluation of this method (Goodwin 1960) lists so many variables involved in patina formation that one must agree that absolute dates cannot be determined. Nevertheless, for certain problems, observation of the amount or color of patina on a stone may be of use. In sites where there is a long sequence, the flints in the bottom levels of a site may have more patina than those found in the upper levels. This difference is especially common in river gravels and terraces of rivers or lakes. When one has a large series of tools from several levels, it is sometimes possible to see clear-cut differences in the relative amounts of patina. With this knowledge it is then possible to assign dependable relative ages to artifacts from the same area. The famous Belzoni, referred to in the third chapter, noted three distinct types of patination on the sculptures on the granite cliffs at Aswan in Egypt, and suggested that by dating the sculpture of one style or age, the age of the other two degrees of patination could be calculated (Belzoni 1820:Vol. 1:360–361).

The variations between areas and even on the same tools greatly limit the use of patina for age determination. When patination is used, it must always be with a firm basis in stratigraphy; it is no substitute for excavation.

Glass that has been buried in soil or submerged under water will undergo surface alteration and form microscopically thick bands or layers, which can be counted. Some studies suggest that these bands are annual, and that their total number is a register of the number of years the glass has been buried or immersed. Ages of nearly 1600 years have thus far been determined for certain archeological specimens (Brill 1961, 1963).

HYDRATION OF OBSIDIAN

Preliminary work with the rate of surface chemical alteration of obsidian shows promise as a dating method. Obsidian, a natural volcanic glass with a high aluminum content, does not weather rapidly, but a freshly exposed surface of obsidian will take up water from the atmosphere to form a hydrated surface level. The dating system is made possible by the fact that the hydration layer builds up at a constant rate. By measuring the thickness of the hydration layer, it is possible to estimate the date when hydration began. Because of the complicated nature of hydration and its great variation under different conditions of temperature, and by reason of the chemical composition of obsidian, universal standards for dating by this method seem to be unattainable. However, series of "hydration dates" from sites in the tropics and temperate zones have yielded results that are comparable to those obtained by other methods. Within restricted geographical areas where temperature and moisture conditions have been uniform the system may have real merit.

A measurement of the amount of hydration on obsidian can be used much as the patina on flint and the relative amounts of fluorine and nitrogen are used (Evans and Meggers 1960). Within one site it is often possible to tell the relative age of samples, but obsidian-hydration dating is plagued with practical problems such as the fact that when it has been burned or has lain exposed on the surface and has been subject to diurnal temperature extremes, as may occur in an archeological site, it cannot be used to determine dates.

One of the principal advantages of obsidian-hydration dating is that it is relatively cheap and easy to do, allowing an archeologist to obtain hundreds of such dates, which allow a more accurate assessment of the reliability of the samples than would be possible with radiocarbon or other techniques. In the past few years progress at a number of laboratories in overcoming the technical problems has been significant, and it is now apparent that obsidian-hydration dating may become a very important tool. However, it is the impression of the present authors that obsidian-hydration dating will never reach a degree of precision that will make it truly reliable for other than relative dating of deposits within a site or between deposits in sites that were exposed to the same environmental conditions. There are simply too many variable factors (such as differing chemical composition within and between obsidian deposits, reuse of implements, short-term fluctuations in temperature, and precipitation in the past) that cannot be anticipated, detected, or compensated for to encourage the hope that a really significant method for absolute dating will be developed.

REFERENCES

General Surveys of Techniques of Archeological Dating: Aitken 1960, 1961; Baud 1960; R. Bowen 1958; Brothwell and Higgs 1969:35–108; Clark 1961; Griffin 1955; Heizer 1953; Michael and Ralph 1971; Oakley 1953, 1964a, 1964b; Pewe 1954; Shapley 1953; Smiley 1955b; Tilton and Hart 1963; Zeuner 1959.

Principles, Techniques and Problems of Radiocarbon Dating: Aitken 1961: Chap. 6; Broecker and Kulp 1956; Catch 1961:Chap. 7; Craig 1954; Dyck 1967; Godwin 1962; Haynes 1966; Johnson 1967; Kamen 1963; Libby 1955, 1961, 1963; Quitta 1967; Renfrew 1968c; Sellstedt, Engstrand, and Gejvall 1966, 1967; Struckenrath 1965; Van der Merwe 1965; Waterbolk 1971; Willis 1969.

Special Problems Encountered in Radiocarbon Dating of Freshwater and Marine Mollusc Shells: M. Bender 1968; Berger, Horney, and Libby 1964; Berger, Taylor, and Libby 1966; Broecker 1964; Craig 1954; Dyck 1967:33–36; J. Evans 1969; Keith and Anderson 1963, 1964; Libby 1955; Rubin, Likens, and Berry 1963; Rafter 1965; Rubin and Taylor 1963; R. Taylor and Berger 1967; Weber and La Rocque 1963; Wickman 1952.

Responsibilities of the Archeologist in Collecting Samples for Radiocarbon Dating, and Problems of Accuracy and Interpretation of Dates: Anderson and Levi 1952; J. Bray 1967; Broecker and Olson 1960; J. Campbell 1965; S. Cook 1964; Dyck 1967; Kovar 1966; Libby 1963; Meighan 1956; Olson and Broecker 1958; Polach and Golson 1966; Ralph and Michael 1967; Ralph 1971; Stuckenrath 1965; Stuiver 1965; Stuiver and Suess 1966; Suess 1965; Tamers and Pearson 1966; Tauber 1958.

The Significance of the Plus-Minus Sigma of Error in Radiocarbon Dates: F. Johnson and others 1951; Spaulding 1958.

Potassium-Argon Dating: Carr and Kulp 1957; Curtis 1961; Curtis and Reynolds 1958; Evernden and Curtis 1965; Evernden, Curtis, and Lipson 1957; Evernden and others 1964; Faul 1971; Gentner and Lippolt 1969; Howell 1962a; Lipson 1958; Schaeffer and Zähringer 1966.

Thermoluminescence (TL) Dating: Aitken 1961:86–87; Dort and others 1965; E. T. Hall 1969; Mazess and Zimmerman 1966; Ralph and Han 1966, 1971; Tite and Waine 1962; Winter 1971.

Natural Low-Level Radioactivity Measurement: Bowie and Davidson 1955; Jelinek and Fitting 1963, 1965; Oakley 1955b, 1961, 1963a, 1963b, 1963c, 1964b; Oakley and Howells 1961; Oakley and Rixon 1958.

Fission Track Dating: Faul and Wagner 1971; Fleischer, Price, and Walker 1965; Fleischer and others 1965; Walker and others 1971; Watanabe and Suzuki 1969; Zimmerman 1971.

Paleomagnetic Dating: Aitken 1960, 1961; R. Cook 1969; Cook and Belshé 1958; Cox, Doell, and Dalrymple 1965; Heizer 1953:20–22; Laming 1952; Thellier and Thellier 1959; Watanable 1959; Weaver 1967.

Fluorine, Uranium, and Nitrogen Content in Bone; Processes of Fossilization: Baud 1960; J. D. Clark and others 1968; S. F. Cook 1951, 1960; S. F. Cook, Brooks, and Ezra-Cohn 1961; Cook and Ezra-Cohn 1959; Cook and Heizer 1952, 1953, 1959; Dallemagne, Baud, and Morgenthaler 1956; Doberenz 1965; Doberenz and Matter 1965; Groff 1971; Heizer and Cook 1952; Oakley 1951, 1955a, 1963c, 1964b, 1969; Oakley and Weiner 1955.

Chemical Extraction of Collagen from Bones for Radiocarbon Dating: Berger, Horney, and Libby 1964; Sinex and Faris 1959; Tamers and Pearson 1965.

Relative Dating of Stone Tools or Petroglyphs by Degree of Patination: Curwen 1940; Engel and Sharp 1958; Goodwin 1960; Hewitt 1915; Higgs 1959:212; Hurst and Kelly 1961; Kelly and Hurst 1956; Schmalz 1960; Sonneville–Bordes 1953.

Obsidian-Hydration Dating: D. L. Clark 1961; L. Davis 1966; V. Dixon 1966; L. Dixon 1966; Evans and Meggers 1960; Friedman and Smith 1960; Friedman, Smith, and Clark 1969; Katsui and Kondo 1965; Meighan, Foote, and Aiello 1968; Michels 1967; Michels and Bolovich 1971.

CHAPTER THIRTEEN

GEOCHRONOLOGY

Because man lives on the earth's surface it is not at all surprising that his bones, tools which he made, and other evidences of his former presence are commonly found on the surface. The houses, buildings, roads, canals, scatters of trash, and everything else that today we strew over the landscape will become, in degrees of varying preservation, the archeological materials of the future. Because the earth's surface is continually subject to change by erosion and deposition, as well as by a multiplicity of other processes which we call geological, we can understand how things that once lay on the surface have been moved or buried, or how things once buried have again been exposed to view. Caves anciently occupied may be abandoned and the living levels become covered with water-laid or wind-borne sediments. In all instances where archeological materials occur in a context that can be called geological, there is presented to the archeologist the possibility that he may be able to determine the chronological placement of the find by one or another of the methods of *geochronology*. The methods are numerous, and the present chapter makes no pretense at doing more than mentioning some of them and referring the student to some of the books that provide the details.

VARVE ANALYSIS

Varve analysis, the oldest technique for geochronology, was described in 1878 by the Swedish Baron Gerard De Geer, who did most of the pioneering work, although somewhat earlier Heer (1863:453–455) had recognized that varves are annually deposited layers of silt. Varve analysis depends on the fact that certain clayey deposits are laminated. These laminations, or *varves*, as they are

269

called in Swedish, are annual layers of sediment deposited in lake basins by the runoff from melting glacial ice. By a process similar to that used in tree-ring analysis; it is possible to measure the relative thickness of the varves and obtain a series to which one can compare and correlate new sections as they are discovered (De Geer 1912; Heizer 1953:9–12).

Varves are composed of a double layer with coarse sediments at the bottom and fine sediments at the top; the finer sediments settle during the winter while the lake is frozen over, and the coarser material is deposited in the summer when it is warmer and melting is increased. Varves may range in thickness from a few millimeters to more than 15 inches, though these maximum and minimum values are seldom reached.

The application of varve dating is restricted by several factors. First, because varves accumulate only near ice, there are no varves in most of the world. Second, in many places where ice was present during the Pleistocene, it has receded and no longer supplies basins with sediments. Therefore, outside Scandinavia it is difficult to find a continuous sequence of varves reaching the present. Varves linked with the present do not extend very far into the past. The longest sequence known goes back only 17,000 years. The explanation is that places where there are now lakes were covered during the height of the Pleistocene glaciation and therefore were not receiving sediments. A final reservation is that varves are not invariably annual; depending on the pattern of melting, layers may be deposited more or less frequently than annually (Flint 1957:293–297).

In spite of the limitations, analyses of varves have been made in the Baltic area, North America, South America, and Africa. Attempts at exact correlations of these several sequences have not been generally accepted. In North America, Ernst Antevs has made several attempts to relate Pleistocene geological formations in the American Southwest to events that produced varves in the northern parts of North America. The dates derived by the varve chronology are generally rather older than those for the same events as determined by the radiocarbon dating method.

Varve analysis can be used indirectly for archeological dating. Sites are not often found in glacial lakes, but sediments in glacial lakes may be correlated with other geological features, such as beaches left by varying water levels. When the sea levels, and hence their beaches, can be dated by reference to varves, it is possible to date archeological material found in the beaches. The method lacks precision, however, because it is possible for archeological materials to have been incorporated into beach deposits long after the beaches were formed.

BEACHES, TERRACES, AND DUNES

When archeological sites are found in association with datable geological phenomena, the archeological materials can be dated indirectly. During the Pleistocene, fluctuations in sea level raised beach lines, which in some areas prove to be useful for archeological interpretation. Great amounts of sea water were periodically locked on land in the form of ice during the cold periods of glacial ice accumulation and advance, and in the warmer inter-glacial times this water was returned to the seas. The alternate raising and lowering of the sea, called eustasy, during the Pleistocene (=glacial epoch or Ice Age) resulted in changes of at least 300 feet in the sea level. Visible records of lower sea levels in the past would have been wiped out by the present high stand of sea level were it not for an accompanying movement of the land masses in some areas, called isostasy. Under the weight of the ice, land masses were depressed, and, when the ice retreated, the land sprang up again. In some places this isostatic action raised the land so high above sea level that traces of old, once much lower, shore lines are visible; without isostasy they would now be submerged. Outside glaciated areas, tectonic action—movement of land masses whether or not they were covered by ice—has exposed Pleistocene shore lines. Some beaches that would have been submerged are now readily seen, but the opposite is also true—some land areas are now submerged that might not have been were it not for tectonic action.

Traces of old sea levels can frequently be dated relative to one another. Extensive work on such correlations has been carried out in the Baltic and Mediterranean, to the great advantage of prehistoric archeology.

Changes in sea level can involve archeological sites in a number of ways. There is good evidence that sea level has risen about 6 meters in the last 6000 years. Scuba divers have found quantities of stone implements on the ocean floor along the coast of Southern California; the only reasonable explanation for their presence is that a rise in sea level submerged earlier sites once situated on the edge of the sea. Teeth of Pleistocene elephants of the sort hunted by Paleo-Indians in North America are occasionally dredged up by fishermen on the continental shelf which has been covered in the last 15,000 years by rising sea levels. Although thus far no stone implements have been found, it is considered highly probable that they do occur as a result of ancient hunters' activities on this now-drowned continental margin. We are just entering a phase of intensive study of the ocean and its floor. The earth having been explored and mapped, attention is now being directed to space exploration (where it is assumed no archeology older than post-Sputnik I "junk" exists) and to the oceans, both areas being essentially unknown. Shipwrecks on the bottom and cities submerged through coastal subsidence are common, but as exploration of the ocean floor proceeds we may expect to hear of finds from the Paleolithic.

At Cape Krusenstern, on the American side of the Bering Sea, Giddings (1965, 1966; see also Giddings and Bandi 1962) has worked out the complicated correlation of a series of successive beach ridges and archeological sites that extend inland for about 3 miles. The oldest ridge (No. 114) lies farthest from the sea, as do the oldest archeological sites; thus the relative chronology of both can be readily determined by counting, if it is assumed that the pattern of site placement next to the ocean prevailed through time.

This continuity could be proved by comparison of the Cape Krusenstern sites with the chronology known elsewhere. The direct chronology is supplied by radiocarbon dating of organic materials recovered from the sites, and it is known that the beach ridges and sites cover a time span of 5000–6000 years. The sequence of cultures noted is

Beach Ridges	Culture Phases
1–8	Modern Eskimo of the past century
9–19	Western Thule culture
29–35	Ipiutak culture
36–50	Norton followed by Choris culture
51–52	Unoccupied
53	Old Whaling culture
54–77	(Unnamed culture)
79–105	Denbigh Flint Complex
+106	"Palisades" Facies

Along the eastern Mediterranean coast it has been possible to relate certain kinds of sand dunes, or weathering horizons within them, to Pleistocene chronology (Howell 1959, 1962b). Sometimes archeological sites can be related not only to beaches but to dunes as well. Even better, in the Baltic, shore lines can sometimes be correlated with varve sequences, and in this way absolute dating can be given to the beaches. In some instances the sinking or rising of shore lines provides a means of dating archeological sites when there is some idea of the rate at which the change in elevation is taking place. These situations have been studied in Tierra del Fuego, Chile, Arctic North America, and New England.

Lakes often form beaches, and where these beaches are controlled by the climate they can be related to a Pleistocene chronology. For example, in western Utah, Jennings found that Danger Cave could not have been occupied before a lowering of Pleistocene "Lake Wendover." Thus he had a date before which the site could not have been occupied. At Leonard Rockshelter in western Nevada, the lowermost cultural layer, which consisted mostly of bat guano, contained a few artifacts left by people who had camped in the protection of the overhanging cliff. Under the guano-artifact layer was a beach sand that contained large numbers of small shells (*Amnicola*) left there when the Pleistocene lake retreated. The radiocarbon age of 11,200 years B.P. for these shells provided a maximum age for the artifact-bearing guano deposits resting on the old beach. This information did not date the cultural materials, but was useful in showing that they must be younger than 11,200 years.

Terraces, former flood plains formed along streams as a result of the changing regime of the river, can be used in the same way that shore lines are used. During periods of aggradation a river will deposit silt and gravel and build up its bed, whereas at other times the river will degrade or cut into its bed. During periods of relative stability a stream may cut a valley sidewise by flooding or meandering. Alternatively, it may build a flood plain by depositing silt and gravel in the river valley. Either process results in a relatively level valley floor over which the stream spreads during floods. Later degradation leaves remnants of the flood plain suspended well above the river. The lowering of the bed of a river ordinarily takes a long time and in the natural course of events the flood plain should wear down at about the same rate as the stream bed. However, sometimes bits of the flood plain are preserved at the margins of the valleys where meanderings of the river have failed to remove them. After a time a series of flood plains at different elevations can be distinguished (Flint 1957: Fig. 12-4). Under certain conditions the heights of these remnants can be used as a means of correlating one terrace with another. This method is the same as that used on shore lines, but it is much more difficult to make correlations with rivers; in practice it is even difficult to identify parts of the same terrace on different stretches of the same river (D. Johnston 1944). If the aggradation or degradation of a river can be directly related to an ocean or lake, it may be possible to date one by the other. Just as archeological material may be found in association with shore lines, so it is often found associated with terraces. A very detailed correlation of archeology with terraces was made along the Nile where a four-year study was undertaken in the late 1920s and 1930s by K. S. Sandford, a geologist, and W. J. Arkell, an archeologist. Before the detailed studies made in connection with the salvage archeology in the Aswan dam basin, the Sandford and Arkell work (1929–1939) was a standard reference, although their results had been questioned because the two investigators sometimes used archeological materials to date terraces, and at other times, terraces to date artifacts. In the Great Basin area of the western United States shorelines of the Pleistocene lakes named Bonneville and Lahontan are marked by prominent beaches and terraces. These are often accompanied by calcareous tufa, a deposit formed by blue-green algae living in the shallow waters of the ancient lake. The tufa, being the product of living organisms, can be dated by radiocarbon assay. Although a considerable number of dates have been secured (Broecker and Orr 1958; Broecker and Kaufman 1965), efforts to associate these with archeological materials have not been very successful (P. Sears and Roosma 1961; Shutler 1961), partly because the scattered surface artifacts are difficult to date relative to the time of formation of the tufa, and partly because of poor collecting techniques of archeologists.

Rivers that flow over a wide flat flood plain may change their course, or meander. At times the meander changes may be unidirectional, with the result that over a long period of time the river will leave behind it a series of abandoned channels which can be detected and plotted either by topographic surveying or aerial photographic mapping (photogrammetry). The most extensive application of a meander chronology to which a rate or tempo has been determined is in the lower Mississippi Valley, where the main stream's former locations have been plotted at 100-year intervals for the last 2000 years (Fisk 1944). The plotting has been done through extrapolation of data on river changes between 1765 and 1940. Sites located on a particular meander channel can be dated as being no older than that of the channel when occupied by the river. Sites on abandoned channels may be much younger than the time when the channel held the main stream of the river. Some abandoned channels, if blocked at two separated points by silting, may collect water and form a lake that will provide an attractive location for settlement. If this did occur, the archeologist might readily recognize it by noting that the water-associated fauna (fish, waterfowl, molluscs) used for food and recovered by him from the site was of the lake rather than river type.

CORRELATION OF PLEISTOCENE FEATURES

The greatest amount of Pleistocene geology has been done in Europe and along the Mediterranean coasts, where some of the best evidence of the Pleistocene climatic succession is preserved. A considerable amount of pre-historic archeology has been done in the same areas; thus European and Russian scholars have been the leaders in correlating Pleistocene events with prehistoric man. By contrast, in North America there was relatively little habitation that can be related to the glacial stages of the Pleistocene. Man probably entered this hemisphere toward the end of the last (Wisconsin) glacial phase. At the present time nothing has been found that is satisfactorily dated older than about 12,000 years in the New World. Many claims of older material denoting man's presence have been advanced, but none has been generally accepted. There may be, even probably is, more ancient evidence of man in the Western Hemisphere, but it awaits either finding or the kind of demonstration called proof.

Moraines of various sorts and outwash features from the melting ice are well-known glacial features. Ordinarily, however, because of their near-ness to glacial ice, which was not a very favorable place for man to live and find his food, they are not directly associated with human habitation. Areas suitable for man lay beyond the immediate margins of the ice. In much of Eurasia this was loessland, in some places several hundred feet thick. Loess "is a sediment commonly nonstratified and commonly unconsolidated, composed dominantly of silt-size particles, ordinarily with accessory clay and sand, and deposited primarily by the wind" (Flint 1957:181). The loess that covers large portions of southwestern Russia, East Europe, and middle-western United States is thought to have been derived from moraines and other glacial debris.

The development of soil horizons in loess is exceptionally important in helping to establish the late Pleistocene chronology of Europe. In theory, loess is deposited during glacial periods, whereas soil horizons are developed in the loess during the warmer phases when plants grow better. When these soils are buried, as they were during the cold (ice advance) and warm (ice retreat) alternations of the Pleistocene climate, a layered sequence is built up. Because some soil horizons are deeper than others, a characteristic sequence of thinner and thicker soils can thus be compared, from one locality to another. Sometimes loesses include fauna that helps to identify them. For example, the snail, *Helicigona banatica* (among others), is found in a soil in central Europe (Movius 1960:359). For a detailed discussion of the correlation of European Pleistocene soils, see G. E. Wright (1961:961–966), Zeuner (1959:35–41), and Butzer (1964:Chap. 6).

Loess regions were grasslands, especially suitable for grazing animals such as bison and mammoths. Hunters of these animals left their camp sites in the loess, and these sites can sometimes be associated with particular loess horizons. A striking example of this association is in southern Moravia, where Dolni Vestonici and Pavlov, both sites of mammoth hunters, are associated with the "Paudorf" soil formation (Zeuner 1955b). The soil, now a marker in the Pleistocene chronology of the area, is estimated to have lasted approximately 4000 years, from about 27,000 to 23,000 B.C. The estimate is based on radiocarbon dates made on charcoal from the sites, as well as humus from the soil (Movius 1963:132).

By slowly compiling knowledge of local time sequences, geologists have begun to establish reliable chronologies for the latter part of the Pleistocene, but for most of the Pleistocene—now thought to be about two million years long—the dating is much less precise (Flint 1957:289–301). There are two reasons for this: either datable remains have not been found, or they do not occur in many areas. Such gross distinctions as the four Alpine glacials—Gunz, Mindel, Riss, and Würm—are of little help to archeologists. In southern areas four "pluvials," presumably contemporary with the Alpine glacials, were identified. Thus in Africa, south of the Sahara, there are the Kageran, Kamasian, Kanjeran, and Gamblian pluvials. These would have been convenient segments to correlate from continent to continent if the events had been strictly contemporaneous; however, they were not. In fact, in Africa, on second look, there is little evidence of widespread pluvial phases (Flint 1959). To add to the difficulty, each Alpine glacial is now subdivided, and it is now known that there are more than four, each of which had its own relatively minor fluctuations of climate. In short, except for the very end of the Pleistocene, when radiocarbon dates and varve sequences are useful in making correlations, chronology based on geologic features is imprecise. This fact is overlooked in many publications on the subject.

RATE OF CHEMICAL CHANGES IN SITE SOILS

Soils undergo changes over time in chemical and physical characteristics. Climatic changes will be reflected in vegetational change, and the soil will modify in accordance with these shifts. Because the chemistry and morphology of soils that have been altered in the past are not readily reversed, soils may contain a record of several past climatic changes. Rates of soil development are variable and not at present well understood, but the known fact that change does occur over time makes soil a potentially useful source of chronology.

Archeologists have been slow to seek the advice and technical assistance of soil experts (pedologists), and the future will probably see increased interest in this subject.

RATE OF ACCUMULATION

Geologists have made inferences about the length of time required for leaching of glacial deposits (Kay 1931; Dreimanis 1957) and archeologists often estimate the duration of a site by its depth of deposit, but any such estimate is likely to be little more than a guess. It is really not useful to say that a deposit in a cave has accumulated at the rate of 15 inches per 1000 years, or that a shell midden accumulated at the rate of 2 feet per 100 years. When such guesses have been checked with radiocarbon or other dating methods, they have usually been proved wrong (Heizer 1953:24–25; 1959:Chap. 9). On the other hand, if the depth of deposit and the length of time it took to accumulate are both known, one can say that, on the average, n centimeters of deposit were added per century. Even with such statistics, however, it is not possible to extrapolate these data from one site to another. There are too many variables to control. Geological deposition is as complex as deposition in an archeological site, and its short-term characteristics are not so easily measured. The lifetime of a human observer is very short compared to the time it takes nature to do most of its work. M. Fowler (1959) has provided us with an instructive example of variable deposition rates in an Illinois rock shelter occupied for a long span of time. He calculates, using radiocarbon-dated levels as a time control, that between 8000 and 5000 B.C. the rate of deposition was about 12 inches per 500 years; between 5000 and 3600 B.C. the rate increased markedly to 102 inches per 500 years, and between 3300 and 2700 B.C. the deposition rate decreased to 15 inches per 500 years. Such fluctuations may be the result of population differences, cultural practices reflected in different amounts of wastes, climatic changes, and so on.

LOCATION OF SITES

In the desert portions of western North America water was scarce; for this reason one usually finds evidences of man's presence in the vicinity of springs or creeks. The presence of chipped flint tools on the shore-line terraces of dry lake basins in the southern California desert has led to the supposition that the stone tools date from the time when the lake held water, and that if one can date the time the water was there, the cultural materials can be dated. This idea seems reasonable, but there are at least two other possibilities that should be considered before the assumption that the age of the lake waters equals the age of the implements can be accepted. First is the known fact that some of these lake basins occasionally fill even today as a result of very heavy rains. In 1938, for example, the basin of normally dry Lake Mohave received enough water in a period of 13 days to form a lake 16 miles long, 2.5 miles wide, and 10 feet deep. In prehistoric times, say as recently as 150 years ago, such a lake would certainly have attracted Indians of the vicinity to its shores, where they would have camped and left traces of their contemporary occupation, however brief, until the lake dried by evaporation. Thus implements found on the surface around the lake margins might be 15,000 years old and date from the Pleistocene when the country was better watered and the lake permanent, or they might be 150 years old. Mere surface associations of this sort between implements and a geological feature may or may not be related in a single way and may refer to only a single event, or to a series of events (Heizer 1965).

A second caution in accepting surface finds of stone implements in desert areas formerly occupied by lakes as proving occupation at a time when a wetter climatic regime prevailed is illustrated by a statement of J. H. Steward (1937:105), who writes,

> In the southern end of Eureka Valley, near the northern end of Death Valley, California, there is a site bordering a playa and extending several miles. Thousands of flint flakes with relatively few artifacts mark it as predominantly a workshop, though the source of the flint is several miles distance in the mountains. The nearest water is a spring 3 to 5 miles away. There is no apparent reason why anyone should choose a place lacking water, having virtually no vegetation, and, in fact, devoid of anything of apparent use to man or beast, for a workshop or other purpose. Nevertheless, the presence here of large spherical stone mortars of the type used by Death Valley Shoshoni and at least one arrow point of the Shoshonean type is presumptive evidence that the Shoshoni visited the site, though it does not, of course, prove that they used it as a workshop. Although Mr. and Mrs. Campbell (1935, p. 26) have never found a camp site more than 3 miles from a water hole in southern California, the writer has repeatedly received accounts from Shoshoni and Paiute informants of camps maintained by entire families and groups of families for days at a time 10 and even 20 miles from water when seeds, salts, flints, edible insects, or other important supplies made it worth while to do so. Water is used sparingly and when the (basketry) ollas in which it is transported are empty one or two persons make the long trip to replenish them. Remoteness from the present water, then, is not, per se, the slightest proof that a site dates from the pluvial period.

Although there is a variety of methods for dating archeological materials by means of geology, none of the methods is simple. It is always better to have several independent methods for dating particular events. Used alone, any method that depends on far-reaching correlations of geologic stratigraphy is likely to be undependable because of weak links in the chain of observations. Archeologists should use geochronologic dating but be aware of its many imprecisions.

REFERENCES

Methods of Geochronology: Butzer 1964:Chaps. 2–3; Flint 1957; Hunt and others 1967; Pewe 1954; Smiley 1955b; H. Wright and Frey 1965; Zeuner 1955b, 1958, 1959.

Glacial and Varve Chronologies; Varve and Radiocarbon Chronologies Compared: Antevs 1948, 1952a, 1953a, 1954, 1957, 1962; De Geer 1912; Flint and Deevey 1951; Heizer 1953:9–10; Smiley 1955a.

Glaciation; Fluctuating Sea Levels; Former Sea-Level Strands; Dunes: Bird 1938:262–264; Deevey 1948; J. Dyson 1962; Fairbridge 1958; Howell 1959, 1962b; Mathiassen 1927:Part I:6–10, 129–130; Russell 1957; Zeuner 1958: Chap. 5, 1959:Chap. 9.

Correlating Former Beaches of Lakes and Archeological Materials: Greenman 1943; Greenman and Stanley 1940; Heizer 1965; Jennings 1957.

Stream Terrace and River Meanders Used for Relative Dating of Archeological Materials: Antevs 1952b; Fisk 1944; J. Ford 1951, 1952; J. Ford, Phillips, and Haag 1955; J. Ford and Webb 1956:116; Greengo 1964:105–107; Horton 1945; Lathrap 1968; Leopold and Langbein 1966; McIntire 1958; Phillips, Ford, and Griffin 1951:295–306; Scully 1953; Sternberg 1960.

Chronology of the Pleistocene Based on Deep-Sea Cores and Terrestrial Geology: Broecker 1966; Butzer 1964; Dorf 1960; Ericson, Ewing, and Wollin 1964; Ericson and Wollin 1964; Kay 1931; Shapley 1953; H. Wright and Frey 1965; Zeuner 1958, 1959.

Changes in Sea Level; Submergence of Archeological Remains: Donn and others 1962; K. Emery and others 1967; K. Emery and Edwards 1966; K. Emery and Garrison 1967; Hopkins 1959; Hume 1966; Redfeld 1967; F. Shepard 1961, 1964; F. Shepard and Suess 1956; Whitmore and others 1967; Zeuner 1952, 1959:350ff.

Underwater Archeology: Kinds of Remains, Their Recovery: Bass 1963; de Borhegyi 1958; Dumas 1962; Folan 1968; Frost 1963; Goggin 1960; Kapitan 1966; Marshall and Moriarty 1964; S. J. Olsen 1961c; Silverberg 1963; J. Taylor 1972; Throckmorton and Bullitt 1963; Tuthill and Allanson 1954.

Rates of Chemical and Morphological Changes in Natural and Archeological Soils: Bryan and Albritton 1943; Carter 1956; Carter and Pendleton 1956; S. Cook 1949a, 1949b, 1964; S. Cook and Ezra-Cohn 1959; S. Cook and Heizer 1962; Cornwall 1958:199–203; U. Cowgill and Hutchinson 1963; Crocker 1952; Dickson and Crocker 1953–1954; Dort 1968; Eckblaw 1936; Eddy and Dregne 1964; Harradine 1949; Jenny 1941; Joeffe 1941; Lotspeich 1961; Lutz 1951; Nikiforoff 1942, 1953; R. Parsons 1962; Pearsall 1952; C. Shaw 1928; Shotten 1969; Simonsen 1954; Siniaguin 1943; Sokoloff and Lorenzo 1953; Storie and Harradine 1950; Thorp 1941.

CHAPTER FOURTEEN

METHODS FOR DATING, USING PLANT AND ANIMAL REMAINS

$\mathbf{M}$an is an intimate part of the natural environment by virtue of the fact that he uses plants and animals, both wild and domestic, for food as well as industrial materials. The residue from this activity, discarded as trash, can often be recovered by an archeologist and used to date the archeological deposit. Further, the natural deposits on which the archeological site rests may yield faunal and/or floral evidence that, if datable, can tell an archeologist the maximum age of the site. When a site has been abandoned and the spot reverts to its original condition as part of the natural environment, there may accumulate faunal and/or floral remains that, if they can be dated, provide the archeologists with the information on when the site was abandoned.

Studies of noncontemporary botanical and zoological materials are termed paleobotany and paleontology, and from their results we learn about distributions of plants and animals of the past. When this information is correlated with that secured by geologists, geographers, climatologists, and ecologists, the natural environment and chronology of the past comes into focus.

There are at least four circumstances that enable archeologists to use plant and animal remains to date sites.

1. If extinct species are present, an archeologist can say definitely that the site is not recent, and he may be a great deal more precise if he knows from other information when the species lived.

2. If plants and animals that are no longer able to live in an area because of climate occur in archeological sites, an archeologist can infer that the climate was different when the site was occupied. If he can determine what the climatic preferences of the species were, he may be able to determine during which period in geologic history the climate would have been suitable to the animals and from this infer the site's age.

3. If some species, especially domesticates, have undergone osteological or morphological changes incident to domestication, it will be possible to say at least that the site was not occupied prior to a certain date. Sometimes enough may be known about the physical changes to enable an archeologist to narrow the time down to a few hundred years. These methods give relative ages that may be capable of refinement, but they are far from precise. Moreover, a person must be very careful of using data derived from one location to make inferences about other areas. For example, at present it is not possible to say that all mastodons became extinct at the same time; there may be a period of several thousand years during which they gradually disappeared, first from one locality, then another, and so on. The same sort of caution must also be applied to climatic changes, especially when they were caused by the advance and retreat of glaciers. Finally, our data on domestication are still too few to permit us to say with confidence that after, say 5000 B.C., all goats looked alike.

4. The most accurate method is tree-ring dating, which gives absolute dates directly correlated with our calendar. These dates are of such precision they are currently being used to check radiocarbon dating (Suess 1965; Stuiver and Suess 1966).

PALYNOLOGY

Pollen analysis (palynology) was first developed in 1916 by the Swedish botanist Lennar von Post, who was interested in forest trees. Twenty years later the technique was extended to all plants that produce and release pollen. It has subsequently been developed into a highly refined method for identifying Quaternary and post-Pleistocene climatic changes and their chronology.

Accurate analysis depends on whether plants distribute their pollen widely and whether the grains are sufficiently well-preserved to be identified. Pollen analysis is tedious and painstaking work. It is based on the microscopic identification of pollen from modern plants. When these have been identified, it is possible to take a standard number of grains from samples in a vertical stratigraphic section and count the number from each species of plant. By plotting the relative frequencies of various species through time, one can make a pollen diagram describing the changing vegetation for the area involved (Fig. 60).

Deevey (1944:138–140) lists four conditions that must be fulfilled in order to apply the technique of pollen analysis to problems of prehistory in any area. These conditions are: (1) there must have been, within the period encompassed by human occupation of the area, vegetational changes resulting from areawide causes; (2) pollen grains must be properly preserved in the deposits; (3) the investigation must first establish a "standard pollen sequence" through study of natural deposits such as lakes and swamps; (4) the investigator must possess a knowledge of the regional plant ecology in order to interpret properly the pollen sequence in terms of vegetational and climatic changes in the past.

If pollen analysis is relatively simple in theory, it is often disappointing in practice, because under many conditions pollen is not preserved. The best conditions are in highly acidic bogs with a pH below 5.0, where pollen has remained damp from the time it was deposited. It is simple to cut sections from peat bogs and plot the pollen diagrams. In Scandinavia, after several hundred such diagrams had been constructed, certain characteristic "zones" in the late glacial and postglacial sequence stood out. These zones are easily identifiable between sites and can be used to indicate climate and chronology. Radiocarbon dating of the peat, combined with pollen analysis, gives the best chronology in the world for the period (Flint 1957: 285–288).

Prehistoric sites found on the edges of bogs or objects found in bogs can thus be dated. However, even though a site is not in a bog, if pollen has

FIG. 60 Diagram showing development of vegetation in Jutland since the retreating ice sheet uncovered the land. The diagram depicts the relative frequencies of pollen from each of the plant species listed. (G. Clark, *Archaeology and Society*, Cambridge: Harvard University Press. London: Methuen and Company, Ltd., 1947.)

CLIMATIC PERIODS	POLLEN ZONES (K. JESSEN)	HERBS	ERICALES	BIRCH	PINE	HAZEL	ALDER	ELM, LIME, OAK, ASH	ASH	ELM	IVY	MISTLETOE	PLANTAIN	RUMEX	CEREALS	BEECH	HORNBEAM	SPHAGNUM
SUB-ATLANTIC	IX																	
SUB-BOREAL	VIII																	
ATLANTIC	VII																	
BOREAL	VI																	
	V																	
PRE-BOREAL	IV																	
YOUNGER DRYAS	III																	
ALLEROD	II																	
OLDER DRYAS	I																	

LATE GLACIAL

been preserved in soil in the cracks of implements collected long ago and stored in museum trays it can often be identified, and the soil layer originally enclosing the artifact can be identified and thus dated (G. Clark 1957:47, 1963). Pollens in soils underlying or overlying archeological areas may be correlated with the already known regional pollen sequence, and the age of the site thus "bracketed."

Intensive studies of pollen are being made in the United States and Canada (for example, Heusser 1960; P. Martin 1963; Schoenwetter 1962), Meso-America (U. Cowgill and others 1966), Southwest Asia (Van Zeist and Wright 1963), and South Africa (Van Zinderen Bakker 1960), but many of the results have not yet been directly applicable to the dating of prehistoric man. Except in England, Scandinavia, and the western United States, well-dated pollen sequences have not been found associated with archeological remains. The problems of beginning pollen studies in an area are enormous. First, one must study the modern flora, and then find good sequences of ancient pollen. The latter is very difficult in arid and semi-arid parts of the world for the reason that pollens in alkaline soil (pH greater than 7.0) are usually destroyed.

Acid peat or bog deposits are ideal sources of ancient pollen, but dry silts, sands, and clays may contain enough pollen to provide a sequence. Oxidation and mineralization frequently destroy pollen, but grains are usually preserved in clays. Methods of extracting pollen from clays are always difficult (and at times impossible) to apply. In the past 10 years pollen analysis has been applied with some success to dry environment soils and to dry cave deposits from which it had been assumed all pollens had disappeared (R. Anderson 1955; Kurtz and Anderson 1955; P. Sears and Roosma 1961; Schoenwetter and Eddy 1964).

Deevey (1951:178) says that "most American pollen stratigraphers have not looked hard enough [for pollen]." A five gram sample of breccia from Locality 1 at Choukoutien, site of the discovery of Peking Man, has yielded 132 pollen grains and 9 spores identifiable as deriving from 16 plants. The floristic assemblage, taken together with the faunal analysis, is considered by Kurtén and Vasari (1960) to indicate a cold (glacial) climate, and the second or Mindel glaciation is identified as the age of the cave deposits. Choukoutien is one of the oldest archeological sites to be pollen-dated. Another good example is Rampart Cave, Arizona, where pollen counts for levels ranging from 10,000–35,000 years ago were obtained (P. Martin, Sabels, and Shutler 1961).

Successful extraction of pollen from open sites in the arid American Southwest is illustrated in papers in the paleoecological monograph on the Llano Estacado region of New Mexico and Texas assembled by F. Wendorf (1961); and by Schoenwetter (1962) on pollen analysis of 18 archeological sites in Arizona and New Mexico.

Deevey's dictum that standard sequences must be established has been partly superseded by careful examination of pollen from archeological sites whose period of use is not long in the usual palynological sense. Studies carried out in the Southwest and in Meso-America show that relatively minor changes in plants around a site can be seen palynologically, with the consequence that accurate relative dating within a small area sometimes can be accomplished.

The problem of pollen analysis in generally unfavorable (that is, dry) areas is to obtain sequences long enough to be of value. When the banks of streams or other sediments have been sampled for pollen they must still be dated. Unlike bogs, inorganic sediments cannot be dated by radiocarbon. There are problems also in taking pollen from caves that man occupied. The pollen frequencies may have been skewed by man's bringing in plants, or by animals bringing in pollen on their fur. The danger of mixing levels in an archeological site is also present, and in a cave with fallen rock, pollen might enter through the interstices and be deposited many feet below its correct level.

However, pollen analysis can be very useful for both relative and absolute dating. Where only broad outlines of the climatic-floral history of a region have been worked out, it is often possible to identify pollen from a warm interglacial or cold glacial period without specifying the date. Where the chronology has been worked out in greater detail, one can place pollen profiles in terms of hundreds of years to give a rough absolute chronology.

Referring back to the discussion of changes in sea level and differences in shore elevation caused by rising or subsidence, we may note here that pollen studies in salt marshes on the coast of eastern United States have helped date these changes (P. Sears 1963; Deevey 1948; K. Emery and others 1967).

PALEONTOLOGY

The study of bones in archeological sites may also give a rough basis for chronology, if it is realized that change in climate can cause migration or extinction as well as bring different animals and different plants into a region. What is more, certain species of animals have become extinct since man appeared. Taking these two factors into account, one may use paleontology to establish relative dates. Thus one can assume a temperate climate if such species as *Elephas antiquus* (a forest elephant) are present, whereas *E. primigenius* (a steppe elephant) indicates a steppe or tundra environment of almost glacial conditions. For some periods during the Pleistocene even such gross estimates of dating as these can prove valuable. For the later stages of the Pleistocene it is often possible to get much finer distinctions. In France, for example, an alternation of the forest and steppe varieties of reindeer suggests the alternation of warm and cold stages during the final glaciation (Movius 1961:564; Bordes 1966).

In North America there was a sequence of extinction of mammals whose remains are found associated with those of early man. The mammoth, horse, camel, and several species of bison all became extinct after the arrival of man in the New World. Although the exact dates for the final extinction of these forms are not yet known, within a margin of error of perhaps 1000 years, it is possible to say that man associated with mammoth remains lived before 6000 B.C. (J. Hester 1960). The problem is that no species of mammal became extinct all at once. Instead, there is good reason to believe that small groups lingered on in isolated refuges long after the main body of the species was extinct. Dating by means of faunal association is thus inexact and may at times be decidedly misleading.

Smaller species of animals may give better evidence. Rodents and birds are often more sensitive indicators of climate than are larger mammals. Some molluscs and forms of snails are exceptionally sensitive to changes in climate (Lais 1939). Their presence or absence in archeological sites may therefore record the changes of climate in an area. When these changes can be related to varves, pollens, or soils, it is frequently possible to date them and the human remains found in association (Sparks 1969). In northern Ireland it has been possible to show changes in coastal environment since the time of human occupation by studying changes in tidal-zone molluscs found in archeological sites (Jope 1960).

One must interpret with caution the chronological and climatic significance of bones found in archeological sites, because the bones were usually brought there by hunters and are not a random sample of the species around the site. If hunters chose one species as their favorite quarry during one period, and then shifted to another species, the findings may appear to indicate climatic change. Such a possible example is provided by caves in the Levant, where early workers reported an alternation in the abundance of *Dama mesopotamica* and *Gazella* (indicating moist and dry habitats, respectively [Garrod and Bate 1937]). Later work by Hooijer on the fauna from Ksar Akil concluded with the statement, "I believe it is only correct to say that what we see reflected in the refuse parts is accessibility of game, and food choice of the men who occupied the rock shelter, rather than climatic changes, the evidence for which is geological" (Hooijer 1961:61).

This warning should be remembered, because many animals can live in a wide range of climate and environment. It is also noteworthy that if the environment is highly varied many different species may live within easy walking distance of a hunter's base camp. The archeological consequence of this remark is that the animal bones in archeological sites may be a partial and selective sample of the total number of zoological species known to, and even used by, man. To use inferences derived from such data as the basis for determining the ages of deposits may therefore be highly inappropriate.

In places where men could choose among many species of game—anything from jackrabbits to mammoths—they may have hunted mainly or even exclusively one species. Thus a hunter living at the base of a mountain might habitually secure his food from the slopes of a mountain rather than from a valley or plain. If the hunter had a choice of food from a forest or plain, the ancient selection of the former would lead the archeologist to believe he is dealing with people living in a forest environment. In reality, both forest and tundra might have been within easy hunting range; yet they imply very different climates. These problems, with examples and citations to the literature, are discussed in more detail in Heizer (1960).

One must also remember that inferences about the climatic tolerance of a species assumes that the tolerance has not changed over the millennia. This is not necessarily a safe assumption. Also, many species have a much greater range of tolerance than of preference. That is, some animals prefer one kind of environment, but under certain conditions may be able to live in a different environment with little visible effect. The preferences and tolerances of various living species, and all the more so for extinct species, are not in fact very well known, and judgments about environment at the time archeological sites were occupied must be made with great caution.

If climate can be deduced from paleontology, it should be obvious that the climatic phase to which it refers may be fitted into a dated sequence derived from other kinds of data.

DENDROCHRONOLOGY

Tree-ring dating, or dendrochronology, is severely restricted in application both in space and time. It has had its greatest use and development in North America, but, as far as prehistoric man is concerned, it allows dating of only the archeology of the last 2000 years.

The method of tree-ring dating now in use was conceived about 1913 by Dr. A. E. Douglass, who was trying to determine whether tree rings held a record of past climate that could be related to sunspot cycles. Knowledge that some trees grew a ring each year and that by counting the rings one could determine the age of the tree had been known since the time of Leonardo da Vinci. In the United States, Reverend Manasseh Cutler in 1788 counted rings of trees growing on archeological sites at Marietta, Ohio, and concluded that the site was about 1000 years old. A similar attempt by M. Fiske, in 1820, yielded an age of 500–600 years for a Tennessee site; Squier and Davis, in their famous report on mounds of the Mississippi Valley, published in 1848, determined the minimum age of certain mounds by counting tree rings; Lapham calculated the minimum age of the aboriginal Wisconsin copper mining dumps at 395 years by counting tree rings; and other early examples of efforts to use this method are given by Fowke. The actual inventor of tree-ring dating of archeological remains was the Englishman Charles Babbage, who published a paper on the subject in 1838.

The method depends on the fact that trees growing in temperate zones have clearly defined annual rings of growth. After a winter period of dormancy, new growth cells are formed in the spring and continue to be added, though at reduced size, during the summer. If a person examines a cross section of a tree trunk he can see these annual increments preserved as a series of concentric rings. To tell how old the tree is, it is necessary only to count the number of rings.

To get a chronology suitable for dating archeological materials it is necessary to match series of rings from trees of various ages. The dendrochronology sequence for the American Southwest, which extends into the first century B.C., was developed by means of cross dating. Because the size of tree rings depends on the weather from year to year, one can match similar series of rings from one tree to another. The relative sizes of rings for a given time will be similar and recognizable in properly selected samples. The system of cross dating is illustrated in Figure 61.

FIG. 61 Diagram illustrating the building of chronology through matching tree rings from successively older samples. (W. Stallings, Jr., 1939, "Dating Prehistoric Ruins by Tree Rings," Santa Fe, N.M.: Laboratory of Anthropology, School of American Research, General Series, Bulletin 8.)

In principle the method is simple, but there are some practical problems. These are listed by Bannister and Smiley (1955:179) as follows:

> The establishment in any given area, of a satisfactory tree-ring chronology, permitting the dating of prehistoric materials, is possible only when the following four conditions are met:
> 1. There must be trees that produce defined annual rings as a result of a definite growing season.
> 2. Tree growth must be principally dependent upon one controlling factor.

3. There must have been an indigenous prehistoric population that made extensive use of wood.

4. The wood must be well enough preserved so that it still retains its cellular structure.

Conifers are the best trees for dating. In the American Southwest, where the system has been used most extensively, the Ponderosa pine (*Pinus ponderosa*) and a few other trees can be used. The longer sequences have come from the giant sequoia in California (*Sequoia gigantea*), and recently the bristlecone pine (*Pinus aristata*) of the White Mountains of eastern California has been found to live more than 4000 years (Schulman 1958). Unfortunately, wood from all these trees does not occur in archeological sites and is thus of no value for direct dating. A second difficulty is that the most dependable sequences come from trees growing in relatively arid climates where tree-ring growth is dependent on soil moisture.

One must also find trees that have not tapped a permanent source of underground water. Trees from hillsides are better than those from river bottoms. The effect of permanent water may sometimes be just the opposite of the expected. In Europe it was found that trees living on the flood plains of rivers put on a very small ring during a wet year. By contrast, trees on the slopes put on large rings. The reason was that the trees on the flood plains were suffering from drowned roots.

When logs for dating are taken from archeological sites, other cautions must be observed. Any terminal date on a log, that is, its last ring, represents the time when the log was cut. It does not necessarily date the time the log was used. In areas where wood was relatively scarce and where it was necessary to cut it with primitive implements, logs were used repeatedly (Judd 1959:56; O'Bryan 1949). Bannister (1962) discusses four possible sources of error often involved in relating a tree-ring date to its associated archeological material.

Dating methods using plant and animal remains include both the most precise and the least exact methods for determining chronology currently at our disposal. It seems safe to say, however, as more evidence accumulates in palynology and paleontology, that in some areas it may become possible to obtain dates on biological species that are nearly as accurate for relative dating as is the cross dating of artifacts today.

REFERENCES

Palynology (Pollen Analysis); Techniques and Illustrative Examples: R. Anderson 1955; Bryant and Holtz 1968; Butzer 1964:Chaps. 16 and 17; M. B. Davis 1963; Dimbleby 1957, 1969; Erdtman 1943; Faegri and Iversen 1964; Gray and Smith 1962; Hill and Hevly 1968; Jelinek 1966; P. Martin 1963; P. Martin and Gray 1962; Mehringer 1967; Wendorf 1961; Wodehouse 1959; H. Wright and Frey 1965:Part II.

Animal Extinction During the Time of Man on Earth: Axelrod 1967; Butzer

1964:Chap. 28; Evernden and others 1964; Forbis 1956; J. Hester 1960; Hubbs 1958; Jelinek 1957; Leakey 1966b; P. Martin 1966; P. Martin and Wright 1967; Osborn 1906.

Early Applications of Tree-Ring Dating (Dendrochronology): Babbage 1838; Fowke 1902:117–128; Lapham 1885:75; Michael 1971; Stallings 1939; Studhalter 1955.

Principles and Practice of Dendrochronological Dating: Bannister 1962, 1969; Bannister and Smiley 1955; Fritts 1965; Giddings 1962; Glock 1937, 1955; McGinnies 1963; Schulman 1940, 1941.

CHAPTER FIFTEEN

OTHER METHODS FOR DATING

Astronomical Dating

For more than 100 years there has been investigation of solar radiation and its effect on the earth's climate. These studies began when a number of early workers who were interested in finding out what had caused the Pleistocene ice advances (Zeuner 1958:134–143) attempted to relate variations in solar radiation to climatic change. This was the origin of the astronomical theory of climate change. Without going into details, the theory is based on the fact that the orbit of the earth undergoes perturbations so that the obliquity of the ecliptic (periodicity of 43,000 years), the eccentricity of the orbit (periodicity of 92,000 years), and the precession of the equinoxes (periodicity of 21,000 years) have changed, owing to the mutual attraction of the planets. In other words, at intervals in the past, the orientation of the earth relative to the sun has shifted. Parts of the earth then received greater or lesser amounts of solar radiation, and the areas receiving the greatest amount of radiation were the warmest.

Today the theory is not accepted generally as an explanation of the cause of the ice advances, but only of the fluctuations during the Pleistocene once the series of glaciations had started. The formulae on which the theory rests were devised by a number of mathematicians, of whom the most prominent is M. Milankovitch. Support for his theory, from which dates can be derived for the various stages of the Pleistocene, comes mainly from

Zeuner in his two major works, *Dating the Past* (1958) and *The Pleistocene Period* (1959: Chap. X). He believes there is a close correspondence between the dates arrived at with Milankovitch's calculations, and elapsed time based on rates of sedimentation and with other time-reckoning methods used in geology (cf. Zeuner 1960). Many authors do not agree with Zeuner's dating of the Pleistocene (cf. E. Carpenter 1955). Even if one assumes that the theory is correct, the calculations themselves can be criticized for failure to take fully into account known sources of error (Flint 1957:300–301, 506–609). More evidence must be secured before the astronomical theory can be proved to be incorrect, correct, or modifiable in such a way that it makes a reliable chronology of the Pleistocene. One relatively sure date is that of the end of the Pleistocene (that is, the age of the Pleistocene-Recent boundary), which has been determined by a very large number of radiocarbon dates at about 11,300 B.P. (9350 B.C.). This date is somewhat older than the Scandinavian varve-analysis calculation made by De Geer (1940) of 7912 B.C.

CALENDARS

Strictly speaking, unless they are calendars, artifacts themselves do not give dates. Prehistoric people did not usually have exact calendars for determining long-range chronology. Simple methods for determining the length of the year and dividing it into months or seasons were in use by preliterate peoples all over the world, who used the winter and summer solstices and the moon's phases. But annual calendars of this sort are only convenient clocks for managing current affairs.

The Bronze Age builders of Stonehenge, Europe's most impressive megalithic monument, are claimed by the Boston University astronomer Gerald Hawkins to have been surprisingly advanced in their achievements in astronomy, eclipse prediction, and calendar system. Such a degree of sophistication by 3000 B.C. in Europe is surprising, though not impossible if one accepts the independent findings of A. Thom (1966, 1967) on the great proficiency of the megalithic peoples of Britain in astronomy and geometry (Fig. 62).

The Olmecs of southeastern lowland Mexico are believed to have had an astronomically based calendar. Part of the evidence for this theory is the precise alignment of the centerline of the La Venta site, which was built about 1000 B.C. and abandoned about 600 B.C. The La Venta pyramid may have served as an astronomical "observatory"—meaning that its elevation permitted a clear view of the true horizon at a distance of about 10 miles (Hatch 1971). It is difficult to prove to everyone's satisfaction that an astronomical calendar was in use in Meso-America as early as 1000 B.C., but there should be nothing surprising about this when we know that the Maya by the second and third century B.C. did possess such knowledge. The Maya, who had an excellent calendric system, are prehistoric in the sense that they wrote

FIG. 62 Stonehenge in southern England has been called a "Neolithic computer" by Gerald Hawkins, an astronomer who has determined the uses to which the megalithic monument may have been put in making astronomical sightings.

no history that can be read. It has not been possible to read very many of the glyphs they used for writing. Most of those that have been read so far pertain to the calendar, but a large number of glyphs appear to be historical in nature, rather than numerical or calendrical. The Maya were therefore literate, but for us they will remain—until their records can be deciphered—prehistoric. Y. V. Knorozov believes that he has deciphered Maya writing, but most Maya scholars do not accept his proposals (Knorozov 1967). R. E. Smith (1955: 3–4, 105–108) has said that Maya stone stelae bearing inscribed dates, which tell one when the city was occupied, can be used to date ceramic sequences only very rarely, because stelae in ceremonial precincts and pottery in trash deposits are not often directly associated. However, as at Tikal, tombs containing pottery are sometimes directly associated with the stelae and both tombs and pottery can be dated by them.

Unfortunately, an exact correlation of the Maya calendar with our own (Christian) calendar is lacking. By the time of the Spanish conquest in the first half of the sixteenth century the Maya had stopped erecting dated stelae at regular intervals. There was, therefore, no direct link between 1520, the time of the Spanish arrival, and the last dated stelae, sculptured and set up sometime just before A.D. 1000.

Various workers have claimed to have the key to the Maya calendar. Even though its cyclic nature is known, authors disagree on its precise relation to our calendar. Two correlations differing by 260 years predominated and vied for approval over the years. When radiocarbon dating was first applied to the solution of the problem, the "Spinden correlation" appeared to be correct. Subsequent reanalysis with refined radiocarbon techniques and a more careful selection of material to be dated indicates that the Goodman-Thompson-Martinez correlation, which makes Maya dates 260 years younger than the Spinden correlation, is probably correct.

When stone stelae that bear dates in the Maya calendar system are found associated with structures, it is generally assumed that the stelae were carved and set up on the date inscribed on the stones. As stelae were often erected at the time pyramids and temples were built and dedicated and are clearly associated with them, one can usually date (that is, within 260 years, depending on which correlation is used) the structure itself and materials contained in it that were placed there at the time of its building. However, this is not invariably the situation; A. Smith (1929) and Ricketson and Ricketson (1937:154–156) point out that dated stelae do not always date the building they are associated with, as older stelae were sometimes moved and re-erected without changing the date glyphs.

A similar problem has been encountered regarding the ancient re-using of beams in Southwestern sites. Although such beams may be dated by dendrochronology, the date may not refer to the age of the building or the room (O'Bryan 1959; Bannister 1962). The point is that even where absolute dating of particular pieces can be determined, such pieces are not always precisely contemporaneous with associated features. A glance at the coins in your pocket or purse will show that there is a range of dates represented. If the coins in your pocket were found archeologically in a group, you would date the find with reference to the latest or most recent minting date. The hoard cannot have been deposited earlier than the most recent coin, and could not have been deposited earlier than the coin bearing the oldest date. It could, however, have been deposited later than the date of the most recent coin.

SEQUENCE DATING

Noncalendrical artifacts themselves do not tell dates, but, if artifacts change in predictable ways through time, it may be possible to date them relative to one another. If one can build up either a generalized temporal sequence of artifact types or associations of artifacts—as are implied in the very elementary "Stone, Bronze, and Iron Age" system, or a more specialized one such as "Mousterian, Aurignacian, Solutrean, Magdalenian, Mesolithic"—he can take isolated examples and fit them into the standard schemes. In this way archeologists can tell that a bronze knife must have been made later than a certain date; they cannot, with equal precision, say that a particular flint tool was not contemporary, as flints were often used together with bronze implements. If an archeologist is familiar with sequences of paleolithic tool assemblages, he can look at a group of tools and tell whether it is representative of the Aurignacian or some other subdivision. By comparative typology he can thus date it within broad limits, because the Aurignacian in general has been dated by radiocarbon. Even without absolute dates an archeologist could readily say that the material was earlier than the Magdalenian and other remains that are consistently found stratigraphically above site layers that produce Aurignacian tools.

Sequences of artifacts are thus a key to relative chronologies, and at their best these tools may be referable to particular dated segments of pre-history. The system of relative dating depends on change that is nonreversible and continuous.

Pottery has traditionally been the most important artifact for purposes of dating. It is durable, being made of fired clay, and therefore accumulates in quantity rather than decays and disappears after it is broken and discarded. It is a medium of artistic and esthetic expression, because the moist clay can be manipulated into different forms and can be decorated by surface impressions in the form of stamping, molding, incising, or painting. Like any aspect of culture, the manufacture and functions of pottery are subject to patterning. That is, any single social group will not make every pot differently (or, of course, every one exactly alike), but will usually settle on a limited variety of shapes and decorative styles so that the pottery becomes definable and recognizable as a ceramic pattern of the society. Like all other parts of a culture, pottery changes over time; by detecting these trends of change, an archeologist can trace associated cultural changes and make short-term time distinctions after careful study of the ceramic remains.

The recognition of the importance of potsherds as a guide to chronology in archeology could not come until reasonably exact excavation methods had been developed. Albright (1957:49ff.) tells us that Furtwängler, who was primarily an art historian, was the first to see and use the significance of painted pottery for chronological purposes in classical studies, and that Petrie, in his report on the excavation of Tell-el-Hesi (Lachish) in 1890, was the first archeologist to appreciate the importance of unpainted pottery for purposes of determining chronology (Petrie 1891:14–15, 40–41). Petrie wrote, "and once settle the pottery of a country, and the key is in our hands for all future explorations. A single glance at a mound of ruins, even without dismounting, will show as much to any one who knows the styles of the pottery, as weeks of work may reveal to the beginner" (cf. Kroeber 1916).

Sir Flinders Petrie, an Egyptologist whose work in Egypt began in 1881, developed the technique known as sequence dating. Predynastic Egypt was almost unknown, and the graves that Petrie excavated at the site of Diospolis Parva could not be dated. The pottery from the graves was varied, but certain types were habitually found together. Petrie reasoned that different assemblages of pottery were of different ages. With this in mind, he analyzed such features as handles on pots and worked out a sequence showing their change, progressing from functional entities to mere decorations. The changes on pots were then correlated with changes in other artifacts from the graves, and he finally ended with a series of numbered pottery stages that he labeled "Sequence Dates." His series ran from s.d. 30 to s.d. 80, but Petrie had no way of telling what this range meant in terms of calendrical dates or elapsed years. He began with s.d. 30 because he assumed (correctly) that he had not found the earliest Egyptian pottery. As a guess, Petrie suggested that s.d. 30 should be about 9000 b.c. We now know that s.d. 30 occurs at about 3500 b.c. (W. Emery 1961:28).

In the New World, local styles of pottery had been identified and named in the Southwest before 1900 by J. W. Fewkes, W. H. Holmes, F. H. Cushing, and other pioneer workers, but no clear idea of how to exploit pottery to extract time ordering was clearly worked out in North America until A. L. Kroeber in 1915, at Zuni Pueblo, collected surface potsherds from local sites and devised the method of surface seriation (Kroeber 1916; reprinted in Heizer 1960:383–393). Although different styles of pottery were recognized and discussed, it did not occur to any of the archeologists working in the United States until 1915 or 1916 that differences in shape and decoration in prehistoric pottery might mean that one style was different in age from another. Kroeber's pioneeering work at Zuni in 1915 showed one method for tracing time differences, and N. C. Nelson's stratigraphic digging in the trash heaps at the Tano ruin in 1916 provided another.

Dating by seriation is a variety of sequence dating; it depends on the fact that types of artifacts change stylistically and in their relative abundance. The fact has been used by many workers to obtain relative dates for the deposits they find in several sites in an area. A simple illustration of the idea behind seriation follows. It frequently happens that in a site of long duration with many stratigraphic levels, certain objects are confined to particular levels. Artifact *a* may occur in levels 1–3, artifact *b* in levels 3–7, artifact *c* in levels 2–5, artifact *d* in levels 4–9, and artifact *e* in levels 4–6. If a nearby site has a stratigraphic unit with artifacts *a,b,c,* one assumes that the unit is contemporary with level 3 in the first site, because this is the only level in which all three artifacts were found (Table 5). If a different combination of

TABLE 5 DISTRIBUTION OF ARTIFACTS BY STRATIGRAPHIC LEVELS

Stratigraphic Levels	Types of Artifacts				
	a	*b*	*c*	*d*	*e*
1	x				
2	x		x		
3	x	x	x		
4		x	x	x	x
5		x		x	x
6		x		x	x
7		x		x	
8		x		x	
9				x	

artifacts had been found, it might not have been possible to relate a level in one site to a single level in another site. For example, *b* and *d* were found alone in levels 7–8, but there may be no other site in which the same combination has been found. If this situation exists, the relative dating cannot be as precise.

The preceding example assumed that the presence or absence of artifacts is the criterion one uses for seriating cross-dating sites, but the method can be somewhat refined by using the frequencies in which artifacts occur in the various levels. Taking artifacts *b* and *d* in Table 6, for example, we find

TABLE 6 RELATIVE FREQUENCIES OF ARTIFACTS OF EACH TYPE IN EACH STRATIGRAPHIC LEVEL

Stratigraphic Levels	Types of Artifacts				
	a	*b*	*c*	*d*	*e*
1	100				
2	75		25		
3	50	40	10		
4		60	5	10	25
5		70		15	15
6		40		50	10
7		30		70	
8		10		90	
9				100	

that they occur in different relative frequencies in the two levels. If, in a comparison of levels, one found 30 percent of *b* and 70 percent of *d,* he would assume that he was dealing with a level contemporary with level 7. When one has enough information (that is, a sufficiently large sample), it is likely that each period can be characterized by the frequencies of artifacts that occur in it (Fig. 63).

The method of sequence dating is implicitly used by most archeologists. One says that an artifact "looks younger" than another, meaning that because of certain stylistic details it looks more recent than another type. This is as though a person were to study pictures of all the automobiles made by one company in 50 years. It would be easy to get sequence dates for the cars because the trends of style from early to late would be apparent. However, cars are not quite the same as pots. The mechanical improvement of cars is shown in their size, shape, and ornament. Pottery is seldom improved; it changes according to the whims of its makers. Furthermore, several "types" may be in use at the same time. It is not always clear, therefore, when one has a hundred pots of different ages, which is the earliest and which is the latest. Petrie was fortunate in being able to anchor one end of his sequence of predynastic Egyptian pots to later pots of known date, but there was much room for error in the earlier periods. At best, sequence dating gives good relative dates. Accurate judgment of the rate of stylistic change is possible only by independent methods.

A final reservation should be mentioned. It is tempting to think of changes in artifacts as progressing from simple to complex and to suggest that simple things are older than more complex things. If this were true, one might assume that flint arrowheads are older than bullets. In general, this

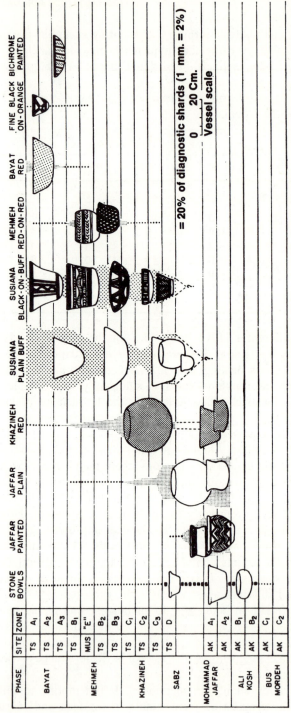

Fig. 63 Frequency polygons showing changes in percentage of various pottery types through time in the Deh Luran sequence, Mohammad Jaffar through Bayat Phases. The phases are characterized by the relative frequency of each type of pottery and also by the presence or absence of certain types. Drawings indicate typical vessels of each period but do not represent the full range of variation. Temporal distribution of stone bowls is shown for comparative purposes, but percentages are not calculated versus pottery. (F. Hole and K. V. Flannery, "The Prehistory of Southwestern Iran: A Preliminary Report," *Proceedings of the Prehistoric Society*, Vol. 33 (1968):Fig. 10.)

may be a correct assumption, but it does not take into account technological lag. People having very crude artifacts may live with others who have a more advanced technology. On typological grounds, the "Stone Age" aborigines of Australia would be placed much earlier than their "Iron Age" white Australian neighbors, but in fact both groups are living at the same time.

CROSS DATING

When an archeologist has established a sequence of artifacts in an area, he then asks how it relates to neighboring sequences. The usual means for establishing relations between areas is through cross dating (cf. Heizer 1959: Chap. 10). Unless there has been widespread trade in exotic items, one can establish only general chronological correspondences between areas. Thus an archeologist might recognize "archaic" sites whether they occurred in New York or Arkansas, but he would have no sure way to determine whether the two sites were contemporary; in fact, they might have been occupied several thousand years apart. When trade items can be found it is often possible to state with certainty that the occupation of one of the sites did not occur before a certain date. If coins or pottery or bronze axes of a known date are found as trade items at undated sites, one can say that the sites were occupied no earlier than the date the objects were known to have been made in their homeland. In this way much protohistoric material from Europe can be dated relative to the centers of civilization in the Mediterranean. This extensional dating of European forms whose origins lie further south in the Mediterranean area has been done in detail by V. G. Childe (1957) and Grahame Clark (1952) in their books on the development of European cultures.

Cross dating works best when two groups exchanged easily identifiable and distinctive objects. If only one part of a trade network can be discovered because some traded artifacts have not been preserved, it is harder to assume close synchronism. That is, if stone axes were traded for sheep wool and grain, no palpable record of the transaction in the form of vegetal food or animal products would remain, or, at least, could be specifically identified. In some instances, perhaps after centuries, axes—being imperishable objects—might find their way a thousand or more miles from their place of origin. The rate of diffusion cannot be easily calculated, but one attempt at calculating the variable speeds at which knowledge of maize agriculture, copper metallurgy, and pottery spread in prehistoric times has been made (Edmonson 1961).

The dependability of cross dating increases proportionately with the amount of foreign trade in which a group engaged. It is most dependable when one can date special trade artifacts, such as coins, beads, or axes, to a narrow range of time, especially when there has been reciprocal trade. In exceptional instances, cross dating can help establish absolute chronologies, as evidenced by the Minoan sequence on Crete that was dated by means of Egyptian trade items (Kantor 1954:11–12, Fig. 1; Weinberg 1954:90), or in the extension of Puebloan-period datings eastward toward the Mississippi Valley (Krieger 1947), or in correlating Great Basin cultures into California cultures on the basis of imported beads of marine shell into the Great Basin (Bennyhoff and Heizer 1958), but more often it merely places certain stages in one sequence opposite their contemporaries in another sequence.

The reader should keep in mind that imported items may have been carried from distant sources by modern collectors, and their apparent association with archeological sites or in an assumed archeological context (for example, as surface finds) is a special situation. Van Riet Lowe (1954) cites the example of a neolithic ax from Norway that was found in South Africa but that could be shown to have been brought there by a recent collector, and soapstone carvings of recent Chinese manufacture that have been found in Mexican sites (Heizer 1953). Rose (1968; also K. Emery and others, 1968) describes the transshipping of flint from Europe as ballast in ocean-going vessels that was dumped in the harbors of the American east coast. A person finding artifacts among these might erroneously assume contact between Europe and America during the paleolithic. Such examples of what have been termed "travelers" or "wayfarers" are, of course, of no value for showing ancient diffusion or cross dating but serve only as traps for the unwary archeologist and the uncritical speculator (Heizer 1968b).

RATE OF ACCUMULATION

Attempts to estimate the rate at which habitation refuse accumulates have been made from the very earliest days of archeology. Petrie estimated that soils of Egyptian sites accumulated about 20 inches a century. Vaillant, excavating the pre-Classic Mexican site of El Arbolillo, compared its refuse dump with that of a Pueblo occupation site in Pecos, New Mexico. Because the Pueblo trash, amounting to 21 feet, had accumulated in 600 years, Vaillant (1935:166–167) suggested that the El Arbolillo dumps, which had somewhat more debris, had probably been used for at least as long. In another instance, Braidwood and Howe (1960:159) estimated that a Near Eastern mound might accumulate at the rate of 2 feet in a generation. Lloyd (1963:73) describes how, some years ago, he computed the age of the first occupation of the site of Hassuna, in Iraq, on what he believed to be the rate of accumulation. He learned after a time, during which the radiocarbon dating method came into use, that his early calculation had been remarkably accurate.

An amusing example of an archeologist who achieved absolute accuracy of dating by utilizing what are known to be incorrect data is that of M. Harrington (1933:171), who calculated the age of the Gypsum Cave culture, associated with extinct ground-sloth remains, as 10,500 years

(8500 B.C.), or three times that of the age of the Basket Maker culture. He used as his measure the assumed age of the Basket Maker culture at 3500 years (1500 B.C.). Since 1933 the tree-ring chronology has corrected the date of the Basket Maker culture to about A.D. 300, and, as Kroeber (1948:681) points out, the age of the Gypsum Cave culture should thereby automatically have been reduced to about 5000 years (3000 B.C.). Radiocarbon age determination of the sloth dung from Gypsum Cave yielded a date of 8505 B.C. (10,505 years old), a figure that checked accurately with the original calculation of 1933. But artifacts made of wood that were believed by the excavators of the cave to be clearly coeval with the sloth-dung deposits prove to have radiocarbon ages of 2400 and 2900 years. The conclusion may be drawn that the ground sloth lived and defecated in the cave between 10 and 11 millennia ago, but man's presence there is not older than 3 millennia. The association of ancient sloth dung and wooden artifacts is therefore fortuitous.

There is no justification for assuming that the rate of the growth of the soil of any particular site was constant throughout its occupation. Increase or decrease in population, the use of several debris dumps, the lateral expansion of a site, and similar factors will all skew deductions. An interesting example is that supplied by Fowler (1959:19–20) with reference to Modoc Rock Shelter in Illinois. Total depth of the archeological deposit was 27 feet, and from the several layers 11 charcoal samples were collected and dated by radiocarbon. Fowler, assuming the correctness of most of the radiocarbon dates, has examined the vertical position of each dated sample with reference to the amount of refuse between it and the next higher dated level in an effort to calculate rate of accumulation. He found that the rate of deposition was constant at about 1 foot per 500 years for the period between 8000–5000 B.C.; increased to about 1 foot per 300 years between 5000 and 3600 B.C.; increased to 1.7 feet per 100 years between 3600–3000 B.C.; and decreased to 1 foot per 400 years between 3300–2700 B.C. These variable rates discourage any attempt in this particular site to apply a single rate of increment, but, having discovered the fluctuations, the archeologist is presented with an intriguing problem of why this variation occurred. Fowler found it necessary to reexamine his total information to learn whether variable rates of accumulation were caused by such factors as climatic conditions, differences over time of number of occupants, variations in living patterns, and so on.

There are times, however, when an archeologist is forced to rely on rate of accumulation because no other means of dating is available to him. Wheeler (1956:45) says about rate of accumulation dating: "Such calculations have, if any, a purely academic or abstract interest. They make no allowance for the intermittencies and vagaries which, alike in human and in geological history, defy the confines of mathematical formulae." This is a rather positive statement, whose effect is to deny any possible validity or utility in increment dating. Actually, Wheeler himself has, in at least one instance, made use of the method in attempting to determine the duration of time involved in the six successive building phases of the platform of the Harappa citadel that he excavated in 1946 (Wheeler 1947:81).

A fair statement about this method of calculating age is that there is no probability that a generally applicable scale or rate of accumulation will be discovered because of the "intermittencies and vagaries . . . in human and geological history," but this denial of a general method should not beguile us into refusing to attempt to determine the rate of accumulation in particular sites in regions where no culture chronology has been earlier determined. Merely by way of illustration, we may cite the observation of Yanine (1960) that refuse accumulated in the city of Novgorod 1000 years ago at a rate of about 1 meter per century. This information might be useful in computing the duration of other, but lesser known, medieval Russian settlements. Atkinson (1956:54–55) calculates the rate of covering the earth of the bluestone chips at the site of Stonehenge at 6–8 inches per century. Here again a possibly useful measure for rough dating of nearby but lesser known megalithic remains is available.

GEOGRAPHIC LOCATION

It is sometimes possible to give a maximum age for a site by noting where it lies in relation to a datable geological feature. The date of the penetration of the Upper Great Lakes area in North America by early hunters using fluted dart points has been estimated in this fashion (R. Mason 1958). Geologists have calculated the dates when the Wisconsin glacial ice receded and when the various glacial lakes waxed and waned; it is therefore possible to say that man could not have lived in certain places before a certain time. A relatively well-known example of this is Danger Cave in western Utah (Jennings 1957:85–98), where the geological history of Lake Bonneville was judiciously correlated with radiocarbon dates for the lowest levels that mark man's presence in the cave. By similar reasoning it has been possible to date Mousterian occupation of caves on the Italian peninsula (Zeuner 1959:243ff.). During the Pleistocene, when the level of the Mediterranean Sea rose, some caves that lie close to the water could not have been occupied. Knowledge of sea levels and their approximate dates thus gives archeologists a date before which the caves could not have been lived in.

Many special dating methods give results that may at times appear to be at variance with the archeological-cultural dating. Unless the contradiction can be resolved either by correcting the dating method or by finding the error in the archeological dating, it is safest to rely on the less precise but better controlled archeological dating. Auxiliary sciences do not always provide dates that are correct or consistent among themselves. An example of a conflict between tree-ring dating and archeological dating is provided by H. S. Gladwin (1943:55–69).

REFERENCES

Astronomical Theory of Pleistocene Chronology: Broecker 1966; Butzer 1964: 35–37; Van Woerkom 1953; Zeuner 1958, 1959, 1960.

Absolute Age of the Pleistocene: Broecker, Ewing, and Heezen 1960; Donnay and others 1966; Emiliani 1966; Ericson, Ewing, and Wollin 1964; Ericson and others 1961; Ku and Broecker 1966; Opdyke and others 1966.

Stonehenge as an Astronomical Observatory: Atkinson 1966; Hawkins 1964, 1965a, 1965b.

The Maya Calendar—Its Principles and Functions, Problems of Correlation with the Christian Calendar: Kelley 1962; Morley 1915; Ralph 1965; Satterthwaite and Ralph 1960; J. Thompson 1950, 1962.

Pottery as a Means of Tracing Temporal Change: Albright 1939; J. Ford 1962; J. Gifford 1960; W. and H. Gladwin 1928b; Peake 1940:23, Quimby 1960.

Sequence Dating or Seriation—Principles and Application: Albright 1957:51–52; M. Ascher and R. Ascher 1963; Brainerd 1951; Cleland 1972; G. Cowgill 1972; J. Ford 1938, 1962; Gelfand 1971; Heizer 1959b:376–383; Hole and Shaw 1967; Jelinek 1967; Kroeber 1916; Kuzara, Mead, and Dixon 1966; Petrie 1901:4–8; W. Robinson 1951; Spier 1917.

Rate-of-Accumulation of Refuse as a Dating Method: F. Hawley 1934:57–58; Heizer 1953:24–25, 1959b:Chap. 9; Heizer and Graham 1967:173–174; Laming-Emperaire 1963:137–138; Rouse 1957:564–566; Sanson 1874:339.

PART V

RECONSTRUCTION AND PROCESSUAL INTERPRETATION

The central concerns of prehistory have always been to document a chronological sequence of man's changes and to describe the variations in ways of life in different places. These reconstructions lead to historical narrative. A more recent approach is to examine the workings of past cultures to determine how and why they operated as they did, and to attempt to find general laws that explain the courses taken by mankind. Some authors, including Willey and Phillips (1958:3–7), see these two approaches as part of a normal sequence of investigation. They refer to three "levels of analysis," only two of which we are concerned with here– "description" and "explanation"; "observation" (the lowest level) was discussed in preceding chapters. These authors say,

> So little work has been done in American archaeology on the explanatory level that it is difficult to find a name for it. . . . Perhaps it is fair to say that there has been a lack of progress in processual interpretation in American archaeology to date precisely because unit formulations have been put together with so little reference to their social aspect (1958:5–6).

As Willey and Phillips have emphasized, American archeologists often fail to

303

appreciate that archeological remains represent the activities of people and that the remains must be interpreted with this fact in mind. In either historical reconstruction or processual interpretation we are making interpretations, but in the two approaches the intents of the studies are different. We discussed some of these differences in Part I and will expand on the concepts relating to reconstruction in Chapter 16. Chapters 17 to 20 describe how prehistorians reconstruct and interpret the history of cultures, and the final chapter deals with concepts and methods of processual interpretation.

It is useful to keep in mind the difference between historical reconstruction on the one hand, and analysis and interpretation of changes on the other. When we excavate a site and describe its contents, we are dealing for the most part with synchronous events. We are observing archeologically a slice of life in the history of a people in much the same way that an ethnologist might study a people over the course of a year or so. We are concerned with the contents of sites and with the interrelations of the things found in them. We describe the houses, burials, work areas, and the artifacts associated with them, and in so doing we gain a glimpse of a way of life. Translated into three dimensions, such a picture is analogous to a museum diorama which is really a scale model of a community with the people engaged in their daily activities.

In contrast with this approach and after some of these slices of life have been described, we may concern ourselves with changes and the processes that enabled them. Our attention turns from the study of things to the study of the way artifacts and sites relate to the behavior of prehistoric people to one another and to the surounding world. Our interest is not in charting the development of ceramic technology, but rather in the reasons for changes in the culture of the people who made the pots. How do we explain the shift from hunting to agriculture? Or from villages to cities? Or why some cultures seem not to change over long periods? These are questions of process which must be answered in the light of theory pertaining specifically to stability and change; they cannot be answered by reference only to the immediate archeological situation. It is for this reason that Flannery (1972) said, "The way data are collected to answer inductive questions of culture history may make it impossible to do processual studies later." In other words, one can do a splendid and convincing three-dimensional reconstruction of a village and yet know nothing of the way it was organized, how the people related to others around them or to their environment, or how they came to be as they were found. Were they in the throes of change? Did they have a long-lasting adaptation? Were they declining from a previous "higher" level? Were they about to become extinct as a viable culture? The question "why a people were as they were" nags at the archeologist interested in process and cannot be answered solely in terms of the immediate situation. Thus studies of process draw on different bodies of theory and express quite different goals from those concerned primarily with reconstruction. It is important to bear in mind that although the two approaches are not mutually exclusive, they are not necessarily complementary either; and one cannot shift readily from one to another unless he has an adequate understanding of how they differ and how they may be mutually supporting.

The studies that reconstruct prehistoric ways of life are more readily understandable than are studies of process for two reasons. First, the former studies deal with things and lend themselves to visual representation; second, they appeal to the common sense. A person can literally imagine himself living in a prehistoric village. Processual studies on the other hand, dealing with organizational interrelationships and changes over long periods of time, lend themselves more to abstract graphic rather than to representational depiction. It would be very hard for a person to imagine himself acting out a thousand generations of a culture's history. For these reasons we shall present the concepts that deal with reconstruction first.

CHAPTER SIXTEEN

CONCEPTS RELATING TO RECONSTRUCTION

Earlier (Chapter 4) we discussed the concepts that make a study of prehistory possible and how they relate to the data and goals of archeology. Now that we have reviewed the ways archeologists obtain and analyze data we must turn to their interpretation. We have also described the controversy in archeology over whether it should be primarily a historical or a scientific discipline. The two points of view implicit in this controversy are not necessarily antithetical, but they usually begin from different sets of premises which lead investigators along different paths in explanation of their data. In this chapter we shall try to make clear the premises on which historical reconstructions are based; in later chapters we show how they are used in specific instances. The basic interpretive concepts are few, but each has a variety of implications that illustrate how the concepts are interrelated and how they may be used in archeological interpretation. The concepts mentioned in Chapter 4 are prerequisite to understanding this chapter.

Although some of the concepts relating specifically to reconstructing the events of prehistory have been mentioned previously, they have not been discussed explicitly in the context of interpretive reconstruction. The concepts are basically concerned with how it was and how we know. They are: data, uniformitarianism, analogy, system, culture, adaptation, ecology, evolution, and model. From most of these concepts there follows a particular view of culture and of data and a set of possible interpretations.

ARCHEOLOGICAL DATA

In many respects, doing archeology is like groping around in a dark and unfamiliar room trying to grab something familiar in order to get oriented. Orientation in a dark room requires fixing on something you can identify that in turn will allow you to predict finding something else, like the presence of a wall or door. Testing of these subsequent predictions will eventually lead to an accurate picture of the room, because the world is predictable—it consists of patterns or relations of objects. Some of the patterns are essentially timeless, having come into being with life itself; others have been added in the long course of human history. But patterns of organization are common to all things and to all life. If we understand this we can use minor clues and incomplete evidence to help us reconstruct prehistoric life.

Archeological data consist of mud, clay, stone, bone, and fibrous objects, and so they will remain unless they are given a cultural interpretation. Then they become bricks, pottery, projectile points, remains of meals, and basketry, used and discarded by living peoples in the normal routine of gaining a livelihood. The proces by which these data are transformed into a picture of life in the past is the subject of the following chapters.

The basic and tangible data we use are derived from the survey and excavation of archeological sites. The data might be treated simply as objects, but if we did so we should not be able to use them in reconstructing prehistoric cultural systems, because the essence of a system is its organization. What we must look for in archeological data, therefore, are the attributes that pertain to organization. They are distribution, relative size, number, spatial arrangement, and hierarchy. These aspects are important with whatever archeological data we are studying, be they sites, houses, artifacts, or burials.

A typology of projectile points, an analysis of settlement patterns, or a reconstruction of the structure of a prehistoric social system—all begin with an analysis of the spatial and quantitative relations of the component parts. In a previous chapter we treated space as one dimension of context, a dimension that could be recorded by measurement and hence become a datum or fact. When we wish to use these data for cultural reconstructions, however, we are concerned with a further dimension-pattern or relation —because these are the attributes that inform on the organization of prehistoric culture systems.

Data are necessary, as we have already mentioned, but they exist only when we think they do and can be obtained only when we have the techniques to find them. The former is the more formidable problem, as was neatly expressed by Mulvaney (1971:239, quoting A. Kenyon 1927:282) in his review of the history of archeological studies in Australia. Work was not done there until recently because it was thought:

Aboriginal material culture was static through time and space, so that excavations were pointless, and in any case sites were shallow and unstratified. "Culture" was a misnomer, because of the essential local causative factors in every instance . . . our black brother . . . was a poor, primitive creature, who allowed the material available to govern him.

If preconceived notions about an entire people and their history could stifle archeological study for half a century, consider how dependent we must also be on conceptions of what is interesting to investigate and what our data will tell. It is also worth reflecting upon the kinds of things we may be systematically overlooking. For example, "It is ironical that archaeology should be so highly prized by votaries of the materialist interpretation of history, when so few of the outstanding monuments or even of the finest artifacts revealed by excavation can, in fact, be explained in material terms" (G. Clark 1970:143).

We should bear in mind Clark's caveat, but a contrary view is usually expressed by new archeologists. For example, in his reconstruction of prehistoric social organization in the American Southwest, J. Hill (1970:48) says,

It would appear . . . that virtually all aspects of prehistoric behavior are amenable to discovery—given appropriate methods and techniques. While I have attempted to argue this and have presented a methodological approach that should be useful in this regard, I am by no means prepared to argue that there are no limits at all! On the other hand, it would be presumptuous to attempt to state with any degree of precision what the limitations actually are; we simply do not know. It is clear, however, that some of the commonly *believed* limitations are not as limiting as they have been thought to be.

Hill (1970:50–52) goes on to state what he thinks the limitations may be. First, most behavioral aspects of behavior are intangible. However,

most of the things the archaeologist is interested in *do* leave . . . remains—the problem is in knowing what kinds of evidence a particular item of behavior might be *expected* to leave in the archaeological remains . . . , and what kinds of methods and techniques can be used to discover this evidence. [Second,] most elements of behavior have more than one or two material correlates, and relatively few of them may be needed to demonstrate the prehistoric existence of behavior. If we begin thinking less about the significance of individual artifacts and more about the *sets* (or clusters) of data that might be associated with a particular element of behavior, we can begin to make (and test) inferences that are presently not believed possible. [See the discussion on analogy in this chapter.]

Third, it has been maintained that we must depend on ethnographic analogy in making inferences. Hill quotes L. Binford (1968b) on this point: "So long as we insist that our knowledge of the past is limited by our knowledge of the present, we are painting ourselves into a methodological corner." Thus Hill maintains that if we are to learn anything *new* about the past we must discard the notion that we are limited by analogy. Finally, it has been stated that inferences we may make are unverifiable but Hill points out that we can test their correctness. In this connection the reader should also see Watson, LeBlanc, and Redman (1971: Chap. 2), and Flannery (1972) who makes the point that the kinds of tests advocated by Hill may reveal "coincident" rather than "causal" relationships.

Hill concludes his discussion of the limitations of data with a statement that is not controversial and with which we would emphatically agree: that we are limited at present not so much by our data as by our theory and by our techniques for gathering and analyzing data.

UNIFORMITARIANISM

In Chapter 4 we discussed the concept of uniformitarianism, especially with regard to geologic processes and ethnographic analogy. The underlying idea is that the present is a clue to the past because all things on earth behave or interact with their environments in ways that are determined by certain principles. The important point is that there are processes that affect all matter. If we can determine what these processes are, we can use this knowledge as a key toward unlocking the unknown. As Sanders and Price (1968: 221–222) put it, "The broad justification for archaeological inference is in effect, the principle of uniformitarianism; but taken alone its explanatory and predictive-retrodictive powers are limited." However, for specific examples they make the point that "similar causes produce similar effects, independently of historical or lineal relationships of cultures." Trigger (1970: 33) says much the same thing: "Products of processes that went on in the past can be interpreted in terms of processes that can be observed at work at the present time." For archeology, of course, the products of the processes are archeological sites and the things that are contained in them, which can be interpreted as residue left by people engaged in their activities, with subsequent modification through the degradation of these remains since they were deposited.

Two concepts are implicit in the foregoing. First, the processes of change are controlled by certain factors. Thus we may speak of cultural evolution, which has been likened to biological evolution and is effected through somewhat analogous processes. Second, people behave in basically similar ways when confronted with certain situations. Thus patterning in site residues can be related to our understanding of the principles of behavior. Here it is that ethnographic analogy is important.

It should be obvious that if it were discovered that uniformitarianism is not a valid concept, all of archeological interpretation would be rendered invalid. The alternative concept is that in relatively recent times all the evidence which we interpret to be indicative of a long history for the earth and its forms of life was spontaneously created. It should also be clear that if uniformitarianism is not correct—if the processes or principles that we can observe today did not pertain in the past—then our interpretations must be skewed. Because cultural change depends in part on the nature of biological man, we cannot assume that all of the principles of behavior that we may discover in today's world pertain to the past. At the same time, the processes of biological change and of changes in the earth itself could follow a strictly uniform line. Because we know that man has not always been either biologically or culturally identical to what he is today, it follows that there are limits to the use of the concept of uniformitarianism in making inferences about material remains and interpretations about the ways of prehistoric peoples.

Still without the concept we would have no guidelines at all toward interpreting cultural changes. We would be left with a study of sequential changes and variety in physical remains, a science of ancient things in their own physical terms alone. In succeeding sections we discuss the ways prehistorians have attempted to overcome the problems posed by the use of analogy and the extent to which it may be used.

ETHNOGRAPHIC ANALOGY

The use of analogy, in which a modern primitive group is used as an example of the way a prehistoric people may have lived, has had a long and useful history beginning as early as 1865, when Lord Avebury wrote *Prehistoric Times, as illustrated by Ancient Remains and the Manners and Customs of Modern Savages.* The technique was popularized and captivated an international audience in Sollas's work, published first in 1911, *Ancient Hunters and Their Modern Representatives.* One of the most recent examples is a well-illustrated book by Grahame Clark, *The Stone Age Hunters,* whose contents are chiefly a description of prehistoric cultures but whose illustrations contain analogous examples drawn from modern peoples living apparently similar ways of life. This approach has the advantage of presenting living examples of ways of life that otherwise are scarcely credible to many people raised in urban-industrial surroundings. Vivid photographs, motion pictures, tape recordings, and examples of artifacts used in hunting or preparing food tell much more to the average student of prehistory than do pages of drawings of projectile points, floor plans of post molds, and tables of bones listed in Latin by genus and species. The expression, "the dry-as-dust facts of archeology," is only too oppressively real to a novice who is working his way for the first time through the tedious presentation of data in a typical site report. For him a boldly drawn analogy with a living people may be his only convincing clue that the whole business is not just an unfathomable and jealously guarded secret kept by a coterie of strange men in pith helmets.

In spite of the obvious value of ethnographic analogy for popularizing prehistory, it must be used with considerable caution, because prehistory deals with the past, and things were different then, the more so as one goes farther back in time. This statement applies both to the environment (even if climate has not changed) and to the ways people lived. Modern-day cultures are the products of their unique histories and inevitably must be different in some respects from all other societies. We should remember also that every human invention and kind of organization had its historical "first." When to this realization we add the fact that communication was far from instantaneous, we realize that prehistoric peoples had far fewer potential alternatives of experience to draw on and were thus more limited in their possible actions than are people today.

Ethnographic analogy is used often to determine the use of artifacts, but probably the most interesting and valuable use of analogy is to gain information about how the artifacts were used in a culture and thereby to learn something about the subsystem of culture in which they were used. Analogy has been used to good effect in interpretations of prehistoric Indians in the Southwest in this manner (Longacre 1970a). In order to use analogy for these purposes, however, one must establish some rules concerning its use. Dozier (1970:203–205) lists six such rules.

> *First*, it is important to have the temporal factor in mind. The shorter the time gap between a prehistoric site and the living site, the more likely that the inference will be a reliable one.
>
> *Second*, . . . the sociocultural level of the prehistoric and ethnologic groups must be matched—at least roughly. For example, analogies between band-level societies and tribal ones may be made only with caution . . .
>
> *Third*, . . . it is important to compare societies having the same type of subsistence economy: hunting-gathering with hunting-gathering ones, agricultural with agricultural ones, . . .
>
> *Fourth*, inferences about societies widely separated in space can be made only with extreme caution . . . The initial work on inferences with analogy to ethnologic groups should be restricted to contiguous areas where the history, prehistory, and distribution of sociocultural and linguistic groups are fairly well known.
>
> *Fifth*, in making inferences, language affiliation should be given low priority, (that is, languages may differ while culture does not).
>
> *Sixth*, . . . some measure of how conservative the ethnologic culture has been over time should be established . . . (that is, those that have changed the least are the most dependable analogs).

CULTURE SYSTEMS

"One of the most important ideas in modern science is the idea of a *system*; and it is almost impossible to define" (Hardin 1968:455). One speaks easily of systems and finds them everywhere he looks but to be useful a concept must be accurately defined. A. Hall and Fagen (1956:18) put it this way: "A system is a set of objects together with relationships between the objects and between their attributes." A system can be subdivided into subsystems. Systems can be physical, biological and cultural;

their common denominator is organization—the way in which the objects interact or relate to one another.

The central concept in scientific and historical studies of cultures or culture, past and present, is system. The term has various shades of meaning which we will discuss below. In anthropology, culture is often said to be patterned; it is systematic in a predictable way. We may also see cultures as examples of life systems that have the same properties and are affected by the same processes as all life systems (Chap. 21). The two uses of the term system are conceptually different and are based on quite different traditions of thought.

The general anthropological view, which is concerned little with long-term changes, sees culture as composed of interrelated parts that are mutually interdependent. Thus anthropologists may see relationships among settlement pattern, subsistence techniques, social organization, and religious beliefs. All these and other aspects (subsystems) of a culture "hang together" in a consistent way lending stability to the way of life and ensuring a measure of predictability in the behavior of individuals in the culture. "If a society is to survive, the gears of its culture must mesh, even though they may growl and grind" (Hoebel 1972:26). A good bit of social anthropology is aimed at describing and interpreting the interactions among the parts of a culture in terms of their mutual effects.

The anthropological view of the systemic nature of culture derives from the fact of variation among cultures and the attempt to understand it. How can we account for the way a people reckon kinship? How does it happen that two peoples speaking closely related languages have quite different cultures, or that peoples who are linguistically unrelated share many basic elements of culture? What is it that makes cultures distinct and how may the distinctions be characterized? These are some of the questions anthropologists have asked and attempted to explain through viewing culture as "the integrated system of learned behavior patterns which are characteristic of the members of a society and which are not the result of biological inheritance" (Hoebel 1972:6). Basic to the concept of culture is that:

1. Every culture represents a limited selection of behavior patterns from the total of human potentialities, individual and collective.
2. The selection tends to be made in accordance with certain postulates (dominant assumptions and values) basic to culture.
3. It follows that every culture exemplifies a more or less complete and coherent pattern, structure, or system of actions and relationships (Hoebel 1972: 26–27).

Culture is thus frequently discussed only in terms of its own properties and without explicit reference to a theory of systems. It is assumed that systematic relationships exist in cultures and that the nature of these relationships is to be found in the particular situations and explained in terms of the overall goals of survival and satisfaction. There typically follows a description of a culture in terms of its central tendencies, norms, or idealized patterns of how things ought to be done. The assumption is that most people behave as they should (at the very least, consistently) or else the culture in question will lack coherence and in the long run endurance.

This "normative" view of culture has been criticized in writings of new archeology because prehistorians cannot observe behavior directly and can know even less of ideals, and values.

> These archeologists have replaced dependence on cognitive explanation with a focus on material remains viewed as a reflection of past behavioral patterns. The logical result of this position is the conviction that one of the major aims of archeology must be to correlate the structure of material remains with the behavioral elements of a cultural system (Watson, LeBlanc, and Redman 1971:63).

It seems there is some confusion inherent in the expressed dichotomy between a normative and a systemic view of culture. Implicit in the quotation above and in other statements of its kind (J. Hill 1970:18; L. Binford 1965:205; Struever 1971:10) is that norms do exist and that these can be discovered archeologically in the patterned remains found in sites. What is important is that a site may not be homogeneous; it may have considerable variability within it. The implication for archeological fieldwork is that one must sample a site to attempt to discover what the intrasite variability is and what it relates to. Thus when J. Hill (1971:18) says, "Analyses of social organization require attention to intrasite and intraregion variability, and a concern for this does not follow from the premise that culture consists of shared ideas and behavior," he is in effect denying a basic concept that he himself uses; namely that such variation as exists is patterned and that the different patterned behaviors represented in archeological remains are related to one another in a systematic fashion that has as its underlying rational the maintenance of the system. This is surely "normative" behavior.

Aberle (1970:216) restates the essential points made by Hill in the following way:

> (1) culture is systemic; (2) it is an energy-harnessing system that articulates a human population with its environment; (3) by virtue of the nature of the productive activities and the social organization of production, there will be nonrandom variation within settlements as a result of (a) different practices in different family or larger kinship groupings, (b) differential locus of various activities, (c) status differentiation, if any, and (d) other reasons; (4) in an archaeological site, these differences appear in nonrandom variability of artifacts, styles, leavings, and so forth. So, (5) it is insufficient for purposes of archaeological analysis to 'type' a site and let it go at that.

The systemic view of culture is described by R. Thompson and Longacre (1966:270).

> We view culture as systemic and thus composed of various highly interrelated subsystems such as the social system, the technological system and the

religious system. . . . All of the material remains in an archaeological site are highly patterned or structured directly as a result of the ways in which the extinct society was organized and the patterned ways in which the people behaved. Thus our first task is to define the archaeological structure at the site and then from that infer the organization of the society and aspects of behavior.

The process of making the inferences may become quite complex, but the goal, of course, is to attempt to explain how a cultural system works.

In examining cultural subsystems we focus our attention for the first time on people, not as individuals, but as members of once-living communities. However, we are not able to comprehend people in all of their facets. We can say little about politics or theology, but we can perceive some of the ways to reconstruct how they were organized. All things are made up of organized parts; it is one of our jobs as social scientists to try to discover the principles of organization that make viable societies of collections of people. As archeologists we must try to reconstruct the organization of the people whose remains we can handle, count, measure, and draw. It is becoming more and more apparent that principles of organization are the basic keys in our understanding of any class of phenomena, including people. This position is taken by General System theorists, and it has been echoed in various forms by anthropologists for many years.

It is probably fortunate that organization has emerged as the focal point of behavioral studies, because archeologists are able to find information in prehistory that relates to organization. The sites, the artifacts in them, and especially the way in which sites and artifacts occur, give clues to the organization of the society that left them. This conviction follows from our belief that cultures are patterned and adaptive. A particular culture represents a system whose parts, largely because of the requirement of adaptation, are in mutual interaction. That is, the parts of the system are organized in a cooperative, mutually beneficial way. Therefore we should be able to discern the patterns of interaction and describe the structure and organization of the system. We state this as a general hypothesis; it clearly needs to be tested with regard to cultures, but it seems to hold true for other communities of biological organisms. The hypothesis has important consequences for anthropology, but its value for archeology may not be obvious at first. Simply stated, it means that objects we find archeologically are remnants of behavior that was carried out in the context of the social system of the time. Therefore, from the artifacts, we can infer human activities. The hypothesis means, moreover, that we can seek interpretations of the material we find, in the expectation that it played an understandable role in an adaptive system. It is here that hypotheses about the operation of systems generally is important, for if we know some of the elements in a culture system we can make reasonable hypotheses, based on our knowledge of how similar systems operate, about other cultures. It needs to be stressed emphatically here, however, that we are talking about hypotheses and not about facts. It is our job to use the hypotheses for the insight they may give us about what to look for and, above all, to use them as accurately phrased questions that are capable of being definitely answered.

We have just written as though the single culture system is the basic unit of our analysis. It is not. Systems operate within systems, and virtually every human group known lived in contact with other human groups and within a context of a circumscribed physical arena. An adequate description of a social system and an understanding of its operation thus require a perspective that transcends the village or tribe and encompasses what we might call the symbiotic, nuclear, or key area that defines the effective universe of interaction for people in the system At this point we find the concepts of human ecology relevant.

ADAPTATION

The centrality of the concept of adaptation can hardly be overstressed in either reconstruction or processual interpretation. Sanders and Price (1968: 221) put the matter succinctly: "What is adaptive survives." Poorly adapted cultures, like biological organisms, are weeded out through natural selection. "The thesis I would seek to propound is quite simply that man and his way of life as this has developed down to the present day are both ultimately the product of natural selection" (G. Clark 1970:61). Freeman (1971:1197) makes the point even more strongly: "In our attempt to understand man's physical and behavioral evolution, we are at long last learning to distinguish Evolution from the concept of Progress and to equate it, as rightfully must be done, with Adaptation."

Alland (1970:40–41) discusses two aspects of adaptation. First are the long-range changes that maintain the viability of a system in relation to its environment. Second are the short-term adjustments which may or may not be carried through in the long term. An analysis of the way of life of a prehistoric people as found in a site describes an adjustment or adaptation to the circumstances of the time. An interpretation of the long-term changes as seen in evidence from many sites is an example of the first sense in which we may analyze adaptation.

Anthropologists, even those who have explicitly disavowed interest in culture history, tend to view social organization as a means of adaptation. A quotation from Radcliffe-Brown (1952:8–9) illustrates this very well.

[Adaptation] is a key concept of the theory of evolution. It is or can be applied both to the study of the forms of organic life and to the forms of social life amongst human beings. A living organism exists and continues to exist only if it is both internally and externally adapted. The internal adaptation depends on the adjustment of the various organs and their activities, so that the various physiological processes constitute a continuing functioning system by which the life of the organism is maintained. The external adaptation is that of the organism to the environment within which it lives. The distinction of external and internal adaptation is merely a way of distinguishing two aspects of the *adaptational system* which is the same for organisms of a single species . . .

When we examine a form of social life amongst human beings as an adaptational system it is useful to distinguish three aspects of the total system. There is the way in which the social life is adjusted to the physical environment (ecological) . . . There are the institutional arrangements by which an orderly social life is maintained (social) . . . there is the social process by which an individual acquires habits and mental characteristics that fit him for a place in the social life and enable him to participate in its activities (cultural) . . . What must be emphasized is that these modes of adaptation are only different aspects from which the total adaptational system can be looked at for convenience of analysis and comparison.

There is a tendency in anthropology to consider almost any kind of behavior adaptive simply because we believe that culture, through its institutions, serves as a means for man to adapt to his environment. Indeed some anthropologists have gone to considerable lengths to justify in adaptive terms what the man on the street would regard as bizarre, stupid, or perhaps offensive behavior. Such studies are usually carried out by cultural ecologists and will be discussed in more detail later. For the present the important consideration is how to judge whether behavior is adaptive. In biology, adaptation is related strictly to reproduction. The more organisms that can be raised to maturity and supported, the better adapted that species is. In cultural terms we might say that the more people a culture can support the better adapted it is.

Although the link between biological and cultural adaptation can thus be measured quantitatively, one should beware of two pitfalls. First, adaptation depends partly on competition. If there is no competition for an ecologic niche, a culture may continue and be considered adapted; however, if competition develops, the former culture may find itself at considerable disadvantage and in the new circumstances cease to exist. This was the case for the native way of life of American Indians after settlement of the continent by Europeans. Second, what gives a momentary advantage may not be viable in the long run. For example, an adaptive change (that is, one that allows for population growth, such as the adoption of firearms by a hunting people) may in the long run result in such a depletion of game that the system cannot withstand the shock when it occurs. Similarly, one could mention intensive farming or grazing practices that have seriously depleted the land, or the drawing of excessive amounts of ground water for irrigation from arid regions. One could also point to the effects of crowding that results from large increases in population; these are problems that have both psychological and physiological implications even if supplies of food and shelter are adequate. In all these cases, short-term advantage may lead to long-term disaster.

ECOLOGY

Ecology is a concept developed in biology to define the relations of an animal to its organic and inorganic environments. The concept implies a concern with how an organism relates to its inanimate environment and also with the interrelationships among organisms who live together in mutual interdependence. The mutual interdependence implies organized relationships and consequently a system, or ecosystem as it is usually called. Parenthetically it should be stressed that the well-advertised concern among conservationists for "ecology" is not the same thing. There is always an environment, whether polluted or not, and there are always organisms adapting to their environments. Ecology cannot be killed, although specific niches may be fouled. Ecologic niche is also a useful concept; it is the particular animate and inanimate sphere within which an organism carries out its life. Classic studies in ecology have often focused upon specific niches—ponds, stumps, forests or grasslands. A culture's niche is likewise circumscribed although usually not so narrowly.

The relationships within a niche may be described in terms of who eats whom or who benefits from the others. We can describe the food chain in these terms; it begins with the lower organisms which convert solar energy through photosynthesis into vegetation, which is then eaten by the animals that constitute the next links in the chain, and are themselves consumed by "higher" forms of life. These are predatory relationships; one animal benefits and the other does not. We may also find commensal relationships which are neutral in effect. Finally there are relationships in which both species gain from their mutual behavior. We might, for example, see animal husbandry as an example of mutualism; in this instance man protects the animals and allows their numbers to increase so that he can harvest them for his advantage.

Cultural ecology is a subfield within anthropology that seeks to understand the workings of culture systems in ecologic terms. It is clear that man has relations with his animate and inanimate environments, but in addition his culture serves to relate him to others of his own species, including people outside his immediate group. The ecologic niche within which people operate is thus typically broader and more complex than among other animate species.

The cultural ecologist sees the culture of a given people as a subsystem in interaction with other subsystems. He argues that the key to understanding the developmental processes of the cultural subsystem lies in this interactive relationship. The total network of relationships between subsystems has been called the "ecological system" or "ecosystem." It includes three subsystems—culture, biota, and physical environment (Sanders and Prince 1968:171).

The focus of attention in cultural ecology is in the interaction among these three subsystems. Sanders (1965) presents eight postulates (somewhat abridged here):

a. Each biological and physical environment offers particular problems to human utilization.

b. Diverse environments offer different problems; therefore, the response by man (that is, the development of a cultural subsystem) will be different.

c. There is an almost unlimited number of possibilities but a limited number of probabilities in the way in which a people may adapt to a given environment. . . .

d. Response to environmental challenges may be technological, social, or ideational. . . .

e. In a broad sense men living in similar environments solve the problem of adaptation in similar ways: in differing environments, in different ways. . . .

f. There is some overlapping of responses and solutions even in cases of strikingly dissimilar environments. . . .

g. Cultures are dynamic, as are all of the components of an ecological system, and the degree of integration of a cultural subsystem to the total ecological system will vary. . . .

h. The culture of a given people, therefore, can be considered essentially as a complex of techniques adaptive to the problems of survival in a particular geographic region. . . .

Cultural ecology is derived from general ecologic studies in biology. Somewhat more restricted in view is an approach pioneered in archeology by Grahame Clark and effectively presented in his classic work, *Prehistoric Europe: The Economic Basis.*

> One of the principal attractions of prehistory is the opportunity it offers for studying the interplay of social aspiration and environing nature over long periods of time. The economy of any community may be considered as an adjustment to specific physical and biological conditions of certain needs, capacities, aspirations, and values. . . . There are thus two sides of the equation . . . the character of the habitat . . . and the kind of life regarded as appropriate by the community (G. Clark 1952:7).

Clark's use of the concepts of ecology can be considered restricted only in the sense that he chose for reasons of the availability of evidence to emphasize the economic aspects (subsistence, trade, technology, and so on) of prehistoric life. Also, he regarded economy as of fundamental importance. "The economy of any community . . . is . . . the product of an adjustment between culture and environing nature" (G. Clark 1952:7). Clark has emphasized the economic subsystem of culture, an approach that has been especially fruitful although not as comprehensive or as informative as studies that examine the ecosystem in its broader aspects. Examples of both approaches are given in succeeding chapters.

MODELS

Models are conceptual structures that (a) organize and guide our thinking (heuristic), (b) describe the relationships between variables (explanatory or legal), or (c) describe a situation in graphic form (illustrative). Most models used in prehistoric interpretation are primarily heuristic and consist of labels like "the Bronze Age," or "the Archaic." This is like saying the Elizabethan Age or the Golden Age of Rome. Such labels are informative in that they connote a vast range of information to a person trained to understand them, but they are of no value to the neophyte. Another kind of heuristic model is exemplified by the concept "pattern." We take as a truism that cultures are patterned and from that it follows that pattern in the distribution of artifacts is meaningful. Thus we have structured our thinking, established some guidelines for fieldwork, and partially determined the results of our analysis by employing the concept "pattern." We have not explained anything; we have only structured our thinking.

Prehistorians often employ ethnographic analogy as illustrative and heuristic models to aid in the interpretation of their data. Present-day Pueblo Indians may serve that purpose for archeologists working in the Southwest; modern hunters and gatherers may even help in understanding prehistoric men who lived thousands of years ago. Thus analogy is a form of model in that it structures our thinking.

As we shall discuss in Chapters 20 and 21, there are models, such as evolution and three-age system, that deal with change in culture. We also have General Systems Theory that serves as a model for understanding the relationships among the parts of a system and for changes in the system itself.

Models, then, are nothing mysterious. We all use them in everyday life. Indeed, it is this ability to conceptualize categories of things and their relationships that enables us to carry out our daily lives effectively. We see this readily in the normative aspects of culture itself, both from the point of view of a participant who knows what ought to be and from the point of view of the outsider who abstracts from observation of collective behavior a model of a culture. These models are called ethnographies.

The remaining chapters are devoted to employing the concepts we have discussed here, sometimes with fuller discussion of their implications.

REFERENCES

Concepts: Bayard 1969; Chang 1967a; D. L. Clark 1968; Deetz 1967; M. Harris 1968; Hole 1972b; Rouse 1972a, 1972b; Trigger 1968, 1970, 1971; Watson, LeBlanc, and Redman 1971.

Ethnographic Analogy: K. Anderson 1969; R. Ascher 1961a, 1962; L. Binford 1967a, 1968b; S. Binford 1968; Blackwood 1950; Chang 1967b; G. Clark 1951, 1957:Chap. 6; J. D. Clark 1968; Driver 1961; Freeman 1969; Gould 1968a, 1968b, 1971; Heider 1967; Isaac 1968; Kehoe 1958; Kosambi 1967; Lafitau 1724; Lee and DeVore 1968; O. Mason 1904; Mulvaney 1971; Orme 1972; Sahlins 1958; Scudder 1971; Service 1962, 1964; M. Smith 1955; R. Thompson 1956; P. Watson 1966; *World Archaeology* Vol. 3, No. 2, 1971.

Ethnohistory and Ethnography as Related to Archeology: L. Binford 1967a; Calnek 1972; Charlton 1969; Cranstone 1971; Dozier 1970; Friedrich 1970; Gould 1968a, 1968b, 1969, 1971; Kroeber 1957b; Lauer 1971; Mulvaney and Golson 1971; C. M. Nelson 1972; E. Parsons 1940; Rowlands 1971; Ucko 1969; Van der Merwe and Scully 1971; C. White and Peterson 1969. See also *Ethnohistory.*

CHAPTER SEVENTEEN

SUBSISTENCE AND ECONOMIC SYSTEMS

In attempting to understand people in prehistory, one might ask, as Childe (1956) did, who the people were, when they lived, what their culture was, and how their culture changed. The questions might be approached frontally in the order given (as they were by Rouse 1965), but our present purposes, which ultimately tend toward the same information, lead us to put the questions in another form. Who, what, when, and how are questions of very different magnitude, requiring different orders of interpretation, and it seems most reasonable to begin with the simpler and work toward the more complex. Moreover, Childe's approach was more nearly in the tradition of historiography, working as he was with European prehistory, which could be linked with historically known peoples. Our approach is more nearly akin to anthropology, where culture, rather than cultures in the specific sense, is important. Accordingly, we are more interested in what was happening and in how ways of life changed than we are in precisely who the people were.

The simplest topics to deal with, and those for which interpretations are the most straightforward, are subsistence and economy. In fact, one can reasonably treat them as aspects of the same thing under the general term "economy."

WHAT IS ECONOMY?

Prehistoric man did not have a money economy such as we are familiar with today. His economy consisted, not of buying, selling, and consuming, but of acquiring, distributing, and consuming. The different words show that basically similar actions and transactions are implied but that the basis of the economy was "do-it-yourself" "reciprocity," and "barter." Prehistoric economy consisted of the way in which man hunted, fished, and collected food; the way he farmed, harvested, and prepared food; the way he used or distributed these products; the shelters in which he lived and the tools he used; the trade he carried on for raw materials; and the manner in which he traveled. In short, prehistoric man's economy was multifaceted, reaching into the technological, environmental, and social spheres of his life.

To begin with the simple, we can consider the landscape, which offered opportunities and set limitations on what man might do. The landscape can be studied easily in the present, but two questions arise when we consider its relation to prehistoric man. First, how does today's landscape compare with that in the past, and second, what skills did man have to exploit the resources that were potentially available? Bearing these two questions in mind, we can consider the role of the landscape in general.

Man lives in a world of plants, animals, minerals, the soil, weather, and people. Taken together, they comprise the elements of an eco-system whose operation or organization archeologists try to reconstruct in their descriptions of prehistoric ways of subsistence and economy (Figs. 64, 65, 66). Plants are basic to man's life, and they in turn depend on climate and soil. Vegetation is dispersed in accordance with climatic zones, and the animals that feed on the plants are thus restricted in their distribution. In turn, man was constrained in his hunting and gathering by the well-defined distribution of species around the world. For most of his prehistory man was not able to move plants and animals from their natural environments to places better suited to his purposes. Such manipulations were possible only after the domestication of plants and animals.

Even with an environment full of plants and animals, man had to be able to use them. He needed the technology for killing his food, for butchering or otherwise preparing it, and for storing and distributing it. Mastery of food procurement came quickly; even today we have not adequately solved the last two problems. Although most of the history of prehistoric man is the story of his increasing efficiency in acquiring food, man still remains at the mercy of his environment to the degree that he can grow only certain crops in any particular area. Where modern man has produced plant hybrids, irrigation, and fertilizer, prehistoric man was largely nonscientific and was forced to get along with what luck and trial-and-error experimentation could produce.

No single environment, delimited by the distance a man might walk

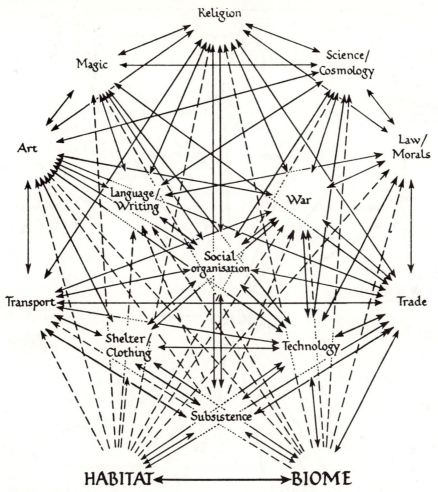

FIG. 64 The habitat-biome-culture network that characterizes the interrelations of man with his environment. (G. Clark 1953b, Fig. 6.)

in his yearly round of hunting or farming, could supply all the material he might wish to use or might require. In many places this limitation meant that he did without or was forced to settle for a substitute. He may have wished for obsidian to make sharp blades but have had to settle for flint. In other areas the acquisition of certain materials was a precondition to life. Prehistoric man could not afford to get himself so far out on a limb that he could not get back, but when man settled into farming villages and became more dependent on one environment, and less mobile as well, he frequently found that he needed to trade for essentials. Salt was prized by farmers who lived exclusively on grain, although it may never have been specially sought by hunters, who found enough salt in the flesh they ate. Wood for fuel (Heizer 1963) and for houses was sometimes traded into areas where there was none. There are few areas in the world so bountiful in agriculture and so

FIG. 65 Simplified diagram of man's exploitation of wild and domestic resources in northern Khuzistan during the seventh and eighth millennia B.C. Also shown are major imports, exports, and a part of the food chain of some of the animal species involved, by "microenvironment."

Abundant deer and acorns (Autumn); maguey (year-round); wild avocado (rainy season)

Small numbers of wood rats and doves (year-round); gophers and cottontails in widest ravines (year-round)

Abundant deer and peccary (Autumn); cottontails, doves, skunks (year-round); cactus fruits (Spring)

Mesquite pods (rainy season); cottontails, jackrabbits, gophers, quails (year-round)

1800 m.

Rio Salado

Eroded Canyons

Thorn Forest

Alluvial Plain

Barren limestone slopes

FIG. 66 The diversity of ecological zones that may be found in a limited area is illustrated by this idealized east-west trans-section of the central part of the Tehuacan Valley, Puebla, Mexico. (See Fig. 32, which shows a Mexican thorn forest.) The seasons in which food is available in each zone are indicated. East is to the left. The length of the area represented is about 20 kilometers. (M. D. Coe and K. V. Flannery, "Microenvironments and Mesoamerican Prehistory." *Science* Vol. 143 (1964): Fig. 1, pp. 650–654. Copyright 1964 by the American Association for the Advancement of Science.)

meager in mineral and plant resources as Mesopotamia, where even stone to build with is lacking on the hot desert plain. In fact, water for farming here often had to be imported by means of irrigation.

However, during most of man's past, trade was not for necessities, because dependence on uncertain supply routes for vital supplies in prehistoric times would often have resulted in death. On the other hand, luxury items were avidly sought and widely traded. Gold, copper, amber, and shells were traded at great distances, and their record provides archeologists with insight into the extent of man's known world. Such trade also tells us something of his acquisitive instincts and esthetic sensibilities. Trade in weapons and luxury goods has left a clear picture of the emergence of class differences and the relation of an "international economy" to the tribal status seekers. For one detailed study of aboriginal intertribal trade in which the particular items exchanged are specified and the complex network of trails is mapped, see the study of trade routes and economic exchange among the Indians of California by J. T. Davis (1961).

A point often overlooked is that trade may consist of more than two people or groups of people exchanging items on an I-will-trade-you-this-for-that basis. W. Hill's (1948) description of Navajo trade, Berndt's (1951) account of Australian ceremonial exchange, and Malinowski's (1932) classic account of the Trobriand "Kula-ring" illustrate the extraordinary amount of social action that may be involved. Archeologists who find the objects that were exchanged will usually think only of commercial trade, having no idea of the interpersonal aspects that had originally been involved. We are not saying that the social actions can always be reconstructed, but familiarity with the fact that they may be involved in trade throws the archeologist's thinking into a quite different perspective. At the minimum, it makes him recognize that all trade need not have been commercial in our sense.

There is scarcely a facet of man's life remaining to be uncovered by the archeologist's shovel that is not in some way tied to economy. For this reason, prehistorians do best when they write the story of man's economic life. However, even if information on economic life comes easier than other knowledge, it is not always found directly. To reconstruct man's economy, one must often infer from what is known to what is not known.

DIET

If preservation is good, we can tell quite a lot about diet, especially of the animals eaten. Because of their poor preservation it is much more difficult to tell what plants were consumed, although some notable exceptions to this rule have been published recently. The identification of species is a routine process of matching bones, seeds, cells, or pollen with examples from the modern flora and fauna. What is much more uncertain, however, is what these remains mean with respect to diet. There are several relevant considerations: what percentage of the total diet was made up of any single source of food, what was the seasonal variation in abundance and in variety, what was the nutritive potential, what was the capacity of the food to be stored and of the people to store it, if we consider their technology and degree of mobility.

We can cite some examples of the ways such kinds of information help in the understanding of subsystems and the processes of culture generally. The relative proportions of meat to plant food, or of wild to domesticated resources, can tell us about the stability of a group, the area it must control or exploit, and its potential for growth. These answers will lead to speculation about the necessity or desirability of trade or interaction between groups of people who exploited somewhat different sets of resources. The data will also permit us to infer the number of people who could be supported, and this estimate in turn gives us some idea of the kind of social organization that might have regulated the population in the acquisition, distribution, and consumption of food. It is only when we consider all these aspects of activity that we can imagine a system operating to satisfy the basic necessities of life for a particular group of people.

Careful scrutiny of the actual details of particular instances is often revealing and clears up certain apparent mysteries. To illustrate this, we can refer to examples drawn from ethnology where the control of data is much more secure. It is sometimes stated that complex developments of culture are possible only with an agricultural base. Without going into the elaborate and necessary qualifying and defining statements about terms, let us simply say that certain hunting and gathering societies have more complex social organizations and more elaborate cultures than certain agricultural societies have. An illustration is the Indians of the Northwest Coast whose culture "seems to be an anomaly, for it was a civilization of the so-called 'hunting-and-gathering' type, without agriculture . . . and possessing no domesticated animals other than the dog" (Drucker 1963:1). In contrast to other hunting and gathering societies it was vastly more complex. Yet we find an agricultural people, the Papago Indians of southern Arizona who, on close examination, were found to "have cultivated only about one-fifth of their food supply, the overwhelming balance of their diet having been derived from native plant and animal foods" (Haury 1950:1966). Papago culture more nearly resembled that of simple hunters and gatherers than it did that of the Northwest Coast Indians. In the same vein, it is surprising to note that the "agricultural" Gwembe Tonga people of Zambia are recorded as collecting 131 wild plants for food, usually in times of poor crops (Scudder 1971); the hunter-gatherer Bushmen studied by R. B. Lee (1968) recognize 113 edible plants; and in Meso-America, a region that has known agriculture for over 5000 years, supplemental hunting and wild vegetal gathering have persisted down to the present data (Lowe 1971:227–230). We should note as well the degree to which insects are used as an important food by many peoples (Bodenheimer 1951). The point to be made here is that one must examine all the evidence; labels such as "agriculturalists" or "hunter-and-gatherer" often set up a chain of thinking that leads to completely erroneous conclusions.

RECOVERING DIETARY INFORMATION

Most bones found in the sites represent animals that were eaten by man, although an exception is made with regard to some rodents and carnivores. It is important, therefore, for a zoologist to identify the bones, for the species, and, more importantly, for the numbers of individuals of each species found (for more details and examples, see Chap. 9). Reports of excavations are replete with lists of fauna (with Latin names), but few go further and try to suggest what cultural practices the array of bones can tell. A review of inferences about the cultural significance of animal bones from prehistoric sites may be found in Heizer (1960) and C. Reed (1963).

As standard practice, C. Reed (1963) recommends recovering all bones from archeological sites. Later a zoologist can sort them, saving and analyzing only the identifiable pieces. For later interpretation a sufficient supply from a site is far more valuable than only a casual sample. Recalling this recommendation, we may refer to Coon's (1957) report on the bones from Belt Cave, a stratified site in northern Iran. Coon recovered 14,006 pieces of bone, horn, antler, and teeth. Inferences on species, age, and sex of the animals were made on a sample of 1170 bones—less than 10 percent of the total. At first glance it looks as though Coon had been unduly careless and that, in view of the important conclusions he proposes, he was remiss in not analyzing the entire collection of bones. We must recognize, however, that not all fragments of bones are identifiable. Most of the pieces Coon counted were unidentifiable scraps and splinters that are of limited value to zoologists; 1170 were suitable for study.

Identification of the species represented by bones is so difficult that it requires detailed analysis by persons thoroughly acquainted with comparative anatomy. In many parts of the world there are no collections of fauna that zoologists can use to compare with the ancient bones. Under such circumstances it is usually necessary for the zoologist to begin his work by making his own collection of the modern fauna and preparing the skeletons so that they can be used for comparative purposes. Manuals of bone identification are of dubious value, especially in the hands of nonzoologists.

Bones that are in bad condition and that are of sufficient interest should be preserved. C. Reed (1963) suggests using some water-soluble glue (gum arabic or carpenter's glue; see also the use of "Elmer's Glue," Wheat 1972:20) to harden them. Reed specifically cautions against the use of shellac, alvar, or celluloid in acetone, because these substances do not penetrate well and often cause damage by peeling the surface of the bone. As a treatment for dry bones, Brothwell (1965) suggests the use of polyvinyl acetate in acetone, or Alvar 1570 in amyl acetate and methylated spirits; for wet bones, an aqueous emulsion of polyvinyl acetate. An excellent preservative for routine use is Bedacryl (Imperial Chemicals, Ltd.), a water-soluble resin that can be applied to wet bones or other organic material. Final cleaning can be easily accomplished in a laboratory. When bones have been treated in the field or laboratory with a preservative this fact should be recorded in the field notebook or collection catalog because future workers may require this information in identifying the solvent required to clean or further mend treated bone, or in subjecting the bones to chemical analysis.

A study of the bones may give some clues about butchering techniques. It was common practice for man to kill the larger animals away from the site and bring back only the best pieces of meat. By noting which parts of the skeleton are present, one can refine the calculation based on a hypothetical maximum amount of meat from each species. A series of excellent articles by T. White (1953a, 1954, 1955b) provides several interesting examples of how an archeologist, working with an osteologist, can reconstruct the method of butchering game animals in the Great Plains area of North America. Furthermore, it is usually possible for the zoologist to tell how old the animals were when they were killed. This information may help him decide at what season the site was occupied and just how good a hunter prehistoric man was.

For example we know the breeding seasons for most animals. The major skeletal changes in them take place within the first year or two. It is often possible, by noting size and whether or not certain bones were fused, to tell within a few months how old an animal was when it was killed. One can often also tell about the season of the hunt by noting such things as whether deer antlers had been shed, because we know at what seasons these animals shed their antlers. In some instances the season can also be inferred if we know the climate. Some animals cannot live in certain places all year round. Migratory animals move between summer and winter pastures, and, if the bones of migratory birds are found, one can tell that the site was occupied during the season of migration. Following are a few examples of the kinds of clues that may lead to inferences about the season in which events happened. Wedel (1961:74) notes that mud-dauber (wasp) nests, presumably broken open to extract the edible larvae, were common in the trash layers of the Allen site in southern Wyoming. Because the mud dauber makes nests from May to September, a summer occupation by man is thus inferable. Winlock (1942: 192) cites the various plant remains found in an Egyptian tomb of the Eighteenth Dynasty that point to the interment as occurring in the month of November, a botanical conclusion confirmed by the inscribed date on the tomb wall of November 25, 1049 B.C. One of the first efforts to determine the season in which an ancient event occurred is Parson's opinion of 1758 that fossil fruits from the Isle of Sheppey were "antediluvian" and that, because the fruits were ascribable to the autumn of the year, the Flood must have occurred at that time (R. Bowen 1958:135). Rudenko (1970:28) details several kinds of evidence that point to late autumn or early winter as the season when the Scythian chiefs were placed in their tombs at Pazyryk in the Altai Mountains (see Fig. 9). A final example is from Muldbjerg, a Danish site where fish traps were made from willow and hazel twigs. Examination of the twigs showed that they were not quite two years old and, more importantly, that they had been cut at the beginning of June (Troels-Smith 1960:593).

Although at times it is relatively easy to show that a site was occupied during a particular season, it is not always so easy to say with equal assurance that a site was not occupied during another season. A review of published papers on seasonal occupation of sites as inferred from the age and species of birds and mammals whose bones are found in the refuse deposits may be found in Heizer (1960: 112–114).

By observing the ages of animals killed, one may learn something about the skills of the hunters. Very old and very young animals were taken more commonly than were mature beasts by some groups. Other groups selected mature individuals as the most desirable quarry. Social, technological, and other reasons must have been factors in such selective hunting, but these are difficult to determine at this distance in time. We can also learn something of the current practices of meatcutting. Split and broken bones argue for the use of heavy cleavers or choppers, both to break off hunks of meat and to extract the marrow. Not all broken bones in archeological sites can be assumed to be the result of human activity. Hyenas and other scavengers, or earth pressure, can break bones in such a way that it is difficult to be certain what specific agency was the cause. Slice marks or scorings indicate the use of knives, and burned bones may tell whether animals were roasted. In some instances oil-rich bones were used as a substitute for firewood (Heizer 1963).

Bones also tell what animals were preferred. For example, some Neanderthal groups ate little except wild cattle (*Bos primigenius*), others wild horses, and still others wild goats. In part this selection was due to availability, but it may also have had to do with what the people thought were good animals to eat. Food taboos, common throughout the world, may have considerable antiquity (Simoons 1961). To give a modern example, we can document the disappearance of the pig from the diet of people in Southwest Asia.

Today, when we find farm animals all over the world, we get the impression that many animals have a wide geographical range. If they have food, protection, and shelter provided by man, this is true, but under natural conditions the range of most species is limited (C. Reed 1959). For example, pigs and cattle were originally restricted to wooded areas, whereas sheep and goats favored hilly or craggy unforested environments. On the other hand, antelopes, horses, and gazelles prefer relatively flat, open grassland. Within certain environments, some animals eat one kind of plants and other animals have quite different diets. These factors, coupled with the fact that many animals migrate seasonally, severely restricted what man found available to hunt in any given area. His specialization on one animal or another might often as well be attributed to availability as to preference. It is just this sort of problem that an archeologist tries to answer, using archeological facts and knowledge of animal ecology to make his decision.

Until man became adept at special techniques for catching animals, he was geographically restricted. The earliest man had no bows and arrows, or even spears; he had to rely on the crippled or small animals he might catch by hand, carrion from the kills of carnivores, or animals trapped in bogs. He could not afford to be too choosy about what he ate. Specialization —in the face of varied possibilities—presupposes considerable know-how and the ability to produce on demand what is needed. The earliest man, therefore, must have been largely omnivorous, depending greatly on plants for food and supplementing his diet with meat when he was lucky. A mouse was important in his diet to a lessening degree as large game animals could be more easily killed.

Man's diet has ranged from almost complete dependence on animal food, as with certain Eskimo groups, to societies, such as Brahmin Indians, who place practically complete dependence on vegetal foods; its scope ranges from the extremes of hunting—or better, scrounging—to full domestication and controlled food production.

It is relatively easier to learn about man's meat diet than about his vegetable diet. Plants are seldom preserved—and then rarely ever beyond 10,000 years. On the other hand, the charred remains of plants may last indefinitely. Charred seeds, for example, retain their morphological characteristics and can thus be identified by a specialist; unless they are subjected to mechanical destruction—breaking or crushing—they should last forever. The problem appears to be one of finding the seeds rather than of having the plants themselves preserved. Recent work by Hole in Iran has demonstrated that a process known as "flotation" or "water separation" is useful even on material 9000 to 10,000 years old, and that theoretically we should be able to recover seeds much older. By this method, which has been used most extensively in American woodland sites, dirt containing carbonized material is immersed in water or a chemical, such as carbon tetrachloride. Carbonized seeds and other organic remains float to the surface and can easily be collected. Unfortunately, flotation does not work in all situations. Apparently it works best where the plant remains have been protected by a cushion of fine-grained dust or alluvium. Coarse-textured matrices crush and abrade the seeds. Until this and similar techniques are developed and exploited extensively, we shall have to depend on our knowledge of the environment for inferences on what men *might* have eaten. For these inferences, geology, paleontology, and paleobotany give us the best clues. When pollen can be found, it is an invaluable clue not only to what was actually eaten but also to available plants that might have been eaten.

For many prehistoric societies we are quite in the dark as to their diet. It is inferred, but not proved, that the Olmec civilization, the oldest of Meso-America, was supported by maize, but though this is highly probable, it is not certain. A similar assumption has been made about the Adena culture of the Upper Mississippi drainages, but only very recently has the first proof been recovered in the form of a carbonized ear of maize from an Ohio burial mound (Murphy 1971). The actual basis for Maya diet is not known, and this lack of knowledge has given rise to a long series of articles, all of them speculative, on the possible basic food resources that supported this civilization (for example, Bronson 1966; U. Cowgill 1971). Maize pollen as old as 2000 B.C. has been recovered from the lowland (Peten) area (U. Cowgill and others 1966:63), but this does not answer the question of whether maize was the major food resource for the Maya. It is therefore premature to cite agricultural failure to account for the collapse, about A.D. 950, of Classic Maya culture when the experts cannot agree on whether the Maya ate manioc, maize, ramon nuts, or marine foods.

With reference to the problem of determining whether the plants and animals eaten by a prehistoric people were wild or domesticated, R. J. Braidwood and his colleagues (1971) suggest that "effective domestication" might be defined when plants and animals can be shown to be morphologically different from wild forms (cf. Drew, Perkins, and Daly 1971). Plants and animals so distinguished would constitute "primary" evidence of food production as contrasted with "secondary" or artifactual evidence such as sickle blades and milling stones which can be used to harvest and grind seeds of both wild and cultivated plants.

People as well as plants were sometimes preserved in bogs, and the stomachs of the preserved bodies have been analyzed to show that early European farmers ate an amazing variety of plant food. It looks as though they gathered anything that was growing and cooked it into a kind of soupy porridge. H. Helbaek's (1950, 1951) analysis of the stomach contents of the Borremose and Tollund bog bodies shows that weeds were an important part of the diet in Iron Age Denmark, even though the Iron Age culture is classed as agricultural. The intestinal duct of Grauballe Man, a bog body from Denmark, contained 59 species of wild plant remains and 7 cultivated plant species (Helbaek 1969:208). Warren (1911) identified the stomach contents of a neolithic body preserved in swampy deposits in England and found that just before his death the man had eaten blackberries, rose haws, and *Atriplex* seeds. W. Emery (1961:243–246) lists the "menu" of a complete meal found preserved in a dry tomb of the Second Dynasty at Sakkara in Egypt. In a grave at the Playa de los Gringos site on the Chilean coast, Bird (1943:222) found a small wooden cup that contained flies and pupae cases. The flies were identified as a species that lives on meat; Bird was thus able to conclude that the cup had been buried with meat in it, perhaps as an offering of food to the deceased. A close parallel is noted by Judd (1954:62) from the site of Pueblo Bonito, New Mexico, where pottery bowls found in graves contained pupae of a muscoid fly (*Caliphoridae*) and body parts of ptinid and darkling beetles (*Niptus sp.; Alphitobius sp.*), whose larvae attack stored cereals. Judd concludes that the bowls contained offering of cornmeal when they were buried. Grahame Clark (1953b:230) cites instances of food found in Bronze Age and Iron Age containers in Europe. Carbonized seeds and grains are sometimes found in storage pits of open sites (Fowke 1902:409–410; Parker 1910:Plate 6; Shetrone 1930:58). A careful sifting of fireplace ash will sometimes reveal these. Pottery and clay sometimes trap the impressions of plants and seeds; such indestructible casts can be identified by a botanist.

Even though actual seed impressions in clay or carbonized seeds are not preserved, there may be ways to determine whether farming was practiced. Ways of doing this are by identifying the function of certain tools as farming implements (hoes and sickles, for example), and by finding prehistoric fields that have survived in the open or that have been buried under earth mounds or refuse deposits. Ancient fields buried under mounds might provide unique opportunities to determine whether fertilizers were used, and the amount of mineral depletion that has occurred. In addition, the fields might contain pollen from which the plants grown in the fields can be identified. Piggott (1959a:99) concluded that the Celts of southern England in the fifth century B.C. probably held farms of about 20 acres, if we are to judge from the number and size of pit silos used for storing crops. Radford (1935) estimated from the dimensions of the granary of a Roman villa at Ditchley,

Fig. 67 Prehistoric diet as determined from identification of food items in coprolites from dry cave and shelter sites in the Humboldt-Carson lakes region of western Nevada. The pie diagrams indicate percentages of types of food: S, seeds; Fi, fiber; Fs, fish; F, fauna; M, miscellaneous; WL, weightloss of coprolite material carried off in solution during rehydration process. Dates are radiocarbon ages. Numbers in parentheses indicate number of coprolites analyzed. (For details see Napton 1969.)

Oxon, that the estate amounted to about 1000 acres. Such estimates, admittedly only estimates, are important in giving some idea of the magnitude of landholdings in antiquity. In some instances ancient fields whose areas can be measured show up clearly in aerial photographs (cf. Bradford 1957).

Fecal remains also provide evidence of diet (Fig. 67). In very dry regions feces are preserved in caves, and their analysis has demonstrated how omnivorous prehistoric man often was. Together with seeds and plant fibers are found bits of bone of fish and rodents that were probably eaten whole (for a review see Heizer 1960:108–109). The size of bone splinters in archeological human feces are often impressive. Callen (1969:243) states that dry feces from caves in Puebla, Mexico, contain bones and bone chips up to 12 by 16 mm. in size. Ethnographers report that a common practice among California Indians was to grind the whole bodies of small rodents into a pulpy mass in a stone mortar and then eat this delicacy raw or cook it in a basket of acorn mush. An ethnographer (Scott 1958:326) relates that the Madakuyan of the Philippines "are used to chewing and digesting tough things and in addition to the bones of small fish and very heavy pieces of cartilage, often masticate and swallow some of the bones of a boiled chicken." Remains of plants may be preserved in yet another way. When plants decay or burn they can leave behind silica "ghosts" of their epidermal cells (Helbaek 1969:211–212). If the ground has not been disturbed, it is sometimes possible to recover these silicate remains and, by microscopic study, identify the plants from which they came.

Thus it is often possible to find out something about the vegetal diet, but it is very difficult to tell just how important it was in relation to the animal diet. Unless we can uncover caches that indicate how much food could have been harvested or collected, we have no good way of estimating surplus production or acquisition. The absence of bones, or the presence of only a few, may indicate that vegetal products were more important than meat. In the few instances where quantitative studies have been made on the bones from several sites, it has been possible to distinguish clear-cut differences in the diets of groups of people who it might otherwise have been assumed lived on identical foods.

J. T. Davis (1959) has critically reviewed a number of generalizations made by Southwestern archeologists about the relative importance of animal versus vegetal food in the diet of the occupants of specific prehistoric sites and has shown that these for the most part rest on very tenuous grounds. The archeologist must not only use judgment in reaching inferences on the basis of what is present, but also keep in mind that a great deal more evidence has disappeared without any trace. It is this requirement—that the prehistorian balance what is known against an indeterminate amount of information that is not known—that makes the job of interpretation so difficult. As A. L. Kroeber once wrote, the training of anthropology consists of "learning to discriminate between better and worse judgments and better or worse evidence."

Archeologists can find useful clues on the food-getting routine of hunter-gatherers by consulting ethnographic descriptions. McCarthy and McArthur (1960:150–180) have written a detailed event-by-event description of the collection of food by an Australian tribe, and we have a similar study for the Bushmen of the Kalahari Desert (R. B. Lee 1968). The economic routine among the dry-land peoples of the peninsula of Lower California was presented by Aschmann (1959) and Malkin (1962). Accounts of the food quest of the Ten'a of the Yukon River described by Sullivan (1942), of the Greenland Eskimo (Krogh and Krogh 1915), the people of Zia Pueblo in New Mexico (F. Hawley 1934) are cited as examples of the kinds of data available to archeologists that are useful in establishing a framework of reasonable possibilities against which the prehistoric data can be projected.

It is probably safer to make inferences from ethnography about subsistence and economy than about any other aspect of prehistoric life, but even these safer inferences are subject to error, as can be shown from an example that combines the use of ethnographic analogy and the direct historical method. The example concerns the data from Lovelock Cave in western

Nevada. Ethnographic studies made around the 1930s of the Northern Paiute Indians indicated that the subsistence pattern involved small groups of people who ranged widely, seasonally collecting pine nuts, kutsavi fly larvae, and cuyui sucker fish, which could then be stored and consumed over the lean winter months. Surprisingly, prehistoric coprolites from the cave showed nearly total dependence on plants and fish present in Humboldt Lake, about 2 miles from the cave; no pine nuts, larvae, or river fish are present in the remains from the cave. A search of historical records showed that the local Indians were dislodged from their prehistoric habitation sites and forced to change their way of life only after 1833. Hence an apparently stable pattern of life, which had been recorded ethnographically and on which many analogous reconstructions were based, is in fact an artifact of the white man's recent encroachment on Indian territory (R. Cowan 1967).

That the subsistence pattern had been inferred incorrectly leads one to question whether other reconstructions of the social organization of the pre-white period are valid. Following Steward's studies in the Great Basin among Shoshonean speakers, most anthropologists conceptualize small family groups scattered over the countryside, moving from grass harvests to grasshopper hunts, to acorn or piñon harvesting as the ripening plants and the seasons dictate. Altogether it is a hand-to-mouth existence. But now it seems that some of the groups, like those at Lovelock Cave, had a much more stable existence. What then does this do to our usual view of the social organization? The wandering bands had a simple family organization having patrilineal descent, with no formal leaders. Can we say the same of a larger settled group? This matter clearly needs further investigation; it is mentioned here chiefly by way of example.

In areas where animals were painted or pecked on rock surfaces one can gain some idea of the species with which the artists were familiar. The great painted caves of southern France and Spain represent, in one sense, ancient zoological libraries whose main purpose was probably religious, but which also inform us of the kinds of animals the Upper Paleolithic peoples were familiar with. The prehistoric pottery of the Mimbres people of New Mexico is well known because animals are frequently depicted, but here it is not so clear that only familiar animals were being painted, because in this fishless region piscatorial representations are common (cf. H. Gladwin 1957: 225–230), and there are composite "monsters" that surely never lived. Here the archeologist is faced with the problem of sorting out real from fanciful forms. That fish-forms portrayed on pottery vessels made and used in a fishless region may have been patterned after actual fish is suggested by the fact that Judd (1959b: 127–128) found scales of the gar pike in a Chaco Canyon (New Mexico) site. Today the nearest occurrence of the pike is in the Rio Grande River, more than 100 miles to the east. A parallel is provided by the occurrence of marine forms represented in rock paintings in the interior of South Africa.

A study has been made of the mammalian forms on Assyrian sculp-

ture (Houghton 1877); there is one review of the ancient fauna of Mesopotamia as evidenced in art by Van Buren (1939); and other works are
available: an entomologist's identification of arthropods portrayed on prehistoric Mimbres pottery from New Mexico (Rodeck 1932), a study of the
domestic and wild animals appearing on cylinder seals (Frankfort 1939),
and a review of animals represented on painted Greek pots (Morin 1911).
North and South African petroglyphs and pictographs cover a very long time
span; a kind of "zoological dating" is therefore possible by identifying styles
and animals represented (Goodall 1946; Wulsin 1941:Chaps. 8, 9). Finally,
a large number of animals known to the ancient Egyptians were mummified
and placed in tombs (Lartet and Gaillard 1907), in effect creating "zoological libraries."   •

An interesting example of inference about prehistoric diet is presented
by Hoyme and Bass (1962) in their analysis of two prehistoric populations
in Virginia. The Tollifero site is Late Archaic in time; its occupants were
either preagricultural or possibly beginning to practice agriculture. The
degree of tooth wear exhibited in the sample of 18 dentitions shows that the
people had a coarse diet that produced rapid tooth wear but relatively little
decay or loss of teeth. The Clarksville site is later in time; its occupants sub-
sisted on agricultural products, chiefly maize. Here the teeth, as judged by
the sample of 38 dentitions, are in much poorer condition, with a low degree
of wear and high incidence of loss of teeth possibly resulting from a soft diet
of corn, which, because it is high in carbohydrates, contributes to dental
decay and tooth loss. Table 7 illustrates the situation.

TABLE 7

	Degree of Wear				
	0 (absent)	1	2	3	4 (greatest)
Tollifero series (18)	—	1	6	9	2
Dentitions with caries	—	0	1	3	2
Dentitions with lost teeth	—	0	1	3	2
Clarksville series (38)	7	17	12	2	—
Dentitions with caries	7	15	12	2	—
Dentitions with lost teeth	2	12	12	2	—

Data indicate that people with agricultural diet at Clarksville site had a higher incidence of dental caries and a greater number of lost teeth than the Tollifero people
whose diet was based largely on wild foods.

The foregoing discussion points up the fact that evidence of diet is
won from the soil only with the most diligent effort and exercise of ingenuity
by the archeologist. Often techniques must be invented or perfected in the
hope that something may be found. A case in point is the flotation process, a
technique that was suggested by a botanist (Hugh Cutler) to an archeologist

(Stuart Struever) to help him find remains that he thought should be in refuse pits but were invisible to the naked eye. In fact, although Struever (1968a) reported that almost all the small seeds and bones had passed unnoticed through the usual dry screen, after flotation at one site, tens of thousands of nut shells, seeds, and fish bones were recovered; the result was a picture of the local subsistence economy that was completely different from what had been imagined. Although these results may seem to have been attained by the use of a simple technique, the process now in use was developed only after several years of work involving many hundreds of man-hours of hard labor.

We might tell much the same story about the botanists who have strained their eyes during thousands of hours at the microscopes to learn the criteria that signal the difference between wild and domestic cereals, or the characteristics of the pollen grains that serve so well to give a picture of the local environment. The important thing is that, before any cultural interpretations can be made, somebody must get the data out of the ground and identify them.

Studies of diet lead directly into studies of technology, because the two aspects of economy are often intimately intertwined. When technology is known in detail, it is possible to infer that certain kinds of hunting or farming were practiced. For example, when an archeologist finds sickles at a settlement he usually infers agriculture, although sometimes sickles may have been used to cut plants other than cultivated grain. Bows and arrows indicate hunting of animals; a study of the kinds of points used may indicate what kind of game was being hunted. Bolas (stones tied to long cords for entangling the feet of game) are an old invention; they were probably nearly as effective as spears or arrows. However, it is not always possible to tell what was hunted just by looking at the tools: absence of a tool may mean nothing. In connection with the use of bolas is the interesting suggestion that their habitual use might leave some skeletal evidence in early man. Wells (1964: 134–135) describes modifications of the humerus that result when slings are used, and it may be that similar motor habits, such as hurling bolas, would leave tangible evidence in the modification of bones.

As we know from a few rare finds, people who lacked spears tipped with stone could have used perishable bone or wood points. One of the Mousterian skeletons at Mt. Carmel, Skhul (IX), showed evidence of having received a hip wound from a four-sided wooden spear (McCown and Keith 1939:2:74–75, 373), and from this we can verify what has seemed highly probable; namely, that the Mousterians used simple wooden spears. What is more, some people may have preferred to snare animals or to catch them in deadfalls or other traps rather than to shoot or spear them. If people had no bows and arrows or atlatls, they were limited to trapping or hunting at close range. Such a situation might altogether preclude the killing of certain types of beasts. Negative evidence for various types of weapons is useful primarily where sites show good preservation and a variety of wooden and bone tools;

then it may safely be inferred that a number of other tools, such as stone spears, were not used.

Without the means for storing food, people had to spend considerable time in its acquisition. This condition probably existed during most of human history, but it was relatively more of a problem for collectors of plants than for big-game hunters. Furthermore, people who had to carry burdens on their backs were limited in the amount they could carry and in the distance they could cover (Steward's [1938] excellent discussion of the daily activities and yearly cycle of a primitive hunting and gathering people should be read carefully by all archeologists). Sometimes the carrying of burdens prevented extreme dependence on one source of food that might have been favored. For example, for many Indian groups the bison was only seasonally important before the use of the horse on the Great Plains. After that time, Plains Indian economy was revolutionized, and the people became almost totally dependent on the bison for the necessities of life (Ewers 1955). This is just one illustration of the interplay between technology and subsistence; and the correlates in social organization are also striking. Lack of certain tools also prevented people from exploiting rich farm land. Before the moldboard plow was invented, people who could not break the sod were prevented from farming the prairie grasslands—and much of the world's best farm land needed first to be cleared of forest with axes and fire.

Such instances serve to illustrate a point: it is difficult to make inferences about diet from technological evidence alone. We know only some of the ways of obtaining food; many others must have been developed and forgotten. Furthermore, we are at the mercy of preservation, and we can rarely be sure that we have the total picture. The biggest and ever-present problem in archeology is how to fill the gaps in the record that have been caused by the disappearance of organic materials.

It is probable that remains of organic matter in archeological deposits can be detected, and often identified, by chemical and physical methods so refined that they have not yet been attempted. Incidentally, this matter of organic residues is a good example of a problem that can be attacked by someone who has the requisite patience and skill. There are methods that are rather gross (in terms of those anticipated for the future), now available, such as determining, from the presence of phosphate, that bone was once present; it is practically certain that in the future much more precise methods for detection of organic residues will be devised. The former presence of some feature such as a human corpse, or wooden beams in archeological sites, may be detectable only as a stain or "silhouette"; special techniques of excavation and recording are required in these situations.

There are many aspects to technology, not all of which relate to the food quest. First and foremost, a study of technology reveals the steady increase of man's skills. Thomsen devised the Three-Age System—Stone, Bronze, and Iron—and it was applied to describe the cultural evolution of man. As Childe (1944b) has pointed out, each of the three ages indicated a significant technological advance that allowed man to do many more things than had been possible before. Today most of the stages of prehistory have been defined on the basis of technology. Put into a series, the stages indicate an ever-better mastery through tools of the environment. As man learned to do new things with the resources about him, his economy was enriched. In some instances it meant that he was able to live better, that is, with less worry about food shortages. In other instances he was able to move into new areas, and in still others he was able to surround himself with luxuries. These advances in technology and the fruits derived from them eventually contributed to craft specialization, population increases, large political groupings, and social hierarchies. The culmination was the increasing complexity of society and the increasing technical mastery of the world that led to civilization as we know it.

The study of technology can lead to inferences about man's cultural progress, but it is also informative about his relations with other people. For more recent prehistoric times it is often possible to trace the spread of technological knowledge into an area and to note the effect it had on the people there. For example, a study of sites in Europe indicates that farming was not accepted by all at first and that a hunting and fishing way of life died slowly (Fig. 68) (G. Clark 1952). Even though a population tries a particular subsistence economy, it may not always be able to count on its productivity. Thus the Hamitic herders between the Nile Valley and the Red Sea, who depend largely on sheep, will sow a field of barley after one of the occasional rains, settle down, and wait for the crop to ripen, and then move on with their flocks (Frankfort 1956:34). Total commitment to a specialized economy by prehistoric men was often hazardous, and such dual economies must have been fairly common; yet they are difficult to identify from archeological materials.

Study of technology may also reveal where and how objects were made. Metal tools, containers, and ornaments as well as some pottery were manufactured by specialists whose skills were beyond those of the common folk. When especially distinctive wares were made, it is possible to trace their trade throughout an area. When this trade has been charted, one must ask what was traded in exchange. Such inquiry may reveal that grains, skins, or raw materials were being exchanged for finished products. Exotic items always imply trade, and because trade—as opposed to tribute—usually follows a two-way road, it gives us the best opportunity for finding direct evidence of the extent to which any particular group of people was isolated. Precise knowledge of the geographic limits of trade enables us to plot the areas of effective intercommunication or interaction for each group of prehistoric people; this knowledge in turn lets us make reasonable guesses about the sources of influence and the nature of the contacts between areas.

Caches of an artisan's tools or paraphernalia of a specialist may throw light on the association of many items that otherwise occur only singly. A few examples may be cited. Mongait (1961:287–288) gives us detailed

FIG. 68 Radiocarbon dating of early agricultural settlements in Europe which illustrate the slow northwestward spread of farming. From G. Clark 1965. (For a recent assessment of the true ages of the dates given here see Renfrew 1970b.)

accounts of the contents of two burned houses in a Russian site, one of an artist, the other of a beadmaker; and MacAlister (1949:134–135) has described in detail an ancient Irish metalworker's hut. W. Wallace (1954) describes the contents of a basketmaker's kit from eastern California (Fig. 69); Elsasser (1961) has collected a great deal of information on medicine-men's kits found in archeological sites in the western United States; pre-historic medicine bags of the Adena culture group of eastern United States are described by Webb and Baby (1957: 72–76); and W. Emery (1948:65) describes a royal tomb in Nubia containing iron ingots and a set of metal-working tools. W. Emery (1961:137–139) mentions a number of burials that were deposited on the perimeter of the tomb of a queen of the First Dynasty of Egypt. The bodies in these graves were those of special craftsmen, such as sculptors, artists, sailors, and butchers, each one accompanied by the characteristic tools of his trade. Dawkins (1880:384–388) provides a list and description of the items in a bronzesmith's hoard found at Larnaud, France. The hoard contained 1485 pieces, of which 163 are items used directly for smelting or working bronze, 266 are tools and implements, 211 are weapons, and the remaining 845 are personal ornaments. This hoard, if

340

analyzed by modern spectrochemical methods and compared with the rich body of museum materials, would yield an important story of where the individual items originated and provide hints as to the ways in which it was accumulated.

Mention may also be made of the marvelous models of daily life, activities, and familiar objects that are found in Egyptian royal tombs and from which much specific and detailed interpretation can be extracted (Winlock 1942:25ff.;1955). The varied activities, such as sowing, reaping, fowling, hunting, and warfare, shown on Egyptian tomb paintings provide us with pictorial evidence of what and how things were done in dynastic times, and we can reconstruct from them many aspects of the technology of these ancient people. W. S. Smith (1958:138) cautions against assuming that the Egyptian paintings and engraved reliefs are always literally exact when he writes,

> Because the Egyptian's pictorial record was unique among his contemporaries, it is now infinitely precious, but his remarkable powers of observation have paradoxically laid him open to criticism for his carelessness. Obviously he was not impelled by a scientific interest in the modern sense and was capable of all sorts of inconsistencies. Hence, there is a danger in drawing too exacting conclusions from his work.

FIG. 69 Basketmaker's kit from Lovelock Cave, Nevada. Foxskin pouch contained the coil of weft material, one complete bone awl, two split bones to be made later into awls, and a sharp edged flint flake which presumably served as a knife.

TRADE

In our own experience we usually think of trade as consisting of buying and selling in the market place or between nations, but more useful connotations for most of prehistory would be exchange, barter, and swapping. Although such dealings are without money they may be far from simple and in fact may require the most delicately balanced sets of conventions or rules. What is more, such exchange literally may be noneconomic in the sense that no gain is expected nor any economic necessity fulfilled. As we can document from ethnographic sources, many modern means of redistributing goods cannot be understood by reference to our own Western industrial concepts of economy (Heider 1969). Yet a careful analysis of trade in a prehistoric context can inform us perhaps more quickly than any other means, of the scope and nature of the effective sphere of interaction in which the people who lived at any one site were participating.

It is easy enough to recognize "foreign" objects in a site, but much harder to demonstrate that they were traded and to pinpoint their origin. The examples that follow will point up some of the problems.

The simplest sort of trade must have involved the casual meeting of two groups of people or their representatives who bartered or exchanged goods. This sort of exchange would be expected among nomadic peoples. Before the use of metal or pottery such trade must have been limited, but we know of instances in which certain kinds of flint, calcite crystals, stalactites, sea shells, and obsidian were traded. None of these were necessities to the people who obtained them, although the imported flint and obsidian made better tools. It is worth noting that we do not find evidence of regular trade before the end of the Pleistocene, but sporadic finds indicate that at least a desultory trade in nonsubsistence items was going on. Saint-Perier (1913:49) lists molluscan species that are present in Upper Paleolithic sites in Lespugne, France, and finds that three species come from the Mediterranean and two from the Atlantic. Here, where there is no other hint of trade relations with these two coastal areas, both of which are about 200 kilometers distant, one cannot make a definite decision on whether the mollusc shells occur at Lespugne through trade or because the occupants happened in the course of time to visit both coasts and collect the shells. A similar find in Pa Sangar, Iran, only piques the curiosity about the mechanism of transmission; the find by itself does not provide the details to fill in the picture (Hole 1970).

In addition to the instances where trade in durable items can be proved (as, for example, between coastal Southern California and the Puebloan Southwest—see Brand 1938; H. Colton 1941; Heizer 1941b; Tower 1945), there probably also was heavy trade in such perishable materials as feathers and skins. When one finds objects of very distant origin in archeological sites, the logical explanation is that they are the result of intergroup trade. However, as one alternative explanation, the possibility should be considered that the items have been transported, in the bodies of migratory animals, from their area of origin to their outland resting place. A number of examples of the transport of artifacts (mainly weapon points) by migratory animals are cited by Heizer (1944, 1968b) and Carneiro (1958).

Objects for decoration and ritual were probably the most favored trade items, because prehistoric man was ordinarily self-sufficient so far as his basic food and tool needs were concerned. Probably to be interpreted as imported luxury items are Mesopotamian cylinder seals of the Uruk-Jemdet Nasr period (sometimes called the Protoliterate period and known to date from 3500–2900 B.C.) that have been found in Gerzean (that is, Late Predynastic) period graves in Egypt. The graves cannot be directly dated but have been relatively dated at falling between S.D. 50–63 (see Chap. 15 for an explanation of the sequence-dating system). These small cylinder seals are therefore highly significant both as evidence of trade and because they permit the fairly precise dating of the Egyptian material just before the First Dynasty (Frankfort 1956:122–123; W. Emery 1961:30; W. S. Smith 1958: 19). From two major source areas, Anatolian Turkey and Armenian Turkey, obsidian was sent throughout the Near East to most of the villages that lay within 600 miles of the sources (Fig. 70). The recent work in spectroscopic analysis of the trace elements in obsidian has gone far toward precisely identifying the finished products with their sources, and consequently opened a new dimension of interpretation concerning the early agriculturalists of the Near East (Renfrew, Dixon, and Cann 1966; J. Dixon, Cann, and Renfrew 1968). The important question remaining is "What was the mechanism of trade and what was traded in return?"

Similar trade routes were established in North America to carry copper and shells. The Ohio Hopewell Indians engaged in trade in obsidian, mica, and other exotic materials from the Atlantic Ocean to the Rocky Mountains, a distance of perhaps 2000 miles or more. Somewhat later, in Aztec times more formal land- and sea-trade routes were established in Meso-America (Fig. 71). The Aztec merchant traders, called *pochteca,* were a hereditary professional class of wealthy and high-status persons. The Aztec ruling elite, who used the valuable foreign luxury goods (feathers, gold, cacao, finely woven cotton cloth, jade) that the *pochteca* secured, protected the traders who operated, as it were, with diplomatic immunity in foreign lands of Meso-America. The *pochteca* served the Aztec state by spying out territories not yet under Aztec control and even acted as agents-provocateurs creating an excuse for military intercession and ultimately absorption of a new area into the Aztec conquest empire (de Cardos 1959; Chapman 1957). In the trade between one Central Mexican metropolitan area and Central American so-called "ports of trade," which were politically neutral commercial exchange towns, figured prominently (Chapman 1959; West, Psuty, and Thom 1969: Fig. 32). With this rich background of the Meso-American trade network, archeologists are testing the evidence of long-distance trade against this model (L. Parsons and Price 1971; T.

Hester, Heizer, and Jack 1971). So far the widespread diffusion of obsidian —the geologic sources of which can be identified through comparison of the trace-element composition of artifacts found in sites with known obsidian deposits—constitutes the best evidence of an ancient trade "network" (Heizer, Williams, and Graham 1965; Jack and Heizer 1968; Stevenson, Stross, and Heizer 1971; Cobean and others 1971; T. Hester, Jack and Heizer 1971).

That the items were not without precedent, however, is evident in the finding of magnetite mirrors in early sites in Oaxaca—seemingly the mirrors were manufactured and traded to Olmec centers on the Atlantic Coast

FIG. 70 The obsidian trade in the Near East from the fifth to the second millennia B.C. (Sources in capitals). Obsidan was one of the first raw materials to be systematically distributed by prehistoric men. The sources from which obsidian came can be determined precisely by several techniques: x-ray fluorescence, optical spectrography, and neutron activation. (C. Renfrew, J. E. Dixon, and J. R. Cann, "Obsidian and Cultural Contact in the Near East," *Proceedings of the Prehistoric Society*, 32 (1966): Fig. 6.)

Fig. 71 Some main trade routes and trade centers in Meso-America at the opening of the Spanish Conquest.

(Flannery and others 1967). In one of these large Olmec sites (La Venta) obsidian, which can be shown to have come from at least five separate sources, three of which are identified as occurring in Guatemala and in the state of Hidalgo north of Mexico City, enlarge our information on the geographical extent of Olmec commerce. A picture of trade contacts extending at least as far distant as 200 miles south, 350 miles east, and 300 miles north thus emerges from these simple facts. Therefore the Olmecs, who lived on the Gulf Coast plain between 1000 and 600 B.C., are seen to have lived in a larger world of contact and communication than might have been supposed, and any interpretation of their culture must take this fact into account.

Unless a site is the indisputable place where trade goods were made, it is often difficult to determine that certain items were traded. For example, pottery could be made by almost anyone, and for the most part trade pieces were probably only the finest wares, which were made by specialists. However, this statement need not necessarily be true. In Meso-America today there are villages where the people make pottery for a whole region, carry it to market periodically, and distribute it widely. In Crete (Xanthoudides 1927:118) and in Peru (Bruning 1898; Donnan 1971) there are itinerant potters who travel about the country and settle down for a time where good clay occurs and a profitable market exists for their wares.

In some cases traveling potters will bring with them a supply of dry, prepared clay. Such pottery, in an archeological context, would not be distinguishable from pottery imported from outside. When their sojourn is no longer profitable, they move on. In antiquity such practices may have occurred and might account for some of the distributions of prehistoric pot forms or styles (cf. K. Dixon 1963). Itinerant Bronze Age smiths (perhaps like the

345

Sleib or Solubiyeh, traveling tinkers of the Syrian desert) in Europe have long been recognized as one of the agencies of diffusion of metal-working techniques, as well as of types of ornaments.

An interesting study by Grace (1961) concerns the ancient wine trade of the Classical period in the Mediterranean as evidenced by two-handled pottery amphoras in which the wine was transported. When pots are not especially distinctive, one might not suspect trade. It is here that routine use of technical analysis is important, because it can give the clue that trade was practiced, and then help in locating the sources of materials. A. Shepard (1948) has written a detailed study of the Meso-American trade pottery called "plumbate" (so named, but incorrectly, on the assumption that it was a lead glaze; however, it proves to be a vitrified surface formed from fine-textured clay of high iron content fired in a reducing atmosphere of about 950 degrees centigrade), which has been found archeologically from Lake Nicaragua in the south to Tepic, Nayarit, in the north. Though the place of manufacture still remains unknown, scientists can determine, from technical analysis of the lustrous vitrified surface and the paste of the pottery, that it all derives from a single source.

Shepard makes a distinction between intrusive pottery, which was secured by trade from an outside area of another ceramic tradition, and trade pottery, which was traded between settlements within the geographical area of a ceramic tradition. The distinction is a useful one, because intrusive pottery can be used to correlate regional chronologies—for an example, see Haury's matching of the Anasazi, Hohokam, and Mogollon cultures of the Southwest (H. Gladwin and others 1937:212–219)—and trade pottery is useful in correlating local sequences.

STANDARDS OF EXCHANGE

Minted metal coins were not used for exchange in prehistory. For the most part, the world was on a barter or exchange system, but there are a few instances in which a form of currency was in use (see Loeb 1936; Bessaignet 1956). The Aztecs and Mayas used the cocoa bean (Chapman 1957). Some Indian groups in California measured wealth in tubular sea shells (*Dentalium indianorum*), the longer being the more valuable. We know that today tribal peoples in many countries reckon wealth in the numbers of livestock they own. When they make large purchases, a certain number of animals is judged to be an equivalent value. For example, in such systems so many chickens may equal a pig, and so many pigs may equal a cow. There is an element of barter economy in this exchange, but at the same time quite arbitrary values are given to things, and these values need have little relation to the intrinsic worth of an object. Thus a pig with particularly well-developed tusks may bring more than one with small tusks.

Without some system of arbitrary value-units, trade would not flourish, because it would be limited by the amount of real worth a man could pack on his back. The use of coins relieved man of having to tote a load of bloody hides home in trade for a copper ax—unless, of course, he happened to want hides. The use of coins enabled much more diversified exchange. A man with hides could sell to a man who wanted hides but who did not have axes to trade. The seller of hides could in turn buy an ax from a man who did not want hides.

On a surprisingly simple cultural level we note specialization of labor, where certain individuals or families work to produce finished products such as arrowpoints, fishnets, and bows and arrows, which they trade to their village mates for other finished items or for food. Ordinarily such craft specialization is found in settled village populations who support themselves by agriculture, but the Indians of central California, whose economy was based on salmon, deer and acorns and who are therefore nonagricultural, did practice craft specialization. An archeologist who assumes too readily that craft specialists come into existence with farming villagers might thereby overlook the possibility of specialization of labor (for additional discussion, see Heizer 1958).

SHELTER

To the degree that people could shelter themselves they could live in areas that were too hot or too cold for constant exposure. Earliest men, like certain peoples living today, were content to lie under a shady bush or tree during the day and to huddle in a burrow during the chill of the night. We do not know when they learned to build shelters or when they learned to clothe themselves with skins. However, once they had done either, they could vastly increase their geographic range. The use of fire not only supplemented their shelter but also enabled them to cook food. What are possibly, though not certainly, the most ancient shelters built by man are the curved stone piles found in Olduvai Gorge at the site of the camping spot of Zinjanthropus, whose age is determined by the potassium-argon method as about 1,750,000 years (Curtis 1961; Gentner and Lippolt 1969). The oldest unequivocal remains of huts occur at Terra Amata, a site in Nice, France, that was salvaged for archeology during the construction of an apartment building. These huts were apparently temporary shelters of poles and skins that were erected seasonally on the beach at a favorable location during the Mindel glaciation some 300,000 years ago (de Lumley 1966). The oldest known use of fire by man is at the site of Choukoutien, where the bones and tools of Peking Man (Sinanthropus), dating from the second, or Mindel, glaciation, were excavated. Attested use of fire by man in Africa came somewhat later in Middle Acheulean times just before the third, or Riss, glaciation (Oakley 1955a; Heizer 1963).

In one sense man's houses show his capabilities as a food getter. The camps of hunters are ordinarily small and temporary. Usually impermanent shelters seem to have been favored. There is some evidence, however, that the reindeer hunters who settled so successfully in the rock shelters of France during the Pleistocene may have constructed a sort of shelter under the rock overhang to give additional protection. At best this would have been a framework of wood overlaid with skins, but it may have lasted from one season to the next. The animal bones in the rock shelter deposits suggest that some of the groups stayed in one place the year round—for all we know, groups may have stayed in one shelter for generations. It is certain that these men could not have carried a shelter very far with them if they migrated, because they had no pack animals. Hunters on the loesslands of Central Europe used the bones of mammoths as framework for their houses and probably roofed them over with skins (Klima 1962; Mongait 1961:91–94). Even wood was scarce there, and the people burned oil-rich mammoth bones for fuel. If these men had not known how to build houses and to make fires, they could not have lived in these regions.

One of the best adaptations to varied climates is the earth-covered house. In prehistoric times some of these houses consisted of pits dug into the ground and roofed over with wood and branches covered with mud or skins. The low-lying houses were sheltered from the wind and were well insulated from heat and cold by the thick layers of dirt on all sides. Of all the houses built in temperate-to-cold climates, these underground houses have enjoyed the longest popularity. In fact, some of the dwellings of the paleolithic mammoth hunters of Russia were essentially pit houses, and our own pioneers in the West built similar houses of sod.

Many kinds of houses are made of mud. Slabs of mud dried in the sun can be piled on one another as bricks, or indeed, bricks can be made in wooden forms and baked. Mud can also be layered on a wall, a little bit being added vertically each day, and allowed to dry in the sun. Another system is to build forms for the walls and to tamp mud between them, allowing it to harden in the sun. Still another way is to build a framework of sticks in the form of loose matting and to plaster this with mud to build up a substantial wall. Such houses are ordinarily roofed with beams laid across the walls. The beams are then covered with sticks or brush and packed over with mud or earth. The result is an economical house that serves admirably in a hot, dry climate. Rain will eventually ruin such houses, but with reasonable care a mud house will last 15 to 50 years. Brick houses, of course, last much longer (see Fig. 48).

When archeologists excavated the floor of the priest's house in the Oval Temple at Khafaje (Iraq), which dates from the twenty-sixth century B.C., they found a number of large mud-wasp nests. The nests had been built in the angles and joints of the complicated wooden beam and mat ceiling. From the negative "casts" of the construction elements, which were preserved in the attachment surface of the wasp nests, a detailed reconstruction of the wooden ceiling could be made (Fig. 72) (Lloyd 1963:Plate 25).

FIG. 72 The outline of a prehistoric house at Nørre Fjand, an early Iron Age site in West Jutland, is revealed by the line of post holes and the shallow wall trench.

The use of stone for building seems to have been a rather late invention, but some of the earliest Mesopotamian and Anatolian mud houses were reinforced, especially at their bases, with stone (see Fig. 42). However, successful stone construction demanded either careful shaping of the blocks so that they could be laid dry, or a knowledge of mortar. Stone houses were often plastered on the inside, but where mud was scarce skins could be hung to keep out drafts.

The kinds of houses depended largely on what building materials were present, but even with limited resources there were alternatives. One of the most unusual villages ever constructed has been excavated at Beersheba in Israel (Perrot 1955a, 1955b). The houses, built entirely underground, resemble an ant colony with passages leading to the rooms. The excavators reported that it was pleasant working underground during the baking heat of the day because there was good ventilation and the heat did not penetrate the earth. In these houses no wood was needed though some passages were lined with stone slabs.

In many parts of the world abandoned houses soon fall down. In Yucatan one finds only a little elevated earth platform on which once stood a thatched house (Bullard 1960). Where there was enough grass or straw and the weather permitted it, houses were built of thatch. The thatch served to keep off the rain and sun but was of little use for conserving heat. Similar structures are built by nomads whose seasonal migrations take them into warm climates. The same group of people occasionally have winter houses that last from year to year, and seasonal houses that are rebuilt every year.

People who live in tents leave characteristic though easily dispersed remains. There is usually a fireplace, often in the form of a little hollow surounded by or lined with stones (Wedel 1961:262). The edges of the tent may be ditched to carry off rain water or they may be outlined by a row of rocks used to hold down the edges of the cover. Inside the house area one may find a platform or layer of rocks on which the people placed objects that they did not want to expose to damp or dirt, and a fireplace. If these remains

349

are on or near the surface they have little chance of preservation if the land is plowed or otherwise disturbed.

Archeologists can misinterpret archeological features as houses. G. Clark (1957:116–117) explains that the excavators of the neolithic settlement of Köln-Lindenthal near Cologne interpreted borrow pits (originally dug to secure earth and later filled with garbage) as houses, but they failed to recognize the rectangular timber structures they found as dwellings. Piggott (1959a:84) shows that the same misinterpretation was made in southern England, partly for the reason that inadequate excavation techniques in the early work did not yield evidence of the presence of timber houses and farm buildings.

As G. Clark (1957:197) has pointed out, there is often a close correspondence between the size of settlement and the kind of economy practiced by prehistoric man. Almost invariably the settlements of farmers are larger than the settlements of hunters (cf. G. Clark 1954:8) because there is a limit to the size of the group that a purely hunting and gathering economy can support. (For some relevant statistics, see Table 8.) The limit depends largely on the number who can live through the worst season or through a succession of bad years. This number, in turn, depends on the amount of game and vegetal food and the efficiency with which the people can secure it.

The size of a settlement is also partly a matter of preference. Some people preferred to live in large groups, whereas others preferred smaller units. We see these differing attitudes in the homesteading farmers of the United States, as opposed to the pueblo-dwelling Indian farmers of the Southwest. On the one hand, each family lives on its plot of land; on the other, all families live in a central village, and the farmer walks to his fields. One system stresses independence of action; the other stresses community living.

The size of a settlement may also depend on other preferences. Some areas were probably always more active socially, whereas others were more isolated or frontier areas. Sites at a distance from established trade routes may have seemed less attractive to some peoples, even though the level of subsistence may have been equally favorable.

Despite all the sociological reasons for the different sizes of settlements, however, other things being equal, there were great inequalities between the lives of hunters and farmers. The latter had an assured food supply unless they had settled on poor land. They could readily grow a surplus and it could be stored against want in the future or traded for goods and services. Population would therefore increase. The history of food-producing people is one of population expansion and the colonization of "underdeveloped" areas.

TRANSPORT AND TRAVEL

Trade, colonization, and migration imply transportation. For most of his history man had to depend on his feet for travel and on his back for trans-

TABLE 8 RELATION BETWEEN ECONOMY AND SIZE OF SITE (AREA IN SQUARE METERS)

Site	Economy		
	Hunter-Gathering (Mesolithic)	Early Farming (Neolithic)	Developed Farming and Technology (Bronze Age)
Nørre Sandegaard II, Denmark	100		
Nørre Sandegaard III, Bornholm, Denmark	290		
Oakhanger, Hants, England	160		
Star Carr, England	240		
Teviec, Morbihan, France	240		
Windmill Hill, England		93,080	
Fort Harrouard, France		68,760	
Aichbühl, Germany		6,300	
Moosseedorf, Switzerland		1,000	
Robenhausen, Switzerland		12,100	
Wasserburg Buchau, Germany			15,000
Gournia, Crete			24,280
Gla, Greece			97,120
Los Millares, Spain			50,590
Troy II, Turkey			8,000
Averages	206	36,248	38,998

The figures listed above should be taken as general indications only. Precise calculations of sizes of settlements are difficult. Comparisons between sites is hazardous because of particular topographic or environmental conditions, and the kind of houses or shelters present. Reports frequently fail to state sizes of settlements, and where sites were occupied over long periods it is hard to state precisely what the size of settlement was for each period. After effective agriculture, there begins a great disparity in the size of sites even within one cultural tradition. Some sites, for economic or social reasons, become more important than others and are not strictly comparable with them.

This chart was taken from a much larger list compiled by Ronald Weber, a student at the University of California. It includes the largest and smallest sites of each economy in Weber's list, together with three of intermediate size.

port. Lack of transportation severely restricted, although it obviously did not prevent, his movements. What it did was to preclude the frequent movement of large amounts of material. Prehistoric man, like most hunters and gatherers around the world, went himself to the supplies or resources rather than bringing them, or having them brought to him. Man's mobility was greatly enhanced when he discovered boats to enable him to cross rivers. The importance of such craft may be forgotten until a person faces the problem of negotiating a body of water that he cannot wade across. The location of towns in our own countries at convenient fords reflects this importance, even to people who have a sophisticated technology. Consider the plight of a westward-moving pioneer in his covered wagon who had to cross one of the major rivers that drain the West. With equipment too heavy to carry and water too deep to ford at most places he was literally incapable of crossing what we all too often think of simply as scenic attractions or sites of recreation. Boats were probably the first improvement in man's means of travel. Simple rafts and dugout canoes were among the first conveyances, and they were followed by vessels with oars and sails. Animal transport, so far as we know, came late, although it is conceivable that the dog was used for packing or traction by the end of the Pleistocene. The animals used for transport include the reindeer, elephant, dog, horse, donkey, ass, ox, water buffalo, sheep, goat, and llama.

The extent to which culture change may be effected by adoption of an efficient means of transport is illustrated by the use of the horse (from Spanish stock) in the Plains-Plateau area of North America. A careful study of the Blackfoot tribe by Ewers (1955) discusses in detail the cultural changes engendered by the horse.

The use of wheeled vehicles caught on very slowly because they require the services of a draft animal and because most areas require extensive preparation (such as roads) before carts can be moved easily. It was also important to have something worth transporting. Forests, mountains, swamps, and sandy areas are virtually impassable for primitive carts. The hard-packed deserts of Mesopotamia and Egypt were most suitable for traverse, and the animals and the incentive to move goods were present there early. It is likely that the first wheeled vehicles in Mesopotamia were reserved for the use of persons with high status and social prerogatives, and not for routine transport of goods (Piggott 1965:92). Even today, as the modern traveler to the area is surprised to learn, the rural villager makes little use of the wheel.

Of course, one might consider all the various devices that have been used to enable or enhance mobility in various parts of the world. Chief among those we have so far omitted are devices that can be used in snowy regions: sleds, skis, and snowshoes for overland travel, and kayaks for water traffic. Incidentally, it should be noted that travel over ice is relatively easy, certainly easier in today's arctic than travel over the spongy expanses of the semithawed tundra that characterizes much of the area in the summer. Travel is easy, provided the ice is firm and not interrupted by crevices or ice wedges. These barriers are as effective in stopping a sled as a river is in preventing the passage of a covered wagon.

The foregoing has considered relatively small-scale movements that were probably typical for most prehistoric man. It is worth noting in addition the deliberate as well as accidental migrations of people who sailed the Pacific in search of islands to settle. In accomplishing these feats with relatively simple boats and navigational equipment they populated the last remaining uninhabited desirable areas of the world which, until some 3000 years ago, were effectively out of reach of man.

By interpreting evidence on climate, geography, plants, animals, and artifacts, the archeologist can learn a great deal about prehistoric man's economy—his struggle to live and improve his lot. However, man's past was not merely a matter of technology and environment; he was a social being. By the painstaking and imaginative examination of archeological evidence, we can learn something about the less tangible aspects of his life.

REFERENCES

Economy: G. Clark 1952; Jarman 1971; R. B. Lee 1968; Malinowski 1932; Mauss 1954; Nash 1966; Polanyi 1957.

Recovering Dietary Information: Aschmann 1959; Bird 1943; R. Bowen 1958; Bradford 1957; Brothwell 1965; Callen 1969; G. Clark 1952, 1953a; Coon 1951; J. Davis and Treganza 1959; W. Emery 1961; Fowke 1902; Frankfort 1939, 1956; Gladwin 1957; Goodall 1946; F. Hawley, Pijoan, and Elkin 1943; Heizer 1960, 1963, 1967; Helbaek 1950, 1951, 1964, 1969; Hough 1930; Houghton 1877; Hoyme and Bass 1962; Isaac 1971a; Judd 1954, 1959b; Krogh and Krogh 1915; Lartet and Gaillard 1907; McCarthy and McArthur 1960; McCown and Keith 1939; Malkin 1962; Morin 1911; Parker 1910; Piggott 1959a; Radford 1935; C. Reed 1959, 1963; J. Robinson 1956; Rodeck 1932; Saffiro 1972; Scott 1958; Shetrone 1930; Simoons 1961; Struever 1962; Sullivan 1942; Troels-Smith 1960; Van Buren 1939; Warren 1911; Wedel 1961; Wells 1964; T. White 1953a, 1954, 1955b; Winlock 1942; W. Wood 1968; *World Archaeology* Vol. 2, No. 3; Wulsin 1941.

Trade: Berndt 1951; Bradly 1971; Brand 1938; Bruning 1898; de Cardos 1959; Carneiro 1958; Chapman 1957; H. Colton 1941; J. Davis 1961; J. Dixon, Cann, and Renfrew 1968; K. Dixon 1963; W. Emery 1961:50; Ewers 1955; Fischer 1963; Flannery and others 1967; Frankford 1956:122–123; H. Gladwin and others 1937; Grace 1961; Haines 1938a, 1938b; Heizer 1941b, 1944, 1963; Herrmann 1968; W. Hill 1948; Hole 1966; Kroeber 1940b; Malinowski 1932; M. Mallowan 1965; Navarro 1925; Pieper 1923; Piggott 1959b; Rathje 1972; Renfrew 1968a, 1969; Renfrew, Dixon, and Cann 1966; Rodden 1966; Sahlins 1965; Saint-Perier 1913; A. Shepard 1948; W. Smith 1958:19; Steward 1938; J. Stone and Thomas 1956; Thompson 1949; Tower 1945; G. A. Wright 1969; Xanthoudides 1927.

Artisan's Tool Kits: Dawkins 1880; Elsasser 1961; W. Emery 1948, 1961; MacAlister 1949; Mongait 1961; W. Wallace 1954; Webb and Baby 1957; Winlock 1942.

Standards of Exchange: Bessaignet 1956; Chapman 1957; Heizer 1958; Loeb 1936.

Shelters: Bullard 1960; Childe 1949, 1950; G. Clark 1954, 1957, 1961; Curtis 1961; Grigor'ev 1967; Klima 1954, 1962; Lloyd 1963; de Lumley 1966; Mongait 1961; Morgan 1965; Oakley 1955b; Perrot 1955a, 1955b; Piggott 1959a; Richmond 1932; Schlette 1958; Wedel 1961; Woodward 1933.

CHAPTER EIGHTEEN

PATTERNS OF SETTLEMENT

In the previous editions we began this chapter with a discussion of the kinds of settlement studies that have been carried out by archeologists. At the end we referred to the field of locational analysis that was becoming important in prehistoric studies. Locational analysis is a special topic within geography and has its own set of concepts and working assumptions, most of which are unfamiliar to prehistorians. However, if we wish to use the ideas of geographers, we need to know what they are based on. Accordingly we will discuss the history and concepts of locational analysis first, then give examples of the kinds of studies being made by archeologists. In this way both the potential of locational analysis and the limited scope of typical archeological studies will be made clear.

Spatial arrangements of man and his works are constantly before us and they make intuitive sense to us all. It is obvious why some things are where they are. The fact that things in space are readily observable lends them to graphic representation, hence the distributional map which can be studied indoors and out and virtually endlessly plotted, copied, colored, and analyzed. Spatial studies reduce some of man's most fundamental traits to graphic two-dimensional expressions; hence the appeal of geography—the "map science"—and its related discipline, settlement archeology.

HISTORY OF SETTLEMENT STUDIES

In his appraisal of *Settlement Archaeology* Willey (1968c:224–225) said,

> It seems safe to say that an interest in, and an awareness of, the settlement dimension will continue and increase. In the past decade, archaeological articles on, and monographs taking account of, site, regional, or areal settlement patterns have appeared with regularity . . . A variety of attitudes or approaches has been addressed to settlement pattern study . . . The prehistoric settlement form or pattern is one important part of this whole past . . . It is now, I think here to stay in archeology. . . .

The term "settlement pattern" has become a part of the vocabulary of archeology and ethnology, and there is general agreement among anthropologists that settlement pattern studies are worth doing. In archeology the settlement approach has encouraged a shift in focus from a study of individual artifacts and sites to culture areas and relationships among sites and areas. Evidence of this shift are papers mentioning settlement patterns or actually relating settlement patterns to environment (Trigger 1968c), social organization (W. Sears 1968), ideology (Trigger 1968c, Vogt 1968), or describing changes in settlement pattern through time (R. Adams 1965; R. Adams and Nissen 1972; W. Adams 1968; Plog 1968; Willey 1953). But although everyone agrees that settlement pattern studies will be part of the more sophisticated investigations of the future, there is no consensus on the concepts necessary for such studies, how they are to be used, what constitutes a settlement or community, what is meant by settlement pattern, or even what we can hope to find out by studying settlement patterns.

Like many terms used in archeology, "settlement pattern" has too many connotations to be useful in scientific discourse. A cursory review of the literature will show that settlement pattern is variously considered (a) a trait indicative of a culture; (b) a valid research objective, for example, "we will survey for settlement pattern"; and (c) a theoretical viewpoint that implies a particular kind of interrelationship among the elements in the distribution of settlements. Collectively these are clearly more conceptual freight than the term can usefully bear in efficient communication. A brief look at archeological history will illustrate how the term has been used.

Following Trigger (1968c:54), we can distinguish two approaches to settlement pattern: the first, often called an ecological approach, deals with the distribution of sites and seeks relationships between sites, subsistence, technology, and environment; the second is more concerned with the distribution of features within a single site and the inferences that can be made from these data about social, political, and religious organization.

Ecological studies are numerous in archeology, having a history that goes back to Julian Steward's suggestion to Gordon Willey that he investigate settlement pattern because of its close relation to subsistence and environment (Willey 1953:xviii). Since the Viru Valley study was published, there has appeared, an impressive list of similar reports that describe the interrelations between environment and settlement pattern. In most of these, "settlement pattern" is considered a trait of the culture or cultures in question, and is as much a characteristic of the culture as its pottery. Struever (1968c:286) sums up the views expressed by most of the authors:

> Culture is viewed as a system of functionally interdependent parts in which change in one aspect is related in specifiable ways to changes in others. Explanation for change in a cultural system requires understanding of these linkages. Cultural variations in space are seen in terms of the differing adaptive requirements of specific environments; accordingly, varying ecological potentialities are linked to different exploitative economies and the latter, in turn, to different integrative requirements and therefore to different forms of social structure, etc.

The theoretical position adopted in ecological studies is that culture is adaptive; consequently its physical manifestations can be seen as examples of adaptation. Although this view clearly oversimplifies the actual situation, it is generally taken as an approximation in ecological studies, without any checks on its accuracy. The assumption of adaptation is a "working conclusion."

The second orientation in archeological studies views the distribution of features within sites as clues to elements of nonmaterial culture.

> It is clear that "there is an obvious relationship between social structure and spatial structure of settlements, villages, and camps" and that social systems may be studied through "objective and crystalized external projections of them" (Fitting 1969:360, quoting Lévi-Strauss 1963:284).

Once again spatial distributions and relationships of architectural features are treated as traits, this time not just of a single culture but as traits revealing behavior that may be common to many cultures. A number of novel and imaginative studies of this kind have emerged. The most convincing are those dealing with Southwestern Pueblos where abundant ethnohistoric data inform on cultural practices of great antiquity and where few substantial changes can be detected in architecture

R. Naroll's work (1962) and similar studies by S. Cook and Heizer (1968) on the correlation between floor space and population in certain California groups are also convincing, based as they are principally on ethnohistorical data. Correlations of data taken from the *Ethnographic Atlas* by Whiting and Ayres (1968:117) are highly speculative but intriguing. They examined correlations between such variables as restrictions on premarital sex and the use of curved as against straight lines in architecture. Three out of four societies requiring premarital virginity use more curved lines! Though such data can doubtless be ferreted out of ethnography they will probably serve more to remind us of the intricacies of our subject than to send us panting in pursuit of the spectrum of prehistoric chastity. Nor is much gained by Eric Reed's (1956:13) speculations on site orientation.

> It surely must reflect something basic in personality structure, outlook, national character—or something comparable to the Spanish inward-facing

patio-type house on the edge of the street and our front-facing dwellings with the lawn on the outside.

Granted there may be aspects of personality in this but most of us will continue to use the information on orientation as a trait and leave the speculation, as Reed suggests, to psychologists, architects, or social commentators.

In the ways in which archeologists have practiced the study of spatial aspects of their data we see two contrasting approaches: the broad ecological overview that stresses man-land relationships, and the view that relates the nature of structures in sites to social and/or psychological factors. Although settlement studies have not stimulated a radical departure from previous practices, they have encouraged examination of regions rather than of single sites and of systematic relations, whether within or among sites. Expressed this way settlement pattern studies are the tool of ecology.

If settlement pattern studies have done no more, one may wonder why they are mentioned so frequently and why there are books with the term "Settlement Archeology" in the title. One answer lies in the visual appeal of distributional maps and the fact that distributions of sites help describe archeological cultures. But probably more important is that geographers have recently been developing a branch called spatial or locational analysis and many archeologists, like Plog (1968:6–7), believe that

> . . . the techniques developed by geographers are directly related to problems of settlement pattern. I believe that anthropologists should take advantage of already proven methods which are applicable to the problems with which they are working.

As a number of current studies (Gumerman 1971) will attest, this view is widely and favorably regarded.

CONCEPTS OF SETTLEMENT ANALYSIS

In view of the interest among prehistorians in settlement studies, it is useful to examine some of the concepts used by geographers. What in their terms is "spatial" or "locational" analysis? It is both a goal and a set of concepts with appropriate techniques. Nystuen (1968:39) expressed the goal this way: "To explain how the elements under study are arranged and associated in space."

Berry (1968:25) amplifies this.

> Geographers are like any other scientists, identified not so much by the phenomena they study, as by the integrating concepts and processes they stress . . . the geographic point of view is spatial . . . the integrating concepts and processes of the geographer relate to spatial arrangements and distribution, to spatial integration, to spatial interactions and organization, and to spatial process.

To analyze the properties of spatial relationships, geographers construct abstract systems which employ the basic concepts *direction, distance,* and *connectivity.*

> To study a system in the abstract has many advantages . . . simplicity . . . clarity . . . the elements in an abstract system possess only those properties explicitly assigned to them . . . the abstract systems which are of use to geographers are precisely those in which the elements in the system retain some geographically significant properties (Nystuen 1968:36).

By *direction*, Nystuen means orientation.

Distance is a deceptively complex element. An example will make this clear.

> In economic, social, or psychological terms, 10 miles is not simply equivalent to 10 times 1 mile, and 10 miles over flat plain is rather different from 10 miles across the Alps. But in models of spatial development we frequently require relationships in which the distance variable is measured quantitatively. If we have to use a distance function in model building, then we need an adequate methodology for understanding distance . . . "Distance" is thus a relative measure (Harvey 1967:599–61).

Note that location is directed distance: the direction and distance from a point of origin.

Connectivity is independent of distance and direction. It is the "functional association of spatially separate elements" (Nystuen 1968:39). The association is expressed in "flow"—"flows of people, goods, or communication . . . flow of words." To study connectivity "requires explicit recognition of the properties of the relationship [connectivity]" (Nystuen 1968:39). In the empirical world such relationships are nearly infinitely varied, and a point that must be kept in mind by archeologists is that the *kind* of relationship is not necessarily revealed by spatial configurations. To put it another way, geographers can use their knowledge of connectivity to interpret spatial distributions, but we cannot willy-nilly turn the matter around and use the spatial distributions to infer the type of connections.

The heart of locational analysis is the use of models based on the concepts enumerated above. As Nystuen remarked, abstract models are easy to use and, if properly constructed, relate closely to the empirical world. Models and theories are both important in locational analysis. A *theory* (hypothesis) is a statement about relationships in the real world whereas a *model* is an abstraction of the working of the relationships. "A theory . . . can be accepted or rejected on the basis of how well it works. . . . A model . . . can only be right or wrong on logical grounds. A model must satisfy only internal criteria; a theory must satisfy external criteria as well" (Chorley 1968:44–45, quoting Coombs, Raiffa, and Thrall 1954). Thus a model is intermediate between theory and the real world. A model can be a mechanical device, a picture, or a mathematical expression.

Direction, distance and connectivity are concepts underlying most geographic models, and there are also six premises which geographers appear to accept as lawlike generalizations (Garner 1967:304–305):

1. The spatial distribution of human activity reflects an ordered adjustment to the factor of distance.

2. Locational decisions are taken, in general, so as to minimize the frictional effects of the distance. (See Lösch 1954, law of minimum effort, and Zipf 1949, principle of least effort.)

3. All locations are endowed with a degree of accessibility but some locations are more accessible than others.

4. There is a tendency for human activities to agglomerate to take advantage of scale economies. (Scale economies mean the savings in costs of operation made possible by concentrating activities at a common location. . . . The concentration of activities to form settlements themselves can be viewed as a reflection of scale economies.)

5. The organization of human activity is essentially hierarchical in character.

6. Human occupation is focal in character.

As an example of how the concepts of distance, direction, and connectivity are used, we cite a study by Nystuen and Dacey (1968), "A Graph Theory Interpretation of Nodal Regions." This study is a procedure for ordering and grouping cities by the magnitude and direction of flow of goods, people, and communication between them. In their work Nystuen and Dacey (1968:408, 410) say,

Cities are viewed as nuclei of specialized activities which are spatially concentrated and functionally associated.

Long-distance telephone communications may be considered a single index of this multidimensional association among cities. . . . This does not deny the existence of other flows or associations to and from each areal unit.

The nodal region describes the relationship between the hinterland which is areal, and the central or nodal city, which is punctiform. In the hinterland concept, the areal units may be abstracted to the level of points, so that the association is in terms of many points being linked to a single central point.

Within the myriad relations existing between cities, the network of largest flows of telephone calls will be the ones outlining the skeleton of the urban organization of the entire region. The term "largest" implies an oriented relation, because a flow between a pair of cities may be the largest in terms of one city but not necessarily in terms of the other city. . . . Using the principle of dominant association, a single out-directed line is assumed to be associated with each point.

Three other properties of the "largest flow" relation are specified (Nystuen and Dacey 1968:410–411):

1. A city is independent if its largest flow is to a smaller city.

2. Transitivity: if a city *a* is subordinate to city *b* and city *b* is subordinate to city *c* then city *a* is subordinate to city *c*.

3. A city is not subordinate to any of its subordinates.

The authors call the largest flow from every subordinate city, the *nodal flow*. In combination these flows form the *nodal structure* of the region (Nystuen and Dacey 1968:411). With these definitions, along with the concepts of direction (outward from a city), distance (measured by phone calls), and connectivity (flow of calls) and the properties specified above, the authors (Nystuen and Dacey 1968:412) prove two theorems.

> Theorem 1: The components of a nodal structure partition a set of cities.
> Theorem 2: Each component of a nodal structure has a unique central city (terminal point).

The authors then applied their model to the urban structure of the State of Washington and found that the nodal regions suggested by the nodal structure agreed in general with their expectations. Moreover, the model helped explain a particular case: "The dominance of Seattle reasserts itself at even greater distances, so that Aberdeen and Centralia are directly associated with Seattle, rather than by a two-link path through the closer and larger city of Tacoma" (Nystuen and Dacey 1968:417).

After this example most archeologists will be willing to concede that locational analysis is different from the study of settlement patterns and that geographers are trying to do something quite different from what archeologists are trying to do. The most striking difference, of course, is that geographers are concerned with building abstract models based on clearly defined concepts and definitions having to do with spatial relations. Archeologists traditionally eschew spatial considerations (except in the simple plotting of distributions) in favor of statements about ecological or other relationships. In neither conception nor practice are these pursuits analogous. In this sense the techniques developed by geographers are not directly related to the problems of settlement pattern. They are not related unless we can state archeological problems in spatial terms; that is, when direction, distance, and connectivity are the principal variables in the expression.

LOCATIONAL ANALYSIS IN ARCHEOLOGY

At this point it is useful to consider again what settlement pattern studies in archeology have tried to do and what concepts have been used. It does not take much study of the literature to discover that archeologists have failed to define concepts analogous to those used by geographers. In other words, they have not developed independently a field of spatial analysis; this suggests that attributes of space per se, especially distance and direction, have never been important in archeological problems. However, connectivity or analogous concepts of relationship have been emphasized. Of these perhaps the most important is *adaptation*.

The fundamental difference in the way archeologists and geographers approach the problem is that while archeologists have been preoccupied with man-land relationships which are believed to operate as part of an adaptive system, geographers have been more concerned with man-man relationships which operate in an economic or information network. The difference, it seems, stems from the following facts. First, archeologists have been primarily concerned with primitive non-Western cultures, whereas geographers have traditionally studied modern Western, economic-oriented societies. Second, while archeology is concerned with real data, manifested principally in sites arrayed over a landscape, locational analysis has dealt with statistical data input into abstract models. Finally, in archeology the fundamental premise of adaptation has overshadowed alternative kinds of relationships that geography routinely uses as instances of connectivity. In a real sense then, spatial analysis in geography has been able to ignore terrain and thus the basis of the man-land relationships that have loomed so large in archeology. The basic difference lies in the approach. Archeologists have traditionally sought to explain the particular instance, whereas geographers have attempted to understand a general class of events through the use of abstract models. In archeology neither the data nor the concepts have been precise enough for constructing analogous models.

If we were to try to define our concepts more clearly, we could readily copy *direction* from spatial analysis. *Distance,* as noted earlier, is more of a problem, and an adequate definition for archeological purposes must consider the kind of relationship as well as the mileage. In order to have an effective way to use both distance and direction, we need to be able to specify the point or area on the map from which we will measure. This involves dealing more meaningfully with some basic matters that are familiar to all of us.

Activity locus, site, settlement, community, and territory are all used to designate the spatial coordinates of certain kinds of human behavior, but they do not all mean the same thing; or perhaps we should say they embody several distinct concepts. Consider the following common archeological problem. A village consisting of an area of closely spaced houses surrounded by miles of terrain without houses is easy to identify as a site and its position on the map is its center. But what is the location of a city 3 by 5 miles in extent? If you want to measure the distance to another city, what point do you use? Or how do you determine the limits of sites marked by seasonal occupations which over the years may accumulate a thin scatter of material over a mile or more? Should we treat as a single site the entire territory occupied by a group of hunters and gatherers over a year? Such a site would consist of many activity loci and campgrounds. These are just some of the issues for which we need operational definitions if we wish to relate spatial analysis to the archeological world.

To return to *connectivity* again, when we speak of settlement patterns we prejudge the matter of relationships. We assume patterns but there are at least three senses in which pattern is used in archeology: (a) a *distribution,* as the simple plotting of locale; (b) a *statement of relationships,* as traits of culture functionally interrelated. In archeology we deal exclusively with physical remains and the relationships among them. For us patterns consist of seeing the same set of variables in different circumstances and we often conclude that the elements in the set are functionally interrelated; (c) a *model,* an abstraction which can include both statements of distribution and of relationship.

In settlement pattern studies the first two uses of pattern are common but the second requires more discussion. As we have noted before, archeologists tend to assume that adaptation or adaptive behavior underlies the man-man or man-land relationships. This is a major assumption that is no less reasonable than the six assumptions ordinarily made by geographers. What is more to the point is that all these assumptions can be stated more profitably as hypotheses to be tested, and explicit effort should be made to find alternative hypotheses. In fact, whether we are interested in settlement patterns or not, it would be useful for archeologists to focus their attention on the general question of connectivity. As archeologists we are often interested in the linkages between peoples in different sites or regions. Trade, diffusion, symbiotic relationships, interaction spheres, warfare, migration, and the like occupy much archeological discussion. These are statements about connectivity, but we understand relatively little about the factors that would go into such relationships. Part of the reason may be that ethnologists have given little attention to such matters; our principal sources in this regard are historical, not anthropological. And part of the reason may be that the questions have not been investigated through the means of testing hypotheses. Archeologists have not assiduously followed the acceptable scientific procedure of zealously trying to *disprove* hypotheses rather than eagerly attempting to prove pet theories. Nor have we devoted sufficient effort to establishing what kinds of evidence we will find acceptable. These are matters of the utmost urgency in archeology.

In summary, settlement archeology grew out of an ecological concern with man-land relationships, and in consequence adaptation has been used to explain observed phenomena. By contrast, locational or spatial analysis has emphasized the spatial arrangement of phenomena and the extensive use of abstract models of settlement systems.

The two fields are not intrinsically incompatible and there is growing evidence that they are converging. Archeologists are beginning to work with models, whereas geographers have shown a growing concern with non-Western, nonindustrial societies; in both fields assumptions are made about the relationships of variables, and in both, hypotheses are tested. However, on balance it would seem that archeology, with its traditional emphasis on sociocultural data of imprecise definition and its attempt to explain the particular, has lagged substantially behind geography which has used accurate quantifiable data that lend themselves readily to abstraction. It is true that archeology has a different set of intellectual concerns from geography but it is one that may be approached in the same manner. If archeology is to develop its own branch of locational analysis, archeologists must first define their basic concepts so as to make them compatible with their intellectual concerns. If this is done, there is room and legitimate need for a science of spatial relationships in both archeology and geography.

ARCHEOLOGICAL STUDIES OF SETTLEMENT

Following the concept of adaptation, most archeologists feel that the location, spacing, size, and kind of sites are determined by the natural environment, by social, and by biological factors. Of these we can deal most effectively with environmental and social factors.

Patterns of settlement can be described statistically; in doing so, size and spacing of sites are emphasized, together with the number of people who live in the sites. This concern with vital statistics is usually called demography. Patterns of settlement can also be interpreted in terms of their relevance to human behavior. In this area concepts of ecology are important.

Trigger (1965:2) writes,

The settlement pattern . . . directs attention toward developing a methodology for the systematic study of the social and economic organization of ancient society. The settlement pattern is the order which the members of a society observe in their utilization of space. It is the plan according to which houses, shelters, fields, markets, temples, forts and cemeteries are distributed across the landscape. When the actors leave the stage, the social, political and economic activities disappear with them, but the settlement pattern, like the set and properties of a play, remains behind. In this basic sense the settlement pattern is an expression of the societal aspects of ancient cultures. The study of changes in settlement patterns thus becomes a study of the development of social and political organization, while the study of change in phase-archaeology is largely a study of the invention and diffusion of various items of material culture.

For archeologists, both description and interpretation of settlement patterns are important, but it should be stressed that interpretation is our ultimate goal. Interpretation must be based on careful recording and description, and the latter can be done effectively only if the archeologist has some idea of how he may want to use his data. This chapter will thus deal with how settlement data are used in archeological interpretation.

DEMOGRAPHY

Demographic data are usually quantities that express the number of persons comprising a certain population, together with the relations among categories (for example, occupation and status) of persons. These can be used to calculate both relative and absolute sizes, as well as rates of changes. Basic to obtaining demographic data in archeology are careful surveys of sites, with an adequate control over dating, and either extensive or sampled excavation of sites to gain an accurate picture of their size and internal structure. Surveys of sites or of areas will reveal the pattern of the space occupied by people and hence represent a description of one area of prehistoric human behavior.

Probably few kinds of archeological interpretation have more systematically built-in sources of potential error than have estimates of population, yet such figures are commonly given and used for making further inferences. It is safe to say that, because our concerns in archeology turn more and more toward reconstructing social systems, we shall have to devise methods of obtaining better demographic data.

Many estimates of population begin with an estimate of the size of sites, because there is some relation between number of people and the area they occupy. The precise relation can be determined through ethnographic analogy, which sometimes may be relatively simple. Such analogies are possible when there is ample ethnohistorical evidence to indicate that the archeological people are direct ancestors of historically known groups. This condition is met, for example, in parts of the Southwest. Here the archeologist can make accurate estimates of the total population if he knows how many houses there are. The problem becomes more difficult when there is no historically known descendant group or, in either instance, when the number of houses occupied at one time is not known.

Several methods have been proposed to calculate the number of people who occupied a site. One method of obtaining a general estimate was proposed by Naroll (1962), who examined a sample of ethnographic sources and determined that the ratio of enclosed floor space per person is a relatively constant 10:1. That is, if there are 100 square meters of floor space there will be 10 people occupying it. Subsequent very careful examination of California data for a large number of sites fully confirms Naroll's conclusions (Cook and Heizer 1965, 1968). These figures probably apply principally to permanent settlements that have substantial houses, but they are likely to be inaccurate if applied to brush huts, tipis, and other forms of impermanent camp shelters. Moreover, the ratios are averages and the range of variation within the samples is large.

Another approach is to try to relate the total surface area of the site to the number of occupants (Cook and Treganza 1950:231–233). A small sample of sites in California showed that there was a relation of the type:

$$\text{log population} = \text{constant} \times \text{log area}.$$

Although the reasons for this relation are not clear, it does seem to hold. Further work (Cook and Heizer 1965, 1968) indicates that the precise relation between surface area of a site and the population is itself related to the ecologic area in which the site is found, and to social factors. Somewhat different relations were obtained for sites in hill, coast, and desert environments and also for sites in which houses were for single families and those in which multi-family dwellings were common. In other words, if archeologists can calculate the relation between area and population they can use this formula for other similar sites in a homogeneous environment. Summarizing their findings on the California sites, the authors say, "As far as village area or space is concerned, there are three very distinct groups, whereas when floor space or house area is considered, all the regions form an unbroken exponential continuum." Fairservis (1967: Table 2) provides a table showing site size in square feet, number of houses per site, and probable prehistoric population of each site based upon present-day modern population density figures for West Pakistan. Such calculations are of course only estimates, but they are important in giving some idea of the numbers of people who originally lived on these sites.

Another important method of roughly estimating the population of a site is to calculate the number of people who could have existed there. This sum can be determined by figuring the amount of food consumed (as represented in the refuse) and determining how many people it would have fed, or by figuring how many people an area could have supported. The former method is illustrated by R. Ascher's (1959) analysis of a California shell midden in which he calculated the amount of protein represented by the shells. Assuming that each person consumed 5 gm. per day, Ascher divided the day-units of protein by the length of occupation of the site, and concluded that over a 25-year period, the population varied between 21 and 53 persons. A similar analysis that considered the amount of meat represented in the bones from Star Carr, an English mesolithic site, is presented by G. Clark (1954: 15–16). One should remember in such interpretations that the remains found in the site may represent only a portion of the total food consumed and may, in fact, represent only a small part of the total diet.

Although these methods are useful, before they are even attempted there are several purely practical problems that must be solved. The first of these is how much to dig. One seldom digs a whole site. For this reason, it is rarely possible to specify the total number of houses, fireplaces or pits, or even the total area of the site. This situation is especially true for large sites and sites in which there are many levels.

Consider the problems in digging a site like Grasshopper Ruin in Arizona, a "masonry pueblo consisting of more than 500 habitation and storage rooms," some of which were two stories high. The site also includes large open courtyards, cemeteries, and numbers of kivas (R. Thompson and Longacre 1966: 259). It would make no sense either scientifically or economically to excavate the whole site; instead, a method for sampling it must be devised. Sampling in itself is no small problem; it requires several years' work, which must be followed by excavation of the sample. The first step is to prepare a map of the site that shows every structure, a task made possible by the fact that the masonry walls lie on or near the surface and can be traced with a minimum of digging. With the number, kinds, and sizes of rooms recorded, it will then be possible to design a technique for sampling them. The judgment of what constitutes a reliable sample will be aided by excavations already completed and by the analysis of mutual variation among the data (R. Thompson and Longacre 1966: 271).

The other practical problem is in judging how many houses or what portions of a site were occupied at one time. The solution to this problem is not obvious for most sites. There may be rare instances where techniques like obsidian-hydration or tree-ring dating will allow one to assign relative dates to separate rooms on one occupation level, but other dating techniques are too coarse to help. Occupation dating is an area in which even modest improvement in techniques will be of great value, and one hopes that further research will result in better methods.

Several unusual methods of estimating population should also be mentioned to illustrate what a perceptive archeologist can do with rather meager data. One is Pericot's (1961:210) effort to estimate the population for Mesolithic Spain from numbers of persons represented in group scenes in cave paintings. The second is a speculative essay on the size of the population that occupied the Scripps Estate site on the southern coast of California between 5500–7400 years ago. Here the amount of shell refuse and numbers of manos (grinding stones for reducing seeds to flour) suggest to the authors (Shumway, Hubbs, and Moriarty 1961:107–108) a population of 30 persons. Although their estimate may not be precisely accurate, these authors feel confident that they have discovered the general magnitude of the population. Even this degree of precision is useful for making further interpretations.

Two examples in which pottery was used as a basis for reconstructing size of population are also instructive. De Borhegyi (1965:13) tells that some 50 million broken vessels were incorporated into the fill that went into the mounds at Kaminaljuyu in Guatemala. If we estimate a time span of 1000 years and that a family of five would break about 10 pots a year, a minimum estimate for the population during an average year would be about 25,000, a figure that generally accords with one based on an estimate of the number of laborers required to build the mounds. The second example treats pottery in quite a different fashion. C. Turner and L. Lofgren studied Northeast Arizona, the area of the western Pueblos, whose archeological record is relatively well known since A.D. 500, when pottery first appeared. These authors suggested that the size and quantity of cooking jars, serving bowls, and ladles might be related to the number of people living in a house.

To test jar capacity (amount of food cooked) and estimate individual portions (from individual serving bowls and ladles), 542 vessels were measured for capacity. These covered a time range from 600–1900 A.D. Judging from ladle capacity (360 cc = 1.5 cups), cooking jars proceed by vessel period as follows: 1 (13.5 cups), 2 (14.4), 3 (15.4), 4 (15.6), 5 (15.4), 6 (21.1). Mean cooking jar capacity runs progressively larger from Period 1 (3107 cc) to Period 6 (4849 cc). This is taken to indicate increasing household size (supported by standardized capacity of ladles and serving bowls). Comparison of room counts of sites multiplied by 4 or 5 persons/family carried out earlier by Colton (1960) with pottery jar-serving bowl ratios multiplied by 4.48 (derived from extensive census data of recent Southwestern Indian groups) shows generally similar results (Turner and Lofgren 1966).

Finally, we consider demographic data obtained from skeletons. The previous methods have used indirect evidence to count the people, whereas this method is direct. It need hardly be pointed out that one can count the bodies in a cemetery to find out exactly how many people lived in a site if one can assume that all bodies were consigned to the grave and if one can control time. Howells (1960) has written the most complete discussion to date of the ways in which burial data can be used for estimating populations. Aside from using such data to estimate populations, however, one can determine age at death and get a life-expectancy curve. This curve will often be interesting for the light it sheds on the conditions under which people lived. To know something of the sex ratio is also important. Occasionally one apparently finds a disproportionate number of skeletons of one sex. An example is at Pecos, a ruin in the Southwest where many more males than females were found buried. Because this proportion runs contrary to what one would expect of a correct sample of the population, it may indicate that the sample is biased because it is incomplete or because the Indians had different burial practices for men and women (Howells 1960). Sexing of skeletons is difficult, and there is also the possibility that some of the Pecos site sex identifications are inaccurate.

Accurate demographic data are hard to obtain even today; yet they are vital if we are to understand trends of stability or change, and they are very useful in helping assess the nature of a particular society. Accordingly, demographic data are one aspect of archeology that needs a good deal more emphasis in the future so that better techniques and more accurate estimates can be developed.

For a general survey of prehistoric demography we refer the reader to S. Cook (1972). Any archeologist dealing with the vital statistics (birth rate, mortality rates, life span) of a prehistoric population will find the recent book by Acsádi and Nemeskéri (1970) indispensable.

FACTORS AFFECTING POPULATION SIZE AND ITS DISTRIBUTION

The size of populations depends on both social and environmental factors. The environmental limitations are clear because, with a given population of plants and animals, there is a theoretical maximum human population that could be supported. If all the food could be used, one would have only to total up the calories, minerals, and vitamins available and calculate how many persons could live on this quantity. However, our knowledge of social factors prevents our even taking the first step in this direction. Man cannot, and may never be able to, use the total food in any environment. In the first place, if he did so, there would be nothing left for the next year; we see this today in places where certain livestock are literally eating themselves out of a future. People could do the same thing.

These considerations reflect certain theoretical parameters affecting population size, but one cannot get very far with such abstract discussions. More meaningful is to deal directly with actual examples. We know that man's use of the land will depend on the resources and on his ability to use them. We are dealing with the interrelations between man and his environment, or, in general terms, an ecosystem. The questions that need to be asked about an area are, "Can man live there? Is it too hot, too cold, too dry, or too wet?" There are a few regions beyond the ability of man to tolerate, but again this is a statement made in the abstract. Much more to the point is whether man can extract from this environment the necessities to sustain life. Is there sufficient food or the potential for agriculture? If wild, how is the food distributed across the landscape, and how is it available seasonally? Are the food sources sufficiently close to drinking water? A good exercise is to take the map of an area, see what resources are available, and then put man there and try to figure how he would exploit the land, granting him several different levels of technological sophistication.

Technology is consequently another important part of the ecosystem. What does man have with which to exploit the resources? Does he have the tools to skin a whale or a hippo? Can he cut, thresh, and grind the wheat? Has he suitable utensils to cook or boil food? Can he rid the acorns or manioc of their poison and thus create for himself a dietary staple? Can man tap the water, provide adequate shelter, and fuel? It was technology that converted a plains hunting ground into the breadbasket of America. Today, with the same environment, but a different technology, the area can support a population many times the size of the total number of Indians in North America at the time of contact.

What we have just said has to do with whether it would be at all possible for man to live in an area, but more usually it is pertinent to ask what limits the environment places on settlement. As many writers have pointed out, hunters make extensive use of the land, ranging far wider on the average than do people who collect plant food or who plant crops. The density of hunting groups depends on the density of animals and the number required to feed the people. That is to say, a human population may fluctuate considerably, because the population of game fluctuates over a period of years. Moreover, if the game is migratory, sometimes it does not migrate near where the people are waiting. Mobility is thus important for hunters and tends to keep the ratio of people to area fairly low. Usually with hunters the social organization is such that it permits both rapid and easy splitting of groups when the occasion demands, and coalescence if desirable. The exigencies of the hunt and the nature of the terrain thus exercise strong controls over the size and distribution of a population. The same is true whether the people are farmers, hunters, or fishers, but it becomes less true as people gain control over the environment by means of technology.

We can also consider the importance of social factors. First, the group must be large enough to carry out all the necessary tasks of subsistence, shelter, and procreation. The size of the group will depend on environmental factors and perhaps also on such intangible factors as the desire for companionship, a consideration that could vary from group to group. The socially acceptable upper limits of settlement size and density probably also vary from group to group. Early villagers in western Iran seem to have split after their communities reach 100 to 200 persons. Subsequently the worldwide trend in the Near East and in many areas has been toward larger and more compact cities. It is relevant to note that external factors such as the encroachment of outsiders may also have an effect on settlement or group size. As Service (1962) has shown, a tribal level of integration is largely a result of external pressure; there seems little reason to doubt, for example, that the density of settlement in the stockaded villages of the Eastern Woodlands had something to do with the threat of attack.

Trade, or commercial activities generally, can affect settlement either by permitting people to live removed from certain vital resources or by creating different types of settlements. Looked at another way, diversification of mutually interdependent types of settlements is one of the characteristics of complex societies. Often there are religious or political capitals, market centers, rural villages, fishing or farming communities, military garrisons, industrial or mining centers, and the like. It is important to note that it is the organization of a social system that permits such specialization and welds the diverse parts into a viable whole. The pattern of settlement thus can be seen to be both a result of, and a contribution to, social complexity.

A final set of factors relates to custom, belief, and religion. Returning to subsistence, we can easily bring to mind a variety of food taboos around the world. We have no idea how old these practices are, but we do know that man today willingly restricts his diet and that there are very few persons who eat the full range of nourishing food found in their environment.

For the most part the reluctance to make use of everything available stems from beliefs in what is good to eat. For example, pigs, snails, snakes, and insects are not eaten by most persons in Southwest Asia. Such exclusion of good food is not always the result of an abundance of other foods. Many peoples have certain animals that are clan totems, and in most instances members of the clans are forbidden to eat these creatures.

Preference rather than taboos also rules out certain food except in unusual circumstances. For example, in Southwest Asia sheep and goats are said to be "warm" animals and good to eat, but cattle are "cold" and not so good to eat. We have records of people who abstain from certain foods that are thought to leave persons with a characteristic odor offensive to themselves and detrimental to hunting. Social reasons for particular choices of food could be listed at great length, but these few illustrations should serve to show that any inferences we might make about hypothetical maximum populations, based only on a simple tally of the available food, are very likely to be wrong.

Warfare, the enslavement of war captives and ritual human sacrifice, were probably not factors of major importance in the regulation of most prehistoric populations but they were in some areas, especially Meso-America. At the time of contact by Spanish conquistadores and for an unknown time before, ritual sacrifice was carried out in highland Mexico on a scale that was certainly consequential for the population. A variety of ethnohistorical sources suggest that there were enough ritually induced deaths to affect population trends. S. Cook (1966:291) estimates that "the mean annual sacrifice rate of 15,000 would have augmented the death rate by roughly fifteen percent, a quantity which, over one or two generations, could have been of material significance in aiding to control the population density." Although recent estimates of the population of Meso-America are considerably higher than the figures Cook used in his calculations, his point still has some validity. We need not think of such numbers of deaths, however, to recognize that even modest-scale warfare could be important. As we describe later on, under trends of change, the calculated growth rate of population during the Neolithic in the Near East would have been offset by one additional death by sacrifice, or a war every 10 years, in a population of 100.

Kroeber (1963:148–149) proposed that warfare among the Indians of the eastern United States was the most potent factor operating to keep the population from expanding and that warfare further prevented the emergence of the state. His discussion, based on ethnographic evidence, constitutes an interpretation which archeologists could test. Kroeber says,

> [The eastern tribes] waged war not for any ulterior or permanent fruits, but for victory; and its conduct and shaping were motivated, when not by revenge, principally by individual desire for personal status within one's society. It was warfare that was insane, unending, continuously attritional, from our point of view; and yet it was so integrated into the whole fabric of Eastern culture, so dominantly emphasized within it, that escape from it was well-nigh impossible. Continuance in the system became self-preservatory. The group that tried to shift its values from war to peace was almost certainly doomed to early extinction. This warfare, with its attendant unsettlement, confusion, destruction, and famines, was probably the most potent reason why population remained low in the East. It kept agriculture in the role of a contributor to subsistence instead of the basis of subsistence. On the other hand, such farming as was practiced yielded enough of added leisure, concentration, and stability to make pretty continuous warfare possible. A population of pure hunter-gatherers would probably, except on the immediate coast, have been too scattered in minute bands, too unsettled in a country of rather evenly distributed food possibilities, too occupied with mere subsistence, to have engaged in war very persistently. . . . Agriculture made their wars possible; but their warfare kept the population down to a point where more agriculture was not needed.

TRENDS OF CHANGE

A useful statistic that may not deal with absolute numbers is that of relative population size at various periods. A time graph of population density for the Jeddito Valley region, Arizona (Hack 1942:78–80), shows relative increase and decrease. Hack assigned a scale of unit values to the size of sites to arrive at a curve of population changes. Rather than showing actual population,

Hack's curve shows the magnitude of changes. An alternate method was adopted to show changing population in Deh Luran, western Iran (Hole and Flannery 1968:Fig. 13; Hole 1968). The curve was based on the number of sites and an estimate of the number of people who lived in them.

It is important to stress here that most such extrapolations are guesses. As S. Cook and Heizer (1965:2) point out, they would be much more convincing if, for example, archeologists gave a "mathematical demonstration that the relation between population and, say, village number actually may be expressed as a linear function." Needless to say, although such a demonstration is desirable, it is often difficult to achieve, but the same authors have shown how it can be done for California data.

Today we are impressed by the rate of population growth and by the dire predictions that accompany it, and we vaguely apprehend that the rate is unusual. But is it? A convenient test of the rate was given by Carneiro and Hilse (1966), when they considered the rate of population increase during the so-called Neolithic revolution when, with the advent of food production, population grew far beyond previous levels. What is surprising in their figures is that the population growth was not rapid; "it was, in fact, only on the order of one-tenth of one percent per year" (Carneiro and Hilse 1966:179). This rate of increase would be unnoticeable to a person whose life expectancy was on the order of 30 years, because in his lifetime there would have been added to a village of 100 only 3 persons.

Such figures are, of course, subject to many errors, including the fact that they are based on the assumption that one rate of change characterized a 4000-year period, but they do have important implications when we consider the effect that an increasing population may have had on social institutions. Today we are faced with many problems brought about by a seemingly endless supply of people who strain existing facilities and for whom adequate planning cannot be effected. Our social institutions are literally being torn by excessive demands. Such would not have been the situation during the Neolithic, when the populations were relatively fixed residentially and the social organization was based on kinship and personal face-to-face relations. The strains would have come when the populations grew beyond the limits of personal recognition and familial control, and when access to wealth or productivity became unequally distributed. In part a contributing factor and in part a by-product, would have been the growth of technological and administrative specialists who eventually comprised an entirely new kind of segment of society. But before this, the first 3000 years of population expansion in Mesopotamia would have seen the budding off of small communities as they reached an optimum size—provided that there was sufficient virgin land available for new settlement under the existing system of extensive, rather than intensive, use of the land (Hole 1966). From an archeological view, the change from many small settlements to a pattern where some if not most became significantly larger would be the clue that a change in social organization was in the offing or already present.

Perhaps no contribution of archeology is more important than its ability to reconstruct the course of change over long periods, but these examples point out clearly that one must look very carefully at the details of the situation before leaping into the realm of speculation and interpretation that might easily be colored by our own experiences during a time of truly exceptional population growth.

COMPOSITION OF SITES

Most sites consist of a number of discrete areas that represent different kinds of activities. Houses, pits, and work areas characterize even simple sites, whereas more complex sites have palaces, temples, aqueducts, wells, houses, and the like. One major archeological problem is to isolate and describe adequately each of the areas of a site and to try to see the whole site as a set of structures and spaces that were used by people. With a site as small as Hatchery West, Illinois, the problem of obtaining a total site plan is not too great, but we have already seen what the comparable problems are for a site as large as Grasshopper. For a very large site, one might question whether extensive sampling is really worth the effort or even possible. A decision would have to depend on the site itself and on what kinds of information a person wants to obtain. There are clearly arguments for and against extensive excavation.

One example is given by the magnificent and unprecedentedly large mound of Çatal Hüyük in Anatolia, which covers some 32 acres (450 meters long and 275 wide) and is at least 19 meters deep (about 60 feet), making it "the largest Neolithic site hitherto known in the Near East" (Mellaart 1967:30). Çatal Hüyük covers an area about 10 times as large as Grasshopper and has a series of buried building levels spanning 600–700 years. How is one to sample Çatal to obtain an intelligent idea of the community pattern? Mellaart did what most archeologists would have done: he picked an area where the walls of burnt buildings were exposed at the surface and began digging down. When this resulted in some of the most spectacular finds in all Near Eastern prehistory, he simply continued to dig in the same area.

> In the area excavated which covers about one acre—a mere thirtieth of the entire surface of the mound—a great number of houses and shrines with their storerooms have been found, but no workshops or public buildings. It must be assumed that these were located in a different part of the mound and the quarter on the west slope was evidently the residential, if not the priestly quarter of the city. One need hardly point out that Çatal Hüyük was not a village (Mellaart 1967:71).

The evidence at Çatal is so well preserved that the excavator can begin his interpretations on much surer footing than was possible at Hatchery West, but no less ingenious sets of postulates and testing of them are required to tease from Çatal the vast amount of information that it must hold. Appropriate models must be conceived to help us understand the many unique features of this site: why is it so precociously large? why is access to the settlement via the roofs rather than through doors? what is the relation between houses and shrines? what kind of social groups occupied the houses? what might the internal differentiation of the community have been? what was the role of Çatal with respect to other contemporary communities? These are only a sample of the questions whose answers will require a careful consideration of the total community pattern, the areal settlement pattern, and the local sources of resources. In short, Çatal must be viewed as the home of a community that lived in the context of a definable and understandable environmental and social system.

No less perplexing examples come from the Americas. Intrasite variation has long interested Maya archeologists, although it is only recently that they have worked out accurate site plans for the major centers, and, more recently, good surveys of regions. The ancient Maya have long confused archeologists because these people seem not to have lived in cities, and remains of domestic structures are relatively rare at the major ceremonial centers. What is more, within the ceremonial centers occur certain buildings that have been called temples and others called palaces. An exceedingly important question that still has not been answered satisfactorily was asked by Willey (1956b: 107) "What were the size and composition of the Maya living community, and what was the relationship between the living community and the ceremonial center?"

Haviland's (1965, 1967, 1969, 1970) work at Tikal and Ricketson's (1937) investigations at Uaxactun, about 10 miles away, have shown that there are large numbers of house mounds surrounding the main temple-plaza zones which are taken to be the religious activity centers of the sites. Another pertinent question concerns the role of different sizes of centers to one another (Bullard 1960). Questions of this kind seem capable of solution by intensive investigation of the community (or better, here perhaps "dispersed community") patterns with special attention to the spacing, size, and mutual variation among all classes of structures and artifacts. An answer to the question of the function of the "palaces" is perhaps less clear, but one has the overriding impression that they have been studied more as examples of architecture than they have as loci of activities. If this is true, one would expect an intensive study of the distribution of artifacts throughout one of the ceremonial centers to reveal patterns of difference among palaces, temples, and domestic structures. To attack the problem in this manner seems more fruitful than simply to repeat something to the effect that the "long, low rectangular structures on plinths surrounding courtyards were palaces." The same might be said of the "nunneries," that are characteristic of the major sites. Because most of these at the major sites have been thoroughly cleaned of artifacts and restored as architectural displays, the information must come from as yet unexcavated lesser sites where the prospects of finding artifacts *in situ* remains.

It seems reasonable to suppose that a great many similar archeological problems would vanish if only they were investigated seriously rather than remarked on in passing. First, the problem must be recognized as one capable of, or worth, solving. Solutions will rarely be found, however, if the archeologists are content to study the objects removed from sites rather than try to determine the social context in which they occur.

INTERPRETING PATTERNS OF SETTLEMENT

The distribution of sites is an important datum for archeological interpretation because it gives the facts, which in turn suggest questions. It tells where the sites are and demands an answer to why they are where they are. Patterns of settlement give us information that is very closely related to environment, technology, and social organization—in short, to the ecologic relations that obtain in any social system.

To illustrate these ecological relations we can take a complex situation, the nature of the Hopewellian occupations that centered in Illinois and Ohio. Various authors have referred to Hopewell as "a culture type, a culture phase, a temporal horizon, and a form of burial complex or cult" (Struever 1964:87). It is represented by mounds, earthworks, villages, and burial sites, and trading centers and identified principally through a shared group of artifacts made of exotic materials that were imported from sources in the Rockies, Great Lakes, and Gulf Coast.

Around 100 B.C. Hopewell appeared abruptly in restricted locales in the Eastern Woodlands. Casting this appearance into ecological terms, Struever (1964:90) suggested that it might attest "to the expansion of a dominant mode of adaptation at the expense of less efficient ones." If this were true, what was the new mode of adaptation? Parenthetically, one should note that when problems are phrased properly they lead to questions that can be answered by finding specific kinds of information—in this example, on subsistence. Supposing that the Hopewell peoples may have initiated agriculture in the area, Struever assessed the distribution of sites with respect to agricultural potential. He found

> that localities manifesting Hopewellian forms can be correlated with a series of ecological zones ranging in increasing specificity from the entire region lying south of the 140-day frost line, to the flood plains of the major rivers, to (in the case of habitation sites) the immediate environs of shallow backwaters and stream banks in and immediately proximal to the alluvium. It can be postulated that this distribution reflects a correlation between these cultural events and the importance of a simple, mud-flat horticulture, an hypothesis that sees a low-level, technologically simple cultivation as an important feature conditioning the degree to which Woodland expressions in different locales underwent a shift to a higher level of complexity exemplified in the Hopewell mortuary expression (Struever 1964:99).

We normally think of agriculture in the New World as involving maize, beans, and squash, but such was clearly not true at many, if any, Hopewell sites. Quite the contrary (and incidentally this is where Struever's experimentation with flotation really paid off), the people in Illinois seem to have been cultivating the locally available wild *Iva* marsh elder. *Chenopodium* lamb's quarter or goosefoot, and *Amaranth,* all plants that do well in the mud-flats bordering streams and sloughs.

The facts fitted the conditions in Illinois very well and immediately suggested that they be tested in other areas. Even at the time of Struever's writing (1964) it could be determined that other nearby contemporary people, who were outside the specific ecological niche of Hopewell, did not participate in the logistics network that distributed exotic raw materials, nor did they have the distinctive burial complex. It seems clear, therefore, that the Hopewell peoples had a more efficient subsistence base, which allowed their population to expand at the expense of other peoples, and that their social organization consequently became more elaborate, as is evidenced in the variety of their artifacts and mortuary practices.

Such conclusions represent only a beginning in understanding Hopewell and contemporary cultures. In particular, such questions as the nature of the social organization responsible for promoting the logistics network, and the nature of the interaction that resulted in raw materials and designs being distributed, remain to be answered. It is obvious, however, that such questions must be approached with a view to the total system as it can be seen in the patterned occurrence of its durable remains.

Another example of the value of studying patterns of settlement is both simple and useful for its practical implications in field work. In Iran, where do you look for caves that may have been occupied by paleolithic hunters? Caves occur in some limestone ridges; it is necessary only to find the ridges to find the sites. A plotting of settlement pattern on a two-dimensional map would, however, be very misleading, for two reasons. First, caves are relatively rare, and people must have lived elsewhere; thus the map really shows the distribution of caves and not the distribution of human settlement. Second, all caves are not the same, as one learns from excavation. Some caves are large, others small; some sites are rock shelters, and others surface scatters in the open. At least three types of settlements occur: base camps, butchering stations, and transitory camps. Had a functional difference between these sites not been seen we should have to consider them separate settlements rather than several loci of activities of one group. Hence an estimate of the total population would have to consider that several sites might be the result of one band of hunters.

Once the interpretation had been made, however, it was possible to calculate roughly how much space was used by each group and thereby to figure a total population for the area. Of course not all the variables have been adequately controlled, and the work on this particular settlement pattern is still in progress.

Another example also comes from Iran. A project was designed on

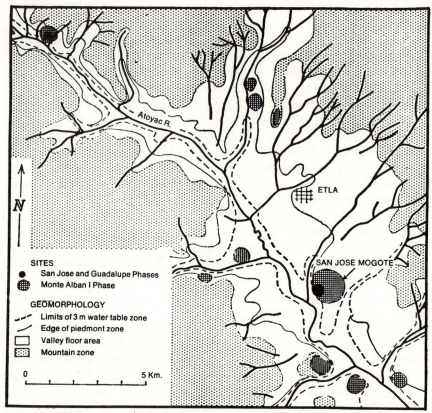

SITES
● San Jose and Guadalupe Phases
◍ Monte Alban I Phase

GEOMORPHOLOGY
‑‑‑ Limits of 3 m water table zone
— Edge of piedmont zone
▢ Valley floor area
▦ Mountain zone

0   5 Km.

FIG. 73 "Pilot" survey area in the northwestern part of the Oaxaca Valley, Mexico, showing the distribution of Formative archeological sites with regard to physiographic areas and water resources. Early Formative sites are found exclusively on the high alluvium, where the water table is within 3 meters of the surface. Later sites spread up the tributaries of the Rio Atoyac into the piedmont zone. (K. V. Flannery, "Farming Systems and Political Growth in Ancient Oaxaca," *Science* Vol. 158 (1967): Fig. 5, pp. 445–454. Copyright 1967 by the American Association for the Advancement of Science.)

the basis of intensive knowledge of the pattern of settlement in one key area, around the city of Kermanshah. On this basis it seemed obvious that the remainder of western Iran should have similar concentrations of sites so long as flat arable land was available. Survey in a carefully selected area to test the hypothesis that settlement pattern of early sites may have been affected by a post-Pleistocene climatic shift yielded no sites whatsoever of the proper age. This was indeed puzzling, until it could be determined that the major variable was the occurrence of surface water rather than arable land— a situation remarkably similar to that in Oaxaca described below (Hole 1962).

In Oaxaca, Mexico, sites of the Early Formative period are located in the center of the valley near the Atoyac River (Fig. 73). The obvious interpretation is that people during the early stages of agriculture preferred to work the good soils of the flood plain and to live close to surface water. The interpretation failed to explain why other areas of the valley that enjoyed the

376

same advantages did not also have Early Formative villages. The apparent explanation emerged following studies in which it was shown that all the early sites are situated on land where the water table is within 3 meters of the surface. The location of the sites was determined by the depth of ground water rather than by quality of soil or availability of surface water (Flannery and others 1967).

Sometimes a careful examination of settlement data will lead to questions or suggest possible lines of investigation. Archeologists often find sites where they do not expect to find them, and this contingency demands an explanation. Such anomalies are regularly overlooked, however, when the total pattern of settlement is not considered. Examples would be trading outposts or mining centers that are far away from the major concentrations of settlement and may in fact be in country so poor that it permits only a precarious existence without the support of subsidies, tribute, or taxes. Such examples are admittedly rare, but few archeologists would be willing to state that all the sites they know of are just where they would have predicted them to be. In short, the archeologist should train himself to look for reasons why things are as they are.

Robert Adams (1962) provides a good example of such speculation. He found in his survey of Khuzistan, southwest Iran, that all early villages were located inside the 300-millimeter rainfall isohyet. This suggested to him that the villagers were still dependent on rainfall farming. In a later period, when he found villages in areas of lower rainfall, he concluded that some farmers were then practicing irrigation. In subsequent years it was possible to prove the correctness of his conjecture by excavating key sites in the area (Hole and Flannery 1968).

Foster (1940:5) observed that the Popoluca of the Tuxtla Mountain region of southern Veracruz, Mexico, have occupied a zone of red volcanic soils, and suggests, since this land will yield only one crop of maize per year and the surrounding black earth soils will yield two, that the Popoluca have been forced onto this less desirable land by the more numerous Nahua-speaking peoples who completely surround them. Such a theory would be susceptible to archeological testing. A similar example is described by Barth (1956) for West Pakistan. Another instance of selective land use comes from Scotland in a study by Henshall (1963:49), who shows the relationship of chambered tombs to grazing lands there and reports the lack of such tombs in forested areas at lower elevations which were apparently avoided as unsuitable.

These examples point up the need for thorough (either complete or sampled) studies of large areas and the testing of a selected range of sites that promise to be useful in the understanding of crucial shifts in way of life. Often when we work in a new and unknown area we have no sure guidelines around which to construct our pattern. Demographic data can often provide us with the first clues to grasp as we grope in the darkened room of prehistory.

TERRITORIALITY

Enough examples have now been cited in this chapter to show what may be done with systematic observation coupled with pertinent hypotheses. In every instance the work leading to the examples was done by archeologists, and inspired either by archeological problems or by ethnographically known situations that were thought to be recognizable archeologically. It remains to consider the role of other fields of study in suggesting suitable approaches and in providing models for testing.

Two of these readily come to mind. The first was mentioned by Vogt (1956:173) as a possible area of inquiry, but it has not been followed up explicitly in archeology. This is the question of "territoriality," which has been studied extensively by ecologists and other students of animal behavior. Territory can mean many different things, and there are consequently various facets to consider. For any particular human group, where does it live? what territory does it exploit, depend on for survival, defend against outsiders, or use for special (for example, ceremonial) purposes? It can be seen that there is a variety of kinds of territories implied in the mere fact of group or community existence. We might also consider hierarchical use of territory or sequential use. The former implies that only certain persons or groups have access to portions of the same territory at different seasons. Finally, we can get down to the individual level and consider how much space a person needs or uses. Edward Hall's book, *The Hidden Dimension* (1966), takes up the psychocultural factors that determine man's interpersonal space requirements. These are not the same in every culture, and because they seem to be deep-seated and enduring, could conceivably be used by archeologists to help in determining historical continuities in populations. The hypothesis would be that if "foreign" people appeared, they would have different spatial arrangements for their daily activities, and the reverse would also be true.

The question of how to define territory archeologically is certainly an important one for archeologists, who usually resort to pottery styles or cultural traits, like the building of burial mounds, as criteria for lumping or segregating people in different sites. The rationale for this tendency, as Klopfer (1962:140) pointed out, is that "the fixity of the territorial boundary implies that there is a training of the young by their parents, a training that involves teaching the offspring the extent of the family territory." In aboriginal Australia and California, for example, children were taken on tours of the territorial border of the tribelet and landmarks such as prominent rocks were pointed out. How common this practice was among hunting-gathering societies we do not know, but it seems probable that most such groups in the prehistoric past did something of the sort. For human beings, such teaching might be aimed at recognizing group-specific styles or artifacts. L. Binford's (1962:219–220) "ideo-technic" artifacts are of this kind. They are

items which signify and symbolize the ideological rationalizations for the social system and further provide the symbolic milieu in which individuals are enculturated, a necessity if they are to take their place as functional participants in the social system. Such items as figures of deities, clan symbols, symbols of natural agencies, etc., fall into this general category.

One might also think of using minute designs on pottery (Cronin, Freeman, and Schoenwetter 1962) to help isolate pots made by certain groups of women. S. Lothrop also did this in his analysis of grave-lots of painted pottery from the tombs at Cocle, Panama, which led him to recognize "lineages" of potters, presumably women. His analysis was aimed primarily at dating the tombs, and he did not capitalize on the social structural implications of his data (Lothrop 1942:183–199). However, this procedure would help define the territory occupied by related females, and the same data can be used to help reconstruct the social organization (Chap. 19).

In addition to the ways already mentioned, territory is denoted by such things as rivers, mountains, field boundaries, walls of cities, walls of dwellings, rooms, courtyards, and fences. A logical question to ask on finding any of these "barriers" is what they mean in the social system. What kind of behavior or necessities caused the people to delimit themselves as they did? Mellaart saw the blank façade of Çatal Hüyük as a defensive mechanism, but one must then ask whom these rich and numerically powerful people had to fear. Courtyards have been suggested by some persons as a way of keeping animals penned and by others as a way to keep the family activities from the prying eyes of inquisitive neighbors. Some have viewed keeping dogs in the house as a means of preventing strangers or unwelcome persons from entering the premises, and the traveler in many parts of the world who has been confronted by one of the snarling beasts would be inclined to agree.

An interesting example of the use of archeological data to infer territoriality is found in Bradley's (1971) article on the relationship between competition in trade and the distribution of artifacts. (Some of the implications of his reasoning are discussed further in Chap. 21.) Bradley has applied the concept of *opportunity* to the study of trade networks. In essence the concept suggests that traders will avoid one another so that they will not be in direct competition. He states that

> the amount of interaction over a given distance will be directly proportional to the opportunities existing at that distance, and inversely proportional to the number of intervening opportunities. In its application to trade, this should have the effect that the field of any particular traded item may be restricted by the presence of a competing business in the area. On the other hand, in a region where there are no "intervening opportunities" of this type, we should see the uninhibited extension of this field. In practical terms its effect should be this: that a trader avoids an area where he must share his business with a competitor and instead extends his operations into an area where he can secure a monopoly. The distributions of the traded items will almost appear to repel one another. (Bradley 1971:347–348)

In a short review of archeological situations where trading was a factor,

Bradley found his principle to operate. Consequently one may see in this behavior some aspects of territoriality.

It is fair to say that concepts of territory are important for all people, but it is by no means clear what they will be or how they will be expressed. If the delineation of territory has been neglected by archeologists, it is to some degree because territory is a more difficult topic to deal with than, for example, the subsistence basis of the Hopewell people.

ATTRIBUTES AND IMPLICATIONS OF SETTLEMENT SYSTEMS

Settlement patterns, as the physical loci of human activity, strongly reflect various aspects of the social systems that used them. We find, for example, that the complexity of social organization can often be inferred from settlement patterns. In illustration of this point, we know from ethnographic studies that one aspect of increasing social complexity is specialization. In a human society this may mean that some persons take over certain activities, that some families are in charge of certain resources or rituals, that one community may manufacture spears and another baskets for trade, that the leaders may have "capitals," that market centers may appear, and so on. Specialization and division of labor among people or subsets of communities are two of the most characteristic features of human social organization. Such specializations occur as aspects of adaptation; it is a reasonable solution to the problem of supply, demand, and distribution.

Speaking generally, there are two things that relate to overall settlement pattern: the activities needed to exploit the resources, and the social organization itself. Even on a very low level of social complexity there may be a differentiated settlement pattern. We noted in the Iranian paleolithic, for example, a minimum of three types of settlements: base camps, butchering stations, and transitory camps. Such a situation would be typical for most hunting and gathering peoples. To take another example, Struever (1965) identified five types of Middle Woodland settlements in the lower Illinois Valley. He found base settlements, summer agricultural camps, regional exchange centers, Hopewellian burial sites (mound groups), and burial sites with associated mortuary camps. Here again we find a settlement system divided into specialized components, but here are clearly implied more differentiation of status and a greater range of activities than we have for the Iranian paleolithic. In both examples the settlements reflect adjustments to patterns of activities carried out in a particular environmental arena. The exact location of the agricultural camp would be related to farming; the base settlement to other considerations, and so on. But wherever the Hopewell settled they had common requirements, and one could expect to find a common set of parts comprising the settlement pattern.

The Yurok tribe of northwestern California provides us with an interesting ethnographic example of land and resource ownership. Here villages are permanent, house sites are owned individually, and each house is named. Private ownership included such economic resources as sections of ocean beach where surf fishes could be dip-netted, sea mammals hunted, and where occasionally a dead whale might be thrown ashore; groves of oak trees which yielded one of the food staples, acorns; pools where salmon could be speared or netted; and favored spots on deer trails where these animals could be snared or noosed. Yurok diet was based on acorns, salmon, and deer, and Yurok territory held these resources in abundance. Villages did not collectively own or control the economic resources in the vicinity of the settlement —rather, choicest hunting, fishing, and collecting locations were individually and exclusively owned. A highly structured system of property rights and inheritance rules encouraged the development of the Yurok system outlined here. Elsewhere among California Indians, similar individual or family usufructuary rights were known, but the Yurok emphasized this more than any other tribe. As an illustration of one man's private resource holdings, see Figure 74.

We do not suggest that situations of this sort are very common among hunter-fisher-gatherers, and we do not know whether they existed in paleo-

Fig. 74 Property and exclusive use rights of one Yurok Indian. A, offshore rock for sea lion hunting; B, C, stretches of ocean beach; D, fifteen groves of acorn-producing oak trees; E, four salmon-fishing pools; F, two deer-snaring localities. G is the man's house in Qo'otep village (after Waterman 1920, Map 3).

lithic times. But if private ownership or exclusive gathering-hunting rights were vested in individuals (or families) in Pleistocene times, it would invalidate attempts such as that of C. Vita-Finzi and E. Higgs (1970) to reconstruct the prehistoric economy in the Mt. Carmel area, Palestine, by their model of "site catchment analysis" which they define as "the study of the relationships between technology and those natural resources lying within the economic range of individual sites."

In reconstructing a settlement pattern an archeologist focuses on the interrelations of the various parts. If, for example, there is a trading center or site of some other specialized activity, it is imperative to try to see it in a context of other communities that support it and in turn take from it. As a general rule, when social organization becomes more complex and wealth (surplus) becomes greater, the area of interaction or influence of any people grows. In other words, there is no way to make a reasonable interpretation of prehistoric life by concentrating one's analysis on a *site*. Environmentally, a site is only a locus on a landscape; socially, the community living there is only one among many that are linked by marriage, trade, or language, and consequently influencing one another. We must make every effort to find the nature of such influences if we are to make any sense of our archeological cultures.

Social organization also directly influences settlement, though its influence may be relatively weaker than economic or subsistence factors. The most notable examples in American archeology would be the Maya pyramids and, to a lesser extent, the Woodland and Mississippian mounds in North America, all of which seem to have something to do with veneration of persons of high status. This association is especially clear in the Maya area, where pyramids are thought by some to be memorials for chiefs and their lineages (some would say rulers and dynasties). The particular kind of structure—private monumental and "nonutilitarian"—can be seen as a normal outcome of at least the following circumstances. The society has the capacity for producing agricultural surplus, but the area is relatively homogeneous and especially lacks the differential distribution of raw materials that characterize some other regions and lend themselves to trade. Therefore wealth is basically 'food, which can be used to "buy" labor. Labor is the universal and abundant commodity because farming takes relatively little time. A person who aspires to status must work with what the system has: unskilled labor. He uses labor to build himself monuments. Pyramids are a natural form because they are impressive and, more importantly, require little skill other than piling up dirt and rubble; only the facades require expertise. The leader of such a system can put his pyramid center wherever he likes, because it bears no important relation to the settlement pattern of the peasants who built it, other than being close to both labor and material.

Quite the opposite is true of commercial centers whose location is very strongly influenced by matters of transportation and politics. (But see the example of territoriality in trade cited earlier.) This aspect of settlement pattern has been studied in great detail by geographers, who have produced a few interesting models of optimization. That is, one can state in very precise terms what the optimum location of settlement will be, given certain circumstances. That these circumstances are really important is underscored by the fact that capital cities are rarely moved if they are commercial as well. According to R. Adams (1965:90), only one such move (from Baghdad to Samarrra) in the Near East was attempted, and that for only 58 years (between A.D. 835–893), after which time the capital reverted to its "natural" location.

The reasons for abandonment of village sites are usually difficult, if not impossible, to determine from archeological evidence alone. A survey of ethnographic information on why villages were abandoned in California (Heizer 1962c) indicates that disease, floods, fear of enemy attacks, bad dreams, dread of ghosts of former inhabitants, accumulation of filth, plagues of fleas, escape from malevolent witchcraft practiced by neighbors, shortage of food in the vicinity, and mere instability of residence patterns are among the causes. This transient occupation in terms of initial settlement, abandonment, and reoccupation, which involved hundreds of villages would also have some effect on tribal territory as a whole. It would be useful to archeologists to have other regional surveys of this sort from other continents in order to gain some perspective of the range of human occupational stability.

Hayes (1964) analyzes the shifting of site locations on Wetherill Mesa, Colorado, from the Piedra Phase (700–900 A.D.) to the Mesa Verde Phase (1250–1350 A.D.) and shows that there was a trend of movement off the mesa top to village locations on the talus slopes and in cliff shelters (Fig. 75 and Table 9). In part this shifting pattern of settlement was due to land

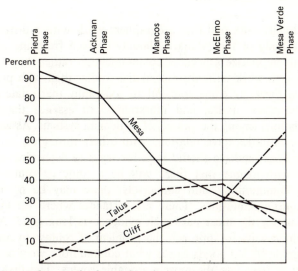

Fig. 75 Changing preference for homesites, in percentages.

TABLE 9   SITES BY PHASE AND LOCATION, WITH ESTIMATED ROOM NUMBERS

Phase	Total Number of Sites	Mesa Sites (%)	Talus and Canyon Sites (%)	Cliff Sites (%)	Estimated Number of Rooms	Number of Rooms in Average Site
La Plata and Piedra	147	91	2	7	1,166	8
Ackmen	208	82	14	4	1,248	6
Mancos	166	47	37	16	996	6
McElmo	60	31	39	30	540	9
Mesa-Verde	168	25	19	66	1,512	9

overuse and the resulting erosion of mesa top fields. A further possible factor was the need to occupy more defensible positions.

The optimization theory of the location of sites is probably valid for all people. The location of a site is based on a number of factors that must be weighed. We can infer some of these factors but can probably never guess all of them. Ethnologists have succeeded in treating settlement pattern as an example of game theory, where the placing of sites is regarded as the best payoff under given circumstances (Barth 1966). To state that there are "natural" patterns of settlement is only to emphasize what we have already said, that there is a predictable pattern in human behavior.

SOME SUGGESTIONS FOR APPLYING LOCATIONAL ANALYSIS

We have already indicated that geographers work with a distinct set of concepts and a body of theory that is largely derived from the modern world. They tend to emphasize aspects of communication rather than ecological relationships and to work with abstract models rather than with particular cases. Nevertheless there are some concepts in geography that relate specifically to ecology: networks, nodes, and hierarchies. In essence these express the ecologic relations among the subsets of settlement systems. As we have already said, all communities have relations with others through a network of communication links, and we should look for ways to determine this archeologically. One can assume that there will be a route or routes between two interacting communities, and conversely, there may be no route between noninteracting communities. There are instances where we know the route of trails, but for the most part such evidence is long gone. Archeologically there are three ways to approach the problem of routes: to note where sites are, to examine traded goods to see what communities were actually in interaction, and to postulate the most reasonable routes. The first two are easy, and the last may be too if a river, a line of springs, a steep cliff, or other natural features predisposed people to movement in certain directions. Geographers point out that roads or trails seldom take what appears to be the fastest route, but they also note—using the theory of optimization—that any route represents a series of compromises and often is a suitable solution to a problem of locating routes that serve several settlements or different purposes. This is especially important if we consider the spread or expansion of population. Where will the people go? Frequently expanding populations must have remained on routes of communication, trade, or irrigation rather than simply heading for the nearest vacant space. Or, vice versa, if we could plot the spread of prehistoric settlements, we might learn something about pre-existing networks of communication. Always, of course, we must bear in mind the dictum "all other things equal."

An interesting archeological problem that would require very intensive survey of a large area, and unusually accurate relative dating of sites, would be to plot the history of settlement starting with the parent communities and working out a "kinship" or descent chart showing the pattern of development. To be considered would be the kind of units that comprised the first settlement, how and where they expanded, whether greater or lesser differentiation followed, whether new units were duplicates of the original settlements, whether some settlements assumed focal points, and whether the sites were in a hierarchy of importance.

Site location also involves the question of nodes, another geographic term meaning "the junctions or vertices" on a network of settlement (Haggett 1965:87). A node is a focal point and, depending on the nature of the analysis, may range from an isolated farmstead to a city.

Geographers struggle with problems of building models to predict where foci will be, but we are interested here more in the fact that there are such things as focal points of settlement. A moment's reflection will indicate that all people have a "center," which is the locus of influence in their lives. A center may be a base camp for hunters; this is the place where the whole group exists in interaction, and it comprises the minimum social unit for the culture. A center may also be a city or even a mobile phenomenon like a chief whose physical residence may change regularly. A center has two aspects; it is a focal point drawing people in, and it is a force that influences people who may not be physically present. It follows, therefore, that centers are different from other kinds of sites; recognizing this fact, we should be able to determine which is which. Such a determination then becomes a statement about the organization of a prehistoric society.

A final consideration is hierarchy. How are the various settlements ranked relative to one another? Three ways to determine rank or importance seem obvious. First, one can regard nodal settlements as more important, evidence of which is that the nodal settlements have subsettlements in their sphere. One might also rank nodal settlements by the same criterion. Second, one can regard relative size of settlements as the criterion of ranking. Finally, internal differentiation of a site may indicate its importance. Hierarchy is important, however, only if it means something. One supposes that its principal meaning is difference in function. This distinction would be especially true of large settlements that, at least in modern times, "have a far greater range of service functions than smaller centers" (Haggett 1965:116).

If a settlement system has a number of sites of different sizes, one may find that there is a regular ratio between the sizes such that, for example, the largest sites are twice as large as the next size. The sizes would imply considerable differences in function, just as a landscape of settlements of uniform size would suggest lack of differentiation in function.

A pattern of settlement is a workable solution to human problems at one moment in history. In time settlement patterns adjust to changes in the working of the social system or to changes in the physical environment. When we examine settlement patterns archeologically, we are therefore coming as close as possible to working with evidence that bears on the processes of culture and of human development.

REFERENCES

Locational Analysis: Berry 1968; Berry and Marble (eds.) 1968; Chorley 1968; Coombs, Raiffa, and Thrall 1954; Garner 1967; Harvey 1967; Lösch 1954; Nystuen 1968; Nystuen and Dacey 1968; Zipf 1949.

Population Statistics: Angel 1947; Ascádi and Nemeskéri 1970; R. Ascher 1959; Birdsell 1957, 1968; Brothwell and Sandison 1967; S. Cook 1972; S. Cook and Borah 1963, 1971; S. Cook and Treganza 1950; Dobyns and Thompson 1966; Durand 1960; Genovés 1969a, 1969b; Goldstein 1953; Haviland 1969, 1970, 1972a, 1972b; Horner 1970; Howells 1960; Kerley and Bass 1967; Kryzwicki 1934; Legoux 1966; McArthur 1970; R. Naroll 1962; Pericot 1961; Senyurek 1947; Shumway, Hubbs, and Moriarty 1961; Turner and Lofgren 1966; Vallois 1960.

Factors Affecting Population Size: Baumhoff 1963; A. Brown 1967; Carneiro 1956, 1961; Charanis 1961; S. Cook 1946, 1947, 1966; S. Cook and Heizer 1965, 1968; U. Cowgill 1961, 1962; Naroll 1962.

Factors Affecting Settlement Pattern: R. Adams 1965, 1970b, 1972; R. Adams and Nissen 1972; W. Adams 1968; Burch 1971; M. Coe 1961; Conklin 1961; Derricourt 1972; Dumond 1961; Flannery and others 1967; Gumerman 1971; Hack 1942; E. Hall 1966; Heizer 1955; Hodder and Hassal 1971; Hole 1962; Meggers 1954; Michels 1968; Steward 1936, 1937; Struever 1965, 1968b.

Intrasite Variation: L. Binford and S. Binford 1966; L. Binford and others 1966; Bordes and de Sonneville-Bordes 1970; Chang 1958; J. Clark 1964; J. Clark and Haynes 1970; S. Cook and Heizer 1965, 1968; S. Cook and Treganza 1950; Cronin, Freeman, and Schoenwetter 1962; Grigor'ev 1967; Haviland 1970; J. Hill 1966; Isaac 1969; Longacre 1964, 1966, 1970a; Marks 1971; P. S. Martin 1962; Mellaart 1967; Mellars 1970; Redman 1972; Robbins 1966; Schiffer 1972; Ucko, Tringham, and Dimbleby 1972; Whallon 1972b; W. Wood 1968.

Trends of Change: Ammerman and Cavalli-Sforza 1972a, 1972b; Carneiro and Hilse 1966; Hole and Flannery 1968; Schwartz 1956, 1970; Wrigley 1966.

Settlement Patterns: R. Adams 1962, 1965:Appendix A, 1970b, 1972; Adams and Nissen 1972; Chang 1958, 1962, 1968; Fitting 1969; Haviland 1965; E. Jones 1966; Nietsch 1939; Struever 1968b; Trigger 1965, 1967; Voorhies 1972; Wagner 1960; Willey 1953, 1956b, 1968b; Young 1966.

Territoriality: Ardrey 1966; Bradley 1971; J. M. Campbell 1968; Friedrich 1970; E. Hall 1966; Klopfer 1962; Vita-Finzi and Higgs 1970; Vogt 1956.

Attributes and Implications of Settlement Systems: Barth 1956, 1959–1960, 1966; Chang 1968; Haggett 1965; E. Hall 1966; Renfrew 1972b.

CHAPTER NINETEEN

SOCIAL, RELIGIOUS, AND INTELLECTUAL SYSTEMS

In the preceding chapters on subsistence and settlement we dealt tangentially with matters of social organization and religion. In this chapter we deal explicitly with how social, religious, and intellectual systems may be deduced from archeological data. It is often difficult to distinguish between social and religious organization because for prehistoric peoples they were frequently aspects of the same thing. Nevertheless, we can make a few inferences about the various religious and ideological matters that can be distinguished from their organizational aspects.

Part of this chapter consists of practical examples of how we deduce information about intangible systems from archeological data, and part is theoretical, in which the reasons for certain organizational forms are discussed. We consider peoples and cultures, socioeconomic units, social differentiation, correlates of social organization, religion, ideology, and intellectual developments.

PREHISTORIC PEOPLES AND CULTURES

When an archeologist finds artifacts he may remark that they belong to the "Basket Maker" culture or to the "Azilian" culture or to one of the many hundred such "cultures" that have been distinguished (See Chap. 4). An archeological culture usually consists of a certain assemblage of artifacts (Childe 1956:15–18). If the archeologist finds the same types of pottery, arrow points, and houses in several sites he will say that they all belong to the same culture. Archeological cultures are thus different from the cultures anthropologists study (Rouse 1965, 1972b:Chap. 2). Anthropological cultures usually consist of people who share a language and various customs and have some feeling of unity, either political or ideological, that separates them from other people. In other words, the people can define the limits of their own group. It often happens that neighboring groups who speak different dialects of a language are antagonistic toward one another. In the minds of the people the neighbors do not share the same culture. They are not the same people. Archeologically, we may not be able to discover such nuances of differences, because the preserved remains of the speakers of two dialects might be identical. It is important to note that the differences we do recognize should bear some relation to the purpose behind our desire to establish cultures. In archeology, as in ethnology, there are times when it is desirable to recognize a general category like "Plains Culture," which denotes a way of life of many distinct peoples who for other purposes should be identified as members of Apache, Cheyenne, or Crow tribes.

The question of the precise identification of prehistoric peoples is only a central concern for most archeologists when their sites have a historical link to modern times. Then archeologists try to define their cultures as ethnologists or historians would. There are relatively few places where such an attempt would have any prospect of success and still fewer where it has been tried. To some extent it has been tried in Europe through tracing the dialects of Indo-European back in time (Crossland 1957, Finley 1970, Gimbutas 1963, Hencken 1955). American archeologists have had considerable success in tracing the prehistory of a number of modern-day Indian cultures. To mention just a few, examples can be found in California (Heizer 1941a), the Plains (Strong 1940), the Southwest (W. Gladwin and H. Gladwin 1928b; J. Hester 1962; Hoijer 1956b; Jett 1964), and the Eastern Woodlands (Caldwell 1958).

The techniques used by these archeologists are ethnohistory and linguistics. The former method was outlined by Steward (1942) and the latter by Traeger (1955) and Sapir (1916). One linguistic technique is to look at the distribution of speakers of a language. If the people are scattered and intermixed with speakers of other languages, it can be assumed that some migration has taken place. A good example is the Navaho, Athabascan speakers, who, with the Apache, represent linguistic foreigners in the Southwest. A linguistic map shows that most Athabascan speakers are in interior Canada, and this is assumed to be the place from which the Navaho originally came. Of practical importance for archeology is the fact that, by using another linguistic technique, glottochronology, the Navaho entry into the Southwest can be dated to about A.D. 1500; sites from an earlier period therefore cannot be Navaho.

Techniques of glottochronology and lexicostatistics allow linguists to tell within limits when groups of people split from other groups. Researchers can do so by measuring the degree of divergence between two dialects or languages. By applying a formula that expresses change in terms of years elapsed since two peoples split, it is possible to get an estimate of the date of migrations or separation of peoples (Hoijer 1956a; Hymes 1960; Kroeber 1955; Swadesh 1960, 1964). We should note, however, that not all authors agree on the validity of the method (Bergsland and Vogt 1962).

Linguistics can also help by finding words in peoples' vocabularies that do not fit their present environment. In the legends of many peoples there are references to places or things that no living person in the group has seen. As an example, which is presently considered an hypothesis rather than a proved case, Thieme (1958) located the homeland of the original Indo-European language community as lying between the Vistula and Elbe Rivers in Europe; and by applying archeological dates to certain words (for example, metals and domesticated animals known to the original speakers) suggested this homeland was occupied toward the end of the fourth millennium B.C. (see also Crossland 1957; Hencken 1955:44ff.; Pulgram 1959). Provable relations in the languages of geographically separated populations may be taken as evidence of migration, a fact no one doubts, although it is often difficult to find archeological proof (MacWhite 1956:16–18).

It is not possible to give the names of modern people or of language groups to most prehistoric cultures; instead, the cultures are usually named after the geographic region, the major site, or characteristic artifacts. For most of prehistory distinct assemblages of artifacts are the criteria used to identify cultures. There remains, however, one more method that has limited application. A person can consider racial characteristics if he has enough skeletons to determine what a population looked like. This area of archeology has received relatively little attention in recent years, but several general reviews by Neumann (1952), in which American Indians are divided into racial groups, illustrate what was at one time considered an important method for identifying genetically related pople. Howells' (1966) recent analysis of the races of Japanese skeletons substantiated the archeological data that differentiated sites of different cultures. Although attempts along this line are scattered and of variable quality, there are many reports in which the skeletal characteristics of populations are discussed and used as a basis for helping reconstruct movements of people, and contact between groups. One difficulty with this approach is that there are relatively few skeletons at most sites; the range of variation of any single population is therefore hard to ascertain.

The purpose of trying to identify separate peoples at all is to reconstruct some details of history in the sense of asking, "What happened?" This question is usually asked when dramatic change is evident in a sequence of events—when a new kind of pottery, house style or settlement pattern appears suddenly in the record. It is often assumed that "outsiders" brought the new traits and that we can tell who they were if we can find the traits manifested earlier elsewhere. Reconstructions of migration thus form a major concern of many archeologists.

Instances of migrations in the American Southwest and South America are detailed in articles in the volume edited by R. Thompson (1958b). Rouse (1958:64) proposes five requirements for the demonstration of a prehistoric migration. These are (1) identify the migrating people as an instrusive unit in the region it has penetrated; (2) trace this unit back to its homeland; (3) determine that all occurrences of the unit are contemporaneous; (4) establish the existence of favorable conditions for migration; (5) demonstrate that some other hypothesis, such as independent invention or diffusion of traits, does not better fit the facts of the situation. Proposed intercontinental diffusions to the New World across the Atlantic or Pacific oceans, such as those of H. Gladwin (1947), Greenman (1963), Heyerdahl (1963), or Heine-Geldern (1954) and Heine-Geldern and Ekholm (1951), and the recently advocated introduction of pottery into Ecuador by Japanese fishermen (Meggers, Evans, and Estrada 1965) have not met with enthusiastic accept-ance by American archeologists, who still prefer to envisage man's entry into the New World from Siberia by the Bering Straits route (Byers 1957; Griffin 1960; Hopkins 1959; Linné 1955), although it must be admitted that there is no archeological proof that this route of entry was used (Giddings 1960). Lacking facts, a good deal of interesting speculation has been done on what the climatic conditions and cultural equipment required for the crossing may have been like (Mather 1954), what kind of men came into the New World from Northeastern Asia (Stewart 1960), and what light linguistic evidence can throw on the old migrations (Swadesh 1962). Problems such as the origin of the American Indians and the source of high cultures in the New World have attracted an unduly large amount of speculative theorizing. Wauchope (1962) has written a thorough review of a number of unacceptable and unsupported theories of origin of the American Indians. The theories include proposals concerning Alexandrian admirals, Phoenicians, Egyptians, and mythical inhabitants of lost continents of Atlantis and Mu as original migrants or culture-bearers to the supposedly ignorant Indians of the Americas.

THE SOCIOECONOMIC UNIT

Basic to any society is its home base, and basic to the home is the family or, put another way, the minimal socioeconomic unit. It is preferable to consider the socioeconomic unit rather than family per se because of the great variety of social arrangements that constitute the family around the world and because the family does not always carry out the social and economic func-tions we have in mind. We cannot generalize from our own typical pattern, in which the family consists of mother, father, and children who together form a residential, economic, reproductive, and socializing unit. We call this the nuclear family. Of course, the pattern in the United States is typical only in the statistical sense, because there are many variations, including a common one in which grandparents and married brothers or sisters and their families live "at home." Still we find that most builders expect nuclear families to occupy their houses. Accordingly they put one kitchen and two, three, or four bedrooms in most houses—just what a nuclear family needs. Even in apartment buildings the individual apartments are divided much like houses for the use of single nuclear families. An archeologist who repeatedly found floor plans of the kind we have in the United States would infer that a basic socioeconomic unit of society resided in the homes.

One archeological task is to identify the spatial context of the minimal socioeconomic unit. For most prehistoric peoples, it consisted of single-room houses; multiroom houses whose rooms can be distinguished functionally; apartmentlike structures made up of separate units; or a group of from two to four rooms around a patio. As we have already mentioned, in many modern societies there is also a constant ratio of floor space to number of people (S. Cook and Heizer 1965). With these two kinds of clues it is relatively easy to make inferences about the minimal group of people who habitually dwell together.

The difficulty is that the people who habitually dwell together may not be either a family or a socioeconomic unit. As D. Bender (1967) and Allen and Richardson (1968) have described at length, there are many possible variations of kinship, residence, economic function, and socialization. As in our own society, they may be combined in the nuclear family, or they may be parceled out to other kinds of social arrangements. It is not easy to judge such things archeologically except when there is good ethnographic evidence for choosing one form of socioeconomic unit over another. Thus, in some of the examples that follow, the archeologists postulated that a social arrangement similar to the one of modern peoples who lived in the same area obtained in the past. This seems the only safe way to proceed, and archeologists who wish to make such reconstructions should carefully read the articles cited earlier for the possible variations they suggest.

We usually assume that the cook for each nuclear family has her own fire, an assumption that is borne out by ethnographic data. In this way Grigor'ev (1967) reconstructed the dwelling pattern at Kostenki, where as many as 10 hearths were found in one presumed shelter. Earlier, Efimenko (1958) inferred that the long dwelling represented a "clan home" that contained all the members in the community who belonged to the particular clan. Reexamination of all the data from several of the important upper paleolithic sites along the Don indicates that the long dwelling was not typical; rather, small, circular, single family huts were. There are also instances where two or three families occupied a larger shelter, but in each shelter the average area of floor that went with each hearth was 5 meters in diameter. Whatever the nature of the aggregations, they seem to comprise nuclear families who lived under a common roof as separate and equal partners.

Grigor'ev suggested as one reason for the aggregation that building materials would have been conserved, a factor that may have been important on the Russian steppe. One can also consider the possibility that the social organization was not exclusively based on the nuclear family. In many societies, it is customary for aged parents, and unmarried or widowed aunts or uncles, to live with a viable nuclear family. These families are called "extended" if the custom is the rule and separate generations habitually live together. In such homes separate fireplaces may be maintained by each of the females. Another possibility is that some of the paleolithic hunters had more than one wife, a practice that we sometimes find even among people who have a simple subsistence economy. Today it is common for extra wives to have their own separate huts in which they raise children and carry out other domestic tasks as though they were a nuclear family, but the same duties could be accomplished under one roof. The reason for not suggesting this possibility earlier for the Kostenki hunters is that plural marriages are usually thought to be a recent innovation. However, if plural marriages are based on economic considerations, there is no reason why the mammoth hunters could not have had extra wives.

Another example, the Hatchery West site, is from the Eastern Woodland, in Carlyle, Illinois. The interpretations derived from this site were much more detailed and extensive, and deserve careful consideration. The project at this site was conceived and carried out by Lewis Binford (1966) as a test of archeological method. The example cited here is therefore relevant to more than just the socioeconomic unit; it should be studied by all archeologists.

This site showed four occupations of the Late Woodland period that were denoted by houses and associated features. The earliest three occupations were of the LaMotte culture, the latest of the Mississippian. Four lodges of the earlier type were distinguished chronologically by stratigraphic evidence and the color of soil in the post molds, which Binford takes to be a function of length of time that they had weathered. Assuming this view to be correct, he found that there were three LaMotte periods of occupation separated by intervals of unknown duration. During the earliest, two lodges were constructed on the edge of a terrace in a clearing; in the second, two new lodges were built to the rear of the clearing; and, in the third, perhaps four families settled in two houses of a different type. One was a single family dwelling; the other a large multifamily structure. Additionally there was a small dome-shaped structure that may have functioned for the seclusion of women during their menses, a practice well attested in the local ethnography. During the Mississippian period another kind of single family house was built on the terrace, one of many similar homesteads representing a dispersed settlement pattern of a different type from the LaMotte culture.

From the fact that the doorways of the keyhole-shaped houses of the LaMotte culture face east the author reasoned that they may have been oriented toward the rising sun. If this interpretation is correct, the houses were built during November, and they may have been, because the earth lodges were shaped like Eskimo igloos and very likely constructed for winter warmth. This inference is also plausible when we consider that the third LaMotte occupation had structures of a different type, which Binford interpreted as spring and summer houses. He made this inference because of the relatively open construction of the walls, reasoning that the spaces between the posts may have been filled with mats or other loosely woven material. That these structures are contemporary with the keyhole lodges is demonstrated by the pottery, although no way was discovered to tell whether the same group of people used the site at different seasons.

Turning now to the associated features, which consist of various kinds of pits, Binford attempted to see whether there was anything in the patterning of pits that would substantiate his postulated four periods of occupation. If there had been four, he reasoned he would find four distinct populations of pits. He said, "In addition, we would expect that the forms of the pits as well as their relative frequencies would vary between the occupations believed to represent different seasons of occupancy as a function of the seasonable variability expected in task performance" (L. Binford and others 1966:108). The analysis of association was complicated, requiring a chain of assumptions, but it substantiated the idea of four occupations. Moreover, Binford concluded (L. Binford and others 1966:106), the pits show a "differentiation with the community into multiple work groups, each performing essentially similar tasks but in different locations."

Because the burials showed two different orientations and postmortem treatment they were susceptible of sociological interpretation. Although the data are limited, it seems that males are oriented with their heads toward the west, whereas adolescents and infants, and probably women, had their heads toward the north. Finally, summarizing the socioeconomic implications of the site, Binford and his associates (1966) said

> If we assume that the orientation of the graves bears some relationship to the symbolism associated with a social segment or sodality, then we would have to infer that membership in the postulated social units was based on matrilineal descent, since the orientations of the children were all alike (suggesting membership in a common social unit), and differentiated from that of the male adult (a presumed affine of the local females) suggesting membership by the adult male in a different social unit. If it is assumed that the persons interred in the small cemetery were all from a single community, we would have to postulate matrilineal descent, with the children belonging to a different membership group from the adult males.

It does not matter a great deal whether these reconstructions stand the test of repeated observations as additional similar sites are excavated. What is important is that they show several ways to improve archeological technique and to phrase pertinent questions about the prehistoric social systems that archeological data can illuminate.

The societies just mentioned were more simple than the Southwestern pueblos studied by J. Hill (1966) and Longacre (1964). There, the size of the community, the durability of the buildings, and the agricultural base of the subsistence system all suggested that the societies should be more complex. Ethnographic evidence shows that the Western Pueblo Indians have clans and matrilineages, social devices for keeping property in the family and for integrating groups of people who may not be closely related biologically. Both Hill and Longacre supposed that lineages and clans might have been present in the prehistoric pueblos, and by means of careful analysis of the mutual variation among types of rooms, features and artifacts within the rooms, and style of pottery designs, they tried to determine whether it was true. Both authors made the assumption that "if there were a system of localized matrilineal descent groups in the village, then ceramic manufacture and decoration would be learned and passed down within the lineage frame, it being assumed that the potters were females as they are today among the Western Pueblos" (Longacre 1964:1454).

At Broken K Pueblo, J. Hill's (1966) use of factor analysis (a mathematical technique of multivariate analysis) of the kinds of data enumerated above showed that the pueblo was divided into five localized residence units. The basis for this statement is that the rooms within each unit showed greater similarity to one another than to rooms in the other units. Hill then used ethnographic analogy with modern Pueblo Indians to conclude that the data suggested five "uxorilocal residence units." This means that "husband and wife live in the vicinity of wife's maternal relatives" (J. Hill 1966:fn.7.) Hill permits himself this inference principally because artifacts related to female activities are distributed nonrandomly in the pueblos. "Of all residence systems known, only uxorilocal and duolocal systems should be reflected by highly nonrandom distributions of female-associated items or stylistic elements; and in the latter case, one would expect male-associated items to distribute in a nonrandom manner also" (J. Hill 1966:21).

Hill was unwilling to declare that descent was matrilineal, although he did conclude, because of the strongly traditional nature of the style of artifacts within each residence unit, that inheritance was within the unit. That is to say, descendants of the original settlers continued to occupy the houses of their birth.

Longacre's (1964) analysis of the Carter Ranch site was similar in technique to Hill's, but it introduced several different kinds of interpretations that are worth noting. At Carter Ranch there were two main groups of rooms, each associated with a kiva (ceremonial room). Analysis of pottery showed that each kiva was associated with a block of rooms, and that certain stylistically distinct vessels were associated with kivas and with burials. Analysis of the burials, which were in three separate areas of the site, showed significant differences in orientation of the bodies and of the ceramics associated with them. Two of the areas pertained to two of the residence units, but the third was mixed, containing bodies from each. The skeletons in the latter area also had twice as many vessels per burial as the burials in the other areas, a discovery suggesting that persons of high status in each main segment of the site were buried in a common plot, whereas the remainder of the people were buried in their "family" plots.

Longacre also found that weaving implements occurred with male burials and in the kivas. This finding shows similarity with modern Pueblo practice, where weaving is largely a male activity that is carried out in the kivas. Continuity in this aspect of culture thus seems to have obtained for some 700 years.

During the occupation of both Broken K and Carter Ranch the environment deteriorated; this factor was used to explain an apparent shift toward intracommunity integration as seen in the development of larger communities but fewer separate settlements after A.D. 1250, and in the shift from lineage kivas to community kivas whose members would have been drawn from all segments of the society. The increase in size of kivas began about A.D. 1000, with an accompanying decrease in the number of kivas, compared with residence rooms. The increase in aggregation of separate settlements and intra-village integration is seen as an adaptive mechanism to cope with decreasing yields of agricultural products, a trend that continued until the time of contact with the Spanish in 1540. At that time there were only three major groups of Pueblos, and ethnographic evidence shows each of them to have a high degree of intragroup integration, which is maintained through various ceremonial societies.

A final example of the way specific aspects of social organization relating to the socioeconomic unit may be inferred from artifact and settlement data is provided by Deetz's (1965) analysis of Arikara archeology and ethnohistory. The archeological problem demanding a cultural explanation was that in a site with three layers the pottery in the earliest layer conformed closely to easily identifiable "types." That is, the pots conformed well to a standard. In the middle and upper levels they became increasingly difficult to put into types. It was apparent that the potters had let their standards slip in the sense that they no longer adhered to a single set of ideal patterns. Deetz, wondering what social factors could have accounted for this change, investigated the known history of the Indians whose site he had dug. He found that, beginning in the sixteenth century, the Arikara had slowly moved up the Missouri River, in the process moving into an environment less thickly forested and into contact with Plains Indians who had horses and with European traders who brought disease.

The early Arikara were food producers who lived in large houses that contained female relatives and their husbands. Such a practice is common if the women do the farming and consequently supply the bulk of the subsistence. As the Arikara moved they became less dependent on farming and less permanent in residence. Just to obtain sufficient firewood they were forced to move their villages as often as every five years. What is more, the men gained economic status when they began to participate as middlemen in trade between Plains Indians, who supplied horses, and Europeans, who supplied guns. Eventually this role in trade broke down, and the population was decimated by smallpox, introduced by Europeans.

The important result of these changes so far as Deetz's archeology is concerned was that women's place in the society changed. The older, large, matrilocal residence units broke up, and settlements came to be mixed.

> Earlier in time, women who resided together, and who were related, would share in idea sets related to pottery which were more or less different from those held by other similar residential groups. . . . But when these groups were broken up, a more random mixing of ideas, and their constituent attributes, would occur (Deetz 1967:112–113).

SOCIAL DIFFERENTIATION

Specialization

Turning from the general question of cultures, we can examine certain social characteristics of cultures and the ways of inferring them archeologically. One of the most basic aspects of society is that people are assigned different tasks. The number of distinct tasks is a measure of the size and complexity of a society, but even in very simple units there is specialization. It is only in a theoretical social sense that "all people are equal." Some are men, some women, some older, some stronger, some more adept, and so forth. Jobs tend to devolve on people who can do them best.

As is true today, there probably never have been skills that could not be mastered by persons of either sex, but it seems likely that in prehistoric times some tasks devolved more on women and others more on men. Hunting was usually but not exclusively a man's job, if we can believe evidence from recent natives (Willoughby 1963). This division of labor, of course, has a biological basis in that women find it hard to chase animals when they are pregnant or caring for young children. The result is that tasks that must be done in and around the home—collecting firewood, caring for children, basket making, cooking meals, and so on—are usually female activities. Necessary activities that require hard work and travel, such as animal hunting and aggressive warfare, are customarily male activities. The fact is that in many societies both cooking and hunting take so much time that one person can hardly be expected to do both. Archeologists usually assume that there was some division of labor based on sex, but because it is practically impossible to determine whether a man or woman made a particular artifact in antiquity, detailed interpretation of archeological materials in this regard has not been done often.

The evidence in some sites suggests that the male and female members of the family specialized in hunting and domestic activities respectively. Some archeological evidence may, however, be misleading. One would normally expect to find male artifacts buried with males and female artifacts with females. That this may not always have been the custom is suggested by data from central California. An examination of artifacts there showed that mortars and pestles (presumably used by women) occurred with about the same frequency in graves of both sexes; the same was true of arrow-points, which were presumably made, owned, and used by men in war and hunting.

Specialization, beyond that which is merely sex-determined or allocated, involves skills known to only a few persons in any community or area. Such things as metalworking, weaving, mining, specialized pottery making, and jewelry manufacture were carried out by persons, either men or women, who traded their handicraft for food. That craft specialization can occur on a very simple cultural level is illustrated by an old Australian man who served as the weapons repairer for his group and was supported in return for his services (McCarthy and McArthur 1960:148).

Another kind of specialization involves whole communities. For example, there is a traditional division between the farmers and herders in many parts of the world, and in the more complex societies the intracommunity specialization can be extreme. Culturally distinct groups might sometimes perform the complementary specialized occupations, but segments of an ethnically homogeneous community can also be employed. Consider our own civilization, in which most persons have a single occupation that is so specialized that they cannot provide themselves directly with the necessities of life, but must have the help of many others. With us, the specialization does not follow any particular ethnic or class lines, but in some civilizations it does. However, in prehistory most persons were much less specialized: herders may have done some farming themselves or had close relatives who did; and persons of whatever specialty were probably capable of gaining their own subsistence livelihood if necessary.

Trading relations that are vital for survival occur among people whose way of life is surprisingly simple, however; thus they provide another example of specialization. When two groups such as farmers and herders depend on one another for products they do not produce, the relation is said to be symbiotic. An extreme example, where the breakdown of such trade resulted in the migration of a people, is related by Spencer (1959:28–29, 201, 203), who describes the disappearance of the inland Eskimo of the Point Barrow region. These Eskimos depended mainly on caribou for food, but could survive in the interior region only if they could secure whale or seal oil for fuel from the coastal Eskimos. In prehistoric times a two-way trade of caribou hides in return for oil was mutually advantageous, but when clothing could be secured by the coastal peoples from whaling ships or traders, they no longer needed the caribou skins. As a consequence, they abandoned trading with their neighbors, leaving the latter in a position where they could not continue to survive. The interior people have thus been forced to migrate to the coast.

Even though specialization was not as extreme in prehistoric times as today, it is something we should look for, but we must admit that recognizing specialization archeologically can be difficult. The difficulty lies in the fact that detection of specialization requires extensive knowledge of intrasite and intersite variation, either through random sampling or complete excavation. There are few examples of either. As evidence of specialization one would expect to find areas within a site where artisans worked, where business or ritual was done, where political or religious leaders lived, and where the common folk resided. For every area one would hope to find a different set of artifacts or features that could be ascribed to the specialized activity. In principle this is in no way different from trying to identify activity areas within sites, although we assume that occupational specialization implies something more in a social sense than the fact that animals were butchered in one place and pottery baked in another.

The kind of variation that indicates full-time specialization will occur only if the population is sufficiently large and wealthy and if the technology is sufficiently well developed to permit the exploitation of different opportunities. Specialization is a consequence of both social and technological factors.

Status and Rank

Specialization may be considered an aspect of status that is closely linked to the roles people play—the jobs they do. Status is the respect or recognition a person earns from playing a certain role, whether the role be that of hunter, chief, or of old man. With every role is a status, and in many societies it is reinforced by tangible "status symbols." As we have already seen, whether or not the status is specifically rewarded, there are likely to be artifacts related to particular roles. Therefore, a way to find out about the roles people played and the status they enjoyed is to see what characteristic artifacts go with the jobs.

Rank is another aspect of social differentiation that implies more social distance between members. In a ranked society "positions of valued status are somehow limited so that not all those of sufficient talent to occupy such statuses actually achieve them" (Fried 1967:109). In these societies we usually find that persons of certain rank have access to prestige items not available to all. Because many of the prestige items are tangible, we stand a good chance of being able to recognize status and rank archeologically.

We are all aware that some of the things we have relate to our work, to our pleasures, to our beliefs, and to our status. Hammers and typewriters, boats and balls, icons, and dress-up clothes or automobiles, are examples. It follows then that, if we can identify artifacts whose type or pattern of occurrence suggests that they were used for one of the classes of activities listed above, we can make a few inferences about the way of life of the people who used them. L. Binford (1962) has indicated this possibility, but in a slightly different way. He says that people have the following classes of artifacts: *technomic,* meaning that they are utilitarian; *sociotechnic,* meaning that they relate to status or rank; and *ideotechnic,* meaning that they are principally symbols or insignia indicating group membership. The important thing stressed by Binford is that artifacts must be considered in the light of our knowledge of their having functioned in one or more of the several subsystems in a particular society. In other words, it is important to view the artifacts as tangible remains of roles enacted in a cultural and environmental context. Their presence is related to something that more often than not can be determined through careful consideration of the alternative explanations.

Binford, when he interpreted an apparent enigma (1962), provided a good example of the way in which one can analyze artifacts with respect to the various subsystems of a culture. The enigma involved the Old Copper culture of the upper Great Lakes in whose sites were often found copper implements. During the Early Woodland period the implements ceased to appear. On the assumption that copper tools were better than stone tools, their disappearance made little sense. Binford proceeded to examine the environmental situation, the setting in which the copper occurred (graves), and relevant models of social behavior as derived from anthropological studies of modern people.

The loctaion of the Old Copper culture sites and the remains in them suggested that the people were pursuing land-based hunting and gathering, whereas in the Early Woodland period a marked shift to exploiting water resources is seen in the settlement pattern, food remains, and subsequent population increase.

By analogy with modern peoples who live in small groups and pursue a hunting-gathering way of life it seemed very likely that the social organization was simple and egalitarian. Looking at it in another way, because the copper was found in graves and in the form of utilitarian objects Binford (1962:222) argued that the Old Copper culture represented an instance of an egalitarian society in which "status symbols are symbolic of the technological activities for which outstanding performance is rewarded by increased status." In other words, a copper knife represented the symbol of achievement of a man whose aspiration did not exceed being recognized for his technological (for example, hunting) proficiency: it was sociotechnic. Had the copper knives been found commonly outside graves, one would have argued that they were primarily utilitarian: that is, technomic. Binford (1962:223) concluded, however, that "the Old Copper copper tools had their primary functional context as symbols of achieved status in cultural systems with an egalitarian system of age grading." Their later disappearance then can be explained by reasoning that there was a shift in the form of society in Early Woodland, a reasonable conjecture in view of the new subsistence pattern and larger population. Thus there is no enigma in their disappearance, and one must look for a different way of expressing status in the new society, a way that may or may not be found among the durable objects recovered by archeologists.

Analyses such as these may prove to be incorrect when there is more information, but it is important for archeologists to learn to try to test their material in the light of the cultural systems that may be operating. It should be clear that there are two facets to such analysis. One is that, knowing certain circumstances, an archeologist can form an hypothesis about what kind of things to expect; or he can work from the pattern of occurrence of artifacts back to general principles of social organization.

That burials, together with the material placed in them alongside the dead, provide information on status and social relationships is not new in archeological thinking. Still there has been relatively little attention paid to the sometimes vast numbers of burials that have been excavated from large sites. Such burials number in the hundreds and sometimes thousands from sites in Southwest Asia, Europe, and America; yet there are few publications documenting and analyzing the associations of material found with each burial and thereby providing useful data for interpretation. Publications tend rather to describe in some detail the "royal" burials or to give illustrations of the finer objects found in all of the burials. In short, archeologists have tended to treat burials descriptively rather than analytically.

In the study of mortuary practices prehistorians are faced once again with a paucity of explicitly stated concepts but no shortage of ad hoc opinions. L. Binford (1971) has reviewed traditional assumptions about burials and found them wanting; he has also pointed to some concepts that are worth noting (Binford 1971:16). First, that burial is both a technical and a symbolic act. It is primarily the symbolic nature of burial customs that interests us here. According to Binford's reasoning, symbols are an arbitrary assigning of meaning to form; therefore the form of the symbol need not denote its meaning, nor need the symbol determine its tangible form. Thus, the same form of symbolic representation may be used in different cultures to denote different social symbols. For example, two peoples may employ the same set of symbols, as in cremation, but one may use it for chiefs and the other for criminals. Thus without additional information one cannot infer status from the fact of cremation.

There are two kinds of information ordinarily conveyed in society and in burials. First, the social persona,

> a composite of the social identities maintained in life and recognized appropriate for consideration at death. Second, is the composition and size of the social unit recognizing status responsibilities to the deceased. We would expect direct correlations between the relative rank of the social position held by the deceased and the number of persons having duty-status relationships vis-à-vis the deceased (L. Binford 1971:17).

With these concepts in mind Binford turned to ethnographic evidence for material with which to test some propositions, two of which are given below.

1. There should be a high degree of isomorphism between (a) the complexity of the status structure in a socio-cultural system and (b) the complexity of mortuary ceremonialism as regards differential treatment of persons occupying different status positions.

2. Among societies of minimal complexity, the major dimensions which serve

for status differentiation are based on the personal qualities of the individuals involved: age, sex and differential capacities for performance of cultural tasks. On the other hand, among more complex socio-cultural systems, status positions may be defined in terms of more abstract characteristics related to the culturally designated and symbolized means employed for partitioning the socially organized human aggregate.

Although the data Binford used and the tests he employed were admittedly crude, his hypotheses appear positively reinforced if not demonstrated. The propositions may seem simple and commonsensical to many readers, but Binford had a clear purpose in stating them. His point was to show that burial data may not be used to support hypotheses of diffusion of ideas or customs surrounding mortuary practices. Rather burial data "must be understood in terms of the organizational properties of the cultural systems themselves" (L. Binford 1971:25).

Probably the clearest evidence of status comes from graves that are unusually well stocked with luxury goods, weapons, food, or religious objects. The Royal Cemetery of Ur, the shaft graves at Mycenae, and King Tutankhamen's tomb are famous examples of rulers' burials that have their less elaborate counterparts in many societies where the implications of status are no less clear. The elaborate tombs found under mounds in North America contained personal and perhaps community wealth that honored the deceased (W. Sears 1954, 1961). The signs of status are not always durable, however, as Rice (1957:116) concluded when she reviewed the historical evidence from Asia and found that tattooing was a sign of rank. The rare find of the tattooed chieftain from Pazyryk corroborates this conclusion (Mongait 1961:170–175). Still higher status seems to be implied in the tombs from many places around the world in which there occur bodies of servants, members of the family, and governmental officials. Of course, these are associated only with complex societies such as the Shang Dynasty of China, in whose capital at Anyang were discovered tombs containing more than 100 sacrificed human beings. The skeletons, always headless, invariably occurred in groups of 10. Evidence that the wrists were tied together behind the back indicates that the decapitation was involuntary. The repeated occurrence of skeletons, knives, axes, and other items in groups of 10 affirms that this was the ritual number of the Shang Chinese of the second millennium B.C. (Creel 1937: 215).

Many of the persons who repose in rich tombs were political leaders who commanded a large following, but religious leaders often have an equally high status and may be as richly buried. Especially in the earlier civilizations and other complex societies, there is good reason to believe that political and religious authority often was vested in the same person, although this custom might not be obvious archeologically. The finding of temples and elaborate ceremonial structures is evidence, however, that the society supported a number of religious specialists and that they or another authority was responsible for organizing the construction of the temples. An example might be the pyramids and buried offerings found at La Venta, which, though difficult to relate to an individual, may have served to commemorate religious beliefs. Whatever the object of the offerings, it is clear that persons of considerable status were responsible for planning and overseeing the construction of the site. The inference that the society was complex enough to support ceremonial specialists and craftsmen is clear, even though the details of the nature of the system itself remain unknown.

Much more common would be shamans or medicine men, who are well known from ethnographic sources to occur in most societies where full-time specialization is not the rule. These are persons who have special powers based on a connection with the supernatural world, but they are not exempt from earning their own subsistence. Thus there is no great difference in status between them and other members of the society. If an archeologist dug the sites where such people lived he would expect to find some religious or magic paraphernalia (medicine bundles, for example) but not expect to find rich tombs or temples. He would more likely find such remains if the society had full-time priests whose knowledge of the supernatural had been gained through long-term study, and who were free of the obligations of sup-porting themselves. Incidentally, this situation would occur only among peoples whose agriculture was capable of producing considerable surplus.

The ancient Maya Indians remain shrouded in mystery in spite of decades of intensive excavation. Although thousands of burials have been excavated, little has been done to relate them to the social structure or to its possible changes. One reason for this neglect may be that burials have been excavated incidentally as they were encountered, rather than systematically for purposes of analysis. Consequently at only one or two sites is there an adequate sample available for analysis. Secondly, there is a great deal of variation in the treatment of the dead in the many Maya sites. Nevertheless, two studies of the relation between Maya burials and social structure have been made (Haviland 1967; Rathje 1970).

Rathje was unfortunately forced to work with burials separated in both time and space; nevertheless, with the skillful use of ethnohistoric, ethnographic, and archeological data, he has been able to suggest some test-able hypotheses. In view of the shortcomings of the data noted above, Rathje's study cannot be considered conclusive, but he does see some support for

a change in emphasis within Classic Maya society (A.D. 300–900) from recruitment of political and religious functionaries from the whole Maya population to the recruitment of officials from small ascribed segments of the population. [The burial] and other data suggest that one of the factors under-lying this change was Classic Maya economic organization and a system involv-ing wealth as a prerequisite for achieving office (Rathje 1970:359).

Without going into all the details and reasoning behind this conclusion we can mention the kinds of archeological data he used. He considered burials at two sites, Barton Ramie in British Honduras and Uaxactun in the Peten of Guatemala, sites some 60 kilometers apart. Barton Ramie was a rural site, occupied during an early and a late period (pre- and post-700 A.D.). The burials came from house platforms. The significant differences between the two periods were these. Early,

> . . . young adult interments were the wealthiest burials placed in house platforms . . . wealthy adults . . . were not interred in the platforms on which they resided. During the later Period, a larger proportion of adults were buried in house platforms. Few individuals living in rural houses were wealthy, and more artifacts were placed in the graves of mature adults. In contrast to wealthy young adult Early Period burials, young adult interments were the poorest found in Late Period houses (Rathje 1970: 362–364).

For comparison Rathje examined data from Uaxactun, a large ceremonial center. He found that the richest burials in both periods were in temple areas and that palaces contained burials similar in age, sex, and artifact distributions to the Late Period Barton Ramie platforms, except that they were richer than their rural counterparts. As he reconstructs the changes, Rathje sees an Early Period in which the wealthy from rural areas were interred in the temple areas. Later with the building of palaces, a resident elite, who no longer recruited personnel from the hinterlands, developed in the ceremonial centers. Thus "socio-political mobility between rural populations and ceremonial center populations had ended" (Rathje 1970: 368).

Rathje's analysis is instructive because it shows how one may approach a problem of this sort. It is equally instructive in that Rathje did not indicate the major shortcomings of the data, nor did he consider alternative hypotheses. In short, whether his conclusions will be shown to be correct or not ultimately, at the present time all he has done is to find evidence that supports his theory.

The analysis of burial data holds a great deal of promise in the areas we have just enumerated, and they can inform on other aspects as well. For a long time, burials have been used to determine racial affinities, although such studies have waned with the realization that there is a great degree of variation within most culturally homogeneous breeding populations. Thus the analysis of a few skulls cannot tell much about kinship. However, striking enough differences may be introduced into local populations to be recognizable in instances of invasion, migration, and colonization, or in the use of slaves. A relatively easy task of identification is in the Americas, where local Indian populations were invaded by Europeans; burials side by side in a cemetery usually leave little doubt of the affinities of the deceased. We might consider too whether such archeologically documented cases of migration and invasion as occurred throughout Europe since the advent of farming might not show up in the skeletons.

Recently, in a dramatic case, the identification of siblings was verified through examination of remains some 3000 years old—the mummies of King Tutankhamen and Smenkhkare, both youths of about 20 years of age. Both had been assigned by Egyptologists to the 18th Dynasty, but considerable debate had ensued over the interrelationships of pharaohs during this period.

An analysis of cranial morphology, stature, and blood grouping "suggest close kinship; in fact a relationship sufficiently close as to suggest that the two pharoahs are brothers" (Harrison and Abdalla 1972:13).

These findings are of more than technical interest, as was explained by Fairman (1972:15). The importance of this identification "lies principally in the contribution it may make to the solution of one of the most intractable and hotly disputed problems in the history of Egypt—the family and chronological relationship of the later kings of the 18th Dynasty. . . ."

CORRELATES OF SOCIAL ORGANIZATION

Social organization is a description of the way people act toward one another, and it can be seen, in turn, as the way a group of people has chosen to behave collectively in adapting to its physical and social environment. Social organization is thus closely related to factors external to the culture. Following anthropological theory, if we can specify some of the external factors, we can infer something of the social organization. When we couple these inferences with archeological data that bear directly on social organization we may be able to make accurate reconstructions of it. Settlement data and the distribution of artifacts within sites are two of the main kinds of data. With regard to the former, Vogt (1956:174) neatly summed up the range of interests we consider in this chapter:

1. The nature of the individual domestic house type or types;
2. The spatial arrangement of these domestic house types with respect to one another within the village or community unit;
3. The relationship of domestic house types to other special architectural features, such as temples, palaces, ball courts, kivas, and so on;
4. The over-all village or community plan; and
5. The spatial relationships of the villages or communities to one another over as large an area as is feasible.

Any environment offers certain opportunities and sets limitations on human behavior, but the way people exploit it depends on their technology and on their social organization. There is abundant evidence from ethnography that among most primitive people social organization is strongly shaped by the environment and by the technological skills of the people. It follows that if we can assess the environment and the technology we can make inferences about social organization, although in more advanced or complex cultures the relations may be less precise. The usual assumption is that there is a limited number of basic types of human organization that can be used to enable the society to adapt to its situation. The stress here is on organization—sets of interlocking roles—rather than on details of kinship, marriage practices, and the like.

Steward's work (1936, 1937, 1938) is basic to this discussion. He found (1937:101–102) that more complex social organization generally goes along with more favorable economic potential. As paraphrased by Eggan (1952:38),

> A low culture and/or unfavorable environment prevents dense population aggregates. It produces groups which, barring special contrary factors, are unilateral, localized, exogamous, and land-owning. Descent is male or female largely according to the economic importance of man or woman in that culture.

It seems to be the rule that people whose subsistence occurs in unpredictable quantity and location from year to year must keep to relatively small groups that will often break down to their lowest denominator, the nuclear family. It follows, therefore, that if we find a settlement pattern of dispersed small camps, that were seasonally occupied at intermittent intervals, the social organization was probably no more complex than the nuclear family, which might be joined seasonally by other families, each preserving its autonomy and flexibility of movement.

Among sedentary agriculturalists there can be found a close correlation between capacity for producing a surplus, distribution of resources throughout the general area, form of social structure, and degree of stratification. As Sahlins put it (1958:247),

> The interaction of a particular technological system with a given environment is the basic adaptation of a culture. It is held that the basic adaptation effected by any culture will be reflected in the social structure, because of the organization requirements of manipulating the technology and distributing life-sustaining goods.

The potential value of this for archeology is given in the following quotation from Sahlins (1958:203):

> If these deductions be correct, empirical evidence (other factors being constant) should show ramified systems in islands in which there is a variety of scattered resource zones differentially exploited by families or small groups of families. Or, inversely, where a single patrilocal extended family could not efficiently exploit the total range of available resources on a high level. However, where resource areas are clustered in time and space so that a single familial group could cope adequately with the total range of available exploitative techniques, descent-line systems would be most frequently found. As a further corollary, we should expect to find ramified systems most often in association with a scattered, hamlet type of settlement pattern, while descent-line systems might frequently be found with a nucleated, village type of settlement arrangement.

Sahlin's survey of ethnographic data from Polynesia showed these relations to hold true, and one might use the facts archeologically to reconstruct possible types of social organization from an evaluation of the resources and a study of settlement pattern.

Michael Coe's (1961) analysis of the Maya takes this kind of inference somewhat further. Following Durkheim (1949), Coe distinguished two types of society, mechanical, or unilateral, and organic. The former societies are relatively undifferentiated in that the subunits are all similar. The solidarity is one of likeness, in which religion provides the sanctions for orderly behavior. Organic societies are those in which the parts of society are different and bound together by their common dependence, which is usually expressed by exchange. "Exchange is the social glue itself, and is ultimately based on the division of labor; in its highest and most effective form it consists of large-scale trade" (M. Coe 1961:66). Although these are recognized as polar types that may have no pure representatives, it is also clear that certain environmental circumstances dispose a society to tend toward one or the other pole.

Organic societies tend to develop in areas that are environmentally differentiated, have a highly productive agricultural system, and adequate transportation. In these areas urban centers develop early as focal points of trade and have a high proportion of merchants and administrators, who exercise political influence in selecting or controlling the leader. The bulk of society consists of peasant farmers.

Unilateral or mechanical societies are found in undifferentiated areas where transportation is difficult; they tend to produce the same crops throughout at the same seasons. Lacking the need for trade, such people are non-urban. Political control devolves unilaterally from the leader, who does not have competition from a group of economically important merchants and administrators.

Following this analysis, Coe found that the Maya correspond to a unilateral society, whereas the people of highland Mexico were organized into organic units. The same kind of comparison can be extended fruitfully to the differences between Mesopotamian and Egyptian societies, which also seem to conform to the two polar types for similar environmental reasons. The old enigma of why some civilizations lacked cities thus seems to have a rational explanation. In an analysis like this it is important to remember that the ideal types pertain to early civilizations; they are early stages of adaptation that became modified, especially under the growing influence of organic civilizations, until some of the "normal" behavior typified by unilateral organization was forced to change to meet the competition.

In the organic civilizations, wealth and prerogatives are spread more widely among the population. Indications of this archeologically would be that "royal" tombs or houses would not be substantially richer or larger than those of rich citizens, and that there would be a continuous gradation from the wealthiest to the poorest citizen. In the unilateral civilizations, the leader would be dramatically richer than even members of his court, and there would be a great difference between the kinds of goods found in his and in his followers' tombs. One characteristic of such societies is that any trade tends to be for luxury goods that emphasize the leader's difference from the populace, and because trade was a royal prerogative, no merchant class developed.

These basic differences between unilateral and organic civilizations may help explain why some civilizations disappear and others continue in one form or another throughout history. In explanation, M. Coe (1961: 83–84) paraphrased Durkheim:

> The relative form of mechanical solidarity is quite weak and powers based on it are subject to rapid overthrow. A social order founded on the sanctions necessary to enforce tribute and corvée labor is extraordinarily brittle to social change, whether internal or external. . . . The unwritten charters of urban, organic civilizations, being based on inter-regional dependence and therefore on interests which are mutual and universal within each society, are by their nature more resilient and adaptable to outside pressure.

RELIGION AND IDEOLOGY

Most archeological inferences about the nature of religion or ideology are highly speculative because they concern areas of behavior for which few rules of interpretation have been developed. Or they may concern the interpretation of artifacts that could be explained by reference to kinds of behavior entirely different from the intellectual. It is an archeological joke that strange things which otherwise cannot be explained are called "ceremonial"; it is probably true that many things that ought to be explained in more mundane ways are called religious.

Perhaps the kinds of artifacts that are most commonly referred to religious belief are figurines and other forms of art on which there is an enormous literature and volumes of published illustrations. In spite of the amount of thought that has been been given to paleolithic art (of Europe during the Upper Paleolithic, some 10,000–30,000 years ago, and to a lesser extent in other parts of the world), there have been few interpretations that seem conclusive to the majority of reviewers. One reason for this situation is that a great deal of art is notoriously hard to date, with the result that a consideration of trends in style or technique is premature. Perhaps a more basic reason is that most art has been studied as art—in terms of its style, design, and composition—and relatively little attention has been given to considering its context in a society. This statement excepts the oft-repeated idea that most cave art is hunting magic. The fact is that until recently no one had systematically analyzed the physical distribution of art in caves. Leroi-Gourhan's (1967, 1968) attempts in this direction now show new ways to date and interpret the pictures. If we can judge from the success archeologists have had in analyzing the spatial occurrence of other kinds of human remains, the prospect of obtaining additional insights into paleolithic art seems good.

Figurines of humans and animals are likewise enigmatic. Most authors refer to the human females as "Venuses," with the obvious implication that they represent female fertility. Somewhat akin to this is the idea that they are "mother goddesses," which would imply that the female was venerated in a religious sense, perhaps as the mother of all living things. If the figurines are fertility symbols, one would expect them to look like the contemporary ideal of feminine sexuality. An exception to this assumption would be made for the figurines that may show pregnancy. If the figurines were mother goddesses, however, they might more reasonably be expected to portray older mature women, as many in fact do.

Because figurines have been made in many areas of the world over tens of thousands of years, in vastly different cultural contexts, it is unwise to generalize very much; this discussion is confined to the European paleolithic. The figurines show a remarkable variety, contrary to what one generally assumes and occasionally reads, "obese naked figurines of women sculptured in the round" (McBurney 1961:110). The fact is, although some are obese, others are slender, and some are in the round, whereas others are simply engraved in rock. They are carved and modeled in a variety of media ranging from limestone to ivory to coal to clay. It seems unlikely that a single interpretation will account for the differences in this group, although it must be admitted that they share the fact of having been made at all, during a relatively short time, by people who are tenuously related (in the sense of sharing certain tools and subsistence). This is a problem, once again, that needs a thorough restudy in the light of the style of the figurines themselves, and the context in which they occur. It may be that there is more pattern in their occurrence than usually meets the eye.

Peter Ucko (1962) gives a useful review of later figurines found in Neolithic Crete and other nearby contemporary cultures. As he pointed out, it is inappropriate to mix periods and cultures when making interpretations. "Any assumption regarding the desirability of numerous children, for example, in an agricultural (neolithic) society may well be quite mistaken for a hunting (paleolithic) society" (Ucko 1962:30). His description of the ways in which figurines are used in modern cultures is especially useful for the range of possible interpretations it suggests. Among these, and the interpretations he suggests as possible explanations of the Cretan figurines, are that they were used as dolls, made by and for children; as teaching devices to instruct initiates; and as vehicles for sympathetic magic (Ucko 1962:47). None of these theories considers that the figurines are mother goddesses, an interpretation that Ucko rejects on several counts. It is important to recognize here again that contextual evidence, coupled with an analysis of the artifacts themselves, ruled out the mother-goddess hypothesis.

A concern with the origins and growth of belief in the supernatural is not evident among Americanists who assume the Indians to have been intellectually advanced when they arrived in the Americas. However, the issue is important in the Paleolithic as man's ancestors gradually acquired the attributes of culture. There is a relative lack of data from this period; about all archeologists have to go on is burials. Concerning burials, it is usually, although not necessarily correctly, assumed that people who interred their dead had a belief in the supernatural, but there is no proof of this. In any event, the beliefs may have been quite different from what we might think. As an example, where the evidence is intact, all skulls, until the Upper Paleolithic, show some signs of mutilation, generally of the basal portion to create access to the brain. Such mutilation of the Neanderthal skull found at Monte Circeo "consists of the careful and symmetric incising of the periphery of the *foramen magnum* (which has been completely destroyed) and the consequent artificial production of a subcircular opening 10–12 centimeters in diameter" (Blanc 1961:126). Many writers have seen these openings as evidence of cannibalism, an explanation suggested by the fact that tribes in New Guinea treat skulls in the same way before ritually consuming the brains. On the other hand, as Brothwell (1965:172) and Wells (1964:139) point out, the base of the skull is fragile and may be broken easily or the *foramen magnum* enlarged by the gnawing of rodents (Brothwell 1965:124, Fig. 49B).

INTELLECTUAL DEVELOPMENTS

The last decade has seen a number of studies that infer the capabilities of prehistoric man in geometry, mathematic, calendrics, and symbolic notation. The best known of these is the study of Stonehenge by an astronomer, Gerald Hawkins, who published a definitive work, *Stonehenge Decoded* (1965a). Stonehenge (see Fig. 62) is a megalithic monument in southern England built in stages during the third millenium B.C. Basically, the monument consists of an outer bank and ditch in the form of a circle with a diameter of 380 feet. Inside this circle the most notable features are: a ring of "Aubrey Holes" just inside the bank; still closer to the center are large standing stones comprising, as one moves toward the center, the "Sarsen Circle"; a "Bluestone Circle," most of whose stones are now missing; the "Trilithon Horseshoe" consisting of enormous upright stones capped with lintels; and finally the "Bluestone Horseshoe." Many legends have surrounded Stonehenge, and it has been used by Druids in recent times to celebrate the annual summer solstice. At this time the sun rises on a line between the center of the circle and the "Heelstone" which lies just outside the encircling bank.

Prevailing archeological theories were that Stonehenge was built by late Neolithic and Early Bronze Age people for reasons that were essentially unfathomable, although the possibility of using the structure to aid in sighting the sun at its solstices was generally accepted.

Hawkins, who had been intrigued with Stonehenge since his youth, investigated its astronomical significance with the aid of a computer which enabled him to make rapid calculation of the correspondence between possible lines of sight through various of the features of Stonehenge and astronomical events. His results were spectacular in that he found it possible to sight all the important solar and lunar cycles and to keep track of them systematically through the years by placing markers in the Aubrey Holes. Further he deduced that one could predict when significant lunar events such as eclipses would take place.

Hawkins' deductions were met at first with stiff resistance from archeologists who felt the sophistication implied far exceeded the capabilities of the people who had built the monument. The consensus now is that Hawkins has showed how Stonehenge might have been used; whether it was used that way is another matter. Still the impressive number of correlations between solar and lunar events and the sight lines within Stonehenge is convincing evidence that the monument was planned to do some if not all of the things Hawkins claims. As he put it (Hawkins 1965a: 1), "If I can see any alignment, general relationship or use for the various parts of Stonehenge, then these facts were also known to the builders."

The implications are that people 5000 years ago, who incidentally built many other similar structures of wood and stone, made systematic and prolonged observations and records of the heavens. The uses to which they may have put this knowledge still escape us. Far from being "howling barbarians" as was once thought, these pastoral and farming peoples were evidently making significant intellectual contributions at about the same time as the great pyramids were being built in Egypt.

Great Britain has many nearly circular alignments of standing stones in addition to Stonehenge, and their study has occupied the attention of Alexander Thom for many years. He has been concerned especially with the method used to align the stones with what seemed an unusual degree of accuracy, apart from the impressive task of transporting and erecting the monoliths themselves. In essence Thom (1964, 1966, 1971) has deduced that the builders had a unit of measurement of 2.72 feet which he calls the "megalithic yard." Thom found that the circular alignments were set in such a way that the circumferences were integrals of the megalithic yard. This is no mean accomplishment today even with the use of calculators, and it certainly required considerable trial and error on the part of the builders who were restricted to the use of stakes, ropes, and perhaps "yardsticks." What this seems to imply is a fascination with proportions, a rather abstract intellectual exercise.

Additionally, Thom (1966), T. Cowan (1970), and Hutchinson (1972) have determined various methods for scribing the rings of standing stones. To construct these, still maintaining the relationship between circumference and the megalithic yard, required the use of the pythagorean triangle or an equilateral triangle depending on how the figure was scribed on the ground.

It is certain that some of the stone rings were used for lunar observations (Thom 1966: 128), but equally impressive is the builder's apparent concern for perfection, so that the measurements were laid out in integral units of "megalithic yards." Thom (1966: 126) said, "One can only surmise that, having no pen and paper, he was building in stone a record of his achievements in geometry and perhaps also in arithmetic."

A final set of examples of prehistoric man's early attempts at symbolic notation and at keeping records goes back into the Upper Paleolithic at a time when peoples were hunting and living in caves and temporary shelters. Alexander Marshack (1964, 1972) has pioneered in the study of engraved bone and stone, some of which he thinks were used to record lunar cycles. His initial study was based on microscopic examination of two bone objects— one from the Magdalenian (some 13,000–16,000 years ago) and one from the Aurignacian (perhaps 10,000 years older)—and of a painting on a rock wall in Spain (between 4000 and 13,000 years old). In each instance a series of marks could be interpreted as denoting the passage of one or more lunar cycles, with the various phases of the moon recorded symbolically.

More recent work by Marshack (1969, 1970a, 1970b, 1970d, 1972) has dealt both with the methods of analysis he has developed and with the interpretations of the significance of the markings on prehistoric objects. One such example is the baton of Montgaudier (Marshack 1970a, 1970c), an engraved antler of Magdalenian age estimated to date to more than 12,000 years ago. On this baton were engraved a salmon, two schematized ibex heads which had been "crossed out," a series of plants in various stages of growth, two seals, and an enigmatic sluglike creature. What is impressive is the extraordinary attention to detail that enables one to follow the growing season from start to finish in the characteristics shown on some of the species. As Marshack (1970a) says,

> What we have, then, is a composition in which diverse species from separate realms (ocean, river, ground and mountain) are differentiated according to their season of appearance, sex, and stage of maturation. All the images are of the spring and summer. We can conjecture that the precision of rendition had a complementary vocabulary for naming and identification, and that it probably also included a lore with which the hunter explained the seasonal reappearance of the species involved and probably the general rebirth of spring and summer.

Marshack (1969) has also shown that other objects were repeatedly engraved, in effect accumulating a record of their use over time. Marshack's interpretations, which have been widely acclaimed for their originality, have been criticized (Rosenfeld 1971; Marshack and Rosenfeld 1972; Marshack 1972).

What is certain is that paleolithic man had skills in drafting that matched his ability to observe anatomical characteristics of the species in his environment. What is uncertain is his motives for making the engravings and paintings. Whether they were hunting magic, art for art's sake, or an attempt to keep permanent records is still open to discussion.

REFERENCES

Prehistoric Peoples and Cultures: Caldwell 1964; Childe 1956; W. Gladwin and H. Gladwin 1928a; Kroeber 1963; Rouse 1965, 1972b:Chaps. 2, 5.
Direct Historical Approach: Caldwell 1958; G. Clark 1957:256–261; Eggan 1952, 1966; H. Gladwin 1934; Heizer 1941a; J. Hester 1962; Hoijer 1956b; Jett 1964; Kossina 1941; Lipe 1970; Murdock 1959; C. Nelson 1972; Rowe 1945, 1946; Steward 1942; Strong 1940; Thieme 1958.

Linguistic Approaches: Baumhoff and Olmsted 1963; Bergsland and Vogt 1962; Crossland 1957; Crossland and Burchell 1972; Finley 1970; Gimbutas 1963; Hencken 1955:44ff; Hoijer 1956a, 1956b; Hymes 1960; Kroeber 1955; Pulgram 1959; Sapir 1916; Swadesh 1953, 1959, 1960, 1962, 1964; D. Taylor and Rouse 1955; Theime 1958; Traeger 1955; Van der Merwe 1966.

Migrations: Byers 1957; Caldwell 1964; Chard 1958; Childe 1957; J. Ford 1966; Genovés 1967; Giddings 1960; H. Gladwin 1947; Greenman 1963; Griffin 1960, 1962; Heine-Geldern 1954; Heine-Geldern and Ekholm 1951; Heizer 1962c; J. Hester 1962; Heyerdahl 1959, 1963; Hopkins 1959; Linné 1955; McBurney 1960; MacWhite 1956:16–18; Mather 1954; Meggers, Evans, and Estrada 1965; Pearson 1968; Rouse 1958; Stewart 1960; Swadesh 1962; R. Thompson 1958b; Wendorf 1966; Willey 1956a.

The Socioeconomic Unit: Allen and Richardson 1968, 1971; Bender 1967; L. Binford 1966; Cornelius 1964; Dean 1970; Deetz 1965, 1967; Efimenko 1958; L. C. Freeman and Brown 1964; Grigor'ev 1967; J. Hill 1966; Longacre 1964, 1966, 1970a; P. S. Martin 1962; A. P. Phillips 1971; Pilling 1965; Vivian 1970.

Specialization: Driver and Massey 1957; Elsasser 1961; Griffin 1930; D. Heath 1958; McCarthy and McArthur 1960; Murdock 1937; A. Shepard 1963; Willoughby 1963.

Status and Rank: L. Binford 1962; Creel 1937; Fleming 1972; Fried 1967; Mayer-Oakes 1963; Mongait 1961:170–175; Rathje 1970; Renfrew 1972b; Rice 1957:116; W. Sears 1954, 1958, 1961.

Skeletal and Burial Evidence: J. Brown 1971; Howells 1966; Kerley and Bass 1967; Lane and Sublett 1972; Neumann 1952; Rathje 1970; Stewart 1960; Stewart and Newmann 1967.

Correlates of Social Organization: Allen and Richardson 1971; Barth 1960; M. Coe 1961; Durkheim 1949; Eggan 1952; E. Evans 1956; Klopfer 1962; Laslett 1965; Lévi-Strauss 1963; Sahlins 1958; Sanders and Price 1968; Service 1962; Steward 1936, 1937, 1938; Vogt 1956.

Religion and Magic: Bergounioux and Goetz 1958; Blanc 1961; Breuil 1951; Coon 1951:36; Elsasser 1961; Engnell 1967; J. Hawkes and Woolley 1963: 208; Heizer 1951b, 1959; Heizer and Baumhoff 1959; Heizer and Hewes 1940; James 1962; Kirchner 1952; Maringer 1960; Mongait 1961:83; W. Sears 1961.

Figurines: Burkitt 1934; J. Davis 1959; Leroi-Gourhan 1967, 1968; McBurney 1961; Pritchard 1966; Ucko 1962; Ucko and Rosenfeld 1967.

Intellectual Developments: Atkinson 1960; Colton and Martin 1969; T. Cowan 1970; Hawkins 1965a, 1965b; Hoyle 1966; Hutchinson 1972; Marshack 1964, 1969, 1970a, 1970b, 1970c, 1970d, 1972; Marshack and Rosenfeld 1972; Rosenfeld 1971; Thom 1964, 1966, 1967, 1971; Vértes 1965.

Astronomy: Atkinson 1960, 1966; Hatch 1971; J. Hawkes 1967; Hawkins 1964, 1965a, and 1965b; Hawkins and others 1967; Hoyle 1966; Marshack 1964.

Psychological Characteristics: Alonzo de Real 1963; Pericot 1961; M. C. Robbins 1966; J. Thompson 1954b; A. Wallace 1950.

CHAPTER TWENTY

HISTORICAL RECONSTRUCTIONS IN ARCHEOLOGY

In this chapter we deal with what happened in history. Before an archeologist can begin to interpret changes in man's past he must first find out something about what the sequence of events was. As we have already indicated and as Wiley and Phillips (1958) pointed out, most archeology is essentially descriptive of what was found in sites and how the sites relate to one another chronologically. With a large enough geographic and chronological perspective such a description amounts to a history of events. But a mere relation of events in their temporal order says nothing about causes; about the best that can be done is to identify moments when major transformations occurred, and some of their characteristics. Working with such data in hand, one can pose hypotheses and then seek relevant data that will prove or disprove them. In any event, most archeological writing has followed the former procedure, and it has remained at an essentially descriptive and inferential level. The various ways in which this work has been done are related here.

From a modern view, prehistory describes foreign lands and faceless people. It may deal with the culture of a people, a region, or the whole world through time. None of us today has the ability to see the past as it was to those who lived it. We can see the past only in ways that are familiar to us, either through our own experience or through our knowledge of other cultures. We judge the artifacts by what we know today. We can describe

414

prehistoric environments and the tools used to cope with them, but we cannot describe what man thought of himself or of the world. We can deal with the past only on our terms, and our terms are not those of prehistoric man.

Prehistoric men had no real sense of history or of their place in the larger world of man, for these imply a conception of the progression of time and events, as well as a familiarity with geography and culture. Most men in prehistory expected tomorrow to be like today and another generation like the last. A prehistorian views the past as a series of changes, and his job becomes one of finding out both what happened and how and why it happened. To learn these things it is first necessary to find out what the chief events of the past were. With this knowledge a prehistorian can see what prehistoric men could not, namely, from whence they came and whither they were going. Having this kind of perspective enables an archeologist to begin making hypotheses concerning how and why certain changes in the past occurred. Such hypotheses depend on a knowledge of the physical environment—its opportunities as well as its changes; of the cultural environment—its pool of technical skill and the possibilities for intercultural exchange; of the interaction between these factors that in the end tell us how cultures change. Knowing how cultures changed is different from knowing why they changed. Ultimate causes of particular events are perhaps unobtainable; yet with our scientific predisposition we are led to ask why, and we try to answer with some statement of cause and effect. It need not invalidate our answer to recognize that prehistoric men would probably not have been able to answer the question. The interpretation of human history is a job for a historian, not for the man who lives, experiences, and inquires about only a small part of it.

Prehistorians try to find reasons not only for the daily life of prehistoric men, but for the existence of the many kinds of prehistoric life and how these related to the gradual development of cultures or civilization. Prehistorians are not interested in the annual rainfall and probable number of frost-free days 20,000 years ago in a valley in France for the sake of this knowledge alone, but for the way changing patterns of weather affected men and their relations with the plants and animals. Prehistorians are interested, not in the quarry from which prehistoric men obtained their flint, but in the development of social and technical skills that enabled them to live in and exploit any environment. Prehistorians are interested, not in the size of a man buried in an African cave, but in man as a biological organism gradually acquiring the features that we recognize as human. Prehistorians examine the relations between culture and biology, and how, in the past two million years, man has become king of the beasts. In short, prehistorians are interested in the history of man, not of particular men.

Historians who deal with literate societies are sometimes impressed with the role played by great men, and their histories therefore emphasized people. Other historians are more interested in the broad outlines of cultural development and see history as a series of technological or social trends. Still others wonder about the influence of environment on man and write their histories to demonstrate a causal relation between the two. Prehistorians have different choices. They cannot see particular persons because their human subjects are impersonal, but they can see societies or cultures in the archeological record.

Both history and prehistory are based on primary documentation. An archeologist's history will stand or fall on the quality of his basic documents —reports on the excavation of sites. If site reports are adequate, it is possible to arrange the data contained in them in a variety of ways, depending on the aims of any particular interpreter. It should be stressed, however, that data gathered solely for descriptive purposes may not lend themselves to processual studies.

SITE REPORTS

Grahame Clark (1957:107) says that "the archeologist with little or no experience of excavation is ill qualified to interpret the results of other people's digging." In spite of Clark's pessimism, there are several criteria that identify good and bad reports. Professional archeologists and even students must try to evaluate the reports they read, both to learn how archeology is done and to see if the writer's conclusions really follow from the evidence presented.

A site report should tell what was found in an excavation. It should include a description of the environment, of the methods by which the site was dug, and of the artifacts found. Finally, there should be a synthesis describing the way people at the site lived. An archeologist will usually include a chapter telling how his material relates to that from other sites and how it fits in the history of a region. All reports should begin with a clear statement of what was attempted and what was accomplished. This statement tells the reader immediately whether the report describes a test excavation, a probing of graves to get a ceramic sequence, the uncovering of a temple complex to determine its development, or the excavation of a whole site, or a portion of it, to get a representative picture of the prehistoric community.

The report should be clear and concise. It should begin with a geographical description and include maps and plans of the site and its environs. The method of excavation should be described in sufficient detail to allow the reader to judge whether, from his knowledge of similar sites, the approach was adequate. It is here that the layman as well as the professional may be seriously misled. The progress of the excavation should be detailed in drawings or photographs, and the stratigraphic relations of one area to another should be clearly shown.

The artifacts and special features—walls, fireplaces, and so on— should be clearly described and illustrated. Sometimes it is possible to refer to other reports and merely say that certain of the new artifacts are similar to others that have been reported before. Usually artifacts are described in accordance with standardized principles of classification. The results should then be tabulated so that quantities can be readily determined.

One can judge a report by the kind of things reported. Certain things are usually present in sites, for example, bones. These should be detailed in a report. If they were discarded or not analyzed, the reader can be sure that valuable information was lost. If an archeologist overlooks information of this kind, he may have overlooked other things as well. For example, preoccupation with burials or houses may have blinded the archeologist to the very small but significant object that can be recovered only by special techniques. Such items as tiny flint tools are often overlooked because the dirt is not screened. Similarly, plant remains are often missed because the archeologist does not recognize the importance of saving them or does not know the techniques for recognizing and recovering them. And, let us emphasize once more, all data must be recorded stratigraphically.

It is well to mention here that many archeologists publish "preliminary" reports summarizing the findings of one season's work, or the essentials of a dig before the fully documented final report can be published. Publication of detailed, well-illustrated reports is both time-consuming and expensive; the preliminary report serves to bridge the gap between the inevitable delay in getting a final report published and the undesirable results of not publishing anything for years after a site has been dug. Many archeologists also publish short articles dealing with a single facet of their excavations. For example, if new types of projectile points are found that the writer believes should be brought to the attention of fellow archeologists, he may simply describe their occurrence. Good examples of the power of such suggestion are the first articles dealing with microblades and burins in America. As an immediate consequence of this work, archeologists suddenly became aware of what to look for, and there has followed a wealth of articles reporting similar finds in other sites.

Interpretation of the evidence in a site report should be presented apart from the description, so that a minimum of bias will be introduced into the basic data. Interpretations can be personal, and even wholly erroneous ones will not affect the quality of the report if they are kept separate from the basic description. There are, in fact, many archeologists who wish to prove pet theories—and do so—but their reports are written in such a way that their interpretations do not alter their data. Other archeologists are then free to interpret the factual data in their own ways.

This discussion avoids the issue of "objectivity" in reporting the results of any investigation. It is clear that no scientist begins his work with an empty head. His method of work, his choice of a subject, and his reporting of the results all depend on what he considers proper and worth while. Some scholars have invented elaborate procedures for recording their data "objectively," but if we examine their position we find that any such attempt represents a sophisticated theoretical bias—the very thing they are trying to avoid. Because we recognize this danger, what we are stressing here is that certain standards of reporting should be observed. These standards are based on what we believe to be the most fruitful approach to prehistory. In any event, we cannot conceive of a reasonable defense for sloppy or incomplete reporting.

REGIONAL HISTORIES

When enough sites in an area have been excavated and reported, archeologists can construct the framework of a regional sequence. For this, one needs only the chronological arrangement of assemblages. It is fair to say that most archeology is concerned with this essential task. The size of a "region" varies, depending on the archeologist's interests. It may be a little valley, a drainage of a major river, such as the Missouri, a major physiographic area, such as the American Southwest, or a continent. Larger regions lend themselves to subdivision, and many archeologists spend their lifetimes studying minor parts of larger areas. If there are suitable ways to date sites, it is easy to set up regional sequences. But establishing relative chronologies bears the same relation to history that the arranging of prime numbers in order of ascending size bears to mathematics.

In the long view, change was pervasive throughout prehistory, and regional sequences document this change. Changes, whether in economy, pottery design, or house type, demand an explanation. In fact, were there no change for a considerable period, one would wonder why there had been none. The prehistorian's task is to answer the question of "how" and "why" about his sequences. Explanation of changes depends on knowing the cultural relations of successive assemblages to one another. Then we can ask how we can account for the differences and similarities in successive assemblages.

As we saw in the preceding chapter, the study of change is complex; yet there are physical clues to change that should trigger an archeologist to look for explanations. Some "explanations" can be simple descriptions of what happened. That is, the descriptions need not consider the ultimate question of why in each instance; however, it is important to stress that they must be based on a systematic areal approach rather than simply on a collection of sites.

Change can result from local invention, influence from another group, or new people bringing in new ideas. If one of these sources can be specified, one might look further to find out the details. Thus, if influences came from another group, it is useful to know from what group and by what means ideas and artifacts were exchanged. Trade, migration, war, or just copying may account for change. Sometimes ideas are diffused. For example, the idea of the throwing stick (atlatl) or potter's wheel might have been diffused to groups that had never seen such implements.

MODELS OF PREHISTORY

Speaking broadly, two quite different kinds of models have been used by archeologists and historians to conceptualize and synthesize their data: descriptive and causal. The former have been used much more extensively and can be subdivided into those that are essentially atemporal in their emphasis (that is, they do not consider change) and those that focus on change.

Descriptive Models

The atemporal descriptive models are best exemplified by Thomsen, who arranged the museum collections of Denmark into stone, bronze, and iron, thereby unwittingly providing terms which, set in chronological sequence, could be used to describe the course of a part of culture history. Although Thomsen devised his organization before accurate dating was known, it was not long before others adopted his divisions as chronological stages, and soon such terms as "Paleolithic," "Mesolithic," and "Neolithic" were coined to describe subdivisions of the Stone Age. From that point most work in the Old World was concerned with describing temporal change.

Quite a different history of work in the Americas led to the widely used "Midwestern Taxonomic Method," first described by McKern (1939). The method resulted when archeologists recognized that they were using terms like "culture" so loosely that it was hard to communicate to one another about what they had excavated. Accordingly, there arose an interest in making more precise systems for classification of artifacts and cultures. The first formal descriptive terminology for use over a wide area reflected this concern for classification, and at the same time the lack of interest in development. The "Midwestern Taxonomic Method" was based entirely on the degree to which an assemblage from one site resembled that from another. In other words, there was no implication of time or space in the taxonomic labels. Beginning with the smallest unit, the system grouped components (assemblages of artifacts from one site or cultural level within a site) into foci. Foci were said to be somewhat equivalent to what ethnologists call tribes. A grouping of similar foci produced an aspect; groups of aspects became phases, which in turn were grouped into patterns, and these finally into bases. A base was the most general classification, and patterns were included in it largely on subsistence similarities; for example, "sedentary-fishing base" or "horticultural base."

A system could hardly be devised that was less adequately directed toward culture history than this one. Even though the sites could be described by this system, its disregard of time and space put the emphasis on classification for the sake of classification. These shortcomings caused arguments over whether something was an aspect or a phase; indeed, the designations had to be changed frequently as more was learned.

Within the Midwestern Taxonomic Method was a designation of cultures that began with "Paleo Indian," "Early Man," or "Big Game Hunter" and was followed by "Archaic," "Desert Culture," and "Woodland." Again there was no necessary implication of development, although the distinctions of time and economy were emphasized.

The lack of a sense of cultural development in much American thinking seems odd to many Old World archeologists, but there were reasons for the prevailing attitude. In the first place, in many areas there was no discernible "development" over the whole time of occupation. That is, economy, being in fine adjustment with the physical and cultural environment, remained stable. The changes that could be seen were stylistic, and their causes could hardly be directly related to the broader development of culture. Perhaps partly responsible for the lack of change in many areas is the relatively short duration of occupation in the Americas, which saw few major climatic changes and gave little time for diffusion of peoples or ideas into more remote areas.

A second factor was that most American Indians, the descendants of the prehistoric men whose remains were being unearthed, had not advanced much beyond savagery or early barbarism on Morgan's (1875) ethnographic scale. Any developments seen archeologically would have seemed relatively minor.

Thirdly, archeologists were greatly influenced by ethnographic descriptions. In many instances their purpose was to produce for prehistory the kind of description that an ethnologist writes of a present-day tribe. For the most part, ethnologists viewed culture without a time dimension. Many archeologists, paralleling the ethnographic use of the "ethnological present," thought of the "prehistoric present" and discounted the importance of historical factors in that momentary slice of life.

Long before the Midwestern Taxonomic Method was devised to describe American Indian cultures, European archeologists had taken the initiative to work out evolutionary models. These followed logically on the discovery that Thomsen's "Three Ages" were in fact chronologically successive in much of Europe, and that biological evolution was a powerful new concept that had far-reaching ramifications.

In ethnology, models were made that described man's progression from savagery through barbarism to civilization (Morgan 1875). The archeological and ethnological models were complementary, dealing with technology and culture. All these early models, based on very scanty evidence, were "in large part the outcome of the doctrines of optimism, the inevitability of progress, and the perfectibility of man current in the eighteenth century" (Piggott 1960:20). It may be worth reiterating here that such models as were introduced in Chapter 19 focus on aspects of human behavior that have analogues in other biological systems or in machines. In a sense these (uncomfortably to some persons) deal with the "inhuman" aspects of man.

For some archeologists, the models were viewed as proofs of cultural laws. To G. de Mortillet (1903) the "law of similar development" was no mere model, nor would Morgan (1875, 1878:vi) have entertained much doubt that man had really advanced by his postulated stages. He contended that "the history of the human race is one in source, one in experience, and one in progress."

Theories of cultural evolution were confined for the most part to the Old World, where the cultural sequence was long enough to contain evidence of man's biological as well as his cultural evolution. In the 1930s archeologists began to see that, even though there was a general increase in technological efficiency in prehistoric times, culture did not everywhere go through precisely the same stages in the same way.

Although this statement is generally true, Soviet archeologists have continued to follow a stricter evolutionary scheme than their colleagues in other countries. Whereas most evolutionary models assume that progressive change is normal or inevitable, the Russians go a step further by declaring that social changes are caused by technological changes. Their model is based on Marx and Engels' incorporation of Morgan's ethnographic data of the late nineteenth century into a picture of the past. It purports to demonstrate the close ties between technology and society. Instead of dividing prehistory into technological stages or economic stages, the Marxist thinkers have set up a series of social stages wherein society changes from a family based on communism to a matrilineal clan, and finally, after techniques of farming are learned, into a series of degenerate class societies. The idea was that the "whole structure of society is determined in the long run by the mode (method) of production which in turn is dependent on the 'means of production'—that is, on the technical forces at the disposal of society for the satisfaction of socially recognized needs" (Childe 1951b:10). As Childe goes on to show, such a viewpoint is untenable in the face of evidence. "The Russian scheme of classification assumes in advance precisely what archaeological facts have to prove" (Childe 1951b:29) and hence is foredoomed. Some sort of causal relation between technology and society is not denied; what is denied is that a kind of technology inevitably results in a kind of society. It is nearer to the truth to say that with a given technology there are certain alternate forms that society may take.

The classic evolutionary approach is often called "unilinear," to emphasize the idea that it purports to describe an invariable chain of events. Even a brief glimpse of human history, however, confirms the fact that there are considerable differences in both the steps by which advanced societies were achieved, and in the complex societies themselves.

Julian Steward in *Theory of Culture Change* proposed a divergent approach to the study of evolution that he calls "multilinear evolution." His approach was "based on the assumption that significant regularities in cultural change occur, and it is concerned with the determination of cultural laws" (1955:18). The approach "simply poses the question of whether any genuine or meaningful similarities between certain cultures exist and whether these lend themselves to formulation" (1955:19).

Steward, like most of the archeologists who have followed his lead

(Adams 1966; Sanders and Price 1968), emphasizes a cultural core of sociocultural integration. In other words, he emphasizes the organizational aspects of society. In his search for regularities in the development of cultures he selects "special constellations of causally interrelated features which are found among two or more, but not necessarily among all, cultures" (1955:23). The real heart of his problem is to determine causal relations that can account for the growth of more complex levels of sociocultural integration. These then become the processes of evolution and can be expressed as laws when they are sufficiently refined.

Robert Adams' book, *The Evolution of Urban Society,* presents a carefully considered alternative to a unilineal evolutionary approach. Adams, like Steward, sees social complexity as the core of the issue rather than such things as temples, international trade, writing-craft specialization, or standing armies. That is, he stresses societal rather than material variables because the latter are symptomatic and often unique, permitting of only limited comparison between separate cultural entities. As he puts it (1966:12),

> Social institutions lend themselves more easily to the construction of a brief paradigm than do the tool types or pottery styles with which the archeologist traditionally works. But I also believe that the available evidence supports the conclusion that the transformation at the core of the Urban Revolution lay in the realm of social organization. And, while the onset of the transformation obviously cannot be understood apart from its cultural and ecological context, it seems to have been primarily changes in social institutions that precipitated changes in technology, subsistence, and other aspects of the wider cultural realm, such as religion, rather than vice versa.

Accordingly, Adams tried to show how the processes of development of two historically separate civilizations were similar, despite their overt and impressive cultural differences. He examined major transformations in detail, reasoning that the growth of civilization was not simply incremental but rather a series of steps by which *qualitatively* different levels of sociocultural complexity were attained. Therefore the subject of his study was what happened at each crucial step; and underlying his analysis was the theoretical position that the adaptation of society within its larger ecosystem was the controlling or guiding factor.

In contrast to those who have constructed universal or particular evolutionary models are many archeologists who have been concerned with stages of development represented in certain areas (Heizer and Graham 1971). The intellectual dependence of these studies on ideas of evolution should be clear, although the authors usually disavow any overt intent at traditional evolutionary thinking. In recent years the trend has been to describe culture history in terms suitable to each geographic or cultural region. That is, archeological stages are named for the places where sites exist rather than for some pancontinental or universal stage of development. This sidesteps the issue of assigning every episode in history to one of the theoretical steps in the evolutionary ladder, but in so doing it also incurs the problem of using specific cultural, rather than presumably universal, aspects of the cultures for description. In other words, it is difficult if not impossible to make direct comparisons among areas. Attempts to avoid this difficulty are seen in Willey and Phillips (1958) and Willey (1966a, 1971) where "stage" *names* are applied across cultures.

At this point it is useful, as an aside, to mention that the practice of describing areas in their own terms was initiated to do away with identifying sites as "middle Paleolithic," "Mesolithic," or "Archaic" when such terms have long since, by indiscriminate use, lost their original precision. Using terms invented in France to describe sites found in the Gobi Desert is sheer nonsense. Among a small group of specialists, shortcut terms may be useful, but they only cause confusion for most of us. To take a notorious example, the word "Neolithic" in various contexts has meant: a self-sufficient food-producing economy; an assemblage in which pottery is found; an assemblage in which polished stone tools are found; and a culture in which the people are settled but have no polished stone or pottery. In short, there are several definitions of "Neolithic," yet many archeologists of sound reputation continue to use the word indiscriminately and wonder what the confusion is all about.

A reaction to evolutionary thinking began with the "direct historical approach" that involved working back through time from the known present to the less well-known prehistoric past. This technique has not yet had the attention it deserves, and much valuable insight has been overlooked (but see McNeal 1972 and C. Nelson 1972). However, it is also possible to begin with the earliest cultures and work toward the present by trying to connect successive archeological periods. The first attempts of this sort were made in nuclear America, where the idea of a "co-tradition" was developed (Rouse 1954, 1957). This was a conscious effort to trace the historic development of the Peruvian civilization. Instead of considering Peruvian history as a number of discrete episodes appearing in time, the workers emphasized the continuity of the episodes. In so doing, they discerned parallel sets of traditions. This was an important step in historical reconstruction because it gave a framework that had meaning in culture as well as in time. But an interest in time and culture alone does not lead to historical interpretation.

The next necessary step was to view the separate traditions and try to understand them against a backdrop of environment and the other traditions with which they came in contact. It is out of this kind of study, based on solidly established regional traditions, that archeologists have been able to discern certain regularities in cultural development. To some persons, these regularities suggest the validity of cultural evolution. The contrast with nineteenth-century archeologists is that today the stages are discovered by examining data. They are not a priori theories to which data are fitted, although the concept that there are stages to discover harks back to earlier approaches.

The stimulus for a nontaxonomic, nonevolutionary approach came largely from the Old World. In America the approach has changed from taxonomy to the process of culture change. The most systematic descriptions of this approach have been made by R. Braidwood (1958) for Southwest Asia, and Willey (1960) for America, the two later making a joint appraisal (R. Braidwood and Willey 1962) of worldwide evidence. It is worth reviewing these efforts and comparing them with a taxonomic approach (Willey and Phillips 1958) to show how they fit into the general studies of culture history.

All thinking about long-range history begins with the obvious assumption that man originally had relatively simple equipment and social organization, and eventually developed the complicated technology and society that we know today. Though some will argue with the use of the term, this change from simple to complex is "progress." It might also be called the "course of culture history," "cultural evolution," or simply "development." Because development (that is, towards more complex, more differentiated, or larger) is undeniable in the long run, any description of culture history must somehow accommodate and, if possible, help explain it.

The most elaborate systematic summaries of New World prehistory to appear have been written by Willey and Phillips (1958), and Willey (1966a, 1971). The former describes culture history by putting all archeological remains into five "stages," which are variously defined on the basis of technology, economy, settlement, society, and esthetics. The stages are ahistorical in the sense that their relative chronological placement is not a primary factor in their definition; yet they are historical in the sense that in some areas they appeared successively. The Willey and Phillips attempt is impressive for its scope, but the fact that its main concern is with classification makes it hard to use for historical interpretation (cf. Caldwell 1959).

While Willey and Phillips were arranging American prehistory into stages, Braidwood was considering the developments that had led to the Old World civilizations. His interest was mainly in Southwest Asia, and the models he devised reflected this interest. In essence he described a series of subsistence-settlement "eras," each of which reflected man's increasing mastery over his environment and his increasing social complexity. The eras were based as much on hindsight as on the evidence at hand. In other words, Braidwood worked from the relatively known to the relatively unknown, but at the same time, as he established each era, he thought of it as a step from the simple to the more complex. Following Braidwood, Willey (1960) described American prehistory in much the same terms. Their jointly edited volume, *Courses toward Urban Life* (1962), clearly demonstrates that although both see progress—but they do not call it that—they recognize that it took place only when the environmental, social, and historical factors were favorable. In other words, they see culture history resulting from a complex interplay of natural and cultural variables. They stress the "cultural alternates" that man could and did choose. Their conclusions clearly indicate that the authors see culture history as a cultural, and not as a biological or supernatural, phenomenon. They also show that there is a discernible direction in man's development that can be understood only by taking a dynamic developmental, rather than a static taxonomic, approach.

Willey's volumes of *An Introduction to American Archeology* (1966a, 1971) take a different tack. This was an attempt to "follow through the histories of the *major cultural traditions* . . . the principal native cultures or major cultural groupings as these can be discerned in geographical space and in chronological time" (Willey 1966a:4). In this book Willey treated the traditions in each area in their own terms so that, whereas in Meso-America he dealt with the Pre-Classic, Classic, and Post-Classic of each civilization, in the Eastern Woodlands he found it useful to describe the Archaic, Woodland, and Mississippian traditions. This approach follows the definitions of significant periods developed by local archeologists; it does not attempt to impose on an area a set of stages that could be considered comparable from one area to another, and universal in scope.

In contrast to these works, the most popular and probably the most influential descriptions of prehistory ever written are *Man Makes Himself* (1951a) and *What Happened in History* (1954) by the late V. Gordon Childe. Childe's success lies as much in his masterly understanding of Old World prehistory—to a degree unparalleled—as in the sheer volume of his work. It is instructive to consider some of his viewpoints.

Childe described culture history by referring to the major technological and social advances as "revolutions" that enabled man to make better use of his environment. For Childe, man's social evolution went hand in hand with his technology. The first revolution, the "Neolithic" (that is, food-producing), allowed man to amass surpluses that allowed a dramatic increase in population and the support of craft specialists. Childe roughly equated his Neolithic stage with Morgan's (1878) "barbarism," but he subdivided it to allow for the effects of other technological advances, such as the use of copper and bronze.

Childe's *Social Evolution* (1951b) is an earlier, one-man summary of the same evidence that was compiled later by Braidwood and Willey (1962), and the conclusions are essentially that cultures have taken diverse roads but are tending in the same direction. In the sense that man has continuously improved his adaptation to his environment and thereby increased his numbers, Childe says that he "progressed," and he calls this progress social evolution. Although their conclusions were similar, Braidwood and Willey were little interested either in progress per se or in revolution.

The descriptive models used by Childe, Braidwood, and Willey attempt to tell what happened in prehistory and how it happened; they do not, except secondarily, try to tell *why* any particular event occurred.

Causal Models

Models of causation are quite different in their intent from descriptive models, although in some descriptive models there may be implied cause, as for example in cultural evolution. Concerning major changes in cultural orientation, causes like stimulus and response, environmental determinism, and racial qualities have been proposed. On a somewhat smaller scale climatic changes, invention, and diffusion have also been suggested as particular causes.

As an example of the broader approach we can cite Arnold Toynbee, who, in his *Study of History* (1934–1960), contended that cultural progress resulted from man's meeting the challenges placed before him. His point of view has strong religious overtones, and for this and other reasons has not been generally accepted. In many instances he relied on data that are now known to be incorrect, and in others he had no data and only assumed certain challenges where there may have been none. In any event, ex post facto it is difficult to know what a "challenge" would have meant to prehistoric man. In short, Toynbee's work fails to give much insight into the course of prehistory.

Ellsworth Huntington, a geographer, also made an attempt to organize culture history (1959). He tried to demonstrate the role of environment in determining civilization. In environment he saw opportunities that would be exploited by people who had the proper genetic makeup. Huntington believed vigorous civilizations could be developed only under rigorous climatic conditions. Albright (1957:121) proposes a series of six stages in the history of culture based on greater or less integration and differentiation through time. According to this approach, "the Graeco-Roman civilization of the time of Christ represented the closest approach to rational unified culture that the world has yet seen and may justly be taken as the culmination of a long period of relatively steady evolution." Culture history has also been written to demonstrate racial superiority. Hitler had his archeologists excavate extensively in Germany to trace the origins of the Aryan race, and he had his historians write histories that showed how the Nordics had led the world from the beginning of time. In expressing the view that Nordics are racially superior and thus bound to advance over their brethren, the Nazi archeologists were stating a biological theory of cultural progress.

Persons who take the view that cultures are basically conservative must often seek explanations for changes in influences from outside the culture. This is the position of many *diffusionists,* who hold that stronger or more advanced cultures exert important influences on lesser cultures. This view says nothing about the development of the strong cultures, but it may help one to understand the direction of transmission of certain ideas and techniques. Gordon Childe's book, *The Dawn of European Civilization* (1957), is a good example of diffusionist thinking. In that volume he attempted to show how Oriental civilization had influenced the course of European history. There is no denying a number of his data, but the more acceptable view today is that there was considerable indigenous development on the part of European peoples. The influence of the diffusionist view of culture is so strong that today many people, especially laymen, can hardly understand the independent invention of such complex cultural items as metallurgy or agriculture in several parts of the world. To adopt the view that all was diffused, however, reduces the problem to ridiculous proportions and leaves one groping for suitable diffusionary mechanisms that could have sped the ideas round the globe.

Migration is one such possible mechanism, and it has been invoked so many times to explain the unexplained that its mere mention is enough to cause one to stop and ask, "Why would people have migrated, and by what route?" Merely finding burned levels in towns and new types of pottery are insufficient to prove a case of migration (or even of invasion). It is very much to the point to consider seriously just what kind of evidence migration would leave. An example from historically documented times is the famous Hyksos invasion of Egypt, which, so far as anyone can tell, left no tangible remains; yet historical records suggest it was of fundamental importance in the disintegration of the thirteenth dynasty. Many authors now wonder whether there ever was a real invasion. There seems no logical home for a large invasion force and no remains other than myth and story to evidence a people who struck terror into the hearts of Egyptians some 3800 years ago.

Migrations and invasions certainly occurred, but the point we wish to make is that they must be proved and based on something more substantial than a wild guess that people may have come from an unexplored part of the prehistoric world. It all too often happens that when the unexplored areas come to be known there is nothing there from which an invasion force could have been mounted. In actual practice it seems most economical to look at each development in its own terms, assuming that most change will have been engendered locally. That is to say, a very close regard to chronology must be paid, and disjunctions in sequences treated from a solid base of evidence rather than from a brave use of guesswork. In Chapter 12 we gave an example of how an incorrect interpretation of dates coupled with the idea of diffusion resulted in an erroneous interpretation of the cultural development of Western Europe in the third and fourth millennia B.C.

Necessity is frequently invoked as the mother of *invention*, but the nature of "necessity" is one that requires considerable thought. Obviously, if ice descended on a previously warm area, people would have to leave or invent ways to stay alive in quite a different environment, but the immanence of most necessities is less obvious. It is well known from anthropological studies that what may seem vital to us would not seem so for other persons. We are gadget-ridden and hence limited in our mobility. It is not stretching the point to say that many people in America would have a hard time adjusting if they were deprived of electricity. It is necessary for them to have power to run their toothbrushes, radios, lawnmowers, and dishwashers. But what are these to a hunter? He feels no necessity to have any of the artifacts mentioned here and would hardly be likely to invent electric generators so that he could have them. It is sufficient to say here that natural events that would impair the ability of a people to survive will usually be counteracted (see Chap. 21 for a discussion of these adaptive adjustments).

People do, of course, invent things in time of crisis, but there is good evidence that more changes, or at least a greater variety of changes, will take place when people are relatively secure (Barnett 1953:81–82).

We have talked at length in previous chapters about adaptation, which is only another way of looking at invention. Inventions are often thought of as new kinds of tools, or houses, but the invention of appropriate forms of society is likewise relevant and must not be overlooked. In the course of human history social adjustments, particularly after basic technology was developed, were probably more important than innovations and style changes in tools. This follows from the concept that organization is what is important in cultural change.

Climatic changes are known to have had effects on human populations, especially during the Pleistocene; however, their effect on hunting peoples may not have been drastic. Of course, if ice covered an area, people would not have been able to live there, but advances and retreats of glaciers were relatively slow compared to the duration of a human generation. In other words, the oscillations of climate during the Pleistocene may have caused people to move without substantially disrupting their lives. When the precise climatic sequence, coupled with detailed archeological evidence, has been worked out in western Europe, it will provide a good case study of the degree to which climate affected the lives of the people. It looks at this time as though the change was not very substantial.

On the other hand, for people who were committed to agriculture, several years of drought and even very minor climatic changes in marginal areas may have had serious consequences within the lifetimes of individuals (Raikes 1967). The more specialized the economic adaptation, the more likely it is that environmental changes will affect the lives of people. This follows closely from theories of ecosystems (Harris 1969). Some of the effects may be seen in technology. For example, it has been suggested that woodworking tools spread with the advance of forests in Africa. We might also expect to find some people shifting the balance of their subsistence according to the proportion of hunting or gathering or farming.

Climatic changes are best understood in limited areas where there are good data on both climate and archeology. That is, we need to know changes in rainfall and temperature in sufficient degree that their precise effect on the distribution of soils, plants, and animals can be specified. And we need archeological dating precise enough to permit us to relate specific horizons in sites to the corresponding environmental conditions. Probably nowhere in the world have data been refined to a sufficient degree, but the best evidence comes from the American Southwest.

Turning now from extracultural to cultural factors, we can discuss the influence of invention and diffusion. These aspects partly represent possible cultural responses to factors like climatic change, but they may, and usually do, take place quite independently. Although many anthropologists and archeologists argue that culture is basically conservative, changing only when necessary, some students of culture change (Barnett 1953, for instance) have pointed out that change is inevitable in the long run. They do not insist, however, that change necessarily takes a continuous path in any particular direction. Changes that might be called inevitable are ordinarily in the realm of unconscious stylistic or dialectic changes (to use an analogy from language). The implications are that there is imperfect transmission of information from one person to another and that it is impossible to duplicate anything precisely. That is to say, the minor changes that have accumulated may, over a period of years, seem striking.

Beginning with some rather simple statements—that is, that cultures change and that on a worldwide basis they tend to change from technologically and socially simple to complex—we can see that in order to understand change we must first find out what happened in the past, but we cannot do so without taking into account what we want to find out.

We can begin by recognizing that most of any culture's artifacts and activities are likely to be only partly, if at all, related to the cause for the general form that culture has developed. This idea suggests that, for understanding trends and long-range changes, there may be aspects of culture that are more important than others. Given our interest in the general history of culture, our problem is twofold: to discover which changes were important in the long run and what caused them. It is here that we find System Theory most relevant, because it emphasizes the organizational aspects of society. By this line of reasoning, for example, we should be more interested in the fact that large groups of laborers were brought together to build the pyramids than in the changes in the architecture of the structures themselves. On the one hand, we have a mobilization for common effort of people who might otherwise have minded their own businesses. On the other hand, we have architectural and artistic changes that, although they may help us identify particular cultures, seem to tell us little about the crucial changes in society itself.

Perhaps we should reemphasize here that we must make our own choices about what is important. For this example we assumed that, over the long run, changes in the organization of society were more important than changes in technological efficiency or in style alone. This assumption in no way minimizes any efforts to trace the causes of the technological and artistic changes; it suggests only that for our present example these efforts seem peripheral.

A number of aspects of the development of human culture might be investigated by archeologists, although perhaps not simultaneously. Changes in technology and subsistence are obvious, and their causes may be discernible. Changes in the organization of society are not directly observable until graphic art and status symbols announce them, but they are "visible" in such structures as pyramids, which imply the mobilization, direction, and maintenance of laborers drawn from outside the range of any single community. We might consider organized warfare as also being closely related to, and an indication of, the establishment of an impersonal and complex status-oriented society.

Still another aspect of human history is the "decline and fall" of certain societies and the changing importance of others relative to neighboring societies. The apparent collapse of the Classic Maya is an example of the former; an example of the latter is the emergence of powerful and colorful societies in the southeast United States or on coastal British Columbia that outstripped their formerly equal neighbors in social organization and wealth. As archeologists, we can ask why these particular changes occurred and, if we can discover their causes, whether our reasons are applicable to general statements about human history. In essence the procedure is to eliminate as many secondary factors as possible so that we can see the more fundamental issues.

We must therefore try to understand particular situations in terms of the situations themselves rather than in terms of some arbitrary set of stages or theories of trends. In any situation there are physical conditions (geographic and demographic) that can be specified. At the same time, it is usually possible to specify many of the technical skills of prehistoric people by observing the tools they used, the things they made, the things they ate, and the things they traded. To this we can add knowledge of social organization and relations to surrounding people. When these factors have been specified, even though we are ignorant of language, customs, and beliefs, we can still, by trying to see how each of these elements relates to the others, make tentative attempts in the direction of understanding. In this way we begin to see how people in the past acted and interacted with their physical and social environments. When we have listed these factors for a number of sites, we may begin to see recurrent situations. This is the traditional approach exemplified by Steward and Adams in their works on the evolution of society, and another good example is the work of Michael Coe (1961), who compared the ancient Maya and Khmer civilizations and found similarities in the environmental situations that suggested possible causes for the form that each society took.

In Coe's view, geographic homogeneity, even distribution of resources, difficulty of travel, and an easily produced surplus of food, predisposed both civilizations to develop "unilineal" societies with a strong religious focus. He contrasts this society with that of highland Mexico and Mesopotamia, where, except for abundant food production, opposite factors prevailed and the civilizations were "organic," held together by economic needs. This analysis, incidentally, relieves one of the problem of trying to relate very similar developments to migration or other sorts of influences of one population on another.

Similar studies might be made—not of moments in time—but of sequences where changes are dramatic, and even of sequences where changes are not evident. In these instances we should focus on determining the causes for change or stability. When dependable data covering long periods of change or stability are not available, archeologists have resorted to picking examples from a variety of places, and trying to account for what they find in the various situations. This task is exceedingly difficult because of the many variables involved. It would seem more fruitful to concentrate these kinds of analyses on sequences where the basic situations remain relatively unchanging and where the influence of specific factors can be assessed. That is, within an unbroken sequence in one region, it is relatively easy to detect things like climatic change, the influx of new people, new technology, and the like, and to see reactions by the local people to them.

This review of the ways archeologists have described and interpreted culture history was intended to show the heuristic value of models and to show how the different kinds of models relate to scientific method. The overall tenor of this book has been that there are ways to do archeology that have more chance of success than others have. The techniques described are only aids or tools that contribute to a realization of the ultimate goals. The proper methods, we reason, are those of science, and the strategies those appropriate to archeological interests. Many problems in human history are too complex to handle today, but the large problems can usually be broken into smaller, more manageable ones. When the small problems are clearly stated in relation to the overall goals, they can often be solved quickly and efficiently. The problem for archeologists is to learn to state the problems accurately, in such a way that they can be solved. Usually this procedure means framing an hypothesis and testing it. On the scaffolding of solid, tested hypotheses we can expect to erect a structure of culture history that will be not only as good as any other but perhaps better. In the end, any structure may fail, but the best structures stand firm in the light of current data and theory. Only revolutionary discoveries and great theoretical advances should call well-built structures into question. But we should remember that "ideas are to be used, not believed." Belief converts ideas to unquestioned ritual, a luxury we can ill afford. Fact is the closest approximation to the truth at any moment, but the world has seen one treasured fact after another fail the test of new ideas.

REFERENCES

General: R. Adams 1966; Bagby 1963; Bernal 1969; Caldwell 1959, 1966; Chang 1967a; G. Clark 1953a, 1953b; Coulborn 1959; Daniel 1968; Deetz 1967; Dray 1957; Heizer and Graham 1971; Kroeber 1953; MacWhite 1956; Melko 1969; Quigley 1961; Renfrew 1968b, 1972a; Riley 1969; Rouse 1953; Sanders and Price 1968; Service 1968; W. Taylor 1948; Willey 1966b; Wolf 1967.

Preparation of Archeological Site Reports: Brodribb 1970; Bryant and Holz 1965; Grinsell, Rahtz, and Warhurst 1966; Lester 1967; Piggott and Hope-Taylor 1965; R. H. Smith 1970; Webster 1963:Chap. V; Wheeler 1956: Chap. XVI.

Regional Histories: For examples, see the list of such books in print in Ancient Peoples and Places Series, London: Thames and Hudson (New York: Praeger).

Descriptive Models: R. Adams 1966; L. Binford 1966; Bordes 1971; R. Braidwood 1958, 1960; R. Braidwood and Reed 1957; R. Braidwood and Willey 1962; A. Bryan 1969; Butler 1965; Caldwell 1958; Childe 1944a, 1944b, 1951a, 1951b, 1954; D. Clarke 1972; J. D. Clark and others 1966; Collins 1970; Daniel 1943, 1971b; Gathercole 1971; Klejn 1972; Kroeber 1962; McKern 1939; Meggers 1959; Morgan 1875, 1878; G. de Mortillet 1903; Piggott 1960; Rouse 1954, 1955, 1957, 1958; Rowe 1966; Sherratt 1972; Steward 1949, 1955, 1968; Vogt 1964; Willey 1960, 1966a; Willey and Phillips 1958.

Causal Models: Albright 1957; Bagby 1963:Chap. 6; Barnett 1953; L. Binford 1968a; Childe 1957; G. Clark 1966; J. D. Clark 1960; M. Coe 1961; Dray 1957; Erasmus 1968; Flannery 1966; Harner 1970; Huntington 1959; Kossina 1941; Raikes 1967; Renfrew 1967, 1968b, 1970a; Sabloff and Willey 1968; Spengler 1926–1928; Tortelot and Sabloff 1972; Toynbee 1934–1960; Willey and Shimkin 1971.

Civilization—Descriptions of and Methods of Analyzing: R. Adams 1966; Bagby 1963; Bernal 1969; Daniel 1968; Heizer and Graham 1971; Hole 1966; Kroeber 1953, 1962; MacNeish 1964; Melko 1969; Quigley 1961; Renfrew 1972a; Riley 1969; Sanders and Price 1968; Wolf 1967.

CHAPTER TWENTY-ONE

CONCEPTS AND METHODS OF PROCESSUAL INTERPRETATION

Our final chapter is primarily theoretical, dealing with concepts that have become important in prehistoric studies only in recent years. At the time of this writing relatively few substantive results have come from the use of new models of thought. We are concerned here primarily with the way cultures operate as systems and the ways in which they change. Most of this book has been concerned with the acquisition and interpretation of data from sites and only the preceding chapter has dealt explicitly with the historical course or development of cultures. In that chapter the methods discussed were derived in part from history and from the historical natural sciences such as paleontology. The emphasis on developing taxonomic frameworks of culture history comes directly out of these fields. What is more, in preceding chapters we dealt principally with particular cultures rather than with general cultural development and the principles that underlie it. Now we turn to unifying concepts based on principles of organization that attempt to place all studies of cultures in a common perspective.

We begin with a discussion of the contrasting viewpoints of science and history as they have been expressed by archeologists, and then we turn to the question of processes. Next we deal with concepts of culture and cultural processes, especially as they relate to general system theory. Finally we give some examples of processual studies in archeology today and some suggestions for further work.

Science and history are two approaches to the study of prehistory, and in order to understand how prehistorians reconstruct and interpret the past it is necessary to examine them more fully. The choice of one or the other of the approaches has an effect upon the concepts that are used and the manner in which they are employed. The two approaches are not antithetical nor mutually exclusive, although they are sometimes so characterized. The historical approach implies a concern for arranging events in the past in sequential order and interpreting the unique events that make each history distinct. Science starts with the premise that the past can be understood rationally, and it attempts to get at general principles of human behavior and explanations of particular events through the testing of hypotheses.

HISTORY

Archeologists have debated whether history is or can be scientific and whether historical explanations are grounded in a well-defined set of concepts and theory. Archeologists sometimes claim that history is basically a descriptive discipline whose chief activity is to set down in chronological order events that happened in the historic past. They also point out that historians usually write about things they think are interesting and so exercise an element of judgment about what to include or leave out (of course archeologists can also be criticized for their selectivity). Thus even a descriptive account must be an interpretation. But most historians do not leave it at that; they go on to tell why they think the course of history was as it is written, and so they enter the realm of explanation. What constitutes explanation in history strikes some archeologists as inadequate, and this would seem to be a fair appraisal if we examine the writings of some authors—chiefly in the nineteenth and early twentieth century—who imposed their own moral or economic doctrines on their accounts of the course of history. Today historians freely employ social science theory and are much less bound by their own cultural heritage in devising explanations.

Trigger (1970:30) criticizes some archeologists' views of the nature of historical research and explains what he thinks is the principal differences between history and the social sciences.

> History differs from the social sciences in that it aims to explain individual situations in all their complexity rather than to formulate general laws for indefinitely repeatable events and processes. . . . This does not mean that historians deny the existence of general rules: rather they seek to employ them to gain an understanding of individual (i.e. unique and non-recurrent) situations. The social sciences, on the other hand, extract recurrent variables from their socio-cultural matrix so that relationships of general validity can be established between them.

Trigger (1970:31) goes on to say that there is no basic dichotomy between science and history. "History and the social sciences are like the two sides of a coin—complementary rather than antagonistic."

In the writing of new archeology, history has been called ideographic (particularizing), and social science, nomothetic (generalizing). These terms usually have been used without explanation but their origin is in the presumed antithesis of the two approaches, an antithesis that serves little useful purpose inasmuch as many archeologists and historians use both.

An article by Sabloff and Willey (1968) has provoked much of the discussion (L. Binford 1968a, Erasmus 1968, Trigger 1970, Watson, Leblanc, and Redman 1971) about the differences in approach and the resulting explanations. It is worth reviewing the arguments for purposes of illustration.

Sabloff and Willey, following the general sequence of investigation advocated by Willey and Phillips in *Method and Theory in American Archaeology* (1958), contend that one must first learn what happened, then determine why. In the case they discuss, the collapse of Lowland Maya civilization is attributed to an invasion, a particular historic event. They find this historic explanation more satisfying than a processual explanation which attempts to account for the reasons an invasion was successful. That is, they were not very concerned with possible problems in the economic, social, technological, or ideological sectors of Maya life that might have allowed an invasion to result in a sudden and widespread collapse. It has rightly been pointed out that total collapse is not a common consequence of invasion. Why in this instance? L. Binford (1968a) argues that Sabloff and Willey have simply offered a common-sense explanation and have not attempted to test its implications; in consequence it stands solely as an opinion, not as fact. We may see the disagreement as concerning two questions: (1) Has an invasion been adequately demonstrated? and (2) If an invasion occurred, does it explain the collapse of the Maya? Watson, LeBlanc, and Redman (1971:33), in a review of the same problem, put Binford's critique into the language of logical positivism:

> If invasion is to explain the collapse of the Lowland Maya, then appeal must be made to a confirmed general law of cultural process, of which the Mayan example is a particular instance. However, no such culture processual law has yet been confirmed. Hence, in order to explain what happened to the Lowland Maya, priority must be given to testing such processual laws to be applied to such cases.

In the meantime there is no "explanation."

Most archeologists—and historians too for that matter—are not prepared to wait around until someone confirms a general law under which the collapse of the Maya can be subsumed. The problem will not be trivial.

> What is the appropriate general law under which we can subsume (and thus explain) the collapse of the Lowland Maya? At the present time no such general law has been confirmed, but if we were to make explicit (formulate as hypotheses) the implicitly assumed laws of cultural process included in

references to invasions as explanations, and then test these hypothetical laws, we could, logically speaking, arrive at confirmed general laws of culture process which might explain the Maya case (Watson, LeBlanc, and Redman 1971:27–28).

Reliance on untested implicit assumptions is disallowed by the methodology of science and should not be condoned by scientific archeologists, who insist on formulating assumptions explicitly in hypothetical explanations to test them in order to confirm or disconfirm them (Watson, LeBlanc, and Redman 1971: 27).

To this attitude, Trigger (1970:35) remarks, "The archaeologist who is primarily interested in formulating laws about sociocultural processes might better become a social anthropologist or an ethnologist and work with existing or historically well-documented peoples rather than with the more refractory material of archaeology." Trigger's opinion is shared by many who feel that if archeology has anything to offer it is the particular and the unique events of the past. Until such time as one can infer all the courses of human history from the present (an unlikely possibility) much of the appeal of archeology will lie in its ability to tell—by reference to the things that remain—what happened in the past.

SCIENCE

In the first chapter we described some of the new approaches in archeology and we have just presented an example of a debate that contrasts stereotypes of the historical and scientific approaches. Watson, LeBlanc, and Redman come out very strongly for a strict scientific approach based on the philosophy of logical positivism, which is, as expressed by philosophers, an ideal view of how some science is practiced. That this approach is not followed by all, even Nobel Prize winners, is dramatically described in *The Double Helix* by James Watson (1968), a point recognized by Watson, LeBlanc, and Redman (1971:15). The essential point, however, is not so much how one does science but what are one's criteria of explanation.

If we can all agree that one important goal is explanation of particular events and processes in the past, then we must agree first on what we mean by explanation. If we agree that explanation means subsumption of the particular events and processes under appropriate general or covering laws, then we must agree on the source of these laws: Do the necessary confirmed laws already exist, or must we formulate and test them? If the former, what are they? If the latter, how do we go about it? Can we use the archeological record to help us formulate and to test hypothetical laws about particular events in human prehistory and processual aspects of human behavior, and about major aspects of culture and cultural processes? Yes, of course, to the extent that archeology is pursued as a science (Watson, LeBlanc, and Redman 1971:171–172).

To the extent that archeology is a science, it must be able to ask the correct questions. "If we ask something without knowing what the possible answers are, then we have not really posed a question; we have instead requested help in formulating a question" (Tribus and McIrvine 1971:179). To the historian interested in explaining why Maya society collapsed, *an* answer is invasion. To Watson and her co-authors, the answer is that the Maya conformed to a general law. In other words, the question as stated has no meaning because it does not suggest answers that might be tested to reduce the uncertainty about which is correct. At least, as L. Binford (1968a) points out, one can test an invasion hypothesis. Similarly one could test whether disease, depletion of the environment, emigration, or internal revolt contributed to the decline. But it is not clear that one can answer the question by invoking a cover law the essentials of which are unfathomed. One might just as well say, "it happened," and let it go at that. For some time we shall probably have to be content to recognize that there are two distinct levels of operation with which we may be concerned: description of particular events and an accurate interpretation of the factors that accompany them; and an attempt to discover underlying principles of human behavior. In the latter we should probably deal with events and processes that are current and readily controlled, while keeping in mind that if they have been correctly interpreted, they should pertain as well to events in the past.

THE SCIENTIFIC METHOD

A scientific approach in prehistory is inextricably linked with the methods of science. For the most part science is analytic and attempts to isolate and explain the relationships between two or more variables. In order to do this it is necessary to reduce problems to the smallest units that have the properties we wish to explain, and to control or hold constant extraneous variables. The next step is to test various hypotheses concerning the causal relationships. If this is carried out successfully, one hypothesis that cannot be rejected will remain. Subsequent tests of other relationships enable a scientist to build up a set of laws that can be combined into a general law covering all the variables that have been under investigation. This procedure has worked exceptionally well in the physical sciences, and it has its applications in the biological social sciences as well, although it has not been so notably effective. Buckley (1968:xvi–xvii) suggests reasons for this. Biology and social science depend on concepts outside the scope of physical concepts: "organism, life, birth, death, sex, viability, adaptation, behavior, cell, organ, evolution, . . . mutation, selection, . . . etc." Although physical sciences are making some contributions toward understanding these things, "still an irreducible residue remains. Biological processes are simply too complex to yield to the scientific method" (Buckley 1968). The problem is even more complex when we try to deal with human behavior where motives play an important role; what we perceive is a person or a group acting in a certain context but we find it virtually impossible to analyze the event into its constituent parts.

The crucial point is that when we are dealing with prehistoric peoples we are concerned with whole entities—tribes, societies, and cultures—or subsets like social organization or economics. What is characteristic about these is that they imply organized relationships among people and among the activities denoted by the subsets. In other words, we are dealing with systems in which the "whole functions as a whole by virtue of the interdependence of its parts" (Buckley 1968: xvii). It follows from this definition that we cannot understand systems simply by analyzing their component parts. Together the parts do not add up to a system. We will take this up in detail in the section on system analysis.

This is not to say that the analytic methods of science have no use in the study of systems; on the contrary, they do, but primarily to test hypotheses about particular happenings. We have mentioned invasion as a happening, and L. Binford (1968a) has given the test implications so that we may verify whether or not it actually occurred. Let us look at another problem of a type that is common in archeology, the solution of which is crucial if we are to make accurate interpretations of culture processes.

Let us say that we find a new type of pottery appearing abruptly in a sequence and we wish to explain its sudden appearance. We make the hypothesis that it was traded into the site from elsewhere. (Until we have determined whether it had an external origin, it is fruitless to consider the factors that may have allowed it to be incorporated into the local inventory.) We should also make the counterhypothesis that the pottery was locally made. Then we can set up some test implications for which we need the following kinds of information.

1. Is the chronological sequence into which the pottery appears complete, or does it have significant gaps?
2. Is there continuity with respect to some types of pottery and perhaps other artifacts in the sequence?
3. Do the "foreign" types of pottery have designs or shapes different from the presumed locally made wares?
4. Are the clays of the "foreign" pots different from the clays used to make the local wares?
5. Are the "foreign" wares functionally similar to the local wares, or are they special types that might have been used in ceremonies?
6. Are the "foreign" wares and local wares found in the same kinds of archeological contexts?
7. If the clays, designs and/or styles of pots are different, can they be shown to be typical of pots made in other areas?
8. Can a mechanism of trade be postulated or demonstrated? That is, what was traded for the pots? For example, if site A manufactured shell beads for trade to site B in exchange for pots, are the beads found at site B?

Answers to this list of questions should show that one of the hypotheses is false and may raise other hypotheses which can be similarly tested. Once the problem of diffusion or local invention has been resolved one can turn to a consideration of the processes that may have accounted for this fact.

PROCESSES

The term "process" or "processes" crops up frequently in the writings of scientific archeology, and it is also used in history, in manufacturing, and in analysis. As we understand the term colloquially it refers to the sequential set of operations that lead from A to B. Thus the process of manufacturing an automobile includes the mining and smelting of the raw materials, the fabrication of parts, the assembly on a moving line, the testing that accompanies the various stages, and finally the road test of the completed car. Similarly, we have referred to the archeological cycle, or the sequential steps involved in a research project. This is the process of doing archeology. In discussing biological evolution we mentioned three processes—natural selection, drift, and mutation—that account for changes in the genetic composition of populations over time. In history certain processes are similarly mentioned: diffusion, invention, warfare, and emigration. One can readily see that process means two quite different things. First, it may refer to a *sequence of events*. Second, it may refer to the *causes* of the sequence of events. In both meanings, process is conceptually linked with the states or conditions of the things under observation at different times.

As process is used in archeology (cf. processual analysis, process archeologists), it refers to an analysis of the factors that cause changes in state; that is, from "barbarism" to "civilization." Processual archeology is an analysis of causes by reference to stated relationships between variables and the testing of these postulated causes with archeological data. The nature of the relationships between variables depends on one's conception of how the thing under observation—in this case prehistoric cultures—works. D. Clark (1968:72–82) sees prehistoric cultures as complex dynamic systems that are regulated by various mechanisms as defined in General System Theory. Although Clarke (1968:22) regards "inevitable variation, multilinear development, invention, diffusion, and cultural selection" as the primary processes, the way he relates them to changes in culture is through the use of system theory.

The so-called "process school" in new archeology is explicitly scientific in the sense described in Watson, LeBlanc, and Redman, *Explanation in Archeology* (1971), although its authors do not discuss processes as such. General statements of process archeology are also found in Flannery (1967a) and Binford (1968a).

GENERAL SYSTEM THEORY

We turn now to concepts of General System Theory that are relevant to adaptive systems. In principle, General System Theory is applicable to other kinds of systems, but our archeological problems generally have to do with adaptation and adaptive changes in cultures. It is important to stress at the outset that we are dealing here with models of organization and behavior that have been derived from analysis of systems generally, rather than particularly from known archeological data. This degree of abstraction from real data is useful because it simplifies a conceptual overview, but the worth of any such models will ultimately have to be demonstrated by careful testing. Because the General System framework of analysis is relatively novel in archeology, the discussion that follows will indicate a latent potential rather than a firmly founded set of facts or procedures.

Boulding (1956b) made the tentative nature of our efforts clear when he reviewed possible levels of theoretical discourse. The levels are arranged in a hierarchy of increasing complexity that begins with static structures like a description of human anatomy or a settlement pattern and then changes to higher levels as more complexity is introduced. Motion and interaction are added to the second level, and then various controls such as feedback and communication, until they ultimately become the self-conscious goal direction of individuals and human societies. At the highest level (level 8), ". . . we must concern ourselves with the content and meaning of messages, the nature and dimensions of value systems, the transcription of images into a historical record, the subtle symbolizations of art, music, and poetry, and the complex gamut of human emotion" (Boulding 1956b:16). Boulding hastens to add that social sciences are about at level 2 empirically, although social scientists aspire to understand level 8. With these caveats in mind, we can now turn to a discussion of the nature of systems.

The Nature of Systems

Fundamentally there are two kinds of systems, open and closed. The closed system is one that tends toward disintegration and entropy, whereas the open system is dynamic and tends toward growth and differentiation. Human societies fall into the latter group and are consequently best understood with concepts derived from the study of other open systems. In other words, models of organization that are based on mechanics are of only limited value in helping us understand human systems. However, in their simplicity they suggest ways of looking at organization that we may regard as a first approximation, although we know ahead of time that they will be insufficient and incomplete for a final analysis (Renfrew 1968b).

It is worth noting here that we can consider different levels of organization. We are concerned with individuals only insofar as they are members of a social system; our analysis focuses on the system rather than on particular people. We have already discussed this in relation to ecology, where we indicated that ecological processes operate only on populations or communities, and not on individuals. The latter are dynamic open systems, whereas the former are closed systems that conform to the thermodynamic principle of entropy as the life processes carry them from birth to death. Populations, species, and cultures, however, exist as systems independently of the life histories of their members and have the characteristic, as systems, of being open, thereby defying the principle of entropy.

It is useful to reiterate some of the characteristics of systems. Hall and Fagen (1956:18) give a terse definition: "A system is a set of objects together with relationships between the objects and between their attributes." For different problems under investigation within the same overall system the set of relations that are important will change. For example, in an archeological study of settlement pattern the color of a house may be considered irrelevant or trivial; however, if it can be shown that color of houses is related to status or ethnic group, it may be a useful attribute of houses to record and consider.

The causal relations among objects in a system must be defined in finite spatial and environmental context. Again A. Hall and Fagen (1956:20) express this well: "For a given system, the environment is the set of all objects a change in whose attributes affect the system and also those objects whose attributes are changed by the behavior of the system." This is another way of saying that we are concerned with only the subset of objects and the relations that have a bearing on our problem—adaptation, because adaptation is concerned with causal relations. It should be obvious, however, that not all objects have an equal effect on all others, and that a change in one need not affect all others. There are degrees to which any set of elements in a system mutually interact. Some things are more important than others.

Some Relevant Concepts

The question now is, "What concepts are relevant to archeological problems?" Most such concepts have to do with an interpretation or explanation of change in organization.

Organizations have some or all of the following properties: wholeness, growth, differentiation, hierarchical order, dominance, control, centralization, and competition.

The wholeness of organizations suggests that they are more than the sum of their parts and therefore not amenable to analysis as *organizations* by considering the parts separately. The emphasis must be on the relations rather than on the parts. This fact was expressed well by Rashevsky (1967:21), who was attempting to isolate the nature of isomorphism between organisms and societies. He said, ". . . one of the difficulties inherent in the question as to whether societies are organisms and vice versa disappears when we keep clearly in mind that such statements are applicable only to the *relational,* but not to the physical and metric aspects of either organisms or societies," This statement underscores the approach taken in General System Theory to seek isomorphic or analogous units of analysis in diverse phenomena to arrive at generally applicable theoretical statements.

In stressing the relational links between elements in the human society (or in any organization) we are concerned with *communication,* a topic that has been intensively studied in relation to regulatory mechanisms of machines. This study, generally called cybernetics, uses communication and feedback to explain how systems regulate themselves to maintain a steady state, or homeostasis. Temperature-controlling mechanisms in mammals are the classic example of homeostatic systems. In these systems, deviations from the norm are counteracted: when the room gets too cool, the thermostat activates the heater. A simple diagram will illustrate this feedback principle of self-regulation (also see Figs. 76–78).

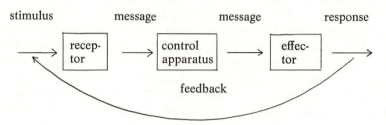

The stimulus "too cold" is received by the thermostat, which acts as a stimulus to initiate the response of turning on the heater. When the temperature has risen to the prearranged degree, the thermostat through the feedback loop initiates the response of turning the heater off. There are many analogous regulatory mechanisms in the human body and in organizations generally. Note, however, that if organizations always operated this way there would be no change without a change in the organization itself. In homeostatic systems the outcome is determined by initial conditions. Obviously, organizations change; hence the simple homeostatic model is insufficient to explain such characteristics as growth or differentiation. The mechanical model covers special conditions, but is too simple for many human situations. This model, however, puts the stress on maintenance of a predetermined condition. Feedback-induced changes are a simple form of adaptation, although they do not allow for a change in structure that is implied in our view that *human organizations are adaptive systems:* ". . . they possess the ability to react to their environmnt in a way that is favorable, in some sense, to the continued operation of the system" (Hall and Fagen 1956:23).

Maruyama (1963) treats this dynamic aspect of organizations under the rubric of "deviation amplifying-mutual, causal processes," the opposite of homeostatic "deviation-counteracting mutual causal processes." These systems are open in the sense that matter is introduced from the outside; that is to say, they are not completely determined by initial conditions. The closed system always reduces differentiation; the open system, on the contrary, tends toward differentiation. This change can be effected because matter (energy) is introduced from the outside. "Such systems can maintain themselves at a high level, and even evolve toward an increase of order and complexity—as is indeed one of the most important characteristics of life processes" (von Bertalanffy 1962:7).

Human organizations are dynamic, containing the potential for change.

> The dynamic-system model denies that the sociocultural system can be adequately characterized as a pre-programmed machine; the notion of complex adaptive organization suggests rather the generation of alternatives which are continually being selected during the process of operation by decision-making units. In this process, sociocultural structures of all levels of complexity may be generated, maintained, elaborated, or changed (Buckley 1967: 159).

Buckley's complex adaptive organizations are "goal-directed," and achieve the direction not only from preprogrammed instructions but also from on-the-spot decision making. According to Ackoff (1960), human organizations consist of two or more people who act in concert to make decisions about possible courses of action. Their actions are effected through communication that ultimately leads to a decision to take one course and not another. As for organizations, decisions will result in behavior that can run the range from adaptive to maladaptive. When the new behavior is significantly more adaptive, a new form of organization may result. This happens in cases where we see increasing differentiation and evolution. In the contrary situation, maladaptive organisms die or, perhaps more realistically with human societies, lose their relative competitive position. Importantly, however, they may be able to regain their position by making more appropriate decisions, if the first mistake did not finish them off.

In the history of human organizations, one of the major variables has been the amount of energy the people were capable of securing for their use. If the organizations were predetermined to a steady state, they would not be able to use, or effectively cope with, infusions of energy above the original levels.

One of von Bertalanffy's most novel concepts was that of *equifinality,* by which he means that "the final state may be reached from different initial conditions and in different ways" (von Bertalanffy 1956:4). This concept is in direct conflict with a model of organization of closed systems which states that the final state is unequivocally determined by the initial conditions. In human history, of course, we find numerous examples of the fact that peoples with different histories do arrive at the same end result, insofar as the organization of society is concerned. The concept of equifinality or convergent development has important implications for the archeological study of the growth of societies.

In system analysis a basic assumption is that *systems are complex* and can only be understood in their complexity. If a system is more than the sum of its parts, if follows that one cannot understand a system by reducing the analysis to the parts alone. It is the relationships among the parts—the organization of the system—that is central to system analysis. In archeology this means that we should study variation in sites and among sites and above all, the relationships among sets of data. It cannot be presumed that any one aspect of the archeological record is necessarily in itself informative about the system that produced it. Artifacts as such are of only minimal interest in system analysis; it is the information that the artifacts may give about the organized behavior which produced them that is important. A system perspective thus shifts our focus from things to relationships that are informative about organization. The degree to which organization is considered important can be judged in two analyses of the emergence of urbanism, in both of which the authors considered the tangible manifestations of civilization decidedly secondary to the organizations that were implied by them (R. Adams 1966; Sanders and Price 1968). We will discuss this in greater detail later.

Buckley's lucid introduction to *Modern Systems Research for the Behavioral Scientist* (1968) calls attention to three perspectives from which systems may be considered. These are especially applicable in archeology. First is the *structure* of the system: "the means by which it is enabled to receive, to store, to process, and to recall information." Second is the *functioning* of the system: "the way in which, by means of processed and stored information, the system responds by 'behavior outputs' to 'sensory inputs' from the environment." Finally, the *evolution* of the system: "structure, function, and evolution (or *being, acting,* and *becoming*) are fundamental aspects of all organized systems" (Buckley 1968:xx).

PRINCIPLES OF GROWTH

In archeology we are often concerned with the development of cultures. Such an interest is expressed in many ways: cultural evolution of several types has been proposed by authors as early as Lewis H. Morgan in *Ancient Society* (1878), and more recently by Robert Adams in his book, *The Evolution of Urban Society* (1966). Another view is to treat the stages through which cultures progressed. Such a view has been treated comparatively in a symposium volume edited by R. Braidwood and Willey, *Courses toward Urban Life* (1962); and this approach is especially prevalent in American archeology. All these attempts stem ultimately from the idea that cultures have tended to become progressively more complex, and the attempt has been to chart this change. The evolutionary nature of such changes is, of course, historically related to similar concepts in biology. However, most of these attempts have been based on a typology of steps rather than on the processes by which the steps were attained, and none was explicitly developed from a general theory of organic growth.

From a study of growth processes in a variety of contexts, system theorists have abstracted some apparently universal characteristics that can serve as testable hypotheses so far as archeological or culture-historical data are concerned. Of course, it is first necessary to have a suitable body of data with which to work. At the time of this writing such data are not available to archeologists, but with the theory in mind it should be relatively easy to construct a research design to test some of the hypotheses.

We can begin with a few simple concepts. In the first place, "growth" should be considered in its two aspects, negative and positive. We ordinarily think of growth as indicating a trend toward larger, but the reverse trend is also pertinent and probably follows the same general rules (see Fig. 78). As Boulding (1956a) developed it, there are three kinds of growth: simple, in which one variable changes; populational, in which there is a change in the birth-death ratio; and structural, in which there is a change in the relations of the parts of the structure. Boulding's article is a convenient point for the following discussion. Simple growth is a change in quantity; for example, more people, more houses, more area of site, and so on. Obviously, these quantitative data can be related to other factors; hence simple expressions of changes are not very revealing. Population changes, defined as a change in birth-death rates, can be treated by various mathematical models of rates that can then be projected in time to arrive at a picture of the age distribution within society at some time in the future; or they may be applied retrospectively to determine how a population attained its present composition. We simply do not have the kind of archeological data now or in the immediate future to allow us this kind of analysis. More interesting for us are structural changes, because there are several specific hypotheses relating to them that can be tested.

The Principle of Progressive Segregation

"The system changes in the direction of increasing division into subsystems and sub-subsystems or differentiation of function. This kind of segregation seems to appear in systems involving some creative processes or in evolutionary and developmental processes" (Hall and Fagen 1956:22).

Returning now to Willey and Phillips (1958), we find a Formative stage in American archeology. If the principle of progressive segregation is correct, we should find that archeological cultures during the Formative stage become increasingly differentiated. That this is true seems assured from results reported from Meso-America, but increasing differentiation is more difficult to prove with the existing data from other areas. In any event, a corollary to the principle might be that if progressive segregation does not appear, the society has reached a point of either equilibrium or of progressive desegregation—it is declining in complexity. Where cultures appear to "fall" (or, perhaps more correctly, to "fade away"), a clue to the onset of such a condition would be at the moment progressive segregation ceases. This aspect has not been examined archeologically thus far in any explicit fashion.

Principle of Systematization

In systematization there is a change toward wholeness, which "may consist of strengthening of preexisting relations among parts, the development of relations among parts previously unrelated, the gradual addition of parts and relations to a system, or some combination of these changes" (Hall and Fagen 1956:22). The process of systematization should be seen archeologically in the development of political orbits of larger size or in the integration of even politically simple societies through a process like the extension of ramified lineages (Sahlins 1958). The former example is more familiar in archeology and is especially pronounced in the growth of city states and empires. On a less spectacular level, we might also expect to find it in the growth of market centers, evidence of systematic interregional trade, or in temple or political centers that drew their support from a wide region.

It is important to note that segregation and systematization can occur simultaneously, but that this need not be the situation. One suspects, for example, that the developing societies in Mesopotamia show both processes, whereas those in Classic Maya area, because of their politico-religious nature, would show more systematization. What is more, the processes may occur in sequence. Following maximum differentiation, systematization could occur. It will be interesting in the future to see whether we can determine what the sequences of development in these terms were in various areas. In this way we may come closer to a crosscultural appreciation of the processes that led to civilization.

Principle of Centralization

In centralization one element becomes dominant in the system to the point that a change in this part greatly affects the whole system (Hall and Fagen 1956:22). A social analogue would be the dictator in a totalitarian regime. M. Coe (1961), following Durkheim, has described a totalitarian society as a mechanical society, and he thinks it can be found in the Maya area. Certainly there is evidence that the ceremonial centers were erected in honor of important political or religious persons (Proskouriakoff 1960), and there is relatively little evidence that there was a substantial group of other persons who comprised anything like a balance of "power." In this sense the chief would be dominant. One would expect, then, that his demise would shake the structure of society, at least in the parts of society that depended on him. Again the Maya offer a possible illustration. Many authors have speculated on the possibility that the end of Classic Maya culture occurred about A.D. 1000, when the ruling class was overthrown. The rapid decline of the Maya in the Peten is suggestive that such a hypothesis (following the principle of centralization) may be correct. Archeological data to support this notion may be hard to find, but if it should be determined that the lineages of ruling families died out, and were not replaced, the hypothesis would seem bolstered, even though not proved because of the great variety of counterhypotheses that could be offered (environmental change, disease, and invasion, for example).

Principle of Nonproportional Change

Many of our archeological data, especially from surface survey, are in the form of numerical expressions of size. It is worth noting that as the linear dimensions of a size doubles, the area enclosed is squared. In other words, a site that is twice as big in outline has four times as much space inside. If we simply divide the area by the assumed amount of space taken up by a house we can arrive at an estimate of the number of houses. However, the geometric increase in areal space raises certain questions about the growth of the structure whose answers are not obvious from surface survey alone. "As some of the essential functions and variables of structure depend on its linear dimensions, some on its areal dimensions, and some on its volumetric dimensions, it is impossible to keep the same proportions between all significant variables and functions as the structure grows" (Boulding 1956a:71).

Especially important is the question of communication among the various parts of the structure. In a small community, face-to-face contact ensures communication. A compensatory change in a larger community, whose total population increases geometrically as a function of its linear dimensions, might be to add to the bureaucracy, whose individual members can maintain face-to-face contacts with the constituents. In any event, it is clear that as any society grows larger there must be increased communication distance between the leader(s) and the followers. In a tribal society, communication is effectively handled through councils, whose members represent their constituent bands or clans, and by heads of families who meet in caucus with the clan leaders. In larger societies a more formal governmental structure is required, but the principle remains: a single representative of government can meet with only so many constituents; therefore, as the population grows, so must bureaucracy. The effectiveness of the communication between government and governed determines the point at which it is no longer feasible to allow the polity to grow. In economic terms, the "law of diminishing returns" applies.

The precise form that government will take to cope with a burgeoning population may be hard to predict, but it is certain, if we follow the principle of nonproportional change, that some compensatory adjustments will need to be made. Archeologically, we should see this in signs—for example, rank becomes more widespread—and perhaps also in the greater distribution of wealth as a bureaucratic middle class emerges.

Another kind of compensatory change would be to make the parts of society functionally separate, following a previous principle of progressive segregation. In this event, needs for communication could be reduced by developing autonomy of parts or rigid and ritualistic patterns of behavior (Boulding 1956a:72). The development of a segment (for example, castes or classes) whose position in society goes unquestioned would be a good example. Archeological evidence of such behavior would be found in clear-cut differences among segments of the society; however, if members of castes were not kept separate spatially, evidence of this kind of social structure might be hard to infer.

Principle That Growth Creates Form, but Form Limits Growth

"This mutual relation between growth and form is perhaps the most essential key to the understanding of structural growth" (Boulding 1956a:72). A structure builds from what it has. Once a structure has certain characteristics, it must take these into account in subsequent changes. Some structures are probably more limiting than others in terms of ultimate growth. In other words, diminishing returns may set in at different stages of growth, depending on the nature of the structure. The truth of this principle is suggested by the principles already discussed.

Archeologically, we might find evidence of the limits of certain forms of structure in the size typically reached. If significantly larger polities came to be incorporated, they might suggest a fundamental change in the structure.

Principle of Equal Advantage

"The advantage of a unit in any location is an inverse function of the relative quantity of units in that location" (Boulding 1956a: 73). That is, it is more advantageous to have no competition. One would therefore expect to find that units of society would bud off until unused space of equal advantage had been used; then units of larger size, accompanied by progressive segregation and/or systematization, would emerge if the population continued to grow.

An archeological example is provided by the spread of prehistoric settlements of fairly uniform size in western Iran following the beginnings of agriculture (Hole and Flannery 1968). In this instance each settlement appears to be self-sufficient and retains in its immediate surroundings enough land to maintain self-sufficiency. In time there was no more land of equal advantage, and compensatory changes had to ensue if the population was to continue growing. The data suggest that nucleation occurred and, with it, progressive systematization (R. Adams 1962), but these beliefs have not yet been demonstrated beyond doubt.

The principles stated above can be considered hypotheses that one can test with data from surface reconnaissance and excavation. They serve to point up the fact that the stating of hypotheses suggests possible things to look for archeologically.

Omitted from consideration above, but obviously important to the structure of any developing society, are rates of change. It is often stated (for instance, Barnett 1953) that rapid change is harder to adjust to than slow change. It might also be assumed that the compensatory structures that are needed to cope with rapid change will be different from those that can handle slow change. There is also the question of what rates of change are "normal." Is there, for example, an equilibrium rate of change under which the structure of a society will remain constant? One might assume, from the example cited above, where villages of approximately equal size budded off from parent communities in West Iran, that there is an equilibrium rate. The subject, of course, needs further investigation.

Most published growth curves are based on the assumption that there was a fairly constant rate during the Paleolithic, when the level of population was low. A more rapid rate ensued after agriculture began; then there was a slowing of the rate until modern times, when it has again speeded up significantly, first following the industrial revolution and then following the advent of modern medicine. What happens to the structure of a society when growth rates change significantly? Are the structural adjustments as severe when growth stops or declines as when the rates speed up? Modern economic analyses suggest that smooth curves of economic growth are rare, and most of us have witnessed periods of economic prosperity and depression that had widespread repercussions. It matters not that we cannot assume analogous economic growth changes in prehistoric times; the point remains that changes in rates of population and technoeconomic development do have wide ramifications in society. If we think in these terms, we may find alternative solutions, or at least hypotheses other than those proposed, to account for declines and falls.

One of the areas in which there has been the greatest use of mathematical models of growth has been in the analysis of rates of growth. These models still remain relatively simple both because of the enormous potential complexity of the problems and because of lack of suitable data. One attempt that has implications in archeology was made by Naroll (1956), who sought allometric relations between the size of the largest settlement in a polity, the number of occupational specialties, and the number of organizational types. He used ethnographic data from several cultures and found that indeed there was a clear allometric relation among these three factors. "Allometric growth is defined as growth of one part relative to another part, or of a part relative to the whole, at such a rate that there is a linear regression of the logarithms of the dimensions" (Naroll 1956:689). That is, the growth of x varies as a function of the growth of y. In Naroll's example, the number of occupational specialties and the number of organizational types changed in a constant ratio with the size of the site.

This ratio could be stated as an archeologically testable hypothesis: the larger the site, the more segregation and differentiation there will be. Referring back to the principle of nonproportional change, we see that the number of potential relations among people in the society increases much more rapidly (exponentially) than sheer size would indicate. Naroll (1956:690) stated it this way:

> My sample suggests that when settlements contain more than about 500 people they must have authoritative officials, and if they contain over a thousand, some kind of specialized organization or corps of officials to perform police functions. . . . the larger the organization the greater the proportion of control officials needed.

Naroll's findings thus suggest that large settlements *must* have greater organizational complexity than small groups. This opinion is something that we should obviously be on the alert to try to recognize and to test.

One of the interesting hypotheses to develop out of the study of biological organisms is that growth rates of populations are functions of the density of the population. In other words, as the density increases, the rate begins to decrease, ultimately approaching a state of equilibrium. This ratio would have interesting implications for archeology if it could be stated as a general law, but a study by Tanner shows that it may not be directly applicable to human populations.

The hypothesis was tested by Tanner (1966), using data drawn from a wide variety of biological forms, with the conclusion that "a population's growth rate is a decreasing function of density" (Tanner 1966:733). But Tanner (1966:740) also found that human populations today are the only groups increasing their rate in spite of increased population density. The obvious question is why the rate of population change is related to density. Tanner adduces a number of standard ecological factors, such as disease, predation, competition, and the like, but he does not suggest an answer to the apparent disconformity of human population rates. In fact, if he were to examine the record of human history, Tanner would find it hard to explain the growth of the species throughout its course of development. The difficulty probably lies in the fact that most biological systems operate with limited resources. Temporarily, at least, this is not so with man, who has found ways of dramatically increasing his energy intake and hence has become more dominant relative to other species. Man appears to be operating in a system that is more "open" than that other species enjoy. This belief is forcefully expressed in several books by V. Gordon Childe, (for example, 1951a, 1954), in which he described the "revolutions" that have changed man's course of history: the Neolithic or food-producing, the urban revolution, and the industrial revolution.

If the hypothesis is true that populations generally, human included, are regulated around an equilibrium and that rates of change are functions of density, we must explain changes in size in spite of density as a function of other factors such as energy intake.

As an example of the kind of reasoning that leads to such a judgment we can cite a study of biological ecosystems by Patten (1959), in which the author used mathematical models based on energy flow in and out of the system. He then related these models to cybernetic concepts of information flow, concluding that "information is the antithesis of entropy, just as organic evolution is antithetical to the general evolution of the cosmos at large. . . . evolution implies increased order and organization, which are the statistical attributes of information" (Patten 1959:226–227). It follows that

> . . . the balance between information gained and entropy generated in a unity of time determines the dynamic state of the ecosystem. If more information is accumulated than used, the excess is converted to biomass. Such a condition of positive balance represents a growing or successional stage. If more entropy is generated than information gained, the system suffers a net loss of order and declines, as in senescence. When an exact balance between negentropy gains and losses is achieved, the ecosystem has reached a stable equilibrium with

respect to other disorder. Such a condition, sustained, marks climax (Patten 1959:231).

In archeology there are numerous situations of stability or equilibrium. Some classic instances have been found in the American West in sites attributed to the Desert Culture (for example, Jennings 1964; W. Taylor 1966). In these places cultures quickly reached a level of adaptation that was maintained throughout some 10,000 years. In terms of the preceding discussion we might regard these people as living in a system whose input energy potential remained constant and who therefore could not attain higher levels of systematization. Of course the contrast is striking with Meso-American peoples who lived in "nuclear" areas (Flannery and others 1967), where the energy potential was much greater and the course of history showed the peoples moving toward increasing differentiation and increased mass (that is, increase in population), reaching a climax in Classic and post-Classic times (see Figs. 76, 77).

CULTURE SYSTEMS

In Chapters 4 and 16 we discussed concepts of culture that put prehistoric studies into a wider intellectual context and that constitute a framework for interpretation. It remains to consider those aspects of culture that are relevant explicitly to a systems analysis of process.

A culture system consists of sets of behavior and the interrelations among them.

For purposes of analysis it is permissible to isolate separate sets, even though they are known to be interrelated. One can conduct analyses on several levels simultaneously, from the organization of the family to the entire society, depending on the purposes of analysis. In contrast, ascertaining the behavior sets involved in the production of a single type of artifact requires different theories and data, and they are directed toward quite different ultimate interpretive ends.

A culture system represents a balance between opportunities and the satisfaction of necessities.

The precise form of a culture system depends on a multiplicity of factors, many of which have never been assessed accurately either archeologically or ethnographically. There are many factors that we may never be able to assess. Among those we might mention, for example only, are a host of perished material culture, precise climatic conditions, and psychological or social factors in the minds of the extinct peoples.

A culture system tends toward higher levels of integration.

That a culture system tends toward higher levels of integration is another way of saying that it strives for greater efficiency, particularly with respect to obtaining food or other energy, and with respect to competition with neighboring peoples. In both contingencies we might expect to see changes in technology and in social organization.

If behavior tends to be adaptive, changes in behavior should be relatable to the factors adapted to.

If behavior is nonadaptive, or any set of behavior is nonadaptive, it should be replaced ultimately by more adaptive behavior.

Cultures change and different aspects of culture (again expressed in sets of behavior) change differentially.

Changes in sets of behavior, such as styles of artifacts, types of artifacts, residence rules, and the organization of society, will require different kinds of explanations.

Cultures tend to change in the direction of least possible effort, but incremental change is pervasive because of the impossibility of exact replication.

As was stated earlier, there are different kinds of changes, and they require different kinds of explanation.

The beliefs about culture remain beliefs for the most part, because in their stated form they are hard to test. We shall see in the final parts of this chapter how these beliefs can be restated as principles of systemic organization, and in such a way that they are amenable to analysis.

COMMUNITIES

Population and Community

The concepts of population and community are key concepts in ecology and are equally applicable in system analysis because the processes of adaptation, growth, diversity, and change operate on aggregates of individuals over time. They do not operate directly on single members of the species. However, as we read in ecology and anthropology, we find that the words "population" and "community" have been used in different ways. This factor may cause confusion unless we recognize that the basic differences in usage have to do with the size of the groups under consideration and the number of different species and inorganic factors that are included in the community.

Populations have the following general characteristics: a finite number of people, likeness of kind, aliveness, and limitation of universe in space and time (Allee and others 1949:265). A living biological population can be defined if we can specify how many persons it comprises, what kind of species are included, and where the members of the population are. We shall use the word "population" here to refer to what ethnologists call bands, tribes, or ethnic entities as distinct and identifiable groups of people.

The word "community" implies several things, and it may be used in different ways for different purposes. At the heart of any definition, however, is the concept that the community has functional integrity. It is composed of "ecologically compatible species populations whose collective ecological requirements of food, shelter, and reproduction are satisfied, in the last analysis, by a certain range of environments" (Allee and others 1949:437). "Community" thus introduces the notions of self-sufficiency that are not claimed for populations. Moreover, it implies that several distinct populations are in mutual interaction. In line with this reasoning, Lawson (1963:111) regards communities as processes or cycles of behavior among the various species or elements that interact in a mutually causal relation. That is, as living communities, the separate species which comprise them cannot be considered in isolation. To understand the processes of culture, then, we must consider the relation between people and the many facets of their self-sustaining world.

If a community embraces more than simply a population of one species or of one village, how big or inclusive need we make it? Here the decision belongs to the person making the analysis, because only he has the intimate knowledge of data necessary to determine the range of factors that will be required to solve his problem. If we take the broadest view of "community," it "may be defined as a natural assemblage of organisms which, together with its habitat, has reached a survival level such that it is relatively independent of adjacent assemblages of equal rank; to this extent, given radiant energy, it is self-sustaining" (Allee and others 1949:436). As stated earlier, this view varies from the usual anthropological or archeological conception of a community, which is taken to be the tribe or village under investigation. In the broadest sense, however, an ecological community (or ecosystem) consists of all the species that interact to form a self-sustaining entity. One or more of the species must be capable of utilizing an inorganic energy source because, obviously, people do not directly convert radiant energy and minerals to food; they do so through the intermediary plants and animals that they consume. Moreover, a village of people ordinarily interacts through marriage, trade, or similar social relations with other villages and groups of people. The concept of the biological community thus forces us to expand our traditional focus to regard things that are not "cultural" as integral parts of any viable cultural system.

In practice, ecologists and archeologists deal mostly with communities that are not too complex or diverse. We may consider, for example, all the people who comprise the sustaining area for one village. That is, all the people who are related through marriage, trade, or political ties form a viable social system that we may liken to a biological community. This is a convenient frame of reference, and we often find that our problems do not require us to consider the rainfall, edaphic conditions, growth of grass, or insect parasites; however, this chapter should serve as fair warning that such factors are important to some aspects of the human community. In archeology we usually select to study from the total ecosystem the portions that we can readily manage and that contribute to the solution of our problems.

Most of us deal "with the local communities comprising groups of animals, the members of which react socially to one another" (Klopfer 1962:130–131). Human communities so defined may contain one homogeneous undifferentiated ethnic group, a single ethnic group structurally differentiated, or several ethnic groups each with structural differentiation. The gamut runs from the simple hunter-gatherer band to complex civilizations with political centers, market towns, trading outposts, and foreign embassies. These can all be examined fruitfully with an ecological perspective.

The Ecology of Social Differentiation

A basic premise of the concept of community is that it has organizational structure. One way in which this structure is accomplished is through differentiation. Within the higher orders of organisms, members of groups are differentiated by sex, age, size, and behavior. Such differentiation is usually expressed in physical distinctiveness and by dominant and submissive behavior. In other words, some animals have greater influence over other animals and consequently gain priority of access to food, females, or other desirable things. In the differentiation of human populations, dominance is important.

Ecologists recognize two basic kinds of social communities—monospecific and polyspecific—referring, respectively, to those composed of one species and to those of more than one species. One cannot relate this directly to human groups, because all humans are of one species, but it is useful to substitute culture for species to see the implications of the distinction.

We find that most human societies are monospecific, being made of members of the same culture, but that most complex societies (especially civilizations) are polyspecific. Both the size of the group and the cultural homogeneity of the population will determine to some degree what sort of dominance hierarchy will obtain. In some societies the hierarchy is linear. In other words, a single person dominates the others. Such a situation is uncommon in human societies, but examples may be found from simple bands to dictator-led civilizations. More common are small populations in which there literally may be no designated "leader," but the larger the groups, the more likely it is that someone will take charge or be designated leader. His status will then be underscored by his dominant behavior and/or by symbols that express his difference. "Once a hierarchy has become established, the ability to recognize individuals greatly reduces the number of conflicts" (Klopfer 1962:133).

In human societies we find that people are usually divided by family and by occupation. Within each family and within each occupation there is a hierarchy, and, finally, each of these units may be ranked relative to all others. That is, some families may be dominant, and some businesses more important. The influence of the various members of the population will ordinarily be in relation to certain tangible aspects of dominance like size and wealth. In most complex societies too much power is held by several segments of the population to make a linear-dominance hierarchy enduringly feasible. Accordingly, we find many gradations along the scale of dominance.

Ecology gives us some reasons why social organization is necessary and some of the basic ways in which organization is accomplished. It alo indicates some of the problems inherent in a differentiated society. A major problem in a human society is to organize the people so that they can do their jobs with a minimum of mistakes and conflicts. In a simple society, where people are jacks-of-all-trades, this is no real problem, but it can be in a society which has many specialized segments. Ecologists have found that, as societies become more complex and statuses and roles (ranked jobs, for example) are added, it becomes more difficult for one person to recognize and react properly toward the statuses of all other people. This condition is especially true in a monospecific community when dominance differences are not physically obvious and when there are more individuals than any one person can know personally. People solve this problem by creating status symbols. These artifacts are to people what size, aggression, and color are to members of other animal communities. We can thus see status as a device to facilitate the orderly operation of a social system.

How do we use these ideas archeologically? In a monospecific culture there are two ways to express status—through the use of symbols and by creating castes or feudal classes. Anthropologists have found that the most elaborate symbols are used in societies where there is the greatest relative difference between the most dominant and the most submissive member. Should the symbols be preserved archeologically, they will be obvious, because they will be restricted to a very few of the total group. In a monospecific society without castes or great relative differences between top and bottom, status symbols will be common objects but perhaps of better quality or different material for the more important people (for instance, copper tools instead of stone). Because they restrict certain kinds of activities to each caste, castes are an alternative way of differentiating people. In this way the society comes to be made up of mutually interacting and interdependent specialized parts. In the most rigid of these societies there is no movement of people between castes. Archeologically, castes would be recognized by the nonrandom distribution of artifacts related to the activities of the caste, and probably also by the relative wealth of members of different castes. Physically, however, the people might all look the same. And it might also be very hard to distinguish members of a caste from persons who belong to occupationally specialized groups.

The most complex societies are multicultural, a situation analogous to different species of animals in a symbiotic relation. An important ecological principle is that two species cannot occupy the same niche; one will drive the other out. If we were to find evidence of two cultural groups coexisting in the same system we should expect to find that they occupied different occupational niches.

A good example of this idea from ethnography is Barth's (1956, 1960) studies of Swat Pakistan, where three distinct culture groups occupied a small area in symbiotic relation to one another. The dominant Pathans engaged in full-time agriculture on the best land, the Kohistanis divided their time between herding and farming, and the Gujars used the left-over space as grazing land for their animals. Collectively and in cooperation, they were able to make efficient use of the area. There is historical evidence that the Pathans drove the less strong Kohistanis out of the best land, providing a convenient example of the idea that cultures cannot remain in competition for the same resources over the long run. Similar examples come from African history and ethnology, where there are multicultural states and "feudal" kingdoms in which there is strict separation between the ruling classes and the peasants, who are ethnically different and remain in a dependent relation.

We should expect to find instances of such behavior archeologically. For example, such an explanation might sometimes be appropriate when peoples are known to have migrated. Then one would expect to find evidence that a dominant people drove out a less powerful group. Archeological evidence of this assumption would be found, let us say, in more efficient agricultural techniques or more complex social organization on the part of the dominant group. Relevant examples are provided by the later prehistory of sub-Saharan Africa, where dominant Bantu-speaking peoples, whose economy was based on cattle herding, moved into areas that had been exploited only by hunters and gatherers. Another example is that of the Plains Indians in the American West who became dominant after they obtained horses.

ECOLOGICAL SYSTEM ANALYSIS

The discussion of differentiation and dominance raises the issue of relations among members of communities or populations. As we stated earlier, human societies and the ecosystems of which they are a part, work in their own self-interest. Behavior is directed toward survival, which is effected only through a balance among cooperation, competition, exploitation, and predation. Klopfer (1962) put this in sharp focus in his chapter, "Why Don't Predators Overeat Their Prey?" The fact is, as students of cybernetics explain it, there are mutual causative factors involved; changes in one factor always cause changes in another factor. If a predator overate his prey he would die also, unless he had an alternative food source. If the number of predators is a function of the number of prey, a decrease in the prey will result in a decrease in the predators; in this way an effective balance is maintained. This is another way of stating that, to ensure survival, mutually beneficial interactions among the total set of factors in an ecosystem must obtain. Of course, this remark does not preclude the fact that the relations between any *two* species may be detrimental to one and advantageous to another.

The interrelations described above are a statement of organization, because the pattern of relations can be abstracted and the links between the elements specified. Consequently, ecology comes under the rubric of General System Theory and is amenable to investigation through the use of its concepts. Inasmuch as the emphasis is on the interrelations among elements, ecology must ignore an analysis that uses culture as its major determinant. It does so because one cannot easily count or describe cultures in ways that are commensurable for comparative or analytic purposes. As Vayda and Rappaport (1968:494) say, one must make a tangible unit, such as population, the focus of ecological studies, because "no such commensurability obtains if cultures are made the units, for cultures, unlike human populations, are not fed upon predators, limited by food supplies, or debilitated by disease."

To an anthropologist, culture is many things; whereas, to an ecologist, culture is an adaptive mechanism expressed in behavior. It is the same kind of variable as body size or speed in running, traits that are selected in the complex interplay of factors that ultimately make any kind of animal better or less suited to survival. In the same fashion, human behavior (culture) is constantly tested and modified in the course of human experience. What is more, culture seems no more important as a primary cause of human behavior (a view espoused by L. White 1948, 1949) than is, for example, climate. To make this statement, however, is only to deny primacy to any *one* cause, not to argue that either culture or climate is all-important or unimportant.

The preceding may sound contradictory, but it is only when you adopt a position that there are clearly specified simple relations of cause and effect. General System theorists and ecologists take the view that there are no such relations, at least in such complex areas as human behavior. They would stress that biological, physical, social, and cultural factors all play parts in affecting final outcomes through a process of mutual causation or circularity. There is no chicken and the egg paradox, because the issue is phrased so that both are necessary for the maintenance of the life system. It also points up the fact that one must consider processes rather than points or static terminal conditions. Processes and organization, rather than causes, lend themselves most readily to archeological and anthropological analysis. We can come much closer to figuring out how an ecosystem works than why it definitely has certain characteristics and not others.

In much archeological writing, ecology is used synonymously with environment. This view was taken by Steward (1937) when he related Great Basin subsistence practices to certain environmental factors. As we have already implied, however, such a view of ecology is overly narrow and, for most purposes, insufficient. A simple example will make this clear. People need water and will therefore live where they can get it. This is an illustration of environmental determinism, which uses a biological fact (that people need water) and couples it with the location of water supplies to predict something about the human settlement pattern. These facts do not, however, allow one to predict exactly where people will live, except under most unusual circumstances, because there are many other factors to consider. For example, how much water is there? how does its volume vary? what is its mineral or bacterial component? how many people are there? to what uses do they put water? what alternative sources are there? how easy is it to get water from the various sources? do other people share the source or have equally good sources? does the water supply have sacred significance? does it supply men's food? is it a route for communication? is it a boundary marker? This brief list includes factors that run the range from purely physical to social to ideological. One might think that the natural thing would be for people to camp on the edge of a spring. But if such a settlement pattern frightened away game, fouled the water, prevented other people from using the water, made it difficult to reach other sources of food, and so on, the relation between settlement and source of water would be much more complicated.

The important point is that ecology involves much more than a set of physical conditions. It is only in the broadest view, where environment is treated as the totality of animate and inanimate objects that affect human societies, that we can equate environment with ecology.

In ecology we are constrained to emphasize adaptation, and from this position we are led to consider certain characteristics of populations or communities that contribute to it. We are also forced to give attention to time, because the processes of adjustment that lead to adaptation run in a chain or a cycle of generations. Not so incidentally, this matter of time raises very serious questions about the usual anthropological approach of spending a year in the field to observe the annual cycle. The annual cycle is a critical segment in the life of a community, but processes of adjustment can seldom be seen in so short a time. Ellefson (1968) has recently advocated 10-year studies of nonhuman primates, but this period may also be too brief. Of course, in archeology we are able to deal effectively with long periods, but we should remember that many of our theories about human behavior in particular are based on short-term observations.

Relevant ecological concepts, in addition to those already mentioned, have to do with populations: the territory they use, their size and structure, and their changes through time.

The term "ecological niche" is used by many archeologists; it implies that people utilize and are adjusted to a particular well-defined environmental area. All species are adapted to certain environments, and this is none the less true for human groups. The way in which people use their land and territory is well described by Coe and Flannery in their article, "Microenvironments and Mesoamerican Prehistory" (1964). To understand effectively the workings of an archeological culture one must ascertain the particular ways in which the environment was used.

No less, one must also consider the space within communities as it concerns relations among individuals. The problem of space has been discussed in Chapter 18, "Patterns of Settlement," but it is useful to reiterate here that space and the objects in it indicate modes of relations among people and the land they live on.

Population density is another concept that has implications of efficiency in exploiting an environment, of relations among people within a village, and of a settlement to those outside it; and vacant spaces or lightly exploited spaces inform on the degree of specialization (narrow-spectrum exploitation of food sources such as agricultural products as opposed to broad-spectrum exploitation exemplified by hunting and collecting), as well as relations among groups of people (buffer zones, territorial boundaries, and the like).

Differentiation of members of a single population or of people who comprise a polyspecific community is likewise an indication of higher levels of integration where the group seeks to maximize its potential through dividing the labor among specialists, thereby gaining an advantage in converting raw materials to energy (principally through farming and manufacturing) or in opposition to outside peoples who impinge with hostile intent.

This division of labor raises the issue of dominance, which has been partly implicit in some of the foregoing remarks. Dominance is expressed when relatively few members of a community have greater access to certain resources than do others, and when one community prevails over another either by eliminating it or by placing it in a subservient position. A most instructive ethnographic example is the one given by Barth (1956), which was related earlier. When only the Kohistanis occupied the land, they exploited it at a relatively low level of efficiency by diversifying their activities. The Pathans raised the level of efficiency by intensively cultivating and subleasing their herding functions to the Kohistanis, who continued to farm at a lower level of efficiency on poorer land. Adding the Gujars to this symbiotic relation allowed still another, albeit poorer, landscape to be exploited. Cumulatively, therefore, the differentiation of labor among the three groups under the dominance of the Pathans permitted a much more intensive exploitation of the land, which was expressed in the vastly increased population that could be supported.

The importance of this example, ecologically stated, is that where there is competition for the same niche, two groups (species) cannot coexist, and one will prevail, owing to its dominance. The less well-adapted group will then have to shift its ecological niche, merge with the dominant group, or be destroyed. Numerous examples of just this situation abound both in historical and ethnographic literature. When a group gains an advantage as did the Plains Indians, who obtained horses early, they were able to dominate pedestrian groups and often to drive them out of the niche that came to be favored by the horsemen. Thus Plains Indian farmers were forced to abandon their villages and adopt the life of nomadic hunters if they were to survive in direct confrontations with the mounted warriors.

The ecological implication in this example is that advantages gained by one group will be exploited to the disadvantage of other groups, who in turn will have to adopt countermeasures if they are to survive. Service (1962) describes this process well in his discussion of the genesis of tribal societies, which he ascribes more to competition among peoples than to any qualities inherent in their physical environmental or social circumstances. Following the expansion of a dominant group, there will be countermeasures and ultimately a return to stable conditions, with new boundaries and new relations, until the next advantage restores the process to a state of disequilibrium. Even over periods measured in the hundreds of years, equilibrium may not be achieved—again, this is a reason why short-term studies can be misleading, and it serves as a warning against a too rapid appraisal of any seemingly adjusted system.

SYSTEMS IN ARCHEOLOGY

Systems have been defined, with respect to their regulatory and adjustive mechanisms (that is, their functioning aspects), as having three general forms. (1) There are equilibrating systems, which maintain themselves without essential change; these have been called "deviation-counteracting mutually causal relationships." (2) There are "deviation-amplifying systems," in which positive feedback causes growth in the system (Maruyama 1963:164). Maruyama has suggested that systems (1) and (2) might be called first and second cybernetics. (3) A third cybernetics has been defined by Kenneth Bailey (1968) in his doctoral dissertation in human ecology. In this third cybernetics the system can neither grow nor remain in equilibrium, but declines into extinction; it might be called a "negative deviation-amplifying system." The applicability of these concepts to archeological and ethnographic situations is given below in examples kindly provided and diagramatically represented by Richard Blanton.

The first example, of a system in equilibrium (the first cybernetics), is based on archeological research in the state of Oaxaca, Mexico by a group headed by Kent Flannery (Flannery 1968; Flannery and Schoenwetter 1970; Flannery and others 1967). In the Early Formative of Oaxaca there is evidence that agricultural peoples were engaged in extensive interactions with neighboring peoples and in long distance trade, often in high-status items such as sea shells and magnetite mirrors. Flannery and Schoenwetter (1970:148–150) suggest this trade is adaptive because

> . . . given the erratic rainfall of semi-arid regions like Oaxaca, unusually good years—and hence maize surpluses—are unpredictable. One way of banking unpredictable maize surpluses (as an alternative to storage) is to convert them into imperishable trade goods which can be used either (1) as "wealth" in times of shortage, or (2) as part of a ritual exchange system, used to establish reciprocal obligations between neighboring peoples. Such exchange systems help to "even out" the differences between good and bad years by circulating foodstuffs and trade goods between regions with different crop cycles.

In ethnographic studies similar explanations of what appear at first to be simply "ritual" exchange have also been made (for example, Lauer 1971).

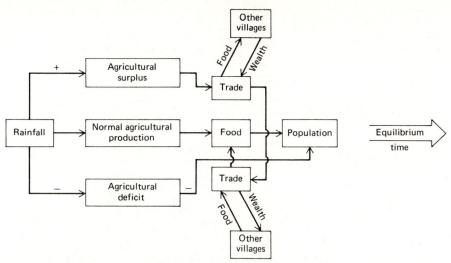

FIG. 76 Diagram of a deviation-counteracting system. (Based on analysis of archeological findings in Oaxaca, Mexico.)

A diagram that describes the deviation-counteracting system described above is shown in Figure 76.

The second example, of a deviation-amplifying system, is based on the work of Richard Blanton (1972) in the Ixtapalapa Region of the Valley of Mexico. With the introduction of maize, which is well adapted to the high, dry environment of the area into local subsistence systems, there followed an increase in population, and farming villages rapidly spread over the easily cultivated and productive land. In time the prime land was occupied and villages began to appear in the less desirable Piedmont zone. It is thought likely that the appearance of hardier varieties of maize enabled farmers to use this land, but there seems no doubt that the overall production was lower and more precarious than on the valley floor adjacent to the lake where the earliest villagers had settled.

Under these circumstances Blanton postulates the development of symbiotic relationships between parent and daughter villages, relationships owing to the differential access to resources enjoyed by the two groups. "While the Piedmont communities did not have access to the deep soil of the alluvial plain and lacustrine resources such as fish, wildfowl, and salt, they were well situated for the cultivation of nopal and mague, and some had ready access to the products of the Sierra zone." Under the circumstances a redistribution system such as described in the first example, and by Sahlins (1958) in an ethnographic situation, may have developed. In turn this redistribution system led to elevated status among those who organized and directed it.

With status differentiation the second "kick" in the deviation-amplifying system could take place—the organization of labor for the construction and maintenance of large-scale irrigation systems. Such systems can be built only in favorable areas of which the Valley of Mexico was one. With

461

FIG. 77 Diagram of a deviation-amplifying system. (Based on analysis of archeological data from the Valley of Mexico.)

irrigation, increases in yield were possible both through ensuring greater predictability annually in the harvest and also by extending arable land. These added yields then allowed for increased population and ultimately for the dense urban center of Teotihuacan which, according to recent estimates (Millon 1970) may have been the residence for more than 200,000 people.

A diagram of the Ixtapalapa system is in Figure 77.

The third example attempts to give the reasons for a rapid decline in the population of the Tapirape tribe of Central Brazil (Wagley 1951). An interpretation in system terms (not Wagley's) follows. After 40 years of contact with Europeans (beginning in the early part of this century) the tribe had reduced in population from an estimated 1000 to 100 and was still declining. In this case the system received European diseases as input and could not counteract them. Inevitably the population declined although this need not necessarily have been catastrophic. The important point is that when the population fell below a critical level (estimated to be 200), certain ceremonial activities which were related to communal subsistence could not be carried out. An important part of Tapirape culture was the mutual interaction; when this could not be carried out, even if people could in fact "survive," for practical purposes the culture was dead.

The situation is diagrammed in Figure 78.

The examples of the three major types of change in systems demonstrate the interconnections between various parts of each system. To be sure, the examples given emphasize only a few of the many possible variables that

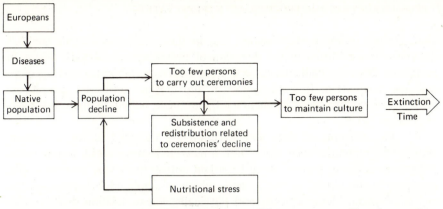

FIG. 78 Diagram of a negative deviation-amplifying system. (Based on ethnographic example from central Brazil.)

are inevitably present in any culture system. (Recently Forrester [1971] constructed a model of the world system using just five variables.) Nevertheless the focus is on the central problem of subsistence and its relationship to population, a relationship that most analysts have thought important since Malthus' dire predictions 150 years ago.

The diagrams are models of what various investigators think is happening in the system under their investigation. The great merit of expressing relationships graphically is that their precision or imprecision becomes clear and the logic of the entire model is open to rapid inspection. The models also show the use of "feedback loops," "the closed path that connects an action to its effect on the surrounding conditions, and these resulting conditions in turn come back as 'information' to influence further action" (Forrester 1971:17) In contrast with the cause-and-effect model, system analysis clearly requires us to consider how the "effect" will influence future "causes." Thus the situations are continually changing.

Much prehistoric research is concerned with cultural evolution, as we mentioned in the previous chapter. Maruyama (1963) treats this as an example of the second cybernetics, a deviation-amplifying mutual positive feedback network. We have already discussed the processes of evolution—mutation, drift, and selection. Let us see how these can be translated into system terms.

Assume a population at some point in its history in which there is an invention (recall our loose equation of invention in culture with mutation in biology). In system terms the invention affords the possibility of deviation from the previous state. Should an innovation like the invention of clothing or the use of fire prove viable, it might allow expansion into new territory. In turn this expansion could result in the growth of population as previously untapped food resources were put to use. In this example we can see how an invention that in itself has nothing to do with the food quest may enable people to use a potential source of food that was previously denied them. The effects of such an invention will then be amplified as people take advantage

463

of it, perhaps refine it still further, and in the process once again amplify
the effect. Once started in the direction of providing extrasomatic forms of
protection from the cold, the culture system further elaborates and develops
this new adaptation. In both biological and cultural terms the people are
evolving: there are more of them and they have added to their inventory
of cultural things.

The concepts of drift and selection are included in the discussion
above. The population that moves into a new environment with a new set of
techniques develops further along lines laid out by the initial invention. The
invention is the "kick" in the system, which is amplified by continued use
and elaboration. Metaphorically and physically, the population drifts farther
and farther away from the parent group. Selection, of course, rests in the
advantage (expressed in the numbers of people who can be supported) gained
by employing the invention.

Human history has seen many such changes and the deviation-
amplifying processes that followed. There is more to this development, however. In human as among other species, there is competition from outside.
Let us say that one group invents firearms and uses them to take advantage
of their neighbors. The group that is being preyed upon may counteract this
situation by also adopting firearms, thus hoping to return to a state of
equilibrium. In this case we would have a deviation-counteracting effect.
However, as we know from modern history, an arms race may ensue, in
which case we have a deviation-amplifying relationship.

The way human societies actually operate to control deviation is
through minor adjustments that are usually not thought to have long-range
implication of their own. However, as Forrester (1971:95) puts it, "There
is usually a conflict between the goals of a subsystem and the welfare of the
broader system." Minor tinkering with the system seems to be characteristic,
but "a policy which produces improvement in the short run is usually one
which degrades the system in the long run" (Forrester 1971:94). This is a
dire prediction that seems not to be borne out by our knowledge of human
evolution, but the apparent paradox is solved by recognizing that as long as
growth is possible, short-term errors may be solved with short-term solutions.
The problem facing mankind today is that continued growth no longer seems
possible.

A systems perspectives forces us to look at the way the subsystems
interact and to consider that as a whole, a culture system will attempt to
counteract deviations and thereby remain stable or in equilibrium. Our
knowledge of human evolution, on the other hand, requires us to take note
of the fact that change is customary. It is instructive to examine situations in
which change cannot be detected in the essentials of a system over a long
duration. Early in human history there were few perceptible changes. Hundreds of thousands of years passed without notable changes in technology or
in biology. Gradually changes that culminated in biologically modern man did
occur and with his appearance so did a great acceleration in the rate of

cultural change as it is expressed in archeological remains. There are circumstances, however, in which even modern peoples seem scarcely to change.

We have seen that culture is transmitted through symbolic communication which allows it to move rapidly and to be cumulative. It is transmitted within and between distinct groups. The fact that it is cumulative means that as time passes there is potentially much more information available to be used and to serve as the basis for inventions. This process of cumulation is accelerated by growth in the total population of mankind. Thus the potential for change has developed at an ever increasing rate, as today's "information" explosion testifies.

Were it not for the potential advantage such changes afforded, however, they would not have been retained. If we recall biological principles, which have been translated into cultural terms by Service (1968) as the "law of evolutionary potential," we see that the larger the inventory of ideas and things a people have, the more likely they will be able to respond to disequilibrating factors. This is another way of saying that diversity, rather than specialization, is adaptive.

If systems tend to counteract deviation, we should expect to find that they change relatively little (except through drift) unless they are faced with disequilibrating factors that cannot be shrugged off. Such factors may be generated internally as with a population that expands to the limits of the system's ability to feed it, or externally as in the case of climatic change or warfare. Archeologically we need to look for potential sources of disequilibration in systems that are known to have been undergoing change and conversely to see what factors inhibit disequilibration in systems that are not changing.

Sanders and Price (1968), in their study of the evolution of Meso-American civilization, see three factors or, as they call them, three "basic ecological processes": population growth, competition, and cooperation.

It is easy to put these into systems terms. Population growth, as we have already shown in examples (see Fig. 77), puts stress on resources and creates a greater density in living arrangements. Consequently there is competition for the resources which may encourage warfare and the elaboration of social stratification. In turn, these effects may lead to increased cooperation, both in the construction of facilities for irrigation, defense, and ceremony on the one hand, and in the unification under central direction of previously separate groups on the other. These actions then feed back upon the population and set up further sources of competition. Thus we find, in very simple outline, a set of factors that result in a deviation-amplifying system, which, expressed in cultural terms, is the evolution of Meso-American civilization.

Methodologically, the use of a systems perspective will ultimately force us to use simulation. The diagrams of feedback loops are a model of the components of the system that one wishes to investigate. Although systems are complex and human societies almost bewildering in their complexity, it has been customary in simulation to look at crucial variables in a subsystem rather than attempting to model the entire system. For example, Forrester's (1971) model of a world system examines five variables: population, capital investment, natural resources, fraction of capital devoted to agriculture, and pollution. "Each of these levels represents the principal variable in a major subsystem of world structure" (Forrester 1971:19). One may also examine each of the subsystems separately. As an example of the *form* of such analysis, "if population P rises, crowding ratio CR increases, the birth-rate-from-crowding multiplier *BRCM declines,* birth rate BR is reduced, and population P is reduced" (Forrester 1971:26).

The model must embody a theory of the structure of the system because it is, in effect, stating assumptions about it. Once the assumptions are clearly stated a computer can be programmed to carry the system through time.

> The computer gives the correct implications of the assumptions that went into the construction of the model. This process of modeling combines the greatest strength of the human mind, its ability to perceive the surrounding world, and eliminates the greatest weakness of the human mind, its inability to estimate the dynamic consequences of even a correct set of system assumptions (Forrester 1971:16).

Simulation also offers the potential for testing our assumptions. We may assume, on the basis of some archeological evidence, that a particular set of factors are operating at time A and that they were the principal causes that led to conditions at time B. If we model the situation at time A and introduce changes at opportune times or at a given rate, we can determine whether they will in fact lead to the conditions we found at time B. In essence this is what Sanders and Price did with their "mental" model of the evolution of the civilization of Meso-America. The crucial problem in simulation, however, is to define the variables in such a way that they can be given values that can be handled mathematically. This has been done with good effect in economics, and we have previously cited an example from archeology in which it was also applied (Ammerman and Cavalli-Sforza 1972a and 1972b).

For two reasons, the problems of using simulation in archeology seem for the moment more difficult than we can easily deal with. First, there has not developed a sufficiently precise body of concepts that lend themselves to mathematical modeling, and second, the mathematics required is formidable and well beyond the capabilities of most archeologists, except for relatively simple models of the kind described by Ammerman and Cavalli-Sforza (1972a, 1972b).

In our discussion of systems we have had no need to mention ceramics, graves, houses, or bone tools, which are what we mostly deal with in archeology. Have we then effectively abandoned archeology as an empirical analytic science, grounded in the observation and analysis of things, in favor of freewheeling theoretical speculation? It may seem so to many readers but this is not the case. The concepts on which system analysis stand are accepted as useful working hypotheses and serve as an embracive framework in which we can view science as a whole. The validity of this model must be tested with empirical evidence dug from the ground in such a manner that we can test specific propositions. This is the direction of new archeology, and it remains to be seen whether it will become only a short-term gain or whether this initial kick in our system of thought will be positively amplified toward the generalizing science that many expect it to become.

REFERENCES

History and Science in Archeology: L. Binford 1968a; Childe 1953b; Erasmus 1968; Kroeber 1957a; Trigger 1970; P. Watson, LeBlanc, and Redman 1971.
Scientific Method: Buckley 1968; Chamberlin 1965; Hayek 1955; Hempel 1951, 1952, 1965, 1966; Kluckhohn 1939; T. Kuhn 1962; Leach 1961; Platt 1962, 1964; Rudner 1966; Tribus and McIrvine 1971; P. Watson 1972a; P. Watson, LeBlanc, and Redman 1971; E. Wilson 1952.
General System Theory: Ackoff 1960, 1963; R. Adams 1968; von Bertalanffy 1956, 1962; Blalock 1971; Boulding 1965b; Buckley 1967, 1968; Forrester 1971; A. Hall and Fagen 1956; Naroll and von Bertalanffy 1956; Rashevsky 1967; Tribus and McIrvine 1971; Watson, LeBlanc, and Redman 1971.
Principles of Growth: R. Adams 1962, 1966; Barnett 1953; Boulding 1965a; R. Braidwood and Willey 1962; Childe 1951a, 1951b, 1954; M. Coe 1961; Flannery and others 1967; Glenn 1966; Hall and Fagen 1956; Hole 1968; Hole and Flannery 1968; Jennings 1964; Lurie 1968; Maruyama 1963; Naroll 1956; Naroll and von Bertalanffy 1956; Patten 1959; Rashevsky 1952; Sahlins 1958; Tanner 1966; W. Taylor 1966; Willey and Phillips 1958; Wolf 1964.
Communities: Allee and others 1949; Barth 1956; Klopfer 1962; Lawson 1963.
Ecological System Analysis: Ammerman and Cavalli-Sforza 1972a, 1972b; Blanton 1972; Bresler 1966; Burnham 1972; Butzer 1972; Carneiro 1961; Ellefson 1968; Eyre and Jones 1966; Flannery 1968; Flannery and Schoenwetter 1970; Forrester 1969, 1971; Frederiksen 1969; Gibson 1972; D. Harris 1972; Hole 1962; Judge 1970; Kemp 1971; Klopfer 1962; Lowe 1971; McNaughton and Wolf 1970; Meighan and others 1958; Odum 1969; Rappaport 1971; Rathje 1972; Renfrew 1972a; Service 1962; Thompson 1949; Trigger 1971; Vayda and Leeds 1965; Vayda and Rappaport 1968; Wallace and Srb 1965; L. White 1948, 1959a; Wood and Matson 1972.

CONCLUDING REMARKS

We have attempted to present a coherent and systematic picture of what archeology is, how it is done, and the rationale underlying its procedures and interpretations. We have followed an expository scheme that moves from the simple and descriptive to the interpretive and explanatory. In this way we have presented what we consider to be a balanced picture of archeology today. In so doing we have included a great deal of material, but we have not treated any subject exhaustively. The references we cite are available to any student who wishes to pursue the discipline further.

Archeology is a developing science that has gone through several important phases. The decade of the sixties saw a rapid development of techniques for obtaining and analyzing data. The decade of the seventies may well emerge as the time of important theoretical advances along the lines we have suggested. The change in format and content with each edition of this book is a reflection of the changes in central concerns of archeology over the past decade and in its own way tells something of the history of prehistoric studies.

Much of archeology is hidden from the view of the layman, who can easily understand and carry out certain aspects of fieldwork, but who seldom sees the much more complex and time-consuming process of formulating problems, selecting appropriate sites to excavate, carrying through analysis, and testing relevant hypotheses. These latter are the concern of professional archeologists, who themselves are finding it increasingly difficult individually to keep up with the latest techniques and ideas.

Many archeologists have become administrators and coordinators rather than diggers, as the swing from the jack-of-all-trades approach has shifted to the multidisciplinary teamwork so essential today in order to extract

468

and analyze the diverse data from a site. To the extent that this trend has taken some archeologists away from direct participation in digging, it is regrettable; however, in the sense that more efficient work is done and more accurate results obtained, it is salutary. Nevertheless, the responsibility for making the decisions and for finally integrating the results rests squarely on the archeologist, who must have enough command of the various facets of his operation to communicate fruitfully with his technical experts and guide their work in ways that will lead to a realizaion of the archeological goals.

In the history of the discipline, most archeologists have been concerned with their site, their region, and the changes they saw expressed in tangible artifacts like settlement patterns, houses, skeletons, and tools. Most archeological effort has been directed toward refining classifications and toward working out the detailed chronological sequences and interrelations of cultures within areas. These data are valuable, because they are readily comprehended and will ultimately provide us with the kind of information we need to test our theories. However, we shall reiterate here what we have said before: that *the facts of prehistory do not speak for themselves*. There are two logical procedures open to us in interpreting prehistory. We can make inferences about the implications of the archeological data, or we can pose hypotheses based on our understanding of cultures or of systems and then test these against our data. The latter approach is directed at exposing the underlying characteristics and causes of cultural phenomena, whereas the former is largely a translation of data into familiar cultural terms. Through inference we see archeological cultures as an ethnologist sees modern peoples. Through the use of testable hypotheses we see the operation of society laid bare although sometimes at the expense of stripping it of its human and particular cultural significance. This approach is more nearly in line with that of scientists working in other fields, who penetrate deeper and deeper into the inner process of organization of their structures.

The larger part of this book has dealt with what archeologists do and have done, but we also have introduced novel and suggestive ideas. In so doing we recognize that many of the ideas presented are difficult to understand, particularly for the beginning student, and some of them are hard to apply. Moreover, some of them will no doubt prove misleading or inaccurate. Our hope is that students of archeology will see our ideas as a challenge and that they will begin to attack the issues squarely. The more nearly they accomplish this goal, the more nearly archeology will enter the mainstream of scientific inquiry and begin to contribute results that will inform us in a more meaningful way of the details of the history of man.

In conclusion we should like to quote a passage from Grahame Clark's book, *Aspects of Prehistory* (1970:127–128).

If one asks why he should want an explanation, one answer might be that he does so in order to meet the apprehensions that accompany self-awareness. The price of knowledge is anxiety or at least an awareness of ignorance. Is this not the nemesis of education? The more we have of it, the more keenly we are or ought to be aware of our ignorance. Yet it is precisely because of this awareness that we feel the need to know more by asking questions and by seeking to understand what we observe. The thirst for knowledge is a direct outcome of self-awareness. And of all the mysteries that confronted man as he emerged from the womb of instinctive life into the world of self-awareness and culture, none can have been more frightening or more poignant than the mystery of time.

BIBLIOGRAPHY

Aberle, D. F., 1970, Comments. In *Reconstructing prehistoric pueblo societies,* W. A. Longacre, ed. Albuquerque: University of New Mexico Press, pp. 214–223.

Ackoff, R. L., 1960, Systems, organizations, and interdisciplinary research. *General Systems* 5:1–8.

———, 1963, General system theory and systems research contrasting conceptions of systems science. *General Systems* 8:107–122.

Adams, R. McC., 1962 Agriculture and urban life in early southwestern Iran, *Science* 136:109–122.

———, 1965, *Land behind Baghdad.* Chicago: University of Chicago Press.

———, 1966, *The evolution of urban society.* Chicago: Aldine.

———, 1968, Archeological research strategies: past and present. *Science* 160: 1187–1192.

———, 1970a, Editorial. *American Anthropologist,* pp. ii–iii.

———, 1970b, The study of ancient Mesopotamian settlement patterns and the problem of urban origins. *Sumer* 25:111–124.

———, 1972, Patterns of urbanism in early southern Mesopotamia. In *Man, settlement and urbanism,* P. J. Ucko, R. Tringham, and G. W. Dimbleby, eds. London: Duckworth, pp. 735–749.

———, and H. J. Nissen, 1972, *The Uruk countryside.* Chicago: University of Chicago Press.

Adams, W. Y., 1968, Settlement pattern in microcosm: the changing aspect of a Nubian village during twelve centuries. In *Settlement archaeology,* K. C. Chang, ed. Palo Alto, Calif.: National Press Books, pp. 174–207.

Aitken, M. J., 1960, Magnetic dating. *Archaeometry* 3:41–44.

——, 1961, *Physics and archaeology.* New York: Interscience.

——, 1969, Magnetic location. In *Science in archaeology,* D. Brothwell and E. Higgs, eds., rev. ed. London: Thames and Hudson, pp. 681–694.

Albright, W. F., 1939, Ceramics and chronology in the Near East. In *So live the works of men,* D. D. Brand and F. E. Harvey, eds. Albuquerque: The University of New Mexico Press, pp. 49–63.

——, 1957, *From the Stone Age to Christianity: monotheism and the historical process,* 2d ed. Baltimore: The Johns Hopkins Press.

Alcock, L., 1951, A technique for surface collecting. *Antiquity* 98:75–76.

Aldred, C., 1961, *The Egyptians.* New York: Praeger.

Alexander, J., 1970, *The directing of archaeological excavations.* New York: Humanities Press.

Alland, A., 1970, *Adaptation in cultural evolution: an approach to medical anthropology.* New York: Columbia University Press.

Allee, W. C., O. Park, A. E. Emerson, T. Park, and K. P. Schmidt, 1949, *Principles of animal ecology.* Philadelphia: Saunders.

Allen, D., 1958, Belgic coins as illustrations of life in the late pre-Roman Iron Age in Britain. *Proceedings of the Prehistoric Society* 24:43–64.

——, and E. P. Cheatum, 1960, Ecological implications of fresh-water and land gastropods in Texas archeological studies. *Bulletin of the Texas Archeological Society* 31:291–316.

Allen, D. C., 1960, The predecessors of Champollion. *Proceedings of the American Philosophical Society* 40:527–547.

——, 1971, The reconstruction of kinship from archaeological data: the concepts, the methods, and the feasibility. *American Antiquity* 36:41–53.

Allen, W. L., and J. B. Richardson III, 1968, Some parameters in the reconstruction of kinship from archaeological data. In *New perspectives in archaeology,* L. Binford and S. Binford, eds. Chicago: Aldine.

Alonso del Real, C., 1963, Notas de sociologia paleolitica. *Journal of World History* 7:675–700.

Alvarez, L., F. Franco, and S. Escobar, 1967, *Analisis quimico de ceramicas arqueologicas.* Mexico City: Instituto Nacional de Antropologia e Historia, *Technologia,* No. 1.

—— and others, 1970, Search for hidden chambers in the pyramids. *Science* 167:832–839.

Ambro, R. D., 1967, Dietary-technological-ecological aspects of Lovelock Cave coprolites. Berkeley: Reports of the University of California Archaeological Survey No. 70:37–48.

Ambrose, W. R., 1967, Archaeology and shell middens. *Archaeology and Physical Anthropology in Oceania* 2:169–187.

Ammerman, A. J., and L. L. Cavalli-Sforza, 1972a, Measuring the rate of spread of early farming in Europe. *Man* 6:674–688.

——, 1972b, A population model for the diffusion of early farming in Europe. In *The explanation of culture change,* C. Renfrew, ed. London: Duckworth.

Andersen, H., 1951a, Det Femte Store Mosefund. *Kuml,* Aarhus, pp. 9–22.

——, 1951b, Tomme Hoje [Empty Tumuli]. *Kuml,* Aarhus, pp. 91–135.

Anderson, E. C., and H. Levi, 1952, Some problems in radiocarbon dating. *Det Kongelige Danske Videnskabernes Selskab,* Copenhagen, 27(6).

Anderson, J. E., 1965, Human skeletons of Tehuacan. *Science* 148:496–497.

Anderson, K. M., 1969, Ethnographic analogy and archeological interpretation. *Science* 163:133–138.

Anderson, R. Y., 1955, Pollen analysis: a research tool for the study of cave deposits. *American Antiquity* 21:84–85.

Angel, Lawrence, 1947, The length of life in ancient Greece. *Journal of Gerontology* 2:18–24.

Angress, S., and C. A. Reed, 1962, An annotated bibliography on the origin and descent of domestic animals, 1900–1955. *Fieldiana, Anthropology*. Chicago: Field Museum of Natural History, 54(1).

Antevs, E., 1948, Climatic changes and pre-white man. Salt Lake City: University of Utah Bulletin 38:168–191.

———, 1952a, Climatic history and the antiquity of man in California. Berkeley: Reports of the University of California Archaeological Survey No. 16:23–31.

———, 1952b, Valley filling and cutting. *Journal of Geology* 60:375–385.

———, 1953a, Geochronology of the Deglacial and Neothermal Ages. *Journal of Geology* 61:195–230.

———, 1953b, Age of the Clovis fluted points with the Naco mammoth. *American Antiquity* 19:15–17.

———, 1954, Teleconnection of varves, radiocarbon chronology and geology. *Journal of Geology* 62:516–521.

———, 1957, Geological tests of the varve and radiocarbon chronologies. *Journal of Geology* 65:129–148.

———, 1959, Geological age of the Lehner Mammoth Site. *American Antiquity* 25:31–34.

———, 1962, Transatlantic climatic agreement versus C_{14} dates. *Journal of Geology* 70:194–205.

Archaeometry. Oxford: Research Laboratory for Archaeology and the History of Art. Annual; Vol. 1, 1958.

Archaeo-physika, 1965, Technische und naturwissenschaftliche Beiträge zur Feld-Archäologie. Bonner Jahrbuch Beiheft 15.

Ardrey, Robert, 1966, *The territorial imperative: a personal inquiry into the animal origins of property and nations*. New York: Atheneum.

Arnold, J. R., and W. F. Libby, 1949, Age determinations by radiocarbon content: checks with samples of known age. *Science* 110:678–680.

Arrhenius, G., 1931, Die Bodenanalyse im Dienst der Archaeologie. *Zeitschrift für Pflanzenerahrung Dungung und Bodenkunde* 10 (Part B):427–439.

———, 1954, Chemical denudation in Sweden. *Tellus* 6:326–341.

Arrhenius, D., 1934, *Fosfathalten i Skånska Jordar*. Stockholm: Sveriges Geologiska Undersökning Ser. C, No. 383 (Årsbok 28, No. 3).

———, 1963, Investigation of soil from old Indian sites. *Ethnos* Nos. 2–4:122–136.

Ascádi, G., and J. Nemeskéri, 1970, *History of human life span and mortality*. Budapest: Akadémìai Kiadó.

Ascher, M., and R. Ascher, 1963, Chronological ordering by computer. *American Anthropologist* 65:1045–1052.

Ascher, R., 1959, A prehistoric population estimate using midden analysis and two population models. *Southwestern Journal of Anthropology* 15:168–178.

———, 1961a, Experimental archeology. *American Anthropologist* 63:793–816.

———, 1961b, Analogy in archaeological interpretation. *Southwestern Journal of Anthropology* 17:317–325.

———, 1962, Ethnography for archeology: a case from the Seri Indians. *Ethnology* 1:360–369.

———, and M. Ascher, 1965, Recognizing the emergence of man. *Science* 148:243–250.

Aschmann, H., 1959, *The central desert of Baja California: demography and ecology.* Berkeley: University of California Press. Ibero-Americana, No. 42.

Ashbee, P., and I. W. Cornwall, 1961, An experiment in field archaeology. *Antiquity* 35:129–135.

Atkinson, R. J. C., 1953, *Field archaeology,* rev. ed. London: Methuen. (1st ed., 1946.)

———, 1956, *Stonehenge.* London: Hamish Hamilton.

———, 1957, Worms and weathering. *Antiquity* 33:219–233.

———, 1960, *Stonehenge.* Baltimore: Penguin.

———, 1966, Moonshine on Stonehenge. *Antiquity* 40:212–216.

———, 1967, Silbury Hill. *Antiquity* 41:259–262.

Axelrod, D. I., 1967, Quaternary extinctions of large mammals. Berkeley: University of California Publications in Geological Sciences Vol. 74.

Babbage, C., 1838, On the age of strata, as inferred from the rings of trees embedded in them. In *The ninth bridgewater treatise: a fragment.* London: J. Murray, Note M, pp. 256–264. (Reprinted in Heizer 1969.)

Baerreis, D. A., 1969, A preliminary analysis of gastropods from the Mill Creek sites. *Journal of the Iowa Archeological Society* 15:333–343.

Bagby, P. H., 1953, Culture and the causes of culture. *American Anthropologist* 55:535–554.

———, 1963, *Culture and history.* Berkeley: University of California Press.

Bailey, K. D., 1968, *Human ecology: a general systems approach.* PhD. dissertation. Austin: University of Texas.

Baker, F. C., 1937, Pleistocene land and fresh-water mollusca as indicators of time and ecological conditions. In *Early man,* G. G. McCurdy, ed. Philadelphia: Lippincott, pp. 67–74.

Baker, P. T., 1962, The application of ecological theory to anthropology. *American Anthropologist* 64:15–22.

Balfet, H., 1952, La vannerie. Essai de classification. *L'Anthropologie* 56:259–280. (English translation in Reports of the University of California Archaeological Survey No. 37:1–21, 1957.)

———, 1965, Ethnographical observations [on pottery making] in north Africa and archaeological interpretation. New York: Viking Fund Publications in Anthropology No. 41:161–177.

Bandi, H. G., 1961, *The art of the Stone Age: forty thousand years of rock art.* London: Methuen.

Bannister, B., 1962, The interpretation of tree-ring dates. *American Antiquity* 27:508–514.

———, 1969, Dendrochronology. In *Science in archaeology,* D. Brothwell and E. Higgs, eds., rev. ed. London: Thames and Hudson, pp. 191–205.

———, and T. L. Smiley, 1955, Dendrochronology. In *Geochronology, with special reference to the southwestern United States,* T. L. Smiley, ed. Tuscon: University of Arizona Bulletin 26:177–195.

Barghoorn, E. S., Jr., 1944, Collecting and preserving botanical materials of archaeological interest. *American Antiquity* 9:289–294.

Barker, P., 1969, Some aspects of the excavation of timber buildings. *World Archaeology* 1:220–235.

Barnes, A. S., 1939, The difference between natural and human flaking in prehistoric flint implements. *American Anthropologist* 41:99–112.

Barnett, H. G., 1953, *Innovation: the basis of cultural change.* New York: McGraw-Hill.

Barrington, D., 1783, Particulars relative to a human skeleton and the garments that were found thereon when dug out of a bog at the foot of Drumkeragh, a mountain in the country of Doron and barony of Kinelearty, on Lord Moira's estate, in the autumn of 1780. *Archaeologia* 7:90–110.

Barth, Fredrik, 1956, Ecologic relations of ethnic groups in Swat, North Pakistan. *American Anthropologist* 58:1079–1089.

———, 1959–1960, The land use patterns of migratory tribes of south Persia. *Norsk Geografisk Tidskrift* 17:1–11. (Bobbs-Merrill Reprint A-11.)

———, 1960, The system of social stratification in Swat, North Pakistan. In *Aspects of caste in South-India, Ceylon, and North-West Pakistan.* Cambridge Papers in Social Anthropology, No. 2:113–148.

———, 1966, *Models of social organization.* London: Royal Anthropological Institute of Great Britain and Ireland, Occasional Papers, No. 23.

Bascom, W., 1971, Deep-water archeology. *Science* 174:161–169.

Bass, G. F., 1963, Underwater archeology: key to history's warehouse. *National Geographic Magazine* 124:138–156.

———, 1966, *Archaeology underwater.* New York: Praeger.

Bastian, T., 1961, Trace element and metallographic studies of prehistoric copper artifacts in North America: a review. Ann Arbor: University of Michigan, Anthropological Papers of the Museum of Anthropology, No. 17:151–189.

Bataille, A., 1952, *Les memnonia.* Cairo: Publications de l'Institut Français d'Archéologie Orientale, Vol. 23.

Baud, C. A., 1960, Dating of prehistoric bones by radiological and optical methods. New York: Viking Fund Publications in Anthropology No. 28:246–264.

Bauer, L. A., 1899, A negative experiment relating to magnetism and the earth's rotation. *Physics Review* 3:34–48.

Baumhoff, M. A., 1963, Ecological determinants of aboriginal California populations. Berkeley: University of California Publications in American Archaeology and Ethnology, 49:155–236.

———, and R. F. Heizer, 1959, Some unexploited possibilities in ceramic analysis. *Southwestern Journal of Anthropology* 15:308–316.

———, and D. L. Olmsted, 1963, Palainihan: radiocarbon support for glottochronology. *American Anthropologist* 65:278–284.

Bayard, D. T., 1969, Science, theory and reality in the 'new archaeology.' *American Antiquity* 34:376–384.

Beals, R. L., 1971, Traffic in antiquities. *American Antiquity* 36:374–375.

———, G. Brainerd, and W. Smith, 1945, Archaeological studies in northeastern Arizona. Berkeley: University of California Publications in American Archaeology and Ethnology, 44(1):1–236.

Beazeley, G. A., 1919, Air photography in archaeology. *The Geographical Journal,* Feb. 20, pp. 331–335.

Beck, C. W., A. B. Adams, G. C. Southard, and C. Fellows, 1971, Determination of the origin of Greek amber artifacts by computer classification of infrared spectra. In *Science and archaeology,* R. H. Brill, ed. Cambridge, Mass.: MIT Press, pp. 235–243.

Bell, R. E., 1958, *Guide to the identification of certain American Indian projectile points.* Oklahoma City: Oklahoma Anthropological Society, Special Publication No. 1.

Belous, R. E., 1953, The central California chronological sequence re-examined. *American Antiquity* 18:341–353.

Belzoni, G., 1820, *Narrative of the operations and recent discoveries within the pyramids, temples, tombs, and excavations in Egypt and Nubia,* 2 vols. London: J. Murray.

Bender, D. R., 1967, A refinement of the concept of household: families. co-residence, and domestic functions. *American Anthropologist* 69:493–504.

Bender, M. M., 1968, Mass spectrometric studies of Carbon 13 variations in corn and other grasses. *Radiocarbon* 10(2):468–472.

Bennett, H. G., 1806, An account of the ancient rolls of papyrus discovered at Herculaneum, and the method employed to unroll them. *Archaeologia* 15:114–117.

Bennett, J. W., 1944, The interaction of culture and environment in the smaller societies. *American Anthropologist* 46:461–478.

Bennyhoff, J. A., and A. B. Elsasser, 1954, Sonoma Mission, an historical and archaeological study of primary constructions 1823–1913. Berkeley: Reports of the University of California Archaeological Survey No. 27.

———, and R. F. Heizer, 1958, Cross-dating Great Basin sites by California shell beads. Reports of the University of California Archaeological Survey No. 42:60–92.

Berger, R., A. B. Horney, and W. F. Libby, 1964, Radiocarbon dating of bone and shell from their organic components. *Science* 144:999–1001.

———, R. E. Taylor, and W. Libby, 1966, Radiocarbon content of marine shells from the California and Mexican west coast. *Science* 153:864–866.

Bergounioux, F.-M., and J. Goetz, 1958, *Les religions des préhistoriques et des primitifs*. Paris: Fayard.

Bergsland, K., and H. Vogt, 1962, On the validity of glottochronology. *Current Anthropology* 3:115–153.

Bernal, I., 1952, *Introduccion a la arqueologia*. Mexico City: Fondo de Cultura Economica.

———, 1969, *The Olmec world*. Berkeley: University of California Press.

Bernand, A., and E. Bernand, 1960, *Les inscriptions Grecques et Latines du Colosse de Memnon*. Cairo: L'institut Français d'Archéologie Orientale.

Berndt, R. M., 1951, Ceremonial exchange in western Arnhem land. *Southwestern Journal of Anthropology* 7:156–176.

Berry, B. J. L., 1968, Approaches to regional analysis: a synthesis. In *Spatial analysis: a reader in statistical geography*, B. J. L. Berry and D. F. Marble, eds. Englewood Cliffs, N.J.: Prentice-Hall, pp. 24–34.

———, and D. F. Marble, eds., 1968, *Spatial analysis: a reader in statistical geography*. Englewood Cliffs, N.J.: Prentice-Hall.

Bertalanffy, Ludwig von, 1956, General system theory. *General Systems* 1:1–10.

———, 1962, General system theory—a critical review. *General Systems* 7:1–20.

Bessaignet, P., 1956, An alleged case of primitive money (New Caledonian beads). *Southwestern Journal of Anthropology* 12:333–345.

Bibby, G., 1956, *The testimony of the spade*. New York: Knopf.

Biddle, M., and B. Kjølbye-Biddle, 1969, Metres, areas and robbing. *World Archaeology* 1:208–219.

Biek, L., 1963, *Archaeology and the microscope*. London: Butterworth.

———, 1969, Soil silhouettes. In *Science in archaeology*, D. Brothwell and E. Higgs, eds., rev. ed. London: Thames and Hudson, pp. 118–119.

Biesele, M., 1968, Faunal remains from the Spring Creek Site. Ann Arbor: University of Michigan, Anthropological Papers of the Museum of Anthropology, No. 38:54–64.

Binford, L. R., 1962, Archeology as anthropology. *American Antiquity* 28:217–225.

———, 1963, A proposed attribute list for the description and classification of projectile points. Ann Arbor: University of Michigan, Anthropological Papers of the American Museum of Anthropology, No. 19:193–221.

———, 1964, A consideration of archaeological research design. *American Antiquity* 29:425–441.

———, 1965, Archaeological systematics and the study of cultural process. *American Antiquity* 31(2):203–210.

Binford, L. R., 1966, The predatory revolution: a consideration of the evidence for a new subsistence level. *American Anthropologist* 68:508–512.

———, 1967a, An ethnohistory of the *Nottoway, Meherrin* and *Weanock* Indians of southeastern Virginia. *Ethnohistory* 14:104–218.

———, 1967b, Smudge pits and hide smoking: the use of analogy in archaeological reasoning. *American Antiquity* 32:1–12.

———, 1968a, Some comments on historical versus processual archaeology. *Southwestern Journal of Anthropology* 24:267–275.

———, 1968b, Methodological considerations of the archeological use of ethnographic data. In *Man the hunter,* R. B. Lee and I. DeVore, eds. Chicago: Aldine, pp. 268–273.

———, 1971, Mortuary practices: their study and their potential. In Approaches to the social dimensions of mortuary practices, J. A. Brown, ed. Salt Lake City: University of Utah, Society for American Archaeology, Memoir No. 25:6–29.

———, 1972, *An archaeological perspective.* New York: Seminar Press.

———, and S. R. Binford, 1966, A preliminary analysis of functional variability in the Mousterian of Levallois facies. *Recent Studies in Paleoanthropology, Special Publications in American Anthropology* 68 (Part 2):238–295. Washington, D.C.: American Anthropological Association.

———, 1968, *New perspectives in archaeology.* Chicago: Aldine.

———, and others, 1966, *Archaeology at Hatchery West, Carlyle, Illinois.* Carbondale: Southern Illinois University, Archaeological Salvage Report No. 25.

———, and others, 1970, *Archaeology at Hatchery West.* Society for American Archaeology, Memoir No. 24.

Binford, S. R., 1968, Ethnographic data and understanding the Pleistocene. In *Man the hunter,* R. B. Lee and I. DeVore, eds. Chicago: Aldine, pp. 274–275.

Bird, J. B., 1938, Antiquity and migrations of the early inhabitants of Patagonia. *Geographical Review* 28:250–275.

———, 1943, Excavations in northern Chile. New York: Anthropological Papers of the American Museum of Natural History 38:171–318.

Birdsell, J. B., 1957, Some population problems involving Pleistocene man. *Cold Spring Harbor Symposia on Quantitative Biology* 22:47–69.

———, 1968, Some predictions for the Pleistocene based on equilibrium systems among recent hunter-gatherers. In *Man the hunter,* R. B. Lee and I. DeVore, eds. Chicago: Aldine, pp. 229–240.

Black, G. A., and R. B. Johnston, 1962, A test of magnetometry as an aid to archaeology. *American Antiquity* 28:199–205.

———, and P. Weer, 1936, A proposed terminology for shape classifications of artifacts. *American Antiquity* 1:280–294.

Blackwood, B., 1950, *The technology of a modern stone age people in New Guinea.* Oxford, England: Oxford University, Pitt-Rivers Museum, Occasional Papers on Technology, No. 3.

Blaker, A. A., 1965, *Photography for scientific publication: a handbook.* San Francisco: Freeman.

Blalock, H. M., ed., 1971, *Causal models in the social sciences.* Chicago: Aldine-Atherton.

Blanc, A. C., 1953, The finest Paleolithic drawings of the human figure—revealed by the demolition of artillery shells in a Sicilian cave. *Illustrated London News* 223:187–189.

———, 1961, Some evidence for the ideologies of early man. In *Social life of early man,* S. L. Washburn, ed. New York: Viking Fund Publications in Anthropology, 31:119–136.

Blanc, A. C., and L. Pales, 1960, Le vestiga umane nella grotta della bàsuore a Toirano. *Rivista di Studi Ligure,* Anno XXVI, 1–90. (Instituto Internazionale di Studi Liguri, Bordighera, Italy.)

Blanton, R., 1972, Prehistoric adaptation in the Ixtapalapa region, Mexico. *Science* 175:1317–1326.

Blinkenberg, C., 1911, *The thunder weapon in religion and folklore: a study in comparative folklore.* London: Cambridge.

Bodenheimer, F. S., 1951, *Insects as human food.* The Hague: Dr. W. Junk Publishers.

Bohmers, A., 1956, Statistics and graphs in the study of flint assemblages. *Palaeohistoria* 5:1–5ff.

———, 1969, A statistical analysis of flint artifacts. In *Science in archaeology,* D. Brothwell and E. Higgs, eds. London: Thames and Hudson, pp. 564–566.

Bonomi, J., 1853, *Nineveh and its palaces.* London: Ingram, Cooke and Co.

deBooy, T., 1915, Pottery from certain caves in eastern Santo Domingo, West Indies. *American Anthropologist* 17:69–97.

Bordaz, J., and V. Bordaz, 1966, A critical examination of data processing in archaeology, with an evaluation of a new inverted data system. *American Antiquity* 31:494–501.

Borden, C. E., 1952, A uniform site designation scheme for Canada. Victoria, B.C.: British Columbia Provincial Museum, *Anthropology in British Columbia,* No. 3:44–48.

Bordes, F., 1947, Étude comparative des differentes techniques de taille du silex et des roches dures. *L'Anthropologie* 51:1–29.

———, 1950, Principes d'une méthode d'étude des techniques de débitage et de la typologie du Paléolithique ancien et moyen. *L'Anthropologie* 54:19–34.

———, 1954, *Les limons quaternaires du Bassin de la Seine.* Archives de L'Institut de Paléontologie Humain, Mémoire No. 26.

———, 1969, Traitement thermique de silex au solutréen. *Bulletin de la société préhistorique française* 66:7:197.

———, 1971, Physical evolution and technological evolution in man: a parallelism. *World Archaeology* 3:1–5.

———, 1972, *A tale of two caves.* New York: Harper & Row.

———, and F. Prat, 1966, Observations sur les faunes du Riss et du Würm I. *L'Anthropologie* 69:31–46.

———, and D. de Sonneville-Bordes, 1970, The significance of variability in Palaeolithic assemblages. *World Archaeology* 2:61–73.

Borhegyi, S. F. de, 1958, Underwater archaeology in Guatemala. *Actas de XXXIII Congreso Internacional de Americanistas,* San Jose, Costa Rica, 2:229–240.

———, 1961, *Ships, shoals, and amphoras: the story of underwater archaeology.* New York: Holt, Rinehart and Winston, Inc.

———, 1965, Archaeological synthesis of the Guatemalan Highlands. *Handbook of Middle American Indians* 2:3–58.

Bouchud, J., 1954, Dents de Rennes, bois de Rennes, et migrations. *Bulletin de la Société Préhistorique Française* 51:340–345.

Boulding, K. W., 1956a, Toward a general theory of growth. *General Systems* 1:66–75.

———, 1956b, General systems theory—the skeleton of science. *General Systems* 1:11–17.

Boule, M., and H. Vallois, 1957, *Fossil men.* New York: Dryden Press.

Bourdier, F., 1953, Pseudo-industries humaines sur galets de quartzite glaciares. *Bulletin de la Société Préhistorique Française* 50:436.

Bowen, H. C., 1967, Corn storage in antiquity. *Antiquity* 41:214–215.

Bowen, R. N. C., 1958, *The exploration of time.* New York: Philosophical Library.

Bowie, S. H. U., and C. F. Davidson, 1955, The radioactivity of the Piltdown fossils. London: *Geology,* Bulletin of the British Museum of Natural History 2(6):276–282.

Bradford, J., 1957, *Ancient landscapes: studies in field archaeology.* London: G. Bell.

Bradley, R., 1971, Trade competition and artifact distribution. *World Archaeology* 2:347–355.

Braidwood, L., 1953, *Digging beyond the Tigris.* New York: Abelard-Schuman.

Braidwood, R. J., 1937, *Mounds in the plain of Antioch: an archeological survey.* Chicago: University of Chicago, Oriental Institute Publications, Vol. 48.

———, 1958, Near Eastern prehistory. *Science* 127:1419–1430.

———, 1960, Levels in prehistory: a model for the consideration of the evidence. In *The evolution of man: mind, culture and society,* Vol. 2, S. Tax, ed. Chicago: University of Chicago Press, pp. 143–151.

———, 1967, *Prehistoric men,* 7th ed. Glenview, Ill.: Scott, Foresman.

———, 1972, Archeology: view from Southwestern Asia. Washington, D.C.: American Anthropological Association Annual Report—1971, pp. 43–52.

———, H. Cambel, C. L. Redman, and P. J. Watson, 1971, Beginnings of village-farming communities in Southwestern Turkey. *Proceedings of the National Academy of Sciences* 68:1236–1240.

———, and B. Howe, 1960, *Prehistoric investigations in Iraqi Kurdistan.* Chicago: Oriental Institute of the University of Chicago, Studies in Ancient Oriental Civilization, No. 31.

———, and C. A. Reed, 1957, The achievement and early consequence of food-production: a consideration of the archeological and natural-historical evidence. *Cold Spring Harbor Symposia on Quantitative Biology* 22:19–32.

———, and G. R. Willey, eds., 1962, *Courses toward urban life: archeological considerations of some cultural alternates.* Viking Fund Publications in Anthropology No. 32.

Brainerd, G. W., 1940, An illustrated field key for the identification of mammal bones. *Ohio State Archaeology Quarterly* 48:324–328.

———, 1951, The place of chronological ordering in archaeological analysis, *American Antiquity* 16:301–313.

Brand, D. D., 1938, Aboriginal trade routes for sea shells in the Southwest. *Association of Pacific Coast Geographers* 4:3–10.

Bray, J. R., 1967, Variation in atmospheric carbon-14 activity relative to a sunspot-auroral solar index. *Science* 156:640–642.

Bray, W., 1972, The biological basis of culture. In *The explanation of culture change,* C. Renfrew, ed. London: Duckworth.

———, and D. Trump, 1970, *A dictionary of archaeology.* London: Alan Lane.

Breasted, C., 1947, *Pioneer to the past; the story of James Henry Breasted, archaeologist.* London: Jenkins.

Breasted, J. H., 1935, *Ancient times,* 2d ed. Boston: Ginn.

Breiner, Sheldon, 1965, The rubidium magnetometer in archeological exploration. *Science* 150:185–193.

Bresler, J. B., ed., 1966, *Human ecology: collected readings.* Reading, Mass.: Addison-Wesley.

Breuil, H., 1912, Les subdivisions du Paléolithique supérieur et leur signification. In Congres International d'Anthropologie et d'Archéologie Préhistoriques, 14 Session, Genève, pp. 165–238.

Breuil, H., 1941, The discovery of the antiquity of man: some of the evidence. Huxley Memorial Lecture for 1941. Published separately by Royal Anthropological Institute, London. (Reprinted in the *Journal for the Royal Anthropological Institute of Great Britain and Ireland,* 1945, 75: 21–31.)

———, 1943, On the presence of quartzites mechanically broken in the Dwyka tillites and their derivation in the older gravels of the Vaal. *South African Journal of Science* 40:285–286.

———, 1951, Pratiques religieuses chez les humanités quaternaires. *Scienza e Civilita,* pp. 45–75.

———, 1952, *Quatre cents siècles d'art pariétal: les cavernes ornées de l'Âge du Renne.* Moñtignac, Dordogue, France: Centre d'Études et de Documentation Préhistorique.

Brew, J. O., 1961a, The threat to Nubia. *Archaeology* 4:268–276.

———, 1961b, Emergency archaeology: salvage in advance of technological progress. *Proceedings of the American Philosophical Society* 105:1–10.

Briggs, L. J., and K. F. Weaver, 1958, How old is it? *National Geographic Magazine* 114:234–255.

Brill, R. H., 1961, The record of time in weathered glass, *Archaeology* 14:18–22.

———, 1963, Ancient glass. *Scientific American* 209:120–130.

———, ed., 1971, *Science and archaeology.* Cambridge, Mass.: MIT Press.

Brion, M., 1959, *La resurrection des villes mortes.* Paris: Plon.

Britton, D., and E. E. Richards, 1969, Optical emission spectroscopy and the study of metallurgy in the European Bronze Age. In *Science in archaeology,* D. Brothwell and E. Higgs, eds., rev. ed. London: Thames and Hudson, pp. 603–613.

Brodribb, C., 1970, *Drawing archaeological finds for publication.* London: John Baker.

Brodrick, A. H., 1948, *Prehistoric painting.* London: Avalon.

Broecker, W. S., 1964, Radiocarbon dating: a case against the proposed link between river mollusks and soil humus. *Science* 143:596–597.

———, 1966, Absolute dating and the astronomical theory of glaciation. *Science* 151:299–304.

———, M. Ewing, and B. C. Heezen, 1960, Evidence for an abrupt change in climate close to 11,000 years ago. *American Journal of Science* 258: 429–448.

———, and A. Kaufman, 1965, Radiocarbon chronology of Lake Lahontan and Lake Bonneville II, Great Basin. *Bulletin of the Geological Society of America* 76:537–566.

———, and J. L. Kulp, 1956, The radiocarbon method of age determination. *American Antiquity* 22:1–11.

———, and E. A. Olson, 1960, Radiocarbon from nuclear tests, II. *Science* 132:712–721.

———, and P. C. Orr, 1958, Radiocarbon chronology of Lake Lahontan and Lake Bonneville. *Bulletin of The Geological Society of America* 69:1009–1032.

Brogger, A. W., H. Falk and H. Schetelig, 1917, *Osebergfundet,* Vol. I. Kristiana, Norway. (Reprinted in part in Heizer 1959:29–53.)

Broholm, H. C., and M. Hald, 1940, *Costumes of the Bronze Age in Denmark.* Copenhagen: Nyt Nordisk Forlag, Arnold Busck.

Bronson, B., 1966, Roots and subsistence of the ancient Maya. *Southwestern Journal of Anthropology* 22:251–279.

Brothwell, D. R., 1965, *Digging up bones.* London: British Museum of Natural History.

Brothwell, D. R., and E. Higgs, eds., 1963, *Science in archaeology.* London: Thames and Hudson.

———, 1969, *Science in archaeology,* revised and enlarged edition. London: Thames and Hudson.

———, and A. T. Sandison, eds., 1967, *Diseases in antiquity: a survey of the diseases, injuries and surgery of early populations.* London: Thomas (Thorson's).

Brown, A. K., 1967, The aboriginal population of the Santa Barbara channel. Berkeley: Reports of the University of California Archaeological Survey, No. 69.

Brown, C. A., 1936, The vegetation of the Indian mounds, middens, and marshes in Plaquemines and St. Bernard parishes. Louisiana Department of Conservation, Geology Bulletin 8:423–440.

Brown, J. A., ed., 1971, *Approaches to the social dimensions of mortuary practices.* Washington, D.C.: Society for American Archaeology, Memoir No. 25:1–5.

Bruce-Mitford, R. L. S., 1968, Sutton Hoo excavation, 1965–1967. *Antiquity* 42:36–39.

Brunett, F. V., 1966, An archaeological survey of the Manistee Basin: Sharon, Michigan to Sherman, Michigan. *The Michigan Archaeologist* 12:169–182.

Bruning, H. H., 1898, Moderne Topferei der Indianer Perus. *Globus* 74:254–260.

Bryan, A. L., 1969, Early man in America and the late Pleistocene chronology of Western Canada and Alaska. *Current Anthropology* 10:339–367.

Bryan, K., and C. C. Albritton, Jr., 1943, Soil phenomena as evidence of climatic changes. *American Journal of Science* 241:461–490.

Bryant, V. M., and R. K. Holtz, 1965, A guide to the drafting of archaeological maps. *Bulletin of the Texas Archaeological Society* 36:269–285.

———, 1968, The role of pollen in the reconstruction of past environments. *Pennsylvania Geographer,* Vol. 6 (reprint, 8 pp., n.p.).

Bucha, V., 1971, Archaeomagnetic dating. In *Dating techniques for the archaeologist,* H. N. Michael and E. K. Ralph, eds. Cambridge, Mass.: MIT Press, pp. 57–117.

Buckley, Walter, 1967, *Sociology and modern systems theory.* Englewood Cliffs, N.J.: Prentice-Hall.

———, ed., 1968, *Modern systems research for the behavioral scientist.* Chicago: Aldine.

Budge, E. A. W., 1920, *By Nile and Tigris.* London: J. Murray.

Buettner-Janusch, J., 1954, Use of infrared photography in archaeological field work. *American Antiquity* 20:84–87.

Builday, J., and P. Parmalee, 1962, Aboriginal butchering techniques at the Eschelman site, Lancaster Co., Pa. *Pennsylvania Archaeological Bulletin of the Society for Pennsylvania Archaeology* 22:59–83.

Bullard, W. R., Jr., 1960, Maya settlement pattern in northeastern Petén, Guatemala. *American Antiquity* 25:355–372.

Burch, E. S., Jr., 1971, The nonempirical environment of the Arctic Alaskan Eskimos. *Southwestern Journal of Anthropology* 27:148–165.

Burchell, J. P. T., 1961, Land shells and their role in dating deposits of postglacial times in southeast England. *Archaeological News Letter,* London 7:34–38.

Burkitt, M. C., 1934, Some reflections on the Aurignacian culture and its female statuettes. *Eurasia Septentrionalis Antiqua,* Helinski, 9:113–122.

———, 1955, *The old Stone Age,* 4th ed. London: Cambridge University Press. (1st ed., 1933.)

Burnham, P., 1972, The explanatory value of the concept of adaptation in studies of culture change. In *The explanation of culture change,* C. Renfrew, ed. London: Duckworth.

Burton, D., J. B. Poole, and R. Reed, 1959, A new approach to the dating of the Dead Sea scrolls. *Nature* 184:533–534.

Butler, B. R., 1965, The structure and function of the old Cordilleran culture concept. *American Anthropologist* 67:1120–1131.

Butzer, K. W., 1964, *Environment and archaeology: an introduction to the Pleistocene.* Chicago: Aldine.

———, 1972, *Environment and archaeology.* London: Methuen.

Byers, D. S., 1957, The Bering-bridge—some speculations. *Ethnos* 22:20–28.

———, ed., 1967, *The prehistory of the Tehuacan Valley.* Austin: University of Texas Press.

———, and F. Johnson, 1940, *Two sites on Martha's Vineyard.* Andover, Mass.: Papers of the R. S. Peabody Foundation for Archaeology, Vol. 1.

Cahen, D., and F. Van Noten, 1971, Stone Age typology: another approach. *Current Anthropology* 12:211–215.

Caldwell, J. R., 1958, *Trend and tradition in the prehistory of the eastern United States.* Washington, D.C.: American Anthropological Association, Memoir No. 88.

———, 1959, The new American archeology. *Science* 129:303–307.

———, 1964, Interaction spheres in prehistory. In *Hopewellian Studies,* J. R. Caldwell and R. L. Hall, eds. Illinois State Museum Scientific Papers 12: 135–143.

———, ed., 1966, *New roads to yesterday: essays in archaeology.* New York: Basic Books.

Caley, E. R., 1949, Archaeological chemistry. *Chemical and Engineering News* 27:2140–2142.

———, 1971, Analyses of some metal artifacts from ancient Afghanistan. In *Science and archaeology,* R. H. Brill, ed. Cambridge, Mass.: MIT Press, pp. 106–113.

Callen, E. O., 1965, Food habits of some Pre-Columbian Mexican Indians. *Economic Botany* 19:335–343.

———, 1967, Analysis of Tehuacan coprolites. In *The prehistory of the Tehuacan Valley,* Vol. 1, D. S. Byers, ed. Austin: University of Texas Press, pp. 261–289.

———, 1969, Diet as revealed by coprolites. In *Science in archaeology,* D. Brothwell and E. Higgs, eds., rev. ed. London: Thames and Hudson, pp. 235–243.

———, and T. W. M. Cameron, 1960, A prehistoric diet revealed by coprolites. *New Scientist,* July 7, pp. 229–234.

Calnek, E. E., 1972, Settlement pattern and chinampa agriculture at *Tenochtitlan. American Antiquity* 37:104–115.

Cameron, H. L., 1958, History from the air. *Photogrammetric Engineering* 24: 366–375.

Campbell, B. G., 1966, *Human evolution: an introduction to man's adaptations.* Chicago: Aldine.

Campbell, J. D., and H. S. Caron, 1964, Data processing by optical coincidence. *Science* 133:1333–1338.

Campbell, J. M., 1965, Radiocarbon dating and far northern [Arctic] archaeology. *Proceedings of the Sixth International Conference on Radiocarbon and Tritium Dating, Pullman, Washington,* pp. 179–186.

———, 1968, Territoriality among ancient hunters: interpretations from ethnography and nature. In *Anthropological Archaeology in the Americas.* Washington, D.C.: Anthropological Society of Washington, pp. 1–21.

Cann, J. R., and C. Renfrew, 1964, The characterization of obsidian and its application to the Mediterranean region. *Proceedings of the Prehistoric Society for 1964* 30:111–133.

Capper, J. E., 1907, Photographs of Stonehenge as seen from a war balloon. *Archaeologia* 60:571.

Cardos de M. A., 1959, El commercio de los Mayas antiguos. *Acta Anthropologica,* Epoca 2, Mexico City, 2(1).

Carneiro, R. L., 1956, Slash-and-burn agriculture: a closer look at its implications for settlement patterns. *Selected Papers of the Fifth International Congress of Anthropological and Ethnological Sciences.* Philadelphia: University of Pennsylvania Press, pp. 229–234.

———, 1958, An instance of the transport of artifacts by migratory animals in South America. *American Antiquity* 24:192–193.

———, 1961, Slash-and-burn cultivation among the Kuikuru and its implications for cultural developments in the Amazon Basin. *Antropologica* (Supplement No. 2), pp. 47–67.

———, and D. F. Hilse, 1966, On determining the probable rate of population growth during the Neolithic. *American Anthropologist* 68:177–181.

Carpenter, E. F., 1955, Astronomical aspects of geochronology. In *Geochronology,* T. L. Smiley, ed. University of Arizona Physical Sciences Bulletin 2:29–74.

Carpenter, R., 1933, *The humanistic value of archaeology,* Martin Classical Lectures IV. Cambridge, Mass.: Harvard University Press.

Carr, D. R., and J. L. Kulp, 1957, Potassium-argon method of geochronometry. *Bulletin of the Geological Society of America* 68:763–784.

Carter, G. F., 1956, On soil color and time. *Southwestern Journal of Anthropology* 12:295–324.

———, 1957, *Pleistocene man at San Diego.* Baltimore: The Johns Hopkins Press.

———, 1971, Compositions of some copper-based coins of Augustus and Tiberius. In *Science and archaeology,* R. H. Brill, ed. Cambridge, Mass.: MIT Press, pp. 114–130.

———, and R. L. Pendleton, 1956, The humid soil: process and time. *Geographical Review* 46:488–507.

Carter, H., and A. C. Wace, 1923–1933. *The tomb of Tut-ank-Amen, discovered by the late Earl of Carnavon and Howard Carter;* Vol. I. London: Cassell.

Caso, A., 1965, Semejanzas de diseno que no indican contactos culturales. *Cuadernos Americanos* No. 6:147–152.

Casson, S., 1939, *The discovery of man: the story of the inquiry into human origins.* London: Hamish Hamilton.

Castellanos, J. de, 1589, *Elegias de varones ilustres de Indias.* Madrid: Biblioteca de autores españoles, Vol. 4 (2d ed., 1850).

Castiglioni, O. C., F. Fussi, and G. D'Agnolo, 1963, Indagini sulla provenienza dell' ossidiana utillizata nelle industrie preistoriche del Mediterraneo Occidentale. Atti della Societa Italiana di Scienza Naturali e del Museo di Storia Naturale, Milan, 102 (Fasc. III):31–322.

Catch, J. R., 1961, *Carbon-14 compounds.* London: Butterworth.

Caton-Thompson, G., and E. W. Gardner, 1934, *The desert Fayum.* London: Royal Anthropological Institute of Great Britain and Ireland.

Ceram (Marek), C. W., 1952, *Götter, Gräber und Gelehrte; Roman der Archäologie.* Hamburg: Rowohlt.

———, 1958, *The march of archaeology,* Richard and Clare Winston, trans. New York: Knopf.

Ceram (Marek), C. W., 1971, *The first Americans*. New York: Harcourt.

Chadwick, J., 1961, *The decipherment of Linear B*. Baltimore: Penguin.

Chamberlin, T. C., 1965, The method of multiple working hypotheses. *Science* 148:754–759. (Originally printed in *Science* [Old Series] 15:92 [1890].)

Chang, K.-C., 1958, Study of the Neolithic social grouping: examples from the New World. *American Anthropologist* 60:298–334.

———, 1962, A typology of settlement and community patterns in some circumpolar societies. *Arctic Anthropology* 1:28–41.

———, 1967a, *Rethinking archaeology*. New York: Random House, Inc.

———, 1967b, Major aspects of the interrelationship of archaeology and ethnology. *Current Anthropology* 8:227–243.

———, ed., 1968, *Settlement archaeology*. Palo Alto, Calif.: National Press.

Chaplin, R. E., 1965, Animals in archaelogy. *Antiquity* 39:204–211.

———, 1971, *The study of animal bones from archaeological sites*. New York: Seminar Press.

Chapman, A. M., 1957, Trade enclaves in Aztec and Maya civilizations. In *Trade and market in the early empires*, K. Polanyi, C. M. Arensberg, and H. W. Pearson, eds. New York: Free Press, pp. 114–153.

———, 1959, *Puertos de intercambio en Mesoamerica prehispanica*. Instituto Nacional de Anthropologia e Historia, Serie Historia No. 3, Mexico.

Charanis, P., 1961, The transfer of population as a policy in the Byzantine Empire. *Comparative Studies in History and Sociology* 3:140–154.

Chard, C. S., 1958, *New World migration routes*. Fairbanks, Alaska: Anthropological Papers of the University of Alaska 7:23–26.

Charlton, T. H., 1969, Ethnohistory and archaeology: Post-Conquest Aztec sites. *American Antiquity* 34:286–294.

Chase, W. T., 1971, Egyptian blue as a pigment and ceramic material. In *Science and archaeology*, R. H. Brill, ed. Cambridge, Mass.: MIT Press, pp. 80–90.

Chenhall, R. G., 1967, The description of archaeological data in computer language. *American Antiquity* 32:161–167.

Chevallier, R., 1957, Bibliographie des applications archéologiques de la photographie aérienne. *Bulletin d'Archéologie Marocaine*. Tome II (Supplement), Edita-Casablanca.

———, 1964, *L'avion et la découverte du passé*. Paris: Fayard.

Chikishev, A. G., 1965, *Plant indicators of soils, rocks, and sub-surface waters*. New York: Consultants Bureau.

Childe, V. G., 1937–1938, The experimental production of the phenomena distinctive of vitrified forts. *Proceedings of the Society of Antiquaries of Scotland* 72:44–55.

———, 1944a, Historical analysis of archaeological method (a review of G. Daniel, "The three ages"). *Nature* 153:206–207.

———, 1944b, *Archaeological ages as technological stages*. London: Royal Anthropological Institute of Great Britain and Ireland, Huxley Lecture. (*Man* 65:19–20.)

———, 1946, Human cultures as adaptations to environment. *Geographical Journal* 108:227–230.

———, 1947, Archaeology as a social science: an inaugural lecture. London: University of London, Institute of Archaeology, Third Annual Report, pp. 49–60.

———, 1949, Neolithic house-types in temperate Europe. *Proceedings of the Prehistoric Society* 15:77–86.

———, 1950, Cave men's buildings. *Antiquity* 24:4–11.

———, 1951a, *Man makes himself*. New York: New American Library.

———, 1951b, *Social evolution*. New York: Henry Schuman.

Childe, V. G., 1953a, The constitution of archaeology as a science. In *Science, medicine and history*, Vol. 1, E. A. Underwood, ed. London: Oxford, pp. 2–15.

———, 1953b, *What is history?* New York: Abelard-Schuman.

———, 1954, *What happened in history*. Baltimore: Penguin.

———, 1956, *Piecing together the past; the interpretation of archaeological data*. New York: Praeger.

———, 1957, *The dawn of European civilization*. New York: Knopf.

———, 1958, *The prehistory of European society*. Baltimore: Penguin.

———, 1962, *A short introduction to archaeology*. New York: Collier.

Chorley, R. J., 1968, Geography and analog theory. In *Spatial analysis: a reader in statistical geography*, B. J. L. Berry and D. F. Marble, eds. Englewood Cliffs, N.J.: Prentice-Hall, pp. 42–52.

Christophe, J., and J. Deshayes, 1964. *Index de l'outillage sur cartes perforées: outils de l'âge du Bronze du Balkans à l'Indus*. Paris.

Clair, C., 1957, *Strong man Egyptologist*. London: Olbourne.

Clark, D. L., 1961, The obsidian dating method. *Current Anthropology* 2:111–116.

Clark, G., 1946, Seal-hunting in the Stone Age of northwestern Europe: a study in economic prehistory. *Proceedings of the Prehistoric Society* 12:12–48.

———, 1947, Sheep and swine in the husbandry of prehistoric Europe. *Antiquity* 21:122–136.

———, 1948a, The development of fishing in prehistoric Europe. *Antiquaries Journal* 28:45–85.

———, 1948b, Fowling in prehistoric Europe. *Antiquity* 21:116–130.

———, 1951, Folk-culture and European prehistory. In *Aspects of archaeology in Britain and beyond*, W. Grimes, ed. London: Edwards, pp. 49–65.

———, 1952, *Prehistoric Europe; the economic basis*. London: Methuen.

———, 1953a, Archaeological theories and interpretations. In *Anthropology today*, A. L. Kroeber, chairman. Chicago: University of Chicago Press, pp. 343–360.

———, 1953b, The economic approach to prehistory. *Proceedings of the British Academy* 39:215–238.

———, 1954, *Excavations at Star Carr*. London: Cambridge.

———, 1957, *Archaeology and society; reconstructing the prehistoric past*. London: Methuen.

———, 1961, *World prehistory: an outline*. London: Cambridge.

———, 1963, Neolithic bows from Somerset, England, and the prehistory of archery in north-west Europe. *Proceedings of the Prehistoric Society* 29:50–98.

———, 1966, The invasion hypothesis in British archaeology. *Antiquity* 40:172–189.

———, 1970, *Aspects of prehistory*. Berkeley: University of California Press.

———, and S. Piggott, 1965, *Prehistoric societies*. New York: Knopf.

Clark, J. D., 1958, The natural fracture of pebbles from the Batoka Gorge, northern Rhodesia, and its bearing on the Kafuan industries of Africa. *Proceedings of the Prehistoric Society* 24:64–77.

———, 1960, Human ecology during Pleistocene and later times in Africa south of the Sahara. *Current Anthropology* 1:307–324.

———, 1961, Fractured chert specimens from the Lower Pleistocene Bethlehem beds, Israel. *Bulletin of the British Museum of Natural History (Geology)* 5(4).

———, 1964, The influence of environment in inducing culture change at the Kalambo Falls prehistoric site. *South African Archaeological Bulletin* 19:93–101.

Clark, J. D., 1965, Culture and ecology in prehistoric Africa. In *Ecology and economic development in tropical Africa,* D. Brokensha, ed. Berkeley: University of California Press, pp. 13–28.

————, 1967, The Middle Acheulian occupation site at Latamne, Northern Syria. *Quaternaria* 9:1–68.

————, 1968, Studies of hunter-gatherers as an aid to the interpretation of prehistoric societies. In *Man the hunter,* R. B. Lee and I. DeVore, eds. Chicago: Aldine, pp. 276–280.

————, D. R. Brothwell, R. Powers, and K. P. Oakley, 1968, Rhodesian Man: notes on a new femur fragment. *Man* 3:105–111.

————, G. H. Cole, G. L. Isaac, and M. R. Kleindienst, 1966, Precision and definition in African archaeology. *South African Archaeological Bulletin* 21:114–121.

————, and C. V. Haynes, 1970, An elephant butchery site at Mwanganda's Village, Karonga, Malawi, and it relevance for Paleolithic archaeology. *World Archaeology* 1:390–411.

————, and F. C. Howell, eds., 1966, Recent studies in paleoanthropology. *American Anthropologist* 68 (2:2). (Special publication.)

Clark, J. G. D., 1965, Radiocarbon dating and the expansion of farming culture. *Proceedings of the Prehistoric Society* 32:58–73.

————, 1967, *The Stone Age hunters.* New York: McGraw-Hill.

Clark, T., and T. Clark, 1903, *Explorations in Bible lands.* Edinburgh: T. Clark.

Clark, W., 1946, *Photography by infrared: its principle and application.* New York: Wiley.

Clarke, D. L., 1962, Matrix analysis and archaeology with particular reference to British Beaker pottery. *Proceedings of the Prehistoric Society* 28:371–382.

————, 1967, Notes on the possible misuse and errors of cumulative percentage frequency graphs for the comparison of prehistoric artifact assemblages. *Proceedings of the Prehistoric Society* 33:57–83.

————, 1968, *Analytical archaeology.* London: Methuen.

————, 1972, *Models in archaeology.* London: Methuen.

Cleator, P. E., 1962, *Lost languages.* New York: New American Library.

Cleland, C. E., 1972, From sacred to profane: style drift in the decoration of Jesuit finger rings. *American Antiquity* 37:202–210.

Clewlow, C. W., 1968, Surface archaeology of the Black Rock Desert, Nevada. Berkeley: Reports of the University of California Archaeological Survey No. 73, Paper No. 1:1–94.

Cobean, R. H., M. D. Coe, E. A. Perry, K. K. Turekian, and D. P. Kharkar, 1971, Obsidian trade at San Lorenzo Tenochtitlan, Mexico. *Science* 174:666–671.

Coe, M. D., 1956, The funerary temple among classic Maya. *Southwestern Journal of Anthropology* 12:387–394.

————, 1961, Social typology and the tropical forest civilizations. *Comparative Studies in Society and History* 4:65–85.

————, 1962, *Mexico.* London: Thames and Hudson.

————, 1967, *The Maya.* New York: Praeger.

————, and K. V. Flannery, 1964, Microenvironments and Mesoamerican prehistory. *Science* 143:650–654.

Coe, W. R., 1959, *Piedras Negras archaeology: artifacts, caches, and burials.* Philadelphia: University of Pennsylvania Museum, Museum Monographs.

Coggins, C., 1969, Illicit traffic of Pre-Columbian antiquities. *Art Journal* 29:94ff.

————, 1970, The Maya scandal: how thieves strip sites of past cultures. *Smithsonian,* October, 2:8–17.

Coghlan, H. H., 1940, Prehistoric copper and some experiments in smelting. *Transactions of the Newcomen Society* 20:49–65.

———, 1960, Metallurgical analysis of archaeological materials: I. New York: Viking Fund Publications in Anthropology No. 28:1–20.

Cohen, Y. A., 1968, Culture as adaptation. In *Man in adaptation: the cultural present,* Y. A. Cohen, ed. Chicago: Aldine, pp. 40–60.

Cole, F. C., and T. Deuel, 1937, *Rediscovering Illinois.* Chicago: University of Chicago Press.

Collins, D., 1970, Stone artefact analysis and the recognition of culture traditions. *World Archaeology* 2:17–27.

Colton, H. S., 1932, Sunset Crater; the effect of a volcanic eruption on an ancient Pueblo people. *Geographical Review* 22:582–590.

———, 1941, Prehistoric trade in the Southwest. *Scientific Monthly* 52:308–319.

———, 1946, *The Sinagua: a summary of the archaeology of the region of Flagstaff, Arizona.* Flagstaff: Museum of Northern Arizona, Bulletin No. 22.

———, 1953, *Potsherds.* Flagstaff: Museum of Northern Arizona, Bulletin No. 25.

———, 1960, *Black sand: prehistory in northern Arizona.* Albuquerque: The University of New Mexico Press.

Colton, R., and R. L. Martin, 1969, Eclipse prediction at Stonehenge. *Nature* 221:1011–1012.

Colwell, R. N., 1956, The taking of helicopter photographs for use in photogrammetric research and training. *Photogrammetric Engineering* 22:613–621.

Colyer, M., and D. Osborne, 1965, Screening soil and fecal samples for recovery of small specimens. *American Antiquity* 31(2:2):186–192.

Conklin, H. C., 1953, Buhid pottery. *University of Manila Journal of East Asiatic Studies* 3:1–12.

———, 1961, The study of shifting cultivation. *Current Anthropology* 2:27–61.

Cook, R. M., 1969, Archaeomagnetism. In *Science in archaeology,* D. Brothwell and E. Higgs, eds., rev. ed. London: Thames and Hudson, pp. 76–87.

———, and J. C. Belshé, 1958, Archaeomagnetism: a preliminary report on Britain. *Antiquity* 32:167–178.

Cook, S. F., 1946, A reconsideration of shellmounds with respect to population and nutrition. *American Antiquity* 12:50–53.

———, 1947, The interrelation of population, food supply, and building in preconquest central Mexico. *American Antiquity* 13:45–52.

———, 1949a, *The historical demography and ecology of the Teotlalpan.* Berkeley: University of California Press, *Ibero-Americana* No. 33.

———, 1949b, *Soil erosion and population in central Mexico.* Berkeley: University of California Press, *Ibero-Americana* No. 34.

———, 1950, Physical analysis as a method for investigating prehistoric habitation sites. Berkeley: Reports of the University of California Archaeological Survey No. 7:2–5.

———, 1951, The fossilization of human bone: calcium, phosphate and carbonate. Berkeley: University of California Publications in American Archaeology and Ethnology, 40(6):263–280.

———, 1960, Dating prehistoric bone by chemical analysis. New York: Viking Fund Publications in Anthropology No. 28:223–245.

———, 1964, The nature of charcoal excavated at archaeological sites. *American Antiquity* 29:514–517.

Cook, S. F., 1966, Human sacrifice and warfare as factors in the demography of precolonial Mexico. In *Ancient Mesoamerica*, J. A. Graham, ed. Palo Alto, Calif.: Peek Publications, pp. 279–298. (Reprinted from *Human Biology* 18:81–102 [1946].)

——, 1972, Prehistoric demography. *McCaleb Module in Anthropology*. Reading, Mass.: Addison-Wesley.

——, and W. Borah, 1963, *The population of central Mexico on the eve of the Spanish Conquest*. Berkeley: University of California Press, *Ibero-Americana* No. 45.

——, 1971, *Essays in population history: Mexico and the Caribbean*, Vol. 1. Berkeley: University of California Press.

——, S. T. Brooks, and H. Ezra-Cohn, 1961, The process of fossilization. *Southwestern Journal of Anthropology* 17:355–364.

——, and H. C. Ezra-Cohn, 1959, An evaluation of the fluorine dating method. *Southwestern Journal of Anthropology* 15:276–290.

——, and R. F. Heizer, 1951, The physical analysis of nine Indian mounds of the Lower Sacramento Valley. Berkeley: University of California Publications in American Archaeology and Ethnology, 40:281–312.

——, 1952, The fossilization of bone: organic components and water. Berkeley: Reports of the University of California Archaeological Survey No. 17.

——, 1953, Archaeological dating by chemical analysis of bone. *Southwestern Journal of Anthropology* 9:231–238.

——, 1959, The chemical analysis of fossil bone: individual variation. *American Journal of Physical Anthropology* 17:109–115.

——, 1962, Chemical analysis of the Hotchkiss site. Berkeley: Reports of the University of California Archaeological Survey No. 57, Part 1:1–24.

——, 1965, The quantitative approach to the relation between population and settlement size. Berkeley: Reports of the University of California Archaeological Survey No. 64:1–97.

——, 1968, Relationships among houses, settlement areas, and population in aboriginal California. In *Settlement archaeology*, K.-C. Chang, ed. Palo Alto, Calif.: National Press, pp. 79–116.

——, and A. E. Treganza, 1947, The quantitative investigation of aboriginal sites: comparative physical and chemical analysis of two California Indian mounds. *American Antiquity* 13:135–141.

——, 1950, The quantitative investigation of Indian mounds. Berkeley: University of California Publications in American Archaeology and Ethnology, 40:223–261.

Cookson, M. B., 1954, *Photography for archaeologists*. London: Parrish.

Coombs, C. H., H. Raiffa, and R. M. Thrall, 1954, Some views on mathematical models and measurement theory. In *Decision processes*, R. M. Thrall and others, eds. New York: Wiley, pp. 25–26.

Coon, C. S., 1951, *Cave explorations in Iran, 1949*. Philadelphia: University of Pennsylvania Museum, Museum Monographs.

——, 1957, *The seven caves; archaeological explorations in the Middle East*. New York: Knopf.

Cooney, J. D., 1963, Assorted errors in art collecting. *Expedition*, University of Pennsylvania Museum 6(1):20–27.

Cornelius, E. S., 1964, *Porter Site #8*. The Totem Pole. Detroit: Bulletin of the Aboriginal Research Club, 47(7).

Cornwall, I. W., 1956, *Bones for the archaeologist*. London: Phoenix House.

——, 1958, *Soils for the archaeologist*. London: Phoenix House.

——, 1960, Soil investigations in the service of archaeology. New York: Viking Fund Publications in Anthropology No. 28:265–299.

Cornwall, I. W., 1963, Soil-science helps the archaeologist. In *The scientist and archaeology,* E. Pyddoke, ed. London: Phoenix House, pp. 31–55.

Cosgrove, C. B., 1947, Caves of the upper Gila and Hueco areas in New Mexico and Texas. Cambridge, Mass.: Harvard University, Papers of the Peabody Museum 24 (2).

Cosner, A. J., 1951, Arrowshaft straightening with a grooved stone. *American Antiquity* 17:147–148.

Cotter, J. L., 1958, *Archeological excavations at Jamestown, colonial national historical park and Jamestown national historic site, Virginia.* Washington, D.C.: National Park Service, Archeological Research Series No. 4.

Cottrell, L., 1957, *Lost cities.* London: R. Hale.

———, ed., 1960, *A concise encyclopedia of archaeology.* London: Hutchinson.

Coulborn, R., 1959, *The origin of civilized societies.* Princeton, N.J.: Princeton University Press.

Cowan, R. A., 1967, Lake-margin ecologic exploitation in the Great Basin as demonstrated by an analysis of coprolites from Lovelock Cave, Nevada. New York: Reports of the University of California Archaeological Survey No. 70: 21–35.

Cowan, T. M., 1970, Megalithic rings: their design construction. *Science* 168: 321–325.

Cowgill, G. L., 1964, The selection of samples from large sherd collections. *American Antiquity* 29:467–473.

———, 1967a, Computer applications in archaeology. In *Computers in humanistic research,* E. A. Bowles, ed. Englewood Cliffs, N.J.: Prentice-Hall, pp. 2–8.

———, 1967b, Computers and prehistoric archaeology. In *Computers in humanistic research,* E. A. Bowles, ed. Englewood Cliffs, N.J.: Prentice-Hall, pp. 47–56.

———, 1968, Archaeological applications of factor, cluster, and proximity analysis. *American Antiquity* 33:367–375.

———, 1970, Sampling and reliability problems in archaeology. In *Archéologie et Calculateurs,* Paris: Éditions du Centre National de la Récherche Scientifique, pp. 161–175.

———, 1972, Models, methods and techniques for seriation. In *Models in archaeology,* D. Clarke, ed. London: Methuen.

Cowgill, U. M., 1961, Soil fertility and the ancient Maya. Transactions of the Connecticut Academy of Arts and Sciences 42:1–56.

———, 1962, An agricultural study of the southern Maya lowlands. *American Anthropologist* 64:273–286.

———, 1971, Some comments on *Manihot* subsistence and the ancient Maya. *Southwestern Journal of Anthropology* 27:51–63.

———, C. Goulden, G. E. Hutchinson, R. Patrick, A. Racke, and M. Tsukado, 1966, *The history of Laguna de Petexil.* New Haven: Memoirs of the Connecticut Academy of Arts and Sciences, Vol. 17.

———, and G. E. Hutchinson, 1963, Ecological and geochemical archaeology in the southern Maya lowlands. *Southwestern Journal of Anthropology* 19:276–286.

Cox, A., R. R. Doell, and G. B. Dalrymple, 1965, Quaternary paleomagnetic stratigraphy. In *The Quaternary of the United States,* H. E. Wright and D. G. Frey, eds. Princeton, N.J.: Princeton University Press, pp. 817–830.

Crabtree, D. E., 1966, A stonemaker's approach to analyzing and replicating the Lindenmeier Folsom. *Tebiwa* 9:3–39. Pocatello: Idaho State College.

———, and Davis, E. L., 1968, Experimental manufacture of wooden implements with tools of flaked stone. *Science* 159:426–428.

Craig, H., 1954, Carbon-14 in plants and relationships between carbon-13 and carbon-14 variations in nature. *Journal of Geology* 62:115–149.

Cranstone, B. A. L., 1971, The Tifalmin: a 'Neolithic' people in New Guinea. *World Archaeology* 3:132–142.

Crawford, O. G. S., 1921, *Man and his past.* London: Oxford University Press.

———, 1953, *Archaeology in the field.* New York: Praeger.

———, 1954, A century of air-photography. *Antiquity* 28:206–210.

———, 1955, *Said and done: the autobiography of an archaeologist.* London: Weidenfeld and Nicolson.

Craytor, W. B., and L. R. Johnson, Jr., 1968, *Refinements in computerized item seriation.* Eugene: University of Oregon, Museum of Natural History, Bulletin No. 10.

Creel, H. G., 1937, *Studies in early Chinese culture.* Washington, D.C.: American Council of Learned Societies, Studies in Chinese and Related Civilizations, No. 3.

Crocker, R. L., 1952, Soil genesis and the pedogenic factors. *Quarterly Review of Biology* 27:139–168.

Crone, D. R., 1963, *Elementary photogrammetry.* London: Edward Arnold.

Cronin, C., L. G. Freeman, and J. Schoenwetter, 1962, Chapters in the prehistory of eastern Arizona I. Chicago: Field Museum of Natural History, Fieldiana, Anthropology, Vol. 53.

Crossland, R. A., 1957, Indo-European origins: the linguistic evidence. *Past and Present* 12:16–46.

———, and A. Burchell, 1972, *Bronze Age migrations in the Aegean.* London: Duckworth.

Cummings, B., 1933, Cuicuilco and the archaic culture of Mexico. *University of Arizona Bulletin* 4(8):1–56.

Cunnington, M. E., 1933, Evidence of climate derived from snail shells and its bearing on the date of Stonehenge. *Wiltshire Archaeological Magazine* 46:350–355.

Curtis, G. H., 1961, A clock for the ages: potassium-argon. *National Geographic Magazine* 120:590–592.

———, and J. H. Reynolds, 1958, Notes on the potassium-argon dating of sedimentary rocks. *Bulletin of the Geological Society of America* 69:151–160.

Curwen, E. C., 1930, Prehistoric flint sickles. *Antiquity* 4:179–186.

———, 1940, The white patination of black flint. *Antiquity* 14:435–437.

Cushing, F. H., 1894, Primitive copper working: an experimental study. *American Anthropologist* (Old Series) 7:93–117.

Custance, A. C., 1968, Stone tools and woodworking. *Science* 160:100–101.

Dallemagne, M. J., C. A. Baud, and P. W. Morganthaler, 1956, Réaction d'échange du calcium dans les os fossiles. *Bulletin de la Société de Chemie Biologique* 38:1207–1211.

Daniel, G. E., 1943, *The three ages; an essay on archaeological method.* London: Cambridge.

———, 1950, *A hundred years of archaeology.* London: Duckworth.

———, 1955, Prehistory and protohistory in France. *Antiquity* 29:209–214.

———, 1959, The idea of man's antiquity. *Scientific American* 201:167–176.

———, 1960, *The prehistoric chambered tombs of France.* New York: McKay.

———, 1962, *The idea of prehistory.* London: Watts.

———, 1963, *The hungry archaeologist in France.* London: Faber.

———, 1967a, Editorial. *Antiquity* 41:169–173.

———, 1967b, The origins and growth of archaeology. Baltimore: Penguin.

———, 1968, *The first civilizations: the archaeology of their origins.* London: Thames and Hudson.

Daniel, G. E., 1971a, Editorial. *Antiquity* 45:246–249.

———, 1971b, From Worsaae to Childe: the models of prehistory. *Proceedings of the Prehistoric Society* 27:140–153.

Dannenfeldt, K., 1959, Egypt and Egyptian antiquities in the Renaissance. *Studies in the Renaissance* 6:7–27.

D'Aquili, E. G., 1972, The biopsychological determinants of culture. *McCaleb Module in Anthropology.* Reading, Mass.: Addison-Wesley.

Dart, R. A., 1949, The predatory implement technique of *Australopithecus. American Journal of Physical Anthropology* (New Series) 7:1–38.

———, 1957, *The osteodontokeratic culture of* Australopithecus Prometheus. Pretoria: Transvaal Museum, Memoir No. 10.

———, 1960, The persistence of some tools and utensils found first in the Makapansgat grey breccia. *South African Journal of Science* 56:71–74.

———, and J. W. Kitching, 1958, Bone tools at the Kalkbank Middle Stone Age site and the Makapansgat Australopithecine locality, central Transvaal: Part 2. The osteodontokeratic contribution. *South African Archaeological Bulletin* 13:94–116.

Daumas, M., 1962, *Histoire générale des techniques:* Vol. 1. *Les origines de la civilization technique.* Paris: Presses Universitaires.

Dauncey, K. D. M., 1952, Phosphate content of soils on archaeological sites. *Advancement of Science* 9:33–36.

Daux, G., 1948, *Les étapes de l'archéologie.* Paris: Presses Universitaires.

David, N. 1971, The Fulani compound and the archaeologist. *World Archaeology* 3:111–131.

———, 1972, On the life span of pottery, type frequencies, and archaeological inference. *American Antiquity* 37:141–142.

Davis, E. L., 1965, Three applications of edge-punched cards for recording and analyzing field data. Washington, D.C.: Society for American Archaeology, Memoir No. 19:216–226.

Davis, H. A., 1972, The crisis in American archaeology. *Science* 175:267–272.

Davis, J. T., 1959, Further notes on clay human figurines in the western United States. Berkeley: Reports of the University of California Archaeological Survey 48:16–31.

———, 1960, An appraisal of certain speculations on prehistoric Pueblo subsistence. *Southwestern Journal of Anthropology* 16:15–21.

———, 1961, Trade routes and economic exchange among the Indians of California. Berkeley: Reports of the University of California Archaeological Survey No. 54.

———, and A. E. Treganza, 1959, The Patterson mound; a comparative analysis of Site Ala-328. Berkeley: Reports of the University of California Archaeological Survey No. 47.

Davis, L. B., 1966, Cooperative obsidian dating research in the northwestern Plains: a status report. *Archaeology in Montana* 7:3–5.

Davis, M. B., 1963, On the theory of pollen analysis. *American Journal of Science* 261:897–912.

Dawkins, W. B., 1880, *Early man in Britain and his place in the Tertiary period.* London: Macmillan.

Dawson, E. W., 1969, Bird remains in archaeology. In *Science in archaeology,* D. Brothwell and E. Higgs, eds., rev. ed. London: Thames and Hudson, pp. 359–375.

Dean, J. S., 1970, Aspects of Tsegi Phase social organization: a trial reconstruction. In *Reconstructing prehistoric pueblo societies,* W. A. Longacre, ed. Albuquerque: University of New Mexico Press, pp. 140–174.

Debenham, F., 1947, *Map making.* Glasgow: Blackie.

Deetz, J., 1965, *The dynamics of stylistic change in Arikara ceramics.* Urbana: University of Illinois Press, Illinois Studies in Anthropology, No. 4.

———, 1967, *Invitation to archaeology.* New York: Doubleday.

———, 1970, Archeology as a social science. Current Directions in Anthropology. Washington, D.C.: *Bulletin of the American Anthropological Association,* 3(32):115–125.

———, and E. Dethlefsen, 1963, Soil pH as a tool in archaeological site interpretation. *American Antiquity* 29:242–243.

Deevey, E. S., Jr., 1944, Pollen analysis and Mexican archaeology. *American Antiquity* 10:135–149.

———, 1948, On the date of the last rise of sea level in southern New England with remarks on the Grassy Island site. *American Journal of Science* 246: 329–352.

———, 1951, Late Glacial and Postglacial pollen diagrams from Maine. *American Journal of Science* 249:177–207.

———, R. F. Flint, and I. Rouse, 1967, *Radiocarbon measurements: comprehensive index, 1950–1965.* New Haven, Conn.: Yale University Press.

de Geer, G., 1912, A geochronology of the last 12,000 years. *Compte Rendus* 1:241–258. (11th International Geological Congress, Stockholm, 1910.)

———, 1940, Geochronologia Suecica Principles. *Konig. Svenska Vetensk. Handl.* (Ser. 3), 18(6).

Delougaz, P., 1933, The treatment of clay tablets in the field. Chicago: Oriental Institute of the University of Chicago, Studies in Ancient Oriental Civilizations, 7(2):39–57.

Dempsey, P., and M. Baumhoff, 1963, The statistical use of artifact distributions to establish chronological sequence. *American Antiquity* 28:496–509.

Derricourt, R. M., 1972, Human ecology and site resource analysis. Capetown, S.A.: South African Archaeological Society Goodwin Series No. 1:21–25.

Dethlefsen, E., and J. Deetz, 1966, Death's heads, cherubs, and willow trees: experimental archaeology in colonial cemeteries. *American Antiquity* 31:502–510.

Detweiler, A. H., 1948, *Manual of archaeological surveying.* New Haven, Conn.: American Schools of Oriental Research, Publications of the Jerusalem School, Vol. 2.

Deuel, L., 1969, *Flights into yesterday: the story of aerial archaeology.* New York: St. Martin's Press.

DeVore, I., ed., 1965, *Primate behavior: field studies of monkeys and apes.* New York: Holt, Rinehart and Winston, Inc.

Dibble, D. S., and E. R. Prewitt, 1967, *Survey and test excavations at Amistad reservoir, 1964–1965.* Austin: Survey Reports of the Texas Archeological Salvage Project, No. 3.

Dickson, B. A., and R. L. Crocker, 1953–1954, A chronosequence of soils and vegetation near Mt. Shasta, California, I–III. *Journal of Soil Science* 4:123–141; 5:173–191.

Dictionnaire archéologique des techniques, 1963–1964. Paris: Éditions de l'Accueil.

Dietz, E. F., 1955, Natural burial of artifacts. *American Antiquity* 20:273–274.

———, 1957, Phosphorus accumulation in soil of an Indian habitation site. *American Antiquity* 22:405–409.

Dimbelby, G. W., 1957, Pollen analysis of terrestrial soils. *New Phytologist* 56:12–28.

———, 1965, Overton Down experimental earthwork. *Antiquity* 39:134–136.

Dimbelby, G. W., 1967, *Plants and archaeology*. London: John Baker.

———, 1969, Pollen analysis. In *Science in archaeology,* D. Brothwell and E. Higgs, eds., rev. ed. London: Thames and Hudson, pp. 167–177.

Dittert, A. E., Jr., and F. Wendorf, 1963, *Procedural manual for archeological field research projects of the Museum of New Mexico*. Santa Fe: Museum of New Mexico, Papers in Anthropology, No. 12.

Dixon, J. E., J. R. Cann, and C. Renfrew, 1968, Obsidian and the origins of trade. *Scientific American* 218:38–46.

Dixon, K. A., 1957, Systematic cordage structure analysis. *American Anthropologist* 59:135–136.

———, 1963, The interamerican diffusion of a cooking technique: the culinary shoe-pot. *American Anthropologist* 65:593–619.

———, 1966, Obsidian hydration dates from Temesco, Valley of Mexico. *American Antiquity* 31:640–643.

Dixon, R. B., 1905, The northern Maidu. New York: Bulletin of the American Museum of Natural History 17(3):119–346.

———, 1928, *The building of cultures*. New York: Scribner.

———, and J. B. Stetson, 1922, Analysis of Pre-Columbian pipe dottels. *American Anthropologist* 24:245–246.

Doberenz, A. R., and P. Matter, 1965, Nitrogen analyses of fossil bones. *Comparative Biochemistry and Physiology* 16:253–258.

Doblhofer, E., 1959, *Le déchiffrement des écritures*. Paris: Arthaud.

Dobyns, H. F., and H. Paul Thompson, 1966, Estimating aboriginal American population: an appraisal of techniques with a new hemispheric estimate (pp. 395–416); a technique using anthropological and biological data (pp. 417–449). *Current Anthropology* 7:395–449.

Dobzhansky, T., 1955, *Evolution, genetics and man*. New York: Wiley.

Dolhinow, P., 1972, *Primate patterns*. New York: Holt, Rinehart and Winston, Inc.

———, and V. M. Sarich, 1971, *Background for man*. New York: Little, Brown.

Donn, W., W. Farrand, and M. Ewing, 1962, Pleistocene ice volumes and sea level lowering. *Journal of Geology* 70:206–214.

Donnan, C., 1971, Ancient Peruvian potters' marks and their interpretation through ethnographic analogy. *American Antiquity* 36:460–466.

Donnay, G., A. N. Thorpe, F. E. Senftle, and R. Sioda, 1966, Pacific Pleistocene cores: faunal analyses and geochronology. *Science* 154:886–890.

Doran, J. E., and F. R. Hodson, 1966, A digital computer analysis of Paleolithic flint assemblages. *Nature* 210:688–689.

Dorf, E., 1960, Climatic changes of the past and present. *American Scientist* 48:341–360.

Dort, W. J., 1968, Paleoclimatic implications of soil structures at the Wasden site (Owl Cave). *Tebiwa* 11:31–36.

Dort, W., and others, 1965, Paleotemperatures and chronology at archaeological cave sites revealed by thermoluminescence. *Science* 150:480–482.

Dorwin, J. T., 1967, Iodine staining and ultraviolet photography field techniques. *American Antiquity* 32:105–107.

———, 1971, *The Bowen site: an archaeological study of culture process in the late prehistory of central Indiana*. Indianapolis: Indiana Historical Society, Prehistory Research Series, 4(4).

Dougherty, R. C., and J. R. Caldwell, 1966, Evidence of early pyrometallurgy in the Kerman Range in Iran. *Science* 153:984–985.

Dowman, E. A., 1970, *Conservation in field archaeology*. London: Methuen.

Downs, J. F., and H. K. Bleibtreu, 1972, *Human variation*. Beverly Hills, Calif.: Benziger Bruce & Glencoe.

Dozier, E. P., 1970, Making inferences from the present to the past. In *Reconstructing prehistoric pueblo societies*, W. A. Longacre, ed. Albuquerque: University of New Mexico Press, pp. 202–213.

Dray, W. H., 1957, *Laws and explanations in history*. London: Oxford.

Dreimanis, A., 1957, Depths of leaching in glacial deposits. *Science* 126:403–404.

Drew, I. M., D. Perkins, and P. Daly, 1971, Prehistoric domestication of animals: effects on bone structure. *Science* 171:280–282.

Drier, R. W., 1961, Archaeology and some metallurgical investigative techniques. Ann Arbor: University of Michigan, Anthropological Papers of the Museum of Anthropology, No. 17:134–147.

Driver, H. E., 1957, Estimation of intensity of land use from ethnobiology: applied to the Yuma Indians. *Ethnohistory* 4:174–197.

———, 1961, Introduction to statistics for comparative research. In *Readings on cross-cultural methods*, F. W. Moore, ed. New Haven, Conn.: HRAF (Human Relations Area File) Press, pp. 303–331.

———, 1962. The contribution of A. L. Kroeber to culture area theory and practice. Bloomington: Indiana University Publications in Anthropology and Linguistics, Memoir No. 18.

———, and W. C. Massey, 1957, *Comparative studies of North American Indians*. Philadelphia: Transactions of the American Philosophical Society 47 (Part 2):312ff., map 106.

Drucker, P., 1943, Archaeological survey of the northern Northwest Coast. Washington, D.C.: Bulletin of the Bureau of American Ethnology, 113:17–142.

———, 1963, *Indians of the Northwest Coast*. New York: Doubleday.

———, and E. Contreras, 1953, Site patterns in the eastern part of Olmec territory. *Journal of the Washington Academy of Science* 43:389–396.

———, R. F. Heizer, and R. Squier, 1959, Excavations at La Venta, Tabasco, 1955. Washington, D.C.: Bulletin of the Bureau of American Ethnology, No. 170.

Duignan, P., 1958, Early Jesuit Missionaries: a suggestion for further study. *American Anthropologist* 60:725–732.

Dumas, F., 1962, *Deep water archaeology*. London: Routledge.

Dumond, D. E., 1961, Swidden agriculture and the rise of Maya civilization. *Southwestern Journal of Anthropology* 17:301–316.

———, 1963, A practical field method for the preservation of soil profiles from archaeological cuts. *American Antiquity* 29:116–118.

Dunlevy, M. L., and E. H. Bell, 1936, A comparison of the cultural manifestations of the Burkett and the Gray Wolf sites. In *Chapters in Nebraska Archaeology*, E. H. Bell, ed. Lincoln: University of Nebraska Press, pp. 151–247.

Durand, J. D., 1960, Mortality estimates from Roman tombstone inscriptions. *American Journal of Sociology* 65:365–373.

Durand-Forrest, J., 1967, Survivance de quelques techniques précolumbiennes dans le Mexique moderne: II. La Poterie. *Journal de la Société des Américanistes de Paris* 56:95–148.

Durkheim, Émile, 1949, *The division of labor in society*. New York: Free Press.

Dyck, W., 1967, *The geological survey of Canada radiocarbon dating laboratory*. Ottawa: Department of Energy, Mines and Resources, Geological Survey of Canada, Paper No. 66–45.

Dyson, J. L., 1962, *The world of ice*. New York: Knopf.

Dyson, R. H., 1953, Archaeology and the domestication of animals in the Old World. *American Anthropologist* 55:661–673.

Eardley, A. J., 1942, *Aerial photographs: their use and interpretation.* New York: Harper & Brothers.

Easby, D. T., and R. Dockstader, 1964, Requiem for Tizoc. *Archaeology* 17:85–90.

Eckblaw, E. W., 1936, Soil geography and relationship of soils to other dynamic processes. *Proceedings of the Soil Science Society of America* 1:1–5.

Eddy, F. W., and H. W. Dregne, 1964, Soil tests on alluvial and archaeological deposits, Navajo reservoir district. *El Palacio* 71:5–21.

Edeine, B., 1956, Une méthode pratique pour la détection aérienne des sites archéologiques, en particulier par la photographie sur films en couleurs et sur films infrarouges. *Bulletin de la Société Préhistorique Française* 53:540–546.

Edmonson, M. S., 1961, Neolithic diffusion rates. *Current Anthropology* 2:71–102.

Efimenko, P. P., 1958, *Kostienki I.* Leningrad: Akademia Nauk SSSR, Institut istorii materialnoi kulturj.

Eggan, F., 1952, The ethnological cultures of eastern United States and their archaeological backgrounds. In *Archeology of eastern United States*, J. B. Griffin, ed. Chicago: University of Chicago Press, pp. 35–45.

———, 1966, *The American Indian.* Chicago: University of Chicago Press.

Eggers, H. J., 1959, *Einführung in die Vorgeschichte.* Munich: Piper.

Einarsen, A. S., 1948, *The pronghorn antelope and its management.* Washington, D.C.: Wildlife Management Institute.

Eisenberg, L., 1972, The *human* nature of human nature. *Science* 176:123–128.

Ekholm, G. F., 1964a, The problem of fakes in Pre-Columbian art. *Curator* 7:19–32.

———, 1964b, Transpacific contacts. In *Prehistoric man in the new world*, J. D. Jennings and E. Norbeck, eds. Chicago: University of Chicago Press, pp. 489–510.

Ellefson, J. O., 1968, Personality and the biological nature of man. In *The study of personality*, E. Norbeck, D. Price-Williams, and W. M. McCord, eds. New York: Holt, Rinehart and Winston, Inc., pp. 137–149.

Ellis, Florence M., 1934, *The significance of the dated prehistory of Chetro Ketl.* Albuquerque: University of New Mexico Bulletin, Monograph Series, 1(1).

Ellis, Henry, 1847, On the ruins of a city submerged in the sea on the coast of Pomerania. *Archaeologia* 32:419–422.

Ellis, H. H., 1940, *Flint-working techniques of the American Indian; an experimental study.* Columbus: Ohio State Museum Lithic Laboratory.

Elmendorf, W. W., and A. L. Kroeber, 1960, *The structure of Twana culture, with comparative notes on the structure of Yurok culture.* Pullman: Washington State University, Research Studies, Monographic Supplement No. 2.

Elsasser, A. B., 1961, Archaeological evidence of shamanism in California and Nevada. Berkeley, Calif. Kroeber Anthropological Society Papers, 24:38–48.

Emery, I., 1966, *The primary structure of fabrics: an illustrated classification.* Washington, D.C.: The Textile Museum.

Emery, K. O., and R. L. Edwards, 1966, Archaeological potential of the Atlantic continental shelf. *American Antiquity* 31:733–737.

———, and L. E. Garrison, 1967, Sea levels 7000 to 20,000 years ago. *Science* 157:684–687.

———, C. A. Kaye, D. H. Loring, and D. J. G. Nota, 1968, European Cretaceous flints on the coast of North America. *Science* 160:1225–1228.

———, R. L. Wigley, A. S. Bartlett, M. Rubin, and E. Barghoorn, 1967, Freshwater peat on the [Atlantic] Continental Shelf. *Science* 158:1301–1307.

Emery, W. B., 1948, *Nubian treasure*. London: Methuen.

———, 1961, *Archaic Egypt*. Baltimore: Penguin.

Emiliani, C., 1966, Isotope paleotemperatures. *Science* 154:851–857.

———, and others, 1964, Paleotemperature analysis of fossil shells of marine mollusks (food refuse) from the Arene Candide Cave, Italy, and the Haua Fteah Cave, Cyrenaica. In *Isotopic and Cosmic Chemistry*, H. Craig, S. L. Miller, and G. J. Wasserburg, eds. Amsterdam: North-Holland, pp. 133–156.

Emlen, J. M., 1966, Natural selection and human behavior. *Journal of Theoretical Biology* 12:410.

———, 1967, On the importance of cultural and biological determinants in human behavior. *American Anthropologist* 67:513–514.

Engel, C. G., and R. P. Sharp, 1958, Chemical data on desert varnish. *Bulletin of the Geological Society of America* 69:487–518.

Engnell, I., 1967, *Studies in divine kingship in the ancient Near East*. Oxford: Blackwell.

Eppel, F., 1958, Funktion und Bedeutung der Lochstäbe aus dem Magdalénien. *Praehistorisches Zeitschrift*, Berlin 36:220–223.

Epstein, J. F., 1964, Towards the systematic description of chipped stone. Mexico City: Actas y Memorias, XXXV Congreso Internacional de Americanistes 1:155–169.

Erasmus, C. J., 1968, Thoughts on upward collapse: an essay on explanation in anthropology. *Southwestern Journal of Anthropology* 24:170–194.

Erdtman, G., 1943, *An introduction to pollen analysis*. New York: Ronald.

Ericson, D. B., M. Ewing, and G. Wollin, 1964, The Pleistocene epoch in deep-sea sediments. *Science* 146:723–732.

———, M. Ewing, G. Wollin, and B. Heezen, 1961, Atlantic deep-sea sediment cores. *Bulletin of the Geological Society of America* 72:193–286.

———, and G. Wollin, 1964, *The deep and the past*. New York: Knopf.

Estrada, E., B. J. Meggers, and C. Evans, 1962, Possible transpacific contact on the coast of Ecuador. *Science* 135:371–372.

Evans, A., 1921–1935, *The palace of Minos*, Vol. 4. London: Macmillan.

Evans, A. C., and V. H. Fenwich, 1971, The Graveny Boat. *Antiquity* 45:89–96.

Evans, C., and B. J. Meggers, 1960, A new dating method using obsidian: II. An archaeological evaluation of the method. *American Antiquity* 25:523–537.

Evans, E. E., 1956, The ecology of peasant life in western Europe. In *Man's role in changing the face of the earth*, W. L. Thomas, ed. Chicago: University of Chicago Press, pp. 217–239.

Evans, J., 1897, *Ancient stone implements, weapons and ornaments of Great Britain*, 2d ed. London: Longmans.

Evans, J. G., 1969, Land and freshwater molluscs in archaeology: chronological aspects. *World Archaeology* 1:170–183.

Evans, Joan, 1943, *Time and chance; the story of Arthur Evans and his forebears*. New York: McKay.

Evernden, J. F., and G. H. Curtis, 1965. The potassium-argon dating of late Cenozoic rocks in east Africa and Italy. *Current Anthropology* 6:343–385.

———, ———, and J. Lipson, 1957, Potassium-argon dating of igneous rocks. *Bulletin of the American Association of Petroleum Geologists* 41:2120–2127.

———, D. E. Savage, G. H. Curtis, and G. T. James, 1964, Potassium-argon dates and Cenozoic mammalian chronology of North America. *American Journal of Science* 262:145–198.

Ewers, J. C., 1955, The horse in Blackfoot Indian culture. Washington, D.C.: Bulletin of the Bureau of American Ethnology, No. 159.

Eyre, S. R., and G. R. J. Jones, eds., 1966, *Geography as human ecology: methodology by example.* London: E. Arnold.

Faegri, K., and J. Iversen, 1964, *Textbook of modern pollen analysis.* Copenhagen: E. Munksgaard.

Fagan, B. M., 1972, *In the beginning.* Boston: Little, Brown.

Fairbridge, R. W., 1958, Dating the latest movements of the Quaternary sea level. Transactions of the New York Academy of Sciences (Series II) 20: 471–482.

Fairman, H. W., 1972, Tutankhamun and the end of the 18th Dynasty. *Antiquity* 44: 15–18.

Fairservis, W. A., 1967, The origin, character, and decline of an early civilization. New York: American Museum of Natural History, Novitiates, No. 2302.

Falkenstein, Adam, 1936, *Archaische Texte aus Uruk. Ausgrabungen der Deutschen Forschungsgemeinschaft in Uruk-Warka.* Vol. 2. Berlin: Deutsche Forschungsgemeinschaft.

Farabee, W. C., 1919, Indian children's burial place in western Pennsylvania. *Museum Journal,* University of Pennsylvania, 10: 166–167.

Farmer, M. F., 1939, Lightning spalling. *American Antiquity* 4: 346–348.

Faul, H., 1971, Potassium-Argon dating. In *Dating techniques for the archaeologist,* H. N. Michael and E. K. Ralph, eds. Cambridge, Mass.: MIT Press, pp. 157–163.

———, and G. A. Wagner, 1971, Fission track dating. In *Dating techniques for the archaeologist,* H. N. Michael and E. K. Ralph, eds. Cambridge, Mass.: MIT Press, pp. 152–156.

Feldhaus, F. M., 1914, *Die Technik der Vorzeit.* Leipzig: W. Engelmann.

Fields, P. R., J. Milsted, E. Henrickson, and R. Ramette, 1971, Trace impurity patterns in copper ores and artifacts. In *Science and archaeology,* R. H. Brill, ed. Cambridge, Mass.: MIT Press, pp. 131–144.

Finkelstein, J. J., 1937, A suggested projectile point classification. *American Antiquity* 2: 197–203.

Finley, M. I., 1970, *Early Greece: The Bronze and Archaeic Ages.* London: Chattos & Windus.

———, 1971, Archaeology and history. *Proceedings of the American Academy of Arts and Sciences* 100: 168–186.

Fischer, E., 1963, Die Topferei bei der Westlichen Dan [of Liberia]. *Zeitschrift für Ethnologie* 88: 100–115.

Fisk, H. N., 1944, *Summary of the geology of the lower alluvial valley of the Mississippi River.* Mississippi River Commission, War Department, Corps of Engineers, United States Army.

Fitch, J. E., 1969, Fish remains, primarily otoliths, from a Ventura, California Chumash village site (Ven-3). Memoirs of the Southern California Academy of Sciences, 8: 56–71.

Fitting, J. E., 1968, The Spring Creek site. Ann Arbor: University of Michigan, Anthropological Papers of the Museum of Anthropology, No. 32, Part 1: 1–78.

———, 1969, Settlement analysis in the Great Lakes region. *Southwestern Journal of Anthropology* 25: 360–377.

FitzHugh, E. W., and R. J. Gettens, 1971, Calcite and other efflorescent salts on objects stored in wooden museum cases. In *Science and archaeology,* R. H. Brill, ed. Cambridge, Mass.: MIT Press, pp. 91–102.

Flannery, K. V., 1965, The ecology of early food production in Mesopotamia. *Science* 147: 1247–1256.

———, 1966, The Postglacial "readaptation" as viewed from Mesoamerica. *American Antiquity* 31: 800–805.

Flannery, K. V., 1967a, Culture history v. cultural process: a debate in American archaeology. *Scientific American* 217:119–122.

———, 1967b, The vertebrate fauna and hunting patterns [in Tehuacan Valley]. In *The prehistory of the Tehuacan Valley.* Vol. 1, D. S. Byers, ed. Austin: University of Texas Press, pp. 132–177.

———, 1968, Archeological systems theory and early Mesoamerica. In *Anthropological archeology in the Americas,* B. J. Meggers, ed. Washington, D.C.: The Anthropological Society of Washington, pp. 67–87.

———, 1969, Origins and ecological effects of early domestication in Iran and the Near East. In *The domestication and exploitation of plants and animals,* P. J. Ucko and G. W. Dimbleby, eds. Chicago: Aldine, pp. 73–100.

———, 1972, Archeology with a capital S. In *Archeology today,* C. L. Redman, ed. New York: Wiley.

———, A. V. T. Kirkby, M. J. Kirkby, and A. W. Williams, Jr., 1967, Farming systems and political growth in ancient Oaxaca. *Science* 158:445–454.

———, and J. Schoenwetter, 1970, Climate and man in formative Oaxaca. *Archaeology* 23:144–152.

Fleischer, R. L., P. B. Price, and R. M. Walker, 1965, Tracks of charged particles in solids. *Science* 149:383–393.

———, and L. S. B. Leakey, 1965, Fission track dating of a Mesolithic knife. *Nature* 205:1138.

Fleming, A., 1972, Models for the development of aristocratic society in the Early Bronze Age. In *The explanation of culture change,* C. Renfrew, ed. London: Duckworth.

Flint, R. F., 1957, *Glacial and Pleistocene geology.* New York: Wiley.

———, 1959, Pleistocene climates in eastern and southern Africa. *Bulletin of the Geological Society of America* 70:343–374.

———, and E. S. Deevey, Jr., 1951, Radiocarbon dating of late-Pleistocene events. *American Journal of Science* 249:257–300.

Folan, W. J., 1968, *El cenote sagrado de Chichen-Itza.* Mexico: Instituto Nacional de Antropologia e Historia, Informes No. 15.

Follett, W. I., 1967, Fish remains from coprolites and midden deposits at Lovelock Cave, Churchill County, Nevada. Berkeley: Reports of the University of California Archaeological Survey No. 70:93–116.

———, 1970, Benthic fishes cast ashore by giant waves near Point Joe, Monterey County, California. San Francisco: Proceeedings of the California Academy of Sciences, Fourth Series 37, No. 15.

Fontana, B. L., 1965, On the meaning of historic sites archaeology. *American Antiquity* 31:61–65.

———, W. J. Robinson, C. W. Cormack, and E. E. Leavitt, Jr., 1962, *Papago Indian pottery.* Seattle: University of Washington Press.

Forbes, R. J., 1955–1958, *Studies in ancient technology,* Vols. 1–6. London: Brill.

Forbis, R. G., 1956, Early man and fossil bison. *Science* 123:327–328.

Ford, J. A., 1938, A chronological method applicable to the Southeast. *American Antiquity* 3:260–264.

———, 1951, Greenhouse: a Troyville-Coles Creek period site in Avoyelles Parish, Louisiana. New York: Anthropological Papers of the American Museum of Natural History 44 (Part 1).

———, 1952, Mound builders of the Mississippi. *Scientific American* 186:23–27.

———, 1954a, Comment on A. C. Spaulding, "Statistical techniques for the discovery of artifact types." *American Antiquity* 19:390–391.

———, 1954b, On the concept of types. *American Anthropologist* 56:42–54.

Ford, J. A., 1959, Eskimo prehistory in the vicinity of Point Barrow, Alaska. New York: Anthropological Papers of the American Museum of Natural History 47 (Part 1).

———, 1962, A quantitive method for deriving cultural chronology. Pan American Union, Technical Manual, No. 1.

———, 1966, Early formative cultures in Georgia and Florida. *American Antiquity* 31:781–799.

———, W. Phillips, and W. Haag, 1955, The Jaketown site in west-central Mississippi. New York: Anthropological Papers of the American Museum of Natural History 45 (1).

———, and C. H. Webb, 1956, Poverty Point, a Late Archaic site in Louisiana. New York: Anthropological Papers of the American Museum of Natural History 46:5–136.

———, and G. R. Willey, 1949, Surface survey of the Viru Valley, Peru. New York: Anthropological Papers of the American Museum of Natural History 43 (Part 1).

Ford, R. I., 1971, Looting the past: an international scandal. *Science* 174:727.

Forrester, J., 1969, *Urban dynamics.* Cambridge, Mass.: MIT Press.

———, 1971, *World dynamics.* Cambridge, Mass.: Wright-Allen Press.

Foster, G. M., 1940, *Notes on the Popoluca of Veracruz.* Mexico, D. F.: Instituto Panamericano de Geografia e Historia, Publication No. 51.

———, 1945, *Sierra Popoluca folklore and beliefs.* Berkeley: University of California Publications in American Archaeology and Ethnology, 42 (2).

———, 1948, Some implications of modern mold-made pottery. *Southwestern Journal of Anthropology* 4:356–370.

———, 1955, Contemporary pottery techniques in southern and central Mexico. New Orleans, La.: Tulane University, Publications of the Middle American Research Institute 22:1–48.

———, 1956, Pottery-making in Bengal. *Southwestern Journal of Anthropology* 12:395–405.

———, 1960a, Archaeological implications of the modern pottery of Acatlan Pueblo, Mexico. *American Antiquity* 26:205–214.

———, 1960b, Life-expectancy of utilitarian pottery in Tzintzuntzan, Michoácan, Mexico. *American Antiquity* 25:606–609.

Fowke, G., 1902, *Archaeological history of Ohio: the mound builders and later Indians.* Columbus: Ohio State Archaeological and Historical Society.

Fowler, M. L., 1959, *Summary report of Modoc Rockshelter 1952, 1953, 1955, 1956.* Springfield: Illinois State Museum, Report of Investigations, No. 8.

Franken, H. J., 1965, Taking the baulks home. *Antiquity* 39:140–142.

Frankfort, H., 1939, *Cylinder seals.* London: Macmillan.

———, 1956, *The birth of civilization in the Near East.* N.Y.: Doubleday.

Frantz, A., 1950, Truth before beauty: or the incompleat photographer. *Archaeology* 3:202–215.

Frederiksen, H., 1969, Feedbacks in economic and demographic transition. *Science* 166:837–847.

Freeman, L. C., and J. A. Brown, 1964, Statistical analysis of Carter Ranch pottery. *Fieldiana Anthropology.* Chicago: Field Museum of Natural History 55:126–154.

Freeman, L. G., 1968, A theoretical framework for interpreting archeological materials. In *Man the hunter,* R. B. Lee and I. DeVore, eds. Chicago: Aldine, pp. 262–267.

———, ed, 1971, New research in paleoanthropology: introduction. *American Anthropologist* 73:1195–1197.

Freeman, L. G., and J. Gonzales Echegaray, 1970, Aurignacian structural features and burials at Cuero Morin (Santander, Spain). *Nature* 226:722–726.

Fried, M. H., 1967, *The evolution of political society*. New York: Random House.

Friedman, A. M., and others, 1966, Copper artifacts: correlations with source types of copper ores. *Science* 152:1504–1506.

Friedman, I., and R. L. Smith, 1960, A new dating method using obsidian: I. The development of the method. *American Antiquity* 25:476–493.

———, ———, and D. L. Clark, 1969, Obsidian dating. In *Science in archaeology*, D. Brothwell and E. Higgs, eds., rev. ed. London: Thames and Hudson, pp. 62–75.

Friedrich, M. H., 1970, Design structure and social interaction: archaeological implications of an ethnographic analysis. *American Antiquity* 35:332–343.

Frison, G. C., 1968, A functional analysis of certain chipped stone tools. *American Antiquity* 33:149–155.

Fritts, H. C., 1965, Dendrochronology. In *The Quaternary of the United States*, H. E. Wright and D. G. Frey, eds. Princeton, N.J.: Princeton University Press, pp. 871–879.

Fritz, J. M., and F. Plog, 1970, The nature of archaeological explanation. *American Antiquity* 35:405–412.

Frost, H., 1963, *Under the Mediterranean*. Englewood Cliffs, N.J.: Prentice-Hall.

Fry, R. E., 1972, Manually operated post-hole diggers as sampling instruments. *American Antiquity* 37:259–260.

Fryxell, R., and D. Daugherty, 1963, *Late Glacial and Post Glacial geological and archaeological chronology of the Columbia Plateau, Washington*. Pullman: Washington State University, Laboratory of Anthropology, Report of Investigations, No. 23.

Gabel, C., 1964, *Man before history*. Englewood Cliffs, N.J.: Prentice-Hall.

———, 1967, *Analysis of prehistoric economic patterns*. New York: Holt, Rinehart and Winston, Inc.

Gadow, H., 1908, *Through southern Mexico: being an account of the travels of a naturalist*. London: Witherby.

Gann, T. W. F., 1927, *Maya cities*. London: Duckworth.

———, 1928, *Discoveries and adventures in Central America*. London: Duckworth.

Garcia Cook, A., 1967, *Análisis tipológico de artefactos*. Mexico City: Instituto Nacional de Antropologia e Historia, Investigaciones, No. 12.

Gardin, J.-C., 1958, Four codes for the description of artifacts: an essay in archeological technique and theory. *American Anthropologist* 60:335–337.

Garner, B., 1967, Models of urban geography and settlement location. In *Models in geography*, R. J. Chorley and P. Haggett, eds. London: Methuen, pp. 303–361.

Garrod, Dorothy A. E., 1946. *Environment, tools, and man*. London: Cambridge.

Garrod, D., and D. M. A. Bate, 1937, *The Stone Age of Mount Carmel*, 2 vols. London: Oxford.

Gathercole, P., 1971, 'Patterns in prehistory': an examination of the later thinking of V. Gordon Childe. *World Archaeology* 3:225–232.

Gebhard, P., 1949, An archaeological survey of the blowouts of Yuma County, Colorado. *American Antiquity* 15:132–143.

Gelfand, A. E., 1971, Seriation methods for archeological materials. *American Antiquity* 36:263–274.

Genovés, S. T., 1967, Some problems in the physical anthropological study of the peopling of America. *Current Anthropology* 8:297–312.

Genovés, S. T., 1969a, Sex determination in earlier man. In *Science in archaeology*, D. Brothwell and E. Higgs, eds., rev. ed. London: Thames and Hudson, pp. 429–439.

————, 1969b, Estimation of age and mortality. In *Science in archaeology*. D. Brothwell and E. Higgs, eds., rev. ed. London: Thames and Hudson, pp. 440–452.

Gentner, W., and H. J. Lippolt, 1969, The potassium-argon dating of Upper Tertiary and Pleistocene deposits. In *Science in archaeology*, D. Brothwell and E. Higgs, eds., rev. ed. London: Thames and Hudson, pp. 88–100.

Germain, L., 1923, Les climats des temps quaternaires d'après les mollusques terrestres et fluviatiles. *L'Anthropologie* 33:301–322.

Gettens, R. J., and B. M. Usilton, 1955, Abstracts of technical studies in art and archaeology. Washington, D.C.: Smithsonian Institution, Freer Gallery of Art, Occasional Papers, 2(2).

Geyer, D., 1923, Die Quartarmollusken und die Klimafrage. *Paleontologisches Zeitschrift* 5:72–94.

Gibson, G. E., 1972, Cultural dynamics and the development of the Oneota lifeway in Wisconsin. *American Antiquity* 37:166–185.

Giddings, J. L., 1960, The archeology of Bering Strait. *Current Anthropology* 1:121–138.

————, 1962, Development of tree-ring dating as an archeological aid. In *Tree growth*, T. T. Koslowski, ed. New York: Ronald, pp. 119–132.

————, 1965, Archaeology [of Alaska]. In *The Quaternary of the United States*, H. E. Wright and D. Frey, eds. Princeton, N.J.: Princeton University Press, pp. 367–374.

————, 1966, Cross-dating the archaeology of northwestern Alaska. *Science* 153:127–135.

Giddings, J. L., and H. G. Bandi, 1962, Eskimo-archäologische Strandwalluntersuchungen auf Kap Krusenstern, Nordwest-Alaska. *Germania* 40:1–21.

Giffin, N. M., 1930, The roles of men and women in Eskimo culture. Chicago: University of Chicago Publications in Anthropology, Ethnology Series, Vol. 13.

Gifford, E. W., 1916, Composition of California shellmounds. Berkeley: University of California Publications in American Archaeology and Ethnology, 12:1–29.

————, 1951, Archaeological investigations in Fiji. Berkeley: University of California Anthropological Records 13:189–288.

Gifford, J. C., 1960, The type-variety method of ceramic classification as an indicator of cultural phenomena. *American Antiquity* 25:341–347.

Gimbutas, M., 1963, The Indo-Europeans: archeological problems. *American Anthropologist* 65:815–836.

Gladwin, H. S., 1934, The archaeology of the Southwest and its relation to the cultures of Texas. *Bulletin of the Texas Archeological and Paleontological Society*, Abilene, 6:19–35.

————, 1943, *A review and analysis of the Flagstaff culture*. Globe, Ariz.: Gila Pueblo Medallion Papers, No. 31.

————, 1947, *Men out of Asia*. New York: McGraw-Hill.

————, 1957, *A history of the ancient Southwest*. Portland, Me.: Bond Wheelwright.

————, E. W. Haury, E. B. Sayles, and N. Gladwin, 1937, *Excavations at Snaketown: material culture*. Globe, Ariz.: Gila Pueblo Medallion Papers, Nos. 25–26, 30, 38.

Gladwin, W., and H. S. Gladwin, 1928a, *A method for the designation of cultures and their variations*. Globe, Ariz.: Gila Pueblo Medallion Papers, No. 15.

————, 1928b, *The use of potsherds in an archaeological survey of the Southwest*. Globe, Ariz.: Gila Pueblo Medallion Papers, No. 2.

Glass, B. P., 1951, *A key to the skulls of North American Mammals*. Minneapolis: Burgess.

Glemser, M. S., 1963, Palaeoserology. In *Science in archaeology*, D. Brothwell and E. Higgs, eds. London: Thames and Hudson, pp. 437–446.

Glenn, E. S., 1966, A cognitive approach to the analysis of cultures and cultural evolution. *General System* 11:115–132.

Glob, P., 1954, Lifelike man preserved 2,000 years in peat. *National Geographic Magazine* 105:419–430.

————, 1969, *The bog people*. London: Faber and Faber.

Glock, W. S., 1937, *Principles and methods of tree-ring analysis*. Washington, D.C.: Carnegie Institution of Washington, Publication No. 486.

————, 1955, Tree growth: growth rings and climate. *The Botanical Review* 21:73–188.

Godwin, H., 1962, Half-life of radiocarbon. *Nature* 195:984.

Goggin, J. M., 1960, Underwater archaeology: its nature and limitations. *American Antiquity* 25:348–354.

Goldstein, M. S., 1953, Some vital statistics based on skeletal material. *Human Biology* 25:3–10.

Goodall, E., 1946, Domestic animals in rock art. *Transactions of the Rhodesia Science Association, Salisbury* 41:57–62.

Goodwin, A. J. H., 1953, *Method in prehistory*. Capetown: South African Archaeological Society Handbook, Series No. 1.

————, 1960, Chemical alteration (patination) of stone. *Viking Fund Publications in Anthropology* No. 28:300–312.

Gordon, C. H., 1970, *Before Columbus*. New York: Crown.

Gordon, D. H., 1953, Fire and the sword: the technique of destruction. *Antiquity* 27:149–153.

Gordus, A. A., 1971, Rapid nondestructive activation analysis of silver in coins. In *Science and archaeology*, R. H. Brill, ed. Cambridge, Mass.: MIT Press, pp. 145–155.

————, J. B. Griffin, and G. A. Wright, 1971, Activation analysis identification of the geologic origins of prehistoric obsidian artifacts. In *Science and archaeology*, R. H. Brill, ed. Cambridge, Masss.: MIT Press, pp. 222–234.

Gorenstein, S., 1965, *Introduction to archaeology*. New York: Basic Books.

Gould, R. A., 1968a, Chipping stones in the outback. *Natural History* 77:42–49.

————, 1968b, Living archaeology: the Ngatatjara of Western Australia. *Southwestern Journal of Anthropology* 24:101–122.

————, 1969, Subsistence behavior among the Western Desert aborigines of Australia. *Oceania* 39:253–274.

————, 1971, The archaeologist as ethnographer: a case from the Western Desert of Australia. *World Archaeology* (2):143–177.

Grace, V. R., 1961, *Amphoras and the ancient wine trade*. Princeton, N.J.: American School of Classical Studies at Athens.

Graham, J. A., R. F. Heizer, and T. R. Hester, 1972, *A bibliography of replicative experiments in archaeology*. Berkeley: University of California, Archaeological Research Facility, pp. 1–26.

Grant, C., 1965, *The rock paintings of the Chumash*. Berkeley: University of California Press.

Grant, J., 1966, *A pillage of art*. New York: Roy.

Grant, M., 1958, *Roman history from coins*. London: Cambridge.

Gray, J. and W. Smith, 1962, Fossil pollen and archaeology. *Archaeology* 15:16–26.

Graziozi, P., 1956, *L'Arte Antica età della Pietra*. Sansioni.

———, 1960, *Palaeolithic art*. New York: McGraw-Hill.

Green, R. C., R. R. Brooks, and R. D. Reeves, 1967, Characterization of New Zealand obsidians by emission spectroscopy. *New Zealand Journal of Science* 10:675–682.

———, and others, 1967, Archeology on the island of Mo'orla, French Polynesia. New York: Anthropological Papers of the American Museum of Natural History, 51 (Part 2).

Greengo, R., 1954, Archaeological marine shells [from the Monagrillo site, Panama]. Cambridge, Mass.: Harvard University, Papers of the Peabody Museum, 49:141–150.

———, 1964, Issaquena: an archaeological phase in the Yazoo Basin of the lower Mississippi Valley. *American Antiquity* 30(2:2).

Greenman, E. F., 1943, The archaeology and geology of two early sites near Killarney, Ontario. Ann Arbor, Mich.: Papers of the Michigan Academy of Science, Arts and Letters 28:505–530.

———, 1957, An American Eolithic? *American Antiquity* 22:298.

———, 1963, The Upper Paleolithic in the New World. *Current Anthropology* 4:41–91.

———, and Stanley, 1940, A geologically dated camp site, Georgian Bay, Ontario. *American Antiquity* 5:194–199.

Greenwood, R., 1961, Quantitative analysis of shells from a site in Goleta, California. *American Antiquity* 26:416–420.

Griffin, J. B., 1955, Chronology and dating processes. In *Yearbook of Anthropology*. New York: Wenner-Gren, pp. 133–148.

———, 1959, The pursuit of archeology in the United States. *American Anthropologist* 61:379–389.

———, 1960, Some prehistoric connections between Siberia and America. *Science* 131:801–812.

———, 1962, A discussion of prehistoric similarities and connections between the Arctic and the temperate zones of North America. In *Prehistoric cultural relations between the Arctic and temperate zones of North America*, J. M. Campbell, ed. Montreal: Arctic Institute of North America, Technical Paper No. 11, pp. 154–163.

———, and C. W. Angell, 1935, An experimental study of the techniques of pottery making. Ann Arbor, Mich.: Papers of the Michigan Academy of Science, Arts and Letters 20:1–6.

Griffiths, J. G., 1956, Archaeology and Hesoid's five ages. *Journal of the History of Ideas* 17:109–119.

Grigor'ev, G. P., 1967, A new reconstruction of above-ground dwelling of Kostenki I. *Current Anthropology* 8:344–349.

Grimes, W. F., 1954, The scientific bias of archaeology. *The Advancement of Science*, London 10:343–346.

Grinsell, L., P. Rahtz, and A. Warhurst, 1966, *The preparation of archaeological reports*. London: J. Baker.

Groff, D. W., 1971, Gas chromatography methods for bone fluorine and nitrogen composition. In *Science and archaeology*, R. H. Brill, ed. Cambridge, Mass.: MIT Press, pp. 272–278.

Grüss, J., 1932, Die beiden ältesten Weine unserer Kulturwelt. *Forschungen und Fortschritte* 8:2:23–24.

Gumerman, G. J., ed, 1971, *The distribution of prehistoric population aggregates.* Prescott, Ariz.: Prescott College Press.

———, and T. R. Lyons, 1971, Archeological methodology and remote sensing. *Science* 172:126–132.

Gunda, B., 1949, Plant gathering in the economic life of Eurasia. *Southwestern Journal of Anthropology* 5:369–378.

Guthe, C. E., 1925, *Pueblo pottery making: a study at the village of San Idlefonso.* New Haven, Conn.: Yale University Press.

Hack, J. T., 1942, The changing physical environment of the Hopi Indians of Arizona. Cambridge, Mass.: Harvard University, Papers of the Peabody Museum, 35(1).

Hadleigh-West, F., 1967, A system of archaeological site designation for Alaska. *American Antiquity* 32:107–108.

Haggett, P., 1965, *Locational analysis in human geography.* London: E. Arnold.

Haines, F., 1938a, Where did the Plains Indians get their horses? *American Anthropologist* 40:112–117.

———, 1938b, The northward spread of horses among the Plains Indians. *American Anthropologist* 40:429–437.

Hall, A. D., and R. E. Fagen, 1956, Definition of system. *General Systems* 1:18–28.

Hall, E. T., 1969, Dating pottery by thermoluminescence. In *Science in archaeology,* D. Brothwell and E. Higgs, eds., rev. ed. London: Thames and Hudson, pp. 106–108.

———, 1971, Two examples of the use of chemical analysis in the solution of archaeological problems. In *Science and archaeology,* R. H. Brill, ed. Cambridge, Mass.: MIT Press, pp. 156–164.

Hall, Edward T., 1966, *The hidden dimension.* New York: Doubleday.

Halloway, R. L., 1969, Culture: a human domain. *Current Anthropology* 10:395–412.

Hallowell, A. I., 1960, The beginnings of anthropology in America. In *Selected papers from the American Anthropologist 1888–1920,* F. de Laguna, ed. New York: Harper & Row, pp. 1–90.

Hammond, A. L., 1971a, The new archeology: toward a social science. *Science* 172:1119–1120.

———, 1971b, Tools for archeology: aids to studying the past. *Science* 173:511–512.

Hammond, P. C., 1963, *Archaeological techniques for amateurs.* Princeton, N.J.: Van Nostrand.

Hamy, E. T., 1870, *Precis de paléontologie humaine.* Paris: J.-B. Ballière.

———, 1963, The fishhook industry of the ancient inhabitants of the archipelago of California. Berkeley: Reports of the University of California Archaeological Survey No. 59:61–69. (Originally printed in *Revue d'Ethnographie* 4:6–13.)

Hardin, G., 1968, The cybernetics of competition: a biologist's view of society. In *Modern systems research for the behavioral scientist,* W. Buckley, ed. pp. 449–459.

Hargrave, L., 1939, Bird remains from abandoned Indian dwellings in Arizona and Utah. *Condor* 41:206–210.

Haring, A., A. E. De Vries, and H. De Vries, 1958, Radiocarbon dating up to 70,000 years by isotopic enrichment. *Science* 128:472–473.

Harlan, J. R., 1967, A wild wheat harvest in Turkey. *Antiquity* 20:197–201.

———, 1971, Agricultural origins: centers and non-centers. *Science* 174:468–474.

Harner, M. J., 1956, Thermo-facts vs. artifacts: an experimental study of the Malpais industry. Berkeley: Reports of the University of California Archaeological Survey No. 33:39–43.

Harner, M. J., 1970, Population pressure and the social evolution of agriculturalists. *Southwestern Journal of Anthropology* 26:67–86.

Harradine, F. F., 1949, The variability of soil properties in relation to stages of profile development. *Proceedings of the Soil Science Society of America* 14:302–311.

Harrington, J. C., 1952, Historic site archeology in the United States. In *Archeology of eastern United States,* J. B. Griffin, ed. Chicago: University of Chicago Press, pp. 335–344.

———, 1955, Archeology as an auxiliary science to American history. *American Anthropologist* 57:1121–1130.

Harrington, M. R., 1933, *Gypsum Cave, Nevada.* Los Angeles: Southwest Museum Papers, No. 8.

Harris, A. H., 1963, *Vertebrate remains and past environmental reconstruction in the Navajo reservoir district.* Santa Fe: Museum of New Mexico, Papers in Anthropology, No. 11.

Harris, D. R., 1969, Agricultural systems, ecosystems and the origins of agriculture. In *The domestication and exploitation of plants and animals,* P. J. Ucko and G. W. Dimbleby, eds. Chicago: Aldine, pp. 3–16.

———, 1972, The prehistory of tropical agriculture: an ethnoecological model. In *The explanation of culture change,* C. Renfrew, ed. London: Duckworth.

Harris, M., 1968, *The rise of anthropological theory.* New York: Crowell.

Harrison, R. G., and A. B. Abdalla, 1972, The remains of Tutankhamun. *Antiquity* 44:8–14.

Harriss, J. C., 1971, Explanations in prehistory. *Proceedings of the Prehistoric Society* 37:38–55.

Harrisson, T., and L. Medway, 1962, A first classification of prehistoric bone and tooth artifacts (based on material from Niah Great Cave). *Sarawak Museum Journal* 10:335–362.

Harvey, D., 1967, Models of the evolution of spatial patterns in human geography. In *Models in geography,* R. J. Chorley and P. Haggett, eds. London: Methuen, pp. 549–609.

Hatch, M. P., 1971, An hypothesis on Olmec astronomy with special reference to the La Venta site. Berkeley: University of California, Archaeological Research Facility, Contribution 13:1–64.

Haury, E. W., 1931, Minute beads from prehistoric pueblos. *American Anthropologist* 33:80–87.

———, 1958, An alluvial site on the San Carlos Indian reservation, Arizona. *American Antiquity* 23:2–27.

———, and others, 1950, *The stratigraphy and archaeology of Ventana Cave, Arizona.* Tucson: University of Arizona Press. (Also, Albuquerque: The University of New Mexico Press.)

———, E. Antevs, and J. F. Lance, 1953, Artifacts with mammoth remains, Naco, Arizona. *American Antiquity* 19:1–24.

———, E. B. Sayles, and W. W. Wasley, 1959, The Lehner mammoth site, southeastern Arizona. *American Antiquity* 25:2–30.

Haviland, W. A., 1965, Prehistoric settlement at Tikal, Guatemala. *Expedition* 7:14–23.

———, 1967, Stature at Tikal, Guatemala: implications for ancient Maya demography and social organization. *American Antiquity* 32:316–325.

———, 1969, A new population estimate for Tikal, Guatemala. *American Antiquity* 34:429–433.

———, 1970, Tikal, Guatemala and Mesoamerican urbanism. *World Archaeology* 2:186–198.

———, 1972a, Family size, prehistoric population estimates, and the ancient Maya. *American Antiquity* 37:135–139.

Haviland, W. A., 1972b, Estimates of Maya population: comments on Thompson's comments. *American Antiquity* 37:261–262.

Hawkes, C. F. C., 1954, Archaeological theory and method: some suggestions from the Old World. *American Anthropologist* 56:155–168.

———, 1957, Archaeology as science: purposes and pitfalls. *The Advancement of Science,* No. 54.

Hawkes, J., 1967, God in the machine. *Antiquity* 41:174–180.

———, 1968, The proper study of mankind. *Antiquity* 42:255–262.

———, and L. Woolley, 1963, *History of mankind:* Vol. 1. *Prehistory and the beginnings of civilization.* New York: Harper & Row.

Hawkins, G. S., 1964, Stonehenge: a Neolithic computer. *Nature* 202:1258–1261.

———, 1965a, *Stonehenge decoded.* New York: Doubleday.

———, 1965b, Sun, moon, men and stones. *American Scientist* 53:391–408.

———, R. J. C. Atkinson, Alexander Thom, C. A. Newham, D. H. Sadler, and R. A. Newall, 1967, Hoyle on Stonehenge: some comments. *Antiquity* 41:91–98.

Hawley, A., 1944, Ecology and human ecology. *Social Forces* 22:398–405.

Hawley, F. M., 1934, *The significance of the dated prehistory of Chetro Ketl.* Albuquerque: University of New Mexico Bulletin, Monograph Series, 1(1).

———, 1937, Reversed stratigraphy. *American Antiquity* 2:297–299.

———, M. Pijoan, and C. A. Elkin, 1943, An inquiry into the food economy of Zia Pueblo. *American Anthropologist* 45:547–556.

Hayden, J. D., 1959, Notes on Pima pottery making. *The Kiva* 24:10–16.

Hayek, F. A., 1955, Degrees of explanation. *British Journal of Philosophical Science* 6:209–225.

Hayes, A. C., 1964, *The archaeological survey of Wetherill Mesa.* Washington, D.C.: National Park Service, Archeological Research Series, No. 7-A.

Haynes, C. V., 1966, Radiocarbon samples: chemical removal of plant contaminants. *Science* 151:1391–1392.

Heath, D. W., 1958, Sexual division of labor and cross-cultural research. *Social Forces* 37:77–79.

Heath, G. R., 1957, Improvements in the stereo-mosaic. *Photogrammetric Engineering* 23:536–542.

Heer, O., 1863, *Die Urwelt der Schweiz.* Zürich: F. Schulthess.

Heider, K. G., 1967, Archaeological assumptions and ethnographical facts; a cautionary tale from New Guinea. *Southwestern Journal of Anthropology* 23:52–64.

———, 1969, Visiting trade institutions. *American Anthropologist* 71:462–471.

Heine-Geldern, R., 1954, Die Asiatische Herkunft der Südamerikanischen Metalltechnik. *Paideuma* 5:347–423.

———, and G. Ekholm, 1951, Significant parallels in the symbolic arts of southern Asia and Middle America. In *The civilizations of ancient America,* Sol Tax, ed. Selected Papers of the 29th International Congress of Americanists, pp. 299–309.

Heinzelin, J. de, 1962, *Manual de typologie des industries lithiques.* Bruxelles: Institut Royal des Sciences Naturelles de Belgique.

Heizer, R. F., 1941a, The direct-historical approach in California archaeology. *American Antiquity* 7:98–122, 141–146.

———, 1941b, Aboriginal trade between the Southwest and California. *Southwest Museum Masterkey* 15:185–188.

———, 1944, Artifact transport by migratory animals and other means. *American Antiquity* 9:395–400.

Heizer, R. F., 1951a, The sickle in aboriginal western North America. *American Antiquity* 16:247–253.

———, 1951b, A prehistoric Yurok ceremonial site (Hum-174). Berkeley: Reports of the University of California Archaeological Survey 11:1–4.

———, 1953, Long-range dating in archaeology. In *Anthropology today*, A. L. Kroeber, chairman. Chicago: University of Chicago Press, pp. 3–42.

———, 1955, Primitive man as an ecologic factor. Berkeley: Kroeber Anthropological Society Papers 13:1–31.

———, 1958, Prehistoric central California: a problem in historical-developmental classification. Berkeley: Reports of the University of California Archaeological Survey 41:19–26.

———, ed., 1959, *The archaeologist at work*. New York: Harper & Row.

———, ed., 1960, Physical analysis of habitation residues. In *The application of quantitative methods in archaeology*. Viking Fund Publications in Anthropology, No. 28:93–157.

———, 1961, Inferences on the nature of Olmec society based on data from the La Venta site. Berkeley: Kroeber Anthropological Society Papers, No. 25:43–57.

———, 1962a, The background of Thomsen's three age system. *Technology and Culture* 3:259–266.

———, 1962b, Village shifts and tribal spreads in California prehistory. *Southwest Museum Masterkey* 36:60–67.

———, 1962c, *Man's discovery of his past: literary landmarks in archaeology*. Englewood Cliffs, N.J.: Prentice-Hall.

———, 1963, Domestic fuel in primitive society. *Journal of the Royal Anthropological Institute* 93:186–193.

———, 1965, Problems in dating Lake Mojave artifacts. *Southwest Museum Masterkey* 39:125–134.

———, 1966, Salvage and other archaeology. *Southwest Museum Masterkey* 40:54–60.

———, 1967, Analysis of human coprolites from a dry Nevada cave. Berkeley: Reports of the University of California Archaeological Survey, No. 70:1–20.

———, 1968a, Suggested change in system of site designations. *American Antiquity* 33:254.

———, 1968b, Migratory animals as dispersal agents of cultural materials. *Science* 161:914–915.

———, 1969, *Man's discovery of his past*. Palo Alto, Calif.: Peek Publications.

———, and M. A. Baumhoff, 1959, Great Basin petroglyphs and prehistoric game trails. *Science* 129:904–905.

———, 1970, Big game hunters in the Great Basin: a critical review of the evidence. Berkeley: University of California, Archaeological Research Facility, Contribution 7:1–12.

———, and R. Berger, 1970, Radiocarbon age of the Gypsum Cave culture. Berkeley: University of California, Archaeological Research Facility, Contribution 7:13–18.

———, and S. F. Cook, 1952. Fluorine and other chemical tests of some North American human and fossil bones. *American Journal of Physical Anthropology* 10:289–304.

———, and J. Graham, 1967, *A guide to field methods in archaeology*. Palo Alto, Calif.: National Press.

———, eds., 1971, *Observations on the emergence of civilization in Mesoamerica*. Berkeley: University of California, Archaeological Research Facility, Contribution No. 11.

Heizer, R. F., 1972, Replicative experiments in archaeology—an introductory bibliography. In *Bela Gunda Festschrift Volume*, Debrecen, Hungary: University of Debrecen.

——, and G. W. Hewes, 1940, Animal ceremonialism in central California in the light of archaeology. *American Anthropologist* 42:587–603.

——, and A. D. Krieger, 1956, The archaeology of Humboldt Cave, Churchill County, Nevada. Berkeley: University of California Publications in American Archaeology and Ethnology, 47:1–190.

——, and L. K. Napton, 1970, *Archaeology and the prehistoric Great Basin subsistence regime as seen from Lovelock Cave, Nevada*. Berkeley: University of California, Archaeological Research Facility, Contribution No. 10.

——, and H. Williams, 1965, Stones used for colossal sculpture at or near Teotihuacan. Berkeley: University of California, Archaeological Research Facility, Contribution No. 1, pp. 55–70.

——, ——, and J. A. Graham, 1965, Notes on Mesoamerican obsidians and their significance in archaeological studies. Berkeley: University of California, Archaeological Research Facility, Contribution No. 1, pp. 94–103.

Helbaek, H., 1950, Tollund manden Sidste Maaltid. *Aarböger for Nordisk Oldkyndighed og Historie*, pp. 311–314.

——, 1951, Seeds of weeds as food in the pre-Roman Iron Age. *Kuml*, 1951: 65–74. Aarhus.

——, 1953, Archaeology and agricultural botany. University of London, Institute of Archaeology, Ninth Annual Report, pp. 44–59.

——, 1959, Domestication of food plants in the Old World. *Science* 130:365–372.

——, 1964, Early Hassunan vegetable food at Tell es Sawwan near Samarra. *Sumer* 20:45–48.

——, 1966, Commentary on the phylogenesis of *Triticum* and *Hordeum*. *Economic Botany* 20:350–360.

——, 1969, Paleo-ethnobotany. In *Science in archaeology*, D. Brothwell and E. Higgs, eds., rev. ed. London: Thames and Hudson, pp. 206–214.

Helm, J., 1962, The ecological approach in anthropology. *American Journal of Sociology* 47:630–639.

Hempel, C. G., 1951, General system theory and the unity of science. *Human Biology* 23:313–322.

——, 1952, Fundamentals of concept formation in empirical science. Chicago: University of Chicago Press, *International Encyclopedia of Unified Science, Foundations of the Unity of Science*, 2(7).

——, 1965, *Aspects of scientific explanation, and other essays in the philosophy of science*. New York: Free Press.

——, 1966, *Philosophy of natural science*. Englewood Cliffs, N.J.: Prentice-Hall.

——, and P. Oppenheim, 1948, Studies in the logic of explanation. *Philosophy of Science* 15:135–175.

Hencken, H. O., 1955, Indo-European languages and archeology. Washington, D.C.: *American Anthropological Association, Memoir* No. 84.

Henshall, A. S., 1951, Textiles and weaving appliances in prehistoric Britain. *Proceedings of the Prehistoric Society* 16:130–162.

——, 1963, *The chambered tombs of Scotland*, Vol. I. Edinburgh: Edinburgh University Press.

Herre, W., 1969, The science and history of domesticated animals. In *Science and archaeology*, D. Brothwell and E. Higgs, eds., rev. ed. London: Thames and Hudson, pp. 257–272.

Herrmann, Georgina, 1968, Lapis lazuli: the early phases of its trade. *Iraq* 30:21–57.

Hesse, A., 1966, *Prospections géophysiques à faible profondeur: applications à l'archéologie.* Paris: Dunod.

Hester, J. J., 1960, Late Pleistocene extinction and radiocarbon dating. *American Antiquity* 26:58–77.

———, 1962, *Early Navajo migrations and acculturation in the Southwest.* Santa Fe, N.M.: Museum of New Mexico, Papers in Anthropology, No. 6.

———, and K. J. Conover, 1970, Ecological sampling of middens on the Northwest Coast. *Northwest Anthropological Research Notes,* 4:2:137–152.

Hester, T. R., 1970, A study of wear patterns on hafted and unhafted bifaces from two Nevada caves. Berkeley: University of California, Archaeological Research Facility, Contribution No. 7, pp. 44–54.

———, 1972, *Prehistoric lithic technology: an introductory bibliography.* Berkeley: University of California, Archaeological Research Facility.

———, and R. F. Heizer, 1972, Problems in the functional interpretation of artifacts: scraper planes from Mitla and Yagul, Oaxaca. Berkeley: University of California, Archaeological Research Facility, Contribution No. 14: 107–123.

———, ———, and R. N. Jack, 1971, Technology and geologic sources of obsidian from Cerro de las Mesas, Veracruz, Mexico, with observations on Olmec trade. Berkeley: University of California, Archaeological Research Facility, Contribution No. 13, pp. 133–142.

———, R. M. Jack, and R. F. Heizer, 1971, The obsidian of Tres Zapotes. Berkeley: University of California, Archaeological Research Facility, Contribution No. 13, pp. 65–132.

Heusser, C. J., 1960, *Late-Pleistocene environments of north Pacific North America.* New York: American Geographical Society, Special Publication No. 35.

Hewitt, H. D., 1915, Some experiments on patination. *Proceedings of the Prehistoric Society of East Anglia* 2:1:45–50.

Heyerdahl, T., 1959, *Aku-Aku; the secret of Easter Island.* New York: Rand McNally Cardinal Giant Pocket Book.

———, 1963, Feasible ocean routes to and from the Americas in pre-Columbian times. *American Antiquity* 28:482–488.

———, and E. Ferdon, 1961, *Archaeology of Easter Island.* Sante Fe: Monographs of the School of American Research and the Museum of New Mexico, No. 24.

Higgs, E. S., 1959, Excavations at a Mesolithic site at Downton near Salisbury, Wiltshire. *Proceedings of the Prehistoric Society* (New Series) 25: 209–232.

———, 1965, Faunal fluctuations and climate in Libya. In *Background to evolution in Africa,* W. J. Bishop and J. D. Clark, eds. Chicago: University of Chicago Press, pp. 149–157.

———, 1968, Archaeology—where now? *Mankind* 6:617–620.

———, and D. Webley, 1971, Further information concerning the environment of Palaeolithic man in Epirus. *Proceedings of the Prehistoric Society* 37(2):367–380.

———, C. Vita-Finzi, D. R. Harris, and A. E. Fagg, 1967, The climate, environment and industries of Stone Age Greece: Part III. *Proceedings of the Prehistoric Society* 33:1–29.

Higham, C. W., 1968, Stock rearing as a cultural factor in prehistoric Europe. *Proceedings of the Prehistoric Society* 33:84–106.

Hill, J. N., 1966, A prehistoric community in eastern Arizona. *Southwestern Journal of Anthropology* 22:9–30.

Hill, J. N., 1967, The problem of sampling. *Fieldiana, Anthropology,* Chicago: Field Museum of Natural History 57: 145–157.

———, 1970, Prehistoric social organization in the American Southwest: theory and method. In *Reconstructing prehistoric Pueblo societies,* W. A. Longacre, ed. Albuquerque: University of New Mexico Press, pp. 11–58.

———, 1971, Report on seminar on the explanation of prehistoric organizational change. *Current Anthropology* 12: 406–408.

———, and R. H. Hevly, 1968, Pollen at Broken K pueblo: some new interpretations. *American Antiquity* 33: 200–210.

Hill, W. W., 1937, *Navajo pottery manufacture.* Albuquerque: University of New Mexico Bulletin, Anthropological Series 2 (3).

———, 1948, Navajo trading and trading ritual: a study of cultural dynamics. *Southwestern Journal of Anthropology* 4: 371–396.

Hinsdale, W. B., 1931, *Archaeological atlas of Michigan.* Ann Arbor: University of Michigan Press, Michigan Handbook Series, No. 4.

Hiroa, Te Hangi (P. Buck), 1930, *Samoan material culture.* Honolulu: Bernice P. Bishop Museum, Bulletin No. 73.

Hodder, I., and M. Hassal, 1971, The non-random spacing of Romano-British walled towns. *Man* 6: 391–407.

Hodges, H. W., 1964, *Artifacts; an introduction to early materials and technology.* London: J. Baker.

Hodgson, J., 1822, On the study of antiquities. *Archaeologia Aeliana* 1: 9–19.

Hodson, F. R., 1969, Searching for structure within multivariate archaeological data. *World Archaeology* 1: 90–105.

Hoebel, E. A., 1972, *Anthropology: the study of man,* 4th ed. New York: McGraw-Hill.

Hoijer, H., 1956a, Lexicostatistics: a critique. *Language* 32: 49–60.

———, 1956b, The chronology of the Athapaskan languages. *International Journal of American Linguistics* 22: 219–232.

Hokr, Z., 1951, A method of quantitative determination of the climate in the Quaternary Period by means of mammal association. *Paleontology, Sbornik Geological Survey, Czechoslovakia* 18: 209–218.

Hole, F., 1962, Archeological survey and excavation in Iran 1961. *Science* 137: 524–526.

———, 1966, Investigating the origins of Mesopotamian civilization. *Science* 153: 605–611.

———, 1968, Evidence of social organization in western Iran: 8000–4000 B.C. In *New perspectives in archeology,* S. Binford and L. Binford, eds. Chicago: Aldine, pp. 245–266.

———, 1970, The paleolithic culture sequence in western Iran. Proceedings, VII International Congress of Prehistoric and Protohistoric Sciences, Prague, 1966, pp. 286–292.

———, 1971, Approaching typology rationally. *The Record* 27: 3.

———, 1972a, The goals and structure of archeology and their relation to student training. In *Archeology today,* C. L. Redman, ed. New York: Wiley.

———, 1972b, Questions of theory in the explanation of culture change in prehistory. In *The explanation of culture change,* C. Renfrew, ed. London: Duckworth.

———, and K. V. Flannery, 1962, Excavations at Ali Kosh, Iran, 1961. *Iranica Antiqua* 2: 97–148.

———, 1968, Prehistory of southwestern Iran: a preliminary report. *Proceedings of the Prehistoric Society* 33: 147–206.

Hole, F., K. V. Flannery, and J. A. Neely, 1969, *Prehistory and human ecology of the Deh Luran Plain.* Ann Arbor: University of Michigan, Museum of Anthropology, Memoirs No. 1.

——, and M. Shaw, 1967. *Computer analysis of chronological seriation.* Houston: Rice University Studies, 53(3).

Holmes, G. W., 1951, The regional significance of the Pleistocene deposits in the Eden Valley, Wyoming. Philadelphia: University of Pennsylvania Museum, Museum Monographs, pp. 95–102.

Holmes, W. H., 1881, Prehistoric textile fabrics of the United States, derived from impressions in pottery. Washington, D.C.: Annual Report, Bureau of American Ethnology, No. 3:393–425.

——, 1893, Vestiges of early man in Minnesota. *The American Geologist* 11:219–240.

——, 1897, *Archeological studies among the ancient cities of Mexico.* Chicago: Field Columbian Museum, Anthropological Series, 1(8).

——, 1913, The relation of archeology to ethnology. *American Anthropologist* 15:566–567.

——, 1919, Handbook of aboriginal American antiquities. Washington, D.C.: Bulletin of the Bureau of American Ethnology, No. 60.

Holmquist, J. D., and A. H. Wheeler, 1964, *Diving into the past.* St. Paul: The Minnesota Historical Society and the Council of Underwater Archaeology.

Hood, M. S. F., 1967, The Tartaria tablets. *Antiquity* 41:99–113.

Hooijer, D. A., 1961, The fossil vertebrates of Ksar 'Akil, a Paleolithic rock shelter in Lebanon. *Zoologische Verhandelingen,* No. 49.

Hope-Taylor, B., 1966, Archaeological draughtmanship: Part II. *Antiquity* 40:107–113.

——, 1967, Archaeological draughtmanship: Part III. *Antiquity* 41:181–189.

Hopkins, D. M., 1959, Cenozoic history of the Bering Land Bridge. *Science* 129:1519–1528.

Horton, R. E., 1945, Erosional development of streams and their drainage patterns. *Bulletin of the Geological Society of America* 56:275–370.

Hough, W., 1897, Stone-work at Tewa. *American Anthropologist* (Old Series) 10:191.

——, 1930, Ancient Pueblo subsistence. New York: Proceedings of the Twenty-Third International Congress of Americanists, pp. 67–69.

Houghton, W., 1877, On the mammalia of the Assyrian sculptures. London: Society of Biblical Archaeology Transactions 5:229–383.

Howell, F. C., 1959, Upper Pleistocene stratigraphy and early man in the Levant. *Proceedings of the American Philosophical Society* 103:1–65.

——, 1962a, Potassium-argon dating at Olduvai Gorge. *Current Anthropology* 3:306–308.

——, ed., 1962b, Early man and Pleistocene stratigraphy in the circum-Mediterranean regions. *Quaternaria,* Vol. 6.

Howells, W. W., 1960, Estimating population numbers through archaeological and skeletal remains. New York: Viking Fund Publications in Anthropology No. 28:158–180.

——, 1966, Population distances: biological, linguistic, geographical, and environmental. *Current Anthropology* 7:531–540.

Hoyle, F., 1966, Speculations on Stonehenge. *Antiquity* 40:262–276.

Hoyme, L. E., and W. M. Bass, 1962, Human skeletal remains from Tollifero (Ha-6) and Clarksville (Mc-14) sites, John H. Kerr Reservoir Basin, Virginia. Washington, D.C.: Bulletin of the Bureau of American Ethnology, 182:329–400.

Hrdlicka, A., 1937, Man and plants in Alaska. *Science* 86:559–560.

Hubbs, C., ed., 1958, *Zoogeography*. Washington, D.C.: American Association for the Advancement of Science, Special Publications, No. 51.

Hudson, K., 1967, *Handbook for industrial archaeologists*. London: J. Baker.

———, 1971, *A guide to the industrial archaeology of Europe*. Bath: Adams & Dart.

Hulse, F. S., 1965, *The human species: an introduction to physical anthropology*. New York: Random House.

Hume, J. D., 1966, Sea level changes during the last 2000 years at Point Barrow, Alaska. *Science* 150:1165–1166.

Hunt, C. B., W. L. Straus, Jr., and M. G. Wolman, eds., 1967, *Time and stratigraphy in the evolution of man*. Washington, D.C.: National Academy of Sciences, National Research Council, Publication No. 1469.

Huntington, E., 1959, *Mainsprings of civilization*. New York: Mentor Books. (Originally published New York: Wiley, 1945.)

Hurst, V. J., and A. R. Kelly, 1961, Patination of cultural flints. *Science* 134:251–256.

Hutchinson, G. E., 1972, Long Meg reconsidered. *American Scientist* 60:24–31, 210–219.

Huxley, J. S., 1955, Evolution, cultural and biological. In *Yearbook of anthropology, 1955*. New York: Wenner-Gren Foundation for Anthropological Research, pp. 3–25.

Hyams, E., 1952, *Soil and civilization*. London: Thames and Hudson.

Hymes, D. H., 1960, Lexicostatistics so far. *Current Anthropology* 1:3–44.

———, 1963, Conference in the use of computers in anthropology. *Current Anthropology* 4:123–129.

———, 1965, *The use of computers in anthropology*. The Hague: Mouton.

Irwin, H. T., D. J. Hurd, and R. M. LaJeunesse, 1971, Description and measurement in anthropology. Pullman: Washington State University, Laboratory of Anthropology Report of Investigations, No. 48.

Isaac, G., 1967, Towards the interpretation of occupation debris: some experiments and observations. Berkeley: Kroeber Anthropological Society Papers, No. 37:31–57.

———, 1968, Traces of Pleistocene hunters: an East African example. In *Man the hunter*, R. B. Lee and I. DeVore, eds. Chicago: Aldine, pp. 253–261.

———, 1969, Studies of early culture in East Africa. *World Archaeology* 1:1–28.

———, 1971a, The diet of early man: aspects of archaeological evidence from Lower and Middle Pleistocene sites in Africa. *World Archaeology* 2:278–279.

———, 1971b, Whither archaeology? *Antiquity* 45:123–129.

———, R. E. F. Leakey, and A. K. Behrensmeyer, 1971, Archeological traces of early hominid activities, east of Lake Rudolf, Kenya. *Science* 173:1129–1134.

Isham, L. B., 1965, Preparation of drawings for paleontologic publication. In *Handbook of paleontological techniques*. San Francisco: Freeman, pp. 459–468.

Itek Corporation, 1965, *Archaeological photo interpretation*. Technical Report No. 65–8458.

Iverson, J., 1956, Forest clearance in the Stone Age. *Scientific American* 194:36–41.

Jack, R. N., and R. F. Heizer, 1968, "Finger-printing" of some Mesoamerican obsidian artifacts. Berkeley: University of California, Archaeological Research Facility, Contribution No. 5, Paper V:81–100.

Jacobsen, T., and R. McC. Adams, 1958, Salt and silt in ancient Mesopotamian agriculture. *Science* 128:1251–1258.

James, E. O., 1962, *Prehistoric religion: a study in prehistoric archaeology.* New York: Barnes & Noble.

Jarman, M., 1971, Culture and economy in the North Italian Neolithic. *World Archaeology* 2:255–265.

Jay, P. C., ed., 1968, *Primates.* Studies in adaptation and variability. New York: Holt, Rinehart and Winston, Inc.

Jelinek, A. J., 1957, Pleistocene faunas and early man. Ann Arbor, Mich.: Papers of the Michigan Academy of Science, Arts and Letters 42:225–237.

———, 1962a, Use of the cumulative graph in temporal ordering. *American Antiquity* 28:241–243.

———, 1962b, An index of radiocarbon dates associated with cultural materials. *Current Anthropology* 3:451–477.

———, 1966, Correlation of archaeological and palynological data. *Science* 152:1507–1509.

———, 1967, *A prehistoric sequence in the middle Pecos Valley, New Mexico.* Ann Arbor: University of Michigan, Anthropological Papers of the Museum of Anthropology, No. 31.

———, and J. E. Fitting, 1963, Some studies of natural radioactivity in archaeological and paleontological materials. Ann Arbor, Mich.: Papers of the Michigan Academy of Science, Arts and Letters 48:531–540.

———, 1965, eds., *Studies in the natural radioactivity of prehistoric materials.* Ann Arbor, Mich.: University of Michigan, Anthropological Papers of the Museum of Anthropology, No. 25.

Jennings, J. D., 1957, *Danger Cave.* Salt Lake City: University of Utah, Society for American Archaeology, Memoir No. 14.

———, 1964, The desert west. In *Prehistoric man in the New World,* J. D. Jennings and E. Norbeck, eds. Chicago: University of Chicago Press (for William Marsh Rice University), pp. 149–174.

———, 1968, *Prehistory of North America.* New York: McGraw-Hill.

———, and E. Norbeck, eds., 1964, *Prehistoric man in the New World.* Chicago: University of Chicago Press.

Jenny, H., 1941, *Factors of soil-formation.* New York: McGraw-Hill.

Jett, S. C., 1964, Pueblo Indian migrations: an evaluation of the possible physical and cultural determinants. *American Antiquity* 29:281–299.

Jewell, P. A., 1958, Buzzards and barrows. *The South African Archaeological Bulletin* 13:153–155.

———, 1961, An experiment in field archaeology. *Advancement of Science,* London, 17:106–109.

———, and G. W. Dimbleby, 1966. The experimental earthwork on Overton Down, Wiltshire, England. *Proceedings of the Prehistoric Society* 32:313–342.

Joeffe, J. S., 1941, Climatic sequence of the post-Wisconsin glacial age as revealed by the soil profile. *Proceedings of the Soil Science Society of America* 6:368–372.

John, D. H. O., 1965, *Photography on expeditions.* New York: Focal Press.

Johnson, F., 1942, *The Boylston Street fishweir.* Andover, Mass.: Papers of the R. S. Peabody Foundation for Archaeology, Vol. 2.

———, 1966, Archeology in an emergency. *Science* 152:1592–1597.

———, 1967, Radiocarbon dating and archeology in North America. *Science* 155:165–169.

———, F. Rainey, D. Collier, and R. F. Flint, 1951, Radiocarbon dating, a summary. *American Antiquity* 27(1:2):58–65.

Johnson, I. W., 1967, Textiles. In *The prehistory of the Tehuacan Valley:* Vol. 2. *Nonceramic artifacts,* R. S. MacNeish, A. Nelken-Terner, and I. W. Johnson, eds. Austin: University of Texas Press, pp. 189–226.

Johnson, L., 1968, Item seriation as an aid for elementary scale and cluster analysis. Eugene: Museum of Natural History, University of Oregon, Bulletin No. 15.

———, 1972, Problems in "avant-garde" archaeology. *American Anthropologist* 74:366–377.

Johnson, R. A., and F. H. Stross, 1965, Laboratory-scale instrumental neutron activation for archaeological analysis. *American Antiquity* 30:345–347.

Johnson, T., 1957, An experiment with cave-painting media. *The South African Archaeological Bulletin* 47:98–101.

Johnston, D. W., 1944, Problems of terrace correlation. *Bulletin of the Geological Society of America* 55:793–818.

Johnston, R. B., 1964, *Proton magnetometry and its application to archaeology: an evaluation at Angel site.* Indianapolis: Indiana Historical Society. Prehistory Research Series, 4(2).

Jones, A. C., J. R. Weaver, and F. H. Stross, 1967, Note on Indian wood carving in the form of a grasshopper found in Lovelock Cave, Nevada. Berkeley: Reports of the University of California Archaeological Survey No. 70, Paper No. VIII:123–128.

Jones, E., 1966, *Human geography: an introduction to man and his world.* New York: Praeger.

Jones, T. B., 1967, *Paths into the ancient past.* New York: Free Press.

Jope, E. M., 1953, History, archaeology and petrology. *Advancement of Science* 9:432–435.

———, 1960, The mollusca and animal bones from the excavations at Ringneill Quay. In *The Quaternary deposits at Ringneill Quay and Ardmillan, County Down,* N. Stephens and A. E. P. Collins, eds. Proceedings of the Royal Irish Academy 61:6:2:41–77.

Jorgensen, S., 1953, Skovryoning med Flintokse [Forest Clearance with Flint Axes]. *Nationalmuseets Arbejdsmark,* pp. 36–43, 109–110.

Judd, N. M., 1930, The excavation and repair of Betatakin. Washington, D.C.: Proceedings of the United States National Museum 77:1–77.

———, 1954, The material culture of Pueblo Bonito. Washington, D.C.: Smithsonian Institution, Miscellaneous Collections, Vol. 124.

———, 1959a, The braced-up cliff at Pueblo Bonito. Washington, D.C.: Smithsonian Institution Annual Report for 1958, pp. 501–511.

———, 1959b, Pueblo del Arroyo, Chaco Canyon, New Mexico. Washington, D.C.: Smithsonian Institution, Miscellaneous Collections, 138(1).

Judge, W. J., 1970, Systems analysis and the Folsom-Midland question. *Southwestern Journal of Anthropology* 26:40–51.

Judson, S., 1953, Geology of the San Jon site, eastern New Mexico. Washington, D.C.: Smithsonian Institution, Miscellaneous Collections, 121(1).

———, 1961, Archaeology and the natural sciences. *American Scientist* 49:410–414.

Kamen, M. D., 1963, Early history of carbon-14. *Science* 140:584–590.

Kantor, H. J., 1954, The chronology of Egypt and its correlation with that of other parts of the Near East in the periods before the Late Bronze Age. In *Relative chronologies in Old World archaeology,* R. W. Ehrich, ed. Chicago: University of Chicago Press, pp. 1–27.

Kapitan, G., 1966, *A bibliography of underwater archaeology.* Chicago: Argonaut Inc.

Katsui, Y., and Y. Kondo, 1965, Dating of stone implements by using hydration layers of obsidian. *Japanese Journal of Geology and Geography* 36:45–60.

Kay, G. F., 1931, Classification and duration of the Pleistocene period. *Bulletin of the Geological Society of America* 48:425–466.

Kedar, Y., 1958, The use of aerial photographs in research in physiogeographic conditions and anthropogeographic data in various historic periods. *Photogrammetric Engineering* 24:584–587.

Kehoe, T. F., 1958, Tipi rings: the "direct ethnological" approach applied to an archaeological problem. *American Anthropologist* 60:861–873.

———, 1967, *The Boarding School bison drive site.* Lincoln, Neb.: Plains Anthropologist, Memoir No. 4.

———, and A. B. Kehoe, 1960, Observations on the butchering technique at a prehistoric bison kill in Montana. *American Antiquity* 25:420–423.

Keiller, A., S. Piggott, and F. S. Wallis, 1941, First report of the sub-committee of the South-Western Group of Museums and Art Galleries on the petrological identification of stone axes. *Proceedings of the Prehistoric Society* 7:50–72. (Reprinted in part in Heizer 1959:450–456.)

Keisch, B., 1968, Dating works of art through their natural radioactivity: improvements and applications. *Science* 160:413–415.

———, R. L. Feller, A. S. Levine, and R. R. Edwards, 1967, Dating and authenticating works of art by measurement of natural Alpha emitters. *Science* 155:1238–1242.

Keith, M. L., and G. M. Anderson, 1963, Radiocarbon dating: fictitious results with mollusk shells. *Science* 141:637–638.

———, 1964, Radiocarbon dating of mollusk shells: a reply. *Science* 144:890.

Kellan, J. H., 1958, *An archaeological survey of Perry County [Indiana].* Indianapolis: Indiana Historical Bureau.

Kelley, D. H., 1962, A history of the decipherment of Maya script. *Anthropological Linguistics* 4(8):1–48.

Kelly, A. R., and V. J. Hurst, 1956, Patination and age relationship in south Georgia flint. *American Antiquity* 22:193–194.

Kemp, W. B., 1971, The flow of energy in a hunting society. *Scientific American* 224:105–115.

Kendall, D. G., 1969, Some problems and methods in statistical archaeology. *World Archaeology* 1:68–76.

Kennedy, G., and L. Knopff, 1960, Dating by thermoluminescence. *Archaeology* 13:147–148.

Kenyon, A. S., 1927, Stone implements on aboriginal camping grounds. *Victorian Naturalist* 43:280–285.

Kenyon, K., 1957, *Digging up Jericho.* London: Ben.

———, 1960, *Archaeology in the Holy Land.* New York: Praeger.

———, 1961, *Beginning in archaeology.* Rev. ed. New York: Praeger.

Kerley, E. R., and W. M. Bass, 1967, Paleopathology: meeting ground for many disciplines. *Science* 157:638–643.

Key, C. A., 1963, Note on the trace-element content of the artifacts of the Kfar Menash hoard. *Israel Exploration Journal* 13:289–290.

Kidder, A. V., 1958, Pecos, New Mexico: archaeological notes. Andover, Mass.: Papers of the R. S. Peabody Foundation for Archaeology, Vol. 5.

Kim, Won-Yong, 1966, Fieldwork planned and begun. *Current Anthropology* 7:99.

King, D. G., 1966, The Lanhill Barrow, Wiltshire, England: an essay in recon-struction. *Proceedings of the Prehistoric Society* 32:73–85.

King, T. F., 1971, A conflict of values in American archaeology. *American Antiquity* 36:255–262.

Kirchner, H., 1952, Ein archäologischer Beitrag zur Urgeschichte des Shamanismus. *Anthropos* 47:244–286.

Kleindienst, M. R., 1961, Variability within the Late Acheulian assemblage in eastern Africa. *South African Archaeological Bulletin* 16:35–62.

Klejn, L., 1972, Marxism, systemic approach and archaeology. In *The explanation of culture change,* C. Renfrew, ed. London: Duckworth.

Klima, B., 1954, Palaeolithic huts at Dolni Věstonice. *Antiquity* 28:4–14.

———, 1962, The first ground-plan of an upper Paleolithic loess settlement in middle Europe and its meaning. In *Courses toward urban life,* R. J. Braidwood and G. R. Willey, eds. Chicago: Aldine, pp. 193–210.

Kloiber, A., 1957, *Die Gräberfelder von Lauriacum; das Ziegelfeld.* Linz und Donau, Austria: Oberösterreichischer Landesverlag.

Klopfer, P. H., 1962, *Behavioral aspects of ecology.* Englewood, N.J.: Prentice-Hall.

Kluckhohn, C., 1939, The place of theory in anthropological studies. *Philosophy of Science* 6:328–344.

———, and W. Kelly, 1945, The concept of culture. In *The science of man in the world crisis,* Ralph Linton, ed. New York: Columbia University Press, pp. 78–106.

Knorozov, Y. V., 1967, *Selected chapters from the writing of the Maya Indians.* Cambridge, Mass.: Harvard University, Russian Translation Series of the Peabody Museum, Vol. 4.

Knowles, F. H. S., 1944, *The manufacture of a flint arrowhead by a quartzite hammer-stone.* Oxford: Oxford University, Pitt-Rivers Museum, Occasional Papers on Technology, No. 1.

Kobayashi, T., and P. Bleed, 1971, Recording and illustrating ceramic surfaces with *Takuhon* rubbings. *Plains Anthropologist* 16:219–221.

Koby, F. E., 1943, Les soi-disant instruments osseux du paléolithique alpin et le charriage à sec des os d'ours des cavernes. *Verhandlungen der Naturforschenden Gesselschaft in Basel* 54:59–95.

Kosambi, D. D., 1967, Living prehistory in India. *Scientific American* 216:104ff.

Kossinna, G., 1941, *Die Deutsche Vorgeschichte.* Leipzig: Barth (Mannus Bücherei). No. 9. Printed 1912, 1914, 1921, 1925, 1933, 1934, 1936.

Kovar, A. J., 1966, Problems in radiocarbon dating at Teotihuacan. *American Antiquity* 31:427–430.

Kragh, A., 1951, Stenalderens Flintteknik. *Kuml,* 1951:49–64.

Krieger, A. D., 1944, The typological concept. *American Antiquity* 9:271–288.

———, 1947, The eastward extension of Puebloan datings toward cultures of the Mississippi Valley. *American Antiquity* 12:141–148.

———, 1960, Archaeological typology in theory and practice. In Selected Papers of the Fifth International Congress of Anthropology and Ethnological Sciences, Philadelphia, pp. 141–151.

———, 1964, New World lithic typology project: Part II. *American Antiquity* 29:489–493.

Kroeber, A. L., 1916, Zuni postherds. New York: Anthropological Papers of the American Museum of Natural History, 18(1).

———, 1925, Handbook of the Indians of California. Washington, D.C.: Bulletin of the Bureau of American Ethnology, No. 78.

Kroeber, A. L., 1936, Culture element distributions: III. Area and climax. Berkeley: University of California Publications in American Archaeology and Ethnology, 37(3).

———, 1940a, Statistical classification. *American Antiquity* 6:29–44.

———, 1940b, Stimulus diffusion. *American Anthropologist* 42:1–20.

———, 1948, *Anthropology.* New York: Harcourt.

———, 1952, *The nature of culture.* Chicago: University of Chicago Press.

———, 1953, The delimitation of civilizations. *Journal of the History of Ideas* 14:264–275.

———, 1955, Linguistic time depth results so far and their meaning. *International Journal of American Linguistics* 21:91–104.

———, 1957a, An anthropologist looks at history. *Pacific Historical Review* 26:281–287.

———, 1957b, What ethnography is. Berkeley: University of California Publications in American Archaeology and Ethnology 47:191–204.

———, 1962, *A roster of civilizations and culture.* New York: Viking Fund Publications in Anthropology, No. 33.

———, 1963, *Cultural and natural areas of native North America.* Berkeley: University of California Press. (Originally published in University of California Publications in American Archaeology and Ethnology 38:1–242.)

———, and C. Kluckhohn, 1952, Culture: a critical review of concepts and definitions. Cambridge, Mass.: Harvard University, Papers of the Peabody Museum, 47(1).

———, 1963, *Culture: a critical review of concepts and definitions.* New York: Random House.

———, and W. D. Strong, 1924, The Uhle pottery collection from Ica. Berkeley: University of California Publications in American Archaeology and Ethnology, 21:95–133.

Krogh, A., and M. Krogh, 1915, A study of the diet and metabolism of Eskimos undertaken in 1908 on an expedition to Greenland. *Meddelelser om Grönland* 2:1–52.

Krumbein, W. C., 1965, Sampling in paleontology. In *Handbook of paleontological techniques,* B. Kummel and D. Raup, eds. San Francisco: Freeman, pp. 137–149.

Kryzwicki, L., 1934, *Primitive society and its vital statistics,* H. E. Kennedy and A. Truszkowski, trans. London: Macmillan.

Ku, T.-L., and W. S. Broecker, 1966, Atlantic deep-sea stratigraphy: extension of absolute chronology to 320,000 years. *Science* 151:448–450.

Kühn, H., 1955, *On the track of prehistoric man.* London: Hutchinson.

Kuhn, E., 1938, Zur quantitativen Analyse der Haustierwelt der Pfahlbauten der Schweiz. *Vierteljahresschrift der Naturforschenden Gesellschaft Zürich* 83:253–263.

Kuhn, T. S., 1962, *The structure of scientific revolutions.* Chicago: University of Chicago Press.

Kurtén, Björn, and Yrjö Vasari, 1960, On the date of Peking Man. *Commentationes biologicae,* Societas Scientiarum Fennica, 23(7).

Kurtz, E. B., Jr., and R. Y. Anderson, 1955, *Pollen analysis.* Tucson: University of Arizona, Physical Science Bulletin, No. 2:113–125.

Kushner, G., 1970, A consideration of some processual designs for archaeology as anthropology. *American Antiquity* 35:125–132.

Kuzara, R. S., G. R. Mead, and K. A. Dixon, 1966, Seriation of anthropological data: a computer program for matrix ordering. *American Anthropologist* 68:1442–1455.

Lacaille, A. D., 1931, Aspects of intentional fracture. *Transactions of the Glasgow Archaeological Society* 9:313–341.

Laet, S. de, 1957, *Archaeology and its problems*. London: Phoenix House. (New York: Macmillan.)

Lafitau, Père, 1724, *Moeurs des sauvages américains comparées aux moeurs des premiers temps*. Paris.

Lais, R., 1939, Molluskenkunde und Vorgeschichte. Berlin: *Deutsches Archäologisches Institut, Römische-Germanische Kommission,* Ber. 26:5–23.

Lamberg-Karlovsky, C. C., 1970, Operations problems in archeology. Current Directions in Anthropology. Washington, D.C.: Bulletin of the American Anthropological Association, 3(3:2):111–114.

Lambert, R. J., 1960, Review of the literature of ethno-conchology pertinent to archaeology. *Sterkiana* 2:1–8.

Laming, A., 1952, L'alimentation thermoremanente des terres cuites. In *La découverte du passé*. A Laming, ed. Paris: Picard, Chap. 10.

Laming-Emperaire, A., 1962, *La signification de l'art rupestre paléolithique*. Paris: Picard.

——, 1963, *L'Archéologie préhistorique*. Paris: Editions du Seuil.

——, 1964, *Origines de l'archéologie préhistorique en France: des superstitions médiévales à la découverte de l'homme fossile*. Paris: Picard.

Lancaster, J. B., 1968, On the evolution of tool-using behavior. *American Anthropologist* 70:56–66.

Lancaster, O., 1949, *Draynefleete revisited*. London: J. Murray.

Lane, R. A., and A. J. Sublett, 1972, Osteology of social organization: residence pattern. *American Antiquity* 37:186–201.

Lantier, R., 1961, *L'Arte préhistorique*. Paris: Massin.

Lapham, I. A., 1855, Antiquities of Wisconsin. Washington, D.C.: Smithsonian Institution, Contributions to Knowledge, 7(Article IV):1–95.

Lartet, E., 1860, Sur l'ancienneté géologique de l'espéce humaine *Comptes Rendus de l'Academie des Sciences* 50:790–791.

——, and C. Gaillard, 1907, La faune momifée de l'ancienne Egypte. Archives du Musée Historie Naturelle de Lyon 9:1–130.

Lasker, G. W., 1961, *The evolution of man: a brief introduction to physical anthropology*. New York: Holt, Rinehart and Winston, Inc.

Laslett, Peter, 1965, The history of population and social and social structure. *International Social Science Journal* 17:582–593.

Lathrap, D. W., 1968, Aboriginal occupation and changes in river channel on the central Ucayali, Peru. *American Antiquity* 33:62–79.

Laudermilk, J. D., and T. G. Kennard, 1938, Concerning lightning spalling. *American Journal of Science* (Series 5) 25:104–122.

Lauer, P. K., 1971, Changing patterns of pottery trade to the Trobriand Islands. *World Archaeology* 3:197–209.

Laughlin, W. S., 1968, Hunting: an integrating biobehavior system and its evolutionary importance. In *Man the hunter,* R. B. Lee and I. DeVore, eds. Chicago: Aldine, pp. 304–320.

Lawrence, B., 1951, *Mammals found at the Awatovi site*. Cambridge, Mass.: Papers of the Peabody Museum, 35(3).

Lawson, C. A., 1963, Language, communication, and biological organization. *General Systems* 8:107–116.

Layard, A. H., 1849, *Nineveh and its remains*. New York: Putnam.

——, 1853, *Discoveries in the ruins of Nineveh and Babylon,* New York: Putnam.

Layard, A. H., 1903, *Sir A. Henry Layard, G. C. B.; D. C. L.; Autobiography and letters.* London: J. Murray.

Layard, N. F., 1922, Prehistoric cooking places in Norfolk. *Proceedings of the Prehistoric Society of East Anglia* 3 (Part 4):483–498.

Leach, E., 1961, *Rethinking anthropology.* London University School of Economics and Political Science. Monographs of Social Anthropology, No. 22. (London: Athlone Press.)

Leakey, L. S. B., 1954, Working stone, bone, and wood. In *A history of technology.* Vol. 1, C. Singer, E. J. Holmyard, and A. R. Hall, eds. London: Oxford.

————, 1960, *Adam's ancestors,* 4th ed. New York: Harper & Row.

————, 1966a, *White African.* Cambridge, Mass.: Schenkman.

————, 1966b, Africa and Pleistocene overkill? *Nature* 212:1615–1616.

————, R. Simpson, and T. Clements, 1968, Archaeological investigations in the Calico Mountains, California: preliminary report. *Science* 160:1022–1023.

————, and H. van Lawick, 1963, Adventures in the search for man. *National Geographic Magazine* 123:132–152.

Lechtman, H. N., 1971, Ancient methods of gilding silver: examples from the Old and the New Worlds. In *Science and archaeology,* R. H. Brill, ed. Cambridge, Mass.: MIT Press, pp. 2–31.

Lee, G. B., 1969, Pedological investigations at Mill Creek Iowa archaeological sites. *Journal of the Iowa Archaeological Society* 15:318–332.

Lee, R. B., 1968, What hunters do for a living, or, How to make out on scarce resources. In *Man the hunter,* R. B. Lee and I. DeVore, eds. Chicago: Aldine, pp. 30–48.

————, and I. DeVore, eds., 1968, *Man the hunter.* Chicago: Aldine.

Lee, R. F., 1970, *The Antiquities Act of 1906.* Washington, D.C.: National Park Service, Office of History and Historic Architecture, Eastern Service Center.

Leechman, D., 1931, Technical methods in the preservation of anthropological museum specimens. Ottawa: National Museum of Canada, Annual Report for 1929, pp. 127–158.

————, 1950, *Aboriginal tree-felling.* Ottawa: National Museum of Canada, Bulletin No. 118.

Legoux, P., 1966, *Détermination de l'age dentaire des fossiles de la lignée humaine.* Paris: Maloine.

Le Gros Clark, W. E., 1967, *Man-apes or ape-men?* New York: Holt, Rinehart and Winston, Inc.

Lehmer, D. J., 1952, Animal bone and plains archaeology. *Plains Archaeological Conference Newsletter* 4:53–55.

————, 1954, *Archeological investigations in the Oahe Dam area, South Dakota, 1950–1951.* Washington, D.C.: Bulletin of the Bureau of American Ethnology, No. 158.

Leonhardy, F., 1966, *Domebo: a paleo-Indian kill in the prairie-plains.* Lawton, Oklahoma: Museum of the Great Plains, Contribution No. 1.

Leopold, L. B., and W. B. Langbein, 1966, River meanders. *Scientific American* 214:60–70.

Lerici, C. M., 1959, Periscope camera pierces ancient tombs to reveal 2,500 year old frescoes. *National Geographic Magazine* 116:336–351.

————, 1962, New archaeological techniques and international cooperation in Italy. *Expedition* 4:5–10.

Leroi-Gourhan, A., 1952, L'étude des vestiges zoologiques. In *La découverte du passé,* A. Laming, ed. Paris: Picard.

————, 1964, *Les religions de la préhistoire (paléolithique) mythes et religions.* Vol. 2. Paris: Presses Universitaires.

Leroi-Gourhan, A., 1967, *Treasures of prehistoric art.* New York: Abrams.

————, 1968, The evolution of Paleolithic art. *Scientific American* 218:58ff.

Lester, J. D., 1967, *Writing research reports: a complete guide.* Glenview, Ill.: Scott, Foresman and Clark.

Levey, M., ed., 1967, *Archaeological chemistry.* Philadelphia: University of Pennsylvania Press.

Lévi-Strauss, C., 1963, *Structural anthropology.* New York: Basic Books.

Lewis, T. M. N., and M. Kneberg, 1946, *Hiwassee island.* Knoxville: University of Tennessee Press.

Libby, W. F., 1955, *Radiocarbon dating,* 2d ed. Chicago: University of Chicago Press.

————, 1961, Radiocarbon dating. *Science* 133:621–629.

————, 1963, Accuracy of radiocarbon dates. *Science* 140:278–280.

Limbrey, S., 1972, *Soil science in archaeology.* New York: Seminar Press.

Linington, R. E., 1961, Physics and archaeological salvage. *Archaeology* 14:287–292.

————, 1963, The application of geophysics to archaeology. *American Scientist* 51:48–70.

Linné, S., 1955, The Bering Isthmus—bridge between Asia and America. *Ethnos* 20:210–215.

Lipe, W. D., 1970, Anasazi communities in the Red Rock Plateau, Southeastern Utah. In *Reconstructing prehistoric pueblo societies,* W. A. Longacre, ed. Albuquerque: University of New Mexico Press, pp. 84–139.

Lipson, J., 1958, Potassium-argon dating of sedimentary rocks. *Bulletin of the Geological Society of America* 69:137–150.

Lloyd, S., 1955, *Foundations in the dust: a story of Mesopotamian exploration.* Baltimore: Penguin.

————, 1963, *Mounds of the Near East.* Edinburgh: Edinburgh University Press.

Locke, L. L., 1912, The ancient quipu, a Peruvian knot record. *American Anthropologist* 14:325–332.

Loeb, E. M., 1936, The distribution and function of money in early societies. In *Essays in anthropology,* R. H. Lowie, ed. Berkeley: University of California Press, pp. 153–168.

Lösch, A., 1954, *The economics of location.* New Haven, Conn.: Yale University Press.

Loftus, W. K., 1858, Warkah: its ruins and remains. Transactions of the Royal Society of Literature (Series No. 2) 6:1–64.

Longacre, W. A., 1964, Archeology as anthropology: a case study. *Science* 144:1454–1455.

————, 1966, Changing patterns of social integration: a prehistoric example from the American Southwest. *American Anthropologist* 68:94–102.

————, ed., 1970a, *Reconstructing prehistoric pueblo societies.* Albuquerque: University of New Mexico Press.

————, 1970b, A historical review. In *Reconstructing prehistoric pueblo societies,* W. A. Longacre, ed. Albuquerque: University of New Mexico Press, pp. 1–10.

————, 1970c, Current thinking in American archeology. Current Directions in Anthropology. Washington, D. C.: Bulletin of the American Anthropological Association, 3(3:2):126–138.

————, and J. E. Ayres, 1968, Archeological lessons from an Apache wickiup. In *New perspectives in archeology,* S. R. Binford and L. R. Binford, eds. Chicago: Aldine, pp. 151–159.

Lorandi de Gieco, A. M., 1965, Sobre la aplicacíon de métodos estadísticós al estudio del arte repestre. Mendoza, Argentina: Universidad Nacional de Cuyo, *Anales de Arquelogia y Ethnologia,* 20:7–26.

Lorch, W., 1939, *Methodische Untersuchungen zur Wüstungsforschung.* Jena: Vol. 4. Arbeiten zur Landes-und Volksforschung.

Lothrop, E. B., 1948, *Throw me a bone: what happens when you marry an archaeologist.* New York: McGraw-Hill.

Lothrop, S. K., 1942, Pottery of the Sitio Conte and other archaeological sites. Cambridge, Mass.: Harvard University, Memoirs of the Peabody Museum, Vol. 8.

Lotspeich, F. B., 1961, *Soil science in the service of archaeology.* Santa Fe, N.M.: Fort Burgwin Research Center, Publication No. 1:137–144.

Loud, L. L., and M. R. Harrington, 1929, Lovelock Cave. *University of California Publications in American Archaeology and Ethnology* 25:1–183.

Lovejoy, C. O., A. H. Burstein, and K. G. Heiple, 1972, Primate phylogeny and immunological distance. *Science* 176:803–805.

Lovett, E., 1877, Notice of the gun flint manufactory at Brandon, with reference to the bearing of its processes upon the modes of flint-working practiced in prehistoric times. *Proceedings of the Society of Antiquaries of Scotland* 21:206–212.

Lowe, G. W., 1971, The civilizational consequences of varying degrees of agricultural and ceramic dependency within the basic ecosystems of Mesoamerica. Berkeley: University of California, Archaeological Research Facility, Contribution No. 11:212–248.

Lowery, P. R., R. D. A. Savage, and R. L. Wilkins, 1971, Scriber, graver, scorper, tracer: notes on experiments in bronzeworking technique. *Proceedings of the Prehistoric Society* 37:167–182.

Lucas, A., 1962, *Ancient Egyptian materials and industries.* London: E. Arnold.

Lumley, Henri de, 1966, Les fouilles de Terra Amata à Nice (A.-M.). *Bulletin du Musée d'Anthropologie Préhistorique de Monaco* 13:29–52.

Lurie, N. O., 1968, Culture change. In *Introduction to cultural anthropology,* J. A. Clifton, ed. New York: Houghton Mifflin, pp. 275–303.

Lutz, H. J., 1951, The concentration of certain chemical elements in the soils of Alaskan archaeological sites. *American Journal of Science* 249:925–928.

Lyell, C., 1872, *Principles of geology,* 11th ed., 2 vols. New York: Appleton.

Lynch, B. D., and T. F. Lynch, 1968, The beginnings of a scientific approach to prehistoric archaeology in seventeenth and eighteenth century Britain. *Southwestern Journal of Anthropology* 24:33–65.

Lyne, W. C., 1916, The significance of the radiographs of the Piltdown teeth. *Proceedings of the Royal Society of Medicine* 9 (Part 3):33–62.

MacAdam, W. I., 1882, On the results of a chemical investigation into the composition of the "bog butters" and of "adipocere" and the "mineral resins" with notice of a cask of bog butter found in Glen Gell, Morvern, Argyllshire. *Proceedings of the Society of Antiquaries of Scotland* (New Series) 4:204–223.

————, 1889, Notes on the analysis of samples of bog butter found in different parts of Scotland. *Proceedings of the Society of Antiquaries of Scotland* 23:433–434.

MacAlister, R. A. S., 1949, *The archaeology of Ireland.* London: Methuen.

McArthur, N., 1970, The demography of primitive populations. *Science* 167:1097–1101.

McBurney, C. B. M., 1960, *The Stone Age of northern Africa.* Baltimore: Penguin.

————, 1961, Aspects of Palaeolithic art. *Antiquity* 35:107–114.

McCarthy, F. D., and M. McArthur, 1960, The food quest and the time factor in aboriginal economic life. Melbourne: University of Melbourne Press Records of the American-Australian Scientific Expedition, 2: 145–194.

McConnell, D., 1962, Dating of fossil bones by the fluorine method. *Science* 136: 241–244.

McCown, T. D., and A. Keith, 1939, *The Stone Age of Mt. Carmel,* Vol. 2. London: Clarendon.

McCrone, A. W., D. South, R. Ascher, and M. Ascher, 1965, Stone artifacts: identification problems. *Science* 148: 167–168.

MacDonald, G. F., and David Sanger, 1968, Some aspects of microscope analysis and photomicrography of lithic artifacts. *American Antiquity* 33: 237–239.

McEwen, J. M., 1946, An experiment with primitive Maori carving tools. *Journal of the Polynesian Society* 55: 111–116.

McFadgen, B. G., 1971, An application of stereophotogrammetry to archaeological recording. *Archaeometry* 13: 71–81.

McGimsey, C. R., 1972, *Public archeology.* New York: Seminar Press.

McGinnies, W. G., 1963, Dendrochronology. *Journal of Forestry* 61: 5–11.

McGregor, J. C., 1965, *Southwestern archaeology,* 2d ed. Urbana: University of Illinois Press.

McGuire, J. D., 1891, The stone hammer and its various uses. *American Anthropologist* 4: 301–312.

McIntire, W. G., 1958, *Prehistoric Indian settlements of the changing Mississippi River Delta.* Baton Rouge: Louisiana State University Press.

McKern, W. C., 1939, The Midwestern taxonomic method as an aid to archaeological culture study. *American Antiquity* 4: 301–313.

McKusick, M., 1963, Identifying Iowa projectile points. *Journal of the Iowa Archaeological Society,* 12 (3, 4).

McNaughton, S. J., and L. L. Wolf, 1970, Dominance and the niche in ecological systems. *Science* 167: 131–139.

McNeal, R. A., 1972, The Greeks in history and prehistory. *Antiquity* 46: 19–28.

MacNeish, R. S., 1958, *Preliminary archaeological investigations in the Sierra de Tamaulipas, Mexico.* Philadelphia: Transactions of the American Philosophical Society (New Series) Vol. 48, Part 6.

———, 1964, Ancient Mesoamerican civilization. *Science* 143: 531–537.

———, 1967a, An interdisciplinary approach to an archaeological problem. In *The prehistory of the Tehuacan Valley: Vol. 1. Environment and subsistence,* D. S. Byers, ed. Austin: University of Texas Press, pp. 14–24.

———, 1967b, A summary of the subsistence. In *The prehistory of the Tehuacan Valley,* Vol. 1. *Environment and subsistence,* D. S. Byers, ed. Austin: University of Texas Press, pp. 290–310.

———, A. Nelken-Terner, and I. W. Johnson, 1967, Nonceramic artifacts. In *The prehistory of the Tehuacan Valley.* Vol. 2., D. S. Byers, ed. Austin: University of Texas Press, pp. 164–187.

McPherron, A., 1967, *The Juntunen site and the Late Woodland prehistory of the Upper Great Lakes Area.* Ann Arbor: University of Michigan, Anthropological Papers of the Museum of Anthropology, No. 30.

MacWhite, E., 1956, On the interpretation of archaeological evidence in historical and sociological terms. *American Anthropologist* 58: 3–25.

Mairui, A., P. V. Bianchi, and L. E. Battaglia, 1961, Last moments of the Pompeians. *National Geographic Magazine* 120: 651–670.

Malinowski, B., 1932, *Argonauts of the western Pacific.* New York: Dutton.

Malkin, B., 1962, *Seri ethnozoology.* Pocatello: Occasional Papers of the Idaho State College Museum, No. 7.

Mallowan, A. C., 1946, *Come, tell me how you live*. New York: Dodd, Mead.

Mallowan, M. E. L., 1965, The mechanics of ancient trade in western Asia. *Iran* 3:1–7.

Mangelsdorf, P., R. MacNeish, and W. Galinat, 1964, Domestication of corn. *Science* 143:538–545.

March, B., 1934, *Standards of pottery description*. Ann Arbor: University of Michigan, Occasional Contributions from the Museum of Anthropology, No. 3.

Maré, E. de, 1962, *Photography*. Baltimore: Penguin.

Marek, K. W. (Ceram, C. W.), 1964, *Archaeology*. New York: Odyssey.

Maringer, J., 1960, *The gods of prehistoric man*. New York: Knopf.

Marks, A. E., 1971, Settlement pattern and intrasite variability in the Central Negev. *American Anthropologist* 73:1237–1244.

Marshack, A., 1964, Lunar notation on Upper Paleolithic remains. *Science* 146: 743–745.

————, 1969, New techniques in the analysis and interpretation of Mesolithic notation and symbolic art. Capo di Ponte: Centro Camuno de Studi Preistorici, Valcamonica Symposium, Actes de Symposium International d'Art Préhistorique.

————, 1970a, The baton of Montgaudier. *Natural History* 79:56–63.

————, 1970b, Polesini: a reexamination of the ingraved mobilary materials by a new methodology. *Rivista di Scienze Preistoriche* 24:219–281.

————, 1970c, Le bâton de commandement de Montgaudier (Charente). Réexamen au microscope et interprétation nouvelle. *L'Anthropologie* 74:321–352.

————, 1970d, Notation dan les gravures du paléolithique supérieur. Bordeaux: Publications de l'Institut de Préhistoire de l'Université de Bordeaux, Mémoire No. 8.

————, 1972, *The roots of civilization: a study in prehistoric cognition; The origins of art, symbol and notation*. New York: McGraw-Hill.

————, and A. Rosenfeld, 1972, Paleolithic notation: Marshack and Rosenfeld. *Antiquity* 46:63–65.

Marshall, N. F., and J. R. Moriarty, 1964, Principles of underwater archaeology. *Pacific Discovery* 17:18–25.

Martin, M., 1936, Comment vivait l'homme de La Quina à l'époque mousterienne. *Préhistoire* 5:7–23.

Martin, P. S. [Chicago], 1962, Archeological investigations in east central Arizona. *Science* 138:826–827.

————, 1970, Explanation as an afterthought and as a goal. In *Reconstructing prehistoric pueblo societies*, W. A. Longacre, ed. Albuquerque: University of New Mexico Press, pp. 194–201.

————, 1971, The revolution in archaeology. *American Antiquity* 36:1–8.

————, J. B. Rinaldo, E. Bluhm, H. C. Cutler, and R. Grange, 1952, *Mogollon cultural continuity and change: the stratigraphic analysis of Tularosa and Cordova Caves*. Chicago: Field Museum of Natural History, Fieldiana, Anthropology, Vol. 40.

Martin, Paul [Arizona], 1961, Pollen analysis of animal coprolites. In *A survey and excavation of caves in Hidalgo County, New Mexico*, M. F. Lambert and R. Ambler, eds. Sante Fe, N.M.: School of American Research, Monograph 25.

————, 1963, *The last 10,000 years: a fossil pollen record of the American Southwest*. Tucson: University of Arizona Press.

————, 1966, Africa and Pleistocene overkill. *Nature* 212:339–342.

Martin, Paul [Arizona], and J. Gray, 1962, Pollen analysis and the Cenozoic. *Science* 137:103–111.

––––––, B. E. Sabels, and D. Shutler, 1961, Rampart Cave coprolite and ecology of the Shasta ground sloth. *American Journal of Science* 259:102–127.

––––––, and F. W. Sharrock, 1964, Pollen analysis of prehistoric human feces: a new approach to ethnobotany. *American Antiquity* 30:168–180.

––––––, and H. E. Wright, Jr., 1967, *Pleistocene extinctions. The search for a cause.* New Haven: Yale University Press, Proceedings of the VII Congress of the International Association for Quaternary Research, Vol. 6.

Maruyama, Magoroh, 1963, The second cybernetics: deviation-amplifying mutual causal processes. *American Scientist* 51:164–179.

MASCA Newsletter, Applied Science Center for Archaeology, The University Museum, University of Pennsylvania, Philadelphia, Pa. 19104. (Reports on current developments in techniques.)

Mason, O. T., 1891, Aboriginal skin dressing; a study based on material in the U.S. National Museum. Washington, D.C.: Smithsonian Institution, Report for 1888–1889, pp. 553–589.

––––––, 1904, Aboriginal American basketry: studies in a textile art without machinery. Washington, D.C.: U.S. National Museum Report for 1902, pp. 171–548.

Mason, R. J., 1958, *Late Pleistocene geochronology and the Paleo-Indian penetration into the lower Michigan peninsula.* Ann Arbor: University of Michigan, Museum of Anthropology, Anthropological Papers, No. 11.

Mather, J. R., 1954, The effect of climate on the New World migration of primitive man. *Southwestern Journal of Anthropology* 10:304–321.

Mathiassen, T., 1927, *Archaeology of the Central Eskimos.* Copenhagen: Report of the Fifth Thule Exposition, 1921–1924, 4(1).

––––––, 1935, Blubber lamps in the Ertebølle culture? *Acta Archaeologica* 9:224–228.

Matson, F. R., 1951, Ceramic technology as an aid to cultural interpretation: techniques and problems. Ann Arbor: Anthropological Papers of the University of Michigan, No. 8:102–116.

––––––, 1960, The quantitative study of ceramic materials. New York: Viking Fund Publications in Anthropology No. 28:34–51.

––––––, ed., 1965, *Ceramics and man.* New York: Viking Fund Publications in Anthropology No. 41.

––––––, 1971, A study of temperatures used in firing ancient Mesopotamian pottery. In *Science and archaeology,* R. H. Brill, ed. Cambridge, Mass.: MIT Press, pp. 65–79.

Matteson, M. R., 1959, Land snails in archeological sites. *American Anthropologist* 61:1049–1096.

––––––, 1960, Reconstruction of prehistoric environments through the analysis of molluscan collections from shell middens. *American Antiquity* 26:117–120.

Matthews, J. M., 1965, Stratigraphic disturbance: the human element. *Antiquity* 39:295–298.

Matthews, S. K., 1968, *Photography in archaeology and art.* London: J. Baker.

Maudsley, A. C., and A. P. Maudsley, 1899, *A glimpse at Guatemala.* London.

Mauss, M., 1954, *The gift.* New York: Free Press.

Mayer-Oakes, W. J., 1963, Complex society archaeology. *American Antiquity* 29:57–60.

Mayes, S., 1961, *The great Belzoni (archeologist extraordinary).* New York: Walker & Co.

Mazess, R. B., and D. W. Zimmerman, 1966, Pottery dating by thermoluminescence. *Science* 152:347–348.

Meggers, B. J., 1954, Environmental limitation on the development of culture. *American Anthropologist* 56:801–824.

————, ed., 1959, *Evolution and anthropology: a centennial appraisal*. Washington, D.C.: Anthropological Society of Washington.

————, 1972, *Prehistoric America*. Chicago: Aldine.

————, and C. Evans, 1957, *Archaeological investigations at the mouth of the Amazon*. Washington, D.C.: Bulletin of the Bureau of American Ethnology, No. 167.

————, ————, and E. Estrada, 1965, *Early formative period of coastal Ecuador*. Washington, D.C.: Smithsonian Institution, Contributions to Anthropology, Vol. 1.

Mehringer, P. J., Jr., 1967, *Pollen analysis of the Tule Springs area, Nevada*. Carson City: Nevada State Museum, Anthropological Papers, No. 13, Part 3.

Meighan, C. W., 1956, *Responsibilities of the archaeologist in using the radiocarbon method*. Salt Lake City: University of Utah, Anthropological Papers, No. 26:48–53.

————, and others, 1958, Ecological interpretation in archaeology. *American Antiquity* 24:1–23, 131–150.

————, 1966, *Archaeology: an introduction*. San Francisco: Chandler Publishing.

————, L. J. Foote, and P. V. Aiello, 1968, Obsidian dating in west Mexican archaeology. *Science* 160:1069–1075.

Meigs, P., 1938, Vegetation on shell mounds, lower California. *Science* 87:346.

Melko, M., 1969, *The nature of civilizations*. Boston: Porter Sargent.

Mellaart, J., 1959, Notes on the architectural remains of Troy I and II. *Anatolian Studies* 9:131–162.

————, 1963, Early cultures of the South Anatolian Plateau. *Anatolian Studies* 13:199–236.

————, 1967, *Çatal Hüyük: a Neolithic town in Anatolia*. London: Thames and Hudson.

Mellars, P., 1970, Some comments on the notion of 'functional variability' in stone-tool assemblages. *World Archaeology* 2:74–89.

Mellor, D. H., 1972, On the existence of cultures. In *The explanation of culture change,* C. Renfrew, ed. London: Duckworth.

Merrill, R. H., 1941a, Photo-surveying assists archaeologist. *Civil Engineering* 11:233–235.

————, 1941b, Photographic surveying. *American Antiquity* 6:343–346.

Mertz, H., 1964, *The wine dark sea: Homer's heroic epic of the North Atlantic*. Chicago.

Metraux, A., 1959, The revolution of the ax. *Diogenes* No. 25:28–40.

Mewhinney, H., 1957, *Manual for Neanderthals*. Austin: University of Texas Press.

Michael, H. N., 1971, Climates, tree rings, and archaeology. In *Dating techniques for the archaeologist,* H. N. Michael and E. K. Ralph, eds. Cambridge, Mass.: MIT Press, pp. 49–56.

————, and E. K. Ralph, 1971, *Dating techniques for the archaeologist*. Cambridge, Mass.: MIT Press.

Michels, J. W., 1967, Archaeology and dating by hydration of obsidian. *Science* 158:211–214.

————, 1968, Settlement pattern and demography at Sheep Rock Shelter: their role in culture contact. *Southwestern Journal of Anthropology* 24:66–82.

————, 1971, The colonial obsidian industry of the Valley of Mexico. In *Science and archaeology,* R. H. Brill, ed. Cambridge, Mass.: MIT Press, pp. 251–271.

Michels, J. W., and C. A. Bebrich, 1971, Obsidian hydration dating. In *Dating techniques for the archaeologist,* H. N. Michael and E. K. Ralph, eds. Cambridge, Mass.: MIT Press, pp. 164–221.

Miller, W. C., 1957, Uses of aerial photographs in archaeological field work. *American Antiquity* 23:46–62.

Millon, R., 1964, The Teotihuacan mapping project. *American Antiquity* 29: 345–352.

———, 1970, Teotihuacan: completion of map of giant ancient city in the Valley of Mexico. *Science* 170:1077–1082.

———, and B. Drewitt, 1961, Earlier structures within the Pyramid of the Sun at Teotihuacan. *American Antiquity* 26:371–380.

———, ———, and J. Bennyhoff, 1965, *The Pyramid of the Sun at Teotihuacan.* Philadelphia: Transactions of the American Philosophical Society (New Series), 55 (Part b).

Miner, H. C., 1936, The importance of textiles in the archaeology of the eastern United States. *American Antiquity* 1:181–192.

Mitchell, S. R., *Stone-Age craftsmen.* Melbourne, Australia: Tait.

Moberg, C.-A., 1961, *Mängder av Fornfynd* (with English summary: *Trends in the present development of quantitative methods in archaeology).* Göteborg; Göteborgs Universitets Arsskrift, Acta Universitatis Göthoburgensis, 47(1).

Mongait, A. L., 1961, *Archaeology in the U.S.S.R.* Baltimore: Penguin.

Montgomery, R. G., W. Smith, and J. O. Brew, 1949, *Franciscan Awatovi.* Cambridge, Mass.: Harvard University, Papers of the Peabody Museum, Vol. 36.

Moorehead, A., 1961, A reporter at large: the temples of the Nile. *New Yorker,* September 23, pp. 106–137.

Moran, H. A., and D. H. Kelley, 1969, *The alphabet and the ancient calendar signs,* 2d ed. Palo Alto, Calif.: Daily Press.

Morgan, L. H., 1875, Ethnical periods. *Proceedings of the American Association for the Advancement of Science* 24:266–274.

———, 1878, *Ancient society.* New York: Holt, Rinehart and Winston, Inc.

———, 1965, *Houses and house-life of the American aborigines.* Chicago: University of Chicago Press. (Originally published as *Contributions to North American Ethnology,* Washington, D.C.: Government Printing Office, Vol. IV, 1881.)

Morin, J., 1911, *Les dessins des animaux en Grèce d'après les vases peints.* Paris.

Morley, S. G., 1915, *An introduction to the study of the Maya hieroglyphs.* Washington, D.C.: Bulletin of the Bureau of American Ethnology, No. 57.

———, 1946, *The ancient Maya.* Palo Alto, Calif.: Stanford University Press.

Morris, A. A., 1931, *Digging in Yucatan.* New York: Doubleday.

———, 1933, *Digging in the Southwest.* New York. Doubleday.

Morris, E. H., 1939, *Archaeological studies in the La Plata district.* Washington, D.C.: Carnegie Institution, Publication No. 519.

———, and R. F. Burgh, 1941, *Anasazi basketry: Basket Maker II through Pueblo III.* Washington, D.C.: Carnegie Institution, Publication No. 533.

———, 1954, *Basket Maker II sites near Durango, Colorado.* Washington, D.C.: Carnegie Institution, Publication No. 604.

Morrison, H. F., 1971, High-sensitivity magnetometers in archaeological exploration. Berkeley: University of California, Archaeological Research Facility, Contribution No. 12:6–20.

———, C. W. Clewlow, and R. F. Heizer, 1970, Magnetometer survey of the La Venta pyramid. Berkeley: University of California, Archaeological Research Facility, Contribution No. 8:1–20.

Mortillet, A. de, 1908, *La classification paléthnologique.* Paris: Schleicher Frères.

Mortillet, G. de, 1867, *Promenades préhistoriques à l'Exposition Universelle: a guide to the prehistoric collections at the Paris exposition of 1867*. Paris.

———, 1903, *Le préhistorique: antiquité de l'homme*. 3d ed. Paris: Reinwald.

Moss, J. H., 1951a, *Glaciation in the Wind River Mountains and its relation to early man in the Eden Valley, Wyoming*. Philadelphia: University of Pennsylvania Museum, Museum Monographs, pp. 9–94.

———, 1951b, *Early man in the Eden Valley*. Philadelphia: University of Pennsylvania Museum, Museum Monographs.

Moss, R. J., 1910, Chemical notes on a stone lamp from Ballyetagh and other similar stone vessels in the Royal Irish Academy Collection. *Proceedings of the Royal Irish Academy* 28:162–168.

Movius, H. L., Jr., 1950, A wooden spear of Third Interglacial Age from Lower Saxony. *Southwestern Journal of Anthropology* 6:139–142.

———, 1960, Radiocarbon dates and Upper Paleolithic archaeology in central and western Europe. *Current Anthropology* 1:355–391.

———, 1961, The Proto-Magdalenian of the Abri Pataud, Les Eyzies (Dordogne). Hamburg: Fifth International Congress for Pre- and Proto-History, 1958, pp. 561–566.

———, 1963, L'Age du périgordien, de l'Aurignacien et du Proto-Magdalenien en France sur la base des datations au carbone 14. Bulletin de la Société Méridionale de Spéléologie et de Préhistoire, Centenaire de fouilles d'Edouard Lartet, pp. 131–142.

———, 1966, The hearths of the Upper Perigordian and Aurignacian horizons at the Abri Pataud, Les Eyzies (Dordogne), and their possible significance. *American Anthropologist* 68(2:2):296–325.

———, and A. S. Brooks, 1971, The analysis of certain major classes of Upper Paleolithic tools: Aurignacian scrapers. *Proceedings of the Prehistoric Society* 37:253–273.

———, and S. Judson, 1956, *The rock-shelter of La Colombiere*. Cambridge, Mass.: Harvard University, Peabody Museum, American School of Prehistoric Research, Bulletin No. 19.

———, and others, 1968, The analysis of certain major classes of Upper Paleolithic tools. Cambridge, Mass.: Harvard University, Peabody Museum, American School of Prehistoric Research, Bulletin No. 26.

Müeller-Beck, H., 1957, *Das Obere Altpaläolithikum in Süddeutschland*. Bonn: Habelt.

———, 1965, Seeberg Burgäschisee-Süd: Part 5. Holzgeräte und Holzbearbeitung. *Acta Bernensia*, Berne, 2(Part 5).

Müller-Karpe, H., 1966, *Handbuch der Vorgeschichte*. München: Beck & Sohn.

Mulvaney, D. J., 1971, Prehistory from Antipodean perspectives. *Proceedings of the Prehistoric Society* 37:228–252.

———, and J. Golson, 1971, *Aboriginal man and environment in Australia*. Canberra.

Munger, P., and R. M. Adams, 1941, Fabric impressions of pottery from the Elizabeth Herrel Site, Missouri. *American Antiquity* 7:166–171.

Murdock, G. P., 1937, Comparative data on division of labor by sex. *Social Forces* 15:551–553.

———, 1959, *Africa*. New York: McGraw-Hill.

Murie, O. J., 1951, *The elk of North America*. Washington, D.C.: Wildlife Management Institute.

Murphy, J. L., 1971, Maize from an Adena mound in Athens County, Ohio. *Science* 171:897–898.

Murray, J., 1970, *The first European agriculture*. Chicago: Aldine.

Nagel, W., 1966, Index de l'outilage. *Berliner Jahrbuch für vor-und frühge-schichte* 6:189–193.

Napier, J. R., 1964, Profile of early man at Olduvai. *New Scientist* 22:86–89.

Napton, L. K., 1969, *Archaeological and paleobiological investigations in Love-lock Cave, Nevada; further analysis of human coprolites.* Berkeley: Kroeber Anthropological Society, Special Publication No. 2.

Naroll, R., 1956, A preliminary index of social development. *American Anthro-pologist* 58:687–715.

———, 1962, Floor area and settlement population. *American Antiquity* 27:587–589.

Naroll, R. S., and L. von Bertalanffy, 1956, The principle of allometry in biology and the social sciences. *General Systems* 1:76–89.

Nash, M., 1966, *Primitive and peasant economic systems.* San Francisco: Chandler Publishing.

Nathan, R., 1960, *The Weans.* New York: Knopf.

Navarro, J. M. D., 1925, Prehistoric routes between northern Europe and Italy defined by the amber trade. *Geographical Journal* 66:481–504.

Negbi, O., 1964, A contribution of mineralogy and palaeontology to an archae-ological study of terracottas. *Israel Exploration Journal* 14:187–189.

Neill, W. T., 1952, The manufacture of fluted points. *Florida Anthropologist* 5:9–16.

Nelson, C. M., 1972, Prehistoric culture change in the intermontane plateau of Western North America. In *The explanation of culture change,* C. Renfrew, ed. London: Duckworth.

Nelson, N. C., 1909, Shellmounds of the San Francisco Bay region. Berkeley: University of California Publications in American Archaeology and Ethnol-ogy, 7:309–348.

———, 1916, Chronology of the Tano Ruins, New Mexico. *American Anthro-pologist* 18:159–180. (Reprinted in Heizer 1959:222–238).

———, 1928, Pseudo-artifacts from the Pliocene of Nebraska. *Science* 67:316–317.

———, 1938, Prehistoric archaeology. In *General anthropology,* F. Boas, ed. New York: Heath, Chap. V, pp. 146–237.

Neumann, Georg K., 1952, Archeology and race in the American Indian. In *Archeology of eastern United States,* James B. Griffin, ed. Chicago: Uni-versity of Chicago Press, pp. 13–34.

Newcomer, M. H., 1971, Some quantitative experiments in hand-axe manufacture. *World Archaeology* 3:85–94.

Niemeyer, H., and V. Schiappacasse, 1971, Analisis cuantitativo de un sitio habitacional: sitio El Pimiento, Prov. de Coquimbo. Museo Arqueologica de La Serena, Chile: Actas del V Congreso Nacional de Arqueologia, Oct. 16–20, 1969, pp. 207–220.

Nietsch, H., 1939, *Wald und Siedlung im vorgeschichtlichen Mitteleuropa.* Leip-zig: Mannus-Bücherei.

Nikiforoff, C. C., 1942, Fundamental formula of soil formation. *American Journal of Science* 240:847–866.

———, 1953, Pedogenic criteria of climatic changes. In *Climatic change,* H. Shap-ley, ed. Cambridge, Mass.: Harvard University Press, pp. 189–200.

Noel-Hume, I., 1969, *Historical archaeology.* New York: Knopf.

Nordenskiöld, G. E. A., 1895, *The cliff dwellers of the Mesa Verde, Southwestern Colorado: their pottery and implements,* trans. by D. L. Morgan. Stockholm: P. A. Norstedt and Söner.

North, F. J., 1937, Geology for archaeologists. *Archaeological Journal* 94:73–115.

Nylander, C., 1967, A note on the stone cutting and masonry of Tel Arad. *Israel Exploration Journal* 17:56–59.

Nylen, E., 1963, A turret for vertical photography. *Antikvarist Arkiv,* Stockholm.

Nystuen, J. D., 1968, Identification of some fundamental spatial concepts. In *Spatial analysis: a reader in statistical geography,* B. J. L. Berry and D. F. Marble, eds. Englewood Cliffs, N.J.: Prentice-Hall, pp. 35–41.

———, and M. F. Dacey, 1968, A graph theory interpretation of nodal regions. In *Spatial analysis: a reader in statistical geography,* B. J. L. Berry and D. F. Marble, eds. Englewood Cliffs, N.J.: Prentice-Hall, pp. 407–418.

Oakley, K. P., 1950, *Man the tool-maker.* London: British Museum.

———, 1953, Dating fossil human remains. In *Anthropology Today,* A. L. Krober, chairman. Chicago: University of Chicago Press, pp. 43–57.

———, 1955a, *Further contributions to the solution of the Piltdown problem.* London: British Museum of Natural History, Vol. 2, Bulletin 6.

———, 1955b, Fire as a paleolithic tool and weapon. *Proceedings of the Prehistoric Society* 21:36–48.

———, 1959, Radiocarbon dating of the Piltdown skull and jaw. *Nature* 184:224–226.

———, 1961, Radiometric assays [of uranium content of bones from the Llano Estacado region]. In *Paleoecology of the Llano Estacado,* F. Wendorf, ed. Santa Fe, N.M.: Fort Burgwin Research Center, Publication No. 1:136.

———, 1963a, Relative dating of Arlington Springs man. *Science* 141:1172.

———, 1963b, Dating skeletal material. *Science* 140:488.

———, 1963c, Fluorine, uranium and nitrogen dating of bone. In *The scientist and archaeology,* E. Pyddoke, ed. London: Phoenix House, pp. 111–119.

———, 1964a, *The problem of man's antiquity; an historical survey.* London: British Museum of Natural History, Geology, Vol. 9, Bulletin 5.

———, 1964b, *Frameworks for dating fossil man.* Chicago: Aldine.

———, 1969, Analytical methods of dating bones. In *Science in archaeology,* D. Brothwell and E. Higgs, eds., rev. ed. London: Thames and Hudson, pp. 35–45.

———, and W. W. Howells, 1961, Age of the skeleton from the Lagow sand pit, Texas. *American Antiquity* 26:543–545.

———, and A. E. Rixon, 1958, The radioactivity of materials from the Scharbauer site near Midland, Texas. *American Antiquity* 24:185–187.

———, and J. S. Weiner, 1955, Piltdown Man. *American Scientist* 43:573–583.

O'Brien, P., 1968, Doctrinaire diffusion and acts of faith. *American Antiquity* 33:386–388.

O'Bryan, D., 1949, Methods of felling trees and tree-ring dating in the Southwest. *American Antiquity* 15:155–156.

Odum, E. P., 1969, The strategy of ecosystem development. *Science* 164:262–270.

Olin, J. S., and E. V. Sayre, 1971, Compositional categories of some English and American pottery of the American Colonial period. In *Science and archaeology,* R. H. Brill, ed. Cambridge, Mass.: MIT Press, pp. 196–209.

Olsen, S. J., 1961a, A basic annotated bibliography to facilitate the identification of vertebrate remains from archeological sites. *Bulletin of the Texas Archeological Society* 30:219–222.

———, 1961b, The relative value of fragmentary mammalian remains. *American Antiquity* 26:538–540.

———, 1961c, SCUBA as an aid to archaeologists and paleontologists. *Curator* 4:371–378.

Olsen, S. J., 1964, Mammal remains from archaeological sites: Part 1. Southeastern and southwestern United States. Cambridge, Mass.: Harvard University, Papers of the Peabody Museum, 56(1).

———, 1971, *Zooarchaeology: animal bones in archaeology and their interpretation*. Addison-Wesley Module in Anthropology.

Olson, E. A., and W. Broecker, 1958, Sample contamination and reliability of radiocarbon dates. *Transactions of the New York Academy of Sciences* (Series 2) 20:593–604.

O'Neale, L. M., 1937, Archaeological explorations in Peru: Part III. Textiles of the early Nazca period. Chicago: Field Museum of Natural History, Anthropology Memoirs 2(3):119–218.

———, 1947, Note on an *Apocynum* fabric. *American Antiquity* 13:179–180.

Opdyke, N. D., B. Glass, J. D. Hays, and J. Foster, 1966, Paleomagnetic study of Antarctic deep-sea cores. *Science* 154:349–357.

Orchard, W. C., 1925, Pottery repairing and restoration. New York: Indian Notes, Heye Foundation, Museum of the American Indian, 2:297–308.

Ore, H. T., 1968, Preliminary petrographic analysis of the sediments at the Wasden site (Owl Cave). *Tebiwa* 11:37–47.

Orme, B., 1972, Archaeology and ethnography. In *The explanation of culture change,* C. Renfrew, ed. London: Duckworth.

Osborn, H. F., 1906, The causes of extinction of mammalia. *American Naturalist* 40:769–795, 829–859.

Osborne, C. M., 1965, The preparation of yucca fibers: an experimental study. *American Antiquity* 31(2:2):45–50.

Oswalt, W. H., and J. W. Van Stone, 1967, The ethnoarcheology of Crow Village, Alaska. Washington, D.C.: Bulletin of the Bureau of American Ethnology, No. 199.

Outwater, J. O., 1957, Pre-Columbian wood-cutting techniques. *American Antiquity* 22:410–411.

Oxenstierna, E., 1967, The Vikings. *Scientific American* 216:67ff.

Page, D., 1959, *History and the Homeric Iliad*. Berkeley: University of California Press.

Pallis, S. F., 1956, *The antiquities of Iraq*. Copenhagen: E. Munksgaard.

Pallottino, M., 1968, *The meaning of archaeology*. London: Thames and Hudson.

Paor, L. de, 1967, *Archaeology: an illustrated introduction*. Baltimore: Penguin.

Papworth, M. L., and L. R. Binford, 1962, A guide to archaeological excavations. *Southwestern Lore* 28:1–24.

Parker, A. C., 1910, *Iroquois uses of maize and other food plants*. Albany: New York State Museum, Bulletin No. 144.

Parkington, J. E., 1972, Stone implements as information. Capetown, S.A.: South African Archaeological Society, Goodwin Series, No. 1:10–20.

Parkinson, A. E., 1951, The preservation of cuneiform tablets by heating to a high temperature. *Museum News* 27:6–8.

Parks, G. A., and T. T. Tieh, 1966, Identifying the geographical source of artifact obsidian. *Nature* 178(5046):289–290.

Parrot, A., 1939, *Malédictions et violations des tombes*. Paris: Paul Guethner.

Parsons, E. C., 1940, Relations between ethnology and archaeology in the Southwest. *American Antiquity* 5:214–220.

Parsons, L. A., and B. J. Price, 1971, Mesoamerican trade and its role in the emergence of civilization. Berkeley: University of California, Archaeological Research Facility, Contribution No. 11, pp. 169–195.

Parsons, R. B., 1962, Indian mounds of northeast Iowa as soil genesis bench-marks. *Journal of the Iowa Archeological Society*, 12(2).

Partington, J. R., 1947, History of alchemy and early chemistry. *Nature* 159: 81–85.

Patten, B. C., 1959, An introduction to the cybernetics of the ecosystem: the trophic-dynamic aspect. *Ecology* 40:221–231.

Payne, S., 1968, The origins of domestic sheep and goats—a reconsideration in light of the fossil evidence. *Proceedings of the Prehistoric Society* 34:368–384.

Peake, H. J. E., 1940, The study of prehistoric times. *Journal of the Royal Anthropological Institute* 70:103–146.

Pearsall, W. H., 1952, The pH of natural soils and its ecological significance. *Journal of Science* 3:41–51.

Pearson, R., 1968, Migration from Japan to Ecuador: the Japanese evidence. *American Anthropologist* 70:85–86.

Peet, T. E., 1943, *The great tomb robberies of the twentieth Egyptian dynasty.* Oxford: Clarendon.

Pei, W. C., 1938, *Le rôle des animaux et des causes naturelles dans la cassure des os.* Nanking: Geological Survey of China, Paleontologica Sinica, n.s.d., No. 7 (Whole Series No. 118).

Perez, J. R., 1935, Exploracion del tunel de la Piramide del Sol. *El Mexico Antiguo* 3:91–95.

Pericot, L., 1961, The social life of Spanish Paleolithic hunters as shown in Levantine art. New York: Viking Fund Publications in Anthropology No. 31:194–213.

Perkins, D., 1960, The faunal remains of Shanidar Cave and Zawi Chemi Shani-dar: 1960 season. *Sumer* 5:77–78.

———, 1969, Fauna of Catal Huyuk: evidence for early cattle domestication in Anatolia. *Science* 164:177–179.

Perlman, I., and F. Asaro, 1971, Pottery analysis by neutron activation. In *Science and archaeology*, R. H. Brill, ed. Cambridge, Mass.: MIT Press, pp. 182–195.

Perrot, J., 1955a, The excavations at Tell Abu Matar, near Beersheba. *Israel Exploration Journal* 5:17–40ff.

———, 1955b, Les fouilles d'Abu Matar. *Syria* 34:1–38.

Peterson, F. A., 1953, Faces that are really false. *Natural History* 62:176–180.

Petrie, W. M. F., 1891, *Tell-el-Hesy (Lachish).* London: Palestine Exploration Fund.

———, 1899, Sequences in prehistoric remains. *Journal of the Royal Anthro-pological Institute* 29:295–301.

———, 1901, *Diospolis Parva.* London: Egyptian Exploration Fund Memoirs, No. 20.

———, 1931, *Seventy years in archaeology.* London: Low, Marston.

Petsche, J. E., 1968, *Bibliography of salvage archeology in the United States.* Washington, D.C.: Smithsonian Institution, River Basin Surveys, Publica-tions in Salvage Archeology, No. 10.

Pewe, T. L., 1954, The geological approach to dating archaeological sites. *Ameri-can Antiquity* 20:51–61.

Phillips, A. P., 1971, Attribute analysis and social structure of Chassey-Cortalliod populations. *Man* 6:341–352.

Phillips, P., 1970, *Archaeological survey in the lower Yazoo Basin, Mississippi,* 1949–1955, Cambridge, Mass.: Harvard University, Papers of the Peabody Museum, Vol. 60.

Phillips, P., J. A. Ford, and J. B. Griffin, 1951, *Archaeological survey in the lower Mississippi alluvial valley, 1940–1947.* Cambridge, Mass.: Harvard University, Papers of the Peabody Museum, Vol. 25.

Pieper, W., 1923, Der Pariastamm der Slêb. *Le Monde Orientale* 17:1–75.

Piggott, S., 1951, The framework of prehistory. *Man* 51:88 (Art. 152).

———, 1959a, *Approach to archaeology.* Cambridge, Mass.: Harvard University Press.

———, 1959b, A Late Bronze Age wine trade? *Antiquity* 33:122–123.

———, 1960, Prehistory and evolutionary theory. In *Evolution after Darwin,* Sol Tax, ed. Chicago: University of Chicago Press, pp. 85–98.

———, 1965, *Ancient Europe.* Chicago: Aldine.

———, and B. Hope-Taylor, 1965, Archaeological draughtsmanship: I, principles and practice. *Antiquity* 39:165–176.

Pilling, A. R., 1965, Life at Porter Site 8, Midland County, Michigan. *The Totem Pole,* Detroit: Bulletin of the Aboriginal Research Club, 48 (4).

Pittioni, R., 1960, Metallurgical analysis of archaeological materials. II. New York: Viking Fund Publications in Anthropology No. 28:21–33.

Planck, M., 1949, *Scientific autobiography and other papers.* New York: Philosophical Library.

Platt, J. R., 1962, *The excitement of science.* Boston: Houghton, Mifflin.

———, 1964, Strong inference. *Science* 146:347–353.

Plenderleith, H. J., 1952, Fakes and forgeries in museums. *Museum Journal* 52:143–148.

———, 1956, *The conservation of antiquities and works of art; treatment, repair, and restoration.* London: Oxford.

———, and A. E. A. Werner, 1971, *The conservation of antiquities and works of art,* 2d ed. London: Oxford University Press.

Plog, F., 1968, *Archeological surveys: a new perspective.* Unpublished MA thesis, University of Chicago.

———, 1972, Laws, systems of law, and the explanation of observed variation. In *The explanation of culture change,* C. Renfrew, ed. London: Duckworth.

Polach, H. A., and J. Golson, 1966, *Collection of specimens for radiocarbon dating and interpretation of results.* Canberra: Australian Institute of Aboriginal Studies, Manual No. 2.

Polanyi, K., 1957, The economy as instituted process. In *Trade and market in the early empires,* K. Polanyi, C. M. Arensberg, and H. W. Pearson, eds. New York: Free Press, pp. 243–262.

Pond, A., 1930, Primitive methods of working stone: based on experiments by Halvor L. Skavlem. Beloit, Wis.: Beloit College, Logan Museum Bulletin, 2 (1).

Poole, L., and Gray, 1966, *One passion, two loves: the story of Heinrich and Sophia Schliemann, discoverers of Troy.* New York: Crowell.

Pope, G. D., Jr., 1960, Aims and methods of projectile point typology. Trenton, N.J.: Eastern States Archeological Federation, Bulletin No. 19:13.

Posnansky, A., 1945, *Tihuanacu, the cradle of American man,* James F. Shearer, trans. Locust Valley, N.Y.: Augustin.

Potratz, J. A. H., 1962, *Einführung in die Archäologie.* Stuttgart: A. Kröner.

Poulik, J., 1956, *Prehistoric art.* London: Spring Books.

Powell, J. W., 1961, *The Colorado River and its canyons.* New York: Dover Books T94.

Powell, T. G. E., 1951, The framework of prehistory. *Man* 51:147 (Art. 248).

———, 1966, *Prehistoric art.* London: Thames and Hudson.

———, and G. E. Daniel, 1956, *Barclodiad y Gawres.* Liverpool: Liverpool University Press.

Powers, S., 1877, Centennial mission to the Indians of western Nevada and California. Washington, D.C.: Smithsonian Institution Annual Report for 1876, pp. 449–460.

Pradenne, A. V. de, 1932, *Les fraudes en archéologie préhistorique*. Paris: Émile Nourry.

Pritchard, J. B., 1966, Palestinian figurines in relation to certain goddesses known through literature. *American Oriental Series*, Vol. 24.

Proskouriakoff, T., 1960, Historical implications of a pattern of dates at Piedras Negras, Guatemala. *American Antiquity* 25:454–475.

Prospezioni Archeologiche, 1966, Vol. 1, Turin: Fondazione Lerici, Commissionaria Editori.

Puleston, D. E., 1971, An experimental approach to the function of Classic Maya *Chultuns. American Antiquity* 36:322–335.

Pulgram, E., 1959, Proto-Indo-European; reality and reconstruction. *Language* 35:421–426.

Pyddoke, E., 1961, *Stratification for the archaeologist*. London: Phoenix House.

———, 1964, *What is archaeology?* New York: Roy.

———, ed., 1963, *The scientist and archaeology*. London: Phoenix House.

Quigley, C., 1961, *The evolution of civilizations*. New York: Macmillan.

Quimby, G. I., 1960, Rates of culture change in archaeology. *American Antiquity* 25:416–417.

Quitta, H., 1967, The C_{14} chronology of the central and SE European neolithic. *Antiquity* 41:263–270.

Rachlin, C. K., 1955, The rubber mold technic for the study of textile-impressed pottery. *American Antiquity* 20:394–396.

Radcliffe-Brown, A. R., 1952, *Structure and function in primitive society*. Glencoe, Ill.: Free Press.

Radford, C. A. R., 1935, A Roman villa at Ditchley, Oxon. *Antiquity* 9:472–476.

Radiocarbon. New Haven, Conn.: American Journal of Science. Annual; Vol. 1, 1959.

Rafter, T. A., 1965, C14 variations in nature and the effect on radiocarbon dating. *New Zealand Journal of Science and Technology*, Section B 37:20–38.

Ragir, S., 1967, A review of techniques for archaeological sampling. In *A guide to field methods in archaeology*, R. F. Heizer and J. A. Graham, eds. Palo Alto, Calif.: National Press, pp. 181–198.

Raikes, R., 1967, *Water, weather and prehistory*. London: J. Baker.

Rainey, F. G., 1966, New techniques in archaeology. *Proceedings of the American Philosophical Society* 110:146–152.

Rainey, F., and E. K. Ralph, 1966, Archeology and its new technology. *Science* 153:1481–1491.

Ralph, E., 1965, Review of radiocarbon dates from Tikal and the Maya calendar correlation problem. *American Antiquity* 30:421–427.

———, 1971, Carbon-14 dating. In *Dating techniques for the archeologist*, H. N. Michael and E. K. Ralph, eds. Cambridge, Mass.: MIT Press, pp. 1–48.

———, and M. C. Han, 1966, Dating of pottery by thermoluminescence. *Nature* 210:245–247.

———, 1971, Potential of thermoluminescence dating. In *Science and archaeology*, R. H. Brill, ed. Cambridge, Mass.: MIT Press, pp. 244–250.

———, and H. N. Michael, 1967, Problems of the radiocarbon calendar. *Archaeometry* 10:3–11.

Randall, E. O., 1908, The mound builders and the lost tribes: the "Holy Stones of Newark." Columbus: Ohio Archaeological and Historical Society, Publication No. 17:208–218.

Rands, R. L., 1953, The water lily in Maya art: a complex of alleged Asiatic origin. Washington, D.C.: Bulletin of the Bureau of American Ethnology, 151:79–153.

Rappaport, R. A., 1971, The flow of energy in an agricultural society. *Scientific American* 224:117–132.

———, and A. Rappaport, 1967, Analysis of coastal deposits for midden content. New York: Anthropological Papers of the American Museum of Natural History 51(2):201–215.

Rashevsky, N., 1952, The effect of environmental factors on the rates of cultural development. *Bulletin of Mathematical Biophysics* 14:193–201.

———, 1967, Organismic sets: outline of a general theory of biological and social organisms. *General Systems* 12:21–28.

Rassam, H., 1897, *Asshur and the Land of Nimrod*. Cincinnati: Curtis and Jennings.

Rathgen, F., 1926, *Die Konservierung von Altertumsfunden*, 2 Vols. Leipzig: Walter de Gruyter.

Rathje, W. L., 1970, Socio-political implications of lowland Maya burials: methodology and tentative hypotheses. *World Archaeology* 1:359–374.

———, 1972, Models for mobile Maya: a variety of constraints. In *The explanation of culture change*, C. Renfrew, ed. London: Duckworth.

Rau, C., 1881, Aboriginal stone drilling. *American Naturalist* 15:536–542.

Rawlinson, H. C., 1850, Notes on the inscriptions of Assyria and Babylonia. *Journal of the Royal Asiatic Society of Great Britain and Ireland* 12:401–483.

Redfield, A. C., 1967, Postglacial change in sea level in the western north Atlantic Ocean. *Science* 157:687–692.

Redman, C. L., 1972, Multivariate approach to understanding changes in an early farming community in Southeast Anatolia. In *The explanation of culture change*, C. Renfrew, ed. London: Duckworth.

———, and P. J. Watson, 1970, Systematic, intensive surface collection. *American Antiquity* 35:279–291.

Reed, C. A., 1959, Animal domestication in the prehistoric Near East. *Science* 130:1629–1639.

———, 1960, A review of the archaeological evidence on animal domestication in the prehistoric Near East. Chicago: Oriental Institute of the University of Chicago, Studies in Ancient Oriental Civilization, No. 31:119–145.

———, 1961, Osteological evidences for prehistoric domestication in southwestern Asia. *Zeitschrift für Tierzüchtung und Züchtungsbiologie* 76:31–38.

———, 1962, Snails on a Persian hillside: ecology, prehistory, gastronomy. New Haven, Conn.: Yale University, Peabody Museum of Natural History, *Postilla* 66.

———, 1963, Osteo-archaeology. In *Science in archaeology*, D. Brothwell and E. Higgs, eds. London: Thames and Hudson, pp. 204–216.

Reed, E., 1956, Types of village-plan lay-outs in the Southwest. In *Prehistoric settlement patterns in the New World*, G. R. Willey, ed. New York: Viking Fund Publications in Anthropology, No. 23:18–25.

Reed, N. A., J. W. Bennett, and J. W. Porter, 1968, Solid core drilling of Monks Mound: technique and findings. *American Antiquity* 33:137–148.

Reeves, D. M., 1936, Aerial photography and archaeology. *American Antiquity* 2:102–107.

Renaud, E. B., 1941, *Classification and description of Indian stone artifacts*. Gunnison: Colorado Archaeological Society. Reprinted in *Southwestern Lore*, 1960, 26(1).

Renfrew, C., 1967, Colonialism and *Megalithismus. Antiquity* 41:276–288.

———, 1968a, Obsidian and the origins of trade. *Scientific American* 218:38ff.

———, 1968b, Models in prehistory. *Antiquity* 42:132–134.

———, 1968c, Wessex without Mycenae. Athens: Annual of the British School of Archaeology at Athens 63:277–285.

———, 1969, Trade and culture process in European prehistory. *Current Anthropology* 10:151–169.

———, 1970a, New configurations in Old World archaeology. *World Archaeology* 2:199–211.

———, 1970b, The tree ring calibration of radio-carbon: an archaeological evaluation. *Proceedings of the Prehistoric Society* 36:280–311.

———, 1972a, *The emergence of civilization.* London: Methuen.

———, 1972b, Monuments and social organization in Neolithic Wessex. In *The explanation of culture change,* C. Renfrew, ed. London: Duckworth.

———, 1972c, *The explanation of culture change.* London: Duckworth.

———, J. R. Cann, and J. E. Dixon, 1965, Obsidian in the Aegean. Athens: Annual of the British School at Athens 60:225–242.

———, J. E. Dixon, and J. R. Cann, 1966, Obsidian and early cultural contact in the Near East. *Proceedings of the Prehistoric Society for 1966* 32:30–72.

Rice, T. T., 1957, *The Scythians.* New York: Praeger. (London: Thames and Hudson.)

Rich, C. J., 1819, *Second memoir on Babylon.* London.

Richards, H. G., 1937, Marine Pleistocene mollusks as indicators of time and ecological conditions. In *Early Man,* G. G. McCurdy, ed. Philadelphia: Lippincott, pp. 75–84.

Richmond, I. A., 1932, The Irish analogies for the Romano-British barn dwelling. *Journal of Roman Studies* 22:96–106.

Ricketson, O. G., 1937, *Uaxactun, Guatemala Group E—1926–1931. Part I: The excavations.* Washington, D.C.: Carnegie Institution, Publication No. 477: 1–180.

Ridgeway, J. C., 1938, *Scientific illustration.* Palo Alto, Calif.: Stanford University Press.

Riesenfeld, A., 1950, *The Megalithic culture of Melanesia.* Leiden: Brill.

Rieth, A., 1970, *Archaeological fakes.* New York: Praeger.

Riley, C. L., 1969, *The origins of civilization.* Carbondale: Southern Illinois University Press.

———, C. W. Pennington, J. C. Kelley, and R. L. Rands, eds., 1970, *Man across the sea.* Austin: University of Texas Press.

Riley, D. N., 1946, The technique of air-archaeology. *Archaeological Journal* 101:1–16.

Ritchie, P. R., and J. Pugh, 1963, Ultra-violet radiation and excavation. *Antiquity* 37:259–263.

Ritchie, W. A., 1954, *Dutch Hollow, an early historic period Seneca site in Livingston County, New York.* Albany: Transactions and Researches of the New York State Museum, 13(1).

———, 1961, *A typology and nomenclature for New York projectile points.* Albany: New York State Museum, Bulletin No. 384.

———, and R. J. MacNeish, 1949, Pre-Iroquoian pottery of New York state. *American Antiquity* 15:97–123.

Robbins, M. C., 1966, Material culture and cognition. *American Anthropologist* 68:745–748.

Robbins, M., and M. B. Irving, 1965, *The amateur archaeologist's handbook.* New York: Crowell.

Roberts, F. H. H., 1935, A Folsom complex. Washington, D.C.: Smithsonian Institution, Miscellaneous Collections, 94(4).

Robertson, M. G., 1972, Monument thievery in Mesoamerica. *American Antiquity* 37:147–155.

Robinson, J. T., 1956, *The dentition of the Australopithecinae.* Pretoria: Transvaal Museum Memoirs, No. 29.

Robinson, W. S., 1951, A method for chronologically ordering archaeological deposits. *American Antiquity* 16:293–301.

Rodden, R. J., 1966, The spondylus-shell trade and the beginnings of the Vinča culture. VIIth International Congress of Prehistoric and Protohistoric Sciences, Prague, 1966.

Rodeck, H. G., 1932, Arthropod designs on prehistoric Mimbres pottery. *Annals of the Entomological Society of America* 25:688–693.

Rogers, M. J., 1936, *Yuman pottery making.* San Diego, Calif.: San Diego Museum Papers, No. 2.

Römisch-Germanisches Zentralmuseum zu Mainz, 1959, *Technische Beiträge zur Archäologie,* Vol. 1.

——, 1965, *Technische Beiträge zur Archäologie,* Vol. 2.

Rootenberg, S., 1964, Archaeological field sampling. *American Antiquity* 30:181–188.

Rose, F. P., 1968, A flint ballast station in New Rochelle, New York. *American Antiquity* 33:240–243.

Rosenfeld, A., 1965, *The inorganic raw materials of antiquity.* New York: Praeger.

——, 1971, Review of Notation dan les gravures du paléolithique supérieur. A. Marshack. *Antiquity* 45:317–319.

Rouse, I., 1952, *Puerto Rican prehistory.* New York: Academy of Science, Scientific Survey of Puerto Rico and the Virgin Islands, 18(3, 4).

——, 1953, The strategy of culture history. In *Anthropology today,* A. L. Kroeber, chairman. Chicago: University of Chicago Press, pp. 57–76.

——, 1954, On the use of the concept of area co-tradition. *American Antiquity* 19:221–225.

——, 1955, On the correlation of phases of culture. *American Anthropologist* 57:713–722.

——, 1957, Culture area and co-tradition. *Southwestern Journal of Anthropology* 13:123–133.

——, 1958, The inference of migrations from anthropological evidence. Tucson: University of Arizona, Social Science Bulletin, No. 27:63–68.

——, 1960a, The classification of artifacts in archaeology. *American Antiquity* 25:313–323.

——, 1960b, *Theoretical concepts underlying projectile point classification.* Trenton, N.J.: Eastern States Archeological Federation, Bulletin 19, p. 20.

——, 1965, The place of "peoples" in prehistoric research. *Journal of the Royal Anthropological Institute* 95:1–15.

——, 1972a, Analytic, synthetic, and experimental archeology. In *Archeology today,* C. L. Redman, ed. New York: Wiley.

——, 1972b, *Introduction to prehistory.* New York: McGraw-Hill.

Roust, N. L., 1967, Preliminary examination of prehistoric human coprolites from four western Nevada caves. Berkeley: Reports of the University of California Archaeological Survey No. 70:49–88.

Rowe, J. H., 1944, An introduction to the archaeology of Cuzco. Cambridge, Mass.: Harvard University, Papers of the Peabody Museum 27(2).

Rowe, J. H., 1945, Absolute chronology in the Andean area. *American Antiquity* 10:265–284.

———, 1946, Inca culture at the time of the Spanish conquest. Washington, D.C.: Bulletin of the Bureau of American Ethnology, 2(143):183–330.

———, 1953, Technological aids in anthropology: a historical survey. In *Anthropology Today*, A. L. Kroeber, chairman. Chicago: University of Chicago Press, pp. 895–941.

———, 1954, Archaeology as a career. *Archaeology* 7:229–236.

———, 1961, Stratigraphy and seriation. *American Antiquity* 26:324–330.

———, 1962, Worsaae's Law and the use of grave lots for archaeological dating. *American Antiquity* 28:129–137.

———, 1966, Diffusionism and archaeology. *American Antiquity* 31:334–337.

———, 1971, Site designation in the Americas. *American Antiquity* 36:477–480.

Rowlands, M. J., 1971, The archaeological interpretation of prehistoric metal-working. *World Archaeology* 3:210–224.

Royal Society of London, 1970, *A symposium on the impact of the natural sciences on archaeology.* Philosophical Transactions of the Royal Society of London 269:1–185.

Rubin, M., R. C. Likens, and E. G. Berry, 1963, On the validity of radiocarbon dates from snail shells. *Journal of Geology* 71:84–89.

———, and D. W. Taylor, 1963, Radiocarbon activity of shells from living clams and snails. *Science* 141:637.

Rudenko, S. I., 1970, *Frozen tombs of Siberia: the Pazyryk burials of Iron Age horsemen.* Berkeley: University of California Press.

Rudner, R. S., 1966, *Philosophy of social science.* Englewood Cliffs, N.J.: Prentice-Hall.

Ruhe, R. V., 1965, Quaternary paleopedology. In *The Quaternary of the United States,* H. G. Wright and D. Frey, eds. Princeton, N.J.: Princeton University Press, pp. 755–764.

Ruppé, R. J., 1966, The archaeological survey: a defense. *American Antiquity* 31:313–333.

Russell, R. J., 1957, Instability of sea level. *American Scientist* 45:414–430.

Ryan, E. J., and G. F. Bass, 1962, Underwater surveying and draughting—a technique. *Antiquity* 36:252–261.

Ryder, M. L., 1966, Can one cook in a skin? *Antiquity* 40:225–227.

———, 1969, Paunch cooking. *Antiquity* 43:218–220.

Sabloff, J., and G. R. Willey, 1968, The collapse of Maya civilization in the Southern Lowlands: a consideration of history and process. *Southwestern Journal of Anthropology* 23:311–336.

Sackett, J. R., 1966, Quantitative analysis of Upper Paleolithic stone tools. *American Anthropologist* 68(2:2):356–394.

Saffirio, L., 1972, *Food and food problems in prehistory.* New York: Seminar Press.

Sahlins, M. D., 1958, *Social stratification in Polynesia.* Seattle: University of Washington Press.

———, 1965, On the sociology of primitive exchange. American Sociological Association, Monograph No. 1:139–236.

Saint David's, Lord Bishop of, 1859, On some traditions relating to the submersion of ancient cities. *Transactions of the Royal Society of Literature* (2d Series) 6:387–415.

St. Joseph, J. K. S., 1951, A survey of pioneering in air-photography. In *Aspects of archaeology in Britain and beyond, essays presented to O. G. S. Crawford,* W. F. Grimes, ed. London: H. W. Edwards.

———, 1966, *The uses of air photography.* London: J. Baker.

Saint-Perier, R. de, 1913, Gravure à contours decoupés en os et coquilles perforées de l'époque Magdalénienne. Paris: Société d'Anthropologie de Paris Bulletin et Mémoires (Series 6) 4:47–52.

Salim, S. M., 1962, *Marsh dwellers of the Euphrates Delta.* London: London School of Economics, Monographs on Social Anthropology, No. 23. (London: Athlone.)

Salisbury, R., 1962, *From stone to steel.* Melbourne: Melbourne University Press.

Samolin, W., 1965, Technical studies of Chinese and Eurasian archaeological objects. *Technology and Culture* 6:249–255.

Samuels, R., 1965, Parasitological study of long-dried fecal samples. In D. Osborne ed., Contributions of the Wetherill Mesa archeological project. Salt Lake City: Society for American Archaeology, Memoir No. 19:175–179.

Sandars, N. K., 1951, The framework of prehistory. *Man* 51:88 (Art. 153).

Sanders, W. T., 1965, *The cultural ecology of the Teotihuacan Valley.* University Park: Pennsylvania State University, Department of Anthropology.

———, and J. Marino, 1970, *New World prehistory.* Englewood Cliffs, N.J.: Prentice-Hall.

———, and B. J. Price, 1968, *Mesoamerica: the evolution of a civilization.* New York: Random House.

Sandford, K. S., and W. J. Arkell, 1929–1939, *Prehistoric survey of Egypt and western Asia.* Vols. 1–4. Chicago: University of Chicago, Oriental Institute Publications, Vols. 10, 17, 18, 46.

Sandin, B., 1962, Gawai Batu: the Iban whetstone feast. *Sarawak Museum Journal* 10:392–408.

Sanson, A., 1874, Le cheval de Solutré. *Materiaux pour l'histoire . . . de l'homme* (Series 2) 5:332–342.

Sapir, E., 1916, *Time perspective in aboriginal American culture: a study in method.* Ottawa: Canada Department of Mines, Geological Survey, Memoir 90. (Reprinted in *Selected writings of Edward Sapir,* D. G. Mandelbaum, ed. Berkeley: University of California Press, 1949.)

Satterwaite, L., and E. Ralph, 1960, New radiocarbon dates and the Maya correlation problem. *American Antiquity* 26:165–184.

Saucier, R. T., 1966, Soil-survey reports and archaeological investigations. *American Antiquity* 31:419–422.

Sayce, R. U., 1963, *Primitive arts and crafts: an introduction to the study of material culture.* New York: Biblo and Tannen.

Sayles, E. B., 1935, *An archaeological survey of Texas.* Globe, Ariz.: Gila Pueblo Medallion Papers, No. 17.

Sayre, E. V., and Lui-Heung Chan, 1971, High-resolution gamma ray spectroscopic analyses of fine orange pottery. In *Science and archaeology,* R. H. Brill, ed. Cambridge, Mass.: MIT Press, pp. 165–177.

Schaber, G. G., and G. J. Gumerman, 1969, Infrared scanning images: an archeological application. *Science* 164:712–714.

Schaeffer, O. A., and J. H. Zähringer, 1966, *Age determination by Potassium-Argon-method.* New York: Springer.

Schaller, G. B., and G. R. Lowther, 1969, The relevance of carnivore behavior to the study of early hominids. *Southwestern Journal of Anthropology* 25:307–341.

Schiffer, M. B., 1972, Archaeological context and systemic context. *American Antiquity* 37:156–165.

Schlabow, K., and others, 1958, Zwei Moorleichen Funde aus dem Domlandsmoor. *Praehistorische Zeitschrift,* Berlin, 26:44–49.

Schlette, F., 1958, Die ältesten Haus-und Siedlungsformen des Menschen auf Grund des steinzeitlichen Fundmaterials Europas und Ethnologischer Vergleiche. *Ethnographisch-archäologische Forschungen,* Berlin, 5:7–185.

Schmalz, R. F., 1960, Flint and the patination of flint artifacts. *Proceedings of the Prehistoric Society* 26:44–49.

Schmid, E., 1969, Cave sediments and prehistory. In *Science in archaeology,* D. Brothwell and E. Higgs, eds., rev. ed. London: Thames and Hudson, pp. 151–166.

Schmidt, E. F., 1928, Time-relations of prehistoric pottery types in southern Arizona. New York: Anthropological Papers of the American Museum of Natural History 30:245–302.

Schoenwetter, J., 1962, The pollen analysis of eighteen archaeological sites in Arizona and New Mexico. Fieldiana, Anthropology. Chicago: Field Museum of Natural History, 53:168–209.

———, and F. W. Eddy, 1964, *Alluvial and palynological reconstruction of environments.* Santa Fe, N.M.: Museum of New Mexico, Papers in Anthropology, No. 13.

Schoute-Vanneck, C. A., 1960, A chemical aid for the relative dating of coastal shell middens. *South African Journal of Science* 56:67–70.

Schroeder, D. L., and K. C. Ruhl, 1968, Metallurgical characteristics of North American prehistoric copper work. *American Antiquity* 33:162–169.

Schulman, E. A., 1940, A bibliography of tree-ring analysis. *Tree Ring Bulletin,* Tucson: University of Arizona, 6:1–12.

———, 1941, Some propositions in tree-ring analysis. *Ecology* 22:193–195.

———, 1958, Bristlecone pine, oldest known living thing. *National Geographic Magazine* 113:353–372.

Schultz, G. B., G. C. Lueninghoener, and W. D. Frankforter, 1948, Preliminary geomorphological studies of the Lime Creek area. Lincoln, Neb.: University of Nebraska State Museum Bulletin 3:31–42.

Schwartz, D. W., 1956, Demographic changes in the early period of Cohonina prehistory. New York: Viking Fund Publications in Anthropology 23:26–31.

———, 1970, The postmigration culture: a base for archaeological inference. In *Reconstructing prehistoric pueblo societies,* W. A. Longacre, ed. Albuquerque: University of New Mexico Press, pp. 175–193.

Schwarz, G. T., 1965, Stereoscopic views taken with an ordinary single camera—a new technique for archaeologists. *Archaeometry* 7:36–42.

———, 1967, *Archäologische Feldmethode [Field Archaeology]. Anleitung für Heimat Forscher, Sammler und Angehende Archäologen.* München: O. Verlag.

Scott, W. H., 1958, Economic and material culture of the Kalingas of Madukayan. *Southwestern Journal of Anthropology* 14:318–337.

Scudder, T., 1971, *Gathering among African woodland savannah cultivators.* University of Zambia, Institute for African Studies, Zambia Papers, No. 5.

Scully, E. G., 1953, Extinct river channels as a method of dating archaeological sites in southwest Missouri. *Missouri Archeologist* 15:84–91.

Sears, P. B., 1952, Palynology in southern North America: I. Archaeological horizons in the Basin of Mexico. *Bulletin of the Geological Society of America* 63:225–240.

———, 1953a, An ecological view of land use in Middle America. *Ceiba* 3:157–165.

———, 1953b, The interdependence of archeology and ecology with examples from Middle America. *Transactions of the New York Academy of Science* (Series 2) 15:113–117.

Sears, P. B., 1963, Vegetation, climate, and coastal submergence in Connecticut. *Science* 140:59–60.

——, and A. Roosma, 1961, A climatic sequence from two Nevada caves. *American Journal of Science* 259:669–678.

Sears, W. H., 1954, The sociopolitical organization of pre-Columbian cultures on the Gulf coastal plain. *American Anthropologist* 56:339–364.

——, 1958, Burial mounds on the Gulf coastal plain. *American Antiquity* 23:274–284.

——, 1961, The study of social and religious systems in North American archaeology. *Current Anthropology* 2:223–246.

——, 1968, The state and settlement patterns in the New World. In *Settlement archaeology*, K. C. Chang, ed. Palo Alto, Calif.: National Press Books, pp. 134–153.

Seborg, R. M., and R. B. Inverarity, 1962, Preservation of old, waterlogged wood by treatment with polyethylene glycol. *Science* 136:649–650.

Sellstedt, H., L. Engstrand, and N. G. Gejvall, 1966, New application of radiocarbon dating to collagen residue in bones. *Nature* 212:572–574.

——, 1967, Radiocarbon dating of bone. *Nature* 213:415.

Semenov, S. A., 1964, *Prehistoric technology,* M. W. Thompson, trans. London: Cory, Adams & Mackay.

Senyurek, M. S., 1947, Duration of life of the ancient inhabitants of Anatolia. *American Journal of Physical Anthropology* 5:55–66.

Service, E. R., 1962, *Primitive social organization.* New York: Random House.

——, 1964, Archeological theory and ethnographic fact. In *Process and pattern in culture,* R. Manners, ed. Chicago: Aldine, pp. 364–375.

——, 1968, The prime-mover of cultural evolution. *Southwestern Journal of Anthropology* 24:396–409.

Shaeffer, J. B., 1960, The county grid system of site designation. *Plains Anthropologist* 5(9):29–31.

Shapley, H., ed., 1953, *Climatic change: evidence, causes and effects.* Cambridge, Mass.: Harvard University Press.

Shaw, C. F., 1928, Profile development and the relationship of soils in California. *Proceedings of the First International Congress of Soil Science* 4:291–317.

Shaw, T., 1970, Methods of earthwork building. *Proceedings of the Prehistoric Society* 36:380–381.

Sheldon, H. H., 1933, *The deer of California.* Santa Barbara, Calif.: Santa Barbara Museum of Natural History, Occasional Papers, No. 3.

Shepard, A. O., 1948, *Plumbate: a Mesoamerican trade ware.* Washington, D.C.: Carnegie Institution, Publication No. 573.

——, 1956, *Ceramics for the archaeologist.* Washington, D.C.: Carnegie Institution, Publication No. 609.

——, 1963, *Beginnings of ceramic industrialization: an example from the Oaxaca Valley.* Washington, D.C.: Carnegie Institution, Notes from a Ceramic Laboratory, No. 2.

——, 1966, Problems in pottery analysis. *American Antiquity* 31:870–871.

——, 1971, Ceramic analysis: the interrelations of methods: the relations of analysts and archaeologists. In *Science and archaeology,* R. H. Brill, ed. Cambridge, Mass.: MIT Press, pp. 55–64.

Shepard, F. P., 1961, Sea level rise during the past 20,000 years. *Zeitschrift für Geomorphologie* 3:30–35.

——, 1964, Sea level changes in the past 6000 years: possible archeological significance. *Science* 143:574–576.

Shepard, F. P., and H. Suess, 1956, Rate of postglacial rise of sea level. *Science* 123: 1082–1083.

Sherratt, A., 1972, Models, theories and hypotheses. In *The explanation of culture change,* C. Renfrew, ed. London: Duckworth.

Shetrone, H. C., 1930. *The mound builders.* New York: Appleton.

Shorer, P., 1964, A method for the transfer of archaeological soil sections on to a flexible rubber backing. London: International Institute for the Conservation of Museum Objects, Studies in Conservation. Abstracts of the Technical Literature on Archaeology and the Fine Arts, Vol. 9.

Shorr, P., 1935, The genesis of prehistorical research. *Isis* 23:425–443.

Shotten, F. W., 1969, Petrological examination. In *Science in archaeology,* D. Brothwell and E. Higgs, eds., rev. ed. London: Thames and Hudson, pp. 571–577.

Shumway, G., C. L. Hubbs, and J. R. Moriarity, 1961, Scripps Estate site, San Diego, California: a La Jolla site dated 5640 to 7370 years before the present. *Annals of the New York Academy of Sciences* 93:39–132.

Shutler, R., 1961, Correlation of beach terraces with climatic cycles of pluvial Lake Lahontan, Nevada. *Annals of the New York Academy of Sciences* 95:513–520.

Silverberg, R., 1963, *Sunken history: the story of underwater archeology.* Philadelphia: Chilton.

———, 1966, *Frontiers in archaeology.* Philadelphia: Chilton.

Simonsen, R. W., 1954, Identification and interpretation of buried soils. *American Journal of Science* 252:705–722.

Simoons, F. J., 1961, *Eat not this flesh: food avoidances in the Old World.* Madison: University of Wisconsin Press.

Simpson, D. D. A., and F. M. B. Cooke, 1967, Photogrammetric planning at Grantully, Perthshire. *Antiquity* 41:220–221.

Simpson, G. C., 1964, Comment on Ascher and Hockett: The human revolution. *Current Anthropology* 5:151.

Simpson, G. G., 1967, *The meaning of evolution.* New Haven, Conn.: Yale University Press.

Sinex, F. M., and B. Faris, 1959, Isolation of gelatin from ancient bones. *Science* 129:969.

Singer, C., E. J. Holmyard, and A. R. Hall, 1954–1958, *A history of technology,* Vols. 1–4. London: Oxford.

Siniaguin, I. I., 1943, A method for determining the absolute age of soils. *Comptes Rendus, Academy of Sciences, U.S.S.R.* 40:335–336.

Slosson, E. E., 1963, The science of the city dump. In *Archaeology,* S. Rapport and H. Wright, eds. New York: New York University Press, pp. 366–367.

Smiley, T. L., 1955a, Varve studies. Tucson: University of Arizona Bulletin, Series No. 26:135–150.

———, ed., 1955b, *Geochronology.* Tucson: University of Arizona Press.

Smith, A. L., 1929, Report on the investigation of stelae. Washington, D.C.: Carnegie Institution of Washington Yearbook, No. 28:323–325.

Smith, C. E., Jr., 1965, Agriculture, Tehuacan Valley. *Fieldiana, Botany.* Chicago: Field Museum of Natural History, 31(3).

Smith, C. S., 1971, The techniques of the Luristan smith, with post-symposium notes. In *Science and archaeology,* R. H. Brill, ed. Cambridge, Mass.: MIT Press, pp. 32–54.

Smith, G. V., 1891, The use of flint blades to work pine wood. Washington, D.C.: Smithsonian Institution, Annual Report for 1891, pp. 601–605.

Smith, H. W., R. H. McCreery, and C. D. Moodie, 1952, Collection and preservation of soil profiles: II. *Soil Science* 73:243.

Smith, H. W. and C. D. Moodie, 1947, Collection and preservation of soil profiles. *Soil Science* 64:61–69.

Smith, M., 1960, Blood groups of the ancient dead. *Science* 131:699–702.

Smith, M. A., 1955, The limitations of inference in archaeology. *Archaeological Newsletter* 6:1–7.

Smith, R. E., 1955, *Ceramic sequences at Uaxactun.* New Orleans: Tulane University, Middle American Research Institute, Publication No. 20.

Smith, R. H., 1970, An approach to the drawing of pottery and small finds for excavation reports. *World Archaeology* 2:212–228.

Smith, W. S., 1958, *The art and architecture of ancient Egypt.* Pelican History of Art Series. Baltimore, Penguin.

Society for American Archaeology, 1971, Society action against illicit antiquities traffic. *American Antiquity* 36:253–254.

Soergel, W., 1939, Unter welchen klimatischen Verhältnissen lebten zur Bildungzeit der alt-diluvialen Kiese von Süssenborn, Rangifer, Ovibus, und Elephas trogontherii in Mittel- und Norddeutschland. *Zeitschrift Deutsches Geologisches Gesellschaft* 91:829–835.

———, 1940, *Zur biologischen Beurteilung diluvialer Saugetierfaunen.* Sitzungsberichte Heidelberg: Heidelberg Akademie der Wissenschaften, No. 4.

Soil Survey Staff, 1962, *Soil survey manual: identification and nomenclature of soil horizons.* Washington, D.C.: Supplement to the U.S. Department of Agriculture Handbook, 18:173–188.

Sokoloff, V. P., and G. F. Carter, 1952, Time and trace metals in archaeological sites. *Science* 116:1–5.

———, and J. L. Lorenzo, 1953, Modern and ancient soils at some archaeological sites in the Valley of Mexico. *American Antiquity* 19:50–55.

Solecki, R. S., 1949, The trinomial classification system [of sites] for West Virginia. *West Virginia Archaeologist* 1:5–6.

———, 1951, Notes on soil analysis and archaeology. *American Antiquity* 16:254–256.

———, 1953, *Exploration of an Adena mound at Natrium, West Virginia.* Washington, D.C.: Bulletin 151, Anthropological Papers, Bureau of American Ethnology, 40:313–396.

———, 1957, Practical aerial photography for archaeologists. *American Antiquity* 22:337–351.

Solheim, W. G., 1960, The use of sherd weights and counts in the handling of archaeological data. *Current Anthropology* 1:325–329.

Sollas, W. J., 1911, *Ancient hunters and their modern representatives.* London: Macmillan.

Sonnenfeld, J., 1962, Interpreting the function of primitive implements. *American Antiquity* 28:56–65.

Sonneville-Bordes, D. de, 1953, Le Paléolithique supérieur du plateau Baillart à Gavaudun (Lot-et-Garonne). *Bulletin de la Société Française Préhistorique* 50:356–364.

———, 1960, *Le Paléolithique supérieur en Périgord,* 2 vols. Paris: Delmas.

Soudsky, B., 1967, *Principles of automatic data treatment applied on Neolithic pottery.* Prague: Czechoslovak Academy of Sciences, Archaeological Institute.

South, S., 1955, Evolutionary theory in archaeology. Chapel Hill, N.C.: Southern Indian Studies, 7:10–32.

Sparks, B. W., 1969, Non-marine mollusca and archaeology. In *Science in archaeology,* D. Brothwell and E. Higgs, eds., rev. ed. London: Thames and Hudson, pp. 395–406.

Spaulding, A. C., 1951, Recent advances in surveying techniques and their application to archaeology. Ann Arbor: University of Michigan, Anthropological Papers of the Museum of Anthropology, No. 8:2–16.

———, 1953, Statistical techniques for the discovery of artifact types. *American Antiquity* 18:305–313, 391–393.

———, 1958, The significance of differences between radiocarbon dates. *American Antiquity* 23:309–311.

———, 1960, Statistical description and comparison of artifact assemblages. New York: Viking Fund Publications in Anthropology, No. 28:60–92.

Spencer, R. F., 1959, *The North Alaskan Eskimo: a study in ecology and society.* Washington, D.C.: Bulletin of the Bureau of American Ethnology, No. 171.

Spengler, O., 1926–1928, *The decline of the West.* New York: Knopf.

Speth, J. D., 1972, Mechanical basis of percussion flaking. *American Antiquity* 37:34–60.

Spier, L., 1917, New data on the Trenton argillite culture. *American Anthropologist* 18:181–189.

Squier, E. G., and E. H. Davis, 1848, *Ancient mounds of the Mississippi valley.* Washington, D.C.: Smithsonian Institution, Contributions to Knowledge, Vol. 1.

Squier, R. J., 1953, The manufacture of flint implements by the Indians of northern and central California. Berkeley: Reports of the University of California Archaeological Survey 19:14–44.

Stallings, W. S., 1939, Dating prehistoric ruins by tree-rings. Santa Fe, N.M.: School of American Research, Laboratory of Anthropology, Bulletin No. 8.

Staniland, L. N., 1953, *The principles of line illustration with emphasis on the requirements of biological and other scientific workers.* Cambridge, Mass.: Harvard University Press.

Stanislawski, M. B., 1969, The ethno-archaeology of Hopi pottery making. *Plateau* 42:27–33.

Staub, G., 1951, Die Geographische Fixierung historischer Objekte und Örtlichkeiten. *Jahrbuch 41 der Schweizerischen Gesellschaft für Urgeschichte,* pp. 191–195.

Steele, R. H., 1930, Experiments in Kaitahu (Ngai-Tahu) methods in drilling. *Journal of the Polynesian Society* 39:181–188.

Steensberg, A., 1943, *Ancient harvesting implements: a study in archaeology and human geography.* Copenhagen: Nationalmuseets Skrifter, Arkeologisk-Historisk Raekke 1.

Steffannson, V., 1937, Food of the ancient and modern Stone Age man. *Journal of the American Dietetic Association* 13:102–119.

Stein, W. T., 1963, Mammal remains from archaeological sites in the Point of Pines region, Arizona. *American Antiquity* 29:213–220.

Stephens, J. L., 1842, *Incidents of travel in Central America, Chiapas and Yucatan,* 2 vols. New York: Harper & Row. (Reprint of one volume: *Incidents of travel in Yucatan,* with intro. by V. von Hagen, ed., new ed. Norman: University of Oklahoma Press, 1962.)

Sternberg, H. O'R., 1960, Radiocarbon dating as applied to a problem of Amazonian morphology. Brazil: Comptes Rendus du XVIII Congrès International de Géographie Rio de Janeiro 2:399–424.

Sterud, G., 1972, A paradigmatic view of prehistory. In *The explanation of culture change,* C. Renfrew, ed. London: Duckworth.

Stevenson, D. P., F. H. Stross, and R. F. Heizer, 1971, An evaluation of X-ray fluorescence analysis as a method for correlating obsidian artifacts with source location. *Archaeometry* 13:17–25.

Steward, J. H., 1936, The economic and social basis of primitive bands. In *Essays in anthropology presented to A. L. Kroeber*. Berkeley: University of California Press, pp. 331–350.

——, 1937, Ecological aspects of Southwestern society. *Anthropos* 32:87–104.

——, 1938, *Basin-Plateau aboriginal sociopolitical groups*. Washington, D.C.: Bulletin of the Bureau of American Ethnology, No. 120.

——, 1942, The direct historical approach to archaeology. *American Antiquity* 7:337–343.

——, 1949, Cultural causality and law: a trial formulation of the development of early civilizations. *American Anthropologist* 51:1–27.

——, 1955, *Theory of culture change: the methodology of multilinear evolution*. Urbana: University of Illinois Press.

——, 1968, Causal factors and processes in the evolution of pre-farming societies. In *Man the hunter*, R. B. Lee and I. DeVore, eds. Chicago: Aldine, pp. 321–334.

Stewart, T. D., 1960, A physical anthropologist's view of the peopling of the New World. *Southwestern Journal of Anthropology* 16:259–273.

——, and M. T. Newman, 1967, Physical types of American Indians. In *The North American Indians, a sourcebook*, R. C. Owen, J. F. Deetz, and A. D. Fisher, eds. New York: Macmillan, pp. 53–67.

Stickle, E. G., and J. L. Chartkoff, 1972, The nature of scientific laws and their relation to law-building in archeology. In *The explanation of culture change*, C. Renfrew, ed. London: Duckworth.

Stirling, M. W., F. Rainey, and M. W. Stirling, Jr., 1960, Electronics and archaeology. Philadelphia: University of Pennsylvania Museum, Expedition, 2(4): 19–29.

Stone, E. H., 1924, *Stones of Stonehenge*. London: Scott.

Stone, J. F. S., 1958, *Wessex before the Celts*. New York: Praeger.

——, and L. C. Thomas, 1956, The use and distribution of faience in the ancient East and prehistoric Europe. *Proceedings of the Prehistoric Society* 22:37–84.

Storie, R. E., and F. Harradine, 1950, An age estimate of the burials unearthed near Concord, California, based on pedologic observations. Berkeley: Reports of the University of California Archaeological Survey No. 9:15–17.

Straffin, D., 1971, A device for vertical archaeological photography. *Plains Anthropologist* 16:232–234.

Strong, W. D., 1940, From history to prehistory in the northern Great Plains. Washington, D.C.: Smithsonian Institution Miscellaneous Collections, 100: 353–394.

——, 1952, The value of archeology in the training of professional anthropologists. *American Anthropologist* 54:318–322.

——, and J. M. Corbett, 1943, *A ceramic sequence at Pachacamac*. New York: Columbia University Studies in Archeology and Ethnology, 1(2).

Stross, F. H., 1960, Authentication of antique stone objects by physical and chemical means. *Analytical Chemistry* 32:17A–24A.

——, ed., 1971, *The application of the physical sciences to archaeology*. Berkeley: University of California, Archaeological Research Facility, Contribution No. 12.

——, D. P. Stevenson, J. R. Weaver, and G. Wyld, 1971, Analysis of American obsidians by X-ray fluorescence and neutron activation analysis. In *Science and archaeology*, R. H. Brill, ed. Cambridge, Mass.: MIT Press, pp. 210–221.

——, J. R. Weaver, G. E. A. Wyld, R. F. Heizer, and J. A. Graham, 1968, Analysis of American obsidians by X-ray fluorescence and neutron activation analysis. Berkeley: University of California, Archaeological Research Facility, Contribution No. 5, Paper 4:59–80.

Struever, S., 1962, Implications of vegetal remains from an Illinois Hopewell site. *American Antiquity* 27:584–587.

——, 1964, The Hopewell interaction sphere in riverine-western Great Lakes culture history. Springfield, Ill.: Illinois State Museum Scientific Papers 12:85–106.

——, 1965, Middle woodland culture history in the Great Lakes riverine area. *American Antiquity* 31:211–223.

——, 1968a, Flotation techniques for the recovery of small-scale archaeological remains. *American Antiquity* 33:353–362.

——, 1968b, Woodland subsistence-settlement systems in the lower Illinois valley. In *New perspectives in archeology*. S. Binford and L. Binford, eds. Chicago: Aldine, pp. 285–312.

——, 1968c, Problems, methods and organization: a disparity in the growth of archeology. In *Anthropological Archeology in the Americas*. Washington, D.C.: Anthropological Society.

——, 1971, Comments on archaeological data requirements and research strategy. *American Antiquity* 36:9–19.

Stuckenrath, R., 1965, On the care and feeding of radiocarbon dates. *Archaeology* 18:277–281.

Studhalter, R. A., 1955, Tree growth: some historical chapters. *The Botanical Review* 24:1–72.

Stuiver, M., 1965, Carbon-14 content of 18th and 19th century wood: Variations correlated with sunspot activity. *Science* 149:533–535.

——, and H. Suess, 1966, On the relationship between radiocarbon dates and true sample ages. *Radiocarbon* 8:534–540.

Sturtevant, W. C., 1958, *Anthropology as a career*. Washington, D.C.: Smithsonian Institution.

Suess, H., 1965, Secular variations of the cosmic ray produced carbon-14 in the atmosphere and their interpretations. *Journal of Geophysical Research* 70:5937–5992.

Suhm, D. A., and A. D. Krieger, 1954, *An introductory handbook of Texas archaeology*. Abilene: Texas Archaeological Society.

Sullivan, R. J., 1942, *The Ten'a food quest*. Washington, D.C.: Catholic University of America Press, Anthropological Series, No. 11.

Swadesh, M., 1953, Archaeological and linguistic chronology of Indo-European groups. *American Anthropologist* 55:349–352.

——, 1959, Linguistics as an instrument of prehistory. *Southwestern Journal of Anthropology* 15:20–35.

——, 1960, *Estudios sobre lengua y cultura*. Mexico City: Acta Anthropologica, Epoca 2, Vol. 2, No. 2.

——, 1962, Linguistic relations across Bering Strait. *American Anthropologist* 64:1262–1291.

——, 1964, Linguistic overview. In *Prehistoric man in the New World*, J. D. Jennings and E. Norbeck, eds. Chicago: University of Chicago Press, pp. 527–556.

Swanson, E. H., and B. R. Butler, 1962, *The first conference of western archaeologists on problems of point typology*. Pocatello: Idaho State College Museum, Occasional Papers, No. 10.

Swanton, J. R., 1942, Source material on the history and ethnology of the Caddo Indians. Washington, D.C.: Bulletin of the Bureau of American Ethnology, No. 132.

Swartz, B. K., 1967, A logical sequence of archaeological objectives. *American Antiquity* 32:487–497.

Sweeney, E. A., 1965, Dental caries in Tehuacan skeletons. *Science* 149:1118.

Tamers, M. A., and F. J. Pearson, 1965, The validity of radiocarbon dates on bone. *Nature* 208:1053–1056.

Tanner, J. T., 1966, Effects of population density on growth rates of animal populations. *Ecology* 47:733–745.

Tanzer, H. H., 1939, *The common people of Pompeii*. Baltimore: Johns Hopkins University Studies in Archaeology, No. 29.

Tauber, H., 1958, Difficulties in the application of C14 results in archaeology. *Archaeologia Austriaca* 24:59–69.

Taylor, D., and I. Rouse, 1955, Linguistic and archaeological time depth in the West Indies. *International Journal of American Linguistics* 21:105–115.

Taylor, J. Du P., ed., 1972, *International journal of nautical archaeology and under-water exploration*, Vol. 1. London: Institute of Archaeology, Council for Nautical Archaeology.

Taylor, R. E., and R. Berger, 1967, Radiocarbon content of marine shells from the Pacific coasts of Central and South America. *Science* 158:1180–1182.

Taylor, W. W., 1948, *A study of archeology*. Washington, D.C.: American Anthropological Association Memoir No. 69, 50 (312).

———, 1954, Southwestern archaeology: its history and theory. *American Anthropologist* 56:561–570.

———, 1966, Archaic cultures adjacent to the northeastern frontiers of Mesoamerica. In *Archaeological frontiers and external connections*, Vol. 4, *Handbook of Middle American Indians*, G. F. Ekholm and G. R. Willey, eds. Austin: University of Texas Press, pp. 59–94.

Terrell, J., 1967, Galatea Bay—the excavation of a beach-stream midden site on Ponui Island in the Hauraki Gulf, New Zealand. Wellington, New Zealand: General Transactions of the Royal Society of New Zealand, 2:31–70.

Thellier, E., and O. Thellier, 1959, Sur l'intensité du champ magnétique terrestre dans le passé historique et géologique. *Annales Géophysiques* 15:285–376.

Thenius, E., 1961a, Über die Bedeutung der Paläokologie für die Anthropologie und Urgeschichte. In *Theorie und Praxis der Zusammenarbeit zwischen den anthropologischen Disziplinen*, J. Haekel, ed. Horn: F. Berger.

———, 1961b, Palazoölogie und Prähistorie. *Mitteilungen der Urgeschichte und Anthropol. Gesellschaft*, Vienna, 12 (3, 4):39–61.

Thieme, F. P., 1958, The Indo-European language. *Scientific American* 199 (October):63–74.

———, and C. M. Otten, 1957, The unreliability of blood typing aged bone. *American Journal of Physical Anthropology* 15:387–398.

Thom, A., 1964, Megalithic geometry in standing stones. *New Scientist* 21:690–691.

———, 1966, Megaliths and mathematics. *Antiquity* 40:121–128.

———, 1967, *Megalithic sites in Britain*. London: Oxford.

———, 1971, *Megalithic lunar observations*. Oxford: Clarendon Press.

Thomas, C., 1971, Ethics in archaeology, 1971. *Antiquity* 45:268–274.

Thomas, D. H., 1971, On distinguishing natural from cultural bone in archaeological sites. *American Antiquity* 36:366–371.

Thomas, D. W., 1961, *Documents from Old Testament times*. New York: Harper & Row.

Thomas, H. H., 1923, The source of the stones of Stonehenge. *Antiquaries Journal* 3:239–260.

Thomas, W. L., ed., 1956, *Man's role in changing the face of the earth*. Chicago: University of Chicago Press.

Thompson, D. F., 1939, The seasonal factor in human culture. *Proceedings of the Prehistoric Society* 5:209–221.

Thompson, D. F., 1949, *Economic structure and the ceremonial exchange cycle in Arnhem Land.* Melbourne: Macmillan.

Thompson, J. E. S., 1950, *Maya hieroglyphic writing: introduction.* Washington, D.C.: Carnegie Institution, Publication No. 589.

———, 1954a, *The rise and fall of Maya civilization.* Norman: University of Oklahoma Press.

———, 1954b, The character of the Maya. Cambridge, England: Proceedings of the 30th International Congress of Americanists, pp. 36–40.

———, 1962, *A catalogue of Maya hieroglyphs.* Norman: University of Oklahoma Press.

———, 1963, *Maya archaeologist.* Norman: University of Oklahoma Press.

Thompson, R. H., 1956, The subjective element in archaeological inference. *Southwestern Journal of Anthropology* 12:327–332.

———, 1958a, *Modern Yucatecan Maya pottery making.* Beloit, Wis.: Society for American Archaeology, Memoir No. 15.

———, 1958b, *Migrations in New World culture history.* Tucson: University of Arizona, Social Science Bulletin No. 27.

———, and W. A. Longacre, 1966, The University of Arizona Archaeological Field School at Grasshopper, East Central Arizona. *Kiva* 31:255–275.

Thorp, J., 1941, The influence of environment on soil formation. *Proceedings of the Soil Science Society of America* 6:39–46.

Thorvildsen, E., 1952, Menneskeofringer i Oldtiden Jarnalderligene fra Borremose i Himmerland. [Human offerings in antiquity.] *Kuml* 1952:32–48.

Throckmorton, P., and J. M. Bullitt, 1963, Underwater surveys in Greece: 1962. *Expedition,* University of Pennsylvania Museum 5:17–23.

Tilton, G. R., and S. R. Hart, 1963, Geochronology. *Science* 140:357–366.

Tite, M. S., 1972, *Methods of physical examination in archaeology.* New York: Seminar Press.

———, and J. Waine, 1962, Thermoluminescent dating: a reappraisal. *Archaeometry* 5:53–79.

Tolstoy, P., 1958, *Surface survey of the northern valley of Mexico: the classic and post-classic periods.* Philadelphia: Transactions of the American Philosophical Society 48 (Part 5).

———, 1966, Method in long range comparison. Madrid: Actas de XXXVI Congreso de Americanistas, 1964 1:69–89. Seville.

Tortellot, G., and J. A. Sabloff, 1972, Exchange systems among the ancient Maya. *American Antiquity* 37:126–134.

Toulouse, J. H., Jr., 1949, *The Mission of San Gregorio de Abo.* Santa Fe, N.M.: Monographs of the School of American Research, No. 13.

Tower, D. B., 1945, *The use of marine mollusca and their value in reconstructing prehistoric trade routes in the American Southwest.* Cambridge, Mass.: Papers of the Excavators' Club, 2 (3).

Toynbee, A. J., 1934–1960, *A study of history,* 12 vols. London: Oxford University Press.

Traeger, G. L., 1955, Linguistics and the reconstruction of culture history. In *New interpretations of aboriginal American culture history.* Washington, D.C.: Anthropological Society of Washington, pp. 110–115.

Treganza, A. E., 1956, Sonoma Mission: an archaeological reconstruction of the Mission San Francisco de Solano Quadrangle. Berkeley: Kroeber Anthropological Society Papers 14:1–18.

———, and S. F. Cook, 1948, The quantitative investigation of aboriginal sites: complete excavation with physical analysis of a single mound. *American Antiquity* 13:287–297.

Treganza, A. E., and L. L. Valdivia, 1955, The manufacture of pecked and ground stone artifacts: a controlled study. Berkeley: Reports of the University of California Archaeological Survey 32:19–29.

Tribus, M., and E. C. McIrvine, 1971, Energy and information. *Scientific American* 224:179–190.

Trigger, B. G., 1965, *History and settlement in Lower Nubia.* New Haven, Conn.: Yale University Publications in Anthropology, No. 69.

———, 1967, Settlement archaeology—its goals and promise. *American Antiquity* 32:149–160.

———, 1968a, *Beyond history: the methods of prehistory.* New York: Holt, Rinehart and Winston, Inc.

———, 1968b, Major concepts of archaeology in historical perspective. *Man* 3:527–541.

———, 1968c, The determinants of settlement patterns. In *Settlement archaeology,* K. C. Chang, ed. Palo Alto, Calif.: National Press Books, pp. 53–78.

———, 1970, Aims in prehistoric archaeology. *Antiquity* 44:26–37.

———, 1971, Archaeology and ecology. *World Archaeology* 2:321–336.

Troels-Smith, J., 1960, The Muldbjerg dwelling place: an early Neolithic archaeological site in the Aamosen Bog, West-Zealand, Denmark. Washington, D.C.: Smithsonian Institution, Annual Report for 1959, pp. 577–601.

Troike, R. C., 1957, Time and types in archeological analysis: the Brainerd Robinson technique. *Bulletin of the Texas Archaeological Society* 28:269–284.

Tugby, D. J., 1965, Archaeological objectives and statistical methods: a frontier in archaeology. *American Antiquity* 31:1–16.

Tuggle, H. D., N. P. S. Price, B. Trigger, 1971, Trigger and prehistoric archaeology. *Antiquity* 45:130–134.

———, A. H. Townsend and R. J. Riley, 1972, Laws, systems, and research design: a discussion of explanation in archaeology. *American Antiquity* 37:3–12.

Turner, C. G., and L. Lofgren, 1966, Household size of prehistoric western Pueblo Indians. *Southwestern Journal of Anthropology* 22:117–132.

Tuthill, C., and A. Allanson, 1954, Ocean-bottom artifacts. *Southwest Museum Masterkey* 28:222–232.

Ucko, P. J., 1962, The interpretation of prehistoric anthropomorphic figurines. *Journal of the Royal Anthropological Institute* 92:38–54.

———, 1969, Ethnography and archaeological interpretation of funerary remains. *World Archaeology* 1:262–280.

———, and G. W. Dimbleby, eds., 1969, *The domestication and exploitation of plants and animals.* Chicago: Aldine.

———, and A. Rosenfeld, 1967, *Palaeolithic cave art.* London: World University Press. (Weidenfeld & Nicholson.)

———, R. Tringham and G. W. Dimbleby, eds., 1972, *Man, settlement and urbanism.* London: Duckworth.

Vaillant, G. C., 1935, *Excavations at El Arbolillo.* New York: Anthropological Papers of the American Museum of Natural History 35 (Part 2).

Vallois, H. V., 1928, *Étude des empreintes de pieds humains du Tuc d'Audoubert, de Cabrerets, et de Ganties.* Amsterdam: Institut Internationale d'Anthropologie, 3e session, September 20–29, 1927.

———, 1960, Vital statistics in prehistoric populations as determined from archaeological data. *Viking Fund Publications in Anthropology* No. 28:186–222.

Van Buren, E. D., 1939, The fauna of ancient Mesopotamia as represented in art. *Analecta Orientalia* 18:1–113.

Van der Merwe, N. J., 1965, Carbon-14 dating of iron: a new archeological tool. *Current Anthropology* 6:475.

——, 1966, New mathematics for glottochronology. *Current Anthropology* 7:485–500.

——, and R. T. K. Scully, 1971, The Phalaborwa story: archaeological and ethnographic investigation of a South African Iron Age group. *World Archaeology* 3:178–196.

——, and P. H. Stern, 1972, Soil chemistry of postmolds and rodent burrows: identification without excavation. *American Antiquity* 37:245–253.

Van Reit Lowe, C., 1950, Prehistory and the humanities. *South African Journal of Science* 47:3–11.

——, 1954, Pitfalls in prehistory. *Antiquity* 28:85–90.

Van Woerkom, A. J. J., 1953, The astronomical theory of climatic changes. In *Climatic change*, H. Shapley, ed. Cambridge, Mass.: Harvard University Press, pp. 147–157.

Van Zeist, W., and H. E. Wright, Jr., 1963, Preliminary pollen studies at Lake Zeribar, Zagros Mountains, southwestern Iran. *Science* 140:65–69.

Van Zinderen Bakker, E. M., ed., 1960, *Palynology in Africa*, 6th report. Bloemfontein, South Africa: University of Orange Free State.

Vayda, A., and A. Leeds, 1965, *Man, culture and animals.* Washington, D.C.: American Association for the Advancement of Science, Publication No. 78.

——, and R. A. Rappaport, 1968, Ecology, cultural and noncultural. In *Introduction to cultural anthropology*, J. A. Clifton, ed. Boston: Houghton Mifflin, Chap. 18, pp. 477–497.

Vértes, L., 1965, "Lunar calendar" from the Hungarian Upper Paleolithic. *Science* 149:855–856.

Vescelius, G., 1955, Archaeological sampling: a problem in statistical inference. In *Essays in the science of culture*, G. E. Dole and R. L. Carneiro, eds. New York: Crowell, pp. 457–470.

Vestine, E. H., L. LaPorte, C. Cooper, I. Lange, and W. C. Hendrix, 1947, Description of the earth's main magnetic field and its secular changes, 1905–1945. Washington, D.C.: Carnegie Institution, Department of Terrestrial Magnetism, Publication No. 578.

Vita-Finzi, C., and E. S. Higgs, 1970, Prehistoric economy in the Mount Carmel area of Palestine: Site catchment analysis. *Proceedings of the Prehistoric Society* 36:1–37.

Vivian, R. G., 1970, An inquiry into prehistoric social organization in Chaco Canyon, New Mexico. In *Reconstructing prehistoric pueblo societies*, W. A. Longacre, ed. Albuquerque: University of New Mexico Press, pp. 59–83.

Vogt, E. Z., 1956, An appraisal of "Prehistoric settlement patterns in the New World." In *Prehistoric settlement patterns in the New World*, G. R. Willey, ed. New York: Viking Fund Publications in Anthropology, No. 23:173–182.

——, 1964, The genetic model and Maya cultural development. *Desarrollo Cultural de Los Mayas*, ed. por E. Z. Vogt y Alberto Ruz L. Mexico City: Universidad Nacional Autónoma de Mexico, pp. 9–48.

——, 1968, Some aspects of Zinacantan settlement patterns and ceremonial organization. In *Settlement archaeology*, K. C. Chang, ed. Palo Alto, Calif.: National Press Books, pp. 154–173.

Von Bothmer, D., and J. V. Noble, 1961, *An inquiry into the forgery of the Etruscan terracotta warriors in the Metropolitan Museum of Art.* New York: Metropolitan Museum of Art, Occasional Papers, No. 11.

Von Hagen, V. W., 1947, *Maya explorer.* Norman: University of Oklahoma Press.

Von Koenigswald, G. H. R., 1956, *Meeting prehistoric man.* London: Thames and Hudson.

Voorhies, B., 1972, Settlement patterns in two regions of the southern Maya lowlands. *American Antiquity* 37:115–125.

Voss, O., 1966, Dokumentationsproblemer Indenfor Arkaeologien [Problems of documentation in archaeology]. *Kuml,* Aarhus. (English version, pp. 122–134.)

Vynckier, J., 1966, Note on the treatment of the waterlogged wooden objects excavated at Gwisho hot-springs. *Proceedings of the Prehistoric Society* 32:260–261.

Wace, A. J. B., 1949, *The Greeks and Romans as archaeologists.* Paris: Société Royale d'Archéologie d'Alexandrie, Bulletin No. 38. (Reprinted in Heizer 1962a.)

Wagley, C., 1951, Cultural influences on population. Sao Paulo: Revista do Museu Paulista 5:95–104.

Wagner, P. L., 1960, The human use of the earth. New York: Free Press.

Wakeling, T. G., 1912, *Forged Egyptian antiquities.* London: A. and C. Black.

Walker, R., M. Maurette, R. Fleischer, and P. Price, 1971, Applications of solid-state nuclear track detectors to archaeology. In *Science and archaeology,* R. H. Brill, ed. Cambridge, Mass.: MIT Press, pp. 279–283.

Wallace, A. F., 1950, A possible technique for recognizing psychological characteristics of the ancient Maya from an analysis of their art. *American Imago* 7:239–253.

Wallace, B., and A. M. Srb, 1965, *Adaptation.* Englewood Cliffs, N.J.: Prentice-Hall.

Wallace, W. J., 1954, A basket-weaver's kit from Death Valley. *Southwest Museum Masterkey* 28:216–221.

———, and D. Lathrap, 1959, Ceremonial bird burials in San Francisco Bay shellmounds. *American Antiquity* 25:262–264.

Wallis, F. S., 1955, Petrology as an aid to prehistoric and medieval archaeology. *Endeavor* 14:146–151.

The War Office, 1956, *Manual of map reading, air photo reading, and field sketching: Part 1. Map reading 1955.* London: Her Majesty's Stationery Office. (Reprinted 1961.)

———, 1958, *Manual of map reading, air photo reading, and field sketching: Part 2. Air photo reading.* London: Her Majesty's Stationery Office. (Reprinted 1965.)

Ward, J., 1900, *Pyramids and progress.* London: Eyre & Spottiswoode.

Waring, A. J., Jr., 1968, *The Waring papers,* S. Williams, ed. Cambridge, Mass.: Papers of the Peabody Museum, Vol. 58.

Warnica, J. M., 1966, New discoveries at the Clovis site. *American Antiquity* 31:345–357.

Warren, S. H., 1911, On a prehistoric interment near Walton-on-Naze. *Essex Naturalist* 16:198–208.

———, 1914, The experimental investigation of flint fracture and its application to problems of human implements. *Journal of the Royal Anthropological Institute* 44:412–450.

———, 1923, Sub-soil pressure flaking. *Proceedings of the Geologists Association* 34:153–175.

Washburn, S. L., 1959, Speculations on the interrelations of the history of tools and biological evolution. *Human Biology* 31:21–31. (Also printed in *The evolution of man's capacity for culture,* J. N. Spuhler, ed. Detroit: Wayne State University Press, 1959.)

Washburn, S. L., 1960, Tools and human evolution. *Scientific American* 203:62–75.

———, 1968, Behavior and the origin of man. *Rockefeller University Review,* January–February, 1968, pp. 10–19.

———, and F. C. Howell, 1960, Human evolution and culture. In *Evolution after Darwin,* Vol. 2. Sol Tax, ed. Chicago: University of Chicago Press pp. 33–56.

———, and P. C. Jay, 1968, *Perspectives on human evolution 1.* New York: Holt, Rinehart and Winston, Inc.

———, and C. S. Lancaster, 1968, The evolution of hunting. In *Man the hunter,* R. B. Lee and I. DeVore, eds. Chicago: Aldine, pp. 293–303.

Watanabe, H., 1949, Natural fracture of pebbles from the fossil-bearing Pleistocene deposits near Akashi. *Zinruigaku Zassi,* Tokyo, 60:121–142.

———, 1959, The direction of remanent magnetism of baked earth and its application to chronology for anthropology and archaeology in Japan. *Journal of the Faculty of Science, University of Tokyo* (Section 2) 2:1–188.

———, 1966, Ecology of the Jomon people: stability of habitation and its biological and ethnohistorical implications. *Journal of the Anthropological Society of Japan* 74:21–32.

Watanabe, N., and M. Suzuki, 1969, Fission track dating of archaeological glass materials from Japan. *Nature* 222(5198):1057–1058.

Waterbolk, H. T., 1971, Working with radiocarbon dates. *Proceedings of the Prehistoric Society* 37:15–33.

Waterman, T. T., 1920, Yurok geography. Berkeley: University of California Publications in American Archaeology and Ethnology, No. 16:177–314.

Watson, J. D., 1968, *The double helix: a personal account of the discovery of the structure of DNA.* New York: Atheneum.

Watson, P. J., 1966, Clues to Iranian prehistory in modern village life. Philadelphia: University of Pennsylvania Museum, *Expedition* 8:9–19.

———, 1969, *The prehistory of Salts Cave, Kentucky.* Springfield, Ill.: Illinois State Museum, Report of Investigations No. 16.

———, 1972a, Explanations and models: the prehistorian as philosopher of science and the prehistorian as excavator of the past. In *The explanation of culture change,* C. Renfrew, ed. London: Duckworth.

———, 1972b, The future of archeology in anthropology: culture history and social science. In *Archeology today,* C. L. Redman, ed. New York: Wiley.

———, S. A. LeBlanc, and C. L. Redman, 1971, *Explanation in archeology: an explicitly scientific approach.* New York: Columbia University Press.

———, and R. A. Yarnell, 1966, Archaeological and paleontological investigations in Salts Cave, Mammoth Cave National Park, Kentucky. *American Antiquity* 31:842–849.

Watson, R. A., and P. J. Watson, 1969, *Man and nature: an anthropological essay in human ecology.* New York: Harcourt.

Watson, V., 1955, Archaeology and proteins. *American Antiquity* 20:288.

Watson, W., 1950, *Flint implements: an account of Stone Age techniques and cultures.* London: British Museum.

Watts, E. W., 1965, *Archaeology: exploring the past.* New York: Metropolitan Museum of Art. (Also Greenwich, Conn.: N.Y. Graphic Society.)

Wauchope, R., 1962, *Lost tribes and sunken continents.* Chicago: University of Chicago Press.

———, 1965, Alfred Vincent Kidder, 1885–1963. *American Antiquity* 31:149–171.

———, 1966, *Archaeological survey of northern Georgia.* Beloit, Wis.: Society for American Archaeology, Memoir 21.

Waugh, F. W., 1916, *Iroquois foods and food preparation.* Ottawa, Can.: Department of Mines, Geological Survey, Anthropological Series, Memoir 86, No. 12.

Weaver, K. F., 1967, Magnetic clues help date the past. *National Geographic Magazine* 131:696–701.

Webb, W. S., 1946, *Indian Knoll.* Lexington, Ky.: University of Kentucky Reports in Anthropology, 4(3).

———, and R. S. Baby, 1957, *The Adena people,* No. 2. Columbus: The Ohio Historical Society, Ohio State University Press.

———, and W. G. Haag, 1939, *The Chiggerville site.* Lexington: University of Kentucky Reports in Anthropology, Vol. 4.

———, and D. L. de Jarnette, 1942, *An archeological survey of Pickwick Basin in the adjacent portions of the states of Alabama, Mississippi and Tennessee.* Washington, D.C.: Bulletin of the Bureau of American Ethnology, No. 129.

Weber, J. N., and A. La Rocque, 1963, Isotope ratios in marine mollusk shells after prolonged contact with flowing fresh water. *Science* 142:1666.

Webster, G., 1963, *Practical archaeology.* London: A. & C. Black.

Wedel, W. R., 1936, *An introduction to Pawnee archeology.* Washington, D.C.: Bulletin of the Bureau of American Ethnology, No. 112.

———, 1938, *The direct-historical approach in Pawnee archeology.* Washington, D.C.: Smithsonian Institution, Miscellaneous Collections, 97(7).

———, 1951, The use of earth-moving machinery in archaeological excavation. Ann Arbor: University of Michigan, Anthropological Papers of the Museum of Anthropology, No. 8:17–33.

———, 1961, *Prehistoric man on the Great Plains.* Norman: University of Oklahoma Press.

———, 1967, Salvage archeology in the Missouri River basin. *Science* 156:589–597.

Weinberg, S. S., 1954, The relative chronology of the Aegean in the Neolithic period and the Early Bronze Age. In *Relative chronologies in Old World archaeology,* R. W. Ehrich, ed. Chicago: University of Chicago Press, pp. 86–107.

Weiner, J. S., 1955, *The Piltdown forgery.* London: Oxford.

Weiss, L. E., 1954, Fabric analysis of some Greek marbles and its application to archaeology. *American Journal of Science* 252:641–662.

Wells, C., 1964, *Bones, bodies, and disease.* London: Thames and Hudson.

Weltfish, G., 1930, Prehistoric North American basketry and modern distributions. *American Anthropologist* 32:454–495.

———, 1932, *Preliminary classification of southwestern basketry.* Washington, D.C.: Smithsonian Institution, Miscellaneous Collections, 87(7).

Wendorf, F., assembler, 1961, *Paleoecology of the Llano Estacado.* Santa Fe: Museum of New Mexico Press.

———, 1962, *A guide for salvage archaeology.* Santa Fe: Museum of New Mexico Press.

———, 1966, Early man in the New World: problems of migration. *American Naturalist* 100:253–270.

———, A. D. Krieger, C. C. Albritton, and T. D. Stewart, 1955, *The Midland discovery.* Austin: University of Texas Press.

Wertenbaker, T. J., 1953, The archaeology of colonial Williamsburg. *Proceedings of the American Philosophical Society* 97:44–50.

Wertime, T. A., 1964, Man's first encounters with metallurgy. *Science* 146:1257–1267.

West, R. C., N. P. Psuty, and B. G. Thom, 1969, *The Tabasco lowlands of south-eastern Mexico*. Baton Rouge: Louisiana State University Coastal Studies Series No. 27.

Wettstein, E., 1924, Die Tierreste aus dem Pfahlbau am Alpenquai in Zürich. *Vierteljahrschrift der Naturforschenden Gesellschaft Zürich* 69:78–127.

Weyer, E. M., Jr., 1964, New World lithic typology project: Part 1. *American Antiquity* 29:487–489.

Whallon, R., 1972a, A new approach to pottery typology. *American Antiquity* 37:13–33.

——, 1972b, Spatial analysis of occupation floors: the application of dimensional analysis of variation. In *The explanation of culture change*, C. Renfrew, ed. London: Duckworth.

Wheat, J. B., 1967, A Paleo-Indian bison kill. *Scientific American* 216(1):44–52.

——, 1972, The Olsen-Chubbuck site: a Paleo-Indian bison kill. Society for American Archaeology, Memoir No. 26.

Wheeler, M., 1947, Harappa 1946: the defences and cemetery R 37. *Ancient India* No. 3:59–130.

——, 1955, *Still digging*. London: M. Joseph.

——, 1956, *Archaeology from the earth*. Baltimore: Pelican.

White, C., and N. Peterson, 1969, Ethnographic interpretations of the prehistory of Western Arnhem Land. *Southwestern Journal of Anthropology* 25:45–67.

White, J. P., 1967, Ethno-archaeology in New Guinea. *Mankind* 6:409–414.

White, L. A., 1947, Evolutionary stages, progress, and the evaluation of cultures. *Southwestern Journal of Anthropology* 3:165–192.

——, 1948, Man's control over civilization: an anthropocentric illusion. *Scientific Monthly* 66:235–247.

——, 1949, *The science of culture, a study of man and civilization*. New York: Farrar, Straus. (Also Grove.)

——, 1959a, *The evolution of culture: the development of civilization to the fall of Rome*. New York: McGraw-Hill.

——, 1959b, The concept of culture. *American Anthropologist* 61:227–251.

White, R. C., 1963, *Luiseño social organization*. Berkeley: University of California Publications in American Archaeology and Ethnology, 48(2).

White, T. E., 1952, Observations on the butchering techniques of some aboriginal peoples, No. 1. *American Antiquity* 17:337–338.

——, 1953a, Observations on the butchering techniques of some aboriginal peoples, No. 2. *American Antiquity* 19:160–164.

——, 1953b, A method for calculating the dietary percentage of various food animals utilized by aboriginal peoples. *American Antiquity* 18:396–398.

——, 1954, Observations on the butchering techniques of some aboriginal peoples, Nos. 3, 4, 5, 6. *American Antiquity* 19:254–264.

——, 1955a, Observations on the butching techniques of some aboriginal peoples, Nos. 7, 8, 9. *American Antiquity* 21:170–178.

——, 1955b, The technique of collecting osteological materials. *American Antiquity* 21:85–87.

——, 1956, The study of osteological materials in the Plains. *American Antiquity* 21:401–404.

Whiteford, A. H., 1947, Description for artifact analysis. *American Antiquity* 12:226–239.

Whiting, J. W. M., and B. Ayres, 1968, Inferences from the shape of dwellings. In *Settlement archaeology*, K. C. Chang, ed. Palo Alto, Calif.: National Press Books, pp. 117–133.

Whitmore, F. C., K. Emery, H. Cooke, and D. Swift, 1967, Elephant teeth from the Atlantic continental shelf. *Science* 156:1477–1481.

Whittlesey, J., 1966a, Photogrammetry for the excavator. *Archaeology* 19:273–276.

———, 1966b, Bipod Camera Support. *Photogrammetric Engineering*, November, pp. 1005–1010.

Wickman, F. E., 1952, Variations in the relative abundance of the carbon isotopes in plants. *Geochimica Acta*, London 2:243–254.

Willey, G. R., 1939, Ceramic stratigraphy in a Georgia village site. *American Antiquity* 5:140–147.

———, 1953, *Prehistoric settlement patterns in the Virú Valley, Peru*. Washington, D.C.: Bulletin of the Bureau of American Ethnology, No. 155.

———, 1955, The prehistoric civilizations of Nuclear America. *American Anthropologist* 57:571–589.

———, 1956a, An archaeological classification of culture contact situations. Beloit, Wis.: Society for American Archaeology, Memoir No. 11:1–30.

———, 1956b, *Prehistoric settlement patterns in the New World*. New York: Viking Fund Publications in Anthropology, No. 23.

———, 1960, New World prehistory. *Science* 131:73–86.

———, 1961, Volume in pottery and the selection of samples. *American Antiquity* 27:230–231.

———, 1966a, *An introduction to American archaeology*, Vol. 1. Englewood Cliffs, N.J.: Prentice-Hall.

———, 1966b, Postlude to village agriculture: the rise of towns and temples and the beginnings of the great traditions. Spain: XXXVI International Congress of Americanists 1964, pp. 267–277.

———, 1968a, One hundred years of American archaeology. In *One hundred years of anthropology*, J. O. Brew, ed. Cambridge, Mass.: Harvard University Press, pp. 29–56.

———, 1968b, Settlement archaeology: an appraisal. In *Settlement archaeology*, K. C. Chang, ed. Palto Alto, Calif.: National Press Books, pp. 208–226.

———, 1971, *An introduction to American archaeology*, Vol. 2. Englewood Cliffs, N.J.: Prentice-Hall.

———, and P. Phillips, 1958, *Method and theory in American archaeology*. Chicago: University of Chicago Press.

———, and D. B. Shimkin, 1971, The collapse of classic Maya civilization in the southern lowlands: a symposium summary statement. *Southwestern Journal of Anthropology* 27:1–18.

Williams, H., 1956, Petrographic notes on tempers of pottery from Chupicuaro, Cerro del Tepelcate and Ticoman, Mexico. Philadelphia: Transactions of the American Philosophical Society 45(5):576–580.

———, and R. F. Heizer, 1965a, Sources of rocks used in Olmec monuments. Berkeley: University of California, Archaeological Research Facility, Contribution No. 1:1–40.

———, 1965b, Geological notes on the ruins of Mitla and other Oaxacan sites, Mexico. Berkeley: University of California, Archaeological Research Facility, Contribution No. 1:41–54.

Willis, E. H., 1969, Radiocarbon dating. In *Science in archaeology*, D. Brothwell and E. Higgs, eds., rev. ed. London: Thames and Hudson, pp. 46–57.

Willoughby, N. C., 1963, Division of labor among the Indians of California. Berkeley: Reports of the University of California Archaeological Survey 60:7–79.

Wilmsen, E. N., 1965, An outline of early man studies in the United States. *American Antiquity* 31:172–192.

Wilmsen, E. N., 1968a, Functional analysis of flaked stone artifacts. *American Antiquity* 33:156–161.

———, 1968b, Lithic analysis in paleoanthropology. *Science* 161:982–987.

Wilson, E. B., 1952, *An introduction to scientific research.* New York: McGraw-Hill.

Wilson, T., 1898, Beveled arrow heads. *American Archaeologist*, Vol. 2.

———, 1899, The beginnings of the science of prehistoric anthropology. *Proceedings of the American Association for the Advancement of Science* 48:309–353.

Wiltshire, J. R., 1967, A pole for high viewpoint photography. *Industrial Commercial Photography* 7:53–56.

Wiltshire, T., 1859–1863, On ancient flint implements of Yorkshire, and the modern fabrication of similar specimens. *Proceedings of the Geologist's Association* 1:215–226.

Winlock, H. E., 1942, *Excavations at Deir El Bahri, 1911–1933.* New York: Macmillan.

———, 1955, Models of daily life in ancient Egypt from the tomb of Meket-Re at Thebes. Cambridge, Mass.: Harvard University Press for the Metropolitan Museum of Art.

Winter, J., 1971, Thermoluminescent dating of pottery. In *Dating techniques for the archaeologist,* H. N. Michael and E. K. Ralph, eds. Cambridge, Mass.: MIT Press, pp. 118–151.

Wissler, C., 1916, The application of statistical methods to the data on the Trenton argillite culture. *American Anthropologist* 18:190–197.

Witherspoon, Y. T., 1961, A statistical device for comparing trait lists. *American Antiquity* 26:433–436.

Witthoft, J., 1955, Worn stone tools from Southeastern Pennsylvania. *Pennsylvania Archaeologist* 25:16–31.

———, 1967, Glazed polish on flint tools. *American Antiquity* 32:383–388.

Wodehouse, R. P., 1959, *Pollen grains: their structure, identification and significance in science and medicine.* New York: Hafner.

Wolf, E. R., 1964, The study of evolution. In *Horizons of anthropology,* Sol Tax, ed. Chicago: Aldine, pp. 108–119.

———, 1967, Understanding civilizations: a review article. *Comparative Studies in Society and History* 9:446–465.

Wood, E. S., 1963, *Collins field guide to archaeology.* London: Collins.

Wood, F. D., 1945, Color photography applied to stratigraphy. New Haven, Conn.: Connecticut Academy of Arts and Sciences Transactions 36:879–882.

Wood, J. J., and R. G. Matson, 1972, Two models of socio-cultural systems and their implications for the archaeological study of change. In *The explanation of culture change,* C. Renfrew, ed. London: Duckworth.

Wood, W. R., 1968, Mississippian hunting and butchering patterns: bone from the Vista shelter, 23R-20, Missouri. *American Antiquity* 33:170–179.

Woodall, J. N., 1968, The use of statistics in archaeology—a bibliography. *Bulletin of the Texas Archaeological Society,* No. 38:25–38.

Woodbury, R. B., 1954, *Prehistoric stone implements from northeastern Arizona.* Cambridge, Mass.: Harvard University, Papers of the Peabody Museum, Vol. 34.

———, 1960, Nels C. Nelson and chronological archaeology. *American Antiquity* 25:400–401.

Woodward, A., 1933, Ancient houses of modern Mexico. Los Angeles, Calif.: *Bulletin of the Southern California Academy of Sciences* 32:79–98.

Woolley, C. L., 1932, *Dead towns and living men.* London: J. Cape. (Rev. ed., 1959, New York: Philosophical Library.)

———, 1952, *Spade work in archaeology.* New York: Philosophical Library.

———, 1953, *Spadework: adventures in archaeology.* London: Lutterworth.

———, 1958, *History unearthed.* London: Benn.

———, 1959, *Digging up the past,* 2d ed. Baltimore: Pelican.

World Archaeology, 1971, Archaeology and Ethnography issue, 3(2).

Wormington, H. M., and D. Ellis, eds. 1967, *Pleistocene studies in southern Nevada.* Carson City: Nevada State Museum, Anthropological Papers, No. 13.

Wright, G. A., 1969, *Obsidian analyses and prehistoric Near Eastern trade: 7500 to 3500 B.C.* Ann Arbor: University of Michigan, Anthropological Papers of the Museum of Anthropology, No. 37.

Wright, G. E., ed., 1961, *The Biblical archaeologist reader.* New York: Doubleday. (Also Chicago: Quadrangle Books.)

Wright, H. E., Jr., 1962, Late Pleistocene geology of coastal Lebanon. *Quaternaria* 6:525–539.

———, and D. G. Frey, eds., 1965, *The Quaternary of the United States.* Princeton, N.J.: Princeton University Press.

Wright, T., 1844, On antiquarian excavations and researches in the Middle Ages. *Archaeologica* 30:438–457.

Wrigley, E. A., 1966, *An introduction to English historical demography from the sixteenth to the nineteenth century.* London: Weidenfeld & Nicholson.

Wulsin, F., 1941, *The prehistoric archaeology of northwest Africa.* Cambridge, Mass.: Harvard University, Papers of the Peabody Museum, 19(1).

Wylie, J. C., 1959, *The wastes of civilization.* London: Faber.

Wynne, E. J., and R. F. Tylecote, 1958, An experimental investigation into primitive iron-smelting technique. *Journal of the Iron and Steel Institute* 191:339–348.

Xanthoudides, S., 1927, Some Minoan potter's-wheel discs. In *Essays in Aegean archaeology presented to Sir Arthur Evans in honour of his 75th birthday,* C. S. Casson, ed. Oxford: Clarendon, pp. 111–128.

Yanine, V. L., 1960, Modern methods in archaeology: the Novgorod excavation. *Diogenes* 29:82–101.

Yao, T. C., and F. H. Stross, 1965, The use of analysis by x-ray fluorescence in the study of coins. *American Journal of Archaeology* 69:154–156.

Yarnell, R. A., 1964, *Aboriginal relationships between culture and plant life in the Upper Great Lakes Basin.* Ann Arbor: University of Michigan, Anthropological Papers of the Museum of Anthropology, No. 23.

———, 1965, Implications of distinctive flora on pueblo ruins. *American Anthropologist* 67:662–674.

———, 1969, Contents of human paleofeces. In P. J. Watson, *The prehistory of Salts Cave, Kentucky.* Springfield, Ill.: Illinois State Museum, Report of Investigations No. 16:41–55.

Young, T. C., Jr., 1966, Survey in Western Iran, 1961. *Journal of Near Eastern Studies* 25:228–239.

Zehren, E., 1962, *The crescent and the bull,* James Cleugh, trans. New York: Hawthorn.

Zeiner, H. M., 1946, Botanical survey of the Angel Mounds site, Evansville, Indiana. *American Journal of Botany* 33:83–90.

Zeuner, F. E., 1952, Pleistocene shore lines. *Geologisches Rundschau* 40:39–50.

———, 1954, The Neolithic-Bronze Age gap on the tell of Jericho. *Palestine Exploration Quarterly.* May–October, pp. 64–68.

Zeuner, F. E., 1955a, Notes on the Bronze Age tombs of Jericho I. *Palestine Exploration Quarterly,* October, pp. 118–220.

————, 1955b, Loess and Paleolithic chronology. *Proceedings of the Prehistoric Society* 21:51–64.

————, 1958, *Dating the past; an introduction to geochronology,* 4th ed. London: Methuen.

————, 1959, *The Pleistocene period.* London: Hutchinson.

————, 1960, Advances in chronological research. New York: Viking Fund Publications in Anthropology No. 28:325–350.

————, 1963, *A history of domesticated animals.* New York: Harper & Row.

Ziegler, A., 1965, *The role of faunal remains in archaeological investigations.* Sacramento, Calif.: Sacramento State College, Sacramento Anthropology Society, Paper 2, pp. 47–75.

Zimmerman, D. W., 1971, Uranium distributions in archeologic ceramics: dating of radioactive inclusions. *Science* 174:818–819.

Zipf, G. K., 1949, *Human behavior and the principle of least effort.* Reading, Mass.: Addison-Wesley.

NAME INDEX

SUBJECT INDEX

KEY TO PLACES MENTIONED IN THE TEXT—
THE AMERICAS